William R. Holm 9/84

Career Information, Career Counseling, and Career Development

FIFTH EDITION

LEE E. ISAACSON
Professor Emeritus, Purdue University

DUANE BROWN
University of North Carolina at Chapel Hill

ALLYN AND BACON
Boston   London   Toronto   Sydney   Tokyo   Singapore

Series Editor: *Ray Short*
Series Editorial Assistant: *Christine Shaw*
Production Administrator: *Annette Joseph*
Production Coordinator: *Susan Freese*
Editorial-Production Service: *WordCrafters Editorial Services, Inc.*
Manufacturing Buyer: *Louise Richardson*
Cover Administrator: *Linda K. Dickinson*
Cover Designer: *Suzanne Harbison*

Previous editions of this book were published under the title *Career Information
in Counseling and Career Development,* by Lee E. Isaacson.

Library of Congress Cataloging-in-Publication Data

Isaacson, Lee E.
    Career information, career counseling, and career development
    / Lee E. Isaacson, Duane Brown. — 5th ed.
      p. cm.
    Includes bibliographical references and index.
    ISBN 0-205-14645-7
    1. Vocational guidance. 2. Vocational guidance—Bibliography.
  3. Vocational guidance—Information services. 4. Information
storage and retrieval systems—Vocational guidance. I. Brown,
Duane. II. Title.
HF5381.I675 1993
371.4′25′07—dc20   92–1610
                                               CIP

Printed in the United States of America

10 9 8 7 6 5 4   97 96 95 94

To
Ardis and Sandra

___ Overview _____

Contents

16   Job Placement, Outplacement, and the Job Search Process   433

PART SIX SPECIAL SETTINGS AND FUTURE POSSIBILITIES

17   Career Development in Business and Industry   455

Preface

Purpose

As this fifth edition goes to press, changes in the American workplace are much in evidence. Competition from Japan, Germany, and other countries in our full-blown global economy has made many of our businesses noncompetitive. The unexpected end of the cold war has brought demands to decrease expenditures for defense and to increase monetary outlay to rebuild the infrastructure of this country. Because of the increased pressure to compete, innovations such as the use of robots in manufacturing are increasingly in evidence. Similarly, as managers in the service sector, which dominates our economy, look for cheaper, faster ways to get things done, change occurs with increasing rapidity. A new restructuring—the new euphemism for reduction in force—is announced daily, or is at least predicted. Adult workers, some of whom are nearing the ends of their careers, are suddenly without jobs. Young workers, particularly those who are undereducated or lacking in skills, find employment difficult to obtain.

Career counselors and other career development workers are faced with enormous challenges as they attempt to help those workers undergoing chaotic change and to prepare young workers to cope with a workplace characterized by uncertainty. A significant part of the challenge is assisting women and minorities as they cope with choosing, entering, and changing careers, as well as with the discriminatory attitudes that have long existed in the workplace. Because of the new complexities of our economy—the changes that must inevitably occur as we dismantle a substantial portion of our defense industry, the realities of a multicultural workplace, and a workplace where women are assuming a role equal to that of men—there is a great need for systematic career counseling and development programs that will help people make informed career decisions. Accordingly, the purposes of this book are to help students understand:

- the career development of all people across the life span.
- the sources of career information and how these can be organized.
- how career development programs can be developed and delivered to facilitate self-understanding and how that self-knowledge can be

coupled with information about jobs to enhance the career choice process.
- the intricacies of the career counseling process.
- the trends that will shape the world of work.

Audience

This book is intended to help those who are now engaged, or who expect to be engaged, in facilitating the career development process. It is written expressly with school counselors, rehabilitation counselors, counseling psychologists, employment counselors, placement officers, and career counselors in mind. However, teachers, media specialists, social workers, and others who are influential in the career development process can benefit from the contents of the book.

Approach

This edition, like the previous ones, includes both theory and practical applications. The theoretical background is included as one means of helping the reader understand why certain practical approaches may be useful and why work is an important aspect of people's lives. The practical tools allow the reader to gain specific knowledge and skills needed to assist with career development problems. The practical applications also help the reader understand how to design and deliver career development programs in various settings.

Organization

This book is divided into six sections. Part One, Foundations of Career Development, examines career development theory and the factors that influence workers in their careers. Part Two, The World of Work, contains discussions of the occupational structure in existence today and the trends that will influence it tomorrow, along with presentations about classifying and describing the world of work. Information about the World of Work is the title of Part Three. In this section various approaches to gathering, organizing, and disseminating occupational information are presented, including an in-depth discussion of computerized systems. Part Four, The Career Development Process, contains four chapters that deal with career development programming across the life span. Chapter 12 deals with the needs of special groups and populations. Part Five, Career Development Procedures, deals with the vital processes of preparation for the workplace, appraisal and assessment, career counseling, and job placement. Part Six is titled Special Settings and Future Possibilities. The special settings discussed are business and industry and private practice. Chapter 19, focusing on future possibilities, includes predictions about the changes in career development theorizing, career counseling, the development and utilization of occupational information, and career development programming.

The Fifth Edition

This edition includes a number of additions, as well as updates of all material included in the fourth edition. Subjects of some chapters are:

- Appraisal and assessment in career development
- Career counseling
- Career development programming in business and industry
- Establishing a career counseling private practice
- Trends and issues in career development.

Every attempt has been made to be sensitive to the issues surrounding the career development of women, minorities, and people who are disabled. Extended discussions of these concerns appear throughout the book.

Also included is updated information on the *Dictionary of Occupational Titles* and the National Career Development Guidelines Project, along with newly revised occupational projections from the Department of Labor. Information from the two Gallup Polls sponsored by the National Career Development Association and the National Occupational Information Coordinating Committee is also included.

Readers should also note a change in editorial style made in this edition. To avoid any type of gender bias, the pronouns *he* and *she* are used alternately to mean a single individual.

Acknowledgments

Many groups and individuals deserve special thanks for making this volume possible. These include, among others, many graduate students whose questions often started the search for better or more complete information; professional colleagues who have been both supportive and challenging; and a host of other authors whose writings stimulated our thinking and helped us understand career development.

We also wish to thank those reviewers who evaluated this book at various stages: John Dagley, University of Georgia at Athens; Dennis Engels, University of North Texas; and Jan Jirouch, Northern State University (Aberdeen, South Dakota).

Finally, a few individuals must be recognized for their special contributions, including Karen Bray, Evelyn Ross, and Karen Thigpen for their skill and patience in deciphering illegible work and turning it into pages of typed manuscript.

We also want to thank our wives, Ardis and Sandra, who have encouraged us throughout our careers, been patient when writing took precedence over what probably should have been more important matters, and willingly given of their time and talent to make this volume and other accomplishments possible.

L. E. I.
D. B.

1

Gaining a Perspective on Work and Career

Many historical events or trends occurring in the 1990s appear likely to influence work both now and in the future. For many workers, the impact will be marginal or undetectable; for others, the effect may range from devastation to great opportunity. In some cases, changes may occur for only isolated individuals or small occupational groups; for others, it may be felt throughout the regional, national, or even international economy.

One trend, if it continues, is the reduction of Cold War tensions. Mutual distrust between capitalist and communist countries has resulted in large military forces on both sides, with huge portions of national income devoted to the support of those forces. The continued relaxation of that hostility and distrust not only will move many workers from military assignments to the civilian work force but also will cause great changes in the so-called defense industries that produce the supplies and equipment for the military forces, as well as in other more peripheral industries.

Another trend is the movement toward regional internationalization. The European Economic Community creates a free-trade area with a common currency and nonrestrictive borders encompassing most of Western Europe. As the Eastern European countries change to more capitalistic and democratic societies, they may join. Similarly, a free-trade zone for all of the western hemisphere has been suggested and may parallel the format of the European Economic Community. Comparable action in Asia is possible. These changes influence workers in polarizing ways: While markets expand and offer new opportunities for the sale of products and services, competitive forces will intensify.

Another example is increasing international concern for the environment. The clear cutting of rain forests, failure to control acid rain, and increases in automotive exhaust fumes wipe out or seriously restrict some occupations, modify others, and create some new ones. The development and promotion of efficient mass transportation in urban areas may reduce the

1

number of service station attendants, auto repairers, and parking lot workers but likely will increase bus drivers and vehicle maintenance workers. Concern for the Northern Spotted Owl as a threatened species in 1990 resulted in restricting the timber industry in the Northwest, thereby reducing the number of loggers and supporting workers.

Many factors unique to work in the United States concern an increasing number of individuals and organizations. Our inability to control illegal immigration brings us large numbers of potential workers with limited education and language, as well as little or no work skills. The relocation of factories and assembly plants to other countries with large, cheaply paid work forces causes unemployment that requires retraining for American workers before reentry to work in another job. The continuing trade deficit and our inability to cope with national budget deficits cause industry and business to move cautiously in planning expansion or new developments.

Many business and industry leaders are expressing concern about the difficulty of finding workers who either have the skills required in new jobs or are trainable to meet the demands of those positions. As advancing technology takes over assembling, painting, welding, and other activities, workers are expected to operate or monitor the robot or computer that does the task. Increasing industrial competitiveness demands higher efficiency and productivity in these more technical occupations.

Since the mid-1980s, numerous organizations have released studies focusing on the interrelated problems of work and education. Johnston and Parker (1987) discuss the problems to be faced in the work force after the turn of the century. Both of the reports from the National Alliance of Business (1986) and the W. T. Grant Foundation (1988) urge the formation of cooperative efforts among community organizations, business, labor, and government to resolve developing problems. The report by the Commission on the Skills of the American Work Force (1990), based on extensive interviews with management and workers in several European and Asian industrial nations, recommends vast changes in our educational system to prepare workers for the increasingly competitive future.

A survey by the National Alliance of Business (1990) states that 64 percent of the 1,200 largest U.S. corporations reported dissatisfaction with the reading, writing, and reasoning skills of high school graduates entering the work force. Defining reading competency as beyond the seventh-grade level and math competency at a fifth-grade level, the companies report having to interview seven to eight applicants to find one that meets this level of skill.

Keller and Piotrowski (1987) indicate that only about one tenth of the *Fortune* 500 companies had career development programs for their employees. Modernizing the work force, upgrading skills, increasing worker satisfaction, and remaining competitive in a changing world require the attention of all institutions and organizations in our society, both public and private. In addition, government agencies and schools must make these goals a priority.

WORK IN RETROSPECT AND PROSPECT

The earliest prehistoric people maintained themselves by hunting and fishing. Anthropologists have shown how this simple, essentially nomadic life was replaced, as cultures became less primitive, by a system of division of labor, in which men were primarily occupied as hunters, fishermen, herdsmen, and traders. As social structures became more sophisticated, the occupations of farmers and craftsmen evolved. During this social change, individual family involvement in task specialization was a limited, part-time, almost incidental activity, perhaps growing out of individual interest or group recognition of an unusual skill. Nevertheless, the trend toward focusing effort on a specific group of tasks had started, and at that point the concept of *career* was born.

From prehistoric times, work has been a crucial factor in social organization. Greek and Roman civilizations each had a complex occupational structure. Many of the turning points in history were a result of changing relationships between humans and work. The early medieval craft guilds were created for occupational purposes, but the guilds exerted a social force that further weakened the semislavery of the feudal period. The Hanseatic League and similar groups of free cities organized, at least in part, to promote trade. The medieval university developed essentially to provide educational preparation for certain professional fields. The Protestant Reformation laid the foundation for a new view of humanity, and the historic period of discovery and exploration provided a vision of new opportunities. The Industrial Revolution accelerated occupational specialization and provided the means of transforming resources into new forms of wealth. The opening of vast geographic areas in the Western Hemisphere for settlement and development suggested that almost any man could, if he wished, acquire some of the ingredients of independence and self-actualization—a homestead, a business, a mine, a factory, a profession, or a job.

Recent decades have produced tremendous expansion in the number and nature of jobs. New relationships between human and machine, employer and employee, society and citizen have evolved and, in the dynamic structure of today's world, will continue through endless mutations and modifications. The continuous interaction between work and society modifies both. Often, transitions can be seen well in advance, and the principal uncertainty focuses on the timing of the event. The transformations, usually gradual and anticipated, are occasionally sudden and unexpected. Some possible imminent changes have been described by Toffler (1980), Naisbitt and Aburdene (1990), and Johnston and Parker (1987).

Two large sectors of the work world are changing extensively as a result of technological advancement. Employment in manufacturing is declining as that industry modernizes, with increasing use of computer-controlled machinery and robots. This transition is particularly obvious in the so-called smokestack industries that produce durable goods such as steel and automobiles. At the same time, new positions are expanding in service and information-processing areas because technological advancements in computers and computer-related equipment permit wider application to materials, processes, and data in these areas.

In some work activities, the increased application of computers and word processors may reduce the need for a centralized work force. Decentralization may occur, with workers performing their duties in many different places. In one application of this concept, workers may perform their work at home. Similarly, the nine-to-five workday may disappear as the worker is able to complete assigned tasks according to a personally adjusted schedule. Another likely extension of such individualization is increased job sharing, in which two or more workers divide work originally anticipated to be performed by a single worker.

Women have been expanding their participation in the paid work force, and Department of Labor projections indicate that this trend will persist. Decentralization of the work force, variable time schedules, and job sharing will facilitate that participation, even for women at home raising children. The current trend toward two-paycheck families is likely to continue.

Existing population factors will influence work in many ways. Not only does a decreasing birth rate reduce the demand for baby food and car seats, it soon results in fewer kindergartens and elementary school classes, and later it provides fewer applicants for jobs in fast-food restaurants. At the other end of the continuum, improved health care may mean that more senior citizens will desire jobs that supplement limited retirement incomes or that provide involvement in activities they consider worthwhile.

Because one's occupation generally determines where and how one lives, the community activities and organizations in which one participates, and many other aspects of life, social status has long been associated with one's job. It is difficult to predict whether this relationship will become more or less intense. If, as some writers predict, technological change results in a small group of highly trained technical experts and a great mass of low-skilled workers who work infrequently at uninteresting and unrewarding positions, then it is likely that social status will become detached from occupation and will shift to some other basis. On the other hand, if technological change produces a general upgrading of most workers and provides most people with an opportunity to participate in activities that not only appear to be worthwhile but *are* challenging and satisfying, then social status may become even more closely related to one's job.

In addition to technological change, population factors, and changing social status, many other pressures in present-day society influence both work and society. Some of these factors include the number of scientists whose research has an impact on everyday life; the availability and application of energy sources; increased innovation and the shortened time between discovery and general application; the uneven distribution of population, food, and natural resources on a worldwide basis; and the accelerated rate of industrialization in underdeveloped countries.

Some generalizations about the impact of these forces can be stated with confidence:

1. Work will continue to change and will be drastically different in the future.
2. Many new jobs will develop, and many present jobs will decline and disappear.
3. Many workers will change jobs more frequently in the future, and they are likely to change their type of work as well.
4. Greater geographic mobility may be required of workers in the future.
5. Retraining programs will be developed by prospective employers, by governmental units, or by cooperative action of both and will become a significant educational effort.
6. Many workers will participate in retraining programs as a means of moving into new employment opportunities. Some workers will retrain several times to maintain employability.
7. There is likely to be a greater demand for information about occupational change by individuals who wish to capitalize on developing opportunities and by governmental and industrial organizations that must plan and deliver preparatory programs.

WHY PEOPLE WORK

Work is seldom, if ever, only a means by which an individual sustains life. Work has many other functions of equal or sometimes greater importance to both society and the individual. It is one way in which the individual relates to society. Work provides the person, and often the family as well, with status, recognition, affiliation, and similar psychological and sociological products essential for participation in a complex society.

Work has religious and theological meanings. In early Hebrew writings, work was viewed as punishment. Early Christians were offended by work for profit, but this view was reversed by the Middle Ages. During the Reformation, work was considered the only way to serve God. Luther and Calvin viewed work positively, and their attitude combined with Social Darwinism and laissez-faire liberalism to form the foundation of what is now called the Protestant work ethic.

Another psychological product of work is the development of self-esteem. People feel a sense of mastery in dealing with objects of work, and their self-esteem is enhanced because they are engaging in activities that produce something that other people value. Unemployed people often suffer low self-esteem because they believe that they cannot produce something that other people value.

If we assume that work is one of the central components of life activities for most adults, it is easy to assume that the satisfaction derived from work is an important determinant in an individual's total satisfaction. This is obviously a nebulous concept. One research approach to determining job satisfaction has been to ask workers, "What type of work would you try to get into if you could start all over again?" One might logically infer that workers who choose the same occupation see greater likelihood of satisfaction in their present occupation than in any other field. Occupations named most frequently in response are those in which incumbents appear to have the greatest degree of control and the feeling that what they do is recognized as important by others. Such studies usually reveal that professions such as university professor, mathematician, biologist, and chemist show high percentages (80 or 90 percent) stating that they would choose the same occupation again. Unskilled and blue-collar workers show the lowest percentages (in the teens or low 20 percent level), and white-collar and skilled workers fall in the middle range.

HOW PEOPLE LOOK AT WORK

It is work which gives flavor to life.
　　　　　—Amiel

To youth I have but three words of counsel—work, work, work.
　　　　　—Bismarck

All work, even cotton-spinning, is noble; work is alone noble. . . . A life of ease is not for any man, nor for any god.
　　　　　—Carlyle

There is no substitute for hard work.
　　　　　—Edison

I look on that man as happy, who, when there is question of success, looks into his work for a reply.
　　　　　—Emerson

Work is love made visible. And if you cannot work with love but only with distaste, it is better that you should leave your work and sit at the gate of the temple and take alms of those who work with joy.
　　　　　—Gibran

Every child should be taught that useful work is worship and that intelligent labor is the highest form of prayer.
　　　　　—Ingersoll

Never is there either work without reward, nor reward without work being expended.
　　　　　—Livy

Though a little one, the master-word (work) looms large in meaning. It is the open sesame to every portal, the great equalizer in the world, the true philosopher's stone which transmutes all the base metal of humanity into gold.
—Osler

Hard work is the best investment a man can make.
　　　　　—Schwab

The Report of the Special Task Force (1973) relates a study showing that workers, when asked to rank-order the aspects of work they considered most important, listed the following: interesting work, enough help and equipment to get the job done, good pay, opportunity to develop special abilities, job security, and seeing the results of one's work. The workers said that the most oppressive features of work were constant supervision and coercion, lack of variety, monotony, meaningless tasks, and isolation. From these data, the report concludes that "an increasing number of workers want more autonomy in tackling their tasks, greater opportunity for increasing their skills, rewards that are directly connected to the intrinsic aspects of work, and greater participation in the design of work and the formulation of their tasks" (p. 13).

Other studies confirm the continuing importance of work in people's lives. Yankelovich (1982, p. 5) describes a survey of workers who were asked to select which of three concepts of work most closely reflected their view. Their options included the following:

1. People work only because they would not otherwise have the resources to sustain themselves.
2. Work is a straight economic transaction in which people relate effort to financial return: The more money they get, the harder they work; the less money they receive, the less effort they give.
3. Work carries a moral imperative to do one's best apart from practical necessity or financial remuneration.

The study reports that 78 percent of the workers questioned selected the third response, whereas only 15 percent and 7 percent, respectively, chose the first or second choice. Yankelovich also cites a 1977 survey by the University of Michigan showing that 75 percent of the group surveyed stated they would continue to work even if they could live comfortably without working for the rest of their lives. One can only conclude that most people consider work an essential component of their lives, one that they would choose to retain even if it were optional.

The National Career Development Association (formerly called the National Vocational Guidance Association), in cooperation with other agencies, commissioned the Gallup Organization to conduct a 1987 survey of public attitudes toward work. The responses to this 20-question survey were published as *Planning For and Working in America* (1988). The National Career Development Association has since published a monograph (edited by Brown and Minor, 1989) discussing the 1987 results in greater detail and including chapters by such well-known experts in the career development field as Hoyt, Hansen, and Drier. Another survey covering the same 20 questions was completed with a different national sample in 1989 (Brown and Minor, 1992). Several of the questions relate directly to how workers look at their jobs. Some are included here, with an abbreviated tabulation of the responses obtained for each (unless indicated differently, figures are for 1989).

Q: *In the past year, did you need help in selecting, changing, or getting a job?*

Ten percent (1987) and seven percent (1989) answered in the affirmative. In 1989, 15 percent of African Americans and 19 percent of Asians said yes compared to 6 percent of whites and 8 percent of Hispanics. Logically, younger age groups expressed more need for help, with 14 percent of the 18–25 group, 9 percent of the 26–40 group, 4 percent of 41–55, 2 percent of 56–65, and 4 percent of the 65+ group saying yes.

Q: (Asked of those who needed assistance) *Did you seek help from any of the following, or didn't you know where to go for help?*

The following responses were obtained (the total exceeds 100% because of multiple responses):

Job service worker	33%
Friends	24%
Professional counselor	22%
Relatives	18%
Community leader	7%
Teacher/school staff member	5%
Didn't know where to go for help	10%
Didn't actually look for help	9%
Don't know	5%

Q: *Which one of the following phrases best describes how you first got started in your present job or career?* (Respondees were employed adults.)

	1989 (%)	*1987 (%)*
I made a conscious choice–followed a definite plan.	41	39
I got started through a set of chance circumstances.	18	23
I was influenced by my parents or relatives.	12	10
I was influenced by friends or associates.	11	10
I took the only job that was available.	12	13
Don't know/not sure/other.	6	5
N =	(1,052)	(735)

Q: *If you could start over and plan your worklife, would you try, or not try, to get more information about the job or career options open to you than you did the first time?*

	Yes, Would (%)	*No, Would Not (%)*	*Not Sure (%)*	*Number of Interviews*
Total	65	31	4	(1,350)
Whites	63	32	5	(737)

	Yes, Would (%)	No, Would Not (%)	Not Sure (%)	Number of Interviews
Blacks	79	19	2	(310)
Asians	71	24	5	(255)
Hispanics	75	19	6	(269)
College graduate	59	36	5	(398)
College incomplete	70	27	3	(299)
HS graduate	64	32	4	(414)
Less than HS graduate	66	27	7	(227)
Employed	62	34	4	(1,052)
Not employed	74	21	5	(289)
18–25	74	25	1	(238)
26–40	72	24	4	(503)
41–55	61	37	2	(342)
56–65	44	45	11	(163)
66 and over	66	28	6	(89)

Q: *In your present or most recent job, would you say your skills and abilities are being used very well, fairly well, not very well, or not at all well?*

	Very Well (%)	Fairly Well (%)	Not Very Well (%)	Not at All Well (%)	Number of Interviews
1989	55	37	4	3	(1,052)
1987	50	37	7	4	(735)

Q: *Thinking ahead for the next three years, which one of the following best describes what is most likely to happen with regard to your present job?*

	1989 (%)	1987 (%)
I will stay with my current employer.	56	61
I will be forced to change jobs because of job termination.	9	4
I will choose to change jobs.	20	21
I will leave the labor force permanently.	7	7
I will leave the labor force temporarily.	5	4
Not sure/don't know	3	3
Number of interviews	(1,052)	(735)

	Stay with Current Job (%)	Choose to Change Job (%)	Forced to Change (%)	Leave Permanently (%)	Leave Temporarily (%)	Don't Know (%)	Number of Interviews
Total	56	20	9	7	5	3	(1,052)
Married	61	15	12	6	3	3	(610)
Nonmarried	48	28	5	8	7	4	(442)
Whites	57	19	10	6	5	3	(579)
Blacks	50	23	7	10	6	4	(232)
Asians	47	29	8	8	6	2	(207)
Hispanics	63	20	6	4	3	4	(199)
18–25	33	43	9	3	10	2	(193)
26–40	63	22	10	—	2	3	(439)
41–55	69	10	7	4	7	3	(288)
56–65	47	4	14	27	4	4	(101)

Q: *In your opinion, which of the following would cause you to accomplish more on your job?*

If I received higher pay	40%
If I received more recognition	31%
If I had additional training	25%
If doing well led to advancement	24%
If I had more control over my job	21%
If I felt my job were more important	11%
Nothing	7%
Don't know	5%
Number of interviews	(1,052)

Q: *I am going to read off some of the areas to which public high schools devote attention in educating students. . . . Tell me whether you feel the high schools in your community devote too much attention, not enough attention, or about the right amount to that area.*

	Too Much (%)	Not Enough (%)	About Right (%)	Don't Know (%)
Helping students choose their careers	2	44	33	21
Helping students who do not go to college develop skills so they can get jobs	2	53	23	22
Helping students develop skills in identifying jobs that open in their communities	2	46	27	25

	Too Much (%)	Not Enough (%)	About Right (%)	Don't Know (%)
Placing students who have dropped out or graduated into jobs	2	51	18	29
Helping students learn how to use occupational information about salary and working conditions	2	41	31	26
Helping students develop the skills they need to get jobs, such as interviewing techniques	1	43	32	24
Preparing students for college	5	31	47	17

One must exercise caution in drawing inferences from a limited sample, but it appears reasonable to conclude the following:

1. About 10 percent of those interviewed needed help in looking for work, with ethnic groups and younger individuals needing more help.
2. Those seeking help in a job search turned to job service workers, friends, professional counselors, and relatives, in that order.
3. The largest number of interviewees made a conscious choice when they started their present job, and the next highest number said that chance was the major factor.
4. Approximately two thirds said they would seek more information if they were to start over.
5. About half thought their skills were very well used in their present job, and another third said their skills were fairly well used.
6. In the next 3 years, over half expected to stay with their present employer, and one fifth will change.
7. The incentives leading to greater accomplishment on the job were higher pay, greater recognition, additional training, and opportunity for advancement.
8. Half said that schools do not do enough to help students prepare for future careers, one fifth to one third said about the right amount of help is given, and only 2 percent said too much help is provided.

DEFINITIONS

Dictionaries often define work as "physical or mental effort or activity directed toward the promotion or accomplishment of something; toil; labor; employment." One sometimes hears the term *real work* applied to jobs involving strenuous physical exertion, implying that jobs requiring only mental effort are certainly different, if not somewhat less demanding, from the others. A prevalent belief is that a task is not work unless one is reimbursed in some way for the expended effort. Thus worth is often correlated with work-produced pay, and it is an easy step from there to the viewpoint that the person who is not earning income is worthless. A broader view that emphasizes purpose would be more appropriate.

Terkel (1974), in his introduction to *Working*, summarizes a broader view:

> Perhaps it is time the "work ethic" was redefined and its idea reclaimed from the banal men who invoke it. In a world of cybernetics, of an almost runaway technology, things are increasingly making things. It is for our species, it would seem, to go on to other matters. Human matters. Freud put it one way. Ralph Helstein puts it another. He is president emeritus of the United Packinghouse Workers of America. "Learning is work. Caring for children is work. Community action is work. Once we accept the concept of work as something meaningful—not just as the source of a buck—you don't have to worry about finding enough jobs. There's no excuse for mules any more. Society does not need them. There's no question about our ability to feed and clothe and house everybody. The problem is going to come in finding enough ways for man to keep occupied, so he's in touch with reality." Our imaginations have obviously not yet been challenged. (p. xxviii)

More recently, Sears (1982) reports the definition adopted by a panel for the National Vocational Guidance Association (NVGA), now known as the National Career Development Association. This panel of experts agreed to define *work* as follows:

> Conscious effort, other than that having as its primary purpose either coping or relaxation, aimed at producing benefits for oneself and/or for oneself and others. (p. 142)

The term *career* has been interpreted or defined in various ways in the professional literature. Some authors favor a broad definition, essentially equating career with the sum of all life experiences including education, work, leisure activities, social and civic memberships and responsibilities, and family membership. This view holds that all life development is an aspect of career.

Others have restricted the term to the individual's lifelong work pattern—that is, the way in which the individual expresses self and relates to society through work. In this view, one's career consists of the chronological sequence of the person's work-related activities. This would include educational experiences designed to prepare oneself for work as well as participation in work itself. The NVGA panel (Sears, 1982, p. 139) suggests that the term be defined as "the totality of work one does in his/her lifetime." This definition is used in this book.

Three other terms defined by the NVGA panel are used frequently throughout this book. They are discussed in detail later but are listed here:

Career counseling: A one-to-one or small group relationship between a client and a counselor with the goal of helping the client(s) integrate and apply an understanding of self and the environment to make the most appropriate career decisions and adjustments

Career development: The total constellation of psychological, sociological, educational, physical, economic, and chance factors that combine to shape the career of any given individual over the life span

Career information: Information related to the world of work that can be useful in the process of career development, including educational, occupational, and psychosocial information related to working (e.g., availability of training, the nature of the work, and status of workers in different occupations)

Shartle (1959, p. 23) defines a *position* as a group of tasks performed by one person; a *job* as a group of similar positions in a single plant, business establishment, educational institution, or other organization; and an *occupation* as a group of similar jobs found in several establishments. Thus there are as many positions as there are workers, and the difference between *job* and *occupation* is determined by degree of dispersion. The NVGA panel recommends a similar view.

CAREER DEVELOPMENT: A LIFELONG PROCESS

We have briefly considered the importance of work in individuals' lives. We have seen how work provides both physical and psychological sustenance, affiliations with society, and status within the group and sets the lifestyle of the individual and the family. Any activity of such major importance must concern most people contemplating the assumption of work roles. It thus seems logical to expect elementary and secondary students to begin to express interest in their future relationship with work and to plan with varying degrees of effectiveness for their entrance into the world of work.

In accepting a developmental approach to career development, we expect to focus on the decisions or adjustments commonly met at each developmental level or those about to be encountered at the next level. On this basis, we may reasonably conclude that high school and college students who will soon leave school will show primary concern for areas related to their postschool life, such as vocational problems and further education. Several studies confirm this conclusion.

Biggers (1971) reports that he found high school seniors as limited in their ability to use information in vocational decision making as they were in the fourth grade. Increased age and school experience did not appear to improve the students' use of occupational information. Biggers concludes that more attention must be focused on helping students use such materials in the career choice process.

Prediger, Roth, and Noeth (1974) report a national study, sampling eighth, ninth, and eleventh graders in 33 states in the spring of 1973. Seventy-eight percent of the eleventh graders in the sample reported a need for more help in making career plans compared to 30 percent who desired help with personal problems. Results for eighth graders were similar: 73 percent were concerned about help with career plans, and 39 percent wanted help with personal problems. Prediger and Sawyer (1986) describe a follow-up study conducted 10 years later in 1983 sampling eighth-, tenth-, and twelfth-grade students. Fewer eleventh graders (71 percent) reported a need for more help. However, 66 percent of the 1983 eleventh graders reported receiving either "some" or "a lot" of help with career planning, compared to 50 percent in 1973.

Another extensive study, completed by the National Assessment of Educational Progress, collected career and occupational development data from a broader group including 9-, 13-, and 17-year-olds and a group of adults (ages 26 to 35). Two divisions of the American Personnel and Guidance Association (the National Vocational Guidance Association and the Association for Measurement and Evaluation in Guidance) formed a commission to prepare a series of publications presenting the results of the study on career and occupational development and suggesting the implications of these data for professionals who work in career development. Miller (1977) reports the data for 9-year-olds. The study found the following:

1. Gender-role stereotyping had already started (more boys could identify newscasters, more girls could identify secretaries).
2. Parental educational background appeared related to the child's occupational knowledge.
3. Most of the group felt that responsibility for selecting their future work belonged to someone else.

Aubrey (1977, pp. 13–43) describes the results for the 13-year-olds. Some of the points he discusses include the following:

1. Descriptions of personal strengths and limitations tended to cluster in topics, such as sports, art and music, and school or academic matters.
2. Thirteen-year-olds knew highly visible occupations reasonably well in terms of physical requirements but knew very little about earning power.
3. There were gender differences in knowledge about specific jobs. Males could identify locksmith, bank teller, carpenter, watch repairman, plumber, and chemist. Females could identify social worker, secretary, accountant, and physician.
4. They considered group and individual sports as the most useful way to obtain a job. Only 3 percent considered academic pursuits as useful in obtaining a future job.
5. Mathematics was perceived as more useful in future jobs than all 10 other academic areas combined.

6. Most could list only two things to consider in choosing a job or a career when asked to name ten. Less than half could list more than five.
7. Counselors and teachers were rarely considered as sources of information about occupations.
8. Most did think about future jobs. Their first choices usually required college or other lengthy preparatory programs.
9. Most (87 percent) had some kind of paid work experience.
10. Most felt that eventually they should make the final decision on what job they would choose to make a living.

Mitchell (1977, pp. 16–51) reviews the results obtained from the 17-year-olds. Some of the significant points in her report include the following:

1. Most 17-year-olds had talked seriously with someone about their future plans, most commonly with parents, and girls more frequently than boys.
2. Most could match at least five of nine occupations with physical characteristics or skills, but less than 10 percent could do all nine correctly.
3. Prestige and status were the most frequent reasons for accepting a promotion, and too much responsibility was the main reason for refusing one.
4. Only 2.2 percent saw school or academic areas as activities that might be useful for a job.
5. Most said they had taken a subject in school that might be useful for a job, with business education, mathematics, vocational education, science, English, and industrial arts named in that order.
6. They believed that observation of the job field was the principal resource for finding out the requirements of a job.
7. Most had thought about the kind of job they would like to have in the future. Most females saw themselves as clerical workers, in service occupations, or as homemakers and housewives. Males saw themselves as craftsmen, farmers, laborers, managers, military personnel, operatives, proprietors, or in protective services.
8. Nearly half accepted sex, age, and marital status discrimination quoted in one of the exercises.
9. Most failed to include educational and training qualifications in preparing a letter of application.
10. Most felt that lack of experience or training would be the main reason that a person willing to work might find it hard to get a job.
11. Fewer than half felt that it would be possible for a worker to like a repetitive job.

Westbrook (1978, pp. 12–23) presents the results obtained from the adult group. One should note that the three younger groups included samples of 28,000, 38,000, and 35,000 respondents, whereas the adult sample included only 2,000 people. Some of the significant points in Westbrook's summary include the following:

1. When asked to indicate one thing they enjoyed doing that they would like to do better, most named an activity from their nonwork time.
2. About two thirds of the adults had taken a test to help them decide on their career or job plans, but only a fifth of these had discussed the results with someone.
3. Most adults had a high level of knowledge of characteristics and training requirements for a variety of jobs. This knowledge level was directly related to their educational and income level.
4. Adults considered working conditions the most important factor when making occupational choices. This was followed by personal satisfaction, prestige, qualifications, personal ability, availability, and responsibility.
5. Adults in occupations other than housewife (80 percent) indicated that their major source of job satisfaction was the ability to do the best they could, followed by interpersonal relations, feeling the job was worthwhile, pay, and specific job duties. Housewives (19 percent of the sample) listed sense of accomplishment, taking care of family, and time spent with family.
6. Most adults who had participated in some type of continuing education saw it as helpful in present or past work.
7. Few adults were able to write a job application letter that included all important elements.

These findings emphasize a need, at all age levels, for a better understanding of work, the qualifications and training needed to perform the work, how to apply for and obtain a desired job, how one's job affects one's life, and the kind of satisfaction or payoff derived from work. Among the various age groups, teenagers have the highest unemployment rate and thus the greatest need to acquire salable skills and techniques for gaining entry to available positions. The impact of technology on work increases the number of workers whose occupations are likely to change drastically or even disappear, thus requiring new skills and reentry in another field. Changing lifestyles for older workers increase the likelihood of their active participation in work for longer periods. The opening of almost all occupations to both men and women, to racial and ethnic minority groups, and to both younger and older applicants increases the need for information and help in applying that information so career development can be positive and satisfying for each individual.

Teachers and other students of human learning report that insight develops as an expansion of the knowledge and understanding that the person already has conceptualized. Career information is meaningful and useful for individuals only if it relates to where they are and where they want to go. In other words, career information must be accessible and useful as well as relevant and understandable. Generally, the individual is forming impressions and fitting together various ideas to form a bigger picture that is broad in scope but probably lacking in detail. The information must fit this kind of situation: It should sketch out the major points; show the important relationships and the unique, identifying factors; and indicate where more facts can be obtained. Materials for a third grader, a high school junior, a widow reentering the labor market, and a worker with a disability must vary according to the individual being served.

Whether one approaches career development from the perspective of general and traditional education, vocational education, career counseling, or adult social services and agencies, certain concepts are basic to all approaches. One of these concepts is the general recognition of the developmental or process aspect. If the heart of the process is decision making, then guidance is needed at all life stages involving decisions. This begins to appear in the elementary school years, when every child makes certain decisions and adjustments, and builds toward a peak during the secondary school years and the few years immediately following high school. These are the years when most individuals face frequent decisions that have both immediate implications and long-range effects on their lives. With increased education, maturity, and experience, individuals can be expected to become more self-directive as they enter adulthood. Thus the need for guidance services decreases, although it probably never disappears entirely. The increasing rapidity with which occupational change occurs suggests that in the years ahead many adults will need access to career counseling to assist them in reorienting career plans.

There may be differences in the clientele served, the particular services supplied, and the setting used. Nevertheless, the commonalities among the counselors serving these various groups in these various settings furnish a basic point of departure for our consideration of career information, counseling, and development. The counselor, in or out of school, is involved in all phases of career development.

REFERENCES

Aubrey, R. F. (1977). *Career development needs of thirteen-year-olds: How to improve career development programs.* Washington, DC: National Advisory Council for Career Education.

Biggers, J. L. (1971). The use of information in vocational decision-making. *Vocational Guidance Quarterly, 19,* 171–176.

Brown, D., & Minor, C. W. (eds.). (1989). *Working in America: A status report on planning and problems.* Alexandria, VA: National Career Development Association.

Brown, D., & Minor, C. W. (eds.). (1992). *Career needs in a diverse workplace: Implications of the NCDA Gallup Survey.* Alexandria, VA: National Career Development Association.

Commission on the Skills of the American Work Force. (1990). *America's choice: High skills or low wages?* New York: National Center on Education and the Economy.

Johnston, W., & Parker, A. (1987). *Workforce 2000: Work and workers for the twenty-first century.* Indianapolis, IN: The Hudson Institute.

Keller, J., & Piotrowski, C. (1987). Career development programs in Fortune 500 firms. *Psychological Reports, 61,* 920–922.

Miller, J. V. (1977). *Career development needs of nine-year-olds: How to improve career development programs.* Washington, DC: National Advisory Council for Career Education.

Mitchell, A. M. (1977). *Career development needs of seventeen-year-olds: How to improve career development programs.* Washington, DC: National Advisory Council for Career Education.

Naisbitt, J., & Aburdene, P. (1990). *Megatrends 2000.* New York: Morrow.

National Alliance of Business. (1986). *Employment policies: Looking to the year 2000.* Washington, DC: Author.

National Alliance of Business. (1990). *Survey of competency level of new job applicants.* Washington, DC: Author.

National Career Development Association. (1988). *Planning for and working in America.* Ellicott City, MD: NCDA.

Prediger, D. J., Roth, J. D., & Noeth, R. J. (1974). Career development of youth: A nationwide study. *Personnel and Guidance Journal, 53,* 97–104.

Prediger, D. J., & Sawyer, R. L. (1986). Ten years of career development: A nationwide study of high school students. *Journal of Counseling and Development, 65,* 45–49.

Sears, S. (1982). A definition of career guidance terms: A National Vocational Guidance Association perspective. *Vocational Guidance Quarterly, 31,* 137–143.

Shartle, C. L. (1959). *Occupational information—Its development and application* (3rd ed.). Englewood Cliffs, NJ: Prentice Hall.

Special Task Force to the Secretary of Health, Education and Welfare. (1973). *Work in America.* Cambridge, MA: The MIT Press.

Terkel, S. (1974). *Working—People talk about what they do all day and how they feel about what they do.* New York: Pantheon Books.

Toffler, A. (1980). *The third wave.* New York: Morrow.

Westbrook, B. W. (1978). *Career development needs of adults: How to improve career development programs.* Washington, DC: National Vocational Guidance Association and the Association for Measurement and Evaluation in Guidance.

W. T. Grant Commission on Work, Family, and Citizenship. (1988). *The forgotten half: Pathways to America's youths and young families.* Washington, DC: Author.

Yankelovich, D. (1982). The work ethic is underemployed. *Psychology Today,* May, 5–8.

2

Theories of Career Choice and Development

Fundamental to our concern about career development is the assumption that our society generally hopes to help its members want to work, to acquire the necessary skills for work, and to find satisfaction in the work they do. Thus the individual's objectives include finding work possible, meaningful, and satisfying.

A wide spectrum of clients need help in career planning. Adolescents who are only beginning to contemplate what they would like to do as life work are at one end of that range; retirees who would like to find something worthwhile to do for several hours a week are at the other end. Most adults who encounter occupational change, either voluntarily or involuntarily, fall between these two extremes. In some cases (e.g., the adolescent), the focus is on long-range planning with short-term implications. That is, even though actual entry into the work setting might be a decade away, the plan is relevant in the immediate future because of its effect on selection of school subjects or preparatory programs. Others (e.g., the factory worker whose job suddenly becomes obsolete) face a situation that emphasizes short-term planning with long-term implications. The unexpected disappearance of a job often finds workers unprepared, both economically and psychologically; they often respond by scrambling for any position that is immediately available. This action solves the short-term need for employment but may simply keep the worker in a situation that will repeat itself again and again. More careful planning in the short term—exploring possible retraining programs or placement in occupations that offer greater durability—might offer more desirable long-term dividends. Each career development professional, regardless of setting, must understand individuals, their situations, and the career development process to provide effective help as individuals make decisions. This

19

understanding and assistance is more likely to be potent when the counselors can apply a foundational network of theoretical concepts.

BUILDING A FRAME OF REFERENCE

Every profession, as well as many skilled crafts, requires a thorough grounding in pertinent knowledge—both developed and theoretical. For example, the physician must understand not only biology, chemistry, and physics, but also anatomy, kinetics, optics, and enzymology. Similarly, the automobile mechanic must know basic physics as well as the theories related to the internal combustion engine, aerodynamics, hydraulics, and structures. Whether dealing with the complexities of the human body or the modern automobile, one must have a theoretical basis on which understanding and insight can be developed. To understand either a malfunctioning liver or a broken steering mechanism, it is necessary to know first how these units operate in normal situations, how they interact with related parts, how the behavior of each part can be influenced and modified, what factors or events can produce malfunction, and how to identify basic information in the presenting situation. From this basic theoretical position, the specialist can then analyze the pertinent data, evaluate appropriate alternatives, and anticipate likely results accruing from each choice.

Counselors in training and others concerned with career development are inclined to overlook the significance of this fundamental principle—that one can perform effectively in a professional position only when one has mastered the knowledge and theory on which that profession is based. For the beginner concerned with building skill or competency—*how* to do something—it is easy to overlook the more essential factor—*why* something is done. The *why* is based on the theoretical or factual background that serves as the frame of reference with which the professional approaches each student, client, or patient. Without that frame of reference, one operates only as a technician even though one's skill may be superb.

Shertzer and Stone (1980) identify four functions of theories appropriate to our discussion. They point out, first, that theory summarizes and generalizes a body of information; second, that theory facilitates understanding and explanation of complex phenomena; third, that theory serves as a predictive function by helping one to estimate what will happen under certain conditions; and finally, that theory stimulates further research and fact finding. All these functions are necessary for the professional practitioner.

Unlike the physical and biological sciences, in which centuries of study and research have contributed to a vast reservoir of knowledge and theory, the behavioral sciences are still in a developmental stage. There has been and will be an increasing effort to understand how careers are built. The professional literature of recent decades includes many articles and books that deal with career choice and development. Our lack of psychological and sociological sophistication has prevented development of a definitive description of career development.

Several authors have asked serious questions about the appropriateness of existing career development position papers or theories. For example, Warnath (1975) raises several issues that a counselor must resolve before focusing on theoretical positions. He describes several conditions in the workplace beyond the control of the individual, such as the simplification of many jobs through technological change, the trend toward larger organizational units at the expense of small companies and entrepreneurships, and the subservience of individual needs to those of the employer. Warnath contends that because so many uncontrollable factors interrupt or impede personal career decisions, counselors and theorists should be helping individuals look for alternatives to paid employment as sources of life satisfaction.

Baumgardner (1977) takes a similarly pessimistic view, contending that fully rational career decisions may be neither possible nor desirable. Because technological change is making much work routine, meaningful work is becoming harder to find. He concludes that because counselors cannot change the workplace, they should help clients to recognize that only minimal planning is possible and that uncertainty and conflict will constitute a major portion of their relationship to work. Baumgardner's position has been challenged by Osipow (1977) and Herr (1977). Osipow agrees that many influencing conditions are immune to personal intervention but says that, nevertheless, individuals can make numerous choices that affect their lives. Herr insists that most vocational theories allow for individual variation in choice-making style and that the aim of career counseling is not to eliminate all uncertainty but to reduce unnecessary uncertainty to a minimum.

Both Warnath and Baumgardner criticize existing theoretical positions as inadequate or, at best, incomplete. Earlier, Carkhuff, Alexik, and Anderson (1967) found shortcomings in each of the vocational choice theories they examined. Similarly, Fitzgerald and Crites (1980) emphasize the lack of comprehensiveness; and Collin and Young (1986) stress the lack of agreement on the definitions of *career* and the tendency to use an objective approach to career development. Most writers in the field would admit that similar charges are still appropriate in the 1990s.

The reader may wonder if serious attention to these position papers is justified. Why not wait until research presents us with a complete and usable theory of career development? Osipow (1983) presents an excellent response. He points out that counselors and teachers face clients and students daily, that they work with actual situations in the here and now. They must take actions, make decisions, and develop plans. Unless the professional offers no more than sympathetic listening and good wishes, some basis must be found for action. Thus, even incomplete theory is far better than none at all. Further, Osipow states that theory precedes and accompanies empirical knowledge and orients it while it is developing, thus gradually separating folklore from theory.

This chapter presents a brief summary of several more widely accepted views of career development. Some views are solidly based on extensive research; others are primarily empirically based. The goal is to give the reader a theoretical base that at least partially answers the *why* for every subsequent chapter. The reader need not develop a thorough and comprehensive understanding of each writer's position. Such an understanding properly belongs in advanced classes and seminars, for which this book is not intended.

The reader who desires more detail about the theoretical positions discussed in this chapter has several options. Recent statements by theorists describing the current status of their viewpoints can be found in Brown, Brooks, and Associates (1990). Earlier scholarly analyses can be found in Osipow (1983), Pietrofesa and Splete (1975), Weinrach (1979), and Whiteley and Resnikoff (1972). (Of course, the reader is encouraged to go to the source—the writings of the theorists.) The major thrust of theory proposals began in the 1950s, with modification and refinement continuing to the present.

Efforts to classify the various career development theories are usually disappointing. The positions often have certain degrees of commonality, slightly different interpretations of some basic assumptions, and often contradictory views of other data. In any attempt to group several theorists, there is some danger of misunderstanding. Nevertheless, it is usually easier for a reader to deal with a cluster of somewhat similar concepts than to struggle with the unique aspects of many. The classifications used here are based on convenience and best fit. In this chapter we consider the following:

1. Trait and factor theory
2. Personality-based theories
3. Developmental theories
4. Social learning theory
5. Economic and sociological theories

TRAIT AND FACTOR THEORY

An oversimplified description of trait and factor theory might be "putting the right peg in the right hole." The crucial component of this approach is the joining of the concepts of individual differences and job analysis. Each individual is seen as possessing a unique set of characteristics, or *traits*, many of which can be identified and measured by tests or other instruments. Thus the counselor's task, in the simplest terms, is to identify the pattern of client traits and match this pattern against known requirements for successful job performance. Each of us holds stereotypes of individuals who are perfect fits in their occupation—the strict, demanding Marine drill sergeant; the glib, assertive, controlling used-car salesperson; the aloof, quiet, reserved computer hacker.

The early development of the trait and factor approach is usually attributed to Parsons (1909). He suggested that a wise vocational choice requires a clear understanding of oneself, including one's attitudes, abilities, interests, ambitions, resources, and limitations; a knowledge of the requirements and conditions in various lines of work; and, finally, the application of true reasoning to discover the relation between the two sets of data.

Many individuals played a significant role in the development of this concept. D. G. Paterson and others at the Minnesota Employment Stabilization Research Institute were instrumental in the development of tests to identify individual traits. Some of their products, such as the Minnesota Clerical Test, the Minnesota Paper Form Board Test, the Minnesota Rate of Manipulation Test, and the Minnesota Test of Spatial Relations, are still widely used today. Industrial psychologists such as Frederick Taylor, Elton Mayo, and Frank and Lillian Gilbreth refined job analysis procedures. The United States' participation in World War II accelerated research and application of the trait and factor approach in both civilian and military life. These early activities provided the foundation for much of the current research in career counseling.

During the years immediately following World War II, Jones (1945) and Williamson (1949) were spokesmen for the trait and factor approach. Jones (1970), revised and updated by Stefflre and Stewart, lists five assumptions basic to the trait and factor position:

1. Vocational development is largely a cognitive process in which individuals use reasoning to arrive at decisions.
2. Occupational choice is a single event.
3. There is a single right goal for everyone making decisions about work.
4. A single type of person works in each job.
5. There is an occupational choice available to each individual (p. 182).

If one reads these assumptions narrowly and precisely, they must be rejected as faulty. Many people use very little reasoning in career choice, frequent job changes require multiple decisions, and there is a broad range of individual differences within every occupational group. Loosely interpreted, however, these assumptions are still generally acceptable today. Most would agree that reasoning is a crucial ingredient in sound career development, that an opportunity for occupational choice does occur at least once for most people, that every individual has sufficient assets to be able to perform some work, and that each person's characteristics are compatible with some occupation.

Williamson (1939) suggests that counseling involves six steps: (1) analysis, (2) synthesis, (3) diagnosis, (4) prognosis, (5) counseling, and (6) follow-up. Taken consecutively, these steps require (1) collecting data about the client from all available sources; (2) organizing and summarizing the data to identify client strengths and weaknesses; (3) drawing inferences from the data that help to explain the client and the client's problem; (4) attempting to predict the degree of success the client might encounter; (5) helping the client to understand the different possibilities and their potential likelihood of success; and (6) checking later with the client to ascertain what happened. Williamson also sees career counseling clients as usually presenting one of four types of problems: no choice, uncertain choice, unwise choice, or a discrepancy between interests and aptitudes. The diagnostic step in counseling focuses on identifying which, if any, of these categories apply to the client.

Trait and factor theory has been responsible for at least two major contributions to career counseling. Its emphasis on identifying such individual characteristics as attitude, ability, interest, and personality has influenced the development of many assessment instruments and techniques. Similarly, the emphasis on knowing and understanding occupational possibilities has encouraged the development of occupational information. Probably no one would advocate that test data alone provide a sufficient basis for occupational choice, nor would anyone contend that exhaustive study of occupational information alone provides a basis for choice. Nevertheless, both activities are important parts of more recent theoretical approaches. The reader will see in the following pages that trait and factor theory provides basic components on which most of the other theories rely.

PERSONALITY-BASED THEORIES

In this section, we look at the viewpoints proposed by two widely respected theorists, Anne Roe and John Holland. Both suggest that the appropriateness of an occupation for a specific individual depends on that individual's personality, which in turn is primarily the product of early experience.

Roe's Theory of Career Choice

Roe bases her theory primarily on the writing of Maslow (1954), who proposed a hierarchy of psychological need. This concept suggests that lower-order needs, those essential for maintaining life, are so strong that higher-level needs will not be addressed until lower-order needs are reasonably well satisfied. Further, the hierarchy suggests the order in which this priority occurs. Maslow lists eight basic needs, arranged in order from lowest to highest as follows:

1. Physiological needs
2. Safety needs
3. Need for belongingness and love
4. Need for importance, respect, self-esteem, and independence
5. Need for self-actualization
6. Need for information
7. Need for understanding
8. Need for beauty

Roe's early research as a clinical psychologist focused on the factors that made an impact on occupational choice among groups of artists and scientists. These studies resulted in a number of publications reporting results (Roe, 1949a, 1949b, 1950, 1951a, 1951b, 1951c, 1951d, 1952a, 1952b, 1953). Roe became convinced that there were real differences in the way in which members of these groups deal with people. Further, she concluded that the differences she observed grew out of early childhood experiences. Roe (1957) published a statement describing her theory of the influence of early childhood experience. Roe and Siegelman (1964) revised and elaborated this earlier statement. These two articles provide the best statement of Roe's position on how early childhood experiences reinforce or weaken higher-order needs and thereby influence career development.

The following quotation, from the monograph that Roe prepared with Siegelman (1964, p. 5), provides a brief summary of Roe's revised theoretical position:*

> *Proposition 1*: Genetic inheritance sets limits to the potential development of all characteristics, but specificity of the genetic control and the extent and nature of the limitations are different for different characteristics.
>
> It is probable that the genetic element is more specific and stronger in what we call intellectual abilities and temperament than it is in such other variables as interests and attitudes.
>
> *Proposition 2*: The degrees and avenues of development of inherited characteristics are affected not only by experience unique to the individual, but also by all aspects of the general cultural background and the socioeconomic position of the family.
>
> *Proposition 3*: The pattern of development of interests, attitudes, and other personality variables with relatively little or non-specific genetic control is primarily determined by individual experiences through which involuntary attention becomes channeled in particular directions.
>
> The important word here is involuntary. The elements in any situation to which one gives automatic or effortless attention are keys to the dynamics of behavior. This proposition is clearly related to hypotheses concerning the relations between personality and perception.
>
> a. These directions are determined in the first place by the patterning of early satisfactions and frustrations. This patterning is affected by the relative strengths of various needs and the forms and relative degrees of satisfaction which they receive. The two latter aspects are environmental variables.
>
> b. The modes and degrees of need satisfaction determine which needs will become the strongest motivators. The nature of the motivation may be quite unconscious.
>
> Possible variations are:

*Source: Roe, A. and Siegelman, M., (1964). The origin of interests. *APGA Inquiry Studies*, No. 1. Washington, D.C.: American Personnel and Guidance Association. Copyright AACD. Reprinted with permission. No further reproduction authorized without further permission of AACD.

1. Needs satisfied routinely as they appear do not become unconscious motivators.
2. Needs, for which even minimum satisfaction is rarely achieved, will, if higher order (as used by Maslow, 1954), become expunged or will, if lower order, prevent the appearance of higher order needs and will become dominant and restricting motivators.
3. Needs, the satisfaction of which is delayed but eventually accomplished, will become (unconscious) motivators, depending largely upon the degree of satisfaction felt. Behavior that has received irregular reinforcement is notably difficult to extinguish (C. B. Ferster and B. F. Skinner, 1957).

The degree of satisfaction felt will depend, among other things, upon the strength of the basic need in the given individual, the length of time elapsing between arousal and satisfaction, and the values ascribed to the satisfaction of this need in the immediate environment.

Proposition 4: The eventual pattern of psychic energies, in terms of attention directedness, is the major determinant of interests.

Proposition 5: The intensity of these needs and of their satisfaction (perhaps particularly as they have remained unconscious) and their organization are the major determinants of the degree of motivation that reaches expression in accomplishment.

Roe proposes that the emotional climate in the home—the relationship between parent and child—is one of three types: emotional concentration on the child, avoidance of the child, or acceptance of the child. These emotional climates are thought to have a circular relationship, with each type shading into the others. Each type is also thought to have two subdivisions that shade into each other and into the adjacent subcategory of the other types. The relationship among these types and subdivisions is demonstrated by the figure that Roe first proposed in her 1957 article.

Emotional concentration on the child includes subdivisions in which the parents are overprotecting and overdemanding. Overprotecting parents encourage dependency in the child and limit exploratory behavior. Parents are indulgent, allow special privileges, and show affection. They limit the child's friendships and protect her from other children. They intrude into the child's life and expect to be told everything that she thinks or experiences. Overdemanding parents set high standards for the child and enforce conformity to the standard. They expect the child to be constructively busy, and they select friends for the child in accordance with their own standards. They tell her what to think and feel.

A climate of avoidance has two extremes: rejection and neglect. Emotionally rejecting parents are more extreme in behavior than are demanding parents. Their attitude toward the child is one of coldness, hostility, derogation, and ridicule. They may leave the child alone and may prevent contact with other children. They establish rules to protect themselves from intrusions by the child into their lives. Neglecting parents do not express hostility or ridicule—they simply ignore the child. They provide a minimum of physical care, but no affection. They leave the child to shift for herself but make no effort to avoid her (see Figure 2.1).

The acceptance category includes the subdivisions of casual acceptance and loving acceptance of the child. Casually accepting parents pay some attention to the child and are mildly affectionate. They accept the child as part of the general situation, and are responsive if not occupied with other matters. They are easygoing, make few rules and exert little effort to train the child, and do not enforce rules or training efforts. Loving, accepting parents give the child warmth and affection. They help with things that are important

FIGURE 2.1 *Roe's Circular Model*

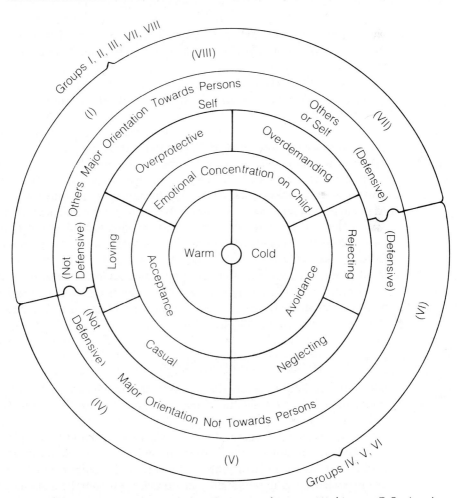

Source: Roe, A. and Siegelman, M. (1964). *Origin of Interest.* Washington, D.C.: American Personnel and Guidance Association. Copyright AACD. Reprinted with permission. No further reproduction authorized without further permission of AACD.

without being monopolistic. They tend to reason rather than punish. They give praise when warranted and try to help with problems. They invite the child's friends to the home, encourage independence, and allow the child to take chances in growing up.

Roe suggests that these six subdivisions produce two types of behavior. The approximate categories of loving, overprotective, and overdemanding produce a major orientation toward people. The areas of casual, neglecting, and rejecting result in a major orientation away from people. Both of these range from defensive to nondefensive. Person-oriented occupational areas include service, business contact, organizations, general culture, and the arts and entertainment. Occupations that are not person oriented are in the categories of technology, the outdoors, and science. Thus an individual whose family provided an accepting or protective environment is likely to seek an occupation working with others in service or business contact or some similar work situation, whereas the individual whose background was casual or neglecting is more likely to move toward a technical or scientific occupation.

Roe's proposal has generated considerable research, only a small part of which has supported her position. Several problems doubtless contribute to the lack of research support. First, an accurate evaluation would necessitate a long-term study following the individual through childhood, adolescence, and well into maturity. Second, many of Roe's proposals are generalizations and, thus, are vague and ambiguous. Third, parental behavior is inconsistent, not only between parents, but even within a specific parent. Fourth, many influences other than the home environment bear on the child.

Another significant aspect of Roe's theory is a classification system for occupations. She proposes that occupations can be divided into eight groups: I—Service, II—Business Contact, III—Organization, IV—Technology, V—Outdoor, VI—Science, VII—General Culture, and VIII—Arts and Entertainment. These are represented by Roman numerals in the outer circle of Figure 2.1. Each of these eight groups is further divided into six levels based on degree of responsibility, capacity, and skill. We discuss this classification system in further detail in Chapter 6.

Holland's Theory of Vocational Choice

Like Roe, Holland developed a theoretical position gradually revealed in a series of published theoretical and research studies (Holland, 1959, 1962, 1963a, 1963b, 1963c, 1963d, 1966a, 1966b, 1968, 1972, 1973, 1985, 1987; Holland & Gottfredson, 1976; Holland & Lutz, 1968; Holland & Nichols, 1964).

Holland assumes that a person expresses personality through the choice of a vocation, and that the devices we usually describe as interest inventories are really personality inventories. Further, he assumes that each person holds stereotypical views of various vocations. These stereotypes have psychological and sociological relevance for the individual, and many of them have demonstrable validity. Holland says that members of a vocation have similar personalities and therefore will respond to many situations and problems in similar ways, thereby creating what he labels a *characteristic interpersonal environment*. Finally, he assumes that vocational satisfaction, stability, and achievement depend on the extent to which the individual's personality and work environment are compatible.

Proceeding from these assumptions, Holland states that we can classify individuals into a limited number of personality types, and that work situations or environments can similarly be classified into a few categories. Personality types include realistic, investigative, artistic, social, enterprising, and conventional.

Realistic people deal with environment in an objective, concrete, and physically manipulative manner. They avoid goals and tasks that demand subjectivity, intellectual or artistic expressions, or social abilities. They are described as masculine, unsociable, emotionally stable, and materialistic. They prefer agricultural, technical, skilled-trade, and engineering vocations. They like activities that involve motor skills, equipment, machines, tools, and structure, such as athletics, scouting, crafts, and shop work.

Investigative people deal with environment by the use of intelligence, manipulating ideas, words, and symbols. They prefer scientific vocations, theoretical tasks, reading, collecting, algebra, foreign languages, and such creative activities as art, music, and sculpture. They avoid social situations and see themselves as unsociable, masculine, persistent, scholarly, and introverted. They achieve primarily in academic and scientific areas and usually do poorly as leaders.

Artistic individuals deal with environment by creating art forms and products. They rely on subjective impressions and fantasies in seeking solutions to problems. They prefer musical, artistic, literary, and dramatic vocations and activities that are creative in nature. They dislike masculine activities and roles such as auto repair and athletics. They see themselves as unsociable, feminine, submissive, introspective, sensitive, impulsive, and flexible.

Social people handle environment by using skills in handling and dealing with others. They are typified by social skills and the need for social interaction. They prefer educational, therapeutic, and religious vocations and such activities as church, government, community services, music, reading, and dramatics. They see themselves as sociable, nurturant, cheerful, conservative, responsible, achieving, and self-accepting.

Enterprising people cope with environment by choices expressing adventurous, dominant, enthusiastic, and impulsive qualities. Characterized as persuasive, verbal, extroverted, self-accepting, self-confident, aggressive, and exhibitionistic, they prefer sales, supervisory, and leadership vocations and activities that satisfy needs for dominance, verbal expression, recognition, and power.

Conventional people deal with the environment by choosing goals and activities that carry social approval. Their approach to problems is stereotyped, correct, and unoriginal. They create a good impression by being neat, sociable, conservative. They prefer clerical and computational tasks, identify with business, and put a high value on economic matters. They see themselves as masculine, shrewd, dominant, controlled, rigid, and stable and have more mathematical than verbal aptitude.

According to Holland, a person can be typed into one of these categories by expressed or demonstrated vocational or educational interests, by employment, or by scores obtained on such instruments as the Kuder Preference Record, the Strong–Campbell Interest Inventory, or the Self-Directed Search. The last, an instrument developed by Holland, consists of occupational titles and activities that can be divided equally among the six type areas. An individual can be expected to demonstrate a primary pattern (highest score) and secondary directions (other high scores). Consistency between primary and secondary areas usually indicates stability, whereas inconsistency usually produces change from one category to another. A consistent pattern not only relates to the individual's vocational direction but also may suggest the level of vocational aspiration or achievement.

Holland proposes that the six personality types are related to personal needs as described by Murray (1938). In other words, the various types are indicative of the needs felt by the individual. Murray was concerned not only with personal needs, but also with environmental presses. Holland accounts for these environmental factors by developing a set of environmental models that he defines as the situation or atmosphere created by the people who dominate a given environment. His environmental models are built on the assumption that their dominant features are created by individuals who control the situation. The environmental conditions of the models reflect the personality attributes of those in control.

The *realistic* environment involves concrete, physical tasks requiring mechanical skill, persistence, and physical movement. Only minimal interpersonal skills are needed. Typical realistic settings include a filling station, a machine shop, a farm, a construction site, and a barber shop.

The *investigative* environment requires the use of abstract and creative abilities rather than personal perceptiveness. Satisfactory performance demands imagination and intelligence; achievement usually requires a considerable time span. Problems encountered may vary in level of difficulty, but they will usually be solved by the application of intellectual skills and tools. The work is with ideas and things rather than with people. Typical settings include a research laboratory; a diagnostic case conference; a library; and a work group of scientists, mathematicians, or research engineers.

The *artistic* environment demands the creative and interpretive use of artistic forms. One must be able to draw on knowledge, intuition, and emotional life in solving typical problems. Information is judged against personal, subjective criteria. The work usually requires intense involvement for prolonged periods. Typical settings include a play rehearsal, a concert hall, a dance studio, a study, a library, and an art or music studio.

The *social* environment demands the ability to interpret and modify human behavior and an interest in caring for and dealing with others. The work requires frequent and prolonged personal relationships. The work hazards are primarily emotional. Typical work situations include school and college classrooms, counseling offices, mental hospitals, churches, educational offices, and recreational centers.

The *enterprising* environment requires verbal skill in directing or persuading other people. The work requires directing, controlling, or planning activities of others, and an interest in others at a more superficial level than in the social environment. Typical settings include a car lot, a real estate office, a political rally, and an advertising agency.

The *conventional* environment involves systematic, concrete, routine processing of verbal and mathematical information. The tasks frequently call for repetitive, short-cycle operations according to an established procedure. Minimal skill in interpersonal relations is required, since the work is mostly with office equipment and materials. Typical settings include a bank, an accounting firm, a post office, a file room, and a business office.

Holland suggests that each model environment is sought by individuals whose personality type is similar to those controlling the environment. It is assumed that they will be comfortable and happy in a compatible environment and uneasy in an environment suited to a different personality type. A congruent person–environment match presumably results in a more stable vocational choice, greater vocational achievement, higher academic achievement, better maintenance of personal stability, and greater satisfaction.

Individuals are rarely pure prototypes of any one of the six personality types. Many people express a predominant similarity to one of the patterns, supplemented by a lesser similarity to another of the groups. Some groups are more compatible, or consistent, with each other than other combinations might be. For example, a high correlation between social and enterprising is thought to be consistent and reflects a sociable, dependent type of person; on the other hand, a low relationship between these two areas appears to be inconsistent.

Further research by Holland has revealed that the interrelationships among the six occupational classes can be demonstrated by arranging the six classes in a hexagonal pattern, as illustrated in Figure 2.2. If connecting lines are drawn from each point to each of the others and intercorrelations are then placed on each connecting line, one finds that the highest correlations tend to be on the shortest lines. Thus the hexagonal pattern places those classes most closely related in nearest proximity and those least related at opposite points. In other words, adjacent corners are most alike; opposite corners (Realistic and Social, Investigative and Enterprising, Artistic and Clerical) are least alike; and the intermediate corners have an intermediate relationship with the base corner (R and A, R and E, and so on).

Holland has developed an occupational classification system based on the model environment construct. Occupations are categorized according to the extent to which they involve activities representing the different points on the hexagon. An occupation that is mainly realistic in nature but involves some investigative activities and a lesser amount of conventional character-

FIGURE 2.2 *Holland's Hexagonal Relationship of Occupational Classes*

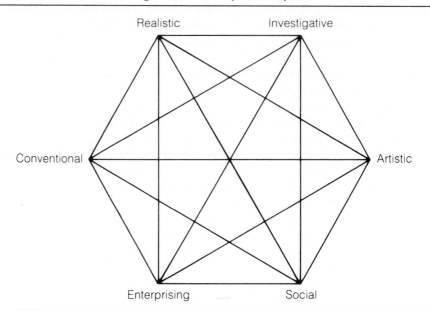

Source: Adapted from J. L. Holland, D. R. Whitney, N. S. Cole, and J. M. Richards, Jr., "An Empirical Occupational Classification Derived from a Theory of Personality and Intended for Practice and Research," *ACT Research Report,* no. 29 (Iowa City: American College Testing Program, 1969). Reprinted with permission.

istics would be labeled as RIC. These letter combinations are referred to as *Holland codes*. This code would be considered consistent because the types are adjacent on the hexagon. A code of RSC, however, would be inconsistent because it involves opposites.

Holland's theory has had great impact on career counseling. Research reporting journals such as the *Journal of Vocational Behavior* and the *Journal of Counseling Psychology* rarely publish an issue that doesn't include at least one article related to Holland's work. An annotated bibliography prepared by Holland and Gottfredson (1990) lists nearly 500 publications relating to Holland's theory.

DEVELOPMENTAL THEORIES: SUPER'S LIFE SPAN APPROACH

Probably no one has written as extensively about career development or influenced the study of the topic as much as Donald Super. His earliest theoretical statements were influenced by researchers in differential psychology, developmental psychology, sociology, and personality theory.

Super's writing on career development is so extensive that even the highly motivated student faces a major challenge in reviewing all of it. The references listed here provide considerable depth but are not intended to be all-inclusive (1951, 1953, 1954, 1955, 1957, 1960, 1961a, 1961b, 1964a, 1964b, 1969, 1972, 1974, 1977, 1980, 1981, 1983, 1984, 1990; Super & Bachrach, 1957; Super et al., 1957; Super & Hall, 1978; Super & Kidd, 1979; Super, Starishevsky, Matlin, & Jordaan, 1963).

Super has often stated that his view is a "segmented" theory consisting of several related propositions, out of which he hopes an integrated theory will ultimately emerge. He has, from time to time, restated these segments, broadening slightly earlier statements and on two occasions adding more segments. His 1953 article presented the initial 10 postulates. He added two more in the 1957 book written with Bachrach. The 1990 article expands the list to 14 propositions. We use this latest listing as the basis for our consideration of Super's life span theory. In this sequence, the original 10 propositions are listed as 1–6 and 9–12, with 7, 8, 13, and 14 being later additions. Super's 1990 statements are listed in italics, followed, where appropriate, with a brief discussion of the proposition.

1. *People differ in their abilities and personalities, needs, values, interests, traits, and self-concepts.* The concept of individual differences is so widely recognized and accepted that no one seriously challenges it. The range of personal characteristics varies widely both within each individual and between individuals. Within each person are traits or abilities so pronounced that often these are used to caricature the individual. At the same time there are areas in which the person is relatively weak or inept. Although most of us are more or less like other people in many traits, the uniqueness of the person is apparent in the individualized combination of strengths and weaknesses.

2. *People are qualified, by virtue of these characteristics, each for a number of occupations.* The range of abilities, personality characteristics, and other traits is so wide that every person has within his or her makeup the requisites for success in many occupations. Research in the field of rehabilitation has demonstrated that even severely disabled individuals have a choice of many occupations in which they can perform satisfactorily. For people without serious physical or emotional impairment, the gamut of possibilities is wide indeed.

   Few occupations require special abilities, skills, or traits in excessive quantity. Just as most athletic activities involve only certain muscles or muscle groups, so too most jobs require only a few specific characteristics. A person, then, can perform successfully in any occupation for which he has the qualifying characteristics. The lack of a certain skill, or its presence in minute quantities, excludes the person from an occupation only if that skill is important in meeting the demands of that occupation.

3. *Each occupation requires a characteristic pattern of abilities and personality traits—with tolerances wide enough to allow both some variety of occupations for each individual and some variety of individuals in each occupation.* For each ability or trait required in the performance of a particular occupation, one might expect to find a modal quantity that best fits the nature of the work. On either side of this amount, however, is a band or range of this characteristic that will meet satisfactorily the demands of the work. For example, picture an extremely simple task that requires, hypothetically, only a single characteristic. In studying this task, we might ascertain the quantity of this trait that would best meet the requirements of the job. We would also expect that a person could perform satisfactorily even though she possessed less than the ideal amount of the trait, as long as she surpassed the minimum demanded by the job. On the other hand, we could also expect satisfactory performance even if the worker possessed more of the trait than was required for optimum performance.

Since the patterns of abilities required in various occupations will rarely be unique, one can expect to find considerable overlap. Thus there will be a number of occupations in which a particular distribution of assets can result in satisfactory performance, just as there will be a number of patterns of ability that can result in satisfactory performance in a given occupation.

4. *Vocational preferences and competencies, the situations in which people live and work, and, hence, their self-concepts change with time and experience, although self-concepts, as products of social learning, are increasingly stable from late adolescence until late maturity, providing some continuity in choice and adjustment.* As individuals exercise certain skills or proficiencies, they may increase or expand them to a higher level. As these higher-level skills develop, workers may be drawn to occupational outlets that provide opportunities to use them. Similarly, as workers perform successfully in given work situations, they may realize that there are more rewarding or more responsible positions in which participation would offer even more satisfaction. On the other hand, there may be work situations that are so demanding on workers that they may look for positions that do not tax the pattern of abilities so heavily.

Since the pattern of skills and preferences, as well as the work situation, undergoes constant change, it is likely that the job that the worker once found entirely satisfactory is no longer viewed in that way. As the individual's self-concept changes, she may also find that the once satisfactory job is no longer so. Either of these changes may result in the worker seeking a new work situation or attempting to adjust the position held in some way so it will again be comfortable and satisfying. Since neither the worker nor the job is static, either change or adjustment is necessary to keep the two in balance.

Super (1984) emphasizes that self-concept should be defined broadly to include not only an internalized personal view of self, but also the individual's view of the situation or condition in which he exists. This is a significant factor because the situation surrounding the individual always bears on the person's behavior and self-understanding. Super suggests that *personal-construct* might be a more useful term than *self-concept* because it permits this broader definition.

5. *This process of change may be summed up in a series of life stages (a "maxicycle") characterized as a sequence of growth, exploration, establishment, maintenance, and decline, and these stages may in turn be subdivided into (a) the fantasy, tentative, and realistic phases of the exploratory stage and (b) the trial and stable phases of the establishment stage. A small (mini) cycle takes place in transitions from one stage to the next or each time an individual is destabilized by a reduction in force, changes in type of personnel needs, illness or injury, or other socioeconomic or personal events. Such unstable or multiple-trial careers involve new growth, reexploration, and reestablishment (recycling).*

The *growth* stage refers to physical and psychological growth. During this time the individual forms attitudes and behavior mechanisms that will be important components of the self-concept for much of life. Simultaneously, experiences are providing a background of knowledge of the world of work that ultimately will be used in tentative choices and in final selections.

The *exploratory* stage begins with the individual's awareness that an occupation will be an aspect of life. During the early or fantasy phase of this stage, the expressed choices are frequently unrealistic and often closely related to the play life of the individual. Examples can be seen in young children's choices of such careers as cowboy, movie star, pilot, and astronaut. These choices are nebulous and temporary and usually have little, if any, long-term significance for the individual. Some adolescents and even some adults, of course, have not advanced beyond the fantasy phase. Often, the understanding of themselves or of the world of work needed to make more effective choices is either missing or is disregarded.

In the tentative phase of the exploratory stage, the individual has narrowed choice to a few possibilities. Because of uncertainty about ability, availability of training, or employment opportunity, the list may contain choices that will later disappear. The final phase of the exploratory stage, still prior to actual entrance into the world of work, narrows the list to those occupations that the individual feels are within reach and provide the opportunities she feels are most important.

The *establishment* stage, as the name implies, relates to early encounters within actual work experiences. During this period the individual, at first perhaps by trial and error, attempts to ascertain whether choices and decisions made during the exploratory period have validity. Some of this period is simply tryout. The individual may accept a job with the definite feeling that he will change jobs if this one does not fit. As he gains experience and proficiency, the individual becomes stabilized; that is, aspects of this occupation are brought into the self-concept and the occupation is accepted as one that offers the best chance to obtain those satisfactions that are important.

During the *maintenance* stage the individual attempts to continue or improve the occupational situation. Since both the occupation and the individual's self-concept have some fluidity, this involves a continual process of change or adjustment. Essentially the person is concerned with continuing the satisfying parts of the work situation and revising or changing those unpleasant aspects that are annoying but not so repulsive that they drive the individual from the field.

The *decline* stage includes the preretirement period, during which the individual's emphasis in work is focused on keeping the job and meeting the minimum standards of output. The worker is now more concerned with retaining the position than with enhancing it. This period terminates with the individual's withdrawal from the world of work.

Research by Levinson, Darrow, Klein, Levinson, and McKee (1978) and by Gould (1978) on postadolescent male development appears to support Super's life stages approach. Both report patterns of adult male development consisting of relatively stable, structure-building periods separated by transitional, structure-changing periods. The Levinson group found that their subjects made occupational choices between ages 17 and 29 and often made different choices later. This age period is somewhat later than Super theorized. They also report that the preparatory phase of occupational development is completed in the 28–33 age period, also later than previously assumed. The discrepancy in ages may be because data for the Levinson subjects were obtained by interviewing adult men who were recalling earlier events in their lives.

Murphy and Burck (1976), using Super's life stages concept, suggest that the increasing frequency of midlife career changes may indicate that an additional stage, the *renewal stage*, be inserted between the establishment stage and the maintenance stage. During this period, approximately between ages 35 and 45, the individual reconsiders earlier goals and plans, and then either rededicates self to pursuing those goals or decides to move in other directions with a midlife career change.

6. *The nature of the career pattern—that is, the occupational level attained and the sequence, frequency, and duration of trial and stable jobs—is determined by the individual's parental socioeconomic level, mental ability, education, skills, personality characteristics (needs, values, interests, traits, and self-concepts), and career maturity and by the opportunities to which he or she is exposed.*

All factors in the individual's experiential background contribute to attitudes and behavior. Some factors obviously contribute more significantly than others. The socioeconomic level of the individual's parents may be one of these, since the individual's early contact with the world of work is largely brought about through parents, family, and friends. Hearing parents and their friends discuss experiences at work; observing the impact of occupational success, failure, or frustration within the family; and obtaining or losing chances at education, travel, or other experiences because of family circumstances all greatly influence the individual's later work history. The individual's mental ability is an important factor in academic success which will open or close doors to many occupations. Ability to deal with others is important in most work situations. "Being in the right place at the right time" or "getting the breaks" is also important, since the individual must first have an opportunity to demonstrate competency before becoming established in a job.

We often think that, in the Horatio Alger tradition, anyone can attain any goal if she only tries hard enough. In reality, however, factors over which we often have no control set limits that can be surpassed or extended only by Herculean effort, if at all.

7. *Success in coping with the demands of the environment and of the organism in that context at any given life-career stage depends on the readiness of the individual to cope with these demands (that is, on his or her career maturity).* Super identifies *career maturity* as a group of physical, psychological, and social characteristics that represent the individual's readiness and ability to deal with the developmental problems and challenges that face him. These personal aspects have both emotional and intellectual components that produce the individual's response to the situation. When the person's maturity is equal to the problem, he probably resolves it with minimal difficulty or concern; when the maturity is not sufficient for the task, inadequate responses of procrastination, ineptness, or failure are likely to occur.

8. *Career maturity is a hypothetical construct. Its operational definition is perhaps as difficult to formulate as is that of intelligence, but its history is much briefer and its achievements even less definite.* Super's early research (e.g., the 25-year longitudinal study called the Career Pattern Study) included attention to the concept of maturity as related to career or vocational development problems. He and co-workers searched for ways to define and assess this concept. Out of these efforts have emerged Super's Career Development Inventory and Crites's Career Maturity Inventory.

9. *Development through the life stages can be guided partly by facilitating the maturing of abilities and interests and partly by aiding in reality testing and in the development of self-concepts.* Individuals can be helped to move toward a satisfying vocational choice in two ways:

(1) by helping them to develop abilities and interests and (2) by helping them to acquire an understanding of their strengths and weaknesses so they can make satisfying choices.

Both aspects of this postulate emphasize the role of the school and its guidance program in assisting the individual to maximize development as a person. The teacher, with frequent contacts with a young person, has the best opportunity to observe latent or underdeveloped abilities in the classroom. The teacher has numerous chances to challenge the individual to push toward higher, but nevertheless reachable, goals. The counselor, similarly, through data obtained from tests or other guidance techniques may encounter undeveloped potential. Out-of-school adults may need similar types of help.

One of the authors of this book has occasionally found three questions useful in the counseling relationship in providing some indication of the extent to which the counselee has already engaged in some reality testing of vocational aspirations. The first question—"What would you like to be if you could do anything you wanted?"—frequently evokes a fantasy response which the individual usually soon labels as such. The second question—"What do you expect to be 10 years from now?"—often elicits a reply that still includes considerable fantasy, but may also include a sizable display of self-evaluation and insight. The third question—"What is the least you would settle for, 10 years from now?"—requires the client to discard fantasy entirely and to cope with strengths, weaknesses, and potential as she sees them.

10. *The process of career development is essentially that of developing and implementing occupational self-concepts. It is a synthesizing and compromising process in which the self-concept is a product of the interaction of inherited aptitudes, physical makeup, opportunity to observe and play various roles, and evaluations of the extent to which the results of role playing meet the approval of superiors and fellows (interactive learning).*

As the individual develops and matures, she acquires a mental picture of self—a self-concept. Since in U.S. culture one's position in the world of work is important, this becomes a major influence on the individual's self-concept. During the educational period, before actual entrance into work, one's anticipated occupational role plays a part in the development of self-concept. Each person attempts to maintain or enhance a favorable self-concept and thus is led toward those activities that will permit her to keep or improve the self-image she would like to have. As the inner drive toward this ideal self-concept pushes the individual strongly, she encounters restricting factors, which may come from personal limitations or from the external environment. These factors interfere with attainment of the ideal self-concept and result in the individual compromising or accepting somewhat less than the ideal.

Also influential is the extent to which individuals can gain insight into a variety of occupations and see to what extent each occupation permits them to be the kind of person they want to be in their own eyes and in the eyes of family, teachers, peer group, and others whose opinions they value.

Super's (1980) description of a life-career rainbow emphasizes the different roles played by each individual during her lifetime and the influence these roles have on lifestyle and career. Typical roles for most people include child, student, citizen, worker, spouse, homemaker, parent, and pensioner. These roles emphasize the lifelong aspect of career development.

11. *The process of synthesis of or compromise between individual and social factors, between self-concepts and reality, is one of role playing and of learning from feedback, whether the role is played in fantasy, in the counseling interview, or in such real-life activities as classes, clubs, part-time work, and entry jobs.*

Modifications of the vocational aspects of the self-concept may occur in many ways. Since the world of work is so complex and entrance requirements in many areas so difficult, it is not feasible to experiment with actual participation in more than a few actual work situations. This leaves the necessity of matching the self-concept and its demands against what occupations have to offer in a situation that is essentially abstract. This may be a daydream or reverie, it may involve seeking professional assistance through counseling, or it may mean seeking related experiences that will help the individual evaluate the suitability of the occupation in terms of self-concept.

12. *Work satisfactions and life satisfactions depend on the extent to which the individual finds adequate outlets for abilities, needs, values, interests, personality traits, and self-concepts. They depend on establishment in a type of work, a work situation, and a way of life in which one can play the kind of role that growth and exploratory experiences have led one to consider congenial and appropriate.*

The individual who finds pleasure and satisfaction in work does so because the position held permits the use of characteristics and values in a way that is seen as important. In other words, the experiences encountered in work are comparable with the mental image held of self—they give sufficient opportunity to be the kind of person one pictures oneself to be.

If the work performed does not provide the possibility to be the type of person one pictures oneself to be, one becomes discontented. This dissatisfaction will usually cause a person to look for a work situation where the possibility to play the desired role seems likelier.

13. *The degree of satisfaction people attain from work is proportional to the degree to which they have been able to implement self-concepts.* The relationship of the work situation to the individual's role must be thought of in the broad sense. The professions and higher managerial positions probably provide the greatest opportunities, as viewed by

most people, for the intrinsic satisfactions that come from work itself. But many individuals gain great satisfaction from work that to some appears boring and monotonous. Other workers find satisfaction in jobs that they too may consider routine and unchallenging but that provide them the chance to be the kind of people they want to be, to do the things they want to do, and to think of themselves as they wish to think. Super proposes that the amount of satisfaction is directly related to the extent the job fits the self-concept. Super and Kidd (1979) explore career change and modification in adults, recognizing the increase in midlife career change. They suggest that *career adaptability* may be an appropriate term to identify the individual's ability to face, pursue, or accept changing career roles.

14. *Work and occupation provide a focus for personality organization for most men and women, although for some persons this focus is peripheral, incidental, or even nonexistent. Then other foci, such as leisure activities and homemaking, may be central. (Social traditions, such as gender-role stereotyping and modeling, racial and ethnic biases, and the opportunity structure, as well as individual differences, are important determinants of preferences for such roles as worker, student, leisurite, homemaker, and citizen.)*

Essentially, this proposition says that most adults are what they do—the individual is a reflection of that person's job or major role. To a large degree this proposition relates to the Life-Career Rainbow proposed by Super (1980) as representative of life-span, life-space career development. As indicated in this proposition, Super believes that the various segments of his theory apply to both men and women, if modified slightly to provide for women's childbearing role.

In addition to the numerous publications of Super and his colleagues, two other teams made significant contributions to the early formation of the developmental approach to career theory. Ginzberg, Ginsburg, Axelrad, and Herma (1951) reported an early study of a small group of boys, ages 11 to 23, from high socioeconomic backgrounds compared with a contrasting group of boys whose fathers were unskilled or semiskilled workers, and a second group consisting of women students in an elite women's college. They identified four variables that bear on vocational choice—a reality factor, the educational process, emotional factors, and personal values. Like Super, the group was obviously influenced by the life stages concept of Buehler (1933). They envisioned three primary periods that they called fantasy, tentative, and realistic. Ginzberg (1972) later restated their earlier position to include three modifications: (1) The decision-making process is parallel to the individual's work life; (2) decisions are not always irreversible and can be delayed or even modified; and (3) the worker continually tries to *optimize* the work situation, seeking changes and adjustments that improve the fit between worker and job.

Tiedeman (1961), Tiedeman and O'Hara (1963), Tiedeman and Miller–Tiedeman (1984), and Miller–Tiedeman and Tiedeman (1990) present the work of the second group. Early work on this approach was done by Tiedeman and O'Hara. After the untimely death of O'Hara, others have worked with Tiedeman in refining the view. Tiedeman suggests that career development is a process of organizing an identification with work through the interaction of one's personality with society. Decision is seen as crucial in vocational development. Each decision, as well as the total lifetime process, includes two periods or aspects, each of which has several substages. The major periods are anticipation and implementation. The anticipation period is subdivided into exploration, crystallization, choice, and specification. The period of implementation and adjustment is divided into induction, transition, and maintenance. Vocational development is seen as the sum of a complex series of decisions made over considerable time, with each previous decision having an impact on later choices and each experience affecting subsequent choices as well.

SOCIAL LEARNING THEORY

Krumboltz (1979), Krumboltz, Mitchell, and Jones (1976, 1978), and Mitchell and Krumboltz (1984, 1990) describe a social learning theory of career selection based on the behavioral theory of Bandura (1977) and others, emphasizing reinforcement theory.

Krumboltz identifies four kinds of factors that influence career decision making:

1. *Genetic endowment and special abilities.* Krumboltz recognizes that certain inherited characteristics can be restrictive influences on the individual, as Tiedeman similarly identifies biological constitution. Some examples are race, gender, and physical appearance. There are other factors for which inheritance, at least in part, may set limits, including various special abilities such as intelligence, musical and artistic ability, and physical coordination.

2. *Environmental conditions and events.* This factor includes those influences that may lie outside the control of anyone but that bear on the individual through the environment in which the individual exists. Some influences may be synthetic in the broadest sense; others may be due to natural forces. These human or natural elements may cause events to occur that also bear on the individual in the educational and career decision process. Examples of influences of this type include the existence of job and training opportunities, social policies and procedures for selecting trainees or workers, rate of return for various occupations, labor and union laws and regulations, physical events such as earthquakes and floods, the existence of natural resources, technologi-

cal developments, changes in social organization, family training experiences and resources, educational systems, and neighborhood and community influences.

3. *Learning experiences.* All previous learning experiences influence the individual's educational and career decision making. Recognizing the extreme complexity of the learning process, Krumboltz identifies only two types of learning as examples: instrumental learning experiences and associative learning experiences. He describes *instrumental learning experiences* as those situations in which the individual acts on the environment to produce certain consequences. *Associative learning experiences* are described as situations in which the individual learns by reacting to external stimuli, by observing real or fictitious models, or by pairing two events in time or location.

4. *Task approach skills.* The skills that the individual applies to each new task or problem are called *task approach skills.* Examples of these include performance standards and values; work habits; and such perceptual and cognitive processes as attending, selecting, symbolic rehearsing, coding, and so on. The application of these skills affects the outcome of each task or problem and in turn is modified by the results.

Krumboltz sees the individual as constantly encountering learning experiences, each of which is followed by rewards or punishments that in turn produce the uniqueness of the individual. This continuous interaction with learning experiences produces three types of consequences, which Krumboltz labels as self-observation generalizations, task approach skills, and actions. A *self-observation generalization* is an overt or covert self-statement that evaluates one's own actual or vicarious performance in relation to learned standards. The generalization may or may not be accurate, just as one's self-concept may or may not coincide with the concept others have of an individual. *Task approach skills* are thought to be efforts by the person to project into the future self-observation generalizations to make predictions about future events. They include work habits, mental sets, perceptual and thought processes, performance standards and values, and the like. *Actions* are implementations of behavior such as applying for a job or changing major field of study. The behavior produces certain consequences that affect future behavior.

In summary, an individual is born into the world with certain genetic characteristics: race, gender, physique, and special abilities or disabilities. As time passes, the individual encounters environmental, economic, social, and cultural events and conditions. The individual learns from these encounters, building self-observations and task approach skills that are applied to new events and encounters. The successes and failures that accrue in these encounters influence the individual in choosing courses of action in subsequent learning experiences, increasing the likelihood of making choices similar to previous ones that led to success and of avoiding choices similar to those that led to failure. The process is complicated by aspects of instability, since the individual changes as a result of the continuous series of learning experiences, and the situation also changes because environmental, cultural, and social conditions are dynamic.

ECONOMIC AND SOCIOLOGICAL THEORIES

The theories considered thus far are basically psychological—they assume that individuals exert control over their lives, although most theorists would agree that the degree of self-control is variable from person to person and situation to situation. Most also would affirm that one, if not the, basic goal of career counselors is to increase that degree of self-direction.

Researchers in related fields such as economics and sociology, however, are often inclined to use more of a conglomerate view, seeing relationships in terms of large groups such as society, race, gender, and so forth. This broad-brush approach often puts greater emphasis on factors that lie outside the control of the individual or, sometimes, of any individual. Warnath (1975) suggests that powerful external forces are increasing and exerting greater influence than in the past.

Economists often identify the laws of supply and demand (sometimes referred to as the freedom of the marketplace) as powerful forces in determining job opportunities and worker availability. Assuming that special skills or training, prior experience, licensure, and other qualifying factors are not operative, this concept proposes that employers will offer only enough pay to attract the required number of workers, and will continue to increase the pay offered until all positions are filled. As the pay escalates, more workers are attracted to the position than are required to fill existing vacancies. This surplus of workers leads the employer to reduce the pay being offered. If pay is reduced too far, workers look elsewhere for better opportunities and, in time, the employer again faces a shortage of workers. This dilemma is solved by raising the pay offered, and the cycle repeats itself.

Many work situations are sensitive to variations in economic conditions, and slight changes in either direction can influence employment. At the same time, it is important to remember that many factors exist that impede the operation of a free market; supply–demand factors are usually moderated by these other conditions. These moderating factors, including social custom as well as legislation or governmental regulation, may have developed to protect the public, the workers, the employers, or others.

Hotchkiss and Borow (1990), reviewing sociological research related to career development, report an increasing emphasis on (1) social structure factors that influence career choices, (2) status attainment research, and (3) the sociology of labor markets. The latter emphasis draws on the areas of economics and sociology.

Sociological research, such as Caplow's early study (1954), may focus on the impact of work on the life of the individual or, as with Hall (1983), may concentrate on factors such as social status or income. Often the emphasis is on how various social influences bear on the work activities of individuals. Again, one sees greater emphasis on the influence of chance—"being in the right place at the right time." Hotchkiss and Borow (1984) identify four ways in which social institutions influence career activity: (1) socializing the individual as a member of the work force, (2) determining interpersonal affiliations, (3) permitting pursuit of certain material and social lifestyles, and (4) giving direction to the career pattern via mobility and advancement.

Lipsett (1962) identifies several social factors that influence career development, such as social-class membership, home influences, school, community, pressure groups, and role perception. Borow (1964) mentions the influence of family and social class and, to a lesser extent, school and community in determining the social and psychological motives on which the individual's behavior is based. Blau and Duncan (1967) developed a formal model of occupational attainment in which father's education and father's occupation were important determinants of the individual's education, which in turn was a major determinant of the individual's occupation. Later work has led to the development of a scale of occupational prestige. A significant imponderable arises when one considers the clash between so-called traditional social values and the pressures created by changing social conditions, such as increases in the number of women at work and serving as heads of household; greater efforts to eliminate barriers based on race, ethnic group, gender, age, and so forth; and the increasing impact of technological change on the workplace.

THEORIES OF DECISION MAKING

Each theory discussed in this chapter incorporates decision making as an important aspect of career choice and career development. However, with the exception of Krumboltz's social learning theory, most give little attention to how individuals make those decisions. The purpose of this section is to alert the reader to the importance of this process, to review briefly a few of the major approaches to understanding the decision-making process, and to direct the reader to more extended discussions of the topic.

Jepsen and Dilley (1974) and Wright (1984) provide discussions of several relevant models useful to the reader. Jepsen and Dilley separate the models they discuss into two groups: *prescriptive models* that describe how decisions ought to be made, and *descriptive models* that describe how decisions are actually made. They also state that the process involves a decision maker and a situation in which two or more alternatives exist that carry potential outcomes of variable significance to the decision maker. The essence of the process is for the decision maker to identify and assign relative values to the alternatives and their consequences so she can maximize the outcome. We examine briefly two models of each type.

Mitchell (1975) modifies a model proposed earlier by Restle (1961) so it can be applied to the career decision-making process. Restle states that the decision maker matches the confronting situation to his view of an ideal one and then chooses the alternative that most closely resembles that ideal situation. Mitchell identifies four elements of preferences held by the décision maker:

1. *Absolute constraints* are the factors that must be present or absent for the alternative to be viable.
2. *Negative characteristics* are undesirable aspects.
3. *Positive characteristics* are desirable aspects.
4. *Neutral characteristics* are aspects present but irrelevant to the choice to be made.

The decision maker can use these elements in a variety of ways, such as comparing only positive characteristics; considering alternatives singly; matching positive versus negative characteristics; rejecting an alternative because of negative characteristics; and other combinations.

Tversky (1972) proposes a model that he names *elimination by aspects*. This approach focuses on all choices simultaneously, with each choice having a variety of characteristics. In this model, the characteristic (e.g., job security) for each alternative is matched, and those that fail to meet the decision maker's minimum standard are eliminated.

Examples of descriptive models include Vroom's expectancy model and Janis and Mann's conflict model. Vroom (1964) uses two key terms in developing his model: *valence*, which can be equated with preference, and *expectancies*, which are comparable to the belief that choices can be realized. Both aspects are crucial to each decision and interact in the process. The force or pressure to make a particular choice is directly related to the sum of the valences of all outcomes and the strength of the expectancies that the choice will result in the attainment of desired outcomes.

Janis and Mann (1977) assume that conflict is caused whenever a person is faced with making a decision, thus producing stress and uncertainty. The process starts when the decision maker becomes aware of a threat that she feels compelled to consider (e.g., the sounding of a fire alarm). The process continues through several steps that can be illustrated by a series of questions that, when answered positively, require action leading to the next question and when answered negatively interrupt the decision-making process. The questions are as follows:

1. Are there risks involved if I do not change?
2. Are the risks serious if I do not change?
3. Can I hope to find a viable solution to the problem?
4. Is there sufficient time to search for viable alternatives?

The individual who answers the final question affirmatively is considered to be in a state of vigilance, where attention can be given to acquiring information about alternatives and to weighing the advantages and disadvantages of each. This is considered to be the most favorable situation for reaching an appropriate decision.

The career counselor faces a serious dilemma in helping clients in the decision-making process. At present, none of the models described has been incorporated into the prevalent theories. It appears likely that one model may fit some clients and some situations better and another may be more satisfactory in different circumstances. The irony is that the counselor must apply a model in deciding which model is likely to be most useful to this client at this time.

Some of the major difficulties for the counselor focus on the inability to be certain of judgments of client characteristics (e.g., one cannot be certain of the client's motivation, clarity of self-understanding, and precision of values ascribed to various factors). It is often impossible to be sure that the client has incorporated his most important values and has weighted them properly. Nevertheless, the client must be helped and the counselor must choose a model or combination of models that appears most viable.

THEORIES FOR SPECIFIC GROUPS

It seems entirely natural to raise questions relative to the appropriateness of the various career development theories for groups such as women and ethnic groups. After all, most of the major theories were first enunciated in the 1950s and 1960s. At that time, the U.S. labor force was overwhelmingly male and Caucasian. During the last two decades there has been a large influx of both women and ethnic groups into the work force, with neither group expecting to limit participation to simple, unskilled, temporary positions, therefore, the question must be confronted.

To date, research on women and career choice has been sketchy and mostly focused toward their participation in work and family activities. Examples of this research include studies by Rand and Miller (1972) and Richardson (1981). Other research has looked for, and usually found, gender differences in both career aspirations and career choices. Examples of this research include studies by Astin and Myint (1971), Brown (1982), Farmer (1976), and O'Leary (1977). Excellent discussions of the general problem of relating the prevalent theories to women's career choice and development can be found in Astin (1984), Fitzgerald and Crites (1980), and Hackett and Betz (1981). Brooks (1990) provides a succinct review of these and other theories focusing on women's career choice.

Astin (1984) emphasizes four constructs in her need-based socio-psychological approach. She stresses motivation, expectations, sex-role socialization, and opportunity structure. Motivation is seen as essentially similar in men and women, based on primary needs of survival, pleasure, and contribution. Because sex-role socialization and opportunities differ between genders, she envisions different expectations for women.

Gottfredson (1981) proposes a theory of occupational aspiration that emphasizes developmental factors and accounts for gender differences because of differing influences in four childhood developmental stages. She sees individuals viewing occupations according to gender, level of work, and field of work. The suitability of an occupation is largely determined by one's self-concept, which has been heavily influenced by experiences in the four developmental stages ranging from approximately age 3 to the mid-teens.

Hackett and Betz (1981) present a self-efficacy theory based largely on earlier views of Bandura. Briefly stated, they suggest that women have lower career-related efficacy expectations than do men, mainly because the gender-role socialization process has prevented women from access to information that would help them build higher expectations.

Research on ethnic minority groups and career development has been even more limited. A few studies have appeared since the 1970s, with most involving African Americans and a few concerning Asian Americans, Hispanics, and Native Americans. Examples of such research can be seen in Smith (1975, 1976, 1977), Scott and Anadon (1980), and Sue (1975). Discussion of the broader topic of specific groups, especially ethnic minorities, can be found in Osipow (1975) and Smith (1983).

Some writers note that many of the research studies do reveal group differences in career choices and developmental patterns. Often they conclude that the variations can be credited to divergences in psychological and sociological factors. Astin (1984) identifies differences in career behavior between men and women as caused by internal factors such as self-concept, achievement motivation, values, attitudes, and interests or external factors such as socioeconomic background, education, and the career counseling received.

Some writers propose that the differences between white male American workers and both women and ethnic minority workers are great enough to justify and require separate career development theories. To date, little has been done to propose such a theoretical position. Before such a step can be taken, much more research must be completed, reported, and evaluated.

A brief review of the theoretical positions we have considered in this chapter raises some question about the validity of narrowly-based theories for specific groups. Roe, for example, bases her theory largely on psychological need, which she considers to be an outgrowth of social and psychological factors in the parental environment that surrounds the individual during the early developmental years. Holland uses personality, personal need, and environmental press as the significant motivators in career choice. Super's approach also is essentially nongender oriented and focuses on self-concept and role-play experiences as crucial factors in choices. Krumboltz builds directly on social learning and uses genetic endowment, environmental conditions, and learning as contributing factors. Each of these theories is essentially nongender oriented. If we add individual differences to the picture, we can easily conclude that differences within the white male group may be as great for most factors as the intergroup differences. If the counselor is fully cognizant of the uniqueness of every individual, attention will be paid consistently to those psychological and sociological factors that are central to each of the theories. This approach makes gender, ethnicity, and all other individual aspects simply important personal characteristics to be considered in the counseling process.

REFERENCES

Astin, H. S. (1984). The meaning of work in women's lives: A sociopsychological model of career choice and work behavior. *Counseling Psychologist, 12,* 117–126.

Astin, H. S., & Myint, T. (1971). Career development of young women during the post-high school years. *Journal of Counseling Psychology, 18,* 369–393.

Bandura, A. (1977). *Social learning theory.* Englewood Cliffs, NJ: Prentice Hall.

Baumgardner, S. R. (1977). Vocational planning: The great swindle. *Personnel and Guidance Journal, 56,* 17–22.

Blau, P. M., & Duncan, O. D. (1967). *The American occupational structure.* New York: Wiley.

Borow, H. (Ed.). (1964). *Man in a world at work.* Boston: Houghton Mifflin.

Brooks, L. (1990). Recent developments in theory building. In D. Brown, L. Brooks, & Associates, (Eds.), *Career choice and development* (2nd ed.). San Francisco: Jossey-Bass.

Brown, D., Brooks, L., & Associates. (1990). *Career choice and development* (2nd ed.). San Francisco: Jossey-Bass.

Brown, M. (1982). Career plans of college women: Patterns and influences. In P. J. Perun (Ed.), *The undergraduate woman: Issues in educational equity.* Lexington, MA: Lexington Books.

Buehler, C. (1933). *Der menschliche lebenslaut als psychologisches problem.* Leipzig: Hirzel.

Caplow, T. (1954). *The sociology of work.* Minneapolis, MN: University of Minnesota Press.

Carkhuff, R. R., Alexik, M., & Anderson, S. (1967). Do we have a theory of vocational choice? *Personnel and Guidance Journal, 46,* 335–345.

Collin, A., & Young, R. A. (1986). New directions for theories of career. *Human Relations, 39,* 837–853.

Farmer, H. S. (1976). What inhibits achievement and career motivation in women? *The Counseling Psychologist, 6,* 12–14.

Ferster, C. B., & Skinner, B. F. (1957). *Schedules of reinforcement.* New York: Appleton-Century-Crofts.

Fitzgerald, L. F., & Crites, J. O. (1980). Toward a career psychology of women: What do we know? What do we need to know? *Journal of Counseling Psychology, 27,* 44–62.

Ginzberg, E. (1972). Toward a theory of occupational choice: A restatement. *Vocational Guidance Quarterly, 20,* 169–176.

Ginzberg, E., Ginsburg, S. W., Axelrad, S., & Herma, J. L. (1951). *Occupational choice: An approach to a general theory.* New York: Columbia University Press.

Gottfredson, L.S. (1981). Circumscription and compromise: A developmental theory of occupational aspirations. *Journal of Counseling Psychology Monograph, 28,* 545–579.

Gould, R. L. (1978). *Transformations: Growth and change in adult life.* New York: Simon & Schuster.

Hackett, G., & Betz, N. E. (1981). A self-efficacy approach to the career development of women. *Journal of Vocational Behavior, 18,* 326–339.

Hall, R. H. (1983). Theoretical trends in the sociology of occupations. *Sociological Quarterly, 24,* 5–23.

Herr, E. L. (1977). Vocational planning: An alternative view. *Personnel and Guidance Journal, 56,* 25–27.

Holland, J. L. (1959). A theory of vocational choice. *Journal of Counseling Psychology, 6,* 35–45.

Holland, J. L. (1962). Some explorations of a theory of vocational choice: I. One- and two-year longitudinal studies. *Psychological Monographs, 76,* (26, Whole No. 545).

Holland, J. L. (1963a). Explorations of a theory of vocational choice and achievement: II A four-year prediction study. *Psychological Reports, 12,* 547–594.

Holland, J. L. (1963b). A theory of vocational choice: Part I. Vocational images and choice. *Vocational Guidance Quarterly, 11,* 232–239.

Holland, J. L. (1963c). A theory of vocational choice: Part II. Self descriptions and vocational preferences. *Vocational Guidance Quarterly, 12,* 17–24.

Holland, J. L. (1963d). A theory of vocational choice: Part IV. Vocational daydreams. *Vocational Guidance Quarterly, 12,* 93–97.

Holland, J. L. (1966a). A psychological classification scheme for vocations and major fields. *Journal of Counseling Psychology, 13,* 278–288.

Holland, J. L. (1966b). *The psychology of vocational choice.* Waltham, MA: Blaisdell.

Holland, J. L. (1968). Explorations of a theory of vocational choice: Part VI. A longitudinal study using a sample of typical college students. *Journal of Applied Psychology, 52* (Monograph Suppl.).

Holland, J. L. (1972). The present status of a theory of vocational choice. In J. M. Whiteley & A. Resnikoff (Eds.), *Perspectives on vocational development.* Washington, DC: American Personnel and Guidance Association.

Holland, J. L. (1973). *Making vocational choices: A theory of careers.* Englewood Cliffs, NJ: Prentice Hall.

Holland, J. L. (1985). *Making vocational choices: A theory of vocational personalities and work environments* (2nd ed.). Englewood Cliffs, NJ: Prentice Hall.

Holland, J. L. (1987). Current status of Holland's theory of careers: Another perspective. *Career Development Quarterly, 36,* 31–44.

Holland, J. L., & Gottfredson, G. D. (1976). Using a typology of persons and environments to explain careers: Some extensions and clarifications. *Counseling Psychologist, 6,* 20–29.

Holland, J. L., & Gottfredson, G. D. (1990). *An annotated bibliography for Holland's theory of vocational personality and work environment.* Baltimore: Johns Hopkins University.

Holland, J. L., & Lutz, S. W. (1968). The predictive value of a student's choice of vocation. *Personnel and Guidance Journal, 46,* 428–436.

Holland, J. L., & Nichols, R. C. (1964). Explorations of a theory of vocational choice: III. A longitudinal study of change in major fields of study. *Personnel and Guidance Journal, 43,* 235–242.

Hotchkiss, L., & Borow, H. (1984). Sociological perspectives on career choice and attainment. In D. Brown, L. Brooks, & Associates (Eds.), *Career choice and development*. San Francisco: Jossey-Bass.

Hotchkiss, L., & Borow, H. (1990). Sociological perspectives on work and career development. In D. Brown, L. Brooks, & Associates (Eds.), *Career choice and development* (2nd ed.). San Francisco: Jossey-Bass.

Janis, I. L., & Mann, L. (1977). *Decision making: A psychological analysis of conflict, choice, and commitment.* New York: Free Press.

Jepsen, D. A., & Dilley, J. S. (1974). Vocational decision-making models: A review and comparative analysis. *Review of Educational Research, 44,* 331–349.

Jones, A. J. (1945). *Principles of guidance.* New York: McGraw-Hill.

Jones, A. J. (1970). *Principles of guidance* (6th ed., revised and updated by B. Stefflre and N. R. Stewart). New York: McGraw-Hill.

Krumboltz, J. D. (1979). A social learning theory of career decision making. In A. M. Mitchell, G. B. Jones, & J. D. Krumboltz (Eds.), *Social learning and career decision making.* Cranston, RI: Caroll Press.

Krumboltz, J. D., Mitchell, A. M., & Jones, G. B. (1976). A social learning theory of career selection. *Counseling Psychologist, 6,* 71–81.

Krumboltz, J. D., Mitchell, A. M., & Jones, G. B. (1978). A social learning theory of career selection. In J. M. Whiteley & A. Resnikoff (Eds.), *Career counseling.* Monterey, CA: Brooks/Cole.

Levinson, D. J., Darrow, C. N., Klein, E. B., Levinson, M. H., & McKee, B. (1978). *The seasons of a man's life.* New York: Knopf.

Lipsett, L. (1962). Social factors in vocational development. *Personnel and Guidance Journal, 40,* 432–437.

Maslow, A. H. (1954). *Motivation and personality.* New York: Harper & Row.

Miller–Tiedeman, A., & Tiedeman, D. V. (1990). Career decision making: An individualistic perspective. In D. Brown, L. Brooks, & Associates (Eds.), *Career choice and development* (2nd ed.). San Francisco: Jossey-Bass.

Mitchell, L. K., & Krumboltz, J. D. (1984). Social learning approach to career decision making: Krumboltz's theory. In D. Brown, L. Brooks, & Associates (Eds.), *Career choice and development.* San Francisco: Jossey-Bass.

Mitchell, L. K., & Krumboltz, J. D. (1990). Social learning approach to career decision making: Krumboltz's theory. In D. Brown, L. Brooks, & Associates (Eds.), *Career choice and development* (2nd ed.). San Francisco: Jossey-Bass.

Mitchell, W. D. (1975). Restle's choice model: A reconceptualization for a special case. *Journal of Vocational Behavior, 6,* 315–330.

Murphy, P. P., & Burck, H. D. (1976). Career development of men at midlife. *Journal of Vocational Behavior, 9,* 337–343.

Murray, H. A. (1938). *Explorations in personality.* New York: Oxford University Press.

O'Leary, V. E. (1977). *Toward understanding women.* Monterey, CA: Brooks/Cole.

Osipow, S. H. (1975). The relevance of theories of career development to special groups: Problems, needed data, and implications. In J. S. Picou & R. E. Campbell (Eds.), *Career behavior of special groups: Theory, research, and practice.* Columbus, OH: Merrill.

Osipow, S. H. (1977). The great expose swindle: A reader's reaction. *Personnel and Guidance Journal, 56,* 23–24.

Osipow, S. H. (1983). *Theories of career development* (3rd ed.). Englewood Cliffs, NJ: Prentice Hall.

Parsons, F. (1909). *Choosing a vocation.* Boston: Houghton Mifflin.

Pietrofesa, J. J., & Splete, H. (1975). *Career development: Theory and research*. New York: Grune & Stratton.

Rand, L., & Miller, A. L. (1972). A developmental cross-sectioning of women's careers and marriage attitudes and life plans. *Journal of Vocational Behavior, 2,* 317–331.

Restle, F. (1961). *Psychology of judgment and choice*. New York: Wiley.

Richardson, M. S. (1981). Occupational and family roles: A neglected intersection. *The Counseling Psychologist, 9,* 13–23.

Roe, A. (1949a). Analysis of group Rorschachs of biologists. *Journal of Projective Techniques, 13,* 25–43.

Roe, A. (1949b). Psychological examination of eminent biologists. *Journal of Consulting Psychology, 13,* 225–246.

Roe, A. (1950). Analysis of group Rorschachs of physical scientists. *Journal of Projective Techniques, 14,* 385–398.

Roe, A. (1951a). A psychological study of eminent biologists. *Psychological Monographs, 65,* (14, Whole No. 331).

Roe, A. (1951b). A psychological study of eminent physical scientists. *Genetic Psychology Monograph, 43,* 121–239.

Roe, A. (1951c). Psychological tests of research scientists. *Journal of Consulting Psychology, 15,* 492–495.

Roe, A. (1951d). A study of imagery in research scientists. *Journal of Personality, 19,* 459–470.

Roe, A. (1952a). Analysis of group Rorschachs of psychologists and anthropologists. *Journal of Projective Techniques, 16,* 212–224.

Roe, A. (1952b). Group Rorschachs of university faculties. *Journal of Consulting Psychology, 16,* 18–22.

Roe, A. (1953). A psychological study of eminent psychologists and anthropologists and a comparison with biological and physical scientists. *Psychological Monographs, 67,* (2, Whole No. 352).

Roe, A. (1957). Early determinants of vocational choice. *Journal of Counseling Psychology, 4,* 212–217.

Roe, A., & Siegelman, M. (1964). The origin of interests. *APGA Inquiry Studies* (No. 1). Washington, DC: American Personnel and Guidance Association.

Scott, T. B., & Anadon, M. (1980). A comparison of the vocational interest profile of Native American and Caucasian college-bound students. *Measurement and Evaluation in Guidance, 13* (1), 35–42.

Shertzer, B. E., & Stone, S. C. (1980). *Fundamentals of counseling* (3rd ed.). Boston: Houghton Mifflin.

Smith, E. J. (1975). Profile of the black individual in vocational literature. *Journal of Vocational Behavior, 6,* 41–59.

Smith, E. J. (1977). Work attitudes and job satisfactions of black workers. *Vocational Guidance Quarterly, 25,* 252–263.

Smith, E. J. (1976). Reference group perspectives and the vocational maturity of lower socioeconomic black youth. *Journal of Vocational Behavior, 8,* 321–336.

Smith, E. J. (1983). Issues in racial minorities' career behavior. In W. B. Walsh & S. H. Osipow (Eds.), *Handbook of vocational psychology* (Vol. 1). Hillsdale, NJ: Erlbaum.

Sue, D. W. (1975). Asian-Americans: Social-psychological forces affecting their life styles. In J. S. Picou and R. E. Campbell (Eds.), *Career behavior of special groups: Theory, research, and practice*. Columbus, OH: Merrill.

Super, D. E. (1951). Vocational adjustment: Implementing a self-concept. *Occupations, 30,* 1–5.

Super, D. E. (1953). A theory of vocational development. *American Psychologist, 8,* 185–190.

Super, D. E. (1954). Career patterns as a basis for vocational counseling. *Journal of Counseling Psychology, 1,* 12–20.

Super, D. E. (1955). Personality integration through vocational counseling. *Journal of Counseling Psychology, 2,* 217–226.

Super, D. E. (1957). *The psychology of careers.* New York: Harper & Row.

Super, D. E. (1960). The critical ninth grade: Vocational choice or vocational exploration. *Personnel and Guidance Journal, 39,* 106–109.

Super, D. E. (1961a). Consistency and wisdom of vocational preference as indices of vocational maturity in the ninth grade. *Journal of Educational Psychology, 52,* 35–43.

Super, D. E. (1961b). Some unresolved issues in vocational development research. *Personnel and Guidance Journal, 40,* 11–14.

Super, D. E. (1964a). A developmental approach to vocational guidance. *Vocational Guidance Quarterly, 13,* 1–10.

Super, D. E. (1964b). Goal specificity in the vocational counseling of future college students. *Personnel and Guidance Journal, 43,* 127–134.

Super, D. E. (1969). Vocational development theory. *The Counseling Psychologist, 1,* 2–30.

Super, D. E. (1972). Vocational development theory: Persons, positions, processes. In J. M. Whiteley & A. Resnikoff (Eds.), *Perspectives on vocational guidance.* Washington, DC: American Personnel and Guidance Association.

Super, D. E. (Ed.). (1974). *Measuring vocational maturity for counseling and evaluation.* Washington, DC: American Personnel and Guidance Association.

Super, D. E. (1977). Vocational maturity in mid-career. *Vocational Guidance Quarterly, 25,* 294–302.

Super, D. E. (1980). A life-span, life-space approach to career development. *Journal of Vocational Behavior, 16,* 282–298.

Super, D. E. (1981). A developmental theory: Implementing a self-concept. In D. H. Montros & C. J. Shinkman (Eds.), *Career development in the 1980s: Theory and practice.* Springfield, IL: Thomas.

Super, D. E. (1983). Assessment in career guidance: Toward truly developmental counseling. *Personnel and Guidance Journal, 61,* 555–562.

Super, D. E. (1984). Career and life development. In D. Brown, L. Brooks, & Associates (Eds.), *Career choice and development.* San Francisco: Jossey-Bass.

Super, D. E. (1990). A life-span, life-space approach to career development. In D. Brown, L. Brooks, & Associates (Eds.), *Career choice and development* (2nd ed.). San Francisco: Jossey-Bass.

Super, D. E., & Bachrach, P. B. (1957). *Scientific careers and vocational development theory.* New York: Teachers College, Columbia University.

Super, D. E., Crites, J. O., Hummel, R. C., Moser, H. P., Overstreet, P. L., & Warnath, C. F. (1957). *Vocational development: A framework for research.* New York: Teachers College, Columbia University.

Super, D. E., & Hall, D. T. (1978). Career development: Exploration and planning. *Annual Review of Psychology, 29,* 333–372.

Super, D. E., & Kidd, J. M. (1979). Vocational maturity in adulthood: Toward turning a model into a measure. *Journal of Vocational Behavior, 14,* 255–270.

Super, D. E., Starishevsky, R., Matlin, R., & Jordaan, J. P. (1963). *Career development: Self-concept theory.* New York: College Entrance Examination Board.

Tiedeman, D. V. (1961). Decision and vocational development: A paradigm and its implications. *Personnel and Guidance Journal, 40,* 15–20.

Tiedeman, D. V., & Miller–Tiedeman, A. (1984). Career decision making: An individualistic perspective. In D. Brown, L. Brooks, & Associates (Eds.), *Career choice and development.* San Francisco: Jossey-Bass.

Tiedeman, D. V., & O'Hara, R. P. (1963). *Career development: Choice and adjustment.* New York: College Entrance Examination Board.

Tversky, A. (1972). Elimination by aspects: A theory of choice. *Psychological Review, 79,* 281–299.

Vroom, V. H. (1964). *Work and motivation.* New York: Wiley.

Warnath, C. F. (1975). Vocational theories: Direction to nowhere. *Personnel and Guidance Journal, 53,* 422–428.

Weinrach, S. G. (Ed.). (1979). *Career counseling.* New York: McGraw-Hill.

Whiteley, J. M., & Resnikoff, A. (Eds.). (1972). *Perspectives on vocational development.* Washington, DC: American Personnel and Guidance Association.

Williamson, E. G. (1939). *How to counsel students.* New York: McGraw-Hill.

Williamson, E. G. (1949). *Counseling adolescents.* New York: McGraw-Hill.

Wright, G. (1984). *Behavioral decision theory.* Newbury Park, CA: Sage.

3

Factors Influencing
Workers and Their Careers

The concept of individual differences confirms the uniqueness of each individual. These differences result from the interaction of each individual's biological inheritance and specific characteristics with the particular and general environment that surrounds the person. The theories of career development considered in Chapter 2 include the principle of individual differences. Roe emphasizes the influence of an individualized psychological need in vocational choice. Super's postulates clearly specify the relevance of individual differences. Tiedeman stresses the unique interaction between personality and the surrounding environment. This acceptance of the concept of individual differences carries with it the assumption that such differences are identifiable.

The spectrum of personal characteristics of the individual is broad enough for the typical person to meet the patterns required in a wide variety of jobs. Conversely, the pattern demanded by the specific job has sufficient flexibility and tolerance to accommodate a wide variety of prospective job holders. This set of premises may be misinterpreted in two ways. If it is taken erroneously in the broadest possible context, one might say that each individual has the personal characteristics that make success possible in *any* job and that the pattern required by *every* job is a universal one found in all people. The indefensibility of such a position is obvious when one contemplates the possibility of a color-blind paint mixer or an accountant without numerical aptitude. At the other extreme, one might postulate that each individual is entirely unique so there is only one job or, more precisely, one position, that one can fill successfully, and that each position is so demanding that only one individual can perform it successfully. If such specificity were widespread, our complex society would be totally immobilized by the impossible task of matching individuals and positions.

A more realistic viewpoint assumes that most human characteristics, like most job requirements, are spread out over a normal distribution. A few individuals, and some jobs, do have such unique characteristics that only a few possible matches exist at any give time (e.g., the position of a soloist at the Metropolitan Opera). A few characteristics are so universal and a few tasks so elemental that practically every person meets at least the minimum requirements for some jobs. Most people and most occupations fall somewhere between these two extremes; we conclude, therefore, that some consideration must be given to balancing human characteristics against occupational demands, if success and satisfaction are to be maximized for the individual and productivity and effectiveness assured for the occupation.

One helpful way to approach the idea that each job requires certain personal attributes of the worker, if he is to perform the work successfully, is to consider briefly the data-people-things concept that is incorporated in the *Dictionary of Occupational Titles (DOT)*. This approach is based on the premise that in every job the worker is involved at some level of complexity with these three entities and, further, that everything the worker does on the job can be assigned to one of these three categories. A counselor, for example, might be expected to deal with data (information, knowledge, and conceptions, including numbers, words, symbols, and ideas) at a very complex level, as well as with people at a very complex level and with things (inanimate objects, machines, tools, equipment) at a fairly simple level. On the other hand, an automobile mechanic would deal with fairly complicated data of a different kind; would have very little involvement with people other than conversation with the auto driver about the difficulty being experienced; and would deal with things, especially tools and machines, at a very complicated level. We will consider the *Dictionary of Occupational Titles* in more detail in Chapter 5. The reader who desires more information about the data-people-things idea may either turn ahead to that chapter or consult the appendix (pages 1369–1371) in the fourth edition of the *Dictionary*. Our present purpose is to establish unequivocally the idea that jobs, like people, do have identifiable characteristics that, in turn, require certain attributes or traits of workers who would perform that work successfully.

The objective of this chapter is to identify and to discuss briefly some of these human and work differences that influence the likelihood of a given individual selecting an occupation, preparing for it, entering it, succeeding at the work, and gaining satisfaction from that participation. Those factors that relate directly to the individual are labeled *internal factors* and are subdivided into three categories—generic, personal-psychological, and personal-sociological. Those factors that relate to the job, work setting, or societal items are labeled *external factors* and also are divided into three categories—work situation, sociological, and economic.

INTERNAL FACTORS

Generic Characteristics

Grouped under this heading are those characteristics that are broadly shared with many other individuals but that contribute significantly to the uniqueness of the individual. Among the many that can be subsumed here, we discuss briefly three examples—gender, ethnicity, and physique.

Gender

Gender was used for many years to restrict participation in many work areas. In spite of equal employment opportunity laws and changing public attitudes, one would be on shaky ground to contend that such restriction is now ancient history.

Astin (1984) and Huston (1983) describe the early childhood socialization that leads to later gender differences, such as competitive games and puzzles for boys, and dolls and make-believe school for girls. This leads to the identification of "traditional" gender work, with teaching, nursing, and allied health fields as feminine, and business, engineering, medicine, law, and scientific research as masculine. Astin believes that recent changes in opportunity, rather than changes in socialization practices, have led to the influx of women into so-called nontraditional fields. Castro (1990) reports that nearly 18 percent of physicians are women, as are 22 percent of lawyers, 32 percent of computer systems analysts, and nearly half of the accountants and auditors. However, among *Fortune* 1000 companies, only 3 percent of the top five jobs below CEO were filled by women, compared to 1 percent 10 years earlier.

Physical differences between men and women that affect work success are primarily related to size and upper body strength. Harris (1976) emphasizes that other gender physical differences are mostly differences of degree. However, upper body strength is an important factor in jobs that require heavy lifting, carrying, pushing, and pulling. Although there are women who can engage in these activities at a level superior to many men, the average man will have more upper body strength as well as more height and weight than the average woman.

Ethnicity

Smith (1983) summarizes the major occupational problems that relate to ethnic minority membership. One of the most critical is the much higher unemployment rate of ethnic groups than Caucasian majority members. Smith reports figures showing unemployment rates for African-American youth in the 16–19 and 20–24 age groups about three times higher than for white youth, and rates for Hispanic youth only slightly better than the figures for African-Americans.

Closely related to the problem of high unemployment are such factors as limited education for many minority groups in our society. This leads, even for those members obtaining employment, to large numbers in "fringe" work situations that lack regularity of work, upgrading opportunities, and such advantages as seniority, and pension rights.

The pattern for Asian Americans appears to be somewhat different from that for African-Americans or Hispanics. Smith credits this difference largely to factors such as different reasons for coming to the United States; preservation of family, language, and cultural patterns; and independence from governmental economic support. In recent years, educational attainment by Asian American youth has exceeded norms for the white majority group, resulting in greater participation in professional and technical occupations.

Smith identifies several career development needs of ethnic minority groups. Near the top of her list are these items: (1) better education and higher achievement, (2) greater occupational awareness, (3) more occupationally diversified role models, (4) fewer environmental and racial constraints, and (5) change in the opportunity structure for ethnic minorities.

Physique

Differences between individuals in height and weight are immediately obvious. Other physical differences may be less apparent, but their existence can be demonstrated easily. Certain physical capacities must be present if the person is to meet the minimum requirements for some jobs. In a later section of this chapter, we consider in more detail the physical requirements for various jobs. Professional athletes provide an example of how this factor relates to qualifications for different occupations; picture for a moment a stereotypical jockey, basketball player, weight lifter, and a marathon runner. It is most unlikely that the jockey could compete successfully in basketball or in weight lifting, or that participants in those activities could bring a horse to the winner's circle of a derby. Most people have sufficient amounts of the various physical capacities to meet the minimum requirement in a wide range of occupations; nevertheless, the absence of a needed capacity can exclude that individual from successful participation in an occupation.

We refer to an individual as *disabled* or *impaired* when certain physical or mental capacities are nonexistent or severely limited. The presence of such conditions can influence career participation in many ways. Often unwarranted assumptions are made about people with disabilities (e.g., if the person cannot walk, then there is no work he can do). If one really pushed, it would be possible to identify some physical or mental capacity that approaches zero for each of us, but we work around it in some way that usually satisfies the situation and do not think of ourselves as people with disabilities. The term *disability* usually refers to a more serious impairment such as loss of a limb or its use. Of course, such disability is serious, frustrating, and inconvenient, often limiting participation in a wide range of activities. It requires the individual to focus on those fields where the absent capacity is not needed. Inability to walk is irrelevant vocationally if the work setting and the job do not require that ability.

Kraus and Stoddard (1989) describe the extent of physical disability and its impact on work. For example, about 20 percent of noninstitutionalized people over age 15 have a physical limitation. Over 18 million people in the United States are unable to lift and carry a 10-pound bag of groceries, nearly 13 million are unable to see words or letters in newsprint, and 2.5 million are unable to speak clearly because of physical restrictions. About 8.6 percent of the working-age population has some form of work disability. Among African-American workers, 13.7 percent have a work disability, and among Hispanics the figure is 7.9 percent. The impact of disability is dramatic, with 19.7 percent of those with a work disability being employed full time compared to 59.4 percent of those without a work disability.

Personal-Psychological Characteristics

In this section we look at some of the psychological requirements that affect the individual's career choice and participation. Our examples include aptitude, interests, and personality (including temperament and values).

Aptitude

Aptitudes are defined as specific capacities and abilities required of an individual to learn or adequately perform a task or job duty. Much psychological research has focused on this topic for over half a century. An early classic work by Bingham (1937), *Aptitudes and Aptitude Testing*, describes the state of the art at that point. Later work includes books by Super and Crites (1962), Cronbach (1970), Goldman (1971), and Anastasi (1982).

Recent research suggests that *aptitude* refers to specific psychological factors that contribute in varying degrees to success in various occupations. It is a capacity or potential that has stability, unity, and independence. Different authors report varying numbers of aptitudes, partly due to variable input factors such as types of psychological measurements, statistical treatment, and subjective factors (e.g., groupings or classifications).

There are several ways to estimate or identify aptitude. The individual who consistently enrolls in the most difficult mathematics courses and easily earns high grades is demonstrating numerical aptitude. The person who always beats all challengers in solving a puzzle like Rubik's Cube is displaying spatial aptitude and some manual dexterity. The skillful crossword fan shows a high verbal aptitude.

The U.S. Employment Service published the General Aptitude Test Battery in 1947 and has continued research on the instrument since that time. Although there are 12 tests in the battery, only nine aptitudes are identified by the test. These, with brief definitions, include the following:

> *G—Intelligence:* General learning ability. The ability to understand instructions and underlying principles; the ability to reason and make judgments. Closely related to doing well in school.
>
> *V—Verbal:* The ability to understand meanings of words and ideas associated with them and to use them effectively; to comprehend language, to understand relationships between words, and to understand meanings of whole sentences and paragraphs; to present information or ideas clearly.
>
> *N—Numerical:* The ability to perform arithmetic operations quickly and accurately.

S—Spatial: The ability to comprehend forms in space and understand relationships of plane and solid objects. May be used in such tasks as blueprint reading and solving geometry problems.

P—Form perception: The ability to perceive pertinent detail in objects or in pictorial or graphic material; to make visual comparisons and discriminations and see slight differences in shapes and shadings of figures and widths and lengths of lines.

Q—Clerical perception: The ability to perceive pertinent detail in verbal or tabular material; to observe differences in copy, to proofread words and numbers, and to avoid perceptual errors in arithmetic computation.

K—Motor coordination: The ability to coordinate eyes and hands or fingers rapidly and accurately in making precise movements with speed; to make a movement response accurately and quickly.

F—Finger dexterity: The ability to move the fingers and manipulate small objects with the fingers rapidly or accurately.

M—Manual dexterity: The ability to move the hands easily and skillfully; to work with the hands in placing and turning motions.

Norm groups for the test consist of successful workers in a wide range of occupations. Occupational Aptitude Patterns (OAPs) that include the scores on the two, three, or four most important aptitudes have been developed for many occupations. The OAPs were established by testing large numbers of workers in the selected occupations between the ages of 18 and 54 and identifying the point on each test above which two thirds of the workers scored. In addition to using the total test to identify 66 broad occupational options with OAPs, it is possible to use various combinations of the 12 tests to form Specific Aptitude Test Batteries (SATBs) to produce scores on those aptitudes involved in a single occupation. Droege and Boese (1982) relate OAPs and SATBs to the work groups included in the *Guide for Occupational Exploration* (discussed in Chapter 5).

High schools frequently use a somewhat comparable test based on school grade norms, entitled the Differential Aptitude Test. The first edition appeared in 1947, and the test has been revised regularly since that time, with the fifth edition appearing in 1990. Each of the eight tests produces a score indicating the person's strength or weakness in that particular aptitude. In addition, two scores are combined to produce a ninth score. Scores on the Differential Aptitude Test appear to be effective predictors of future academic grades. Little is known about relating scores directly to occupational success. The eight parts include the following:

Verbal reasoning ⎫
Numerical ability ⎬ Scholastic ability
Abstract reasoning ⎭
Clerical speed and accuracy

Mechanical reasoning
Space relations
Spelling
Language usage

Examples of other tests that are generally classified as aptitude tests include the Armed Services Vocational Aptitude Battery (ASVAB), the Career Ability Placement Survey (CAPS), the Flanagan Aptitude Classification Tests (FACT), and the Graflex Vocational Evaluation System. The last of these is a work sample test, often used in rehabilitation centers and job retraining programs.

Interests

When individuals begin to think of possible future occupations, many first consider their interests with questions such as, "What activities do I enjoy?" and "What occupational group has the same likes and dislikes that I have?" The underlying assumptions are that if a person likes an activity, she will be more highly motivated, will work harder, and hence is more likely to succeed at the activity. The idea of compatible likes and dislikes assumes that a person will feel more comfortable with like-minded co-workers and hence is more likely to feel satisfied and to be successful. Aspects of Roe's and Holland's theories, described in Chapter 2, speak directly to this concept.

Super (1957) describes four types of interests, varying primarily with the method of assessment:

Expressed interests: Verbal statements or claims of interest

Manifest interests: Shown through actions and participation

Inventoried interests: Estimates of interest based on responses to a set of questions concerning likes and dislikes

Tested interests: Revealed under controlled situations

Each of these methods of assessment provides useful information in appropriate situations. The individual with a wide range of experiences and some skill in self-evaluation should be able to *express* interest with some reliability. Perhaps even more reliable is the interest that is *manifest* in the activities in which the person engages. *Inventoried* interests are most commonly seen by counselors because of the widespread use of several interest inventories. By carefully structuring choice situations where the person must choose between two relatively equal situations, we can *test* the strength of the individual's interests.

Many research studies have focused on the relationship between interest and occupational choice or satisfaction. Only a few of these studies, however, have focused on the predictive validity of expressed vocational choice, which could be assumed to be identical with expressed interest. Whitney (1969), reviewing the various studies related to expressed choice, concludes that expressed choice has as much predictive validity as do various measures of interest, aptitude, and socioeconomic factors. Rose and Elston (1970) tend to support this view with their conclusion that scores obtained on the Strong Vocational Interest Blank by high school seniors appear to corroborate their expressed vocational choices. On the other hand, Nelson (1971) was unable to find that Kuder Preference Record scores would confirm the expressed vocational choices of eleventh-grade boys. Whitney makes a strong point in favor of expressed choice when he states that an individual expressing a preference for an occupation usually has some awareness of both the aptitudes required in the work and her own aptitudes. This type of information is beyond the scope of the best of the interest inventories. Nevertheless, most recent research has focused on inventoried interests.

Instruments that are used widely to assess career-related interests include the following: Career Assessment Inventory, California Occupational Preference Survey, Jackson Vocational Interest Survey, Kuder General Interest Survey, Kuder Occupational Interest Survey, Ohio Vocational Interest Survey, Self-Directed Search, Strong Vocational Interest Blank, Vocational Interests, Experience and Skill Assessment. Several of these inventories are discussed in Chapter 13.

Personality, Temperament, and Values

The theoretical positions of Roe, Holland, Super, and Tiedeman include specific statements referring to a relationship between personality or temperament and occupation. Each of us also holds stereotypes of the typical personality characteristics of members of many occupational groups—the meek, reticent librarian; the loquacious, dominating sales representative; the caring nurse; the vague, absent-minded professor. Nevertheless, research in relating personality characteristics to success in various occupations is clearly less well developed than that focusing on aptitude or interest. There are two possible reasons for this discrepancy. First, measurement instruments in the area of personality are generally less precise than in several other areas; and second, occupations may tolerate a wider latitude of personality differences than of aptitude, interest, or other characteristics.

Manuals for several widely used personality tests include data based on specific occupational groups. Examples include the California Psychological Inventory, the Guilford–Zimmerman Temperament Survey, and the Edwards Personal Preference Schedule. Professional schools such as theological seminaries sometimes require applicants to complete personality inventories as part of the admissions process. Personnel offices for some large companies may also use personality instruments as they attempt to fill certain positions.

Perhaps a more useful approach in considering relationships between personality and occupations would be to think in terms of the kind of personality or temperament characteristics stipulated or suggested by the nature of the work situation. As extreme examples of this concept, consider the need for a fire lookout to work in isolation for long periods of time, or for an air traffic controller to work under stress and deal with constantly changing situations. The third edition (1965) of the *Dictionary of Occupational Titles* introduced such an approach, but it was not included in the fourth edition (1977). A modified form has been used in the *Guide for Occupational Exploration*.

The concept of *values* is closely related to the broader and more widely used term *personality*. Often the term *values* is juxtaposed with *needs*. The idea of values as representative of personality types was proposed by Spranger over half a century ago (1928). He suggested that men could be classified according to their value types as theoretical, economic, social, political, aesthetic, and religious.

A more philosophic approach to values is taken by Peterson (1970, p. 9):

> A value is a learned conception, explicit or implicit, of what is desirable. It is a hypothetical construct, a criterion upon which choice, either by an individual or a group, is justified and also serves to motivate commitment and action. Value represents more than needs, goals, beliefs, attitudes, interests, or preferences (terms frequently confused with value), although it may be closely related to them.

The focus of this definition is on the individual's view of what is desirable. Peterson points out that today's youth often receive conflicting messages about what is good and therefore encounter difficulty in developing values. The counselor often encounters youth who are seeking identity and thereby attempting to clarify their values. Peterson suggests that values are hypothetical constructs that have motivational force and that represent the desirable in the sense of what one ought to do or what is perceived as the right thing to do in this situation. Attention often has focused on attempts to relate values to attitudes of individuals toward work. One monograph of particular significance in relating values to work and career is *Decisions and Values* by M. Katz (1963).

Personal-Sociological Characteristics

This category includes those characteristics that are personal in the sense that they have an impact on a particular individual, but they involve others close to that person. We consider three examples: family socioeconomic status, access to education, and lifestyle.

Family Socioeconomic Status

Sociological literature from its beginning has included studies of relationships between family and work, social status and work, and the impact of family status on individuals. Oppenheimer (1982) studied census records to compare family data for eight different occupational groups. She further divided the sample into income levels to identify periods of economic stress. She found that most families face three periods of such stress, labeled life-cycle squeezes. These usually occur when the couple establishes an independent household, when children reach adolescence, and when the couple reaches the postretirement period. The strategies used by the family to resolve the financial crunch appear to be related to the occupational status of the father. For example, during the second squeeze (children at the late adolescent period), children of low-income, blue-collar families frequently discontinued schooling and went to work either to help with family finances or to provide self-support, usually at low-level jobs, while children of high-income, white-collar families continued their education, thus increasing their eligibility for higher level jobs.

Higher socioeconomic status of parents provides many opportunities for children that may influence their later career planning. In addition to longer and richer educational advantages, they are more likely to engage in travel, summer camp, or similar enrichment experiences and to have contact with a wide range of occupational role models within the family circle of friends and acquaintances. Meantime, their peers from lower status families are restricted from such contacts not only by financial factors but by lack of access to such opportunities. Blau and Duncan (1967) and Sewell and Hauser (1975) are classic sociological studies showing the relationship between family status and later occupational attainment. Hotchkiss and Borow (1990) review many of the sociological studies on this topic.

Access to Education

Americans commonly take pride in their free public education system, implying that equal opportunity for quality elementary and secondary education exists for all. There are at least two problems in this assumption: first, access to education may not be uniformly equal; and second, the quality available may not be equal.

Statewide competency testing programs have demonstrated regularly a wide discrepancy in the percentage of students from different schools and school systems who pass the test successfully. Undoubtedly, many factors produce this variation, but those schools with higher failure rates consistently have limited funding, crowded classes, lower quality staff, restricted facilities and resources, and other aspects that reflect lower quality education. Statewide, such schools are frequently found in two locations—isolated rural areas with limited financial resources, or inner-city urban areas with high ratios of low-income and welfare families. Such schools also frequently show poor attendance records, high dropout rates, and a limited number of educational programs. Recent court rulings in several states have required reorganization of state educational systems to reduce obvious discrepancies.

We oversimplify when we assume that because a school exists and tuition fees are not charged, it is accessible to all. There are numerous hidden costs in most school attendance situations, such as book fees, activity fees, transportation costs, and clothing expenses. Some potential students are absent because they must care for family members, either younger siblings or ill adults, or because they must engage in work that is often irregular, seasonal, or part time. Increasing numbers of nonattending or irregularly attending students are members of single-parent families, and sometimes that parent is dysfunctional or lacks parental skills.

Several researchers have explored the impact of school tracking, where students are assigned to programs such as college preparatory or vocational. Among these are studies by Alexander and McDill (1976), Garet and DeLany (1988), Gamoran and Mare (1989), and Vanfossen, Jones, and Spade (1987). The research shows a close relationship between family status and the track to which a student is assigned. This, in turn, has a direct impact on subsequent career participation.

There are striking exceptions to these generalizations. Every school teacher and counselor can identify individual students who face overwhelming odds in getting to school and staying in school and who nevertheless succeed academically. However, it often is the comparison between this unusual, highly motivated student and the generally typical student that makes the stark reality so apparent.

Our discussion, thus far, has focused on the elementary and secondary levels. Access to postsecondary education is restricted by a number of factors, including geographic location, costs, eligibility for admission, and limitation of enrollment.

Lifestyle

Lifestyle factors in the parental home influence the childhood and adolescent years in ways that carry over into adulthood and have an impact on career. One example, mentioned earlier, is the single-parent family. In many such families, especially where finances are adequate, child care or other resources fill the gap caused by the absent parent. In other situations, particularly in low-income settings, the result may be little or no supervision, involvement with high-risk activities, lack of encouragement and motivation, absence of role models, and lack of access to developmental and enlightening experiences. Smith (1983) describes the many problems faced by inner-city poor black children, many of whom live in single-parent families. These conditions discourage, and sometimes prevent, motivated involvement in education, thus later severely restricting successful career involvement.

An example of lifestyle influence on adult career behavior is the rapidly growing phenomenon of the dual-career family. The trend during the past decade has clearly been an increase in two-earner families. This appears likely to increase in the years ahead. Dual-career families find both positive and negative aspects to their status. On the plus side, these families report a greater degree of flexibility in partners being able to relinquish unsatisfactory career paths and either search for new opportunities or take up a training program that might open new paths. This is obviously the result of the security provided by the second income. On the negative side are reports that dual-career families must sometimes forgo career opportunities that require relocating because such a move would be disruptive for the partner's career. Indirectly related to career development are other problems faced by dual-career families, such as increased pressure on time allocation, the difficulty of finding time for family activities, and the sharing of household tasks.

EXTERNAL FACTORS

Work Situation

In this section we consider factors influencing career participation that are direct outgrowths of the job or the work situation. The training time required for various jobs, the physical demands required to do the work, and the environmental conditions imposed by the work are examined.

Training Time
Except in very simple occupations, the acquisition of general and specialized knowledge and skills is necessary for successful performance by the worker. The particular mix of general and specific knowledge and skill obviously varies from occupation to occupation.

A companion volume to the *DOT* entitled *Selected Characteristics of Occupations Defined in the Dictionary of Occupational Titles* provides information about the amount of both types of preparation required by each occupation included in the *DOT*. We consider this volume along with the *DOT* in Chapter 5.

General educational development includes the broad academic preparation acquired in elementary and secondary school and in college that does not have a specific occupational objective. It usually refers to aspects of education that develop reasoning and adaptability to environment, ability to understand and follow directions, and such tool knowledges as mathematics and language.

Six levels of complexity have been identified in both mathematical development and language development. These range from very basic arithmetic computation and very simple reading, writing, or speaking at the lowest level, to abstract mathematics such as advanced calculus and statistical inference and intricate language usage at the highest level. An occupation is classified at the level equivalent to its most complex activity in each of the two tool areas.

The complete classification system can be found in Appendix C of *Selected Characteristics*. Level 3 (High School Diploma) is included here to illustrate the system.

Level	*Mathematical Development*	*Language Development*
3	Compute discount, interest, profit, and loss; commission, markups, and selling price; ratio and proportion; and percentages. Calculate surfaces, volumes, weights, and measures.	*Reading:* Read a variety of novels, magazines, atlases, and encyclopedias. Read safety rules, instructions in the use and maintenance of shop tools and equipment, and methods

Algebra: Calculate variables and formulas; monomials and polynomials; ratio and proportion variables; and square roots and radicals.

Geometry: Calculate plane and solid figures, circumference, area, and volume. Understand kinds of angles, and properties of pairs and angles.

and procedures in mechanical drawing and layout work.

Writing: Write reports and essays with proper format, punctuation, spelling, and grammar, using all parts of speech.

Speaking: Speak before an audience with poise, voice control, and confidence, using correct English and well-modulated voice.

Specific vocational preparation is training time required to learn the techniques and knowledge and to develop the skills needed for average performance in a specific job-worker situation. The training includes the acquisition of skills and knowledge needed to do the job, but it does not include the orientation training that is usually required to familiarize the worker with the special conditions or procedures existing at the specific work site. Specific vocational preparation is usually obtained in one or a combination of the following:

1. Vocational education
2. Apprentice training
3. In-plant training
4. On-the-job training
5. Essential experience in other jobs

Nine levels are used to categorize specific vocational preparation:

Level	Time
1	Short demonstration
2	Anything beyond short demonstration up to and including 30 days
3	Over 30 days up to and including 3 months
4	Over 3 months up to and including 6 months
5	Over 6 months up to and including 1 year
6	Over 1 year up to and including 2 years
7	Over 2 years up to and including 4 years
8	Over 4 years up to and including 10 years
9	Over 10 years

The following occupations have been chosen randomly from *Selected Characteristics* and from the 1982 supplement to the *DOT* to illustrate how occupations are classified for general educational development and specific vocational preparation (SVP):

Occupation	*Math*	*Language*	*SVP*
Fast-foods worker	2	2	2
Mail carrier	2	3	4
Nuclear-fuels research engineer	6	6	8
Tree surgeon	2	2	6
Word-processing-machine operator	1	3	4
Zoo veterinarian	5	5	8

Physical Demands

Every work situation requires some physical involvement of the worker; conversely, every worker brings to the work situation certain physical capacities that are used in the process of performing the work. Just as one might expect the physical characteristics of individuals to vary, so too might one expect the physical demands associated with different types of work to vary. Some occupations require minimum output of physical activity, some require vigorous action of one or two types, and others involve strenuous activity across a broad range. *Selected Characteristics* identifies the demands imposed on the worker in each job listed in the *DOT*. The description of the factors as listed in Appendix A of *Selected Characteristics* is as follows:

> The physical demands listed in this publication serve as a means of expressing both the physical requirements of the job and the physical capacities (specific physical traits) a worker must have to meet those required by many jobs (perceiving by the sense of vision), and also the name of a specific capacity possessed by many people (having the power of sight). The worker must possess physical capacities at least in an amount equal to the physical demands made by the job.

The Factors

1. *Strength:* This factor is expressed in terms of *Sedentary, Light, Medium, Heavy,* and *Very Heavy.* It is measured by involvement of the worker with one or more of the following activities:
   a. Worker position(s):
      (1) *Standing:* Remaining on one's feet in an upright position at a workstation without moving about.
      (2) *Walking:* Moving about on foot.
      (3) *Sitting:* Remaining in the normal seated position.
   b. Worker movement of objects (including extremities used):
      (1) *Lifting:* Raising or lowering an object from one level to another (includes upward pulling).
      (2) *Carrying:* Transporting an object, usually holding it in the hands or arms or on the shoulder.
      (3) *Pushing:* Exerting force upon an object so that the object moves away from the force (includes slapping, striking, kicking, and treadle actions).
      (4) *Pulling:* Exerting force upon an object so that the object moves toward the force (includes jerking).

The five degrees of Physical Demands Factor No. 1 (strength), are as follows:

S—Sedentary Work: Lifting 10 lbs. maximum and occasionally lifting and/or carrying such articles as dockets, ledgers, and small tools. Although a sedentary job is defined as one which involves sitting, a certain amount of walking and standing is often necessary in carrying out job duties. Jobs are sedentary if walking and standing are required only occasionally and other sedentary criteria are met.

L—Light Work: Lifting 20 lbs. maximum with frequent lifting and/or carrying of objects weighing up to 10 lbs. Even though the weight lifted may be only a negligible amount, a job is in this category when it requires walking or standing to a significant degree, or when it involves sitting most of the time with a degree of pushing and pulling of arm and/or leg controls.

M—Medium Work: Lifting 50 lbs. maximum with frequent lifting and/or carrying of objects weighing up to 25 lbs.

H—Heavy Work: Lifting 100 lbs. maximum with frequent lifting and/or carrying of objects weighing up to 50 lbs.

V—Very Heavy Work: Lifting objects in excess of 100 lbs. with frequent lifting and/or carrying of objects weighing 50 lbs. or more.

2. *Climbing and/or Balancing:*
   (1) Climbing: Ascending or descending ladders, stairs, scaffolding, ramps, poles, ropes, and the like, using the feet and legs and/or hands and arms.
   (2) Balancing: Maintaining body equilibrium to prevent falling when walking, standing, crouching, or running on narrow, slippery, or erratically moving surfaces; or maintaining body equilibrium when performing gymnastic feats.
3. *Stooping, Kneeling, Crouching, and/or Crawling:*
   (1) Stooping: Bending the body downward and forward by bending the spine at the waist.
   (2) Kneeling: Bending the legs at the knees to come to rest on the knee or knees.
   (3) Crouching: Bending the body downward and forward by bending the legs and spine.
   (4) Crawling: Moving about on the hands and knees or hands and feet.
4. *Reaching, Handling, Fingering, and/or Feeling:*
   (1) Reaching: Extending the hands and arms in any direction.
   (2) Handling: Seizing, holding, grasping, turning, or otherwise working with the hand or hands (fingering not involved).
   (3) Fingering: Picking, pinching, or otherwise working with the fingers primarily (rather than with the whole hand or arm as in handling).
   (4) Feeling: Perceiving such attributes of objects and materials as size, shape, temperature, or texture, by means of receptors in the skin, particularly those of the fingertips.
5. *Talking and/or Hearing:*
   (1) Talking: Expressing or exchanging ideas by means of the spoken word.
   (2) Hearing: Perceiving the nature of sounds by the ear.
6. *Seeing:* Obtaining impressions through the eyes of the shape, size, distance, motion, color, or other characteristics of objects. The major visual functions are: (1) acuity, far and near, (2) depth perception, (3) field of vision, (4) accommodation, and (5) color vision.
   The functions are defined as follows:

(1) Acuity, far—clarity of vision at 20 feet or more.
Acuity, near—clarity of vision at 20 inches or less.
(2) Depth perception—three-dimensional vision. The ability to judge distance and space relationships so as to see objects where and as they actually are.
(3) Field of vision—the area that can be seen up and down or to the right or left while the eyes are fixed on a given point.
(4) Accommodation—adjustment of the lens of the eye to bring an object into sharp focus. This item is especially important when doing near-point work at varying distances from the eye.
(5) Color vision—the ability to identify and distinguish colors.

Obviously, the worker must have sufficient physical capacity to perform the activities required in the occupation. The inability to do certain physical tasks (e.g., lift 100 pounds) is important only if the ability is required to do the work. The reverse is also true: The ability to lift a heavy weight is irrelevant unless this is required to do the work. Some individuals with physical disabilities may generalize their inability to do certain tasks to all activities; other people who do one activity better than most others expect to excel in all. The crucial factor concerning physical demands is that the worker must be able to meet the minimum requirements.

Environmental Conditions

Just as an occupation requires a worker to meet certain physical demands, it frequently requires that the work be performed in a particular setting that may impose certain demands on the worker's physical capacities. Those of us who work in comfortable, climate-controlled, well-lighted offices are likely to give little thought to the minimal demands that our work situation makes of us. Many workers, however, are confronted with specific circumstances, imposed by the location and nature of the work, that place far heavier demands on them. For example, a blast furnace keeper in a steel mill encounters extreme temperatures as a normal part of the work; a coal miner is faced with noise, hazards, dust, and poor ventilation.

The classification for environmental conditions, found in Appendix B of *Selected Characteristics*, is as follows:

1. *Inside, Outside, or Both:*
   I   Inside: Protection from weather conditions but not necessarily from temperature changes.
   O   Outside: No effective protection from weather.
   B   Both: Inside and outside.
A job is considered "inside" if the worker spends approximately 75 percent or more of the time inside, and "outside" if the worker spends approximately 75 percent or more of the time outside. A job is considered "both" if the activities occur inside and outside in approximately equal amounts.

2. *Extremes of Cold Plus Temperature Changes:*
   (1) Extremes of Cold: Temperature sufficiently low to cause marked bodily discomfort unless the worker is provided with exceptional protection.
   (2) Temperature Changes: Variations in temperature which are sufficiently marked and abrupt to cause noticeable bodily reactions.
3. *Extremes of Heat Plus Temperature Changes:*
   (1) Extremes of Heat: Temperature sufficiently high to cause marked bodily discomfort unless the worker is provided with exceptional protection.
   (2) Temperature Changes: Same as 2(2).
4. *Wet and Humid:*
   (1) Wet: Contact with water or other liquids.
   (2) Humid: Atmospheric condition with moisture content sufficiently high to cause marked bodily discomfort.
5. *Noise and Vibration:* Sufficient noise, either constant or intermittent, to cause marked distraction or possible injury to the sense of hearing, and/or sufficient vibration (production of an oscillating movement or strain on the body or its extremities from repeated motion or shock) to cause bodily harm if endured day after day.
6. *Hazards:* Situations in which the individual is exposed to the definite risk of bodily injury.
7. *Fumes, Odors, Toxic Conditions, Dust, and Poor Ventilation:*
   (1) Fumes: Smoky or vaporous exhalations, usually odorous, thrown off as the result of combustion or chemical reaction.
   (2) Odors: Noxious smells, either toxic or nontoxic.
   (3) Toxic Conditions: Exposure to toxic dust, fumes, gases, vapors, mists, or liquids which cause general or localized disabling conditions as a result of inhalation or action on the skin.
   (4) Dust: Air filled with small particles of any kind, such as textile dust, flour, wood, leather, feathers, etc., inorganic dust, including silica and asbestos, which make the workplace unpleasant or are the source of occupational diseases.
   (5) Poor Ventilation: Insufficient movement of air causing the feeling of suffocation; or exposure to drafts.

To continue our earlier illustration, the following are the same six occupations with their physical demands and environmental conditions identified as listed in either *Selected Characteristics* or the 1991 *DOT:*

Occupation	*Physical Demands*	*Environmental Conditions*	
Fast-foods worker	L 456	I	
Mail carrier	L 46	B	
Nuclear-fuels research engineer	L 456	I	
Tree surgeon	M 2,346	O	467
Word-processing-machine operator	S 456	I	
Zoo veterinarian	M 46	B	7

Sociological Influences

The relationship between individuals and their occupations is, in many ways, similar to that between individuals and their spouses. Both partners contribute to meeting each other's needs; both impose demands on the other. If compatibility is to develop, there must be adaptability, mutual interest and concern, tolerance, and acceptance. In an earlier section of this chapter, we discussed the sociological factors in the immediate family environment of the individual. In this section we are concerned with the broad view beyond the family, as sociologists study the impact of work on individuals and their lives. Helpful sources to consult for further information include Terkel (1972); O'Toole, Scheiber, and Wood (1981); Stewart and Cantor (1982); Hall (1986); and Rothman (1987). Recent, relevant sociological research can often be found in professional journals such as *American Journal of Sociology*, the *American Sociological Review*, and *Work and Occupations*. Our examples of this sociological focus include occupational prestige, occupational mobility, regulating admission to occupations, and regulation of worker behavior.

Occupational Prestige

The importance of occupational prestige for the counselor and the teacher can be focused primarily on (1) recognizing the considerable variation in the amount of prestige generally given to various occupations, and (2) recognizing the impact that such prestige values have on individuals who are considering and evaluating occupations.

Occupational prestige has been defined in many ways. In some research studies reported in the literature, specific efforts have been made to avoid definition in order to draw from the respondents their ideas and attitudes concerning the meaning of the term. For the purpose of this chapter, occupational prestige is considered to be the esteem or social status accorded to an occupation by the general population. It is important to recognize that the concern here is the prestige of the occupation, not that of the individual.

Garbin and Bates (1966) studied 20 factors that appear to influence the prestige ranking of an occupation. Of the 20 factors reported, six showed positive correlations of .90 to .95 with occupational prestige. In descending order, these are as follows:

1. Regarded as desirable to associate with
2. Intelligence required
3. Scarcity of personnel who can do the job
4. Interesting and challenging work
5. Training required
6. Education required

Five other factors produced correlations of .80 or better:

1. Work calling for originality and initiative
2. Toil for improving others
3. Having an influence over others
4. Security
5. Opportunity for advancement

Counts (1925) asked a group of 450 people ranging in maturity from high school seniors to high school teachers to rank 45 occupations. In 1946 Deeg and Paterson repeated Counts's earlier study. The study was replicated again in 1967 by Hakel, Hollman, and Dunnette, and by Kanzaki in 1975. Table 3.1 compares the rankings of occupations found in these four studies that span half a century. The most striking result observed is the relative stability of occupations. In 1946 only three occupations changed more than two ranks; in 1967 eight occupations made such moves; and in 1975 nine changed more than two spaces, including five of those that had changed in 1967. Over the 50-year span, only six occupations had moved more than two ranks, and the greatest move was five places. Results are listed in Table 3.1.

A more extensive study, involving 90 occupations and a carefully selected sample of 3,000 respondents selected with concern for region, size of city, age, sex, status, and race, was reported by North and Hatt in 1947 (National Opinion Research Center, 1947), and replicated by Hodge, Siegel, and Rossi in 1963. Results of both studies showed high degrees of consistency with the studies shown in Table 3.1. Reported coefficients are comparable to those included in the table.

The social status of occupations appears to remain relatively stable over long periods of time. It also holds that stability across groups, gender, and national boundaries. Braun and Bayer (1973) compared the ratings made by groups of African-American and white male and female college students and by an adult group. Correlations across the groups were consistently high, as were group ratings matched against the Deeg and Paterson results. Studies by Tuckman (1950) and by Stefflre, Resnikoff, and Lezotte (1968) show that gender is not a factor in ranking the prestige of occupations, since rankings by their samples of women correlated highly with rankings by men and by general population groups.

Occupational Mobility

The Horatio Alger concept of the poor but industrious and ambitious boy who starts at the bottom and rises to the top of his career field has long been a part of U.S. heritage. In the dynamic, expanding, and classless society that has existed in the United States for the past 2 centuries, such opportunities have existed; and every community has within it examples of self-made successes.

Sociologists have assigned the term *vertical mobility* to movement from one occupational stratum to a higher or lower one. When the change is essentially one of function but the person remains at the same level, the term *horizontal mobility* is used.

TABLE 3.1   *Social Status Ranks of 25 Occupations from 1925, 1946, 1967, and 1975*

Occupation	Counts (1925)	Deeg and Paterson (1946)	Hakel, Hollman, & Dunnete (1967)	Kanzaki (1975)
Banker	1	2.5	4	3
Physician	2	1	1	1
Lawyer	3	2.5	2	5
Superintendent of schools	4	4	3	4
Civil engineer	5	5	5	2
Army captain	6	6	8	8
Foreign missionary	7	7	7	9
Elementary school teacher	8	8	6	6
Farmer	9	12	19	7
Machinist	10	9	12	11
Traveling salesman	11	16	13	16
Grocer	12	13	17	13
Electrician	13	11	9	10
Insurance agent	14	10	10	14
Mail carrier	15	14	18	17
Carpenter	16	15	11	12
Soldier	17	19	15	19
Plumber	18	17	16	15
Motorman	19	18	20	22
Barber	20	20	14	18
Truck driver	21	21.5	21	21
Coal miner	22	21.5	23	20
Janitor	23	23	22	24
Hod carrier	24	24	24	23
Ditch digger	25	25	25	25

Source: From G. A. Kanzaki, "Fifty Years (1925–1975) of Stability in the Social Status of Occupations," *Vocational Guidance Quarterly, 25* (1976), 101–105. Copyright AACD. Reprinted with permission. No further reproduction authorized without further permission of AACD.
Note: The rank-order correlations (rho) are as follows: 1925 and 1946, .97; 1925 and 1967, .88; 1925 and 1975, .92; 1946 and 1967, .93; 1946 and 1975, .96; 1967 and 1975, .94.

The biographies of self-made men and women often imply that the individual's success has come about through the persistent application of hard work, faithfulness, and virtue. This view, of course, takes the position that only the individual was active and that the situation in which a person worked was passive and inert. The stories of failures, on the other hand, all too often cast the individual in the role of the helpless, storm-tossed victim of ruthless and uncontrollable circumstances. In such a picture, we must assume that the individual is passive and the situation is all-powerful. If, however, we view people and their work as an interacting relationship, to which both contribute and from which both benefit, then both parties are seen as active. A realistic consideration of mobility must proceed from this assumption of interrelatedness.

Hotchkiss and Borow (1990) summarize sociological research that explores "status attainment"—the sociological term for how individuals pursue and reach status goals such as education, occupation, and income. Most research on status attainment is an outgrowth of earlier research on occupational mobility. The general basis assumed is that parental status heavily influences, both directly and indirectly, the status achieved by their children. Early studies (pre-1967) also identified education, achievement motivation, influence of peers, and intelligence as other important determinants of occupational mobility. Blau and Duncan (1967) established the pattern for current research on status attainment by developing a model of occupational attainment and also a graded scale of occupational prestige.

Blau and Duncan's model showed that the father's occupation (heavily influenced by his education) has an important effect on the son's education and subsequent occupation. Simultaneously, Sewell and others started a longitudinal study in 1957 with Wisconsin high school seniors; they followed the group until 1975 (Sewell & Hauser, 1975). Sewell and others modified the Blau–Duncan model by proposing that family status and certain cognitive variables (such as mental ability and school performance) influence what they call "social-psychological processes" (including such items as educational and occupational aspiration, parental encouragement to attend college, teacher encouragement, and peer plans); these in turn influence educational attainment, which then influences occupational attainment. The so-called Wisconsin model has been applied to other data samples, with supporting results obtained. Factors such as geographic or cultural isolation do appear to reduce aspiration levels. Evidence suggests that economic restraints may also have a negative effect.

Early sociological research (Form & Miller, 1949; Thomas, 1956) showed the influence of first full-time employment on later attained occupational level. Both studies suggest that workers tend to remain at about the same occupational level as the one where they begin to work. More recently, Borow (1981) reemphasizes that one's first job has an important influence on one's entire work history—it can be constrictive and limit future advancement, or it can broaden future options by providing the base from which mobility is facilitated. Borow contends that youth and others should be helped to see what chances each position offers to move on or upward to other jobs. This again emphasizes the interrelatedness of people and work and the importance of information, planning, educational opportunity, and support or encouragement from parents and significant others for effective and satisfying career development.

Regulating Admission to Occupations

Colleges and universities with strong athletic programs have used various techniques to attract outstanding high school athletes. The military services participate vigorously, even competitively, in recruiting practices. Many occupations and professions similarly exert considerable effort to attract new entrants to the field. In some cases, the procedures used are as open and spirited as those of the military. In many other situations, however, the process is performed with subtlety and diplomatic finesse.

Conversely, many occupational groups have established various methods of restricting entrance into the occupation. Most of these regulating devices serve one or the other of two basic purposes. Some of the restrictions are established to protect the public (those outside the occupation) from incompetence and inefficiency and thus are intended to uphold adequate standards. Other regulations are established primarily to protect the group within the occupation, particularly to maintain the level of income by preventing an oversupply of workers.

Some occupations, especially many of the professions, have successfully established formal control of admission procedures. This is usually accomplished by requiring the completion of specific schooling of a particular type and duration, or by demanding that the prospective applicant serve an apprenticeship or internship of a specified period. The imposition of a lengthy training program on potential candidates controls the number of applicants in two ways: first, a long period of preparation discourages some by reducing the attractiveness of the work; and second, the training establishments often serve as a selective instrument, restricting the members admitted to preparatory programs.

As an occupational group becomes strongly established and clearly recognized, it may successfully develop additional means of controlling admission by arranging for legally recognized bodies to have the power to issue licenses or certificates. As the group becomes more professionalized, it may reach the point at which the profession itself controls the preparatory program and the licensing procedure. This concentration of power and control evolves gradually, with the profession increasing its position because of technical complexities in the preparatory program or in the actual practice of the profession.

Shimberg, Esser, and Kruger (1973) emphasize that the establishment of licensing procedures is usually the result of special efforts by practitioners. Customarily, such legislation has resulted in the creation of a regulatory board composed, either primarily or entirely, of practitioners of the occupation itself. Strongly established professions will hold control of the licensing board themselves, whereas those groups who are primarily employed or supervised by another professional group will often find their licensing board dominated by that more powerful group. Weaker, independent groups will often have a majority of members representing the general public.

Certification, registration, and *licensure* are sometimes considered synonymous. There is, however, a significant technical difference. Certification and registration usually represent the granting of recognition of qualification or competence to certain individuals in an occupation or profession, usually by a nongovernmental agency or association, as a result of successful completion of a prescribed preparatory program, of an examination, or of a specified period of work experience. Licensure, on the other hand, includes a legal right to engage in an occupation, usually conferred by a governmental agency.

Shimberg et al. (1973) examine licensing procedures in several states. They describe the use of license regulatory boards by one professional group to control a closely related occupation. For example, the licensing boards for licensed practical nurses (LPNs), in most states included in their study, were primarily populated by registered nurses (RNs), who frequently voted in unison on matters related to control of the other group. Similarly, licensing boards for dental hygienists are made up almost entirely of dentists.

The examination required for certification for some occupations, such as over-the-road driving, is administered by the prospective employer, who also issues the certificate. This procedure obviously permits considerable variability in decisions relative to marginal applicants; perhaps the demand for drivers could be a major criterion.

Both Wilensky (1965) and Hughes (1963) discuss the efforts of many occupations to become professions. One factor that often prompts such groups to move toward professionalization is the desire to obtain greater control over the recruitment and selection of entrants. Both authors emphasize that few occupations undertaking such efforts succeed in winning the status they seek. Hughes also points out that the concept of the professions is changing to include salaried professionals in bureaucratic organizations as well as those in private practice.

Many skilled crafts use an apprenticeship program to regulate admission. Although there is usually nationwide agreement concerning the length and content of the apprenticeship, the extent to which it is actually enforced may vary considerably depending on a number of factors. In extensively organized occupational groups, enforcement is more widespread than in groups that are only partially organized. With the latter groups, apprenticeships may exist in those geographic areas (often in metropolitan or highly industrialized sections) where organization is strong, and may be nonexistent or spotty in areas that are not organized.

Preparatory programs, both formal classroom and practical or applied on-the-job plans, are often used to develop the initiate's identification with the occupational group. This is done by teaching occupational history; identifying significant contributors to the development of the occupation; promoting myths or legends related to the occupation (e.g., Florence Nightingale and the nursing profession, Casey Jones and railroad locomotive engineers); encouraging attitudes and values congruent with those held by practitioners; and teaching the rules that apply to the work.

Regulating Behavior on the Job

Regulations, both formal and informal, exist to control the behavior of workers in most occupations. How apparent these controls are varies from occupation to occupation, and sometimes even from workplace to workplace.

Careful observation of settings that appear to be relatively open will often reveal subtle influences that set limits and thus control worker behavior. The existence of these rules, where they are openly recognized, is usually justified on the same grounds used for rules regulating admission to occupations—protection either of the public or of the occupational group.

Self-regulating professions maintain their self-regulatory status by developing and enforcing a code of ethics for practitioners in the profession. These codes usually include fairly explicit descriptions of prohibited behavior (abuse of clients, antisocial acts, unfair business practices); descriptions of expected or exemplary behavior; and claims to any legal exemptions that are assumed necessary to perform the occupational duties (such as privileged communication or immunity from prosecution in the event of accidents).

Another aspect of on-the-job behavior is the degree of autonomy granted to the worker to determine what she will do, how it will be done, and when it will be done. Assembly line workers have very little control of this type, whereas skilled craft workers and professionals have a great deal. Riemer (1982) has studied this autonomy among building-trades craft workers; he states that individual autonomy arises from three sources—apprenticeship training, tool ownership, and the portable nature of the worker's skills. Group autonomy for building craft workers comes from recruitment control, informal work group control, and formal union control.

Behavior on the job is sometimes established by attitudes and/or behaviors acquired during the formal preparatory programs, so the worker arrives on the job already conditioned in a particular way. Just as physicians are taught (primarily by role model behavior of supervising physicians), during their internship assignments, that their decisions regarding patient care are to be accepted unhesitatingly by other health-care workers, so, too, are nurses and others taught the primacy of the physician's orders. It is difficult for either professional group to accept any other relationship. Haas and Shaffir (1982) describe the process that transpires as medical students attempt to professionalize their behavior—that is, how they attempt to convince fellow students, faculty, and supervising physicians of their *appearance* of competency. Actually possessing skill and knowledge is less important than being able to appear competent.

Employers, or those who control the work site, have considerable input into worker behavior on the job. This is evident in negotiated or decreed work rules, influence in code-of-ethics statements, and involvement in preparatory programs. Fellow workers also influence worker behavior. This can come through the same channels used by employers, or it can appear in informal relationships on the job.

Beginning teachers, office workers, and sales representatives identify the range of acceptable attire either by observing other workers in the workplace or by consulting fellow workers. Although specific dress codes are rarely spelled out, the informal identification of appropriate and inappropriate clothing is well known and followed by the workers. Those who deviate beyond the set limits subject themselves to criticism by fellow workers and, often, by employers or supervisors.

Occupations are occasionally caught up in periods of change and transition during which workers are confused because the role they are expected to play (the on-the-job behavior displayed) is unclear. Such episodes may be produced by the impact of technological change, revised public expectations, or efforts by the occupation to change its activities or public perception. During these periods of turmoil, workers are uncertain as to whether they should behave in the old way or in the new way.

Not long ago, pharmacists were primarily responsible for compounding drugs to fill prescriptions written by physicians. Their place of employment was usually a small pharmacy or apothecary shop, and occasionally a hospital or similar health-care setting. Modern technology multiplied the drugs available for human use and at the same time delivered them ready for sale, already compounded and usually prepackaged as well. The pharmacist faced a transitional period in which the occupation changed roles from scientist-technician to sales-business person.

Similarly, the creation of walk-in medical-care centers in shopping malls and the earlier formation of medical clinics have caused role conflict for physicians caught between the centuries-old concept of a personalized doctor-patient relationship and the new scheme of speedy, efficient delivery of services that applies business practices to maximize the clientele seen by each physician.

Almost every worker can provide illustrations of control exerted on off-the-job behavior. This can result from direct, unequivocal demands made by the employer, or from very subtle, unexpressed social pressures of public expectation, or from any step between these two extremes. Public school teachers, especially in smaller communities, are often expected to maintain standards of decorum usually exceeding the established level of the community. Principals or school board members often are very explicit about what is acceptable behavior in the community. Successful lawyers and physicians may encounter public expectations that require them to maintain expensive automobiles, homes, or club memberships as symbols of their professional success. Business executives and governmental administrators are often expected to contribute both time and money to local United Fund campaigns.

Economic Aspects

In this section, we look primarily at the elements affecting the income workers obtain from their efforts. Surprisingly little literature bears directly on the economic aspects of careers. Specific statistical information on such items as wages and hours can be obtained from the Bureau of Labor Statistics and other sections of the Department of Labor. These data are published annually in such publications as *Monthly Labor Review* and are sometimes summarized in *Occupational Outlook Quarterly*. State Employment Security offices compile and publish data for both statewide and regional areas. Detailed information for each Standard Metropolitan Statistical Area (SMSA) within the state is collected, collated, and published on a regular basis. Typical publications include occupational employment statistics, industry and occupational employment projections, and compensation and wage data. Most states also now have computerized systems of occupational information that include current economic data. We consider briefly four topics that reflect economic influences: supply and demand, employment and unemployment, payment systems, and the influence of structural changes.

Supply and Demand

Economists generally contend that over the long run in a free economy, the basic determinant of occupational income is the ratio between the supply of a given quality of labor and the demand for it. In other words, wages and salaries are determined by the number of workers with a particular skill who can be induced to sell their skill at a certain rate of pay and the number of employers who desire to purchase that skill and who will make wage offers at a certain rate of pay. Any factor that tends to increase the number of workers willing to sell their skill will usually cause wage levels to go lower. Any factor that decreases the number of available workers will tend to cause wages to rise. Similarly, any factor that increases employer demand for workers will cause wages to rise, whereas any factor reducing employer demand will cause wages to fall. Hotchkiss and Borow (1990) provide a thorough discussion of these economic factors.

In actuality, the basic supply-and-demand ratio is rarely permitted to operate with total freedom. A number of factors exist that control, or at least restrict, the free operation of the supply-demand ratio. Some of these factors have been developed to protect the general public; others have been designed to protect or assist the specific group of workers. Some of these restricting elements are social custom; others have been established as legal regulations. All of them impede the free operation of the supply-demand ratio.

Such interference with the free operation of supply-demand interaction usually comes from one or more of three sources—the public, the employers, or the workers. Control and regulation may take the form of legislation, general practice, or sometimes a combination of both.

Examples of interference or control emerging from the public include both legislation and social practice. Minimum-wage laws and child labor regulations are typical of such action. Minimum-wage laws provide a floor in covered industries below which workers cannot be paid. Obviously, this control has an influence beyond the particular industries specified in the legislation, since noncovered industries must usually offer a competitive wage to attract workers. Child labor laws similarly restrict the number of potential workers available to the employer and thus force the proffered wages to be higher to attract a sufficient number of workers. Legislation specifying that workers must have specific qualifications, through licensure or otherwise, is another restrictive factor of the same sort.

The employer can interfere with the free operation of supply and demand by engaging in certain hiring practices that limit access to the job by certain workers. At first glance, one might assume that such restrictive practices would result in limited supplies of workers and therefore produce higher wages—a situation inimical to the interests of the employer. Such restriction, however, may limit some workers to access to only a very few jobs, thus depressing the wages to be paid in those positions. Though now illegal in most work situations, such practices have not totally disappeared. In previous years, this type of control was sometimes exerted toward female workers or minority-group members. The employer can, in collusion with other employers, engage in establishment of a so-called prevailing wage or going rate that is offered on a take-it-or-leave-it basis, so the position is left unfilled if prospective workers will not accept the standard that has been established.

Equal pay for equal work has been established as a basic principle through passage of several different pieces of national legislation. This concept has made it illegal to pay any worker (usually women or minority-group members) lower rates of pay than that paid to others (usually white males) performing the same task. Although the principle is generally accepted, some employers still use evasion to avoid compliance. For example, an employer might use a different name for a position held by women and minorities, despite only minor differences in assigned duties, to justify a lower rate of pay.

Even more difficult to resolve is the idea of comparable pay for comparable jobs. Several legal cases relating to this problem are working their way through the judicial system, and the issue will remain unresolved until a sufficient body of court decisions provides a foundation for legislation. The basic issue is that many positions that require fairly extensive educational preparation or the development of relatively high levels of skill have rates of pay considerably lower than those for other jobs that require less education and less skill and have no obvious requirements that justify the higher rate of pay. Opponents of the comparable-work concept insist that the differences in pay are due to conditions in the marketplace and are basically related to supply-and-demand factors. Advocates point out that in most cases where the pay differential is great, the higher paid, lower requirement job is overwhelmingly staffed with men, and the lower paid, higher qualification job is predominantly filled with women.

Workers, or their representative, can interfere with the supply-demand equation. Worker groups can insist on establishing wage rates by negotiation—a process that assures that all involved workers will require the same wage rate for the same job, thus eliminating the possibility for single workers to accept employment at lower wage rates. Workers may also control admission to the training programs by which workers become qualified for employment. An example of this is limiting the number of apprentices admitted to a craft to a certain percentage of employed journeymen, regardless of the number of unfilled positions existing in that craft.

The factors listed here establish conditions within which the supply-demand ratio must operate. Additional factors directly affecting the supply of qualified labor include the following:

Qualifications demanded of a given kind and grade of labor: The types of special traits required in all kinds of work are too numerous to mention. Illustrative of these factors would be specific physical or mental skills required in certain work, the amount and type of effort demanded, and the amount and type of responsibility that the work carries.

General appeal of a given kind of work: The more attractive the occupation, the greater the likelihood that a large number of potential workers will attempt to qualify for placement. The effect of some factors related to a given occupation is difficult to evaluate in terms of appeal. What is challenging and interesting to one person may be monotonous and distasteful to another. There are, however, certain characteristics that tend to be commonly evaluated. Remuneration relative to other occupations is one such factor.

Regularity of employment is often an attractive feature, and many workers will accept a lower wage if they can be assured that the work is steady. Another factor that adds to the general appeal of an occupation is the opportunity for advancement. Some fields are stepping stones and training jobs for other, more advanced and attractive occupations. The possibility of moving ahead later to such an opportunity is often sufficient to attract a large supply of workers willing to work for a relatively low wage.

Other factors:
1. Workers are often reluctant to move to other geographic areas. This can affect the labor supply in two ways. First, it may cause a surplus in an area where employment is decreasing, thus forcing wages even lower. Second, the reluctance to move may prevent the solution of a shortage of workers in an expanding labor market, thus forcing wages still higher in an attempt to find sufficient workers.
2. The long-term movement of workers from rural to urban areas in this country has provided a larger supply of unskilled and low-skilled workers for the urban labor market than would exist otherwise.
3. The difficulty of transferring from one occupation to another without extensive retraining affects the labor supply in expanding fields. As the demand for low levels of skill continues to decrease and greater demands are made for skilled workers, this problem will intensify.
4. Unequal access to educational opportunities restricts the labor supply to some extent, since training opportunities are limited and not available to all who might like to take advantage of them. Restricting

factors may be due to location, cost, entrance requirements, discrimination, or other reasons.

5. Organized labor exerts influence and control on the supply of workers available. Restriction on the number of members, apprenticeship or initiation requirements, and conditions of work impose limitations on the supply of workers.

6. Similarly, the labor supply can be influenced by activities of employers and employers' groups. Positive influences would include such things as publicizing opportunities, providing training, and improving wages and working conditions.

7. Government assistance, such as welfare, may influence the supply of labor by reducing the number seeking low-paying jobs.

One factor having a definite effect on the demand for labor is the general status of business. When producers are confident of a continuing or increasing public demand for goods or services, their demand for labor goes up. If producers feel that the business cycle is headed downward toward less demand for goods or services, they reduce their demand for labor.

Employment and Unemployment

One frequently hears on radio or television newscasts or sees in daily newspapers or weekly news magazines statements about changing rates of employment and unemployment and similar information. Although we often do not stop to think precisely who is included in these data, it is important to understand the terminology if the data are to have any meaning.

Considered from the standpoint of the worker, employment appears to be a simple concept that can be identified by asking the worker, "Do you have a job?" If the worker says yes, we would classify her as employed; if the answer is no, we would consider her unemployed. Complications (and there are many of them) arise when the answer is, "Well, yes and no." One of the first complications carries us back to our discussion of work in Chapter 1. For the purposes of state and national statistical data, employment requires pay or the sharing of benefits in a family-operated enterprise. Thus homemakers and volunteers are not considered to be employed on the basis of homemaking and volunteer activities.

A further complication arises in obtaining employment data. There is no way to maintain an accurate count of who is working for pay, so sampling methods must be applied. For governmental purposes, using a nationwide sample of 60,000 households, *employed* people include the following:

1. All civilians who worked for pay anytime during the week that includes the twelfth day in the month for at least an hour, or who worked unpaid for at least 15 hours in a family-operated enterprise.

2. Those who were temporarily absent from their regular jobs because of illness, vacation, industrial dispute, or similar reasons during that week.

3. Members of the armed forces stationed in the United States.

Unemployed people are those who did not work during the survey week but were available for work and had looked for jobs within the preceding 4 weeks. Individuals on layoff who did not look for work or who are expecting to start new jobs within 30 days are counted as unemployed. There are generally thought to be three types of unemployment:

Frictional unemployment is the temporary joblessness of individuals who are between jobs, are engaged in seasonal work, have quit their job and are looking for a better job, or are looking for their first job.

Cyclical unemployment is the situation that arises from changes in the level of business activity during the course of the business cycle. The factory worker on layoff because product demand has fallen is an example.

Structural unemployment is the joblessness that occurs when technological change or similar factors eliminate the need for that worker. The worker can no longer sell his skills because there is no demand for them.

The term *underemployment* is also frequently encountered. The underemployed worker is employed but is in a job below his level of skill or experience, usually because there is no job available at the higher level.

A *discouraged worker* is a person without a job who is no longer looking for work because he believes no job is available. Because he is not looking, this worker is no longer counted as unemployed. Sometimes unemployment figures appear to improve because people stop looking for jobs and are dropped from the figures.

Labor force is another term that is sometimes used in different ways. The total labor force includes all employed civilians and the armed forces within the United States, plus those who are unemployed but seeking work and available to work. Unemployment figures are usually quoted as a percentage of this total figure. Individuals not in the labor force include retirees, those engaged in their own housework, students, the long-term ill, discouraged workers, and those voluntarily idle.

Payment Systems
The income provided to workers for their efforts can be categorized as follows:

> Entrepreneurial withdrawal
> Fees
> Compensation of employees
>   Salaries
>   Wages

Entrepreneurial withdrawal is the income taken by the owner of a business or industry as compensation for the responsibility and risk that she has assumed in establishing and undertaking the business.

Fees constitute the income paid to the various free professions when the worker is engaged in the actual independent practice of the profession. An example is the income of lawyers and physicians in private practice.

Employees of organizations are paid either in the form of salaries or wages. *Salary* is usually a fixed compensation regularly paid for services over a specific period of time, such as a year, quarter, month, or week. *Wages* are similarly compensation for services (usually labor) paid at short, stated intervals. Salaries are usually paid to managerial, administrative, professional, clerical, and supervisory employees. Although the amount of salary may be on the basis of a year, it is often paid in installments each week or month.

Workers described as laborers, even though highly skilled, are usually paid wages. These may be based on either a time rate or a piece rate. *Time-rate wages* pay the worker a fixed rate per unit of time. The time unit ordinarily is 1 hour, and workers often describe their income in terms of so much an hour. The *piece-rate system* compensates the worker in terms of the number of units produced.

In many work situations, some combination of time- and piece-rate wages may be in effect. This permits the worker to gain from the advantages of both systems, but he or she may also be subject to some of the disadvantages of both systems. A combination method usually provides a minimum guarantee and a bonus if the standard output established for that job is exceeded. Many workers and worker groups are suspicious of piece-rate or so-called incentive systems, since they fear that the superior worker who develops a method of higher production may cause either the piece rate to be lowered or the number of needed workers to be reduced. Every organization can point to instances when unscrupulous employers have done exactly that.

Many workers, especially service workers such as waiters and waitresses, receive their income either partly or entirely from tips provided by the customers they serve. Such compensation is based on neither the unit of time nor the unit of work. Similarly, individuals in sales positions may be paid a commission—a percentage of their total sales.

In addition to cash payments received by workers, two other methods of payment are part of the total picture of worker reimbursement: fringe benefits and payment in kind. *Fringe benefits* include indirect payments to workers that can amount to an important part of their total income. Typical fringe benefits include paid vacations and holidays and various types of insurance coverage such as medical, accident, or life. Other examples include retirement programs, supplemental unemployment income, and military or maternity leave with pay. *Payment in kind* includes meals provided without charge by the employer, company housing free or at a reduced rental, expense accounts, free travel, use of a company automobile, uniforms or other clothing, and so forth.

In recent years, several modifications of the basic wage system have appeared. Some companies have adopted a profit-sharing system, in which a certain proportion of the company's annual profit is divided among the workers, often in the form of an end-of-the-year, Christmas, or vacation bonus. Other companies have established a guaranteed annual wage by which workers are assured of a specified income regardless of the number of weeks worked. Still other companies have linked wage rates to a cost-of-living index, so wages are increased to compensate for increases in the cost of living. Presumably, such systems would also lower wages with a declining cost of living.

Influence of Structural Change

In Chapter 4 we examine the world of work in some detail, including its present structure and the causes of changes that are likely to influence its nature in future years. We consider this topic here only to emphasize that one factor influencing workers and their careers is the continuous change that occurs in the occupational format.

For example, the refinement and improvement of the internal combustion engine at the turn of the century brought about the development of the automobile. The rapid acceptance of this invention reduced the demand for buggy makers and harness makers and created an array of automobile manufacturing jobs. Similarly, changes in the food processing industry with the development of the so-called tin can reduced the demand for wooden barrels and almost eliminated the job of cooper.

Change is a persistent part of our lives, and as that change influences the way we live, it also modifies the occupational structure that surrounds us. One change likely to continue through most of the 1990s is the reduction of manufacturing jobs and their replacement by service industry occupations. For example, the jobs expected to experience the most growth between 1982 and 2000 include building custodians, cashiers, secretaries, general clerks, sales clerks, nurses, waiters and waitresses, elementary and kindergarten teachers, truck drivers, and nursing aids. As manufacturing jobs decline, workers are displaced from positions with relatively high rates of pay and favorable fringe benefits such as pension and health insurance programs. If they are to transfer to expanding areas, most will need extensive retraining before qualifying for positions that offer lower rates of pay, greater job insecurity, and fewer fringe benefits.

Appraisal of the individual in terms of ability, temperament, interest, and educational achievement is used routinely in career development. Of equal importance are the factors beyond the individual's psychological self that shape and influence the world of work and the individual's relationship to it. If it is appropriate to discuss ability as it bears on the possibilities of entering a particular field, it is equally sound to look at admission restrictions, social selectivity, and lifestyle. Selection of career goals should include consideration of how the individual fits the occupational mold *and* how the occupation fits the individual.

SUMMARY

One might say that it is obvious that almost every characteristic of the individual and the situation in which that individual lives influence the relationship between the worker and his or her work. Nevertheless, it is often helpful to consider this interaction in an orderly and methodical frame of reference.

Factors that directly relate to the person have been labeled *internal factors;* these factors are subdivided into generic, personal-psychological, and personal-sociological categories. In the generic group we looked at gender, ethnicity, and physique. The psychological sector included aptitude, interests, personality, temperament, and values. The sociological unit consisted of family socioeconomic status, access to education, and lifestyle.

External factors include those influences situated beyond the individual and the immediate family. These are subdivided into the work situation, sociological, and economic aspects. Topics considered under the work situation label included training time, physical demands, and the environmental conditions in which the work is performed. Sociological topics included prestige ratings, mobility, the control of admission to specific occupations, and control of worker behavior on and off the job. Economic items included the effect of supply and demand, the meaning of employment and unemployment, and how workers are paid for their efforts.

REFERENCES

Alexander, L., & McDill, E. L. (1976). Selection and allocation within schools: Some causes and consequences of curriculum placement. *American Sociological Review, 41,* 963–980.

Anastasi, A. (1982). *Psychological testing* (5th ed.). New York: MacMillan.

Astin, H. S. (1984). The meaning of work in women's lives: A sociopsychological model of career choice and work behavior. *Counseling Psychologist, 12,* 117–126.

Bingham, W. V. (1937). *Aptitudes and aptitude testing.* New York: Harper & Row.

Blau, P. M., & Duncan, O. D. (1967). *The American occupational structure.* New York: Wiley.

Borow, H. (1981). Career guidance uses of labor market information: Limitations and potentialities. In D. H. Montross & C. J. Shinkman (Eds.), *Career development in the 1980s: Theory and practice.* Springfield, IL: Charles C. Thomas.

Braun, J., & Bayer, F. (1973). Social desirability of occupations: Revisited. *Vocational Guidance Quarterly, 21,* 202–205.

Castro, J. (1990). Get set: Here they come. *Time,* special issue, Fall 1990, 50–51.

Counts, G. S. (1925). The social status of occupations. *School Review, 33,* 16–27.

Cronbach, L. J. (1970). *Essentials of psychological testing* (3rd ed.). New York: Harper & Row.

Deeg, M. E., & Paterson, D. G. (1947). Changes in social status of occupations. *Occupations, 25*, 205–208.

Droege, R. C., & Boese, R. (1982). Development of a new occupational aptitude pattern structure with comprehensive occupational coverage. *Vocational Guidance Quarterly, 30*, 219–229.

Form, W. H., & Miller, D. C. (1949). Occupational career pattern as a sociological instrument. *American Journal of Sociology, 54*, 317–329.

Gamoran, A., & Mare, R. D. (1989). Secondary school tracking and educational inequality: Compensation, reinforcement, or neutrality? *American Journal of Sociology, 94*, 1146–1183.

Garbin, A. P., & Bates, F. L. (1966). Occupational prestige and its correlates: A reexamination. *Social Forces, 44*, 295–302.

Garet, M. S., & DeLany, B. (1988). Students, courses, and stratification. *Sociology of Education, 61*, 61–77.

Goldman, L. (1971). *Using tests in counseling* (2nd ed.). New York: Appleton-Century-Crofts.

Haas, J., & Shaffir, W. (1982). Ritual evaluation of competence. *Work and Occupations, 9*, 131–154.

Hakel, M. D., Hollman, T. D., & Dunnette, M. D. (1968). Stability and change in the social status of occupations over 21 and 42 year periods. *Personnel and Guidance Journal, 46*, 762–764.

Hall, R. H. (1986). *Dimensions of Work*. Newbury Park, CA: Sage.

Harris, D. V. (1976). Physical sex differences: A matter of degree. *Counseling Psychologist, 6*, 9–11.

Hodge, R. W., Siegel, P. M., & Rossi, P. H. (1964). Occupational prestige in the United States, 1925–63. *American Journal of Sociology, 70*, 286–302.

Hotchkiss, L., & Borow, H. (1990). Sociological perspectives on career development and attainment. In D. Brown, L. Brooks, and Associates, *Career choice and development: Applying contemporary theories to practice* (2nd ed). San Francisco: Jossey-Bass.

Hughes, E. C. (1963). Professions. *Daedalus, 92*, 655–668.

Huston, A. C. (1983). Sextyping. In M. E. Hetherton, (Ed.), *Socialization, personality and social development*, vol. IV of *Handbook of child development*. New York: Wiley.

Kanzaki, G. A. (1976). Fifty years (1925–1975) of stability in the social status of occupations. *Vocational Guidance Quarterly, 25*, 101–105.

Katz, M. (1963). *Decisions and values*. New York: College Entrance Examination Board.

Kraus, L. E., & Stoddard, S. (1989). *Chartbook on disability in the United States*. Washington, DC: U.S. National Institute on Disability and Rehabilitation Research.

National Opinion Research Center. (1947). Jobs and occupations: A popular evaluation. *Opinion News, 9*, 4, 3–13.

Nelson, A. G. (1971). Discrepancy between expressed and inventoried vocational interest. *Vocational Guidance Quarterly, 20*, 21–24.

Oppenheimer, V. K. (1982). *Work and the family: A study in social demography*. New York: Academic Press.

O'Toole, J., Scheiber, J. L., & Wood, L. C. (Eds.). (1981). *Working: Changes and choices*. New York: Human Sciences Press.

Peterson, J. A. (1970). *Counseling and values.* Scranton, PA: International Textbook.

Riemer, J. W. (1982). Worker autonomy in the skilled building trades. In P. L. Stewart & M. G. Cantor (Eds.), *Varieties of work.* Beverly Hills, CA: Sage.

Rose, H. A., & Elston, C. F. (1970). Ask him or test him? *Vocational Guidance Quarterly, 19,* 28–32.

Rothman, R. A. (1987). *Working: Sociological perspectives.* Englewood Cliffs, NJ: Prentice Hall.

Sewell, W. H., & Hauser, R. M. (1975). *Education, occupation, and earnings: Achievement in early career.* New York: Academic Press.

Shimberg, B., Esser, B. F., & Kruger, D. H. (1973). *Occupational licensing: Practices and policies.* Washington, DC: Public Affairs Press.

Smith, E. J. (1983). Issues in racial minorities career behavior. In W. B. Walsh & S. H. Osipow (Eds.), *Handbook of vocational psychology,* vol. 1, *Foundations.* Hillsdale, NJ: Lawrence Erlbaum Associates.

Spranger, E. (1928). *Types of men.* Translated from 5th German edition. Halle: Max Niemeyer.

Stefflre, B., Resnikoff, A., & Lezotte, L. (1968). The relationship of sex to occupational prestige. *Personnel and Guidance Journal, 46,* 765–772.

Stewart, P. L., & Cantor, M. G. (Eds.). (1982). *Varieties of work.* Beverly Hills, CA: Sage.

Super, D. E. (1957). *The psychology of careers.* New York: Harper & Row.

Super, D. E., & Crites, J. O. (1962). *Appraising vocational fitness through psychological means.* New York: Harper & Row.

Terkel, S. (1972). *Working.* New York: Pantheon.

Thomas, L. G. (1956). *The occupational structure and education.* Englewood Cliffs, NJ: Prentice Hall.

Tuckman, J. (1950). Ranking of women's occupations according to social status, earnings, and working conditions. *Occupations, 28,* 290–294.

U.S. Department of Labor, Employment and Training Administration. (1981). *Selected characteristics of occupations defined in the Dictionary of Occupational Titles.* Washington, DC: U.S. Government Printing Office.

U.S. Department of Labor, Employment and Training Administration. (1982). *Dictionary of occupational titles, fourth edition supplement.* Washington, DC: U.S. Government Printing Office.

Vanfossen, E., Jones, D., & Spade, J. S. (1987). Curriculum tracking and status maintenance. *Sociology of Education, 60,* 104–122.

Whitney, D. R. (1969). Predicting from expressed choice: A review. *Personnel and Guidance Journal, 48,* 279–286.

Wilensky, H. L. (1965). The professionalization of everyone. *American Journal of Sociology, 70,* 137–158.

4

Occupational Structure Today and Tomorrow

Both scholars and philosophers have frequently declared that the most constant factor in life is change. Each of us encounters change in some way every day. Even those of us who describe ourselves as young remark regularly that things aren't the way they used to be. In some parts of life, change occurs very slowly and gradually, whereas elsewhere it may be sudden, unexpected, and massive; and there are gradations between these two extremes. The occupational world is also constantly changing and readjusting.

Predicting the future is hazardous business, and even the best estimates often leave many factors unaccounted for. The risk of error increases with the need for precision and the distance projected into the future. For example, in the United States, we can say with some confidence that January is likely to be colder than November or March. But matching high temperature at a given location on January 15 against that of November 15 or March 15 is less reliable. Similarly, we can usually make a better prediction of tomorrow's weather than that of a year from tomorrow. Even though we cannot build a formula that will weight all factors accurately, we can usually identify those factors that are most likely to be influential. Then we can either proceed on the basis of all other things being equal or, as the Bureau of Labor Statistics does, with a best-case and worst-case approach that will identify the range within which reality will likely be found.

In this chapter we discuss four broad topics that relate to anticipated change and present structure in the world of work:

Causes of long-term trends
Causes of short-term trends
The occupational world through the 1990s
Sources of information on change and structure

CAUSES OF LONG-TERM TRENDS

Some changes in the world of work occur slowly and may be anticipated or identified long before their influence becomes significant. Their eventual impact can be massive and can last for a very long time. These big changes are grouped into four categories, but it is important to recognize that these often may be interrelated, so some items could be listed under more than one heading. These causal forces are labeled population, sociological, economic, and technological factors.

Population Factors

Three factors influence the growth of our population: the birth rate, the death rate, and the net immigration (the excess of immigration over emigration). Birth rates began to decline in the mid-1960s and have continued to decline since that time, although they are expected to turn upward in the mid-1990s. The impact of declining birth rates has a delayed effect on the numbers in the labor force because newborns do not go to work. The delayed impact begins to appear 16 to 20 years later, so the children of the baby-boom generation are entering the work force during the 1990s. However, a declining birth rate does influence the existing labor force by reducing the need for child care workers, elementary teachers, factory workers who manufacture school equipment, and so forth.

Improved nutrition, greater access to medical care, and other life-extending factors have also changed the death rate, so people live longer than previously. More older people in the population create a different demand for goods (e.g., leisure equipment) and services (e.g., medical care). This increased longevity, added to a decreased birth rate, compounds the rate at which the average age of our population moves upward.

The 16–24 age group is expected to make up 16 percent of the labor force in the year 2000, down from 19 percent in 1988. The 24–34 age group grew 64 percent from 1976 to 1988 but will decline about 12 percent by 2000. The 35–54 group is expected to increase, and the over-55 group should hold constant. Overall, a 16 percent increase in the number of people available to participate in the labor force is expected to occur during the period from 1988 to 2000, compared with a 26.5 percent growth in the previous 12 years. Thus there will be many fewer workers available for beginning jobs, so some occupations usually filled by workers in this age group (fast-food workers and military personnel, for example) may remain unfilled unless there are competitive activities to attract potential workers. At the same time, the greater number of workers in the 25–54 age range will increase the competition for desirable occupations and reduce the opportunities for promotion. However, this shift could lead to higher productivity because workers in this age range are usually experienced and have high productivity records. The labor force is projected to total 136 to 141 million by 2000. Women comprised 40 percent of the work group in 1976; this percentage is expected to grow to 47 percent by 2000.

Population growth is not uniform across the country. This is mainly the result of movement and relocation rather than significant regional differences in birth and death rates. The 1990 census shows 63 percent of the decade's total population growth accounted for by California, Arizona, Texas, and Florida. States such as West Virginia, Iowa, Wyoming, North Dakota, Illinois, Michigan, and Pennsylvania showed declines from almost 1 percent to over 8 percent.

Another expected change in the 1990s is growth in minority participation in the work force. African Americans made up about 11 percent of the labor force in 1988; this is expected to become 12 percent by 2000. During this same period, the Hispanic percentage of the labor force is expected to grow from 7 percent to 10 percent. The proportion of Asians and others will grow from 3 percent to 4 percent.

Immigration factors are even harder to predict. The Bureau of the Census assumes that documented immigration totals approximately 560,000 annually and emigration totals about 160,000 annually. The Immigration Reform and Control Act was fully implemented at the end of 1988, and this is expected to reduce undocumented immigration to about 100,000 per year by the late 1990s. This would result in a population increase by net immigration of approximately a half million per year. Many will compete for available jobs immediately.

A final aspect of population impact on occupations relates to the average age of workers in a specific occupation. Variation in average age between occupations can be produced by such situations as a large influx of workers within a short period when the occupation was established or when some factor created a sudden demand for workers. If the occupation then stabilizes, as most do, one sees this large cadre of single-age workers move through the working years together, with many withdrawing almost simultaneously at retirement time. Vacancies occur in occupations either because of growth that causes increased demand for workers or because of the need to replace workers who leave the occupation through resignation, retirement, or death. As the average age in an occupation increases, the replacement rate is also likely to increase.

Sociological Factors

The effect of sociological factors is sometimes more difficult to visualize than other causes of long-term trends. Social consciousness usually develops gradually, ultimately causing changes in ethical viewpoints and creating increased social pressures. This may, in time, result in officially sanctioned and enforced changes in human behavior. Even before official action occurs, there can be an observable influence on work and workers.

Forces that relate to lifestyle, social values, attitudes, and similar factors that change group behavior are classified in this group. Some of these factors may be expressed through legislation or by amendment or repeal of earlier legislation. For example, during the past 2 decades, concern for the environment has focused attention on the disposition of hazardous waste and on correcting conditions caused earlier by reckless handling of these materials. Similarly, concern for reducing the effects caused by acid rain can have an impact on jobs in the coal mines of the Midwest and in factories that use high-sulfur coal.

Efforts to reduce our dependence on foreign oil sparked the development of more fuel-efficient automobiles that are both smaller and lighter. The decrease in automobile size, as well as the use of lightweight materials, reduced the demand for steel and thereby the jobs related to steel production at the same time that demand for the substitute materials was increasing. Unfortunately, it is not easy to shift a steel mill or steelworkers to the production of aluminum and plastics.

One example of increased allegiance to the self-fulfillment ethic is greater participation in recreational activities. This interest has created demand for running shoes, warmup suits, and health club facilities as well as for camping equipment, boats, and recreational vehicles. Another example is the extended participation of women in the labor force, which has an effect far beyond the job they hold and the greater income that job produces. That participation influences living patterns for families—kinds of foods consumed and how they are prepared, household tasks and how they are managed, type of housing and transportation used, need for child care, and so on.

Changes in the educational attainment of the general population also affect occupations. The evidence is strong that the least educated have the greatest difficulty in securing and retaining employment and that those with the most educational background have the lowest rates of unemployment. The average amount of completed education is increasing for two reasons: first, older people withdrawing from work often have fewer years of education; and second, younger people entering work generally have completed more years of schooling.

The presence of adequate retirement programs for older workers also influences the number of workers who stay on the job. For several years, there has been a steady reduction in the average retirement age of workers. Recent legislation raising the compulsory retirement age from 65 to 70 may gradually increase the number of workers who continue to work beyond the traditional retirement age. A further increase will occur if the minimum age required to qualify for retirement benefits is also raised. Uncertainties about the cost of living, the threat of inflation, and similar factors will also keep older workers on the job.

Economic Factors

In a totally free market, the supply and demand of workers and raw materials would greatly influence the number and nature of available jobs. In most societies, numerous controls have been developed that interfere with the free operation of the market. Many of these (e.g., minimum-wage laws, licensing requirements, and import controls) came into existence to regulate what had been seen as disruptive surges in that market. Although controls have subdued drastic and sudden fluctuations, there are still discernible trends suggesting upward or downward movements in the marketplace that bear on occupational opportunity.

Changes in capitalization requirements also influence jobs. Undoubtedly one cause of the consistent decline in employment in agriculture relates to this factor. Farming of almost every type now requires such an extensive investment in land and equipment that efficiency becomes the determining factor between success and failure. In other businesses, the constant search for mergers is often related to economic factors that are fundamentally based on productive efficiency—creating more goods with fewer workers. National fiscal policy also influences the number of jobs. Large national deficits create competition for investment dollars, making plant expansion more costly and hence slowing creation of jobs.

Technological Factors

Obvious factors that have a long-term influence on occupations are technological progress, invention, and discovery. Entire industries have come into existence as a result of the relentless march of technology. Sometimes the new discovery or invention creates a new market for itself as the public becomes familiar and accustomed to it. An example of this is air conditioning. Only a few decades old, this invention has brought with it thousands of jobs in the manufacture, distribution, sale, and maintenance of equipment. Similarly, television has created opportunities for vast numbers of workers not only in the fields just mentioned, but also in the broad entertainment and advertising aspects of that industry. For the most part, areas such as these have created entirely new occupations that were nonexistent before.

In many areas of modern life, technological progress (e.g., computers and word processors) has resulted in improvements and refinements, in the replacing of old methods and products with new and better ways. When this happens, some occupations may be drastically reduced and sometimes may disappear altogether, to be replaced by those related to the new technique or product. Examples include the coopers, mentioned in the previous chapter, who were as prevalent as plumbers or pipefitters in the 1890 census but whose numbers had declined so much they were not listed in the 1940 census. Similar changes are occurring in many occupations and industries. The increased use of robots and automated equipment has reduced the number of production line workers in many fields. This is especially apparent in the U.S. automobile industry, where new plants use more machines and fewer workers.

Closely related to invention and discovery is our access to natural resources. The recognition of our dependence on outside sources for such crucial items as petroleum continues to produce vast changes in our lives and in occupational opportunities. The automobile industry has undergone a metamorphosis that, in turn, has affected the production of steel and other supplies. The search for oil has been accelerated, as has the search for alternative sources of energy.

CAUSES OF SHORT-TERM TRENDS

Several examples of factors producing short-term trends can be identified. Viewed objectively, these usually have less effect than do long-term trends. Nevertheless, to individuals who are caught in the crunch produced by transitory factors, the impact can be devastating. Some influences have a generalized effect across almost the entire economy; others may be more specific.

One of the most obvious causes of short-term trends is various types of calamities, either humanly caused or natural. Natural disasters such as earthquakes, floods, and volcanic eruptions can disrupt and change occupational patterns in the area for extended periods of time. Unexpected freezes in citrus-growing areas may not only destroy the current crop but also, if trees are seriously damaged, require new plantings that need several years to become productive.

Human disasters can be just as disruptive. War or the threat of war diverts large numbers of workers from civilian occupations to military assignments. It further affects others by switching manufacturing and other sectors to the production of military goods. It may create serious shortages of workers in fields that are considered less essential to the national welfare.

New directions in fashion, recreation, and other activities can also distort the occupational structure by creating new demands or reducing old ones. Changes in men's hairstyles in recent years have eliminated many barber shops. Similarly, changes in lapel width and hemline height can make clothing obsolete long before it wears out. Imitation of movie idols, popular athletes, or television stars can create demands where none previously existed. Some technological developments occasionally start as fads (e.g., video cassette recorders and personal computers).

Seasonal variations are also influential. Summers tend to increase demand for goods and services in mountain and seaside resorts; winters have the same effect on resorts located in warm areas. The back-to-school season includes buying in retail stores, for which manufacturers have been preparing. Planting time and harvest time change typical patterns in agricultural areas. The annual Christmas shopping season creates demand for temporary sales workers, letter carriers, transportation workers, and other workers.

Short-term economic factors also exert an influence. Although the general business trend over long periods is either upward or downward, small segments of that larger trend will show considerable variation. Factors that create these short-term zigzags include strikes, unexpected surpluses or shortages of raw materials or processed goods, temporary market disruptions, fluctuations in access to short-term capital caused by changes in interest rates, inflationary pressures, changing tax laws, and sometimes even the anticipation of possible events.

THE OCCUPATIONAL WORLD THROUGH THE 1990S

Having identified some of the factors most likely to create occupational change, we are now ready to look briefly at the world of work as it is today and as it may be in the near future. Our previous discussion pointed out the sudden changes that can occur. Major changes usually take some time to transpire; thus a projection based on recent trends is usually the safest estimate of what the near future is likely to hold. Most of our attention in this discussion focuses on the period between 1988 and 2000, for which Bureau of Labor Statistics estimates are available.

In the 1970s and early 1980s, much attention was focused on the changes that would occur as automation became more widespread. The word *automation* referred to the increased control of manufacturing processes by automatic machines directed by computerized programs. Now that automated processes are standard in many industries, we rarely refer to automation. Instead, we talk about high technology, or *high tech*.

The widespread application of high tech has had two massive effects on the world of work. First, automated equipment can operate only when it has been programmed to accomplish the various tasks to be performed. Thus many new openings have been created for individuals to process the information that must be programmed to make the machines work automatically. Second, as production workers have been replaced by machines, they have sought other areas for reentry to work. Only in the service area have jobs been expanding significantly, so many workers have shifted from relatively high-paying production jobs in manufacturing to much lower paying jobs with lower skill levels in service activities.

The exodus of many workers from manufacturing jobs has been intensified by the relocation of many manufacturing plants that are labor intensive to geographic sites where labor can be employed more economically. Within the United States, this has often meant relocation from the Northeast and North Central areas to the South and the West, where labor unions generally are weaker. In many cases, plants have been relocated to underdeveloped countries where pay rates are very low. High-tech equipment, involving computerized control coupled with worldwide communications systems, permits the home office to maintain its direction of operations just as easily as it did when the plant was "out back."

INDUSTRIAL GROUPING

In looking at today's world of work, we consider two perspectives: where the jobs are and what the jobs are. An *industry* is an establishment or group of establishments engaged in producing similar types of goods and services. In earlier paragraphs we referred to *manufacturing*—a term that is understood to mean the process of modifying and converting raw materials into finished, usable products. When we refer to the manufacturing industry, we are including all the establishments that make things. In Chapter 1 we defined *work* as the production of goods and services valued by others. Thus all work involves either goods or services, and all the places where people work must likewise be concerned with producing either goods or services. Goods-producing industries include agriculture, mining, construction, and manufacturing. Service-producing industries include transportation, communication, and public utilities; trade (both wholesale and retail); finance, insurance, and real estate; services; and government. These nine sectors provide the sites where all occupations are located. The reader should be aware that the term *service* is applied to two *industrial* categories as well as an *occupational* category. Service-producing industries are the industries not included in the goods-producing group, and they include the five sectors listed here. One of these sectors is also called the service sector and is described later. In addition, there are service occupations, and we consider this label later when we discuss other occupational groups. Understanding the statistics included in the tables in this chapter requires knowing which of these three images is applicable. For example, Table 4.1 (showing employment in the various industrial areas) lists the service-producing industrial area as probably having 96 million workers by the year 2000; of these, almost 34 million will be in the service sector of that broader industrial area. Most of these workers are not employed in service occupations. Table 4.3 shows that there are expected to be almost 23 million workers in service occupations in the year 2000.

Tables 4.1 and 4.2 provide specific information about the changes that have occurred in the industrial sectors between 1976 and 1988 and estimates of the changes expected to take place between 1988 and 2000. The projections include three sets of figures labeled "low," "moderate," and "high." The "low" column includes figures based on the most conservative estimate; the "high" column reflects the most optimistic data; the "moderate" column represents the average estimate and probably is the most realistic figure to use. We use the "moderate" estimate in our brief review of these data.

The labor force grew by approximately 28 million workers in the 12 years from 1976 to 1988. It is expected to increase by another 18 million by 2000. The slower growth rate is, at least in part, due to the expectation of fewer available workers with expected declines in both the numbers of youth and women entering the labor market. We consider several of the categories listed in Tables 4.1 and 4.2.

The *mining and petroleum* sector produces much of the raw material and energy sources used by industry and private consumers. Within the energy areas are coal mining and the finding and extraction of crude petroleum and natural gas. These industries account for approximately 75 percent of the workers in this sector. Other industries in this sector include iron mining; copper mining; mining of other metals such as gold, stone and clay mining and quarrying; and chemical and fertilizer mineral mining. This sector declined by approximately 7 percent from 1976 to 1988, and another decline of about 2 percent is expected to occur by 2000.

TABLE 4.1 *Employment by Major Industry Division, 1976, 1988, and Projected to 2000 (numbers in thousands)*

Industry	1976	1988	2000 Low	2000 Moderate	2000 High	Change, 1988–2000 Low	Change, 1988–2000 Moderate	Change, 1988–2000 High
Total	89,942	118,104	127,118	136,211	144,146	9,014	18,107	26,042
Nonfarm wage and salary	79,080	104,960	114,154	122,056	128,998	9,194	17,096	24,038
Goods-producing	23,358	25,252	23,512	25,680	27,785	−1,740	428	2,533
Mining	779	721	656	705	827	−65	−16	106
Construction	3,576	5,125	5,504	5,885	6,318	379	760	1,193
Manu-facturing	19,003	19,406	17,352	19,090	20,640	−2,054	−316	1,234
Durable	11,080	11,436	10,160	11,220	12,255	−1,276	−216	819
Nondurable	7,923	7,970	7,192	7,870	8,385	−778	−100	415
Service-producing	55,722	79,708	90,642	96,376	101,213	10,934	16,668	21,505
Transporta-tion and utilities	4,583	5,548	5,713	6,096	6,587	165	548	1,039
Wholesale trade	4,546	6,029	6,463	6,936	7,457	434	907	1,428
Retail trade	13,208	19,110	21,251	22,875	23,812	2,141	3,765	4,702
Finance, insurance and real estate	4,271	6,677	7,306	7,762	8,104	629	1,085	1,427
Services	14,243	24,971	31,644	33,718	35,258	6,673	8,747	10,287
Government	14,871	17,373	18,265	18,989	19,995	892	1,616	2,622
Agriculture	3,371	3,259	2,797	3,125	3,315	−462	−134	56
Private households	1,398	1,163	1,014	1,103	1,166	−149	−60	3
Nonfarm self-employed and unpaid family	6,093	8,722	9,153	9,927	10,667	431	1,205	1,945

The *construction* sector includes the building of new homes, nonresidential buildings, public utilities, highways, all other new construction, and maintenance and repair construction. The sector grew from over 3.5 million workers in 1976 to more than 5 million in 1988, a rate of more than 40 percent. By 2000, the sector will approach 6 million with a growth rate of about 15 percent. Most workers in this sector are so-called blue-collar workers, and more than half of the total group are craft workers such as carpenters, electricians, painters, and plumbers. About half of the workers in this sector are employed by special trade contractors who often subcontract to perform specific parts of a larger construction job. About one third work for general building contractors. The remaining one fifth are involved in heavy construction projects such as dams, bridges, and roads.

TABLE 4.2 *Employment by Major Industry Division, 1976, 1988, and Projected to 2000 (percent distribution and annual rate of change)*

Industry	Percent distribution of wage and salary employment					Annual rate of change			
			2000				Change, 1988–2000		
	1976	1988	Low	Mod-erate	High	1976–88	Low	Mod-erate	High
Total	—	—	—	—	—	2.3	.6	1.2	1.7
Nonfarm wage and salary	100.0	100.0	100.0	100.0	100.0	2.4	.7	1.3	1.7
Goods-producing	29.5	24.1	20.6	21.0	21.5	.7	-.6	.1	.8
Mining	1.0	.7	.6	.6	.6	-.6	-.8	-.2	1.1
Construction	4.5	4.9	4.8	4.8	4.9	3.0	.6	1.2	1.8
Manu-facturing	24.0	18.5	15.2	15.6	16.0	.2	-.9	-.1	.5
Durable	14.0	10.9	8.9	9.2	9.5	.3	-1.0	-.2	.6
Nondurable	10.0	7.6	6.3	6.4	6.5	.0	-.9	-.1	.4
Service-producing	70.5	75.9	79.4	79.0	78.5	3.0	1.1	1.6	2.0
Transportation and utilities	5.8	5.3	5.0	5.0	5.1	1.6	.2	.8	1.4
Wholesale trade	5.7	5.7	5.7	5.7	5.8	2.4	.6	1.2	1.8
Retail trade	16.7	18.2	18.6	18.7	18.5	3.1	.9	1.5	1.9
Finance, insurance and real estate	5.4	6.4	6.4	6.4	6.3	3.8	.8	1.3	1.6
Services	18.0	23.8	27.7	27.6	27.3	4.8	2.0	2.5	2.9
Government	18.8	16.6	16.0	15.6	15.5	1.3	.4	.7	1.2
Agriculture	—	—	—	—	—	-.3	-1.3	-.3	.1
Private households	—	—	—	—	—	-1.5	-1.1	-.4	.0
Nonfarm self-employed and unpaid family	—	—	—	—	—	3.0	.4	1.1	1.7

Source: Personick, 1989.
Note: Dash indicates data not available.

Manufacturing is the second largest industrial sector, employing almost 20 million workers in 1988, and it is expected to shrink slightly by 2000. It is also very diverse, consisting of two large areas: durable goods and nondurable goods. Durable goods include those items that are expected to last for 3 years or more: iron and steel, machinery, automobiles, furniture, and so on. Nondurable goods are those materials that are consumed or used up in a relatively brief time, such as paper, textiles, food products, and leather. Although this sector is very susceptible to changes in the general economy, it held relatively stable at 19 million workers during the 1976–1988 period and is expected to remain level until 2000. Some of these industries—

motor vehicle and apparel, for example—are each larger than the entire mining and petroleum sector. In spite of the tremendous range of products created by the manufacturing sector, 10 industries employ approximately 75 percent of all manufacturing workers:

Durable Goods	**Nondurable Goods**
Machinery, except electrical	Food products
Electrical and electronic equipment	Apparel and other textile products
Transportation equipment	Printing and publishing
Fabricated metal products	Chemicals
Primary metals	Rubber and miscellaneous plastic

As is true of the other sectors, manufacturing has its own unique composition of workers. Nearly two thirds are blue-collar workers; of these the largest group consists of machine operatives, who account for about 40 percent of all manufacturing employees. The next largest section of blue-collar workers is the craft group, amounting to about 20 percent of all workers. Clerical workers (about 12 percent of the total) make up the largest group of white-collar workers, followed by the professional and technical workers, who fill about 10 percent of the jobs.

Transportation, communications, and public utilities provide quite different services and products but are often grouped together because they are considered to be public service activities and are either owned or regulated by governmental agencies. This sector is about the same size as the construction sector, including slightly more than 5.5 million workers in 1988. In addition to the obvious transportation systems—railroads, local and interurban buses, trucks, and air and water transportation—this category includes pipeline transportation and supporting services for each network. The communication area includes radio and television broadcasting and all other communications, the largest part being telephone systems. Utilities include electric, gas, and water and sanitation systems. Within transportation, the largest group of employees is operators, followed by craft and clerical workers. In communications the largest group is clerical workers, and in the utilities most employees are craft workers. The sector increased by about 1 million workers (over 20 percent) between 1976 and 1988 and will probably add another half million, or about 10 percent by 2000.

Wholesale trade is concerned with assembling materials from producers, sometimes recombining them in variously sized lots, and distributing them to retail stores and large users such as schools, hospitals, and industrial firms. The sector expanded by nearly one third in the 1976–1988 period and will likely grow by about 15 percent by 2000.

Retail trade sells goods or services directly to the consumers in stores, by mail and telephone, or through door-to-door contact. Although the customer ordinarily is most likely to have contact with a sales worker, sales jobs account for only about one fifth of the jobs in this sector. Slightly smaller numbers are employed as managers, service workers, and clerical workers. This sector grew by about 45 percent between 1976 and 1988. It is expected to grow by about 20 percent more by 2000.

Finance, insurance, and real estate employed over 6.5 million workers in 1988 and will likely grow to 7.75 million by 2000, an increase of about 16 percent. The finance area includes banking, credit agencies, and financial brokers. The finance and insurance workers are mostly clerical employees. In the real estate section, sales workers predominate.

The *services* sector includes a wide spectrum of activities scattered across several large industries. It is the largest sector and in 1988 was approximately equal to the entire goods-producing group; by 2000 it is likely to exceed that group by nearly one third, and if so this sector will include about one fourth of the total work force. Under this heading one finds hotels and lodging places, barber and beauty shops, advertising agencies, automobile repair shops, amusements, health services, education, and other services. One third of the workers in the service sector are professional and technical, the highest proportion in all the sectors. Other large groups of workers include service workers and clerical workers. Less than one tenth of the employees are blue-collar workers.

The *government* sector employed about 17 million workers in 1988 and will probably increase to nearly 19 million by 2000. Only about one sixth of the workers are employed by the federal government; most work in state or local units, including counties, cities, school districts, and similar governmental units. This sector does not include the military forces because they are not considered part of the civilian labor force. It does include public school teachers, who could justifiably be classified in the services sector.

The *agriculture* division includes farm jobs as well as relatively small numbers of workers engaged in forestry, fishing, hunting, and trapping. It does not include those workers engaged in what is often called agribusiness, who manufacture, sell, and repair the equipment and other materials used by farm workers. Large increases in productivity in agriculture have permitted fewer workers to produce more food and fiber, resulting in a continuing decline in the number of agricultural workers.

The *self-employed* sector includes those individuals who either work for themselves or are part of a self-contained, family-operated enterprise. The more than 40 percent increase from 1976 to 1988 is expected to slow to less than a 15 percent increase by 2000.

OCCUPATIONAL GROUPING

The previous section focused on where workers perform their tasks—the industrial sectors and the various industries. When we think of the various tasks performed by workers regardless of where they are accomplished, we think in terms of occupations. Technically, we use the term *occupation* to represent a set of tasks widely recognized as usually performed by a single worker—for example, a physician, secretary, tile setter, short-order cook, or bus driver.

Because we live in a technologically complex society, we have a very large number of occupations—so many, in fact, that it would be difficult to specify precisely how many there are. The number would depend on how very closely related sets of tasks are grouped or divided. Should one consider "high school teacher" as one occupation, or English teacher, foreign language teacher, biology teacher, chemistry teacher, mathematics teacher, physical education teacher, social studies teacher, and speech teacher as eight occupations? In some cases it is advantageous to group broadly; in others, specificity is best. Printed materials describing the world of work, occupational data, and other information about occupations use various grouping systems, often dependent on the source of the data. Therefore, it is essential that the career counselor be knowledgeable about each of these systems to help a client use information about alternatives in the decision-making process. We consider in detail several of these grouping systems in the next two chapters. Since in this discussion we are concerned only with the broad picture, we apply terminology drawn from two of these systems to describe frequently used occupational groupings. Because both systems cover the same territory, it is helpful to understand the similarity in structure. Although the names vary slightly, the similarity of the two systems is apparent immediately.

Bureau of Labor Statistics	*Dictionary of Occupational Titles*
Executive, administrative, managerial	
Professional specialty occupations	Professional, technical, managerial
Technicians and related support occupations	
Marketing and sales	
Administrative support occupations including clerical	Clerical and sales
Service occupations	Service occupations
Agricultural, forestry, fishing	Agricultural occupations
	Processing occupations
Precision production, craft, and repair	Machine trade occupations
Operators, fabricators, and laborers	Benchwork occupations
	Structural work occupations
	Miscellaneous occupations

Table 4.3 provides information on employment in the major occupational groups in 1988 and projected to 2000 based on the Bureau of Labor

Statistics classification. Moderate alternative information is used for the projections.

Executive, administrative, and managerial occupations are involved in the operation and direction of organizations such as business. Examples include bank officers, buyers, credit managers, and managers of fast-food restaurants. Over 12 million workers were in this category in 1988. The group is expected to grow by approximately 22 percent by 2000.

Professional specialty occupations are concerned with the theoretical aspects of such fields as architecture, the sciences, medicine, education, law, theology, and art. Most of these occupations require lengthy educational preparation at college or other advanced levels. In 1988 there were nearly 15 million professional specialty workers, and the group is expected to increase by nearly one quarter by 2000.

Technicians and support occupations make up the most rapidly expanding group, both in the 1976–1988 period and in the 1988–2000 span, with a growth of nearly 32 percent expected in the 1990s. Workers in health technologies such as laboratory and X-ray technicians, workers in the engineering and science technologies, and computer programmers are examples of this cluster.

Marketing and sales occupations include those who attempt to influence customers in favor of a commodity or service and those workers closely related to this process. Workers are primarily employed in wholesale and retail trade or by manufacturing, insurance, or real estate companies. There were over 13 million workers in 1988 and almost 16 million are expected by 2000, an increase that reflects average growth for the period.

Administrative support occupations, including clerical are those workers who prepare, transcribe, systematize, or preserve written communications and records, distribute information, or collect accounts. Jobs included are computer operators, secretaries, stenographers, and clerical supervisors. This is the largest occupational group, including 21 million workers in 1988 and expecting another 2.5 million by 2000.

Service occupations are the second largest group, with over 18 million workers in 1988 and almost 23 million expected in 2000. This group is also growing rapidly. Examples of subgroups in this category include cleaning and building service jobs, food preparation and service, health service, personal service, private household workers, and protective service occupations.

Agricultural, forestry, fishing, and related occupations are concerned primarily with propagating, growing, caring for, and harvesting plant and animal products. The forestry and fishing sectors are both very small compared to the farm jobs. The area has been decreasing in number for some time, with the 3.5 million workers in 1988 expected to drop another 5 percent by 2000.

Precision production, craft, and repair occupations are skilled jobs, including carpenters, tool-and-die makers, machinists, electricians, and mechanics. The area is expected to grow more slowly than the average for total employment from 1988 to 2000, as it did from 1976 to 1988. Most of the

TABLE 4.3 *Employment by Major Occupational Group, 1988 and Projected to 2000, Moderate Alternative Projection, and Percent Change 1976–88 and 1988–2000 (Numbers in Thousands)*

Occupational Title	1988		2000		Percent Change	
	Number	*Percent*	*Number*	*Percent*	*1976– 88*	*1988– 2000*
Total, all occupations	118,104	100.0	136,211	100.0	29.5	15.3
Executive, administrative, and managerial occupations	12,104	10.2	14,762	10.8	66.4	22.0
Professional specialty occupations	14,628	12.4	18,137	13.3	44.6	24.0
Technicians and related support occupations	3,867	3.3	5,089	3.7	53.9	31.6
Marketing and sales occupations	13,316	11.3	15,924	11.7	46.1	19.6
Administrative support occupations, including clerical	21,066	17.8	23,553	17.3	27.8	11.8
Service occupations	18,479	15.6	22,651	16.6	28.2	22.6
Agricultural, forestry, fishing and related occupations	3,503	3.0	3,334	2.4	–7.7	–4.8
Precision production, craft, and repair occupations	14,159	12.0	15,563	11.4	25.3	9.9
Operators, fabricators, and laborers	16,983	14.4	17,198	12.6	2.9	1.3

Source: Silvestri and Lukasiewicz, 1989.

Note: The 1988 and 2000 employment data, and the projected change 1988–2000, are derived from data from the industry-occupation matrixes for each year. The data on 1976–88 percent change were derived from the Current Population Survey data because a comparable industry-occupation matrix for 1976 is not available. The resulting comparison of change between 1976–88 and 1988–2000 consequently is only broadly indicative of trends.

additional million and a half jobs will be in construction and service industry divisions.

Operators, fabricators, and laborers are mostly semiskilled and unskilled workers who run various machines or processes used primarily in the production of goods. Typical occupations include assemblers, production painters, transport workers, helpers, and laborers. There were about 17 million workers in 1988, and this number will increase by only 200,000 by 2000.

Processing occupations are defined by the *DOT* as those concerned with refining, mixing, compounding, chemically treating, heat treating, or similarly working materials in solid, fluid, semifluid, or gaseous states to prepare them for use as basic materials, stock for further manufacturing treatment, or for sale as finished products to commercial users. Knowledge of a process and adherence to formulas or other specifications are required to some degree. Vats, stills, ovens, furnaces, mixing machines, crushers, grinders, and related machines and equipment usually are involved. The group includes occupations involved in processing metal, ore, food, tobacco, paper, petroleum, chemicals, wood, stone, leather, and other materials.

Machine trades and occupations include those concerned with the operation of machines that cut, bore, mill, abrade, print, and similarly work with such materials as metal, paper, wood, plastics, and stone. A worker's relationship to the machine is of primary importance. The more complicated jobs require an understanding of machine functions, blueprint reading, making mathematical computations, and exercising judgment to attain conformance to specifications. In other jobs, eye and hand coordination may be the most significant factor. Installation, repair, and maintenance of machines and mechanical equipment, and weaving, knitting, spinning, and similarly working textiles are included. Typical jobs in this group include machinists, grinders, punch press operators, automobile mechanics, typesetters, and cabinetmakers.

Benchwork occupations are those concerned with using body members, hand tools, and bench machines to fabricate, inspect, or repair relatively small products such as jewelry, record players, light bulbs, musical instruments, tires, footwear, pottery, and garments. The work is usually performed at a set position or station in a mill, plant, or shop; at a bench, worktable, or conveyor. Workers in more complex jobs may be required to read blueprints, follow patterns, use a variety of hand tools, and assume responsibility for meeting standards. Other jobs may only require workers to follow standardized procedures. Some occupations included in this group are jeweler, silversmith, watch repairer, television and radio repairer, piano tuner, assembler, stonecutter, glassblower, tailor, and shoemaker.

Structural work occupations include those occupations involved with fabricating, erecting, installing, paving, painting, and repairing structures and structural parts such as bridges, buildings, roads, motor vehicles, cables, internal combustion engines, girders, plates, and frames. Generally work is done outdoors, except for factory production line occupations. The worker's relationship to hand tools and power tools is more important than that to stationary machines, which are also used. Knowledge of the properties (stress, strain, durability, resistance) of the materials used (wood, metal, concrete, glass, clay) is often a requirement. Representative occupations include riveter, structural-steel worker, sheet-metal worker, boilermaker, rigger, test driver, electrician, paperhanger, bulldozer operator, carpenter, plumber, and chimney sweep.

Miscellaneous occupations are concerned with transporting people and cargo from one geographical location to another by various methods; packaging materials and moving materials in and around establishments; extracting minerals from the earth; producing and distributing utilities; modeling for painters, sculptors, and photographers; providing various production services in motion pictures and radio and television broadcasting; producing graphic art work; and other miscellaneous activities. Occupations include truck driver, barge captain, automobile service-station attendant, packager, hoist operator, stevedore, jack-hammer operator, miner, motion-picture projectionist, sign painter, photo-engraver, bookbinder, and print-shop helper.

PRESENT AND FUTURE NUMBERS

Table 4.4 shows the composition of the labor force in 1976 and 1988 and a projection to 2000 by gender, age group, and ethnic origin. The table shows that more than three quarters of men age 16 or older were in the work force in 1988, and 56 percent of women in the same age group were in the work force. There appears to be relatively little difference across ethnic groups, with figures varying from 63.8 to 67.4 percent for men and from 53.2 to 58.0 for women in 1988. Variation by age group is much greater, ranging from 56.9 to 94.5 for men and from 43.5 to 75.2 for women, with the 65 and over age group excluded.

Figures 4.1 and 4.2 show the occupations most frequently entered in 1986–1987 by young workers ages 16 to 24 and by older workers age 55 and over. In Figure 4.1 each symbol represents 20,000 new entrants, and in Figure 4.2 each represents only 2,000 workers. It is interesting to note that half of the occupations entered by the two groups are shared, although not in the same order of frequency. Further, as one might expect, half of the occupations for each group are on the list of the occupations with the largest numerical growth for the 1988–2000 period.

Tables 4.1 and 4.3 include projections of expected numbers for 2000 by industry divisions and major occupational groups. The trends seen in the 1976–1988 and the 1988–2000 periods are likely to indicate the situation in the subsequent decade.

During the 1988–2000 period, according to *Occupational Outlook Quarterly* (Fall 1989), the labor force is expected to increase from about 118 million workers to between 136 and 141 million. This is a slower growth rate than occurred from 1976 to 1988. Workers in the 16–24 age span will decline, and the 25–54 age group will increase. Women in the labor force will increase faster than men, especially in the 24–54 age range. Participation by whites will grow more slowly than for African Americans and Asians but will still hold the largest numerical increase. Hispanics will add about 5 million workers to the labor force between 1988 and 2000. Numerical growth will be greatest between 1988 and 2000 in the service and professional specialty occupational groups and least in agriculture, where the decline of previous years continues, and in semiskilled and unskilled jobs in the operators, fabricators, and laborers group.

The contrast between growth in numbers and the percentage growth rate is an important factor when one examines specific occupations. Failure

TABLE 4.4 *Civilian Labor Force and Participation Rates by Sex, Age, Race, and Hispanic Origin, 1976 and 1988, and Moderate Growth Projection to 2000*

Group	Participation Rate (Percent)			Level (in Thousands)			Change (in Thousands)	
	1976	1988	2000	1976	1988	2000	1976–88	1988–2000
Total, 16 and over	61.6	65.9	69.0	96,158	121,669	141,134	25,511	19,465
Men, 16 and over	77.5	76.2	75.9	57,174	66,927	74,324	9,753	7,397
16 to 19	59.3	56.9	59.0	4,886	4,159	4,422	–727	263
20 to 24	85.1	85.0	86.5	7,866	7,594	6,930	–272	–664
25 to 34	95.2	94.3	94.1	14,784	19,742	16,572	4,958	–3,170
35 to 44	95.4	94.5	94.3	10,500	16,074	20,188	5,574	4,114
45 to 54	91.6	90.9	90.5	10,293	10,566	16,395	273	5,829
55 to 64	74.3	67.0	68.1	7,020	6,831	7,796	–189	965
65 and over	20.2	16.5	14.7	1,826	1,960	2,021	134	61
Women, 16 and over	47.3	56.6	62.6	38,983	54,742	66,810	15,759	12,068
16 to 19	49.8	53.6	59.6	4,170	3,872	4,399	–298	527
20 to 24	65.0	72.7	77.9	6,418	6,910	6,705	492	–205
25 to 34	57.3	72.7	82.4	9,419	15,761	15,105	6,342	–656
35 to 44	57.8	75.2	84.9	6,817	13,361	18,584	6,544	5,223
45 to 54	55.0	69.0	76.5	6,689	8,537	14,423	1,848	5,886
55 to 64	41.0	43.5	49.0	4,402	4,977	6,140	575	1,163
65 and over	8.2	7.9	7.6	1,069	1,324	1,454	255	130
Whites, 16 and over	61.8	66.2	69.5	84,767	104,756	118,981	19,989	14,225
Men	78.4	76.9	76.6	51,033	58,317	63,288	7,284	4,971
Women	46.9	56.4	62.9	33,735	46,439	55,693	12,704	9,254
Blacks, 16 and over	58.9	63.8	66.5	9,565	13,205	16,465	3,640	3,260
Men	69.7	71.0	71.4	5,105	6,596	8,007	1,491	1,411
Women	50.0	58.0	62.5	4,460	6,609	8,458	2,149	1,849
Asian and other, 16 and over[1]	62.8	65.0	65.5	1,826	3,709	5,688	1,883	1,979
Men	74.9	74.4	74.6	1,036	2,015	3,029	979	1,014
Women	51.6	56.5	57.5	790	1,694	2,659	904	965
Hispanics, 16 and over[2]	60.7	67.4	69.9	4,279	8,982	14,321	4,703	5,339
Men	79.6	81.9	80.3	2,625	5,409	8,284	2,784	2,875
Women	44.1	53.2	59.4	1,654	3,573	6,037	1,919	2,464

Source: Fullteron, 1989.

[1] The "Asian and other" group includes American Indians, Alaskan Natives, Asians, and Pacific Islanders. The historic data are derived by subtracting "Black" from the "Black and other" group; projections are made directly.

[2] Persons of Hispanic origin may be of any race.

FIGURE 4.1

Almost half of the 7.9 million entrants aged 16 to 24 went into these occupations.

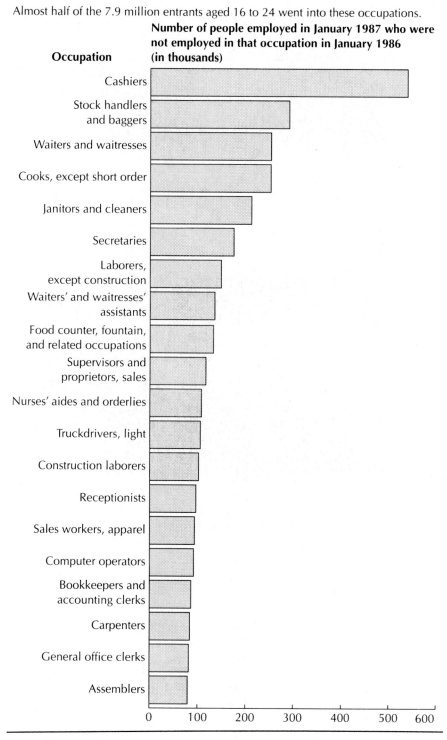

| Occupation | Number of people employed in January 1987 who were not employed in that occupation in January 1986 (in thousands) |

Source: Carey, 1989.

FIGURE 4.2

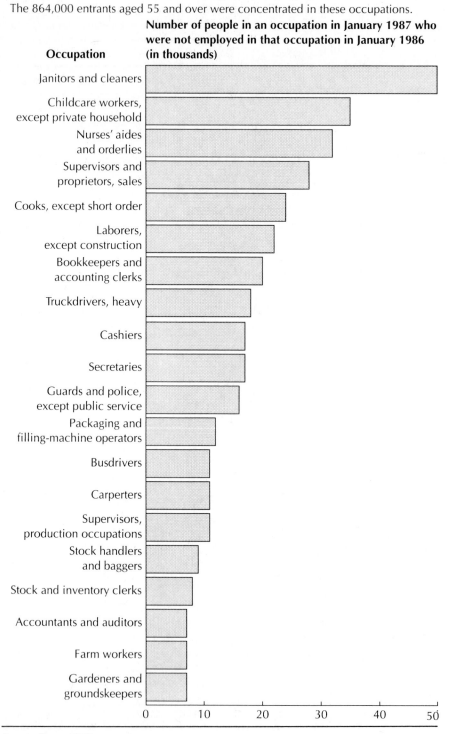

The 864,000 entrants aged 55 and over were concentrated in these occupations.

Occupation

Number of people in an occupation in January 1987 who were not employed in that occupation in January 1986 (in thousands)

Source: Carey, 1989.

to discriminate between actual numbers of increased jobs and percentage increase can lead to erroneous conclusions about where opportunities are greatest. For example, according to Table 4.5, the fastest growing occupation between 1988 and 2000 is expected to be paralegals, with a percentage growth rate of 75.3. According to Table 4.6, the first occupation listed (salespersons, retail) has a percentage growth of only 19 percent; however, its numerical increase during that period is nearly 12 times greater than paralegals, with a numerical increase of 730,000 positions compared to an increase of 62,000 paralegals.

The apparent contradiction between percentage and numerical change can be put in perspective with a simple example. An infant is usually expected to triple its birth weight in the first year of life, growing from approximately 8 pounds to 24 pounds. Thus a weight change of 16 pounds for the infant is a percentage change of 300 percent, although it would be only a 13

TABLE 4.5 *The Fastest Growing Occupations, 1988–2000, Moderate Alternative Projection (numbers in thousands)*

	Employment		Change in Employment 1988–2000	
Occupation	1988	Projected, 2000	Number	Percent
Paralegals	83	145	62	75.3
Medical assistants	149	253	104	70.0
Home health aides	236	397	160	67.9
Radiologic technologists and technicians	132	218	87	66.0
Data processing equipment repairers	71	115	44	61.2
Medical record technicians	47	75	28	59.9
Medical secretaries	207	327	120	58.0
Physical therapists	68	107	39	57.0
Surgical technologists	35	55	20	56.4
Operations research analysts	55	85	30	55.4
Securities and financial services sales workers	200	309	109	54.8
Travel agents	142	219	77	54.1
Computer systems analysts	403	617	214	53.3
Physical and corrective therapy assistants	39	60	21	52.5
Social welfare service aides	91	138	47	51.5
Occupational therapists	33	48	16	48.8
Computer programmers	519	769	250	48.1
Human services workers	118	171	53	44.9
Respiratory therapists	56	79	23	41.3
Corrections officers and jailers	186	262	76	40.8

Source: Silvestri and Lukasiewicz, 1989.

TABLE 4.6 *Occupations with the Largest Job Growth, 1988–2000, Moderate Alternative Projection (numbers in thousands)*

Occupation	Employment		Change in Employment 1988–2000	
	1988	*Projected, 2000*	*Number*	*Percent*
Salespersons, retail	3,834	4,564	730	19.0
Registered nurses	1,577	2,190	613	38.8
Janitors and cleaners, including maids and housekeeping cleaners	2,895	3,450	556	19.2
Waiters and waitresses	1,786	2,337	551	30.9
General managers and top executives	3,030	3,509	479	5.8
General office clerks	2,519	2,974	455	18.1
Secretaries, except legal and medical	2,903	3,288	385	13.2
Nursing aides, orderlies, and attendants	1,184	1,562	378	31.9
Truckdrivers, light and heavy	2,399	2,768	369	15.4
Receptionists and information clerks	833	1,164	331	39.8
Cashiers	2,310	2,614	304	13.2
Guards	795	1,050	256	32.2
Computer programmers	519	769	250	48.1
Food counter, fountain, and related workers	1,626	1,866	240	14.7
Food preparation workers	1,027	1,260	234	22.8
Licensed practical nurses	626	855	229	36.6
Teachers, secondary school	1,164	1,388	224	19.5
Computer systems analysts	403	617	214	53.3
Accountants and auditors	963	1,174	211	22.0
Teachers, kindergarten and elementary	1,359	1,567	208	15.3

Source: Silvestri and Lukasiewicz, 1989.

percent change for an adult weighing 120 pounds and only 10 percent for one weighing 160 pounds.

Although the expanding labor market generally suggests that most jobs will increase in numbers, this is not true for all occupations. In some cases, certain jobs will decline because they are heavily concentrated in industries that are shrinking; in other cases, the job may be widely distributed across industries but still may be declining because of technological change that is replacing the job. In other cases, the loss of jobs in declining industries may be heavy, but the loss is countered by an equal or greater expansion in growing industries. For example, a decline of 44,000 secretaries is expected to occur by 2000 in the so-called declining industries; however, growing industries are expected to employ an additional 428,000 secretaries in that period for an overall growth of 384,000 positions. On the other hand, assemblers and fabricators will decrease by 113,000 in declining industries, and another 3,000 in growing industries, for a total loss of 116,000 jobs.

SOURCES OF INFORMATION ON CHANGE
AND STRUCTURE

Whether one is assisting sixth graders to become more familiar with occupations generally, high school graduates to initiate job searches, workers with disabilities to move to compatible jobs, or structurally unemployed workers to find new directions, both helper and client need information about the present and future structure of the world of work as well as about likely change in the near and distant future. Current, useful information is available in a variety of publications. One can look at data that are as broad and general as the nation as a whole or as detailed as a single industry in a single Standard Metropolitan Statistical Area.

Because they are involved in the process of accumulating, organizing, and interpreting data about changes in the world of work, labor market analysts in the local State Employment Security office are often the best resource close at hand for local or regional information. They can also explain the kinds of data available from regional or state offices. Each state employment service includes a research and analysis section that assembles and publishes locally collected data on a regional or state basis.

In subsequent chapters, we examine in detail many of the materials that counselors, teachers, and other helpers will find useful in obtaining information about the world of work. We list here only a representative group of publications that supply useful data on the change and structure aspects that we have discussed in this chapter. The materials mentioned here are generally available in local libraries and local offices of the state employment service. In addition to the sources listed here, the reader should include publications of NOICC (National Occupational Information Coordinating Committee), SOICC (State Occupational Information Coordinating Committee), and the state CIDS (Career Information Delivery System). These are discussed in Chapter 7.

National Sources

Occupational Outlook Handbook: Published biennially by the Bureau of Labor Statistics (BLS), this publication covers about 185 occupations, including data on job outlook.

Occupational Outlook Quarterly: Published quarterly, also by the BLS, this journal provides updated information related to the *Handbook* and other relevant outlook data.

Occupational Projections and Training Data: Published annually by the BLS, this publication provides data on employment prospects and on training requirements, so one can see not only the likely number of vacancies in an occupation but also the supply of trained individuals who can enter those positions.

U.S. Industrial Outlook: Published annually by the Bureau of Industrial Economics in the Department of Commerce, this publication provides a survey picture of current developments in each industry as well as long-range forecasts of what can be expected over the next decade.

State and Local Sources

Occupational Employment Survey Statistics: Published on a 3-year cycle by each State Employment Security Agency, the survey collects current data on wage and salary employment by industry on a sample basis over 3 years, covering about 2,000 occupations.

OES Employment Outlook: Published irregularly and updated as needed by the State Employment Security Agency, this material includes long-term projections on both occupations and industries and is produced through a federal-state cooperative arrangement.

Covered Employment, Wages, and Contributions: Published quarterly by the State Employment Security Agency, this report provides a detailed summary of employment and wage information for workers covered by state unemployment insurance laws.

Labor Market Information Newsletter: Published monthly by the State Employment Security Agency, this monthly summary shows significant changes in the labor force during the month and the year.

SUMMARY

Although many people view the world of work as a rigid sociological structure, it is, in fact, a dynamic, constantly changing entity. Some of the influences causing long-term changes in the structure include population variables such as changes in birthrate and increasing longevity, and sociological and technological developments. Some events, such as calamities, human disasters, or seasonal variations, create either a beneficial or a depressing influence on a short-term basis.

Even though the work structure is subject to some continual changes, there is sufficient stability to permit classification and analysis. One approach to classifying work is based on an industrial view, that is, the work setting where the task is performed. Another approach is that of occupation—what the worker actually does.

Both industrial and occupational groups continue to change constantly. Nevertheless, the changes usually are not drastic and sudden. Consequently, numbers and trends can be predicted with a fair degree of accuracy, especially over short-term periods of five to ten years.

REFERENCES

Carey, M. L. (1989). Characteristics of occupational entrants. *Occupational Outlook Quarterly, 33* (2), 8–17.

Fullerton, H. N., Jr. (1989). New labor force projections, spanning 1988 to 2000. *Monthly Labor Review, 112* (11), 3–12.

Personick, V. A. (1989). Industry output and employment: A slower trend for the nineties. *Monthly Labor Review, 112* (11), 25–41.

Silvestri, G., & Lukasiewicz, J. (1989). Projections of occupational employment, 1988–2000. *Monthly Labor Review, 112* (11), 42–65.

U.S. Department of Labor. (1989). The labor force. *Occupational Outlook Quarterly, 33* (3), 4–11.

5

The *Dictionary of Occupational Titles* and Related Systems

The world of work continuously grows more complex. It would be difficult, perhaps even impossible, to identify definitively the exact number of different occupations in existence at a given time. As in any complex organism, old cells die and are sloughed off, new cells replicate existing ones and replace them, other new cells develop as slight modifications of existing cells, and some new cells are totally different from any previously existing units and take on new functions. Thus the world of work continuously and simultaneously is involved in the processes of rejuvenation, homeostasis, and evolution.

Precise estimates of the number of different occupations depend on how one defines *different*, since many occupations have common factors and may differ more in degree than in kind. Nevertheless, it is commonly thought that the United States has more than 20,000 occupations sufficiently varied to be thought different. Many of these occupations may be known by more than one name in different regions, or even within a given region.

If one is to help individuals learn about occupations or develop an understanding of their relationship to the world of work, a broad knowledge of occupations is absolutely essential. Yet maintaining a good grasp of 20,000 constantly changing occupations is beyond the competence of most human minds. Some method of classification or grouping must be used to bring this array into manageable proportions.

Even though the number of occupations is large, many of them are related in various ways. Just as human families include brothers, sisters, and cousins, so too do many occupations show similar types of relationships. Classification systems are useful in understanding these relationships within the world of work.

Occupations can be grouped and classified by many systems, each of which has its own advantage or its unique contribution. Since the system that is best for a specific situation or purpose depends on the desired goal, there can be no single overall best method. The method that best achieves the goal is the best one to use. Because situations vary, the person involved in career education or career counseling must understand a variety of systems to make the best choice for the desired purpose. In this chapter and the next, we consider several of the commonly used classification systems. We first consider the *Dictionary of Occupational Titles* and those systems directly related to its concept. In the next chapter, we look at systems that are oriented in other ways.

DICTIONARY OF OCCUPATIONAL TITLES

Of all the publications related to counseling and teaching about occupations, the *Dictionary of Occupational Titles* has been the most widely used. It has provided classification systems for occupations, a basis for filing career materials, a method for relating beginning positions to jobs available for experienced workers, a system for identifying workers whose skills and abilities approximate those needed in fields with shortages, and a brief occupational description developed from job analysis reports.

Originally published in 1939, the *Dictionary of Occupational Titles*, usually called the *DOT*, was brought up to date by a second edition in 1949. The book was totally revised in 1965, with a new coding system and extensive new information provided in its structure. The fourth edition was published in 1977. A revision of the fourth edition was released in 1991. Plans currently call for issuance of the fifth edition in the mid- to late 1990s. This chapter uses the 1991 revision of the fourth edition. It consists of two volumes including 12,741 job descriptions, of which about one fifth are new or revised. A further advantage of the 1991 revision is the incorporation of codes and information from the *Guide for Occupational Exploration (GOE)* and *Selected Characteristics of Occupations Defined in the Dictionary of Occupational Titles.* Both of these publications are discussed later in this chapter.

We discussed the broad occupational categories of the *DOT* in Chapter 4, where we considered occupational groupings starting with "professional, technical, and managerial." These nine categories break into 83 occupationally specific divisions, such as various occupations in medicine and health in the professional category, or "mechanics and machinery repairers" in the machine trades category. The 83 divisions are further subdivided into 564 groups—for example, "dentists" or "registered nurses" in the medicine and health divisions and "motorized vehicle and engineering equipment mechanics and repairers" or "farm mechanics and repairers" in the mechanics and machinery repairer division.

Figure 5.1 presents typical *DOT* definitions and identifies the seven basic parts to be discussed next.

FIGURE 5.1 *Basic Parts of DOT Definition*

1.
Code
number

2.
Occupational
title

3.
Registry
designation

045.107-010 COUNSELOR (profess. & kin.)

5.
Definition

Counsels individuals and provides group educational and vocational guidance services: Collects, organizes, and analyzes information about individuals through records, tests, interviews, and professional sources, to appraise their interests, aptitudes, abilities, and personality characteristics, for vocational and educational planning. Compiles and studies occupational, educational, and economic information to aid counselees in making and carrying out vocational and educational objectives. Refers students to placement service. Assists individuals to understand and overcome social and emotional problems. May engage in research and follow-up activities to evaluate counseling techniques. May teach classes. May be designated according to area of activity as Academic

6.
Undefined
related
titles

Counselor (education); Career Placement Services Counselor (education); Employment Counselor (government ser.); Guidance Counselor (education); Vocational Advisor (education).
GOE: 10.01.02 STRENGTH: S GED: R5 M5 L5 SVP: 7 DLU: 81

045.107-014 COUNSELOR, NURSES'Association (medical ser.)

Offers vocational, educational, and professional counseling to registered professional nurses, licensed practical nurses, and prospective professional and practical nurse students: Compiles credentials and prepares biographies of counselees. Provides information relative to qualifications required, opportunities for placement and advancement, wages, hours, and other data pertaining to selected field of work to assist nurses in determining educational and vocational objectives. Refers qualified nurses to employers for placement. Assists in establishing personnel policies relative to placement. Aids applicants in obtaining vocational, health, or other assistance from community agencies. May

7.
Definition
trailer

assist in recruitment.
GOE: 10.01.02 STRENGTH: S GED: R5 M4 L5 SVP: 8 DLU: 77

045.107-018 DIRECTOR OF COUNSELING (profess. & kin.)
alternate titles: counseling-center manager; director,
counseling bureau; director, vocational counseling;
head counselor

4.
Alternate
Titles

Directs personnel engaged in providing educational and vocational guidance for students and graduates: Assigns and evaluates work of personnel. Conducts in-service training program for professional staff. Coordinates counseling bureau with school and community services. Analyzes counseling and guidance procedures and techniques to improve quality of service. Counsels individuals and groups relative to personal and social problems, and educational and vocational objectives. Addresses community groups and faculty members to interpret counseling service. Supervises maintenance of occupational library for use by counseling personnel. Directs activities of testing and occupational service center. May supervise auxiliary services, such as student learning center. May supervise in-service training programs in counseling, testing, or occupational information for graduate students. May teach graduate courses in psychology, guidance, and related subjects. May participate in appraising qualifications of candidates for faculty positions and eligibility of students for admission to medical, nursing, and engineering schools.
GOE: 10.01.02 STRENGTH: S GED: R5 M5 L5 SVP: 8 DLU: 77

Source: 1991 *DOT,* p. 51.

Occupational Code Number

The *DOT* code number assigned to each defined occupation consists of nine digits divided into three sections, with three digits in each part. The parts have a particular purpose and provide specific information about the occupation. In the first two parts, each digit supplies certain information.

The first three digits reveal the category, division, and group in which the occupation is classified. Figure 5.2 is a page from the *DOT* (p. xxix) listing the occupational categories (first digit) and the divisions in the 0/1 to 7 categories. As one can see, the divisions involve two digits, always starting with the category number. Two numbers (0/1) are used for the "professional, technical, and managerial" category to allow sufficient space for the 16 divisions included. This doubling up also happens twice at the division level, 00/01 and 62/63, for a similar reason. Only three categories (processing occupations, machine trades occupations, and benchwork occupations) use all the spaces that are available in each division. Unused two-digit codes (e.g., 06, 28, and 47) are left vacant to be used as new divisions of occupations emerge. For example, the 03 division is used for the first time in the 1991 revision for computer-related occupations.

Similarly, occupational groups are designated by the first three digits. Figure 5.3 presents a portion of page xxx of the *DOT* and lists the 00/01 to 14 divisions and their respective occupational groups. The 16 divisions in the 00/01 to 19 range include 105 occupational groups ranging from "001—Architectural occupations" to "199—Miscellaneous professional, technical, and managerial occupations, n.e.c." (not elsewhere classified). Thus, we see that the first three digits for counselor, as shown in Figure 5.1, provide the following information:

Category	0	Professional, technical, and managerial occupations
Division	04	Occupations in life sciences
Group	045	Occupations in psychology

The second set of three digits in the code number provides the worker function ratings for the tasks performed in the occupations. The *DOT* assumes that all occupations require the worker to be involved with data, people, or things (d-p-t) in some degree of complexity. The levels of relationship to data, people, and things are as follows:

Data (4th digit)	*People (5th digit)*	*Things (6th digit)*
0 Synthesizing	0 Mentoring	0 Setting up
1 Coordinating	1 Negotiating	1 Precision working
2 Analyzing	2 Instructing	2 Operating-controlling
3 Compiling	3 Supervising	3 Driving-operating

FIGURE 5.2   *Sample Page from DOT Illustrating Categories and Divisions*

Occupational Categories, Divisions, and Groups

One-Digit Occupational Categories

0/1 Professional, technical, and managerial occupations

2 Clerical and sales occupations

3 Service occupations

4 Agricultural, fishery, forestry, and related occupations

5 Processing occupations

6 Machine trades occupations

7 Benchwork occupations

8 Structural work occupations

9 Miscellaneous occupations

Two-Digit Occupational Categories

0/1 Professional, technical, and managerial occupations

00/01 Occupations in architecture, engineering, and surveying

02 Occupations in mathematics and physical sciences

03 Computer-related occupations

04 Occupations in life sciences

05 Occupations in social sciences

07 Occupations in medicine and health

09 Occupations in education

10 Occupations in museum, library, and archival sciences

11 Occupations in law and jurisprudence

12 Occupations in religion and theology

13 Occupations in writing

14 Occupations in art

15 Occupations in entertainment and recreation

16 Occupations in administrative specializations

18 Managers and officials, n.e.c.

19 Miscellaneous professional, technical, and managerial occupations

2 Clerical and sales occupations

20 Stenography, typing, filing, and related occupations

21 Computing and account-recording occupations

22 Production and stock clerks and related occupations

23 Information and message distribution occupations

24 Miscellaneous clerical occupations

25 Sales occupations, services

26 Sales occupations, consumable commodities

27 Sales occupations, commodities, n.e.c.

29 Miscellaneous sales occupations

3 Service Occupations

30 Domestic service occupations

31 Food and beverage preparation and service occupations

32 Lodging and related service occupations

33 Barbering, cosmetology, and related service occupations

34 Amusement and recreation service occupations

35 Miscellaneous personal service occupations

36 Apparel and furnishings service occupations

37 Protective service occupations

38 Building and related service occupations

4 Agricultural, fishery, forestry, and related occupations

40 Plant farming occupations

41 Animal farming occupations

42 Miscellaneous agricultural and related occupations

44 Fishery and related occupations

45 Forestry occupations

46 Hunting, trapping, and related occupations

5 Processing occupations

50 Occupations in processing of metal

51 Ore refining and foundry occupations

52 Occupations in processing of food, tobacco, and related products

53 Occupations in processing of paper and related materials

54 Occupations in processing of petroleum, coal, natural and manufactured gas, and related products

(continued)

FIGURE 5.2   *Continued*

Occupational Categories, Divisions, and Groups

Two-Digit Occupational Categories

55 Occupations in processing of chemicals, plastics, synthetics, rubber, paint, and related products
56 Occupations in processing of wood and wood products
57 Occupations in processing of stone, clay, glass, and related products
58 Occupations in processing of leather, textiles, and related products
59 Processing occupations, n.e.c.

6 Machine trades occupations
60 Metal machining occupations
61 Metalworking occupations, n.e.c.
62/63 Mechanics and machinery repairers
64 Paperworking occupations
65 Printing occupations
66 Wood machining occupations
67 Occupations in machining stone, clay, glass, and related materials
68 Textile occupations
69 Machine trades occupations, n.e.c.

7 Benchwork Occupations
70 Occupations in fabrication, assembly, and repair of metal products, n.e.c.
71 Occupations in fabrication and repair of scientific, medical, photographic, optical horological, and related products
72 Occupations in assembly and repair of electrical equipment
73 Occupations in fabrication and repair of products made from assorted materials
74 Painting, decorating, and related occupations
75 Occupations in fabrication and repair of plastics, synthetics, rubber, and related products
76 Occupations in fabrication and repair of wood products
77 Occupations in fabrication and repair of sand, stone, clay, and glass products
78 Occupations in fabrication and repair of textile, leather, and related products
79 Benchwork occupations, n.e.c.

Source: 1991 *DOT*, p. xxix.

Data (4th digit)	*People (5th digit)*	*Things (6th digit)*
4 Computing	4 Diverting	4 Manipulating
5 Copying	5 Persuading	5 Tending
6 Comparing	6 Speaking-signaling	6 Feeding-offbearing
	7 Serving	7 Handling
	8 Taking instructions-helping	

As one can see from this list, the most complex relationships are assigned the lowest numbers; as complexity decreases, the numbers are higher. The levels are so arranged that, as one moves from the simplest level to the more complex, it is assumed that each succeeding level includes the previous level but is less complex than the next level above. The relationships that are significant in the performance of the occupation are used to evaluate the work, and those incidental relationships that are tangential to the performance of the job are disregarded. Definitions and explanations of each term can be found in the appendix to the *DOT.* Returning to our illustration in

FIGURE 5.3 *Examples of Occupational Divisions and Groups in the Professional, Technical, and Managerial Occupations*

Three-Digit Occupational Groups

Professional, Technical, and Managerial Occupations

00/01 Occupations in Architecture, Engineering, and Surveying
001 Architectural occupations
002 Aeronautical engineering occupations
003 Electrical/electronics engineering occupations
005 Civil engineering occupations
006 Ceramic engineering occupations
007 Mechanical engineering occupations
008 Chemical engineering occupations
010 Mining and petroleum engineering occupations
011 Metallurgy and metallurgical engineering occupations
012 Industrial engineering occupations
013 Agricultural engineering occupations
014 Marine engineering occupations
015 Nuclear engineering occupations
017 Drafters, n.e.c.
018 Surveying/cartographic occupations
019 Occupations in architecture, engineering, and surveying, n.e.c.

02 Occupations in mathematics and physical sciences
020 Occupations in mathematics
021 Occupations in astronomy
022 Occupations in chemistry
023 Occupations in physics
024 Occupations in geology
025 Occupations in meteorology
029 Occupations in mathematics and physical sciences, n.e.c.

03 Computer-related occupations
030 Occupations in systems analysis and programming
031 Occupations in data communications and networks
032 Occupations in computer system user support
033 Occupations in computer systems technical support
039 Computer-related occupations, n.e.c.

04 Occupations in life sciences
040 Occupations in agricultural sciences
041 Occupations in biological sciences
045 Occupations in psychology
049 Occupations in life sciences, n.e.c.

05 Occupations in social sciences
050 Occupations in economics
051 Occupations in political science
052 Occupations in history
054 Occupations in sociology
055 Occupations in anthropology
059 Occupations in social sciences, n.e.c.

07 Occupations in medicine and health
070 Physicians and surgeons
071 Osteopaths
072 Dentists
073 Veterinarians
074 Pharmacists
075 Registered nurses
076 Therapists
077 Dietitians
078 Occupations in medical and dental technology
079 Occupations in medicine and health, n.e.c.

09 Occupations in education
090 Occupations in college and university education
091 Occupations in secondary school education
092 Occupations in preschool, primary school, and kindergarten education
094 Occupations in education of persons with disabilities
096 Home economists and farm advisers
097 Occupations in vocational education
099 Occupations in education, n.e.c.

10 Occupations in museum, library, and archival sciences
100 Librarians

(continued)

FIGURE 5.3 *Continued*

Three-Digit Occupational Groups
Professional, Technical, and Managerial Occupations

101 Archivists
102 Museum curators and related occupations
109 Occupations in museum, library, and archival sciences, n.e.c.
11 Occupations in law and jurisprudence
110 Lawyers
111 Judges
119 Occupations in law and jurisprudence, n.e.c.

12 Occupations in religion and theology
120 Clergy
129 Occupations in religion and theology, n.e.c.

13 Occupations in writing
131 Writers
132 Editors: publication, broadcast, and script
137 Interpreters and translators
139 Occupations in writing, n.e.c.

14 Occupations in art
141 Commercial artists: designers and illustrators, graphic arts
142 Environmental, product, and related designers
143 Occupations in photography
144 Fine artists: painters, sculptors, and related occupations
149 Occupations in art, n.e.c.

Source: 1991 *DOT,* p. xxix.

Figure 5.1, we now see that the 107 in the code number provides the following information:

> 4th DIGIT–DATA–1–*Coordinating* (Determining time, place, and sequence of operations or action to be taken on the basis of analysis of data; executing determination and/or reporting on events)
>
> 5th DIGIT–PEOPLE–0–*Mentoring* (Dealing with individuals in terms of their total personality in order to advise, counsel, and/or guide them with regard to problems that may be resolved by legal, scientific, clinical, spiritual, and/or other professional principles)
>
> 6th DIGIT–THINGS–7–*Handling* (Using body members, hand tools, and/or special devices to work, move, or carry objects or materials. Involves little or no latitude for judgment with regard to attainment of standards or in selecting appropriate tool, object, or material.)

Winer (1981) reports an application of the worker functions system to a group of graduate psychology students. She asked two groups of students to respond to several sets of interest inquiries and to self-report on an array of competencies. She found that the data submitted by students studying in two diverse areas of psychology were separated effectively by a worker functions system.

Prediger (1981) contends that the data factor actually is a mixture of two antipodal components, "ideas" and "data." He suggests that *ideas* are intrapersonal, involving theories, knowledge, and insights, whereas *data* are impersonal—facts, records, files, and numbers. He combines the polarity of these two items with the earlier established concept of a people-things polarity to produce a two-dimensional classification system that we examine in the next chapter.

The last three digits of the code number have been assigned to permit differentiation of those occupations that share the same first six digits. At the time that these digits were assigned (several months before the fourth edition of the *DOT* was published), occupations with the same first six-digit code were arranged alphabetically and were then assigned an identifier code sequentially in multiples of four, starting with 010 for the first occupation in each six-digit code batch. The numbers for each batch run in this order: 010, 014, 018, 022, . . . to the highest number needed. In our example, we see that "counselor" is the first occupation alphabetically among those occupations with the 045.107 code number. By examining *DOT* pages 51 and 52, where occupations with that code number are defined, we see that there are 12 other occupations that share the same first six digits with "counselor." The occasional exceptions to the sequencing are easily explained. For example, apprenticeships, not on the original list, are sometimes assigned a number two units higher than the occupation so that they will be located immediately after that occupation. A missing number in the sequence (010, 014, 022) suggests that the occupation originally assigned the identifier (018 in this case) was deleted after the list was established. An occupation with an identifier code higher than the alphabetical sequence suggests that it is probably one that was added to the list after the sequence had been assigned.

The *DOT* code number identifies and assembles closely related occupations in two ways. First, the initial three digits bring into the occupational group those occupations that share type or field of work within the occupational category. Thus the occupational division 68 brings together all the textile occupations, and within that cluster the occupational group 682 includes all the spinning occupations. The fourth, fifth, and sixth digits cluster occupations within each group according to the occupation's relationship to data, people, and things. Therefore, occupations sharing the same first six digits are closely related by type or field of work within a category *and* involve d-p-t activities at the same level of relationship. Further, other occupations with the same first three digits and very small differences in the second three digits are within the same field or type of work but have slightly different d-p-t relationships. As the differences between d-p-t codes grow larger, the differences between the jobs within the group grow larger.

Occupational Title

The occupational title appears in boldface upper-case letters immediately following the code number. This title, called the *base title*, is the name used most frequently for this specific job. Occupations that have more than one word in the base title will be listed in the index according to the key word in the title. Thus bridge carpenters, mine carpenters, rough carpenters, and ship carpenters are all listed together under "carpenter." On the other hand, career-guidance technician is listed alphabetically at "career" because there is no relationship between most of the various technicians.

Two other types of titles require some additional explanation: *master titles* and *term titles*. A *master title* is simply a means of conserving paper and space. It is used for those occupations that share a great many duties but that also have some specific duties. For example, in both retail and wholesale trade one can find many SALESPERSONS, usually named according to item or service sold, who share many duties in addition to some that relate uniquely to the item or service sold. The duties common to all salespersons are defined once as a *master definition*. Each base title definition then includes only the unique tasks and refers the reader to the master definition for the duties that are common to all salespersons. *Term titles* are common to a wide group of jobs that differ widely in the job knowledge required, the tasks performed, or the job location. The term title includes information about the jobs that are often grouped under this umbrella and suggests how to obtain the appropriate base title. For example, ENTERTAINER represents individuals who act, dance, sing, or perform feats of skill. Except for amusing audiences, they have little in common. The base title for each depends on the type of entertainment provided; thus examples of base titles would be ACTOR or ACTRESS, DANCER, SINGER, COMEDIAN, JUGGLER, and so on.

Industry Designation

Because occupations in different fields may share the same name but perform very different duties or tasks, the industry designation is a crucial part of the title. The industry designation may tell one or more of the following about an occupation:

> Location of the occupation (hotel & rest.; mach. shop)
> Type of duties associated with the occupation (clean; dye & press.)
> Products manufactured (textiles; optical goods)
> Processes used (electroplating; petrol. refin.)
> Raw materials used (nonfer. metal alloys; stonework)

Some occupations occur in a large number of industries and are assigned an industry designation that reflects this dispersion. For example, clerical occupations that are found in almost every industry are labeled (clerical) and most professions are assigned (profess. & kin.). Several occupations are found in a number of industries but not as widely as others. These occupations usually carry an industry designation of (any ind.). A section of the *DOT* lists in alphabetical order all occupations in each industry designation. This listing is helpful when one knows the industry in which a worker is employed but does not know the proper title for the occupation. One can then identify possible titles from the list and check occupational definitions against the duties performed by the worker.

The 1991 revised edition has reduced and revised the number of industrial designations, from 220 in the original fourth edition to 140. The current listings have been aligned more closely with the system used in the Standard Industrial Classification, a system that we examine in the next chapter.

Alternate Title

An alternate title is a synonym for a base title. One might think of this as comparable to a nickname—John Smith may be known as "Jack" or "Smitty." Among the names used for a specific set of tasks, the one most widely used across the country has been selected as the base title, and the others are designated as alternate titles. A given job may have many alternate titles or none at all. Sometimes regional usage may focus on one of the alternate titles. The alternate titles are listed in lower-case type in the definition, in the alphabetical index, and in the listing according to industry designation. In the index and industry listing, alternate titles carry the code number of the base title. Therefore, regardless of the name used, either index or industry listing will refer the searcher to the base title via its code number.

Definition

The definition is a brief description of the job as it most commonly occurs. There are often minor variations from one work site to another in the duties performed by workers who mostly do the same things. It would not be possible to include all local variants in the definitions; therefore, the printed definition must be viewed as a composite or typical listing of duties.

The first sentence of the definition summarizes the essential information about the occupation. The remainder of the definition consists of task element statements that indicate what the worker does to accomplish the overall job purpose.

Some titles (including our illustration in Figure 5.1) contain additional statements introduced by the word *May*. These sentences describe duties that are frequently, but not universally, assigned to the worker.

Any technical terms used in the definition are printed in italics to alert the reader to the fact that the word has a special usage. Such italicized words are defined in the glossary included in the *DOT* following the coded definitions.

Sometimes different occupations within the same industry carry the same name. In earlier editions of the *DOT* this problem was solved by adding a Roman numeral following the industry designation. Although the d-p-t code numbers have eliminated the need for this in most cases, the practice is still continued.

Undefined Related Titles

Whereas an alternate title is a different name for the same job, an undefined related title is a name for a slightly different variant of the same job. It is so similar to the base title that it is properly grouped with it, yet different enough to require some separate recognition. It carries the same code number as the base title and is listed in the alphabetical index and industry listing.

Definition Trailer

The last line of the definition brings into the *DOT* five pieces of information that are most helpful to the user. The first piece ("a" in our illustration) refers to the *Guide for Occupational Exploration*, and the next three pieces (b, c, and d) relate to *Selected Characteristics*. Both of these publications are considered later in this chapter.

In Figure 5.1, the last line in the definition for counselor appears as follows:

GOE:10.01.02   Strength: S   GED R5ML5   SVP: 7   DLU:81)

a   b   c   d   e

The section marked "a" provides the GOE code to which this occupation relates.

The "b" piece indicates the amount of physical exertion required by the occupation.

The "c" code tells the amount of general education in reasoning, mathematics, and language required to perform the work.

The "d" section refers to the amount of specific vocational preparation demanded.

The "e" figure reveals the year in which the definition was last updated.

Information about how the material in the *DOT* is organized and how one can find an occupational title and code number is included in the introductory pages of the *DOT*. Readers who wish to develop some skill in using the *DOT* as a reference should read the introductory section carefully, examine each of the major parts of the book, and then attempt to find base titles and code numbers for a number of jobs with which they are already familiar.

Using the *DOT*

Experienced counselors and career development specialists will recognize at once that the *DOT* is not a panacea to solve instantly all the problems they encounter in career planning and counseling. In fact, the *DOT* alone probably will not solve even one problem. It is, however, a very important tool, the utility and value of which depend on the professional skill of the individual employing it.

The *DOT*, in its present form, has been developed and modified over many years to serve a wide range of users in many different situations. Not all these groups will use the book in the same way, or even for the same purposes. The neophyte should first attempt to understand how the tool is used in the function he or she wishes to perform and then develop skill and competence in this particular application. As one becomes more familiar with the book and its ramifications, additional insight into its other uses will ordinarily increase proficiency in using it for special purposes. Although the employment counselor will use the book often to ascertain a code number for a referred worker or to develop an entry code number for a person entering the labor market, neither the counselor nor the teacher will be much concerned with this application. Even though their understanding of how the book is used for this purpose will be helpful, it will not directly advance their work with students or clients.

Counselors and career development specialists will find the *DOT* helpful in the following ways:

1. It is a useful way of helping individuals, singly or in groups, to develop an understanding of the world of work. All people have some previously acquired knowledge of the world of work. The *DOT* can help them add to their knowledge in several dimensions. Classification systems can be used along with the *DOT* to show both scope and depth in various occupational areas. It is particularly valuable in introductory and exploratory activities in the classroom and in the counseling session. The coding structure and the data-people-things concepts are especially appropriate for helping a person to form some picture of the world of work, and are equally useful in helping to explore the relationship between an occupation and the rest of the working world.

2. The *DOT* clearly demonstrates the interrelationships that exist in the world of work. This is of great importance in working with individuals who may conceive of work as being organized into tight, unrelated compartments. The *occupational group arrangement* is directly related to the *field* concept of occupations and can be used to demonstrate this relationship. The *worker functions arrangement* clearly shows a *level* approach to occupations. Thus promotional routes and transfer lines can be demonstrated and studied so the individual can see the various avenues that lead from each occupation to other parts of the world of work. The industry designation provides further insight by relating each occupation to its industrial location.

3. Both the occupational group arrangement and the worker functions arrangement provide useful bases for filing career materials. Where a file is intended primarily to help the user gain a broader knowledge of the world of work, a system based on occupational groups will often be most useful. If the basic purpose is to help the user relate self and abilities, interests, and goals to the world of work, a system based on the worker functions arrangement will have direct relevance.

4. The *DOT* provides a basis for counselor use in assisting clients to initiate career planning on a broad foundation, and to move forward to more specific objectives as client experience and maturation justify more specific planning.

GUIDE FOR OCCUPATIONAL EXPLORATION

Often one can see a similarity between the relationships that exist among jobs and the kinships that tie people together. In some ways the occupational groups of the *DOT* are like a nuclear family, closely related, sharing some common physical and personality characteristics, and often having the same name. There can be other individuals closely related to this group (half brothers and sisters, and cousins) who share in parts of the relationship but not in other parts. Thus listing those who share one element—a common surname, for example—may leave out much information that might be available if a different base were used. This is also true with occupations; therefore, we need several different systems, some of which may be closely coordinated, to see different types of relationships.

The Department of Labor published the *Guide for Occupational Exploration (GOE)* in 1979 as a companion volume to be used with the *Dictionary of Occupational Titles*. It includes an occupational grouping system based on extensive research with various well-known interest inventories. Droege and Padgett (1979) describe the research procedures followed in the development of the *GOE*. The *GOE* is particularly important to career counselors because it provides a useful bridge between interest inventory results and the *DOT*. A second edition, edited by Harrington and O'Shea (1984) is published by the National Forum Foundation and distributed by the American Guidance Service. A third edition, titled *Enhanced Guide for Occupational Exploration*, compiled by Maze and Mayall, was published by JIST Works in 1991.

The *GOE* grouping is based on 12 interest factors or very broad occupational clusters. Each of these is divided into variable numbers of work groups consisting of closely related activities. The work groups also are divided further into subgroups.

The *GOE* interest factors, briefly defined, are as follows:

1. *Artistic:* Interest in creative expression of feelings or ideas.
2. *Scientific:* Interest in discovering, collecting, and analyzing information about the natural world and in applying scientific research findings to problems in medicine, life sciences, and natural sciences.
3. *Plants and Animals:* Interest in activities involving plants and animals, usually in an outdoor setting.
4. *Protective:* Interest in the use of authority to protect people and property.
5. *Mechanical:* Interest in applying mechanical principles to practical situations, using machines, hand tools, or techniques.

6. *Industrial:* Interest in repetitive, concrete, organized activities in a factory setting.
7. *Business Detail:* Interest in organized, clearly defined activities requiring accuracy and attention to detail, primarily in an office setting.
8. *Selling:* Interest in bringing others to a point of view through personal persuasion, using sales and promotion techniques.
9. *Accommodating:* Interest in catering to the wishes of others, usually on a one-to-one basis.
10. *Humanitarian:* Interest in helping others with their mental, spiritual, social, physical, or vocational needs.
11. *Leading-Influencing:* Interest in leading and influencing others through activities involving high-level verbal and numerical abilities.
12. *Physical Performing:* Interest in physical activities performed before an audience (p. 8).

The 12 interest areas are divided into 66 work groups that are further subdivided into 348 subgroups. The coding system uses a six-digit arrangement, with the first two digits representing interest area, the first four digits identifying the work group, and all six digits designating the subgroup. Each subgroup lists actual *DOT* occupational titles and code numbers so *DOT* information can be used when specific occupations are being considered. Figure 5.4 is a list of the interest areas and the work groups.

Each work group area provides a general description of what workers in the group do and the settings where jobs are found. Additional information is provided as answers to five basic questions asked for each work group as follows:

What kind of work would you do?

What skills and abilities do you need for this kind of work?

How do you know if you would like or could learn to do this kind of work?

How can you prepare for and enter this kind of work?

What else should you consider about these jobs?

Most of the 1991 edition consists of descriptions of 2,500 occupations selected as most important. Those included represent approximately 95 percent of the total work force. The two major criteria for inclusion were, first, "there is a significant labor market for the job," and second, "the occupation is an access point for people who have been working in other fields, or are just starting to work."

In addition to the 1977 *DOT* description of the occupation, several significant items are included in code form with code explanations in various appendices:

1. Office of Employment Statistics (OES) code number
2. General Educational Development code
3. Specific Vocational Preparation code

FIGURE 5.4 GOE *Interest Areas and Work Group Arrangement*

V. Area and Group Arrangement	
01 Artistic	06.03 Quality Control
01.01 Literary Arts	06.04 Elemental Work: Industrial
01.02 Visual Arts	07 Business Detail
01.03 Performing Arts: Drama	07.01 Administrative Detail
01.04 Performing Arts: Music	07.02 Mathematical Detail
01.05 Performing Arts: Dance	07.03 Financial Detail
01.06 Craft Arts	07.04 Oral Communications
01.07 Elemental Arts	07.05 Records Processing
01.08 Modeling	07.06 Clerical Machine Operation
02 Scientific	07.07 Clerical Handling
02.01 Physical Sciences	08 Selling
02.02 Life Sciences	08.01 Sales Technology
02.03 Medical Sciences	08.02 General Sales
02.04 Laboratory Technology	08.03 Vending
03 Plants and Animals	09 Accommodating
03.01 Managerial Work: Plants and Animals	09.01 Hospitality Services
03.02 General Supervision: Plants and Animals	09.02 Barber and Beauty Services
	09.03 Passenger Services
03.03 Animal Training and Service	09.04 Customer Services
03.04 Elemental Work: Plants and Animals	09.05 Attendant Services
04 Protective	10 Humanitarian
04.01 Safety and Law Enforcement	10.01 Social Services
04.02 Security Services	10.02 Nursing, Therapy, and Specialized Teaching Services
05 Mechanical	10.03 Child and Adult Care
05.01 Engineering	11 Leading-Influencing
05.02 Managerial Work: Mechanical	11.01 Mathematics and Statistics
05.03 Engineering Technology	11.02 Educational and Library Services
05.04 Air and Water Vehicle Operation	11.03 Social Research
05.05 Craft Technology	11.04 Law
05.06 Systems Operation	11.05 Business Administration
05.07 Quality Control	11.06 Finance
05.08 Land and Water Vehicle Operation	11.07 Services Administration
05.09 Material Control	11.08 Communications
05.10 Crafts	11.09 Promotion
05.11 Equipment Operation	11.10 Regulations Enforcement
05.12 Elemental Work: Mechanical	11.11 Business Management
06 Industrial	11.12 Contracts and Claims
06.01 Production Technology	12 Physical Performing
06.02 Production Work	12.01 Sports
	12.02 Physical Feats

Source: Guide for Occupational Exploration (1979); p. v–vi.

4. Academic code showing the degree or certification required and the amount of English usage skill
5. Work Field codes showing specific skills used in the job
6. MPSMS code telling what materials, products, subject matter, or services are used in the work

7. Aptitude codes as used with General Aptitude Test Battery (GATB)
8. Temperament codes showing personality characteristics required of the worker
9. Stress codes, listed where the work has a significant degree of stress
10. Physical codes, as used in *Selected Characteristics*
11. Work Environment codes, also from *Selected Characteristics*
12. Salary codes providing information on the average salary range to be expected
13. Outlook codes indicating how long it usually takes to find this type of job

One chapter provides a detailed explanation of how to use the book effectively, and another includes explanations of the various coding systems. Four of the appendices provide helpful lists, such as an alphabetical list of the occupations included in the book, an alphabetical list of industries, the grouping of the 2,500 selected occupations by industry, and the selected occupations by educational level. Other appendices give further information about the OES, MPSMS, and Work Field codes.

Droege and Boese (1982) describe how use of the General Aptitude Test Battery has been integrated with application of the *GOE*. Occupational aptitude patterns (OAP) have been developed for 59 of the 66 work groups included in the *GOE;* these apply to 97 percent of the nonsupervisory occupations. Jones (1980) suggests how the *GOE* can be used with Holland codes and presents a table identifying the primary Holland code for each of the *GOE* work groups.

The *GOE* has great potential value for the career counselor because its foundation of interest areas provides such a useful device for helping clients translate assessment of their interests into relevant occupational fields. Further, information in each work group description about the skills and abilities required and about preparation programs also provides a base for relating the client's evaluation of aptitudes or general educational plans to appropriate occupational groups at the work group level. Those work group areas that appear to be related to client interests, aptitudes, or educational plans can be explored further by considering the narrative descriptions and coded information included in the 1991 edition. One must be aware that the narrative descriptions appear to be drawn from the 1977 edition of the *DOT*. Occupations that have changed extensively since that time are described more accurately in the 1991 revision of the *DOT;* consequently, caution is necessary if one uses the descriptions in the 1991 *GOE*.

SELECTED CHARACTERISTICS OF OCCUPATIONS DEFINED IN THE *DICTIONARY OF OCCUPATIONAL TITLES*

In 1981 the U.S. Department of Labor published the third volume in the series we are considering in this chapter: *Selected Characteristics of Occupations*

Defined in the Dictionary of Occupational Titles, usually referred to simply as *Selected Characteristics*. The characteristics included are the physical demands, environmental conditions, and training time for all *DOT* base titles.

Occupations are listed in Part A according to *GOE* Work Subgroups (six-digit codes). Within each subgroup, occupations are grouped according to exertional level, and within these groups they are arranged by *DOT* code number. Other physical demands, the environmental conditions, and training requirements are listed for each entry. These factors were discussed in Chapter 3 and are identified here only for the convenience of the reader. Part B lists occupations sequentially according to *DOT* code number. Each entry also includes the *GOE* subgroup code, the strength factor, the *DOT* base title, and the *DOT* industry designation.

Examples of entries in Part A are listed in Figure 5.5. As indicated earlier, Part A provides five pieces of information for each occupation classified in each *GOE* Work Subgroup. The *DOT* code, title, and industry designation are self-explanatory. Physical demands for each occupation are rated according to standard *DOT* classifications with the letters S, L, M, H, and V representing lifting and carrying strength factors. The numbers represent the following demands:

2—Climb and balance

3—Stoop, kneel, crouch, crawl

4—Reach, handle, finger, feel

5—Talk, hear

6—See (acuity, depth perception, field of vision, accommodation) (p. 479)

Environmental conditions represent the usual *DOT* definitions for those conditions as follows:

I—Inside (75 percent or more)

O—Outside (75 percent or more)

B—Both

2—Extremes of cold plus temperature changes

3—Extremes of heat plus temperature changes

4—Wet and humid

5—Noise and vibration

6—Hazards

7—Fumes, odors, toxic conditions, dust, poor ventilation (p. 479)

The final columns list the training time required for the occupation. This is provided under three headings. The M and L represent mathematical development and language development, and SVP is the usual *DOT* factor of specific vocational preparation. The *Selected Characteristics* material for tool knowledges provides information for each level ranging from level 6

FIGURE 5.5   Selected Characteristics *Part A, Sample Page (p. 259)*

PART A

Titles are arranged by Guide for Occupational Exploration group and physical demands

10.01 Social Services

Occupations in this group involve assisting people in dealing with problems that are usually personal, social, vocational, physical, educational, or spiritual in nature. Skills and abilities required include: Applying logic and special training to counsel individuals or assist them in defining and solving social, personal, or other related problems; gaining trust and confidence of people by demonstrating interest in and desire to help people; keeping records and writing investigative reports; and communicating effectively with people.

10.01.01 Religious

DOT Code	DOT Title and Industry Designation	Physical Demands	Environmental Conditions	M	L	SVP
129.107-014	Christian science practitioner (profess. and kin.)	S 5	I	2	3	6
129.107-018	Director of religious activities (education)	S 5	I	3	5	8
120.007-010	Clergy member (profess. & kin.)	L 5	I	4	6	8
129.271-010	Mohel (profess. & kin.)	L 4 5 6	I	2	4	6

10.01.02 Counseling and Social Work

DOT Code	DOT Title and Industry Designation	Physical Demands	Environmental Conditions	M	L	SVP
045.107-014	Counselor, nurses' association (medical ser.)	S 4 5	I	4	5	8
045.107-018	Director of counseling (profess. & kin.)	S 5	I	5	5	8
045.107-022	Psychologist, clinical (profess. & kin.)	S 5 6	I	5	6	8
045.107-026	Psychologist, counseling (profess. & kin.)	S 5	I	5	5	8
045.107-034	Psychologist, school (profess. & kin.)	S 5 6	I	5	5	8
045.107-038	Residence counselor (education)	S 5	I	4	5	7
045.107-042	Vocational-rehabilitation counselor (gov. ser.)	S 5	I	3	5	8
090.107-101	Foreign-student adviser (education)	S 5	I	2	5	7
090.117-018	Dean of students (education) I	S 5	I	3	5	8
091.107-010	Dean of students (eduction) II	S 5	i	3	5	8
159.207-010	Astrologer (amuse. & rec.)	S 5	I	4	4	4
166.167-014	Director of placement (education)	S 4 5	I	5	5	8
187.167-198	Veterans contact representative (nonprofit organ.)	S 5	I	4	5	7
195.107-101	Caseworker (social ser.)	S 5	I	4	5	7

(continued)

FIGURE 5.5 *Continued*

DOT Code	DOT Title and Industry Designation	Physical Demands	Environmental Conditions	M	L	SVP
195.107-014	Caseworker, child welfare (social ser.)	S 5	I	3	5	7
195.107-018	Caseworker, family (social ser.)	S 5	I	4	5	7
195.107-022	Social group worker (social ser.)	S 5	I	3	5	8
195.107-030	Social worker, medical (profess. & kin.)	S 5	I	3	5	7
195.107-034	Social worker, psychiatric (profess. & kin.)	S 5	I	3	5	7
195.107-038	Social worker, school (profess. & kin.)	S 5	I	3	5	7
195.137-010	Caseworker supervisor (social ser.)	S 5	I	3	5	7
195.167-030	Parole officer (profess. & kin.)	S 5	I	3	5	7
199.207-010	Dianetic counselor (profess. & kin.)	S 5	I	3	4	6
045.107-010	Counselor (profess. & kin.)	L 4 5 6	I	5	5	7
195.107-026	Social worker, delinquency prevention (social ser.)	L 5	I	3	5	7
195.267-014	Human relations or drug and alcohol counselor (military ser.)	L 4 5	I	3	3	6
195.367-010	Case aide (social ser.)	L 5	I	3	5	6

(most complex) to level 1 (simplest). The more complex levels of M are described in terms of three applications, as follows:

Level 6—Advanced calculus, modern algebra, statistics

Level 5—Algebra, calculus, statistics

Level 4—Algebra, geometry, shop math (p. 469)

Lower levels of M are described in terms of practical applied arithmetic functions. All levels of L are described as skill requirements in reading, writing, and speaking.

Specific vocational preparation represents the amount of time required to learn the techniques, acquire information, and develop the facility needed for average performance in a specific job-worker situation. SVP may include training acquired through vocational education, apprenticeship, in-plant training, on-the-job training, or experience in other jobs. Nine levels are recognized as follows:

1—Short demonstration.

2—Anything beyond short demonstration up to 30 days.

3—Over 30 days up to and including 3 months.

4—Over 3 months up to and including 6 months.

5—Over 6 months up to and including 1 year.

6—Over 1 year up to and including 2 years.

7—Over 2 years up to and including 4 years.

8—Over 4 years up to and including 10 years.

9—Over 10 years (p. 479)

Part B includes material that is self-explanatory. Part B is often helpful in finding the Part A information. If the client or counselor has an occupational title, the alphabetical index in the *DOT* can be used to obtain the *DOT* code; then Part B will provide the *GOE* Work Subgroup code number under which the occupation can be found in Part A. Similarly, given the occupational title, one can look in Appendix D (Alphabetical Arrangement of Occupations) in the 1979 *GOE* where both *DOT* and *GOE* codes are listed, then in Part A of *Selected Characteristics* for information located there.

Using the same illustration of *counselor* listed in Figure 5.1, we can turn to Part B of *Selected Characteristics* and, on page 300, find the following entry.

045.107-010   10.01.02   L COUNSELOR (profess. & kin.)

Turning to page 259 for the 10.01.02 subgroup (see Figure 5.5) we find counselor listed near the bottom of the page. The information shows us that the occupation is considered light (maximum lifting 20 pounds, frequent lifting or carrying of 10 pounds, includes walking and standing), and it requires some manual manipulation and the ability to talk, hear, and see. The work is performed primarily inside. The math and language development required is at level 5, indicating some graduate-level mathematics and the most complex language development. Specific vocational preparation ranges from 2 to 4 years (a master's degree plus some internship or practical experience). We also can observe that there are 26 other occupations closely related to counselor in this subgroup.

SUMMARY

Each of the three volumes discussed here—*DOT, GOE,* and *Selected Characteristics*—serves a particular purpose and provides information not available in either of the other two volumes. The *DOT* is the basic reference that provides the definition, industry designation, occupational grouping, and worker functions information. One can also identify other occupations in the occupational group that have comparable or fairly similar worker functions.

The *GOE*, as its title indicates, was developed to provide assistance in the exploration process. Walker (1980) emphasizes its value for both school counselors and Job Service counselors. Because it provides brief information about basic questions— "What do you do?" "What skills do you need?"—it can be used by clients who are just beginning to match themselves against possible occupations. It is just as valuable for the displaced worker, the reentry worker, or the worker involved in midlife reassessment, who all usually need the same kind of information as they examine occupations for which they have limited knowledge. Grouping occupations, as occurs in the subgroup arrangement, provides a basis for widening horizons by suggesting closely related possibilities that were probably unlikely to be considered.

Selected Characteristics supplies specific answers to questions about physical capacities and so forth that clients must answer as they match themselves against occupational requirements. Counselors and others who assist individuals with physical or educational restrictions that must be reckoned with in the matching process will find this volume especially useful. Rehabilitation counselors searching for occupations to which a worker can transfer existing skills can often find possible alternatives within the same or related subgroup listings.

REFERENCES

Droege, R. C., & Boese, R. (1982). Development of a new occupational aptitude pattern structure with comprehensive occupational coverage. *Vocational Guidance Quarterly, 30*, 219–229.

Droege, R. C., & Padgett, A. (1979). Development of an interest-oriented occupational classification system. *Vocational Guidance Quarterly, 27*, 302–310.

Harrington, T. F., & O'Shea, A. J. (Eds.). (1984). *Guide for occupational exploration* (2nd ed.). Minneapolis: National Forum Foundation.

Jones, L. K. (1980). Holland's typology and the new *Guide for Occupational Exploration:* Bridging the gap. *Vocational Guidance Quarterly, 29*, 70–76.

Maze, M., & Mayall, D. (1991). *Enhanced guide for occupational exploration.* Indianapolis, IN: JIST.

Prediger, D. J. (1981). Getting "ideas" out of the DOT and into vocational guidance. *Vocational Guidance Quarterly, 29*, 293–305.

U.S. Department of Labor. (1977). *Dictionary of occupational titles* (4th ed.). Washington, DC: U.S. Government Printing Office.

U.S. Department of Labor. (1979). *Guide for occupational exploration.* Washington, DC: U.S. Government Printing Office.

U.S. Department of Labor. (1981). *Selected characteristics of occupations defined in the dictionary of occupational titles.* Washington, DC: U.S. Government Printing Office.

U.S. Department of Labor. (1991). *Dictionary of occupational titles* (4th ed., revised 1991). Washington, DC: U.S. Government Printing Office.

Walker, M. J. (1980). Guide for occupational exploration. *Occupational Outlook Quarterly, 24*, 26–28.

Winer, J. L. (1981). Worker functions and intraoccupational specialty in psychology. *Vocational Guidance Quarterly, 30*, 50–60.

__6

Other Classification Systems

We have already established the fact that the world of work is extremely varied and complex. The more than 20,000 occupations included in the *Dictionary of Occupational Titles* are brought together by code numbers into a classification system that has two major parts—the occupational group arrangement and the worker function arrangement. Each part, as we saw in the last chapter, is a complete, self-contained classification system. Each part can be, and often is, used by itself for classification purposes as well as in combination to produce the code number.

If we wish to compare benchwork occupations with processing occupations, we can do so by using the occupational group arrangements to identify the jobs classified in the two categories. Within these two categories, we can use the worker function arrangement if we wish to study how these two categories of occupations relate to the data-people-things concept. The occupational group arrangement permits us to be as broad as a major category or as specific as a three-digit group. Thus we can select the classification system that provides the degree of specificity we need to accomplish our task.

In some situations we need, or perhaps prefer, an extremely broad classification of occupations. The blue-collar/white-collar dichotomy is an illustration of the broadest type of classification. This structure is generally understood, widely used, and often sufficiently specific for a given situation. A moment's reflection, however, shows some serious disadvantages. Each class (white-collar/blue-collar) is so broad as to be almost meaningless; and many occupations can be classified in either division, or often in both, with equally valid arguments for the action. Nevertheless, the terminology is extremely useful in appropriate situations.

At the other extreme, one can hypothesize that grouping as specific as nine-digit *DOT* numbers are too broad and general to meet the need of the moment. All secondary teachers, for example, carry the same code number, as do all secretaries, all carpenters, and all accountants. Yet there may be times when a much finer distinction within each occupation is desirable.

The purpose of this chapter is to identify some of the other widely used and recognized classification system so the reader knows the commonly used arrangements or has sufficient knowledge to develop a system for a specific situation. Exhaustive treatment of the topic would result in a voluminous, too detailed chapter. Obviously, many systems that have significant value for a specific situation have not been included. In this chapter, we consider the following classification systems:

Standard Industrial Classification
Standard Occupational Classification
Two-dimensional Classification
Three-dimensional Classification

Although each classification system described in the previous chapter and in this chapter is complete, one does need occasionally to move from one system to another. This crossover is suggested by the inclusion of Standard Occupational Classification codes in *DOT supplements*. Another publication that partially facilitates this movement from *DOT* codes to those used in other systems is *Vocational Preparation and Occupations*. Published by the National Occupational Information Coordinating Committee, it includes crosswalk tables for several vocational program areas that include *DOT* codes, *Selected Characteristics* data, *Standard Occupational Classification* codes, as well as Occupational Employment Statistics codes and 1980 Census codes.

STANDARD INDUSTRIAL CLASSIFICATION (SIC)

Although counselors are usually seeking information about *jobs*, or what tasks the worker performs, there are times when they can approach this search more effectively by investigating the *setting* where the tasks are performed. This industrial approach can be facilitated by using a classification system that organizes industries rather than occupations.

The most widely used industrial system is called the *Standard Industrial Classification*, developed by the Office of Management and Budget and last revised in 1987. It is now widely used by both state and federal agencies as the structure for compiling industrial statistics. A further advantage arises from its degree of specificity within a classification system that covers our entire economy. The *SIC* is important to counselors because its broad usage by government agencies means that much of the data and information they publish about jobs, trends, future developments, and so on are organized according to the *SIC* structure. Familiarity with the system expedites finding the needed information and also helps in proper interpretation of those data.

The *SIC* divides industries into 10 major divisions plus one miscellaneous group. These divisions were introduced and described in detail in

Chapter 4, so they are only listed here. The 10 major divisions include the following:

A. Agriculture, Forestry, Fishing, Hunting, Trapping
B. Mining (Energy)
C. Construction
D. Manufacturing
E. Transportation, Communication, Public Utilities
F. Wholesale Trade
G. Retail Trade
H. Finance, Insurance, Real Estate
 I. Services
J. Public Administration
K. Nonclassifiable Establishments

These divisions are divided into 83 major groups identified with a two-digit code number. For example, "Division F—Wholesale Trade" is divided into "Major Group 50. Wholesale Trade—Durable Goods" and "Major Group 51. Wholesale Trade—Nondurable Goods." Figure 6.1 consists of a sample page from the *SIC Manual* and shows the coding structure. The Major Groups are divided into Groups that carry three-digit codes and contain closely related industries. An example of a Group can be seen in Figure 6.1 with the heading "501 MOTOR VEHICLES AND MOTOR VEHICLE PARTS AND SUPPLIES." Groups are then subdivided into specific industries, which carry four-digit codes.

Establishments are classified in the *SIC* according to the primary type of activity in which they engage. An illustration of how a peripheral activity might be misleading can be seen in Figure 6.1 in the description of Industry Number 5012. Here one sees a statement about an automobile distributor that occasionally sells vehicles wholesale but ordinarily is engaged in retail sales. Another example can be seen across the Midwest, where many localities consider the local factory to be a part of the automobile industry although it actually produces tires, batteries, wiring systems, or other components. The *SIC* would list that factory according to what it actually manufactures, not according to the ultimate destination of the product. The term *automobile manufacturing* would be reserved for those plants that assemble the components to produce a completed automobile.

STANDARD OCCUPATIONAL CLASSIFICATION (SOC)

Most classification system have been developed to meet a particular need. The *DOT* originated in the Great Depression of the 1930s as the federal employment agencies searched for a system that could be used to match unemployed workers with new vacancies; the *GOE* grew out of an effort to

FIGURE 6.1 *Sample Page from* Standard Industrial Classification Manual

Major Group 50.—WHOLESALE TRADE—DURABLE GOODS
The Major Group as a Whole

This major group includes establishments primarily engaged in the wholesale distribution of durable goods.

Industry
Group   Industry
No.   No.

501   MOTOR VEHICLES AND MOTOR VEHICLE PARTS AND SUPPLIES

   5102   **Automobiles and Other Motor Vehicles**

Establishments primarily engaged in the wholesale distribution of new and used passenger automobiles, trucks, trailers, and other motor vehicles, including motorcycles, motor homes, and snowmobiles. Automotive distributors primarily engaged in selling at retail to individual consumers for personal use, and also selling a limited amount of new and used passenger automobiles and trucks at wholesale, are classified in Retail Trade, Industry 5511.

Ambulances—wholesale	Motorcycles—wholesale
Automobile auction—wholesale	Popup campers—wholesale
Automobiles—wholesale	Recreational vehicles—wholesale
Bodies, automotive—wholesale	Snowmobiles—wholesale
Buses—wholesale	Taxicabs—wholesale
Campers (pickup coaches) for mounting on trucks—wholesale	Trailers for passenger automobiles—wholesale
Mopeds—wholesale	Truck tractors—wholesale
Motor homes—wholesale	Truck trailers—wholesale
Motor scooters—wholesale	Trucks—wholesale
Motor vehicles, commercial—wholesale	Vans—wholesale

   5013   **Motor Vehicle Supplies and New Parts**

Establishments primarily engaged in the wholesale distribution of motor vehicle supplies, accessories, tools, and equipment; and new motor vehicle parts.

Automobile engine testing equipment, electrical—wholesale	Hardware, automotive—wholesale
Automobile glass—wholesale	Motorcycle parts—wholesale
Automobile service station equipment—wholesale	Pumps, measuring and dispensing: gasoline and oil—wholesale
Automotive accessories—wholesale	Seat belts, automotive—wholesale
Automotive engines, new—wholesale	Seat covers, automotive—wholesale
Automotive parts, new—wholesale	Service station equipment, automobile—wholesale
Automotive stampings—wholesale	Testing equipment, electrical: automotive—wholesale
Automotive supplies—wholesale	
Batteries, automotive—wholesale	Tools and equipment, automotive—wholesale
Engine electrical equipment, automotive—wholesale	Wheels, motor vehicle: new—wholesale
Garage service equipment—wholesale	

   5014   **Tires and Tubes**

Establishments primarily engaged in the wholesale distribution of tires and tubes for passenger and commercial vehicles.

FIGURE 6.1   *Continued*

| Repair materials, tire and tube—wholesale | Tires and tubes, new–wholesale |
| | Tires, used—wholesale |

5015   Motor Vehicle Parts, Used

Establishments primarily engaged in the distribution at wholesale or retail of used motor vehicle parts. This industry includes establishments primarily engaged in dismantling motor vehicles for the purpose of selling parts. Estab-

translate interest inventory scores into occupational structure; and the *SIC* was developed to provide a framework for reporting industrial and occupational data collected by various governmental agencies. As more and more local, state, and federal agencies used occupational data in their work, they often selected one of the existing systems and adapted it to their needs, or, in some cases, developed their own classification system to meet the special needs they addressed. Inevitably, each agency accumulated extensive data of great value; but because of the diversity in the systems used, most of the data could not be combined or related effectively. The need for another system that would bridge the differing methods already in use became obvious. This movement covered an extended period of time, starting in the early 1940s with the decennial census of that year, followed by the formation of an interagency committee in the mid-1960s, the publication of the *Standard Occupational Classification* in 1977, and its revision in 1980.

Formed for the express purpose of developing a mechanism that would maximize the analytical usefulness of data on labor force, employment, and income collected by various agencies, the interagency committee established a set of principles that largely identify the advantage incorporated in the system they developed. Those principles comprise the following excerpt from the *Standard Occupational Classification Manual*, 1980 edition (pp. 8, 9):

Principles of Classification

In developing the Classification the following principles were followed:

1. The classification should realistically reflect the current occupational structure of the United States.
2. An occupation should be classified on the basis of work performed. Skill level, training, education, licensing and credential requirements usually associated with job performance should be considered only when an inaccurate picture of the occupational structure would be presented without such consideration.
3. Place of work (industry) should be considered in classifying an occupation when the work setting alters the nature of the work sufficiently to warrant separate classification. For example, cooks in private households and commercial settings were classified in different unit groups because work is significantly dissimilar in their respective work settings.
4. The occupations should be classified in homogenous groups that can be defined so that the content of each group is well delineated.

5. An occupation that combines two distinct activities should be classified in one group on the basis of the primary activity—the one that accounts for the major portion of the worker's time. However, in cases where one activity requires special skills that are crucial in carrying out the duties of the occupation (although not required for as much time as other activities), that activity should determine the classification of the occupation.

6. Each occupation should be assigned to only one group at the lowest level of the classification system (unit group).

7. Large size should not by itself be considered sufficient reason for separate identification of a group.

8. Small size should not be considered sufficient reason for excluding a group from separate identification, although size must be considered, or the system could become too large to be useful.

9. Supervisors should be identified separately from the workers they supervise wherever possible in keeping with the real structure of the world of work.

10. Apprentices and trainees should be classified with the occupation for which training is being taken.

11. Helpers should be identified separately when their work is such that they are not in training for the occupation they are providing help, or if their work is truly different.

12. The need for comparability to *International Standard Classification of Occupations* should be considered in developing the structure, but it should not be an overriding factor.

The original intent was to use the 1977 publication for a 5-year period and then revise it as usage suggested. This plan was changed, and the revision was moved forward to 1980 so the *SOC* could be used for the 1980 decennial census. It was reprinted in 1989. Most readers will encounter the *SOC* in the *Occupational Outlook Handbook (OOH)*, where it has been used to group the occupations included. The major groupings were modified for the 1990–1991 *OOH*. Table 6.1 compares the major groups of the 1980 *SOC* with those titles used in the 1990–1991 *OOH*.

The *SOC* is designed to cover all occupations where work is performed for pay or profit, including work in family-operated enterprises where direct payment may not be made to family members. Both military and civilian workers are included.

The *SOC* uses a four-level system with each level providing finer detail. There are 22 divisions, which in turn are divided into 60 major groups. The major groups are represented by a two-digit code number ranging from "11—Officials and Administrators, Public Administration" to "99—Miscellaneous Occupations."

The major groups are divided into minor groups, which in turn are divided into unit groups. There are 212 minor groups and 538 unit groups. Figure 6.2, a sample page (91) from the *SOC*, illustrates the graduation levels. A *major group* can be seen in the entry "33 EDITORS, REPORTERS, PUBLIC RELATIONS SPECIALISTS, AND ANNOUNCERS." A brief definition describes the workers included in this major group. An example of a *minor*

TABLE 6.1   *A Comparison of 1980 SOC Major Groups and the Modifications Used in the 1990–1991 OOH*

1980 *SOC*	1990–1991 *OOH*
Executive, administrative, or managerial occupations	Executive, administrative, and managerial occupations
Engineers, surveyors, and architects Natural scientists and mathematicians Social scientists, social workers, religious workers, and lawyers Teachers, librarians, and counselors Health diagnosing and treating practitioners Registered nurses, pharmacists, dieticians, therapists, physicians' assistants Writers, artists, entertainers, and athletes	Professional specialty occupations
Health technologists and technicians Technologists and technicians, except health Marketing and sales occupations	Technicians and related support occupations Marketing and sales occupations
Administrative support occupations, including clerical Service occupations Agricultural, forestry, and fishing occupations Mechanics and repairers Construction and extractive occupations	Administrative support occupations, including clerical Service occupations Agricultural, forestry, fishing, and related occupations Mechanics, installers, and repairers Construction trades and extractive occupations
Precision production occupations Production working occupations Transportation and material moving occupations Handlers, equipment cleaners, helpers and laborers Military occupations Miscellaneous occupations	 Production occupations Transportation and material moving occupations Handlers, equipment cleaners, helpers, and laborers Armed forces

group can be seen in the entry "331 EDITORS AND REPORTERS." Here again is a brief definition describing the included workers. A *unit group* is represented by the entry "3312 Editors." In addition to the descriptive definition, a listing of actual occupations is seen arranged according to *DOT* code. The occupational entry typically appears as follows:

Script reader   724   131267022

FIGURE 6.2   *Sample Page from* Standard Occupational Classification Manual

33 EDITORS, REPORTERS, PUBLIC RELATIONS SPECIALISTS, AND ANNOUNCERS

This major group includes occupations concerned with editing and reporting news items and features, writing publicity articles and press releases, and announcing radio and television news, commercials, and station identification. Writers of technical manuals and similar materials are classified in minor group 398.

331   EDITORS AND REPORTERS

This minor group includes occupations involving collecting and analyzing facts about news events by interview, investigation, or observation, and reporting and writing stories for publication or radio and television broadcasting.

3312   Editors

This unit group includes occupations involving coordinating the work of writers and editing writer's material. Editors may plan layout of writer's material according to time or space allocation, to rewrite or reorganize writer's work to insure conformance to company policy, and to make certain all laws and regulations are followed by the writer.

Script reader	724	131267022
Editor, managing, newspaper	699	132017010
Editor, newspaper	699	132017014
Editor, technical and scientific publications	705	132017018
Continuity director	724	132037010
Editor, city	699	132037014
Editor, department	699	132037018
Editor, publications	699	132037022
Story editor	589-724	132037026
Bureau chief	699	132067010
Editor, book	699	132067014
Editor, dictionary	705	132067018
Editor, greeting card	699	132067022
Editor, news	699	132067026
Assignment editor	724	132137010
Editor, telegraph	699-724	132267010
Editorial assistant	699	132267014
Editor, index	699	132367010
Editor, film	589-724	962264010

3313   Reporters

This unit group includes occupations involving collecting and analyzing facts about news events by interview, investigation, or observation, and reporting and writing stories for publication or radio and television broadcasting.

Columnist/commentator	699-724	131067010
Copy writer	705	131067014
Critic	699-724	131067018
Editorial writer	699	131067022
Newscaster	724	131267010
Newswriter	699-724	131267014
Reporter	699-724	131267018

332   PUBLIC RELATIONS SPECIALISTS AND PUBLICITY WRITERS

This minor group includes occupations involving promoting or creating goodwill for individuals or organizations by writing or selecting favorable publicity material and releasing it through various communications media, preparing and arranging for displays, making speeches and performing related pub-

The occupational title is obvious; it is a *DOT* base title. The first column of three or more digits represents the *DOT* industry designation for the industry in which the occupation is found ("724—Radio and TV Broadcasting"). Some occupations (see "Story editor") occur in more than one industry; in that case, additional three-digit codes are listed in this column. The nine-digit code in the right-hand column is the *DOT* code number without decimal and hyphen. Occasional occupations are listed with a Roman numeral. This indicates that there is more than one job with the same title and industry designation. Also, one occasionally sees a three-digit code located approximately at midline without an industry or *DOT* code. These titles are 1970 census titles and are included to provide some insight into how those data fit the *SOC* system.

Occupational definitions in the *Fourth Edition Supplement* of the *DOT* include *SOC* code numbers, so one can move easily from the *DOT* code to the *SOC* code. The presence of that information in the *Supplement* definition suggests that future editions of the *DOT* will incorporate these data.

TWO-DIMENSIONAL CLASSIFICATION

Many criteria can be used to organize occupations into related groups. The next logical step is to join two of these into a combined system. Several authors have used this approach effectively. We consider a few of these as representative of a much larger group.

Roe (1956, 1984) and Roe and Klos (1972) present a two-dimensional system that has been used widely for many years. Roe proposes that a horizontal grouping of occupations can be made on the basis of the primary focus of activity, an idea quite similar to the several systems we have already examined. She suggests that the focus of an occupation may be on personal interactions, the handling or processing of natural resources, the development of knowledge, or similar factors. This has led to a series of eight groups defined by Roe and Klos as follows:

1. *Service*—These occupations are primarily concerned with serving and attending to the personal tastes, needs, and welfare of other persons. Included are occupations such as social work and guidance, and domestic and protective services. The essential element is a situation in which one person is doing something for another.
2. *Business Contact*—These occupations are primarily concerned with the face-to-face sale of commodities, investments, real estate, and services. The person-to-person relation is again important, but it is focused on persuasion to a course of action rather than on helping. The persuader will profit if his advice is followed; the advisee is supposed to.
3. *Organization*—These are the managerial and white collar jobs in business, industry, and government—the occupations concerned primarily with the organization and efficient functioning of commercial enterprises and government activities. The quality of person-to-person relations is largely formalized.

4. *Technology*—This group includes occupations concerned with the production, maintenance, and transportation of commodities and utilities. Here are occupations in engineering, crafts, and the machine trades, as well as in transportation and communication. Interpersonal relations are of relatively little importance, and the focus is on dealing with things.

5. *Outdoor*—This group includes the occupations primarily concerned with the cultivation, preservation, and gathering of crops, of marine or inland water resources or mineral resources, of forest products and of other natural resources, and with animal husbandry. Because of the increasing mechanization of some of these occupations, perhaps particularly those concerned with the petroleum industry, a number of jobs previously classified in this group have been moved to Group 4. There still remain a great many persons, however, whose work is most appropriately classified here. Interpersonal relations are largely irrelevant.

6. *Science*—These are the occupations primarily concerned with scientific theory and its application under specified circumstances other than technology. Even in scientific research (as in physics) that is not at all person-oriented as well as in such fields as psychology and anthropology, it is clear that there is a relationship to the occupations in Group 7, with some return to more specific personal relations in the medical groups that belong here.

7. *General Culture*—These occupations are primarily concerned with the preservation and transmission of the general cultural heritage. Interest is in human activities rather than in individual persons. This group includes occupations in education, journalism, jurisprudence, the ministry, linguistics, and the subjects usually called the humanities. Most elementary and high school teachers are placed in this group. At higher levels teachers are placed in groups by subject matter—e.g., teachers of science in 6, or art in 8, or humanities in 7.

8. *Arts and Entertainment*—These occupations include those primarily concerned with the use of special skills in the creative arts and in the field of entertainment. For the most part, the focus is on a relationship between one person (or an organized group) and a more general public. The interpersonal relation is important but neither so direct nor of the same nature as that in group 1. [*Source:* A. Roe and D. Klos, "Classification of Occupations," in J. M Whiteley and A. Resinkoff (Eds.), *Perspectives on Vocational Development* (Washington, DC: American Personnel and Guidance Association, 1972, pp. 202–203). Copyright AACD. Reprinted with permission. No further reproduction authorized without further permission of AACD.]

The second, or vertical, dimension is based on level of function, including the degree of responsibility, capacity, or skill. When these three factors do not correlate with one another for a specific job, Roe gives basic emphasis to the level of responsibility required in an occupation. The six levels of function are described by Roe and Klos as follows:

1. *Professional and managerial 1:* Independent responsibility—This level includes not only the innovators and creators but also the top managerial and administrative people, as well as those professional persons who have

independent responsibility in important respects. For occupations at this level there is generally no higher authority, except the social group. Several criteria are suggested: (a) important, independent, and varied responsibilities; (b) policy-making; (c) education—when high level education is relevant (it is not required in the creative arts, for example, or a necessity for dictators, or even for our own high government officials), it is at the doctoral level or equivalent.

2. *Professional and managerial 2:* The distinction between this level and the previous one is primarily one of degree. Genuine autonomy may be present but with narrower or less significant responsibilities than in Level 1. Suggested criteria are: (a) medium-level responsibilities, for self and others, both with regard to importance and variety; (b) policy interpretation; (c) education at or above the bachelor level, but below the doctorate or its equivalent.

3. *Semi-professional and small business*—The criteria suggested here are: (a) low-level responsibility for others; (b) application of policy, or determination for self only (as in managing a small business); (c) education, high school and technical school or the equivalent.

4. *Skilled*—This and the following levels are classical subdivisions. Skilled occupations require apprenticeship or other special training or experience.

5. *Semi-skilled*—These occupations require some training and experience, but markedly less than the occupations in Level 4. In addition, there is much less autonomy and initiative permitted in these occupations.

6. *Unskilled*—These occupations require no special training or education and not much more ability than is needed to follow simple directions and to engage in simple repetitive actions. At this level, group differentiation depends primarily upon the occupational setting. [*Source:* A. Roe and D. Klos, "Classification of Occupations," in J. M. Whiteley and A. Resnikoff (Eds.), *Perspectives on Vocational Development* (Washington, DC: American Personnel and Guidance Association, 1972, pp. 208–209). Copyright AACD. Reprinted with permission. No further reproduction authorized without further permission from AACD.]

Figure 6.3 illustrates how Roe combines these two criteria to provide an eight- by six-cell framework for categorizing occupations. An empty cell suggests that an occupation has not been identified that fits that level and group.

The two-dimensional classification system is particularly helpful when used to assist clients or students in grasping both the scope and interrelationships in the world of work. The vastness of the occupational life of our nation is overwhelming to youth and adults alike. The suggestion that there are more than 20,000 different ways to earn a livelihood can easily create despair and frustration. Considering the world of work from the approach of Roe's classification system, however, simplifies the task and also stresses an orderliness in it.

The horizontal dimension is useful in illustrating the broad areas into which occupations can be divided. Even though *primary focus* is the classification factor used for this dimension, this term embraces several characteristics of what people do, how they do it, and where they do it—in general, the

FIGURE 6.3 *Roe's Two-Way Classification of Occupations*

Level	I Service	II Business Contact	III Organization	IV Technology
1 Professional & managerial (ind. responsibility)	Personal therapists Social work supervisors Counselors	Promoters	U.S. President & cabinet officers Industrial tycoons International bankers	Inventive geniuses Consulting or chief engineers Ship's commanders
2 Professional & managerial	Social workers Occupational therapists Probation truant officers (with training)	Promoters Public relations counselors	C.P.A.'s Business and government executives Union officials	Applied scientists Factory managers Ship's officers
3 Semiprofessional and small business	YMCA officials Detectives, police sergeants Welfare workers City inspectors	Salesmen; auto, bond, insurance Dealers, retail & wholesale Confidence men	Accountants, average Employment managers Owners, catering, dry-cleaning, etc.	Aviators Contractors Foremen (*DOT* II) Radio operators
4 Skilled	Barbers Chefs Practical nurses Policemen	Auctioneers Buyers (*DOT* I) House canvassers	Cashiers Clerks Foremen, warehouse Salesclerks	Blacksmiths Electricians Foremen (*DOT* I) Mechanics
5 Semiskilled	Taxi drivers General houseworkers City firemen	Peddlers	Clerks, file, stock, etc. Notaries Runners	Bulldozer operators Truck drivers
6 Unskilled	Chambermaids Hospital attendants Watchmen		Messengers	Helpers Laborers Wrappers Yardmen

field in which they work. An obviously related factor in considering this dimension is an individual's interests—the kinds of things she likes and prefers. In considering Roe's horizontal axis, it is important for the reader to remember that Roe views this plane as a circle, not as a straight line; hence areas VIII and I have the same relationship as I and II. This can be visualized

FIGURE 6.3 *Continued*

V Outdoor	VI Science	VII General Cultural	VIII Arts and Entertainment

Consulting
  specialists
	Research
	  scientists
	Univ., col.
	  faculties
	Medical
	  specialists
	Museum curators
		Supreme Court
		  justices
		Univ., col.
		  faculties
		Prophets
		Scholars
			Creative artists
			Performers, great
			Teachers,
			  university
			  equivalent
			Museum curators

Applied scientists
Land owners and
  operators, large
Landscape
  architects
	Scientists,
	  semi-
	  independent
	Nurses
	Pharmacists
	Veterinarians
		Editors
		Teachers, high
		  school and
		  elementary
			Athletes
			Art critics
			Designers
			Music arrangers

County agents
Farm owners
Forest rangers
Fish, game
  wardens
	Technicians,
	  medical, X-ray,
	  museum
	Weather
	  observers
	Chiropractors
		Justices of the
		  peace
		Radio
		  announcers
		Reporters
		Librarians
			Ad writers
			Designers
			Interior
			  decorators
			Showmen

Laboratory
  testors,
  dairy products,
  etc.
Miners
	Technical
	  assistants
		Law clerks	Advertising artists
			Decorators,
			  window, etc.
			Photographers

Gardeners
Farm tenants
Teamsters
	Veterinary
	  hospital
	  attendants
			Illustrators,
			  greeting
			  cards
			Showcard writers
			Stagehands

Dairy hands
Farm laborers
Lumberjacks
	Nontechnical
	  helpers in
	  scientific
	  organization		

Source: Reprinted with permission from *The Psychology of Occupations* by A. Roe, p. 151. Copyright 1956 by John Wiley & Sons, Inc., New York.

if one mentally rolls the edges of Figure 6.3 so the outer margins overlap. Figure 2.1 in Chapter 2 illustrates Roe's concept of concentric circles, with the outer circle containing the eight occupational groups.

The vertical dimension encourages consideration of such factors as ability, educational preparation, degree of responsibility, and related items. This may be extremely helpful, for example, in showing a person whose possibilities of attaining a college education are limited that the field of, say, technology includes a long list of occupations other than engineering in which a college degree is not a prerequisite for admission. Clients and students sometimes reveal confusion and indecision in vocational planning because they have an interest in an area but lack knowledge of what is available in that area at the level that seems accessible to them. As mentioned earlier, the horizontal axis produces a circle and the vertical axis provides depth so one might view Roe's structure as a cylinder. Roe and Klos (1972) suggest that a shape nearer reality might be an inverse cone.

The two-dimensional approach to occupations emphasizes consideration of both similarities and differences between occupations. It also focuses attention on different factors or traits that relate directly to vocational choice. The system is useful in the classroom, where the teacher may wish to develop a general concept of the world of work. It is equally useful in the counseling room, where the client may be seeking help in matching abilities, interests, and ambitions with the realities of the occupational world.

Studies by Meir (1970, 1978) attempted to determine the extent to which Roe's Primary Focus of Activity classification could be confirmed statistically. Meir discovered that he could identify a graded order of levels in the fields of Service, Business, Organization, Technology, Outdoor, Science, General Culture, and Arts and Entertainment. His investigation produced two structures, one of which included Service, Organization, Business, Technology, and Outdoor. The second structure included Business, Service, General Culture, and Science. Three replications produced the same results. One must conclude that, in general, Roe's two-dimensional system may have considerable validity as an overall representation of the world of work, both horizontally by area and vertically by level. Further, as one might logically suppose, some of the areas and levels can be more clearly circumscribed than others.

The *World of Work Map for Job Families* (Hanson, 1974) is another example of a two-dimensional plan that facilitates understanding the relationships between occupations. This proposal has developed from the research conducted by the American College Testing Program, which indicated that there are two fairly independent sets of dimensions involved in most work activities. These bipolar dimensions include a data/ideas continuum and a people/things continuum. By using one of these sets for a horizontal axis and the other for a vertical axis, it is possible to visualize a map on which each occupational group can be plotted according to the coordinates obtained from the two bipolar continua. Thus occupations requiring considerable involvement with people and with data would be plotted in a quadrant opposite that representing occupations involving major contact with things and ideas; similarly, occupations involving great use of data and only moderate contact with people or things would lie opposite occupations with emphasis on ideas and only moderate contact with people or things. As the research has progressed, the map has been divided into 13 regions. Twelve of these represent 30-degree sectors of the circle; the thirteenth region is a centralized area reflecting no major relationship to any of the four extremes. The regions on the map can then be related to various job clusters and job families.

Figure 6.4 presents the *World of Work Map for Job Families.* Although specific points are plotted to represent the various job families, it should be obvious that each cluster really occupies an area, not a specific point. Thus many job families actually may overlap into an adjacent region. The plotted point must be viewed as representing a general area.

THREE-DIMENSIONAL CLASSIFICATION

The previous section demonstrated how one can classify occupations according to two criteria simultaneously. The discussion of Roe's system suggested that if we view her primary focus as a circle rather than a continuum, we have a three-dimensional cylinder or inverse cone. In this section we examine two systems that are three-dimensional.

The Cubistic classification system, proposed by D'Costa and Winefordner (1969), is an example of direct application of *DOT* concepts. This plan develops a three-dimensional approach to the Worker Functions Arrangement of the *DOT.* Proceeding from the idea that each job can be described in terms of its relationship to data-people-things, this notion considers the world of work as a cube, with each of the three aspects constituting one dimension of the cube.

If we group the seven to nine levels of involvement for the data-people-things relationships into three broader classes of high, average, or low, it becomes easier to visualize. Figure 6.5 shows this reclassification. Thus the original cube can be subdivided each direction into a 3 x 3 x 3 matrix of 27 cells. Each cell can be thought to represent those occupations involving the corresponding attributes of the data-people-things relationships. Viewing the total cube head on, the front left lower cell is designated 000 and represents those occupations with low relationship to all three factors. Similarly, the rear right upper cell is labeled 222 and would involve occupations that require the highest levels of involvement in all three areas.

Figure 6.6 illustrates the composition of the cube and the interrelationship of the cells as proposed by D'Costa and Winefordner (1969). Each *DOT* Worker Function Arrangement code can be transposed into the appropriate cell label representing that degree of involvement with data, people, and things, respectively. For example, the worker function code of .137 encompassing a coordinating (data)—supervising (people)—handling (things) level of involvement reflects a high-average-low level, represented by a code of 210 and the rear middle lower cell. All occupations involving this worker trait arrangement occupy this particular cell. Again, one might expect many dif-

FIGURE 6.4 *World-of-Work Map (2nd Edition)*

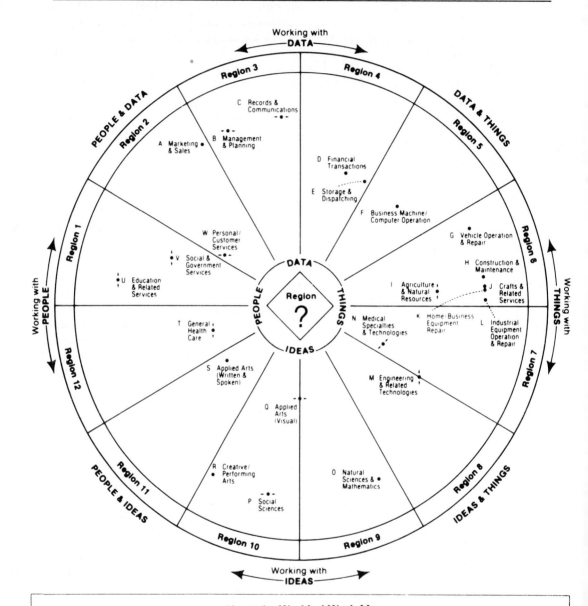

About the World-of-Work Map

The location of a Job Family on the map shows how much it involves working with DATA, IDEAS, PEOPLE, and THINGS. Arrows by a Job Family show that work tasks often heavily involve both PEOPLE and THINGS (◄►) or DATA and IDEAS (↕). Although each Job Family is shown as a single point, the jobs in a family vary in their locations. Most jobs, however, are located near the point shown for the Job Family.

FIGURE 6.5 *Division of Worker Function Codes into High, Average, and Low Groups as Used in the* Ohio Vocational Interest Survey II

Level of Involvement	OVIS II Code	DOT Data Functions	DOT People Functions	DOT Things Functions
High	H	0 Synthesizing 1 Coordinating 2 Analyzing	0 Mentoring 1 Negotiating 2 Instructing	0 Setting-Up 1 Precision Working

Average	A	3 Compiling
		4 Computing
			3 Supervising
			4 Directing
			5 Persuading
				2 Operating-
				  Controlling
				3 Driving-
				  Operating
				4 Manipulating

Low	L	5 Copying
		6 Comparing
			6 Speaking-
			  Signaling
			7 Serving
			8 Taking
			  Instructions-
			  Helping
				5 Tending
				6 Feeding-
				  Offbearing
				7 Handling

Source: From the manual for the Ohio Vocational Interest Survey: 2nd edition. Copyright © 1981 by The Psychological Corporation. Reproduced by permission. All rights reserved.

ferent types of activities to exist within this cell, but all occupations placed there would have the same high data, average people, low things relationship.

The Cubistic system is used by the Ohio Vocational Interest Survey, as illustrated in Figure 6.5. When the test was revised and OVIS II was published in 1983, the same basic system was used; but the 2-1-0 numbering system to represent high-average-low was replaced by the letters H-A-L, as seen in Figure 6.5, column 2. The 23 occupational clusters included in OVIS II and their Cubistic classification are listed in Figure 6.7 to illustrate how occupational groups can be assigned to segments of the cube and also to demonstrate that occupational groups involving quite different interests and skills can occupy the same segment. This is logical when one keeps in mind that worker function levels are concerned with degree of complexity of the relationship to d-p-t, not with type of involvement

Super (1957) proposes a system using a field and level approach for two dimensions that is quite similar to Roe's primary focus and level. In fact, both systems use an eight- by six-cell format. To these two dimensions, Super adds a third, "ENTERPRISE," which corresponds rather closely to the categories used in the *Standard Industrial Classification*. The major advantage of the third dimension is that it illustrates that many jobs occur in several different work settings or industries—in fact, that many industries are large and varied enough to include great numbers of different occupations. This concept is often helpful in both counseling room and classroom to demonstrate the very broad relationship between work and setting, or job and industry.

FIGURE 6.6   *Data-People-Things Dimensions of the World at Work*

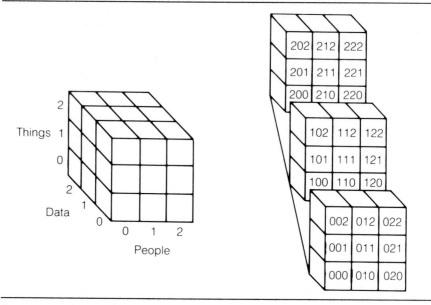

Source: A. G. D'Costa, *The Development of a Vocational Interest Survey Using the Data-People-Things Model of Work.* Paper presented to APGA Convention, Las Vegas, Nevada, 1969. Reprinted with permission.

SUMMARY

In this chapter we have considered several additional classification systems, all of them widely used. None is ideal for every situation, and all have advantages as well as disadvantages. They are important to counselors and teachers, as well as their clients and students, because classification systems provide a frame of reference that is helpful in understanding occupations and how they relate to one another.

REFERENCES

D'Costa, A. G., & Winefordner, D. W. (1969). A cubistic model of vocational interests. *Vocational Guidance Quarterly, 17,* 242–249.

Hanson, G. (1974). *ACT research report 67: Assessing the career interests of college youth: Summary of research and applications.* Iowa City, IA: American College Testing Program.

Meier, E. I. (1970). Empirical test of Roe's structure of occupations and an alternative structure. *Journal of Counseling Psychology, 17,* 41–48.

Meier, E. I. (1978). A test of the independence of fields and levels in Roe's occupational classification. *Vocational Guidance Quarterly, 27,* 124–128.

FIGURE 6.7 *OVIS II Occupational Clusters Showing Cubistic Classification*

1. **Manual Work** (L-L-L)—Using hands and hand tools to do physically active and routine work.
2. **Basic Services** (L-L-L)—Protecting or caring for people or animals.
3. **Machine Operation** (L-L-A)—Driving vehicles, operating heavy equipment, and using machines to make products.
4. **Quality Control** (A-L-L)—Checking the quality of products, materials, and services.
5. **Clerical** (A-L-L)—Typing, filing, recording, key punching, scheduling, and doing other detailed work.
6. **Health Services** (A-L-L)—Providing nursing and related health services to the ill, injured, or handicapped.
7. **Crafts and Precise Operations** (A-L-H)—Doing highly skilled hand and machine work.
8. **Skilled Personal Services** (A-L-H)—Sewing, tailoring, cooking, and cutting and styling hair.
9. **Sports and Recreation** (A-L-L)—Competing and officiating in professional sports and helping to entertain people in their leisure time.
10. **Customer Services** (A-A-L)—Selling products and services, making reservations, and giving information.
11. **Regulations Enforcement** (H-L-L)—Enforcing laws and regulations to protect health, safety, and property.
12. **Communications** (H-L-L)—Writing, editing, reporting, conducting research, and organizing and retrieving information.
13. **Numerical** (H-L-L)—Using mathematics in accounting, banking, data processing, and research.
14. **Visual Arts** (H-L-H)—Creating art through painting, drawing, photography, and other forms.
15. **Agriculture and Life Sciences** (H-L-H)—Conducting research and applying knowledge of the life sciences to raising crops and training animals.
16. **Engineering and Physical Sciences** (H-L-H)—Conducting research and applying knowledge of the physical sciences to construction and manufacturing.
17. **Music** (H-A-L)—Singing, playing an instrument, composing, arranging, teaching, and directing musical groups.
18. **Performing Arts** (H-A-L)—Entertaining an audience through dancing, acting, or announcing, and teaching and directing these activities.
19. **Marketing** (H-A-L)—Advertising, demonstrating, and buying and selling complex products and services.
20. **Legal Services** (H-H-L)—Applying knowledge of the law to preparing contracts and settling disputes.
21. **Management** (H-H-L)—Directing, planning, and managing the major activities of private and government organizations.
22. **Education and Social Work** (H-H-L)—Teaching, counseling, and providing other social services.
23. **Medical Services** (H-H-L)—Preventing or diagnosing and treating diseases and injuries of people and animals.

Source: Winefordner, D. W. (1983). *Manual for Interpreting Ohio Vocational Interest Survey,* 2nd Edition. New York: Harcourt Brace Jovanovich, Inc. (p. 3). From the manual for the Ohio Vocational Interest Survey: 2nd edition. Copyright © 1981 by The Psychological Corporation. Reproduced by permission. All rights reserved.

National Occupational Information Coordinating Committee. (1982) *Vocational preparation and occupations: Vol. 1. Educational and occupational code crosswalk* (3rd ed.). Washington, DC: NOICC.

Roe A. (1956). *The psychology of occupations.* New York: Wiley.

Roe, A. (1984). Personality development and career choice. In D. Brown, L. Brooks, & Associates (Eds.), *Career choice and development.* San Francisco: Jossey-Bass.

Roe, A., & Klos, D. (1972). Classification of occupations. In J. M. Whiteley & A. Resnikoff (Eds.), *Perspectives on vocational development.* Washington, DC: American Personnel and Guidance Association.

Super, D. E. (1957). *The psychology of careers.* New York: Harper & Brothers.

U.S. Department of Commerce, Office of Federal Statistical Policy and Standards. (1980). *Standard occupational classification manual.* Washington, DC: U.S. Government Printing Office.

U.S. Executive Office of the President, Office of Management and Budget. (1987). *Standard industrial classification manual.* Washington, DC: U.S. Government Printing Office.

Winefordner, D. W. (1983). *Manual for interpreting Ohio Vocational Interest Survey* (2nd ed.). New York: Harcourt Brace Jovanovich.

__7__

Finding and Organizing Career Information

Career information, as defined in Chapter 1, includes educational, occupational, and psychosocial information related to work. Simply put, occupational information consists of facts about jobs. It helps individuals gain insight and understanding about the world of work, whether used in industry, government, or education. The major focus of this chapter is on materials that can be used in the counseling office and the classroom to create awareness, encourage exploration, facilitate decision making, enhance preparation, and increase employability.

Occupational information frequently has focused on what the worker does and related matters; less often has it included psychological or sociological information. Even in this apparently factual approach, one must be constantly wary of misinformation, distortion, inaccuracy, and obsolescence. It is essential that those who use educational and occupational materials keep in mind the dynamic, constantly changing nature of the world of work.

Further, one must recognize the variation that can occur within a single occupation as it is encountered in numerous situations across a country as vast as the United States. What is most frequently presented as nationally representative is the mean or median of the range of these variations—the picture most typical of the total range. Despite these limitations, career information is so important to the career development process that special effort must be made to assure accuracy, currency, and usability.

BASIC SOURCES OF OCCUPATIONAL INFORMATION

There are only two basic or primary sources of information about the worker and what he does: the worker and the worker's employer. In some occupa-

159

tional fields, a third primary source might be added—the governmental agency involved in licensing or certifying workers or in controlling worker activity in some other way.

The U.S. Employment Service defines *job analysis* as the activity involved in determining what the worker does in relation to data, people, and things; the methodologies and techniques employed; the materials, products, subject matter, and services involved; the machines, tools, equipment, and work aids used; and the traits required of the worker for satisfactory performance.

From this definition one can deduce that job analysis is a process of observing jobs being performed and reporting pertinent facts. It was developed primarily for industrial purposes beyond our immediate concern. From an industrial viewpoint, however, job analysis is important because it provides knowledge about the requirements for the job, thus helping determine the qualifications workers need. It also is used in industry as a means of seeing the worker in relation to a specific task performed to determine the best way to perform the task or job. In other words, industrial use of job analysis aims at improving the technical proficiency of workers and perfecting techniques for hiring workers. Job analysis is important to counselors, however, as the only accurate source of knowledge about the nature and demands of a job and the qualifications a worker needs to perform that task.

At present, five categories of information are included in a complete analysis of a job. These categories are listed in *Job Analysis for Human Resources Management* (U.S. Department of Labor, 1974) as follows:

1. Worker functions
2. Work fields
3. Machines, tools, equipment, and work aids
4. Materials, products, subject matter, and services
5. Worker traits

Although our major concern with job analysis is based on providing accurate information, it is easy to see many related applications of the procedure. These would include (1) providing a base for training programs for potential workers, (2) restructuring jobs to provide both opportunities for entry-level workers and more challenging activities for higher level workers, and (3) developing career ladders that permit promotion of workers to more advanced levels.

Job analysis, as described here, is obviously intended to answer questions about a specific job. Sometimes, however, one is less interested in acquiring information about a particular job than in developing a general picture of the total work situation in a community or other geographic area. In this case, the questions are more likely to be related to what jobs exist and where they are.

At least part of this information can be acquired from the latest decennial census, if those data can still be considered current. Such a source can probably be used safely in most communities during about the first third of each decade, and then with diminishing confidence in each succeeding year.

Most state employment security agencies routinely collect data for established regions within the state, known as Standard Metropolitan Statistical Areas (SMSAs), on a rotating 3-year cycle. Although possibly not as comprehensive as the information in the decennial census, at least two thirds of the time the information will be more current than census data.

A third source of occupational information has more direct relevance to curriculum evaluation and revision but nevertheless provides data that have great value within a specific school. This source is the follow-up survey of previous students. Properly executed, such a study permits a school to reach some decisions regarding the effectiveness of its program in assisting its students to meet the problems they encounter after leaving school. Information obtained about career experiences should be pertinent for those students about to complete their schooling. To be completely realistic, the study should include dropouts as well as those who have completed the program. Because of possible biases that can result from incomplete returns, every effort should be made to secure as near total returns as possible.

Congress established the National Occupational Information Coordinating Committee (NOICC) in 1976. Nine federal agencies now cooperate in its operation. The purposes of the agency are to improve coordination, cooperation, and communication in the development of occupational information systems at the national and local levels; to standardize definitions, estimating procedures, and occupational classifications that meet common informational needs among various training programs; to assist state-level committees; to improve liaison between developers and users of occupational information; and to give special attention to young people's needs for labor market information. These goals, in simplest terms, are aimed at reducing overlap and preventing gaps in the development of occupational information and improving the quality and availability of materials.

The NOICC has played an important role in the development of career information delivery systems (CIDS) in the various states to meet the needs of clients and students in local settings. The NOICC has also produced the *Occupational Information System Handbook* (1981), which identifies available sources of educational and occupational data and describes methods for aggregating and analyzing information about supply and demand. The NOICC has also funded and sponsored many workshops for career counselors in all settings designed to improve career decision making by clients; the workshops have emphasized obtaining, understanding, and using labor market information with clients. Although the NOICC is primarily a coordinating and enabling agency, its activities and products are extremely important to all counselors who work with clients facing career problems.

The NOICC has also sponsored the publication of materials useful to career counselors. An example of this effort is *Using Labor Market Information in Career Exploration and Decision Making: A Resource Guide*. This volume, published in 1986, contains nearly 300 pages of helpful materials; a second edition was released in 1991.

The legislation that established the national committee also provided for a similar organization at the state and territory level, usually referred to as the State Occupational Information Coordinating Committee (SOICC). The state-level cooperative arrangement and its purposes are generally similar to the national level. Because there is considerable variation in the available funding and identified needs, there is diversity in services delivered. Activities generally have included determining the type of occupational information needed by user groups; identifying the kinds of information already available from state sources and preparing a catalog of existing materials and resources; and, in many states, developing or improving a statewide career information delivery system.

There are several reasons for career counselors knowing the SOICC staff and services in their state. Their assigned role is to assist in finding the kinds of information clients need. They are in a position to draw on the resources of the agencies that produce most of the information prepared at the state level and are knowledgeable about what already exists or how nonexistent data can be acquired. In most states, they are the major force involved in the development of effective delivery systems. Many SOICCs are already involved in providing workshops and training programs intended to familiarize counselors with available materials.

In most states, the SOICC office is located in the state capital. It can be found easily by consulting a state government directory (see the Appendix). Often the nearby State Employment Security Agency office may be the easiest source for information. Several publications—for example, the *Occupational Outlook Handbook*—list the address and telephone number for each SOICC office.

TYPES OF CAREER INFORMATION

Kunze (1967) describes a "spectrum of occupational information data" originally developed by Thompson and proposed in an unpublished report. This spectrum provides a useful system for viewing the varied kinds of occupational information. If one considers these points on Thompson's spectrum from a client's perspective, one might label them as different types, whereas the counselor's view might label them as different delivery systems. In either case, they are ways for an individual to acquire understanding about occupations.

Thompson's spectrum includes the following:

1. Publications (books, monographs, etc.)
2. Audiovisual (AV) aids (films, tapes, slides, etc.)
3. Programmed instructional materials (books, workbooks, etc.)
4. Computer-based systems (storage and retrieval mechanized systems)
5. Interviews with experts (direct questioning of occupational representatives)

6. Simulated situations (career games, role playing, etc.)
7. Synthetically created work environments (artificial reproduction of work settings)
8. Direct observation (visits to work sites)
9. Directed exploratory experiences (work samples, evaluation tasks, etc.)
10. On-the-job (O-T-J) tryout (casual work or work-study programs).

One can group items in this spectrum either according to the degree of contact or activity with work materials or according to the site where the contact is most likely to occur. These divisions then appear as follows:

Degree of Involvement	Item	Site of Contact
Passive	1. Printed matter 2. AV material 3. Programmed material	Career resource center
Interactive	4. Computer-based systems 5. Interviews 6. Simulation 7. Synthetic work	Other sites
Direct contact	8. Direct observation 9. Exporatory experience 10. O-T-J tryout	Work site

In the following sections of this chapter, we consider each of these media types except for computer-based systems. Because computerized systems have expanded so rapidly in the past decade, we devote the next chapter to that topic. In the final sections of this chapter, we discuss organizing and managing the career resource center.

Print Material: Occupational

The structure that probably is most useful for classifying the materials we are concerned with here is one proposed by the National Vocational Guidance Association (NVGA) Career Information Review Service Committee and used in materials prepared by that group, such as the *NVGA Bibliography of Current Career Literature* (NVGA, 1978). The NVGA is now called the National Career Development Association (NCDA). The terms and definitions listed next are from that source. The groupings and headings are added to help the reader grasp the general purpose of the various items. The 12 types proposed by the NVGA and recombined into four groups are as follows:

Recreational Reading

1. Career fiction: An account, portrayed through the experiences of one or more fictional characters, of any occupation which may encompass duties,

qualifications, preparations, conditions and nature of work and advancement.

2. Biography: An account of the life of a successful person in a given field of endeavor, portraying the problems faced in preparing for and advancing his or her career.

Occupational Information

3. Single-job information: Information pertaining to a single job, such as accountant. The length does not matter because the reader can see the length in terms of pages and prices.

4. Jobs in specific businesses or industries: A group of jobs in one business or industry, such as "Careers in the Plastics Industry."

5. Job-family information: Information pertaining to a related group of jobs, such as "Careers in the Medical Field."

Special-Purpose Materials

6. Recruitment literature: Descriptive promotional information pointed at recruiting young men and women into an occupation or career field. Brief coverage of facts.

7. Orientation—the world of work: Information designed to help the reader make occupational choices and enter the world of work. Includes such information as relating one's interest, aptitudes, and abilities to occupations; sources of information regarding occupational opportunities, requirements, and trends; conditions of work; techniques for investigating occupations; information about courses and schools of training; and preparation for job interviews.

8. Special groups: Information indicating the relationship of certain groups to the occupational world—for example, women, handicapped people, the educationally disadvantaged.

Reference Materials

9. Bibliography: A printed listing of materials concerned with career information.

10. Directory: An alphabetic or classified list of institutions, public or private, offering educational and/or training programs.

11. Financial assistance: Information concerning the provision of financial support; may be at any educational level.

12. Other: Includes specialized occupational studies, general occupational reviews, and technical reports or portions thereof if applicable; charts, posters, and other miscellaneous occupational information. Information presented by types other than those listed here should be accounted for here; being certain to specify kind and scope of publication. (pp. 3–4)

An annual issue of *Career Development Quarterly* includes a section prepared by the NCDA Career Information Review Service Committee entitled "Current Career Literature." This section provides basic information about recent relevant publications that have been reviewed by committee members and rated according to degree of adherence with NCDA guidelines. Materials listed in this section are classified according to the following types:

  I. Vocational
    A. Occupations
    B. Trends and outlook
    C. Job training
    D. Employment opportunities
 II. Educational
    A. Status and trends
    B. Schools, colleges
    C. Scholarships, fellowships, grants, and loans
III. Personal
    A. Planning (resume, job search, etc.)
    B. Adjustment

A review of items listed shows that the vast majority of items are categorized as IA (I. Vocational—A. Occupations) but with occasional items from other groups. Thus most of the materials would be assigned to the occupational information section of the earlier listing.

A review of the types of occupational materials defined here reveals that some may be as brief as a single page, others as long as an entire book. Since each client or student has unique needs, the counselor and teacher will obviously require knowledge of a wide range of materials for many occupational fields. The student who is just beginning to explore the world of work is more likely to need access to a wide array of short descriptive statements such as those found in a brief or abstract. On the other hand, the client who is moving toward an appropriate choice may be anxious to read a lengthy description, such as a monograph, to answer specific questions about the occupation.

The study by Chapman and Katz (1981) found that bound reference publications are used more frequently by students in all kinds of schools than any other type of career resource. The most used publications are the *Occupational Outlook Handbook*; the *Dictionary of Occupational Titles*; and occupational briefs (four-to-six-page descriptions of occupations, usually available from commercial publishers). In 1980, rural and small schools were more limited in variety of resources than larger and urban schools.

Occupational information is acquired and developed by means of one of the previously described methods. It is processed and published by numerous agencies and companies—so many, in fact, that some categorization of such sources is essential in order to use them most effectively. This book does not attempt to provide an exhaustive list of either occupational materials or their sources. Major groupings of these sources include those discussed next.

Government Agencies
Many federal agencies publish materials relating directly to occupations. Free publications can be obtained directly from the agency that produces

them. Most materials are sold and can be obtained either from the agency itself or from the Superintendent of Documents, U.S. Government Printing Office. The latter source is usually the better one.

Since the output of the U.S. Government Printing Office is so extensive, it is difficult to keep abreast of new items that might have value for the counselor or teacher. A catalog, published monthly, lists all materials issued during the previous month. The only way to be certain of identifying each government publication that is pertinent to the field is to check each issue of the catalog carefully, an arduous and time-consuming task. Most counselors find it more convenient to be placed on the mailing list of agencies that produce the major portion of occupational materials, or to obtain regularly the price lists of materials (available from either the agency or the Superintendent of Documents) published by those agencies. These lists, though not as comprehensive, will help the counselor keep abreast of most of the materials issued by government agencies. To provide some picture of the scope of pertinent government agencies, three of those that publish more extensively are listed here, with a brief statement of the kinds of materials available from each.

Department of Commerce. Many publications are available related to various aspects of business—both "business" in a broad sense and "business and commerce" in a narrow usage. Important materials for the counselor include the following:

1. *U.S. Industrial Outlook:* Published annually, this provides a survey of U.S. business, showing current developments in each industry as well as long-range forecasts.
2. *County Business Patterns:* Also published annually, this survey shows first-quarter employment and payroll data by industry in each county, SMSA, and state.
3. *Standard Occupational Classification Manual:* This classification system was discussed in Chapter 6.

Department of Defense. Each of the armed services publishes handbooks and brochures describing career opportunities within that specific branch of service. Intended primarily for recruiting purposes, each book provides an indication of the relationship of each military specialty to civilian work.

The *Military Career Guide* (U.S. Department of Defense) is an example of armed services publications. This book covers 134 clusters of enlisted occupations for the five military services using the Standard Occupational Classification discussed in Chapter 6. Information provided includes typical work tasks, work environment, physical demands, training provided, helpful attributes, and special qualifications. Indexes included permit use of DOT numbers, DOT alphabetical listing, and information provided by the Armed Services Vocational Aptitude Battery (ASVAB).

The *Military Occupational and Training Data* (U.S. Department of Defense) publications are revised annually and provide comprehensive information on military occupations, both officer and enlisted. Information included parallels that described for the *Military Career Guide.*

Department of Labor. Many sections of this large department publish materials crucial for counselors and teachers. The publication list would be a useful one to have available. Sample publications from this department include the following:

1. *DOT/GOE/OOH/OOQ/Selected Characteristics:* All these have been discussed in earlier chapters.
2. *Occupational Projections and Training Data:* Published annually, this volume provides information on employment prospects and related needed training. It includes a comprehensive supply-demand analysis for college graduates as well as other training programs.
3. *BLS Wage Surveys:* Published annually, these booklets supply data for occupations in 76 categories based on wage and salary information for workers in most industrial classifications, excluding public service and the relatively small areas of agriculture, mining, and construction.

Many other federal departments and agencies publish materials that are useful in career development activities. Many items relate directly to the purpose of the agency. Obviously, the Department of the Interior provides information about jobs in national parks, and the Office of Personnel Management provides information about career jobs in federal government. State government agencies also publish materials that are directly relevant for counselors and teachers.

Commercial Publishers

Many commercial printing companies produce materials directly related to career development. Some concentrate their efforts on instructional materials, assessment instruments, counseling aids, and materials for special populations. The available materials range from occupational briefs of four to six pages to book-length items including fiction and biography. Several publishers have organized programs for varying age groups and grade levels as well as materials for individual counseling. The media specialist in the local school media center or public library is knowledgeable about the resources that identify these publishers and their materials.

Professional and Industrial Organizations

A variety of occupational materials is available from professional organizations and societies active in career fields. Some of these groups have prepared and published excellent monographs and other materials of real help to the counselor or teacher. The Department of Commerce has published a *Directory of National Associations of Businessmen,* which provides a list of most of the groups that can be classified under this heading. The Department of Labor publishes a similar directory of labor unions. Since the materials published by these groups may be designed to serve the special interests of the sponsoring group, the counselor should evaluate the materials carefully before using them.

Private Companies

A number of private companies in a variety of industries, such as retail merchandising, banking, steel production, and chemical production, publish occupational materials. Ordinarily, this is done by large nationwide corporations whose basic purpose is to use the materials in recruiting potential career workers; thus the publications tend to emphasize the benefits that accrue to the worker. On the other hand, the materials often include copious illustrations and information that make them very useful. The items available from these sources also vary widely, from brief pamphlets to substantial hardback books.

Educational Institutions

Many universities and other educational institutions have prepared materials that describe opportunities in career fields for which the specific school provides preparation. Some of these are brief, four-page abstracts; others are collections of such briefs; and a few are extensive publications covering several fields in depth.

Trade and technical schools often prepare descriptions of the fields for which they offer training; the materials tend to focus specifically on the area within which the school places most of its graduates. A few degree-granting schools prepare lists of occupations in which their graduates are employed.

Periodicals

One often encounters articles in popular national magazines that are pertinent to the field of career information. Many of these articles have been prepared as human interest or feature stories, but they may be highly useful in helping a student understand an occupational field.

Several professional journals regularly read by counselors include career information of value to counselors. Some of the journals primarily report research studies; some focus more on practical, how-to-do-it field reports; and some are factual, statistical reporting publications. Titles that the counselor should review include *American Vocational Journal, Career Development Quarterly, Journal of College Placement, Journal of Counseling and Development, Journal of Counseling Psychology, Journal of Employment Counseling, Journal of Vocational Behavior, Monthly Labor Review, Occupational Outlook Quarterly,* and *Work and Occupations.*

Indexes

As one surveys the wide range of sources from which career information emanates, one is led to conclude that it is difficult to keep abreast of current publications—and so it is. Effective proctoring of the various sources requires close attention to a number of publications designed to notify interested individuals that new materials are available. The listing of recently released materials in *Career Development Quarterly* is one such source.

Indexes published by commercial publishers, public service agencies, and professional organizations are another source. These indexes usually are printed at regular intervals and include lists of articles, pamphlets, or other material related to the field. Many counselors find this type of service especially helpful in locating materials from sources outside the channels they check routinely. The following are examples of indexes:

1. *Career Index.* Published by Chronicle Guidance Publications, Moravia, NY 13118. An annual listing of occupational and educational materials from many organizations.
2. *Educators Guide to Free Teaching Aids.* M. H. Saterstrom, editor. Published by Educators Progress Service, Inc., Randolph, WI 53956. An annual listing of free materials, including audiovisual materials as well as printed matter.
3. *Counselor's Information Service.* Published by B'nai B'rith Career and Counseling Services, Washington, DC 20036. Published four times yearly in newsletter form, this bibliography of current materials also identifies items useful with special populations—adults, aging, and people with disabilities.

Cumulative indexes have certain inherent advantages, particularly in terms of comprehensiveness. On the other hand, publication lag causes some datedness to develop before the item is even ordered. This lag time becomes even more serious when the publication cycle of the index exceeds a year.

Print Material: Educational

One might reasonably expect that occupational information would include explanations of the kinds of education or training needed to qualify for that work. This is often true, but there are at least two reasons for considering information about education and training opportunities separately. First, most occupational materials that include discussions of kinds of preparation needed for entrance and advancement do not identify specific schools or organizations where that preparation is available. Second, a large portion of high school graduates select a school for postsecondary education without first deciding what occupation they are preparing to enter. We consider sources of information for three types of postsecondary preparation: 2- and 4-year colleges and universities, technical and trade schools, and apprenticeship programs.

Colleges and Universities

Obviously, the most precise and up-to-date information about a specific school can be obtained from the institution itself. Colleges and universities, because of changes in enrollments, rapid advances in science and other fields of learning, fluctuating financial resources, and other factors, are in a state of constant change. Consequently, every other source of information must be considered as possibly obsolete because of modifications that might have occurred since the data were obtained. The schools are too numerous and the time required to obtain specific answers too long to consider individual contact with all higher educational institutions. Only when a prospective student has developed a tentative list of schools is such contact appropriate.

Careful reading and study of the catalog and other institutional publications is similarly impossible. However, one should recognize that, next to direct contact with the school itself, the catalog and other publications are probably the best sources of accurate information—barring changes that have occurred since publication. Further, even a carefully prepared catalog cannot answer many of the questions likely to occur to an investigating student.

Because of the scope of the problem, the prospective student and her parents, teachers, and counselor often must rely on secondary sources of information about schools, at least during the early phases of the screening process. This inevitably leads to one of the guides or directories that offer condensed descriptions of the schools. Because up-to-date information is crucial, the latest edition always should be used—with the caution that even this may be out of date for a specific item concerning a particular school.

The list of directories in Table 7.1 includes several of those widely used. They are grouped by publisher and therefore cover both 2- and 4-year institutions. The listing is roughly alphabetical.

Technical and Trade Schools

Obtaining accurate, usable information about a vocational school is often much more difficult than finding similar information about a degree-granting institution, for several reasons. Teachers and counselors, having been professionally prepared in colleges and universities, are more aware of the baccalaureate schools. Intercollegiate athletics and other activities publicize the colleges and universities locally, regionally, and nationally. Most of society's prestigious or high-status occupations require college educations and focus public attention on schools that provide such education. In addition, technical and trade schools usually offer shorter training programs in less conspicuous quarters, have often been in existence for shorter periods, and rarely attract public attention.

The need for current, reliable, and useful information about vocational schools is apparent, but such information is difficult to obtain. Publications similar to the catalog or bulletin of a college, university, or community college are unusual rather than customary for vocational schools. Information often is provided in the form of brochures, briefs, flyers, or other sketchy

TABLE 7.1 *Directories of Colleges and Universities*

Directory	Publisher
Accredited Institutions of Postsecondary Education	American Council on Education
	One Dupont Circle
American Universities and Colleges	Washington, DC 20036
Barron's Profiles of American Colleges	Barron's Educational Series
	250 Wireless Boulevard
	Hauppauge, NY 11788
The College Blue Book	Macmillan, Inc.
	866 3rd Avenue
	New York, NY 10022
The College Handbook	College Board Publications
College Cost Book	Box 886
College Guide for Parents	New York, NY 10101
Comparative Guide to American Colleges	HarperCollins Publishers
	10 East 53rd Street
	New York, NY 10022
Four-Year College Databook	Chronicle Guidance Publications
Two-Year College Databook	Aurora Street
Student Aid Annual	Moravia, NY 13118

statements. In vocational schools, new programs are established and old programs disappear more rapidly than in traditional 2-year and 4-year institutions; this affects routine publication of informational materials. Counselors who need current information about vocational schools may find it helpful to check with the state office of education about opportunities within their state. Additional sources of information include the American Vocational Association in Washington, DC, and the Center for Research in Vocational and Technical Education at Ohio State University, Columbus, Ohio.

The directories listed in Table 7.2 provide information about many trade and technical schools. Because of the great diversity among these schools, directories often are less comprehensive than those that deal with traditional degree-granting institutions.

Apprenticeships

Printed material about specific apprenticeship opportunities is almost non-existent. This is due partly to the nature of apprenticeship programs, in which national, state, and regional offices have mainly coordinating and liaison responsibilities and local offices have administrative and operating functions. Thus detailed information about actual training spaces and the process of filling those spaces usually must be obtained from a local office.

General information about apprenticeship programs can be obtained from the Bureau of Apprenticeships, U.S. Department of Labor, Washington, DC 20210. Information about local and regional offices also can be obtained

TABLE 7.2   *Directories of Trade and Technical Schools*

Directory	Publisher
American Trade Schools Directory	Croner Publications, Inc. 211-03 Jamaica Avenue Jamaica, NY 11428
Directory of the National Association of Trade and Technical Schools	Directory National Association of Trade and Technical Schools 2021 K Street, N.W. Washington, DC 20006
Directory of Post-secondary Schools with Occupational Programs, Public and Private	U.S. Government Printing Office Washington, DC 20402
Vocational School Manual	Chronicle Guidance Publications Aurora Street Moravia, NY 13118

there. If the state government offices include a Department of Labor, that office can provide statewide information. In larger communities, local telephone directories will list numbers for local union representatives who can provide information about local programs for that union.

Audiovisual and Programmed Material

Until recently, AV material referred almost exclusively to films and filmstrips. These materials have been supplemented, and in many cases replaced, by videotapes and audiotapes. In addition, closely related to this field is an array of materials often called mechanized or programmed materials that use microfilm or systems of cards, charts, and similar visual material.

Films, Filmstrips, and Videotapes. Whether one views a film or videotape, one will probably learn more about what a worker does and how it is done in a few minutes than could be acquired from a much longer period of reading.

Since films are costly to produce and many have a more limited usage than printed materials, renting these materials rather than purchasing them may be advisable. Most schools and related agencies regularly use such services through the facilities of city or state educational departments or the visual instruction center of nearby universities.

Audiovisual materials often serve as the core for the many multimedia approaches that are now available to schools and agencies. The well-established trend for school systems to employ media specialists reflects the phenomenal growth in this area. Responsible for an overwhelming array of materials and devices for effective use of the materials, these specialists can be of great help to the counselor in finding and using audiovisual materials as well as more traditional printed library resources.

Laramore (1971) describes a project in which counselors made audiotapes and slides of jobs for use with high school students in Maryland. Many school systems now own portable videotaping equipment that can be applied to the preparation of local career information. The local interest and local color that a homemade production can incorporate may compensate for the lack of professional quality. Johnson, Korn, and Dunn (1975) report a study in which they demonstrated that presentation of occupational information by use of a locally prepared slide-tape format was more effective than presenting the same information either orally or in a written format. Bradley and Thacker (1978) describe the development of slide and tape presentations intended primarily to prepare viewers for later plant visits. The Chapman and Katz (1981) study for the NOICC found that two thirds of the schools in the survey group had audiovisual equipment and that students used these materials about 25 percent of the time available for use. The survey confirms that school counselors and teachers using career development materials use printed matter and AV materials more frequently than they use other types of materials and resources.

Vocational Information for Education and Work (VIEW). The VIEW system was developed to serve high schools and junior colleges within the geographic and political unit of San Diego County. It was expected that the system would overcome weaknesses that had been encountered and reported by school counselors, such as (1) occupational information lacking in authenticity and realism, (2) lack of currency and local application of career material, and (3) difficulty in filing and retrieving data.

Two four-page occupational briefs were prepared for each occupation. The first brief was general and national in nature; the second emphasized local and regional information. Each four-page brief then was transferred to a standard microfilm aperture card into which was punched additional information about the occupation that could be used in sorting and listing according to individual characteristics or needs. As data become obsolete, a new brief is prepared, master microfilm cards are made, and copies are distributed to users to replace the out-of-date cards quickly and inexpensively. Use of the card by the client and the counselor requires either a microfilm reader-scanner or a microfilm reader-printer. The system provides for developing the basic information for relatively small geographic areas, such as states, regions, or metropolitan centers, and permits delivery of information that meets the needs and interests of the user group within that area.

Nearly three quarters of the states have used some form of the VIEW system. Typical of the more advanced applications is the system used in Pennsylvania, named Pennscript. In this project, the state has been divided into 18 areas for which localized labor market information is available. The 260 most common occupations requiring educational preparation, ranging from the eighth grade to beyond the master's degree, are included in the deck. A VIEW (or Pennscript) deck of 260 cards has been developed for each of the 18 labor market areas.

Effective application of a plan such as Pennscript requires commitment by the state educational agency or its designate to provide the services needed to operate such a plan. These include personnel to write the scripts and to prepare and distribute cards to cooperating agencies. Regular revision and updating must be maintained.

Worker Trait Keysort Deck

The Worker Trait Keysort Deck, developed under the direction of Winefordner at the Appalacia Educational Laboratory, is closely related to the *Guide for Occupational Exploration*. The deck uses the 12 interest areas and the 66 work groups of the *GOE;* the latter are called worker trait groups. Each worker trait group is represented by a card in the deck.

The system provides a method for identifying the relationship between certain factors and the occupations grouped in that worker trait group. These factors include the following:

> Work activities
> Work situations
> Worker functions
> Physical demands
> Working conditions
> Aptitudes
> General educational development
> Preparation and training

Each card in the Keysort Deck has numerical or letter codes for five of these factors (work activities, work situations, physical demands, general educational development, and preparation) printed at specific points near the four edges of the card. Each card includes a brief descriptive paragraph for that group (essentially comparable to the description of each four-digit group in the *GOE*). Between each numerical or letter code and the edge of the card is a hole that can be notched when that item relates to the worker trait group represented on the card.

A client can identify each worker trait group that is related to each identified factor by using a sorting needle. The deck is first aligned and then the needle is inserted in the hole representing the characteristic under consideration. Because those cards that relate to the characteristic have been notched, they will drop away, while those groups not related to the characteristic will be held on the needle. Succeeding sorts can be made with identified cards in the same way.

Occupational View-Deck

The *Occupational View-Deck,* marketed by Chronicle Guidance Publications, offers a similar approach to helping clients relate occupations to personal preferences, temperaments, and educational plans. The system consists of a master card with numbers representing about 700 occupations, plus 35 transparencies, one for each of the various characteristics, on which numbers representing occupations not involving that trait have been blocked out. Thus one sees the numbers for occupations that do relate to the specific item. Overlay transparencies can be used singly or in combinations representative of the user. A *Career Profile Guide* provides a brief description of the 700 occupations with *DOT*, *SOC*, and *GOE* codes included.

INTERVIEWS WITH EXPERTS

Every counselor or teacher has encountered problems of credibility when discussing career options outside the educational structure. Even the teacher with many years of significant involvement in a noneducational field is likely to meet the attitude, "How can you know about that job—you're a teacher!" Attempting to dispel that point of view may be futile. Fortunately, a solution is available that is advantageous to all concerned. The logical step is to enlist the assistance of someone with that aura of credibility—someone engaged in the field and thereby automatically regarded as an expert.

Interviews with experts are appropriate experiences in the career development process at all steps, from the awareness level onward. Obviously, they should be adjusted to the level of development of the individuals involved, and other steps should be taken to make the experience valuable. In the awareness and early exploratory phases of career development, such interviews can be used best with groups of students. The career day and career conference programs are examples of such activities commonly used in schools; we consider these shortly. As the person progresses toward a tentative decision, it would be useful to confer individually with such a resource person.

Career Day

On *career day* in most schools, groups of students are given an opportunity for direct contact with representatives of selected occupations in which they have indicated an interest.

The career day program is designed to provide the students with pertinent and accurate information about specific fields of work. If properly organized, it can help them broaden their understanding of fields in which they are interested. It also gives them contact with at least one individual in the occupation from whom they may be able to obtain further information if their interest continues and expands.

Once the date has been set, the next question concerns the best part of the day for the program. Whether morning or afternoon is chosen depends largely on the local situation, the normal school schedule, and which portion of the day best lends itself to the objectives of the program. An evening program should be considered if the school wishes to include parents in the activity. There are many obvious advantages to a schedule that permits the maximum number of parents to be included, and this is more likely to occur outside the usual workday. Including parents in the career day is based on our assumption that the development of sound career plans involves the adults in the youth's immediate environment—parents, teachers, and counselors.

Career day programs sometimes have been criticized because the occupations included have not been representative of student interest. One way to prevent this is to begin planning with a survey of the students who will be involved in the program. Students may be asked to list the occupations they would most like included in a career day program. Sometimes a checklist is used, on which the student indicates from three to five preferences. The list can be compiled from a survey of occupations entered by students from the school or from a listing of the occupations most prevalent in the geographic area. Space should be provided on any checklist to add occupations not listed.

It is rarely possible to include all occupations listed by students in a single school. A tally of the checklists, however, will indicate areas in which student interest is sufficient to plan for one or more groups. Frequently one can meet specialized interests by grouping on a broader base than student response. For example, if only a few indicate interest in carpentry, stonemasonry, and painting, these logically can be grouped as construction trades. When student interest is too small to include the requested occupations, the students making the requests should be helped individually to obtain the desired information in other ways.

Once student interests have been inventoried and tallied, the occupations to be included can be identified. Every effort should be made to cover the entire range of student interests. One occupational area—the professions, for example—should not dominate the program. Securing speakers for each area may be difficult and time-consuming. Members of the faculty may be able to suggest resources or speakers in some areas. Often local service clubs can suggest individuals who might discuss particular fields. Speakers for craft and manufacturing areas may be found by consulting local union representatives or employers.

Speakers should be sought who can present their occupations fairly to interested students. Years of experience in the field may not necessarily be a major concern, particularly of a field in which changes have occurred recently. Giving speakers appropriate materials well in advance can assist them in preparing for their participation. Pamphlets, booklets, pages from the *Occupational Outlook Handbook*, and similar materials may be useful in broadening the individual's perspective of her own field. Student groups—the advisory committee, perhaps—can prepare lists of questions that students are likely to ask in the actual program so speakers can anticipate some of the topics about which they might be questioned.

Since the program is basically a learning activity, students should be prepared properly for their part. If students are provided ample opportunity to read and study material about the occupations of interest before the career day program, they will be in a better position to ask appropriate questions and, thereby, make better use of the speakers' limited time. Groups of students can be encouraged to prepare questions in advance and to complete other preparatory steps that will increase the effectiveness of the program. Serious advance preparation also may help to alleviate the carnival air that sometimes surrounds career day programs.

Once students have indicated their interests on the inventory and the areas to be included in the program have been identified, it is possible to establish a schedule for each student and to see that groups where multiple sessions are needed can be balanced. Students should be informed in advance of their schedule for the day, and a duplicate copy of the schedule should be filed in case of forgetfulness. Rooms should be assigned with the sizes of the groups in mind.

Soon after the program has been held, it should be evaluated by all participants to determine whether such a program should be used in subsequent years and, if so, how it should be modified to improve its effectiveness. Ideally, evaluation should include reactions from students, faculty members, and occupational representatives. Most schools use a brief evaluation form for gathering reactions from students and speakers.

Follow-up is as crucial as preparation of students beforehand. Many opportunities for follow-up exist in every school situation; these should be identified and capitalized on. Several of the classes in which students are enrolled naturally lend themselves to further discussion of the topics in the program. Others, such as English classes, can be used for stimulating student thought and reaction through assigned papers, preparation of letters, role-playing interviews, and similar activities. Counselors should follow up with student interviews to help students obtain further information, discuss tentative career choices, arrange for visits to businesses, industries, or advanced schools; or schedule further activities that help develop career plans.

By bringing together representatives of various occupations for presentations within a prescribed time frame, career days efficiently serve an educational setting, in which one is likely to encounter enough individuals at the same developmental stage to justify using the procedure. It is equally appropriate at all educational levels. Isaacson and Hayes (1980) describe an application of career day to an elementary school in which presenters were asked to show student participants what they did at work rather than using more abstract verbal explanations. It is also used at the college level either in the format described here or with various adaptations. Self and Lopez (1982) describe a seminar for college women in which presenters were women employed in nontraditional occupations. Because the seminar program scheduled one speaker each week, the format approximated the career conference, a plan that we consider next. Pate, Tullock, and Dassance (1981) describe an event that combines a career day with a postsecondary education day organized by a professional group for clientele drawn from several schools and the community at large.

Career Conference

Some schools have used the career conference instead of scheduling a special career day. Arranging a special day obviously interrupts normal school activity and sometimes carries with it a holiday atmosphere that can interfere with its basic purpose. In some schools the career day is advantageous because it briefly concentrates the attention of the entire school, and sometimes even the community, on the school's commitment to career planning.

If a school prefers not to interrupt its schedule, a series of career conferences can be arranged within the framework of the regular school calendar. Basically, the career conference is a segment of the career day program in which an occupational representative is brought together with a group of interested students to discuss a specific field. Often a series of these, extending over a considerable period of time, can be strung together to provide the same coverage as the career day program.

Organizing and developing a series of career conferences involves the same steps as those described for the career day program. The major difference between the two activities is simply that the career day puts the whole program into a single day or portion of a day, whereas the career conferences may number one or two per day over a period of a month or more, depending on the number of occupations to be included.

The flexibility provided in a series of career conferences has certain definite advantages (Hoppock, 1970; Plotsky & Goad, 1974). Individual student scheduling is likely to be easy since students can be scheduled for the number of conferences in which they indicate an interest. Under the career day plan it is difficult to avoid the regimentation of scheduling all students for the number of sessions included in the program. Some students may be seriously interested in exploring only one or two areas, whereas others may wish to participate in five or six conferences. The students included in career conferences are more likely to be truly interested in the area being discussed, with the increased possibility that the session will be more profitable for them. The flexible schedule also may make it easier to obtain occupational representatives who can do the best job of presenting information about their fields.

Warrington and Method–Walker (1981) describe an adaptation of the career conference in which they used the campus radio station to broadcast a weekly interview with a guest resource person representing an occupational area affiliated with various collegial units within the university.

Follow-up and evaluation of the career conference are just as important as for the career day program. Usually the same techniques can be used.

Heppner (1981) describes the application of a program by a university counseling center where the job holders to be interviewed are university alumni volunteers. The program provides levels of intensity of contact, including taped interviews with the job holder, telephone contact with the job holder to acquire information, face-to-face interviews, and an externship extending from a half day to 3 days in length. The latter opportunity exceeds the usual range of interviews with experts, and we consider this type of contact later when we discuss shadowing. This type of career information is also usable in nonschool settings on a group or individual basis.

Post–High School Education Programs

Many high schools have organized programs or special days labeled "College Day" or some similar title. These programs resemble the career day, except that speakers are drawn from educational institutions. Historically, these programs have developed because school and college officials recognize that high school students need an opportunity to discuss post–high school educational plans with representatives of institutions in which they might be interested. Numerous high schools set aside a special day or time when the representatives of the various schools are invited to meet with interested students.

As the name implies, many schools invite only college representatives to participate in their college day programs. Since every school has students whose future plans do not include college, only a portion of the student group is served by such a program. It seems wise, with increased emphasis on post–high school education of many types, to rename the day with a broader term that will permit inclusion of representatives from technical schools, trade and vocational schools, and other similar institutions—perhaps it should be called higher education day.

Although many high schools have overlooked the importance of parental involvement in career days, they have often provided for this in programs related to colleges. Consequently, many of these sessions have been properly labeled "College Night" and scheduled in the evening, to permit parents to attend with the youngsters. Scheduling both types of activities outside regular working hours might encourage greater participation by parents and result in a closer working relationship between school and parent. The format of these programs is similar to that used in career day programs, and the organization and development of such programs should be similar.

A further difficulty may be encountered in the typical higher education day. Student questions to the institutional representative can, of course, cover the entire range of the institution's program. It is difficult for any representative to be equally versed in all phases of an extensive educational program; consequently, she may not always be able to provide the precise information desired by the student.

Many schools have developed a modified version of the higher education day that is particularly advantageous. It involves asking recent alumni of the local school to be institutional representatives. The major advantages are obvious: (1) The former students arouse personal interest among the listeners, since they are probably known to them; (2) their experiences will be accepted by the student groups; and (3) the alumni concerns and problems will have meaning for the students.

SIMULATION AND SYNTHETIC WORK ENVIRONMENTS

In this section, we discuss providing experiences, through artificial means, that are intended to help the student or client understand more completely the decision-making process or the nature of a work situation. This experience can often be encountered in the classroom or learning situation but is by no means limited to the school setting. One type of simulation that everyone has experienced is role playing. Perhaps the simplest definition of simulation is that it is an artificial activity in an artificial setting that provides the participant some understanding of the real activity performed in a real situation.

Simulation has long been recognized by teachers as an effective means of teaching both simple and complex skills. Obviously, simulation offers counselors a comparable opportunity to transmit or develop insight into demands imposed on workers, the nature of the work environment, skills workers need to complete certain jobs successfully, and similar aspects of employment. Strangely, the procedure remains underdeveloped as it relates to counseling and career development activities.

A common example of simulation is the fire drill, encountered by every elementary school pupil. The military services have used the technique extensively with infiltration courses, obstacle courses, and combat training. A more sophisticated example of simulation is the Link Trainer, a device encountered by many who have qualified for a pilot's license.

Many high schools have developed "civil service commissions" (a student-faculty committee that assigns students to tasks in the school) of various types to provide students job experiences through various helper positions in classrooms, laboratories, and elsewhere in the school. These programs usually require completion of an application form, sometimes a job interview, supervisory reports from the responsible faculty member, and similar job-related experiences.

Fifield and Peterson (1978) describe the development and use of 30 simulation units with elementary school pupils. Each unit represents a realistic aspect of a job, with all of the Office of Education career clusters represented. For example, the auto brake repair unit includes an appropriately mounted car fender with backing plate and brake parts on a movable support. Units were developed locally at costs ranging between $200 and $400. Evaluation showed increased learning about occupations, improved attitudes, and greater interest in occupations. Cooperating teachers and parents also responded favorably.

The Singer Vocational Evaluation System, often used in vocational rehabilitation centers to evaluate the aptitudes of clients with disabilities, is another illustration of simulation. Some of the parts of the Vocational Evaluation System can be considered to be actual work samples, a technique we discuss in a later section.

Elementary teachers have used this technique frequently to enhance classroom learning activities; for example, the class establishes a "store" where class members acquire commonly used supplies such as paper, crayons, pencils, and paste, or perhaps a "bank" in which each student maintains a small savings account.

High school vocational education classes also have used the technique extensively to teach specific vocational skills. Many trade and industry departments assign construction craft students to a class project involving the complete building of a home that then is sold to provide the materials for next year's similar project. In the construction process, the students, under proper faculty supervision, actually do the work of a carpenter, an electrician, a plasterer, a plumber, a painter, a mason, and so on.

Almost every elementary and secondary counselor can find within the school numerous activities that can be used effectively in career development. A little ingenuity and consultation with teachers will uncover unlimited possibilities.

DIRECT EXPERIENCES: OBSERVATION, EXPLORATION, AND TRYOUT

We now consider the use of direct contact with workers in natural work settings as the final form of career information media. The advantages of such a technique are immediately apparent. The credibility of reality is always difficult to contest. The student or client is able to see things as they are and to develop impressions and insights that would be impossible to foster in other ways. At the same time, this tremendous advantage also can operate in a negative fashion. Inexperienced observers and participants are not always able to see things as they really are, and misunderstandings can develop. Further, the specimen situation may be atypical for various reasons, so that misconceptions are created. Both difficulties can be counteracted by increasing the number and the time factor for direct contact; if this corrective measure cannot be applied, then the contacts used must be truly representative.

As the world of work has become more complex, many occupations have been removed from public view so that most students have little opportunity to go behind the scenes and actually see how and where certain types of work are performed. The perceptions they have may be developed on limited information and consequently may be unrealistic.

The field trip or industry tour provides many students their first chance to have direct contact with this side of the world of work. Such a trip can be highly motivating to students, encouraging them to explore further both the world of work and their own plans.

The group involved and the purposes to be accomplished are important in planning a field trip of this type. If the group consists of younger students and the purpose is to arouse interest and insight into how people earn their living, the tour probably should be limited to samples of occupations most frequently encountered in the local community. On the other hand, sophomores or juniors in the vocational curriculum will be interested in a different type of trip. They will be anxious to see working conditions, tools and equipment used, actual work processes, company organizations, and similar items that specifically relate to particular occupations. A high school class in occupations may be interested in exploring, but at a much different level from the elementary group.

The individual visit by a single student to a specific industry or business may offer one of the best opportunities to gain insight into a field in which the student is seriously interested. Such a visit often is arranged for an entire working day, and usually the visiting student is assigned to a worker with whom the entire day is spent. Such a visit provides maximum opportunity to see a variety of aspects of the job and to question the worker about what she is doing, as well as why and how. The student may have an opportunity to spend time with two or three workers in the course of the day. This provides a chance to become familiar with the workers' attitude toward their work, opportunities for advancement, and work stability, among other things. This prolonged contact with one or two workers has become known as *shadowing*. Some schools have arranged for classes of elementary or middle school students to shadow a parent, other relative, or close family friend. High school or college students or nonschool adults usually would not require a personal acquaintanceship. Heppner's (1981) description of using alumni contacts to establish an externship of a day or more for college students is an application of the shadowing technique. A similar approach is reported by Sampson (1980) using local alumni. Tomlinson and DiLeo (1980) describe a field trip to local work sites as part of a seminar designed to assist college women considering careers in science. Herr and Watts (1988) describe shadowing as it is currently being used in Britain to help students learn about work. Kelly (1978) and Kelly and Moore (1979) describe the use of shadowing experiences by counselors to assist them in expanding their understanding of the industrial work situation.

The use of the individual industry visit is one way in which the career day program can be supplemented for many students. It should be restricted to students who would find a visit most helpful in developing plans. Arranging visits will be time-consuming for both school personnel and for the cooperating industry, but the benefits to the student are usually worth the effort.

Many colleges and universities have recognized the importance of such visits as part of the educational planning of high school students and have developed programs such as "Day on Campus," in which students from secondary schools are invited to participate in a day's program on campus. If a formal program is scheduled, it usually provides an opportunity to talk with representatives of the curricular areas in which the visitors are interested, to visit educational facilities and housing units, and to talk to one or two students from the visitors' home schools. Even though such a mass program has obvious disadvantages, it does at least permit the student to gain some feeling of the institution and its various programs.

The ideal campus visit occurs when prospective students are not part of a mass inundation, so they can see a typical cross-section of campus life. Individual school tours require more effort for the local counselor or teacher to arrange but usually can be handled without insurmountable problems.

Although the school visit is often considered in making plans for students who are college bound, it is just as important for students whose interests lie in other educational directions. The same arrangements can and should be made for students interested in vocational schools and other noncollegiate institutions. Many arguments can be raised that these visits are even more crucial; for example, many vocational schools provide limited facilities for student activities and housing, so a student may be forced to make individual arrangements to a greater extent than on many college campuses. Some preview of what is available may be helpful in making appropriate plans.

Work experience programs can be exploratory, general, or vocational preparatory. Exploratory programs aim at helping students understand various types of work, work settings, tools and equipment used by workers, demands placed on workers, and similar factors. General work experience programs are designed to assist students develop attitudes and skills that are not narrowly vocational in nature, including punctuality, dependability, acceptance of supervision, interpersonal relations, and similar characteristics that apply to all work situations.

Another example of direct on-the-job experience is the college-level cooperative program, usually associated with academic majors in many technical areas. In some fields these experiences are referred to as field practice or internship. Typically, all of these involve alternating periods of full-time study and work assignments. An experience of this kind usually comes late in the preparatory program and is designed to develop and sharpen work-related skills rather than to provide exploratory insight into the occupation. Nevertheless, it does offer a meaningful contact with work that the individual can use to confirm the appropriateness of an earlier choice or to begin the process of realigning plans.

THE CAREER RESOURCE CENTER

The increased availability of career materials—printed, audiovisual, programmed, and computer based—has emphasized the need for an organized system to handle these items in an orderly way. The answer in most settings has been the development of a *career resource center*, also frequently called a *career information center.*

In the last decade there has been considerable growth of career resource centers. Such centers assemble materials and a professional and paraprofessional staff whose responsibility is to develop in-house and outreach programs. These activities are sometimes referred to as *career information delivery systems*. The combination of materials, staff, and program provide the essentials for a career resource center.

The Chapman and Katz (1981) survey found that 70 percent of the high schools surveyed did not have a central index of the career materials available in the school. One can extrapolate from these data that these schools did not yet have a career resource center. The responsibility for aiding students in locating career information varied somewhat; 64 percent of the schools assigned this to the guidance director and guidance staff, 15 percent to the career education coordinator, 13 percent to the school librarian, and 7 percent to teachers. Ninety percent of the schools, however, said the counselors were involved in directing students to career information materials.

There are many references to which the reader can turn for specific information on establishing a career resource center. Some of the more helpful references include Brown and Brown (1990); Cheshire, B. (1988); Frederickson (1982); Hubbard and Hawke (1987); Jacobson (1972); Martin (1980); Meerbach (1978); Reardon (1973); Reardon and Domkowski (1977); Reardon, Domkowski, and Jackson (1980); and Reardon and Minor (1975). Because there is such a great variability in clientele served, facilities and other resources available, and other relevant factors, our discussion focuses on general principles that are applicable across the variable factors.

Basic Criteria

At least four factors must be considered as plans are made to develop a career resource center: accessibility, attractiveness, ease of operation, and adaptability.

1. *Accessibility.* If career materials are conveniently located, more people will use them. If they are to be used in an educational setting, consideration should be given to student traffic flow and a location that is available to the greatest number of students for the maximum period of time. Although confidentiality is not a major consideration, it should be possible for the student or client to have access to career materials without feeling conspicuous.

   In nonschool settings the problem of accessibility is likely to be a lesser one, since the number of individuals using the materials will probably be considerably fewer and the hours the materials are available will usually coincide with the operating hours of the agencies involved.

2. *Attractiveness.* The setting in which career information is maintained should be inviting to users and stimulate their interest. Furnishings should be tasteful and selected to encourage both casual browsing and serious study.

3. *Ease of operation.* Career materials probably will be used more if they are organized so the user can find items without help. If the filing

system is easily understood and the materials so placed that users can be self-sufficient, they will likely sample what is available. If clients find that obtaining what they want is simple, they are likely to explore further. Perhaps the basic rule is to select the filing system that is easiest for the user and is compatible with the range and variety of available material.

4. *Adaptability*. It is important to collect career materials to fit the needs of the group that the resource center is intended to serve. The filing system also should be tailored to those needs. Because variations can be expected among various groups, the filing system should have enough flexibility to expand in areas that call for stretching and to contract in those areas in which the need is little or nonexistent.

OPERATIONAL DECISIONS

In addition to the general criteria just discussed, several administrative factors bear directly on the development of a career resource center. Most of these must be considered and at least tentative answers obtained before a final decision on a filing plan or system can be reached. The following topics need attention:

1. *Responsibility*. One of the first decisions that should be made is who will be responsible for developing and maintaining the career resource center. In a nonschool agency, this question is usually resolved easily by assigning responsibility to the person who takes leadership in the vocational counseling provided by the agency. If the agency is a large counseling center, each counselor may take primary responsibility for different phases of the program related to his activity, one of which would be the career resource center (others might be the testing program and the research activities).

   Although one can generally assume that a collection of career information materials in a school media center has been developed to meet different uses than the materials found in the counselor's office, one cannot automatically assume that responsibility for the materials should be taken from the librarian or media specialist and given to the counselor. The decision should be based on all the factors in the local situation. One would expect the counselors, the media specialists, and the teachers to work together closely to find the best solution. Often some kind of joint responsibility will offer the best opportunity to provide the broadest service possible.

   Because of increased decentralization on college and university campuses, the responsibility often gravitates to the student personnel division and usually to counseling center staff members. However, the staff should be familiar with resources and materials that may already exist in the library, or in offices of various academic divisions such as schools or departments, especially if those sections have traditionally held responsibility for scheduling and class selection. In noneducational settings, the responsibility usually can be assigned by administrative action.

2. *Staff.* Problems of staffing depend in part on the size and scope of the anticipated career resource center, the extent to which the clientele who will use the materials can operate independently, the volume of acquisitions, and the general usage of the materials and other factors. Professional people will be needed for at least part of the staff. Decisions about materials to be purchased, classification and evaluation, periodic review, and general supervision must all be put in responsible hands.

   Florida remains ahead of the other states by having provided, through legislation, paraprofessionals called *occupational specialists.* The natural habitat for this rare bird is the career resource center, and there is much that such individuals can do effectively. Panther (1975) describes their use with elementary-age youngsters in awareness-stage activities. Myrick and Wilkinson (1976) found them to have a special advantage in working with early school leavers.

3. *Facilities.* The decision to develop a career resource center carries with it the assumption that necessary facilities and equipment can be provided. The following will be needed: a considerable quantity of shelf space, filing cabinets for unbound materials, furniture such as study tables and chairs, a table or desk for checking materials in and out and for processing new materials, small card files for recordkeeping, display racks for new booklets, and bulletin boards. If AV equipment is not initially available, plans should include provisions for or access to such equipment, including videocassette recorders, filmstrip viewers, a slide projector, 8-mm and 16-mm film projectors, and a copier. Most centers now include computer equipment or terminals with connections to larger units for access to on-line data banks.

   Minimum space can be ascertained fairly easily if one visualizes the area required for initial and soon-to-be-acquired equipment, for staff to be assigned to the center, and for clients. In school and university settings, it may be difficult to operate with less than one large classroom or equivalent. In noneducational settings, with fewer clients using the space simultaneously, one might be able to operate in an area of about 500 square feet. The important factor is not number of square feet but what is to be done, how and with what it is to be accomplished, how many people will be involved at a time, and how much space this requires.

4. *Location.* Several factors bear on the location of the career resource center. Not the least of these is available space. The problem is likely to be simple when a new school is being opened. If adequate long-range

planning has gone into the development of the building, a room has been set aside to meet this need. Ideally, there will be a room of adequate size, with direct access from the outer office of the guidance suite. Such a room can be readily available at all times to clients and others wishing to use the materials, as well as to counselors who desire to introduce counselees to the materials. Some supervision also is possible by the clerical or receptionist staff, whose work space is likely to be in the outer office.

5. *Security.* Every effort should be made to provide clients maximum access to the resources on file. The system for obtaining and using career information materials should be made as simple and as easy as possible. Without doubt, efforts to simplify the system may well result in some losses that could have been prevented by more stringent security measures. Generally, however, these losses will not be excessive and should be accepted as part of the operating costs.

6. *Budget.* Establishing an adequate career resource center involves considerable expense; additional funds are needed regularly thereafter to maintain and expand it. Unless the school or agency is willing to accept this double responsibility, it should think carefully before making the original investment. Because the amounts for both purposes depend on many factors, no particular amount can be specified as sufficient for the project.

    Many schools find the support of the career resource center to be a project attractive to local service clubs seeking a worthwhile way to assist the school. It would probably be wise administrative policy to provide basic or minimal support within the regular school budget and to use such outside support for increased or expanded services. Since assurance of continued support may be difficult to obtain, provisions for continuity should probably be based on school support.

7. *Publicity.* A career resource center is meant to be used. Thus provision should be made to keep potential users continually informed of its availability. All agencies that work with adolescents are aware of the constant changes in their clientele as a result of maturation alone. Each school, for example, starts a new freshman class each year. This necessitates some plan for informing this group as well as familiarizing those who have been around before but who have not established contact. In most settings, the need for this communicative effort is continuous.

8. *Operating policies.* Many problems cannot be anticipated. Some person or group must be assigned the responsibility for solving problems as they arise. Even though the general operating framework of the career resource center can be determined ahead of time, there must be provision for flexibility and modification to fit the needs of the group served. Someone must be responsible for establishing procedures and for making changes as needed.

COLLECTING AND EVALUATING MATERIALS

All agencies that work with adolescents and adults in the process of career choice and planning will need a wide range of print and AV career materials. Since the materials will be used with many clients and students, a collection of these items should be compiled in advance so they will be available for use as needed.

Among the changes that have occurred recently is the transformation of the school library into a learning resource center or media center. Techno-logical developments have made possible the inclusion of much material in a variety of forms, both printed and nonprinted, as well as an assortment of equipment used in applying the materials. With increasing frequency, this vital area of the school is staffed by a highly competent, thoroughly trained media specialist.

Since many counselors work in nonschool settings and some work in schools without broadly trained media specialists, the remainder of this chapter is written on the assumption that the counselor must take either sole responsibility for or major leadership in developing and operating a career resource center.

Chapman and Katz (1981) report that the counseling staff has primary responsibility for career materials. Among the schools surveyed, 51 percent said the counseling staff had responsibility for replacing career materials and evaluating new material; 64 percent said counselors held responsibility for helping students find material or advising them where to look; and 57 percent said counselors must decide when to discard old and obsolete material.

Criteria for Collecting Material

Several factors must be considered in assembling the resources for the center:

1. *The group that will make major use of the materials.* Obviously, differ-ent materials would be used in a junior high school, where students are only beginning to explore concepts about the world of work, than in a vocational rehabilitation center for adults. Even where the differences are less extreme, materials should be appropriate to the specific group. Within a school, the grade levels to be served by the career resource center provide some basis for selection. If materials are to be used primarily by junior high school students, a different emphasis is needed than if students from grades 7 through 12 are expected to use the collection, or if only senior high school students are involved. The range of ability and interest in the group also influences the choice of materi-als.

    Most nonschool agencies can almost automatically assume a broad range of interest, ability, and academic background in the clients they serve. These variations will necessitate planning to select as broad a range of career materials as needed. If the agency exists to serve a specific group, its needs must be considered in choosing materials.

2. *The nature of the community.* A knowledge of the community where the school or agency is situated will provide additional information about the group that will use the career resource center. Although the high mobility of Americans decreases the likelihood that they will remain within the community throughout their lives, the range and scope of occupations within the community may provide the framework for the evaluation and consideration of career fields by students and their parents. That is, it will be more difficult to stimulate students to consider a wide range of occupational choice if they have grown up in a stable community dominated by a single industry than if the town has many businesses and factories and the population is constantly changing.

The socioeconomic range within the community and the extent to which community attitudes encourage educational achievement and individual development are other factors to be considered.

3. *The staff that will apply the materials.* Logically, the materials to be used only by the counselor would differ from those to be used by group leaders or teachers. Use of some items—for example, the *Dictionary of Occupational Titles*—presupposes some understanding of the organizational structure of the world of work and of the volume itself, as well as the theoretical and philosophic basis for the book. If materials are purchased that lie beyond the competency of the staff that will use them, they will likely be misused or left unused unless a staff training program is provided.

4. *How the materials will be used.* Closely related to *who* uses the career resource center is the question of *how* the materials are to be used. If career materials will be used only in individual counseling concerning vocational plans, a wide range of items in single or duplicate copies will probably be most appropriate. On the other hand, if materials are to be used for instructional purposes in a group guidance or classroom setting, the range of materials will probably be narrowed to make available the number of copies needed for the entire group.

5. *Existing materials already available.* Even if a counselor were newly appointed in a school that had never previously had a counselor, it would usually be fallacious to assume that the school had no career material on hand. The only time this is likely to be true is when a new school is opened. Whether or not she finds a file of career information in the office, the counselor should check with the school librarian or media specialist to learn what pertinent materials are in the library or media center.

An additional reservoir of career materials may be found in the resource materials collected by teachers for their use in the classroom. Many teachers have encountered student inquiries concerning the relationship between subject area and possible career fields. The classroom bookshelves are a likely source of career materials.

6. *Auxiliary local resources.* Almost every community has agencies that work with youth or adults and hence might have materials that relate to their problems, including career materials. The local public library is an obvious location for materials of this type. Other local resources that may have materials would be 4-H clubs, youth centers, the YMCA, YWCA, and churches or other groups that operate active youth or adult programs.

7. *Funds available.* Obviously, plans for obtaining career information will be influenced by the amount of money available. Rarely does a school or any other agency have an unlimited budget; consequently, the development of a basic library of materials may have to be planned over a period of time. The individual responsible for developing the center should be sure that there are sufficient funds to make a reasonable start and that there will be continuing appropriations in future budgets for extending the project as well as replacing out-of-date items.

Initiating a Collection

A school that includes many students who will complete their formal education at this level must have career materials to serve them. Since this may be their last chance for such help, these students may warrant some priority. In other schools, most students may be college bound. In this case, emphasis should first be given to materials related to occupational fields requiring college training and to educational information about colleges. Similarly, noneducational agencies need to plan according to the nature of the groups they serve that will use the resource center. Young adults in a Job Search Club will want materials far different than will their former schoolmates who are now completing a technical school course.

Once the counselor has collected the materials that are urgently needed to meet the most pressing needs apparent within the user group, it is logical to move toward the development of breadth of materials. The extent or range of materials to be considered is based on the range within the group. After these two needs have been met, at least minimally, one then may move toward acquiring materials related to specialized fields or adding depth to already selected areas.

The counselor should take the following steps, though not necessarily in this order, to gain familiarity with what is currently available:

1. Subscribe to some of the indexes listing occupational materials. Since these do not completely overlap, it often is wise to subscribe to at least two, if possible.

2. Request price lists from federal and state agencies that publish materials related to areas pertinent to the counselor's group. One also may

wish to check with the local library to determine if it subscribes to the U.S. Government Printing Office's *Monthly Catalog.* If so, the counselor may want to check this regularly for useful publications.

3. Check recent professional publications, such as *Career Development Quarterly,* for appropriate materials.

4. Obtain price lists from commercial publishers who have materials directly related to occupations.

5. Ascertain from appropriate professional organizations and societies, private industries, industrial associations, and private companies what materials they have that are appropriate for the user group. O'Neil and Price (1977) describe the use of computerized labels to obtain much free material from this source.

6. Contact educational institutions for publications. Many colleges and universities have career materials available, as well as such items as catalogs and bulletins. Among higher educational institutions, the counselor in a secondary school would probably first contact the colleges within the state or immediate geographic area and then those out-of-state institutions to which students from the school go regularly. Materials from trade and technical schools usually would be requested on the basis of the schools in which students express an interest.

7. Determine which general items or basic resource volumes are essential for immediate use. These might include one or more copies of the latest *Dictionary of Occupational Titles,* the *Guide for Occupational Exploration, Selected Characteristics,* the latest issue of *Occupational Outlook Handbook,* and annual subscriptions to *Occupational Outlook Quarterly* and appropriate educational directories.

Once counselors have completed these steps, they have the basic information needed to make appropriate purchases with the funds at hand. If funds are sufficient, they should hold some in reserve to purchase new materials as they appear or to obtain materials for special needs that develop during the year.

Evaluating materials is an integral part of building a good career resource center. Many of the factors discussed in the two previous sections impinge on decisions to acquire materials for the center. The NVGA (now NCDA) has established, and regularly revises, *Guidelines for the Preparation and Evaluation of Career Information Literature* (NVGA, 1980). These will be helpful in the collecting process. A counselor always should keep in mind the needs of the group of clients or students who will use the materials. Further, one must remember the staff who will use the materials and the ways the materials will be used. Finally, one must remain aware of the costs of the desired items in relation to the funds available.

Additionally, each possible acquisition should be measured against these criteria: accuracy, currency, usability, reader appeal, and comprehensiveness.

1. *Accuracy.* Even if the item being evaluated meets all other criteria, it is valueless if it fails this one. The material must depict the occupation fairly and correctly if the reader is to draw inferences and conclusions that will help in understanding the field. Inaccuracies inevitably will be misleading and could lead to decisions based on fallacy rather than fact. The material should be forthright and honest and should describe the occupation as it is. The publisher who wants to serve both counselor and client will include within a publication information that will help the counselor judge its accuracy. As a minimum, this would include an indication of how the information was collected, the size of the sample on which it is based, its location and extent of dispersion, identification of the person who collected the information and prepared the publication, evidence of that person's competency in unbiased reporting, and the dates when the data were obtained.

   Since most published data presumably are based on a fairly large geographic area, the counselor needs to check not only the general accuracy for the occupation across the country but also the degree of precision with which the local situation is depicted. When the information necessary to determine accuracy is not included, the counselor has little recourse other than to match the information against such sources as the *Occupational Outlook Handbook* and other Department of Labor publications that are based, for the most part, on careful job analyses with relatively large samples.

2. *Currency.* This criterion, though closely related to accuracy, is listed separately to emphasize its importance. *Accuracy* tends to stress precision; *currency* adds the time factor. In other words, as we evaluate career information, we must ask: Is it accurate *now*?

   At any given point, an occupation either may be holding relatively constant or may be involved in very rapid, perhaps even extreme, change; or it may be someplace in between. For example, the present impact of technological modernization is producing extensive change in many of the manufacturing occupations.

   It is difficult for the counselor to predict precisely or even to estimate the degree to which an occupation is caught up in this change at a given moment. The best basis for judgment probably lies in an unending effort to keep abreast of developments and anticipated changes across the entire spectrum of the world of work. Publications from the Bureau of Labor Statistics and the State Employment Security Agency will be of some help in this task, as will materials such as reliable weekly news magazines that keep the counselor informed of economic and technical developments.

3. *Usability.* At least during the preliminary period of collecting career materials, preference should be given to materials that concern the more common occupations, since these are usually of greatest interest to the greatest number.

Similarly, some materials are so organized and prepared that they are of value to a variety of students or clients whose purpose in using them may range from casual perusal to serious study. Certain publications can be used advantageously by a broader group of the staff and perhaps even in a wider variety of situations. When this appears likely, first purchases should include those that have wide usability.

4. *Reader appeal.* Attractive materials are likely to be used by more readers than are materials with an uninviting format. This is probably true to an even greater extent when the users are adolescents. A readable typeface, arranged in a pleasing layout and accompanied by an appealing use of color and illustrations, will result in greater use of the materials. In addition to general appearance, the writing style and the general level of reading difficulty should be considered.

5. *Comprehensiveness.* Occasionally, in evaluating career materials for selection, a counselor will have a special purpose in mind and will be seeking material to fit that purpose. Ordinarily, however, the counselor is concerned with selecting materials that will have general application for the group using the resource center. In the latter case, comprehensiveness should be considered as material is evaluated.

To a large extent, this must be appraised in terms of the group that is to use the career resource center. Comprehensiveness is crucial for upper educational years and later, when users are seriously involved in actual choices and decisions. At this point the counselee or client should have available all information that depicts clearly the occupation considered.

Managing Materials

The fundamental purpose for a career resource center, and for collecting and evaluating the materials deposited there, is to ensure access to high-quality career information when it is needed by clients and those assisting in the career development process. Hence an efficient and easy operational system is crucial. Brown and Brown (1990) discuss this topic from the viewpoint of a high school counselor, and Green (1979) considers it from a librarian's approach. Smith (1983) describes a library management system entitled *Career Key* that provides a microcomputer access system to the cataloging records of a career resource center. This permits clients to obtain a comprehensive listing of all resources available in the center that deal with the specific topic being searched.

As indicated earlier, Chapman and Katz (1981) found that actual management responsibility for helping students locate career materials rested with the guidance director and counselors in 64 percent of the schools and with the librarian only 13 percent of the time. Obviously, the counselors must capitalize on the professional expertise of the librarian or media specialist to devise a system that provides maximum utility.

Educational Materials

Most career information emphasizes either the educational and training aspects or the various occupations themselves. This book follows a similar approach, and we first consider the matter of filing educational materials. Three general topics are considered:

1. Training directories
2. School catalogs and bulletins
3. Miscellaneous educational materials and information

One essential ingredient in every career resource center is a collection of training or educational directories. The number and scope needed will vary with the age and educational range of the users and the breadth of their anticipated educational plans, but even a modest library should include at least one directory for each general educational level. Most centers, especially those serving senior high schools, should provide more than one.

Within the career resource center, the educational directories usually can be handled best by placing all directories together on a conveniently located shelf. If the center has several directories, it may help to divide this shelf according to educational level—for example, a section for college and university directories, one for trade and vocational schools, and so on. In some settings, it may be more appropriate to place the directories with other publications from the kinds of schools included in the directories; that is, the vocational school directories might be located with vocational school bulletins. Ordinarily, however, the centralized location will be more convenient and will permit more efficient use.

School catalogs and bulletins can be organized either on shelves or in filing cabinets. In either case, it is usually desirable to separate them according to broad categories of schools—professional schools, 4-year colleges and universities, community colleges, vocational-technical-trade schools, and others. Since most professional schools are related to a college or university, it may be advantageous to combine the first two categories. If it is anticipated that the range of schools regularly included will not be extensive, it may even be desirable to combine the first three categories so that only two groupings are used, with a general label such as "academic" for one group and "vocational-technical-trade" for the other.

Materials from the vocational-technical-trade schools can be arranged by either of the methods described for the academic institutions. In addition, another alternative is often preferred: These publications can be arranged according to the occupation for which training is provided. Since many schools of this type are likely to be single-purpose institutions, there is often an advantage in this system, which, for example, brings together in a single section all barber schools. When this system is used, the occupational headings are often arranged alphabetically or according to *DOT* number, with each school placed alphabetically within this category.

Unbound Occupational Materials

One major problem in establishing a career resource center is selecting a filing system for occupational materials. Since these materials make up a major portion of the total center, the filing system must be organized to meet the general principles already discussed. A decision about the filing system to be used should be reached before any attempt is made to collect materials, so that all acquisitions can be incorporated into the file as soon as they arrive. Since no system yet devised serves all purposes ideally, a compromise is necessary. The selection should be made in terms of the factors most important in the local situation.

Most occupational materials are published as unbound pamphlets, briefs, or monographs. Obviously, these must be handled differently from bound items. Many attempts have been made to organize unbound materials into some meaningful system. Several systems are in use today, and no one method is generally preferred over others. We briefly discuss alphabetical, coded, and other systems.

Filing systems can be developed locally to meet the needs of a particular agency, or they can be purchased commercially. This decision depends on such factors as available funds, staff time, special local needs, and suitability of commercial systems. The commercial systems take a variety of forms. Some publishers, for example, sell a set of gummed labels and directions for developing the file; others supply printed folders with directions and cross-reference cards or a complete kit including the filing system and an assortment of occupational materials.

Alphabetical System
The simplest method of filing unbound occupational materials is in a series of folders, each labeled with the name of an occupation, arranged in alphabetical order. In schools or agencies where unorganized occupational materials have accumulated over a period of time, an alphabetical system is often an immediate solution.

A simple alphabetical system has certain obvious advantages. First, it is the easiest system to operate and therefore is usable at low educational levels or by clients whose educational background is limited. Second, an alphabetical system is totally adjustable to local conditions, since the number of folders included can be fitted exactly to the materials used in the file. As new materials are obtained on occupations not previously included, the file is expanded easily by simply labeling new folders with the names of the occupations to be added. Third, it requires no key or index to help find materials, which can be filed or found easily and rapidly.

When it is expected that the ultimate size of the file will not exceed one or two file drawers, the alphabetical system is usually more efficient than any other method.

As the occupational file grows larger, the simple alphabetical system becomes less efficient. As the file expands, the problem of alternative titles becomes a serious one. The only feasible solution to the problem actually adds to its complexity. To be sure that clients will locate the material in the file, regardless of the title under which it is placed, it becomes necessary to set up folders for each title that they might use and organize a cross-reference system that will direct them to the folder or folders in which material can be found.

A further criticism of the simple alphabetical system is that it does not provide any way to identify occupational groups or families. Occupations that actually may be very closely related often are filed far apart because of alphabetical order.

Coded System

The *Dictionary of Occupational Titles* has served as a logical base for filing career materials since the first edition appeared in 1939. At one time, a system was proposed based on the literal translation of the *DOT* coding system into a filing plan. With more than 7,000 code numbers in the 1939 edition, it is obvious that such a plan is far too detailed for practical application. Nevertheless, the *DOT* provides an obviously useful base for filing career materials. Consequently, it has frequently served as the model for building filing systems, both privately developed and commercially prepared. One widely used plan of this type is the *Chronicle Occupational Library*, published by Chronicle Guidance Publications, Inc., Moravia, NY 13118.

The *Chronicle Library* includes a filing system of folders for approximately 700 occupational briefs and reprints. The user may select a basic filing system based on either the *Dictionary of Occupational Titles* or the *Guide for Occupational Exploration*. All items are cross-referenced to the *DOT*, the *GOE*, and the *SOC*. One advantage for this type of plan is its use of a widely used classification system. A second advantage is the ability to expand in areas where local circumstances suggest a need for more materials and to contract in areas of little interest or a paucity of material.

The major criticism aimed at such a plan relates to the first advantage listed. Some contend that the plan requires special knowledge and training to operate. Most individuals will find the system somewhat complicated at first encounter, especially if they are exploring on their own. But if we assume that most users will be introduced to the file system by a counselor or someone who understands it, this criticism is immaterial.

The *Careers Desk-Top Kit* published by Careers, Inc., Largo, FL 33540, is an attempt to provide a condensed supplement to the regular occupational file. It includes brief sketches of a fairly wide range of occupations organized in a portable box only 6 inches by 9 inches by 19 inches. The *Desk-Top Kit* can be used easily by the counselor, students, or clients. The material included is filed according to a system based on the *DOT*.

Other Systems

Through the years, a number of proposals have been made for other methods of filing unbound occupational information. Such plans frequently have been based on either areas of interest or academic subject areas. In the first case it has been fairly common to tie the filing system to an interest inventory, often the Kuder General Interest Survey Form E or Holland's Self-Directed Search. In the second case, either high school subjects or college major areas are used as a base for filing.

The major advantage of such plans is fairly obvious, since the filing plan is tied directly to a base that is easily understood by the users of the file. It is very simple to consider a Kuder General Interest or a Self-Directed Search profile, for example, to ascertain the area(s) of highest interest and then turn to a filing system that lists jobs in this same type of classification. On the surface, such a system appears to make sense and appeals to the user.

Such plans have two serious disadvantages, either of which can prevent their adoption. First, interest factors or academic subjects are unrealistic bases for classifying occupations, simply because most fields of work do not have or require a special or unique interest pattern that can be used to differentiate them from other fields. The second disadvantage is the danger that classification by either subject matter or interest area will mislead the user by placing undue emphasis on the base system (either interest or sub-ject) as the primary factor in making a vocational choice.

Filing Bound Occupational Materials

Filing bound occupational information usually does not present the problems encountered with unbound materials. First, probably fewer items are pub-lished in bound form; second, counselors, teachers, and other personnel are more accustomed to working with bound materials.

If all occupational materials are to be located together—in the career resource center, for example—a simple plan for shelf filing usually can be developed to fit the system used for unbound materials. For most users it will be easier if the two types of materials are set up under the same general filing plan. Shelf space can be readily organized in this fashion. Since many of the bound items—such as the *Occupational Outlook Handbook*—include infor-mation that cuts across many occupations, a general shelf will have to be established in addition to the specific areas. The development of microfiche and computerized systems has changed the old card file plan for locating material, but has not eliminated the search for information. Sampson (1982) describes a computer-assisted index system for career materials used in a college setting. The system that best fits local conditions and the users is the ideal system to adopt.

SUMMARY

The aim of this chapter was two-fold: first to consider the various types of career information used in counseling and teaching situations, and second to examine ways to organize and maintain that information in a career resource center so it can be used effectively in all career development activities.

All career-related information arises from two fundamental sources: either the person doing the work or the person for whom the work is being done. Career information coming from the two basic sources is acquired, processed, and distributed by various entities and organizations, such as government agencies, commercial publishers, professional organizations, private employers, and educational institutions. In addition to printed material, career information comes in many other forms, including audio-visual and programmed formats; interview sources; practice and artificial experiences; as well as direct exposure through observation, exploration, and try-out.

Establishing a resource center requires consideration of many problems beyond space, staff, equipment, funding, and maintenance. Among these considerations are the establishment of policies regarding who is to be served and how, and the setting up of operational policies. Before materials can be acquired, decisions about criteria for collecting and maintaining them must be made, as well as decisions about how materials will be stored and accessed.

REFERENCES

Bradley, R. W., & Thacker, M.S. (1978). Developing local sources of career education. *Vocational Guidance Quarterly, 26*, 268–272.

Brown, S. T., & Brown, D. (1990). *Designing and implementing a career information center.* Garrett Park, MD: Garrett Park Press.

Chapman, W., & Katz, M. (1981). *Survey of career information systems in secondary schools.* Princeton, NJ: Educational Testing Service.

Cheshire, B. (1988). *A handbook for guidance counselors.* Statesboro, GA: School of Education.

Fifield, M., & Petersen, L. (1978). Job simulation: A method of vocational exploration. *Vocational Guidance Quarterly, 26*, 326–333.

Frederickson, R. H. (1982). *Career information.* Englewood Cliffs, NJ: Prentice Hall (pp. 48–65).

Green, C. H. (1979). Managing career information: A librarian's perspective. *Vocational Guidance Quarterly, 28*, 83–91.

Heppner, M. J. (1981). Alumni sharing knowledge (ASK): High quality, cost-effective career resources. *Journal of College Student Personnel, 22*, 173–174.

Herr, E. L., & Watts, A.G. (1988). Work shadowing and work-related learning. *Career Development Quarterly, 37*, 78–86.

Hoppock, R. (1970). How to conduct an occupational group conference with an alumnus. *Vocational Guidance Quarterly, 18*, 311–312.

Hubbard, M., & Hawke, S. (1987). *Developing a career information center.* Montreal, Quebec: Guidance Information Center, Concordia University.

Isaacson, L. E., & Hayes, R. (1980). Adapting career day to the elementary school. *Elementary School Guidance and Counseling, 14*, 258–261.

Jacobson, T. J. (1972). Career guidance centers. *Personnel and Guidance Journal, 50*, 599–604.

Johnson, W. F., Korn, T. A., & Dunn, D. J. (1975). Comparing three methods of presenting occupational information. *Vocational Guidance Quarterly, 24,* 62–66.

Kelly, E. W., Jr. (1978). Industrial shadow experiences: Career counseling from an experiential base. *Vocational Guidance Quarterly, 26,* 342–348.

Kelly, E. W., Jr., & Moore, P. R. (1979). Process analysis of industrial shadow experiences. *Vocational Guidance Quarterly, 27,* 244–249.

Kunze, K. R. (1967). Industry resources available to counselors. *Vocational Guidance Quarterly, 16,* 137–142.

Laramore, D. (1971). Counselors make occupational information packages. *Vocational Guidance Quarterly, 19,* 220–224.

Martin, G. M. (1980). A guide to setting up a career resource information center. *Occupational Outlook Quarterly, 24 (3),* 12–17.

Meerbach, J. (1978). *The career resource center.* New York: Human Sciences.

Myrick, R. D., & Wilkinson, G. (1976). The occupational specialist: A study of guidance support personnel. *Vocational Guidance Quarterly, 24,* 244–249.

National Occupational Information Coordinating Committee. (1986). *Using labor market information in career exploration and decision making: A resource guide.* Garrett Park, MD: Garrett Park Press.

National Vocational Guidance Association. (1978). *NVGA bibliography of current career information.* Washington, DC: National Vocational Guidance Association.

National Vocational Guidance Association. (1980). Guidelines for the preparation and evaluation of career information literature. *Vocational Guidance Quarterly, 28,* 291–296.

O'Neil, J. N., & Price, G. E. (1977). Low-cost career information. *Vocational Guidance Quarterly, 26,* 76–78.

Panther, E. E. (1975). Career education's missing link: Support personnel. *Vocational Guidance Quarterly, 24,* 73–76.

Pate, R. H., Jr., Tullock, J. B., & Dassance, C. R. (1981). A regional job and educational opportunities fair. *Personnel and Guidance Journal, 60,* 187–189.

Plotsky, F. A., & Goad, R. (1974). Encouraging women through a career conference. *Personnel and Guidance Journal, 52,* 486–488.

Reardon, R. C. (1973). The counselor and career information services. *Journal of College Student Personnel, 14,* 495–500.

Reardon, R. C., & Domkowski, D. (1977). Building instruction into a career information center. *Vocational Guidance Quarterly, 25,* 274–278.

Reardon, R. C., Domkowski, D., & Jackson, E. (1980). Career center evaluation methods: A case study. *Vocational Guidance Quarterly, 29,* 150–158.

Reardon, R. C., & Minor, C. W. (1975). Revitalizing the career information service. *Personnel and Guidance Journal, 54,* 169–171.

Sampson, J. P., Jr. (1980). Using college alumni as resource persons for providing occupational information. *Journal of College Student Personnel, 21,* 172.

Sampson, J. P., Jr. (1982). A computer-assisted library index for career materials. *Journal of College Student Personnel, 23,* 539–540.

Self, C., & Lopez, F. (1982). Women in nontraditional fields: A career development seminar for college women. *Journal of College Student Personnel, 23,* 545–546.

Smith, E. (1983). Career key: A career library management system. *Vocational Guidance Quarterly, 32,* 52–56.

Tomlinson, E., & DiLeo, J. C. (1980). Broadening horizons: Careers for women in science. *Journal of College Student Personnel, 21,* 570–571.

U.S. Department of Defense. (1984). *Military career guide.* Washington, DC: Author.

U.S. Department of Defense, Office of the Assistant Secretary for Manpower, Installations, and Logistics. (1984). *Military occupational and training data.* Washington, DC: U.S. Government Printing Office.

U.S. Department of Labor, Manpower Administration. (1974). *Job analysis for human resources management: A review of selected research and development.* Manpower Research Monograph No. 36. Washington, DC: U.S. Government Printing Office.

Warrington, D. L., & Method–Walker, Y. (1981). Career scope. *Journal of College Student Personnel, 22,* 169–170.

8

Computer-Assisted Career Guidance Systems

In Chapter 7 we identified a computer-based system as one of several methods by which counselor and client can find and use career information and advance the career development process. In this chapter, we review the present status of this technology and some of the typical programs and materials currently being used.

Harris–Bowlsbey (1990) points out that the present pace of change in computer-assisted career guidance (CACG) systems mandates total redevelopment of programs on a 5- to 6-year cycle. Even if this pace were to slow to a complete change each decade, counselors and other career development specialists would be hard pressed to maintain currency in a field that evolves so rapidly. The purpose of this admonition is twofold: first, to emphasize to the reader the rapidity with which change in computer hardware and software can occur and the difficulty of being certain that available information truly represents the present status; and second, to point out that the time required to design, complete, report, and publish research inevitably means that changes in hardware and/or software have likely occurred since the research was initiated. Therefore, the research reports or descriptive statements, such as this chapter, at best reflect the status of these systems at the time of writing.

Sampson and Reardon (1990) present the proceedings of an international teleconference on technology and career development. The conference occurred in June, 1989 and provides an extremely rich source of information about computer-assisted career guidance systems, as of that date, in both the United States and in western Europe. Especially useful are several papers by individuals who have contributed significantly to the development of this field, including Harris–Bowlsbey, Katz, and McKinlay, each of whom developed one of the early computerized programs still widely used today. The purposes of the conference included reviewing the past, present, and likely future status of CACG and developing recommendations for future actions by systems developers, policy makers, researchers and evaluators, practitioners, and counselor educators that would lead to more effective design and use of future CACG systems. The proceedings include recommendations for these groups developed by the conference participants; these are considered later in this chapter.

COMPUTERS AND CAREER DEVELOPMENT

The career counseling process typically involves four activities that sometimes transpire sequentially, sometimes simultaneously, and sometimes in various combinations:

1. Learning about and knowing oneself and one's psychological world
2. Learning about the world of work
3. Expanding one's options, narrowing choices, and making decisions
4. Making plans

Computers can be employed in each of these activities, although at present they are more useful and efficient in some steps than in others. We examine briefly some of the applications that are practical at this time with existing systems. New developments may permit applications that are now not feasible or may simplify existing applications.

Learning about Oneself

In general, computers have limited value at present for this purpose. Considering the many components of each individual's psychological world, the experiences and events that have made that world unique, and the interaction between the individual and that world, it is evident that attempts to establish categories or ranks must result in either superficial groupings or innumerable and impractical combinations.

Specific personal attributes such as interests, aptitudes and abilities, personality, and values lend themselves to computer applications. Most paper-and-pencil tests can be incorporated into a computerized presentation so that the client answers test items presented by the computer. This approach, however, has few advantages (possibly the only one would be almost instantly available test results) and some serious disadvantages, particularly inefficient use of computer time since the test-taking client prevents the use of the equipment by others for the time periods involved in the various tests. No additional information would ordinarily be available, and most test data warrant some discussion with the counselor to prevent misunderstanding and even error if instructions have not been followed. Several software systems for computerized administration of many commonly used interest and personality tests are now available. Johnston, Buescher, and Heppner (1988) point out the need for the usual psychometric research to establish reliability, validity, and usefulness of computer-presented assessment instruments.

Learning about the World of Work

From the first application of computers to career counseling, they have been most useful in the storage and retrieval of career information. Except for the smaller microcomputers, storage space in most systems is sufficient to provide detailed information on a thousand or more occupations. The occupations included can be arranged in multiple combinations or clusters, using such variables as occupational family, related personal attributes, educational or training requirements, geographic location, and a great many others.

Two very important advantages accrue from maintaining a computerized bank of career information. One is the ability to maintain currency. Unlike printed material, where revision is slow and cumbersome, computer-stored information can be revised readily by replacing present information with new data—much like erasing a chalkboard and then writing a new statement. Second, greater flexibility permits maintaining all data that might be found in the usual print-media file, plus regional or state information that may often contrast significantly with national information. Most computer-assisted programs can capitalize on the existing clustering and grouping systems to permit users to survey occupational information at various levels of detail according to user needs, or to use data on a regional or national level, or to adjust the system in terms of variables of concern to the user.

One word of caution must be emphasized concerning the occupational information data bank. Obviously, the more specific and precise the classification system, the greater the number of categories included in the system. If one were to use all the coded titles included in the *Dictionary of Occupational Titles*, the demand for memory storage would greatly exceed all but the largest mainframe computers. For example, we can compare the generic title *high school teacher* with the specific titles that represent each particular kind of high school teacher—probably 20 or more, depending on how precisely we wish to make distinctions—teacher, social studies teacher, history teacher, world history teacher, and so on. For most of these more exact titles, the data in the memory bank would be practically identical. Thus systems are continually caught in a conflict between exact information versus expediency. Although memory bank capacity is growing rapidly, most systems must still use titles that can best be described as generic or broad. Systems with approximately 1,000 occupational titles have sufficient specificity to claim that they include the occupations pursued by 90 to 95 percent of the working population.

Expanding Options, Narrowing Choices, and Making Decisions

Computerized systems are unequaled in their ability to assist clients in identifying rapidly occupations that relate to specific personal attributes, both singly and in various combinations. It is almost standard practice in computer-assisted systems to include in occupational descriptions such data as relevant interest and ability patterns, physical requirements, working conditions, and so forth. Thus it involves a very simple response for the computer to list all occupations (of those in the data bank) that relate to a preference for mechanical kinds of activities, or those that involve a high level of manual dexterity, or those that are performed entirely indoors.

As indicated earlier, the list drawn from the memory bank is restricted by the degree of detail in that memory. If the total list of occupations is seriously restricted, the occupations identified with each personal attribute will also be restricted. Even with the best present system there has been considerable compacting of occupational titles. Most clients who use the computer to obtain a list of occupations that relate to certain specified personal attributes will need to be advised that the printout includes representative titles only and should not be viewed as comprehensive. Clients may need counselor help in identifying additional titles that are closely related to those on the printout. Although some systems are moving toward providing access to related titles, the client may need to turn to such supplementary sources as the *Dictionary of Occupational Titles*, the *Guide for Occupational Exploration, Selected Characteristics*, or the *Occupational Outlook Handbook* to see titles that are more specific than *teacher*, as used in the preceding illustration.

The computer is equally skillful in the narrowing process, in which the client is ordinarily focusing on identifying those occupational options that relate most closely to a combination of personal attributes. It is a simple step to move from asking the computer "What occupations in the memory bank involve mechanical activities?" to asking "What occupations in the memory bank that involve mechanical activities also involve high manual dexterity, are performed entirely indoors, don't require shift work, pay at least a specified annual income, and exist in this geographic region?" Obviously, the combination of personal attributes and other factors can be manipulated in many ways—including most desired factors, excluding factors the person wishes to avoid, taking any one factor from a group of several, readjusting an earlier command to a more or less demanding level, and so on.

Making Plans

Many parts of the planning phase can be incorporated in computer-assisted systems in ways that are very helpful to the client. Most obvious are those that deal with training and educational programs and those that relate to job search procedures.

Many computer-assisted systems handle information about educational and training programs in a parallel fashion to occupational information. This often means that files exist according to type and level of education—for example, apprenticeship programs, 2-year schools, 4-year schools, graduate and professional schools, and so forth. A user can readily identify schools at the appropriate level that offer desired programs and then, by using other personally important variables, narrow the list as far as he wishes.

Job search procedures vary considerably among the various systems. Many include at least basic information on how one prepares for specific occupations and the types of work settings in which those occupational members are found. The best statewide career information delivery systems (CIDS) incorporate information from the state employment security agency, including such data as actual vacancies, expected hiring numbers, and salary and wage data. Because such information is so volatile, currency and comprehensiveness are still difficult to acquire and maintain.

STATUS OF COMPUTER-ASSISTED CAREER GUIDANCE SYSTEMS

Historical Background

Serious efforts were undertaken as early as the mid-1960s to relate computer technology to career counseling. Some of the early attempts are still operational today, although modernized and expanded. Jo Ann Harris–Bowlsbey was instrumental in the planning that led to the Computerized Vocational Information System (CVIS), placed in operation in 1968. At the same time, Donald Super and Roger Myers of Columbia University were working with Frank Minor of IBM to create the Education and Career Exploration System (ECES), and David Tiedeman of Harvard and his colleagues were developing a system called Information System for Vocational Decisions (ISVD). CVIS provided a method for storing information about approximately 400 occupations arranged in the classification system originally developed by Roe (1956). The information file also included certain items of individual information for each student user, such as class rank, composite achievement and ability test scores, and interest inventory scores, thus permitting some comparison of prior data with requirements for entry and success in occupations. The system was primarily on-line information retrieval, and it effectively capitalized on the technology available at that time. It continued as a pilot program until 1972 and was then established as a demonstration center leading to widespread adoption of the system.

Both ECES and ISVD were more extensive efforts to computerize larger portions of the counseling process. Both provided for development and storage of self-descriptive information that would assist the client in better self-understanding; extensive data about future possibilities (in ECES this included occupations and educational files, and in ISVD these two areas were supplemented by files on military service and family); and procedures for clarifying and developing plans. Both reached the operational stage in the 1969–1970 period. The elaborate program incorporated in each system was theoretically sound, useful to clients, and technologically possible. Both, however, required such heavy use of computer time that they were ahead of reality in terms of cost-effectiveness, considering the developmental state of computers; consequently, neither has been widely adopted. Several of Tiedeman's colleagues on the ISVD project later turned to the development of a simpler system, which has become the Guidance Information System (GIS) in extensive use today.

During the early developmental years, essentially 1965 to 1980, computer technology was basically restricted to large, mainframe systems that were costly to operate both in terms of time and money. Harris–Bowlsbey (1990) identifies 11 systems that were developed and put into usage during that period:

AUTOCOUN
CHOICES
CIS (Career Information System)
COIS (Computerized Occupational Information System)
CVIS (Computerized Vocational Information System)
DISCOVER
ECES (Education and Career Exploration System)
GIS (Guidance Information System)
ISVD (Information System for Vocational Decisions)
SIGI (System for Interactive Guidance Information)
TGIS (Total Guidance Information System)

One can deduce from the names of these early systems that two types of programs were being developed. One group emphasized information and focused on building systems in which one could search easily and rapidly for quality information about occupations and educational or training institutions. The other branch concentrated on the career planning process and provided use of self-information, decision-making strategies, and career development concepts. Very few systems were or are purely one type with total disregard for the other. The difference is primarily one of major emphasis. Recent years have shown movement toward the center; that is, inclusion of both branches. Two from each branch are discussed later in this chapter.

Present Status

The rapid progress of computer technology resulted in the availability of microcomputers by the mid-1980s with the operational and storage capability of mainframe machines of the mid-1960s, and at far less cost. This expansion of power and reduction of cost now makes CACG a practical tool for almost every agency involved in assisting the career development process. Harris–Bowlsbey (1990) points out that the reason most frequently given for not acquiring or using a CACG system is cost. Nevertheless, in 1990, this service could be provided for $2 or less per user hour, including replacement of hardware on a 3-year cycle.

McKinlay (1990), reporting 1987–1988 data obtained from the Association of Computer-Based Systems for Career Information (ACSCI), and Lester (1990), reporting 1988 data obtained by the National Occupational Information Coordinating Committee (NOICC), show general concurrence on the extent of systems and usage for that time. There were 49 state-based career information delivery systems (CIDS) providing information to approximately 14,000 to 15,000 user sites. Of these, about 70 percent were in K-12 schools and served approximately 70 percent of the 5 million users. According to McKinlay, nearly one fourth of the country's high schools are served by systems supplied by state-based system operators (CIDS). Beyond elementary and secondary schools, the next largest user group was correctional institutions, with about 8 percent of the systems. Other groups, such as vocational schools, community colleges, degree-granting colleges or universities, the Employment Service, counseling agencies, and libraries each possessed 4 to 6 percent of the reported systems.

Many state-based systems have developed through NOICC funding, according to McCormac (1988). More than two thirds of the local site systems involve computers in some way. Even though the expansion of CACG systems from the early 1980s to the 1987–1988 period was very rapid, Harris–Bowlsbey (1990) points out that less than 10 percent of the population that needs access to CACG actually has it. She emphasizes a need for systems in all schools as well as postsecondary institutions and other social agencies that serve out-of-school individuals.

Thompson and LaRochelle (1985) describe the Connecticut CIDS. Originally funded by a NOICC grant in 1979, it is representative of many of the state programs that came on line in the early 1980s. The system is named CONSIDER/GIS and is based on the Guidance Information System (discussed in more detail later in this chapter). The system includes 13 files of information on occupations, education, and educational financial aid. Seven of the files are national information. Thompson and LaRochelle report that 60 percent of the clients want to use the system again, 96 percent of the counselors reported that clients were satisfied or very satisfied, and the system was rated superior by 94 percent of the counselors. Most sites included in the report appear to be educational institutions; thus the population included is somewhat narrower than the general population.

Lester (1990) reports that the Maine State Occupational Information Coordinating Committee (SOICC) has already implemented a multisystem program so that different user agencies can have access to the type of system that best fits their needs. She also reports that Michigan has developed a means of integrating information about the state job training and adult education program into its statewide system to assist residents to learn about education and training services, identify interests and skills, develop a career plan, prepare a resume, and obtain placement assistance. In addition, Pennsylvania has a pilot project that establishes career/job resource centers in public libraries and other facilities easily available to adults.

In addition to the systems that exist, there are two other types of computer usage in career development programs. One of these includes specialized software packages, usually focused on a particular aspect of the total process (e.g., resume writing or job hunting). These are usually available from commercial vendors. The second type can be described as "home grown" and consists of locally developed programs, usually designed to meet specific, unusual local situations or to avoid what is thought to be "too costly" commercial programs. Kuhlman (1988), after developing programs for a local site, urges the use of commercially available programs because of the cost in time and funds to develop individual programs.

Gysbers (1990) describes several rationalizations used by counselors who are reluctant to incorporate computerized programs in their career development efforts. These include, "Computers are outside the counseling process," "Computers, like printed materials, are used elsewhere," and "Computer systems take too much time." He also proposes ways by which those counselors can use CACG in each step of the counseling process.

Future Possibilities

Participants in the international teleconference mentioned previously produced a series of recommendations for improving both design and usage of CACG systems. Sampson, Reardon, Lenz, and Morgenthau (1990) summarize and group these proposals into six broad categories. These topics and brief descriptive statements include the following:

1. *Improved design and use of CACG is primarily dependent upon improved training systems.* Better training programs should be directed toward pre-service training in counselor education; better materials and procedures for training support; attention to operational use of CACG systems; better training for paraprofessionals, administrators, and support personnel; dissemination of validated training materials; and identification of training as a priority activity by all involved personnel.
2. *Differential effects and programming of systems for varied client groups, career guidance environments, and levels of counselor support.* Systems should be intentionally designed for, and used with, special populations, such as unemployed youth and adults, children, ethnic minorities, and disabled persons.
3. *Increased local funding, legislative support, and public information for career guidance in general and CACG systems in particular.*
4. *Conceptualizing effective use of CACG within the context of a comprehensive system of career guidance services.*
5. *Needed improvements in software.* This includes better client record keeping, use of video disk technology, more demonstrated validity in self-assessment and search procedures, and improved career information data bases.
6. *Improved dissemination of information about comparative system features, successful implementation models, and outcome studies on the effects of CACG systems.* (pp. 100–102)

WIDELY USED SYSTEMS AND MATERIALS

There are several sources the reader can consult for information about available systems. One obvious source is the distributor for each. The advantage, and a big one, is that information can be expected to be up to date. The disadvantage is the "sales-pitch" slant that is likely to accompany the information. The state CIDS office or the nearest Employment Service Office can provide information on the statewide program. Local educational institutions may have an individually operated system or cooperate with other institutions in a jointly operated system. Descriptive articles and research reports can be found in the professional counseling journals. State and national professional meetings are also likely sources of information on existing systems and new developments.

In this section we examine briefly four of the systems and some of the software packages that were prevalent in 1991.

Career Information System (CIS)

The CIS program was developed as the Oregon state system under an early Department of Labor grant (1969), directed by Dr. Bruce McKinlay. A separate organization, National CIS, now exists to coordinate the application of CIS elsewhere and to provide additional services in the development of software and provision of training. From the beginning CIS has emphasized the use of local or regional information; as a result, each local CIS system has modified and adjusted the basic plan to fit the needs in that user area. The system also has incorporated specific training and preparation for those individuals such as counselors, librarians, and teachers who are involved in helping clients use the system. The system is currently used in educational settings, such as high schools and colleges, and in employment service agencies, prisons, rehabilitation agencies, and training programs. It is the basic system in 16 state CIDS, the largest number for any system.

The system includes several components. The access strategy, called QUEST, is a brief 25-item questionnaire related to self-estimates of physical limitations, geographic preferences, anticipated educational level, aptitudes, interests, and desired beginning wage. Several QUEST items are based on occupational factors identified by Department of Labor analysis of occupations. QUEST is available on line or in a needlesort format (notched cards that can be sorted with a needlelike device). Users are provided a printout of occupations related to their combined QUEST responses. The occupational descriptions are brief 300-word summaries of between 250 and 550 occupations, including duties, pay, aptitudes, work setting, hiring practices, outlook, and current employment. Information is locally, state, and nationally based and updated regularly.

Kjos (1987) reports a study of 100 participants from a base population of 3,000 unemployed in south Chicago. QUEST was administered to each participant; 70 percent of the group had been unemployed for an average of

3 years. The purpose of the study was to determine if the QUEST list of occupations selected by the individual included occupations that directly or indirectly matched prior work experience. Kjos concludes that QUEST was generally reflective of past work experience regardless of age, educational attainment, or preferred beginning wage.

In addition to QUEST and the occupational description file, most CIS systems include a preparation file and a bibliography file in the occupational information section, and a program file and school file in the educational information section. The preparation file identifies ways to prepare for an occupation and includes information on skills needed, licensing information, and a cross-reference to related postsecondary training. The bibliography file lists the most pertinent published sources for further information on each occupation. The program file includes information on postsecondary educational programs in the CIS site area. The information includes a description of degrees offered, specialties, program objectives, courses, and lists of schools that offer the program. The school file contains information on all the 2- and 4-year colleges and proprietary schools in the area. Institutions in the school file can be compared simultaneously, three at a time, on 65 different information topics.

In addition to these files, the Oregon CIS includes six additional files, some of which are used in other CIS programs. These additional files include an attribute file showing QUEST responses related to each occupation, an employment file that aids in job search, a visit file that includes names of local individuals working in each occupation who are willing to discuss the occupations with CIS users, a clubs file, a national school file listing 1,700 four-year colleges, and a financial aid file.

The *User's Handbook* includes instructions for operating the system as well as the QUEST items, and users are expected to complete QUEST and read the instructions before using the system. Additional help is included in the computer system. Most users find the system easy to use, interesting, and helpful. The average on-line time is 30 minutes per use, and many users return for further information at least once within the year.

Maze and Cummings (1982) report that CIS has been adapted to more than 10 models of computers to meet the needs of various regional and state users. Per-user cost is reduced by the relatively brief time needed on the terminal but is increased by the somewhat higher cost of obtaining and updating local data. Because CIS is used in several different settings, there is likely to be considerable variation in charges by participating agencies.

Factors that might be considered as limitations by some evaluators could well be counted as assets by others. The system does not attempt to provide guidance for the user beyond the items in QUEST that are used to narrow the list of occupations the user considers. CIS does not incorporate any on-line assessment; thus clients may be uncertain of personal attributes or characteristics they could profitably identify in the interaction with the computer. Counselor help will often be needed before the user is ready to use the system. Didactic modules that teach the client how to use CIS, or that explain the available system, do not exist on line. This information is available to the client in the *User's Handbook*. A further potential limitation can also arise from the basic concept on which CIS has been developed—that is, the flexibility that allows the system to emphasize local information and adjust to local clientele needs can result in variable quality of information between CIS franchises.

Guidance Information System (GIS)

The Guidance Information System is one of the most widely used of the existing systems, with reported use in 1990 at more than 4,500 locations. Nationally, GIS is operated by Houghton Mifflin. GIS provides access to national data in six files—occupations, 4-year colleges, 2-year colleges, graduate schools, financial aid information, and armed services occupations. The occupations file contains over 1,000 primary occupational listings, with reference to another 2,500 related jobs; the armed services file contains information on over 200 military occupations; the 2- and 4-year college files include information on over 3,400 educational institutions; and the graduate school file has information on 1,500 schools. In addition to these national files, local or regional information files can be developed covering such topics as vocational schools, local sources of financial aid, and local human services. Local occupational information can be incorporated with the national file so that the user obtains both national and local information for those occupations for which local information has been developed. The overall aim of GIS is to deliver to the user information that is useful in the career decision-making process.

Information in the files is arranged according to groups of characteristics or attributes. For example, the occupations file includes data on interests (11 characteristics), aptitudes (10 characteristics), physical demands (12 characteristics), work conditions (9 characteristics), lifestyle (16 characteristics), salary (12 characteristics), employment potential (5 characteristics), education and training (21 characteristics), and other qualifications (5 characteristics). The 4-year college file is arranged according to academic program (approximately 450 characteristics), location (68 characteristics), type of institution (14 characteristics), undergraduate enrollment (11 characteristics), control (2 characteristics), religious affiliation (5 characteristics), accreditation (5 characteristics), faculty (2 characteristics), admissions information (13 characteristics), academic characteristics of first-year students (22 characteristics), admissions policies (15 characteristics), calendar plan (6 characteristics), degree requirements (3 characteristics), student body data (5 characteristics), annual costs (24 characteristics), residence policies (11 characteristics), financial aid (13 characteristics), special programs (27 characteristics), ROTC (4 characteristics), campus life (25 characteristics), athletic programs (129 characteristics), and athletic scholarships (86 characteristics).

Users can obtain general or detailed information about occupations or schools in which they are interested. The PRINT command can be used to obtain general information about a specific occupation or school or about several occupations or schools. The ITEMIZE command can be used similarly to obtain detailed information either about a single occupation or school or about several. If desired, detailed information about specific sets of characteristics can be obtained without itemizing all the information in the file. This request for general or detailed information about one or more occupations or schools is labeled the *direct method*. Obviously, it is most useful when the client has an occupation or school in mind and wants to obtain information about it. The armed services file works only with this method. All other files can also be approached in this way.

The *search method* is probably used more frequently. This approach is designed to help the user who wants to know what occupations or schools would meet characteristics or requirements she might have in mind. Local worksheets for the various files are usually arranged so that they list brief identifiers for each of the characteristics included in the file. The user is asked first to identify those characteristics to be included, those to be excluded, and those that can be combined on an either/or basis. Next the user is asked to arrange these marked items in a hierarchy with the most important item, either inclusion or exclusion, listed first. Summary sheets are often provided for this ranking. The ADD command is used to enter those characteristics to be included, and the SUBTRACT command is used for excluded items. If combined items exist on the list, the EITHER/OR command tells the computer to include any occupation or college that has at least one of the listed characteristics. Starting with all occupations or schools in the file being searched, the system reports after each entry the number that remain. As each ADD or SUBTRACT is made, the number qualifying dwindles. When those occupations or schools remaining in the list number 25 or fewer, the user can ask for the names of those remaining. This list can then be used with the PRINT or ITEMIZE commands described earlier. If the user enters a command that reduces the list too drastically, or if the user changes her mind about the characteristics, the DELETE command eliminates that characteristic from the search. The user has great flexibility in organizing the search and can capitalize on personal preferences as well as change directions during the process. The user also can move from one file to another easily— for example, from the occupations file where possible jobs were identified to one of the school files to explore information about relevant preparatory programs.

Efficient use of terminal time requires the user to give prior consideration to those characteristics that are important to her. This can be done either independently or with the counselor, and many GIS sites have locally developed worksheets that facilitate identifying the characteristics the user wants to include. As the various characteristics are entered, the computer immediately responds with the number of occupations or schools remaining on the list; thus the user can see at once the impact of that particular characteristic. If the user previously has identified the characteristics she is most interested in, the required terminal time is usually not more than 10 or 15 minutes.

The *User's Guide* is a handbook that explains how the system operates and includes a description of each characteristic included in the national files. The *Guide* is revised regularly and distributed to centers using GIS. In addition to the *User's Guide*, there are indexes for each of the national files. Each index is most useful for the user who wishes to apply the direct method. For example, the *Occupations Index* arranges occupations according to a cluster system, the *Dictionary of Occupational Titles* code number, and alphabetically. Additional supplementary materials are available.

A recent GIS format change for microcomputer users permits the presentation of characteristics of all files on screen so that the user can select them from there rather than from the *Guide* or a local worksheet. The major search commands are visible at the bottom of the screen at all times, and a user can type HELP followed by a command letter to obtain an on-screen explanation of how to use that command. In addition, a change has been made in the use of interest inventory data. The Harrington–O'Shea Career Decision-Making System is available on line; after completing the inventory (including items on occupational preference, school subject preferences, future educational plans, job values, and self-reported abilities), the user is presented with titles of career clusters related to the responses. It is also now possible to enter results from eight other interest inventories (California Occupational Preference Schedule, Career Assessment Inventory, Harrington–O'Shea Career Decision-Making, Job-O, Kuder General Interest, Ohio Vocational Interest Survey, Self-Directed Search, and Strong Interest Inventory) taken before using the computer and thus obtain a list of related occupations in the OCCU file.

Most clients will want and/or need counselor help both before and after terminal use. Although the characteristics included in the various files are clear and easily understood, their relationship to the client's psychological world becomes more apparent in a counseling session. Similarly, the final printout of the narrowed list of occupations or schools may well leave the user without a sense of closure. The counselor can help the user consider exploratory steps to acquire additional information on the listed items that will lead to decision making and subsequent planning.

Discover

The development of DISCOVER has been largely the work of Jo Ann Harris–Bowlsbey and, in part, is an extension of her earlier effort on CVIS, one of the earliest systems that gained widespread usage. DISCOVER was developed as a systematic career guidance program to assist in career development activities at the secondary school level. From its earliest days, its emphasis has been on the career planning process. Harris–Bowlsbey (1990) stresses that competitive pressures among the various systems require updating and redevelopment on a fairly short cycle of 5 to 6 years. DISCOVER has followed such a pattern and has been very successful in anticipating market needs and staying abreast of those needs.

DISCOVER, in 1991, offered five different versions for individuals at the junior high level, the high school level, college and adults in transition level, employees and organizations, and a retirement planning version. Each version can stand alone or fit with the others to form an integrated approach as the individual progresses educationally. While the plan to integrate levels is certainly worthy, it does appear to disregard the very high likelihood of revision and modifications as CACG systems continue to evolve.

The junior high school version, designed for students in grades 6 to 9, is focused toward helping them plan for high school. The conceptual approach, based on the ACT World-of-Work Map (described in Chapter 6), is intended to give students a start in career exploration with an overview of the world of work and identification of personal characteristics. The junior high version has an entry/exit section and three major modules. The individual may choose to use any one or all three of the modules.

Entry/Exit

This section explains how to use the system and collect identifying information in order to store student records, and it explains the career planning process used in the modules. When ready to sign off, students can save the results for later use or reference. The modules are as follows:

1. *You and the World of Work:* This module uses the ACT World-of-Work Map described in Chapter 6. Users can participate in a World-of-Work Map game that requires identifying basic work tasks involved in nine job-related activities. They are required to become familiar with basic work tasks (working with people, data, things, or combinations of these) and examples of typical activities for each. Users are asked to identify whether they would enjoy the activity, thus beginning awareness of their reactions to work activities.

2. *Exploring Occupations:* In this module students systematically explore occupations using the World-of-Work Map and Holland's typology. Students can enter their scores on any of several achievement tests, grades earned in selected courses, or self-ratings in several ability areas, to relate specific achievement or ability to various occupational clusters. Occupational information can be accessed by adding the anticipated educational level students hope to attain before going to work.

3. *Planning for High School:* This module uses the student's tentative career and educational aspirations to plan a high school program of studies. If desired, schools can incorporate local graduation requirements and course offerings in this section.

The high school version places primary emphasis on career direction and thereby proposes to offer help to both students whose plans are beginning to crystallize or students who are still undecided or uncertain. This version provides modules at each step of the career planning process. There are seven in all, and each is divided into subparts that can be used independently if desired. Several activities (e.g., interest assessment) are available either on line through the computer or in paper-and-pencil format not requiring computer time. The seven modules are as follows:

1. *Beginning the Career Journey:* In this module the user checks his level of career decision-making maturity to determine which later modules will be most useful. A 36-item inventory, taken either on or off line, is keyed to the remaining modules and provides a list of modules most likely to be helpful.

2. *Learning about the World of Work:* This section presents the ACT World-of-Work Map and explains the concepts of work tasks, map regions, clusters, and job families.

3. *Learning about Yourself:* This module helps the user acquire information about self through a series of exercises, including interest assessment and other devices that also can be completed on or off line. Factors besides interest include abilities, work-related values, and experiences. The module can also accept data from a range of previously completed interest and aptitude measures.

4. *Finding Occupations:* This module generates lists of occupations for consideration and exploration. The user can select suboptions from an array of categories such as employment outlook, job setting, work hours, amount of supervision, job pressure, and education needed.

5. *Learning about Occupations:* This module provides detailed information about any of the 458 occupations included in the file. Information is updated annually. As new occupations become significant in the labor market, they are added to the file. DISCOVER claims that the 458 occupations represent 95 percent of the employment opportunities in the United States.

6. *Making Educational Choices:* This module presents information on educational preparation leading to the occupations identified in Module 5. Appropriate majors or programs of study are also listed for chosen occupations.

7. *Planning Next Steps:* This module provides information about postsecondary educational opportunities. The file includes 2,921 vocational-technical schools, 1,458 two-year colleges, 1,731 four-year colleges, 1,241 graduate schools, 144 external degree programs, and 212 military programs.

The college and adult version of DISCOVER consists of modules 1 through 7 of the high school version, with two additional modules:

8. *Planning Your Career:* This module is designed for adults in transition or others beyond the college age group. It uses Super's Life/Career

Rainbow (1990) as the basis for exploring the various roles in each person's life. Users can apply the module to plan for changes in their future.

9. *Making Transitions:* This module helps users understand career transitions that are increasingly common, the pressures and tensions that one encounters in such transitions, and how to deal with and control these factors.

The organization version of DISCOVER is intended for use by employees in larger business and industrial settings. Its purpose is to assist employees to relate information about themselves to career opportunities in-house, and thus to develop plans to capitalize on available career advancement paths. The system provides a great deal of flexibility, drawing on the modules previously described to help the employee through the following four steps:

1. Reviewing and Organizing What You Know about Yourself
2. Learning about Jobs and Your Organization
3. Identifying Options and Making Plans
4. Putting Plans into Action

The system can be customized to fit the needs of the specific company by incorporating information about personnel policies and procedures, company position descriptions, information about training programs, occupations outside the company, etc.

Like the organization version, the retirement planning system is designed for use in large businesses or organizations to assist employees in making plans for their retirement years. It can be used with or apart from the organization system. It consists of an introductory module followed by four major sections with the following titles:

1. Mastering Your Lifestyle: Changes in Roles, Relationships, and Use of Time
2. Mastering Your Financial Planning
3. Mastering Your Physical Well-being
4. Mastering Your Living Arrangements

Roselle and Hummel (1988) report a study of 12 college students to examine the relationship between intellectual development and effective use of DISCOVER. Students with higher scores on the Measure of Intellectual Development showed higher ability to use DISCOVER as one more tool in career planning, to adapt easily to the system, and to show greater self-knowledge. This suggests that most users will need assistance in using the system for maximum advantage in reverse proportion to intellectual development. Shahnasarian and Peterson (1988) report that having students view a brief videotape explaining Holland's typology improved their thinking about occupational possibilities; however, those who did not view the videotape felt more certain of their vocational choices. Fukuyama, Probert, Neimeyer, Nevill, and Metzler (1988) report that completion of the college system resulted in higher self-efficacy scores for undergraduates. The students who had completed the system were much more certain of their occupational plans than students who had not used DISCOVER. Garis and Niles (1990) report a study using DISCOVER and SIGI with career planning courses matched against students taking the courses without access to CACG. Their results do not show significant increases when computer systems are added.

System of Interactive Guidance and Information (SIGI)

SIGI, now known as SIGI PLUS, is the product of developmental effort by a research group led by Martin Katz at Educational Testing Service. Katz (1990) describes the early activities that resulted in SIGI. It was originally intended for use by students in or about to enter 2-year colleges. It is now applied more broadly, including usage in 4-year schools and with out-of-school adults in a variety of settings.

The philosophic basis for SIGI proposes that values identification and clarification are basic to an effective career decision process involving evaluation of the rewards and risks that accompany each option. The system covers the major aspects of career decision making, using nine separate modules or sections. Each module provides an array of user activities that can be used selectively or entirely. The introductory section can recommend specific pathways based on user-provided personal information about present career status. Like DISCOVER, the system provides a means of storing client records that permits the client to recall information from previous system usage. Included in the following brief descriptions of the nine modules is a question that indicates the purpose of the section, a description of what the client can do, and some of the special features built into the module.

1. ***Introduction*** *What is in SIGI PLUS?*

   Included: An overview of SIGI PLUS and a recommended pathway based on client provided information.

   Features: Clear explanation; directs clients to sections that apply to them; permits requests for additional information about subsequent parts.

2. ***Self-Assessment*** *What do I want? What am I good at?*

   Included: Work-related values and personal choices of most importance; choice of main interest fields; consideration of work activities and evaluation of likes and what they do well; a game to help clarify values.

   Features: Chance to clarify personal values, interests, and skills; helps identify what's most important personally; maintains emphasis on personal values; uses an activities inventory that links interests and skills; relates these to everyday life.

3. ***Search*** *What occupations might I like?*

    Included: Identification of preferred work features; identification of work features client wishes to avoid; creates a list of occupations having the preferred features.

    Features: Helps client develop a personal list of occupational alternatives; allows any combination of values, interests, skills, level of education, and features to be avoided; permits exclusion of occupations client does not want to consider; explains which factor eliminated a specific occupation not on the list.

4. ***Information*** *What occupations might I like?*

    Included: Selection of one or two occupations at a time to match against information such as skills required, advancement possibilities, potential income, national employment outlook, and educational requirements.

    Features: Answers 27 questions about each selected occupation, gives alternate job titles, provides sources for additional information, possible to add local information.

5. ***Skills*** *Can I do what's required?*

    Included: Lists specific skills required for any listed occupation; self-rating on skills required.

    Features: Selection of any included occupation; shows how work skills are applied in the specific occupation; provides examples of how these skills are applied in everyday life; includes information on managerial and supervisory skills.

6. ***Preparing*** *Can I do what's required?*

    Included: Shows typical preparatory paths, estimates client's likelihood of completing preparation.

    Features: Links career planning to preparatory programs; shows typical preparation for each specific field, including courses and course descriptions if desired; considers factors related to acquiring preparation such as finding time, finding money, handling the difficulty, staying motivated.

7. ***Coping*** *Can I do what's required?*

    Included: Suggestions on dealing with issues related to preparation such as finding time and money; arranging care for others; obtaining school credit for present knowledge; learning to handle preparation-related worries.

Features: Specific suggestions for time management; financing alternatives; responds to common preparation worries; information on establishing academic credit; permits addition of local information.

8. **Deciding** *What's right for me?*

Included: Client can match three occupations at a time for rewards, anticipated employment, chances for entrance and success, overall evaluation.

Features: Summarizes information from previous sections; provides a decision-making strategy; permits comparison of occupation with possible new careers; introduces basis for graphic comparison of alternatives.

9. **Next Steps** *How do I put my plan into action?*

Included: Clients can start toward career goal by planning short-term goals such as more education or training; developing new skills; proving they can do the work; building a network of contacts; writing a resume; overcoming obstacles.

Features: Helps identify specific steps; provides concrete suggestions, tips, and models for resume writing; prompts planning immediate first steps.

Maze and Cummings (1982) report that the average user spends 3.5 hours to complete the process. This time is all computer-connect and terminal use time and therefore is relatively costly under present conditions. SIGI software has been developed for use with a variety of computers of all three sizes.

Like other systems, SIGI's strengths and weaknesses depend on how those characteristics are valued by user sites. SIGI is based on a clearly conceived theoretical position. It emphasizes the importance of values, and some will see it as underplaying other important attributes. It focuses on an educationally related clientele, so some will see it as serving other groups less adequately. It requires the user to progress methodically through its conception of the career decision process, so some will see it as more rigid and less flexible than systems that do not adhere to a clear philosophic position.

Other Systems

Two other systems are used widely in the United States. McKinlay (1990) reports that CHOICES (Computerized Heuristic Occupational Information and Career Exploration System), originally developed for Canadian users, has been adopted by five states for their statewide CID system and in 1988 served about 700 sites. Although largely aimed toward information access and retrieval, CHOICES does include aspects of career exploration.

Designed for use on microcomputers, CHOICES has two major sections, called components: occupations and colleges. The occupations component consists of two sections called *Search* and *Information*. Data about the 675 primary occupations included in the system are drawn from the *Occupational Employment Statistics (OES)* discussed in Chapter 4. These data are based on a combination of *Standard Occupational Classification* and *Dictionary of Occupational Titles* systems, and they cover the major portion of the labor market in the United States.

Information about included occupations is divided into four categories, namely, identification data, descriptive data, coded attribute data, and similar occupations data. The coded attribute data section includes 17 *topics*, such as education, work sites, physical demands, temperaments, earnings, aptitudes, and interests. The Explore Route permits the user to hunt for occupations compatible to her evaluation of the personal importance of these topics. The Information Route permits the user either to obtain specific coded attribute information about a particular occupation or to compare two occupations simultaneously on the attributes.

Information about 2,400 two- and four-year colleges is structured in parallel fashion. The general categories of information, again called *topics*, include geographic location, programs, institutional types, tuition, enrollment, community size, athletic programs, and on-campus housing. As with occupations topics, users are asked to complete a personal profile that reports their priority for the topics as well as personal preferences within each one. These responses can then be used to search for institutions that match personal preferences or to obtain specific information about institutions for which they desire further details.

C-LECT (Computer-Linked Exploration of Careers and Training), marketed by Chronicle Guidance Publications, also includes identification of personal temperament and interest patterns in addition to occupational and educational information. Both CHOICES and C-LECT are designed for general use in the career development process and, thereby, are used mainly in educational settings. C-LECT is quite brief compared to the more extensive programs described earlier and usually requires less than an hour to complete.

Some programs or systems are designed for either special purposes or special clientele. Two of these are described briefly as representative of a field that can be expected to expand rapidly.

Career Navigator is a software system designed specifically to assist job seekers, particularly new entrants interested in business and professional careers. The system has been developed by Drake Beam Morin Inc., a consulting firm that has specialized in out-placement—a process of helping discharged employees to find new opportunities elsewhere. The package includes four computer diskettes and a 200-page manual that has quizzes, worksheets, short case studies, examples of resumes, letters, and interview sessions. Sections of the program include the following: Start the Program, Know Yourself, How to Communicate, Develop Your Job Search Tools, Conduct Your Job Search Campaign, and Land the Job. Each section includes a sequence of related activities, skill-developing tasks, time schedules, etc. Garis and Hess (1989) report a study of College of Business juniors and seniors using Career Navigator with a comparable group enrolled in a course dealing with professional development and a control group with access to neither. The Career Navigator group scored higher on a questionnaire related to confidence and progress in career implementation and on a questionnaire about their knowledge of the job search process.

Career Design 1.4 consists of many brief modules that, by questioning the user, increase self-understanding and clarify career goals. It appears to be most useful for individuals in transition, contemplating a job change or even searching for a new direction. The software is self-contained and has no workbook or accompanying manual. Companies such as Jist, Career Aids, or Wintergreen Software offer numerous software packages. A new publication, available from the American Association for Counseling and Development entitled *Counseling Software Guide* and edited by Garry Walz and Jeanne Bleuer, provides a comprehensive review of software related to the counseling field. The *Guide* is to be updated periodically.

SUMMARY

A crucial question often raised as one evaluates a new technique or device is, "What does the research show?" Although it is a fair question to ask, it is very difficult to organize a satisfactory answer when conditions remain in a state of flux. Perhaps a reasonable analogy is the dilemma faced by someone who decides to use reports from a reliable consumer products research agency when purchasing a new automobile. When the model is new, no research is available; by the time the car has been in use for 3 years and repair data are available, the vehicle has been sufficiently modified so that the data cannot be applied to the current model.

Bloch and Kinnison (1989) report the results of ratings of computer-assisted systems in use in New York state. User satisfaction was evaluated by ratings completed by school principals, school counselors, students, and parents in 26 high schools. Comprehensiveness was evaluated by scoring a checklist of items submitted by system vendors. Accuracy was rated on a scale developed for independent evaluation of contents of printouts of occupational and college information. Effectiveness was measured by a review panel of experts who observed actual use of the systems. The three separate components were combined into a cumulative score, with 100 representing a perfect system. The component and cumulative scores are reported in Table 8.1. It should be noted that SIGI was one of the systems in use but was excluded from the study because of equipment failure at the time of the review panel's observation.

Frequent modification of both hardware and software must be expected as computer-based programs are integrated into career resource cen-

TABLE 8.1   *Final Rating of CIDS: Summation of All Factors*

Rank	System	Contents	Information Accuracy	Review Panel	Cumulative Score
1	CIS	94.00	65.26	67.33	75.53
2	GIS	68.00	71.58	81.85	73.81
3	CHOICES	67.34	67.37	84.24	72.98
4	DISCOVER	62.00	67.37	81.48	70.28
5	C-LECT	79.00	43.16	72.76	64.97

Source: Bloch and Kinnison, 1989. Reprinted with permission.

ters, counselors' offices, and classrooms. No one can estimate precisely the time required to reach a plateau where refinement and improvement continues but at a less rapid pace than is occurring today. Until such a plateau becomes evident, research will be restricted by the rapidity of change. Johnston, Buescher, and Heppner (1988) emphasize the need for research related to CACG systems, as does Katz (1990).

McKinlay (1990) identifies several factors that will be crucial in determining the role of CACG systems in the future. He lists quality of information, both accuracy and usefulness, as the major factor. Additional factors include more effective use of technological components; better management of systems by faster delivery of information and more efficient use; and programs that will serve important population segments not currently reached by existing operations.

REFERENCES

Bloch, D. P., & Kinnison, J. F. (1989). A method for rating computer-based career information delivery systems. *Measurement and Evaluation in Counseling and Development, 21,* 177–187.

Fukuyama, M. A., Probert, B. S., Neimeyer, G. J., Nevill, D. D., & Metzler, A. E. (1988). Effects of DISCOVER on career self-efficacy and decision making of undergraduates. *Career Development Quarterly, 37,* 56–62.

Garis, J. W., & Hess, H. R. (1989). Career Navigator: Its use with college students beginning the job search process. *Career Development Quarterly, 38,* 65–74.

Garis, J. W., & Niles, S. G. (1990). The separate and combined effects of SIGI or DISCOVER and a career planning course on undecided university students. *Career Development Quarterly, 38,* 261–274.

Gysbers, N. C. (1990). Computer-based career guidance systems: Their past, present, and a possible future—A reaction. In J. P. Sampson, Jr. and R. C. Reardon (Eds.), *Enhancing the design and use of computer-assisted career guidance systems.* Alexandria, VA: National Career Development Association.

Harris–Bowlsbey, J. (1990). Computer-based career guidance systems: Their past, present and a possible future. In J. P. Sampson, Jr. & R. C. Reardon (Eds.), *Enhancing the design and use of computer-assisted career guidance systems.* Alexandria, VA: National Career Development Association.

Johnston, J. A., Buescher, K. L., & Heppner, M. J. (1988). Computerized career information and guidance systems: Caveat emptor. *Journal of Counseling and Development, 67,* 39–41.

Katz, M. R. (1990). Yesterday, today, and tomorrow. In J. P. Sampson, Jr., & R. C. Reardon (Eds.), *Enhancing the design and use of computer-assisted career guidance systems.* Alexandria, VA: National Career Development Association.

Kjos, D. L. (1987). QUEST: Work experience and the results of an occupational search questionnaire among unemployed adults. *Career Development Quarterly, 35,* 326–336.

Kuhlman, G. A. (1988). Computer and video applications in career services programs. *Career Development Quarterly, 37,* 177–182.

Lester, J. N. (1990). Career information in career development: A public policy reaction. In J. P. Sampson, Jr., & R. C. Reardon (Eds.), *Enhancing the design and use of computer-assisted career guidance systems.* Alexandria, VA: National Career Development Association.

Maze, M., & Cummings, R. (1982). *How to select a computer assisted career guidance system.* Madison, WI: Wisconsin Vocational Studies Center.

McCormac, M. E. (1988). The use of career information delivery systems in the States. *Journal of Career Development, 14* (3), 196–204.

McKinlay, B. (1990). Information systems in career development: History and prospects. In J. P. Sampson, Jr., & R. C. Reardon (Eds.), *Enhancing the design and use of computer-assisted career guidance systems.* Alexandria, VA: National Career Development Association.

Roe, A. (1956). *The psychology of occupations.* New York: Wiley.

Roselle, B. E., & Hummel, T. J. (1988). Intellectual development and interaction effectiveness with DISCOVER. *Career Development Quarterly, 36,* 241–250.

Sampson, J. P., Jr., & Reardon, R. C. (Eds.) (1990). *Enhancing the design and use of computer-assisted career guidance systems.* Alexandria, VA: National Career Development Association.

Sampson, J. P., Jr., Reardon, R. C., Lenz, J. G., & Morgenthau, E. D. (1990). North American conference recommendations. In J. P. Sampson, Jr., & R. C. Reardon (Eds.), *Enhancing the design and use of computer-assisted career guidance systems.* Alexandria, VA: National Career Development Association.

Shahnasarian, M., & Peterson, G. W. (1988). The effect of a prior cognitive structuring intervention with computer-assisted career guidance. *Computers In Human Behavior, 4,* 125–131.

Super, D. E. (1990). A life-span, life-space approach to career development. In D. Brown, L. Brooks, and Associates, *Career choice and development.* San Francisco: Jossey-Bass.

Thompson, D. L., & LaRochelle, D. R. (1985). Implementation and evaluation of a computerized career information delivery system. *Vocational Guidance Quarterly, 34,* 106–115.

9

Systematic Career Development Programming: Application to Elementary and Middle Schools

Historical Background

It has long been theorized that career development is a lifelong process (Ginzberg, Ginzburg, Axelrad, & Herma, 1951; Super, 1957) and that crucial aspects of this development occur during the school years. Over the past 3 decades there have been numerous educational thrusts aimed at promoting career development in elementary, middle, and high school. The most ambitious of these programs was the career education movement that developed during the Nixon administration under the leadership of then Secretary of Education, Sidney Marland. Many prominent counselor educators, including K. B. Hoyt, were prominently involved in this movement, which saw the establishment of extensive programs to help children and adolescents broaden their career horizons, learn decision-making skills, acquire vocational skills, and generally develop an appreciation for themselves. Hoyt (1977, p. 5) defined career education as follows:

> Career education is an effort aimed at refocusing American education and the actions of the broader community in ways that will help individuals acquire and utilize the knowledge, skills, and attitudes necessary for each to make work a meaningful, productive and satisfying part of his or her way of living.

Marland (1974, pp. 100–102) describes the eight elements of career education as identified by the Center for Research in Vocational Education at Ohio State University:

225

1. Career Awareness—knowledge of the total spectrum of careers.
2. Self-Awareness—knowledge of the components that make up self.
3. Appreciations, Attitudes—life roles; feelings toward self and others in respect to society and economics.
4. Decision-Making Skills—applying information to rational processes in order to reach decisions.
5. Economic Awareness—perception of processes in production, distribution, and consumption.
6. Skill Awareness and Beginning Competence—skills in ways in which man extends his behavior.
7. Employability Skills—social and communication skills appropriate to career placement.
8. Educational Awareness—perception of the relationship between education and life roles.

By the mid-1980s, most of the remnants of the career education movement had been swept from American schools by the back-to-basics educational movement. Advocates of back to basics were particularly critical of career education in elementary schools that focused children's attention on workers, developing skills with tools through hands-on approaches, and field trips to work sites because these activities took time away from core subjects. However, the failure of career education in the elementary school cannot be laid solely at the doorstep of the back-to-basics movement. Many mistakes were made in the design and implementation of those programs, including (1) they were funded with monies external to the school district with no plans to provide internal financial support once external funding was withdrawn; (2) they added to the work load of an already overloaded group: teachers; (3) the term *career education* was negatively associated with vocational education by many middle-class parents, who were concerned that their children might be diverted from a college preparatory curriculum; and (4) local political support among educators, parents, and the business community was not carefully developed in many instances.

Even though the career education movement of the seventies has largely dissipated, Hoyt (1985) is still a vigorous advocate for the concept. Interestingly, at about the time of Hoyt's reaffirmation of the viability of career education in our nation's schools, the National Occupational Information Coordinating Committee (NOICC) was funding the first phase of what has become the National Career Development Guideline Project, which has resulted in five extensive publications of guidelines for establishing career counseling and guidance programs in elementary schools, middle and junior high schools, high schools, and postsecondary educational institutions (NOICC, 1989a, b, c, d). In early 1991 these guidelines were being tested in over 30 states. They represent the most comprehensive effort to influence the career development of our citizenry since the seventies. In the sections that follow, a general model for planning career development programs is presented along with an overview of the National Career Development Guidelines.

PROGRAMMING FOR CAREER DEVELOPMENT

As noted earlier, several strategic errors were made in the establishment of career development programs, not the least of which may have been to label them *career education,* because that term was associated with vocational education in the minds of many. However, the focus of current efforts to establish career development programs is to avoid the mistakes of the past while building on the positive experiences from that era. Perhaps the clearest message that came out of the experiences of the 1960s and 1970s was that programs need to be carefully conceptualized, planned, implemented, and evaluated. In this vein, Walz and Benjamin (1984) list several characteristics of what they term a systemic career development program. To paraphrase Walz and Benjamin, the program

1. Is organized and planned by a team of knowledgeable professionals, parents, and representatives from the community.
2. Includes materials and learning experiences that are appropriate for the developmental stage of the students. The delivery of the program is carefully articulated across educational levels.
3. Is based on the needs of the students.
4. Is designed around a set of measurable objectives which are clearly stated at the outset.
5. Has an evaluation plan that includes the measurement of the extent to which goals are achieved and determines the value of the various processes involved in the program.
6. Is delivered by highly skilled personnel who use a wide variety of resources and strategies to achieve program objectives.

The remainder of this chapter includes a general discussion of the principles of change and the steps involved in the development of a comprehensive career development model. A discussion of the NCDG model is presented, as is a review of some of the unique aspects of developing a career development program in elementary and middle schools.

Program Development and Change

Whether a new program is being devised or an old program is being renovated, program planners are engaged in a change process that should follow certain principles. These principles have been set forth by various authors (e.g., Brown, Pryzwansky, & Schulte, 1991; Lippitt, 1973; Lippitt & Lippitt, 1986). Perhaps the primary principle that should be followed when initiating a change process is that the rationale for the change must be clearly communicated to those involved. Two corollaries to this principle are that the people affected by the change process must be involved in designing the changes and their support for them must be engendered. Developing support for change is not an easy task, particularly if there is satisfaction with the status quo or when people involved in the change process see the personal costs (e.g., time spent to bring about the changes) as exceeding the value of the changes. Therefore, it is necessary to assess the extent to which the people most affected by the change are invested in the current program and to develop an approach to change that will not overburden them. In addition, planners often set up resistance to the change process by failing to consider some of the psychological forces that are set in motion by change. One of these is that people who perceive themselves as competent in the current program may be concerned that they will not have the skills they need to be competent in the new program. Program planners must assure those people involved in developing new programs that they will have opportunities to develop needed skills. Finally, program changes need to be endorsed by the educational leaders, and these individuals must systematically reinforce change efforts. Without support and encouragement from the "top," change efforts are likely to be unsuccessful.

Conceptualizing Career Development Programs

Herr and Cramer (1988) suggest that there are a number of conceptual bases for career development programs. Two of the obvious ones can be characterized as theoretical and rational. Career development theories such as Super's (1990) can be used as the conceptual basis for designing a career development program. We might, for example, want all elementary students to develop a vocational self-concept, be aware of the major groups of occupations available to them as workers, develop an awareness of the need to plan for their future occupation, become aware of the types of occupational information, and develop basic decision-making skills. All of these areas would be in line with Super's theoretical propositions.

Another approach to developing a conceptual base for a career development program would be to rationally and/or empirically determine what career development skills and attitudes are needed by students and workers and set up a K–12 program to develop those competencies. We know that women have increasingly entered the work force and will continue to do so in the future, and thus girls and young women should develop those skills and attitudes necessary to enter and succeed in a career. As a result of this same trend, boys and girls need to overcome stereotypes that suggest that some jobs are "women's jobs" and others are "men's jobs." For the most part, those people engaged in conceptualizing career development programs have taken the rational/empirical approach and have tried to ascertain on an a priori basis what students and workers need and then have logically set about to build programs based on their assumptions. This is not to suggest that career development theory has not influenced the conceptualizing of career development programs. Almost all programs include ideas such as enhancing self-concept and developing an awareness of interests, work values, and aptitude—ideas that are derived directly from career development theory.

Developing a Program Philosophy

The conceptual basis of a career development program suggests in general terms what the program planners hope to accomplish (e.g., produce students with marketable skills). The statement of philosophy tells why the program planners believe that a career development program is important (Herr & Cramer, 1988). In a sense, the philosophy statement is a statement about values. A school district can be committed to a host of educational values, some of which may be mutually exclusive, complementary and overlapping, and/or conflicting. Some people see focusing on career development as antithetical to fostering academic achievement because career development activities detract from the amount of time that can be spent on academic pursuits. Other educators see career development programming as complementary to the idea that schooling should first and foremost be preparation for life. They also believe that career development programming enhances the achievement of students by illustrating the relevance of education to work and thus to students' futures. The philosophical statement clarifies these beliefs.

Typically, program philosophy statements are succinct. The following statement might reflect the philosophy of a school district:

> The ultimate goal of education is to enrich the lives of students by providing them with the skills they need to lead happy, productive lives. In modern society quality of life is dependent on having the educational skills needed to participate fully in our society, including those skills required for the citizenship role, the worker role, the family role, and the leisure role. The career development program is aimed at helping students realize the importance of education, to identify personally relevant career options, and to develop the personal, interpersonal, educational, and vocational skills needed to enter and advance in their careers.

Establishing Needs

School districts located in rural West Virginia, suburban Indianapolis, inner-city Chicago, and Chapel Hill, North Carolina will have different types of students and thus the need for different types of career development programs. Many of the students in rural West Virginia will go directly into the military or the civilian workplace, as will the students in inner-city Chicago. However, students in rural West Virginia will probably have to relocate to another geographic area within the state or even outside of the state to find suitable employment. If the students from an inner city are minority students, they are likely to be confronted with varying degrees of discrimination. It is likely that large numbers of students from the Chapel Hill and suburban Indianapolis school districts will attend some form of postsecondary educational institution, and therefore their initial career decision process will be somewhat more protracted. However, all these students need to be able to incorporate career planning into their educational planning processes. To determine the type of program that will best serve the students in these school districts, it is imperative that a full understanding of the characteristics of students and their families be developed. The process of developing this profile is usually termed *needs assessment.*

Data about the needs of students are available from a variety of sources, including demographic data about the community, the results of achievement testing, information about the dropout rate, follow-up of studies of graduates and dropouts, and direct surveys of students, teachers, business leaders, and parents. The questions to be answered through needs assessment are (1) Who are our students?, (2) What are their needs as they relate to the career development process?, and (3) What seems to be the best approach to meeting the needs that are identified? (Herma, Morris, & Fitz-Gibbon, 1987). When data from direct surveys are combined with information such as that collected from graduates and business leaders as well as other sources, planners can begin to get a sense of the type of program that needs to be delivered.

Setting Goals

Once needs have been ascertained, planners of career development programs must assemble the data and begin to establish the overall goals for the program. These are usually stated in rather broad terms such as, "Students will increase their knowledge of the types of careers available to them." Broad goal statements are then broken down into their behavioral objectives, which are sequenced chronologically.

Behavioral objectives contain four components: who will accomplish, what they will accomplish and to what degree they will accomplish it, by when they will accomplish it, and by what means they will accomplish it (Burns, 1972; Morris, Fitz-Gibbon, & Lindheim, 1987). The following is an example of a series of behavioral objectives that might be written for the aforementioned goal:

> *Goal:* Students will increase their knowledge of the careers available to them.
>
> *K*—By the end of kindergarten, students will be able to identify their parents' jobs and be able to list at least three of the duties they perform on those jobs, as a result of homework assignments to interview their parents about their jobs.
>
> *1st grade*—By the end of grade 1, all students will be able to identify three community helpers and three of their duties as a result of a speakers' program featuring community workers.
>
> *2nd grade*—By the end of grade 2, all students will be able to identify three workers who work in their county along with two tasks they perform and how they use reading on their jobs, as a result of classroom unit titled "Workers in Our County."

3rd grade—By the end of grade 3, all students will be able to identify five workers employed by the state, identify their major responsibilities, and tell two ways they use mathematics on their jobs, as a result of a field trip to the state capitol and follow-up activities.

4th grade—By the end of grade 4, all students will be able to identify five workers who are unique to the Southeast, describe their major job responsibilities, and tell how they use information learned in at least two school subjects on their jobs, as a result of completing an out-of-class assignment "Workers in Our Region."

5th grade—By the end of grade 5, all students will be able to identify 10 U.S. workers who hold jobs outside of the Southeast, the major duties they perform, and how they use information from school on their jobs, as a result of writing an essay on jobs in America, viewing filmstrips at a work station established for this purpose, and class assignments.

Middle school—By the end of grade 8, students will have identified three jobs that may be of interest to them in the future, determined what academic skills are needed to enter those jobs, and analyzed how their aptitudes and academic performance may prepare them for or provide a barrier to entering those jobs, as a result of the following activities:

6th grade—Students learn about careers in our hemisphere and the world as a result of infusion in all classes. Students complete an English essay "If I Could Be Anything." Counselor-led monthly seminars will feature speakers who represent international careers.

7th grade—Students complete an interest inventory and then participate in counselor-led groups to discuss the sources of interests and how interests influence career choice making.

8th grade—Students complete a 9-week class on choosing a career that focuses on decision making and using occupational information along with data about self to make career choices. The culminating experience is to select three careers of interest and to do a self-analysis regarding potential to enter those careers and to lay out an educational path to the most desired career.

High school—Each student will make a preliminary career choice along with an alternative choice and construct educational plans to enter those careers, as a result of counselor-directed activities such as career seminars, individual planning sessions, bibliotherapy, job shadowing, participation in career day, interest and aptitude assessment, and so forth.

The construction of behavioral objectives for each facet of the career development program is a laborious task. However, these specific objectives serve as the road map that tells which activities are going to be performed and when and with what expected result. With this type of information, it is relatively easy to design an evaluation of the program.

Program Evaluation

Burck (1978) states that "the aim of [program] evaluation is to establish worth, effectiveness, and efficiency" (p. 179) after reviewing more than half a dozen definitions of the process. He also concludes that evaluation consists of determining the outcomes that have been achieved, examining the processes by which these outcomes were achieved, and finally judging the value not only of the total program but the components of the program as well. These aspects of evaluation are examined in this section.

Process and Product Evaluation

Program evaluation can and should be conducted on two dimensions of the program: product and process. Product or summative evaluation attempts to answer the question, "What were the outcomes of our program?" or, put somewhat differently, "What new skills and attitudes (learning) resulted from students participating in our program?" Process or formative evaluation attempts to answer the question, "Why did students learn (or fail to learn) the things that they did?" In other words, "What contributed to the observed product or outcome?" Traditionally, schools have been more concerned with outcomes and less concerned with why the outcomes occurred. It is important to note that these two types of evaluations are conducted for different reasons. Product evaluation allows us to ascertain that we have accomplished what we set out to do (i.e., influence student career development) and allows us to be accountable to ourselves and our public. Process evaluation gives us the information that we need to make changes in our programs. As suggested earlier, we need to know why programs are successful or unsuccessful so we can alter or delete those parts of programs that are not contributing to the outcomes and perhaps intensify those efforts that are contributing to outcomes.

There are a number of approaches that may be used in evaluating a program (Stecher & Davis, 1987). One of these is to establish an experimental design which allows program developers to compare the outcomes of their program to those in a school that has no program. When establishing this type of evaluation design, it is important that the demographic characteristics of the "control" school be as similar to the one in which the career development program is being developed as possible. The goal-oriented approach to evaluation, which is the primary approach recommended here, focuses on the extent to which specific goals are attained. Often, in a goal-oriented approach to evaluation, the multitude of goals that are inevitably developed will have to be prioritized because it will be impossible to evaluate all of them in a single evaluation effort. Decision-oriented approaches to evaluation may also be conducted to inform key decision-making processes (What type of professional functions most effectively in the program?). User-oriented evaluation focuses on the human factors in the program, such as staff rapport. Responsive evaluation is a more qualitative approach to evaluation and focuses on what various people have at stake in the program and their points of view about the program. When this type of evaluation is conducted, the evaluator spends a great deal of time interacting with the program staff and observing various types of program activities. Stecher and Davis (1987) point out that comprehensive evaluations include several of the aforementioned evaluation approaches.

One of the objectives set forth in a preceding subsection was that each high school student should establish a career goal, develop an alternative goal, and construct an educational path to reach the goals that have been established. If our evaluation indicates that we have achieved this goal, we would want to know which of our activities contributed to goal attainment. Similarly, if our evaluation suggests that we have not attained our objective, we would want to ask which activities had contributed to students' planning and which had not. Process evaluation allows us to keep and strengthen those aspects of our programs that contribute to product (goal) attainment and to delete or alter those that do not.

Establishing Criteria

One issue that must be addressed in goal-oriented evaluation involves establishing the criteria by which success will be judged. We previously discussed an objective that all students would make a career choice, choose an alternative, and then develop an educational plan that would allow them to implement their choices. The word *all* suggests that to be successful, 100 percent of the students must complete the activity, which is one aspect of the criterion. A second part of the criterion issue concerns what constitutes a career choice and an educational plan to implement the choice. Many students have career choices that are unrealistic for a variety of reasons. Perhaps the objective should state that the choice should be attainable, but then the question needs to be posed, "How do we know that the career goal is attainable?" The objective could read that each student will establish a career goal that is attainable as judged by the counselor and in doing so establish that all students will establish an attainable career goal that the counselor perceives to be realistic. It must also be determined how the educational plan mentioned in this objective is constructed so that students will advance toward their goals.

When program objectives are established, they constitute the basis for product evaluation if they are properly written. Thus objectives need to be constructed carefully. It is also important that program objectives are within reach of the staff's ability to attain them. All students may select career options, but it would be unrealistic to expect that all students would prepare for and enter those options. A more realistic objective might be that 50 percent of the students in school would prepare for and enter either their primary or secondary career choice within 6 years of their graduation from high school as determined by a follow-up study of graduates. In this objective, a reasonable criterion has been established along with a time frame in which the objective is to be accomplished and a means of evaluating the extent of goal attainment (student self-reports in a follow-up study).

Program Implementation

Once needs have been ascertained, objectives established, and an evaluation plan designed, the program can be implemented. It is not unusual for school districts to pilot test programs in order to evaluate the procedures that are to be used prior to implementing a program throughout the entire district. In preparation for program implementation, whether it be to pilot test the program or a districtwide implementation, certain steps must be taken to ensure success. These steps are to communicate fully the nature of the program to students, parents, and staff; to develop support for the program among parents and the professional staff; and to make certain that those people who will be implementing the program are fully trained in the procedures required for implementation. These recommendations are in keeping with the principles of change discussed earlier.

The National Career Development Guidelines Model

The National Career Development Guidelines (NCDG) project was initiated to formulate and field test a comprehensive set of guidelines for career guidance and counseling programs at all levels (NOICC, 1989a). Clearly the guidelines are designed to enhance program planning not just in the area of career development but for the total guidance and counseling program. They are also intended to serve as the focal point for the development of professional standards for personnel, legislation and policy, and program accreditation standards at the state and national level. However, the developers of the guidelines also realize that, regardless of the nature of the goals of the project, the delivery of services must occur in individual schools.

The more than 150 people who provided input into the initial development of the NOICC guidelines reasoned that students need competencies related to career development in several areas. Additionally, student indicators have been developed for each of the competencies. These can be seen in Figure 9.1 (NOICC, 1989a, b, c, pp. 5–6) for elementary, middle, and high school students (1989b).

In addition to student competencies, the NCDG developers have enumerated 65 skills and competencies needed by school counselors regarding guidance and counseling generally, including the utilization of information, program implementation, individual and group assessment, management and administrative consultation, and working with special populations. For example, counselors need to have the ability to identify appropriate role models, understand career paths and patterns, identify assessment resources, and help parents assist students to explore career options and alternatives for their children according to the guidelines (NOICC, 1989a). Earlier we listed the ways that career development activities could be delivered to elementary and middle school students. Clearly the NCDG are set up to focus on one of these options: delivery by the school counselor.

The first step in the implementation of the NCDG in elementary and secondary schools is to establish a steering committee that will manage and coordinate the implementation process. It is also recommended that an advi-

FIGURE 9.1 *Career Development Competencies*

	Indicator that Competency Has Been Developed. Student Can:

Elementary School

1. Knowledge of the importance of a positive self-concept to career development
2. Skills for interacting with others
3. Awareness of the importance of emotional and physical development on career decision making
4. Awareness of the importance of educational achievement to career opportunities
5. Awareness of interrelationship of work and learning
6. Skills for understanding and using career information
7. Awareness of the interrelationship of personal responsibility, good work habits, and career opportunities
8. Awareness of how careers relate to needs and functions of society
9. Understanding of how to make decisions and choose alternatives related to tentative educational and career goals
10. Awareness of the interrelationship of life roles and careers
11. Awareness of changing male/female roles in different occupations

Student Can:

1. Describe positive characteristics about self
2. Demonstrate skills in resolving conflicts
3. Identify ways to express and deal with feelings
4. Implement a plan of action for improving academic skills
5. Describe how one's role as a student is like that of an adult worker
6. Describe jobs in his/her community
7. Describe the importance of cooperation among workers for accomplishing a task
8. Describe how careers can satisfy personal needs
9. Describe how decisions affect self and others
10. Identify the value of leisure activities for enriching one's life style
11. Describe the changing roles of men and women in the workplace

Middle School

1. Knowledge of the influence of positive self-concept on career development
2. Skills for interacting with others
3. Knowledge of the importance of emotional and physical development on career decision making
4. Knowledge of the relationship of educational achievement to career opportunities
5. Skills for locating, understanding, and using career information
6. Knowledge of skills necessary to seek and obtain a job
7. Understanding of the attitudes necessary for success in work and learning
8. Understanding of how careers relate to needs and functions of the economy and society
9. Skills in making decisions and choosing alternatives in planning for and pursuing tentative educational and career goals
10. Knowledge of the interrelationship of life roles and careers
11. Understanding of how sex-role stereotyping, bias, and discrimination limit career choices, opportunity, and achievement
12. Understanding of the process of career exploration and planning

Student Can:

1. Assess personal likes and dislikes
2. Demonstrate an appreciation for similarities and differences in people
3. Identify internal and external sources of stress and conflict
4. Relate one's aptitudes and abilities to broad occupational areas
5. Identify various ways occupations can be classified
6. Compile a job application form in a satisfactory manner
7. Demonstrate effective learning habits and skills
8. Discuss the variety and complexity of occupations
9. Describe one's current life context as it relates to career decisions
10. Describe the interrelationships among family, career, and leisure
11. Describe problems, adjustments, and advantages of entering a non-traditional career
12. Identify tentative life and career goals

Source: National Career Development Guidelines: Local Handbook for Elementary Schools. (1989). Washington, D.C.: NOICC, pp. 5–6.

sory committee be formed made up of administrators, counselors, teachers, other pupil support personnel such as school psychologists, parents, representatives from business and labor, counselors from the high school, and perhaps individuals from institutions of higher education and state agencies. The purposes of the advisory committee are to participate in the public relations effort needed to market the program, review all implementation and evaluation processes, and help secure support for the revision of the guidance and counseling program (NOICC, 1989a).

Once the steering and advisory committees are in place and properly oriented to their task, commitments from key personnel such as the Board of Education, the central administration staff, the building principal, teachers, and others must be obtained, a comprehensive career guidance and counseling plan designed, and program implementation time lines established. These organizational tasks are outlined in Figure 9.2 (NOICC, 1988, p. 43).

The actual process of developing a comprehensive career development program follows the general case described earlier and begins with an assessment of the student needs to be served (NOICC, 1989a). Factors such as gender, physical and mental disabilities, socioeconomic status, race and eth-

FIGURE 9.2   *Summary Checklist for Initial Organization of the Career Development Program*

Tasks	Date Completed
1. Form a steering committee	_____
a. Identify and select members	_____
b. Initiate steering committee	_____
c. Gain support and commitments	_____
d. Train steering committee	_____
e. Develop steering committee management plan	_____
2. Form an advisory committee	_____
a. Identify and select members	_____
b. Invite members to serve	_____
c. Schedule and plan first meeting	_____
d. Develop plan for use of advisory committee throughout implementation process	_____
3. Identify benefits	_____
a. Identify ways in which trends and issues are creating local needs	_____
b. Identify benefits of program related to local needs	_____
c. Develop information brief	_____
d. Conduct public relations using information brief	_____
4. Develop a career guidance and counseling plan	_____
5. Develop a task-timeline	_____

Source: National Career Development Guidelines: Local Handbook for Elementary Schools. (1989). Washington, DC: NOICC, p. 43.

nic background, as well as other individual characteristics influence the career development of children (Super, 1990) and must be taken into consideration in the development of the program. The needs assessment instrument should be constructed in a manner that will be sensitive to the special needs of all groups.

Once needs are assessed, objectives can be established and indicators of the achievement of those objectives determined using the student competencies listed in Figure 9.1. These objectives serve as the basis for developing the program. The NOICC (1989a) guidelines offer little in terms of the actual delivery mechanisms to be used in the elementary school program. This was a deliberate attempt by the developers of the guidelines to avoid being prescriptive. The activities used to meet the objectives that have been established will vary depending on the monetary resources available, the preferences of the personnel involved, the degree of administrative support, and the needs of the children.

Once preliminary planning has been completed, an organizational theme adopted, objectives established, and activities to meet the objectives determined, it is time to begin improving the existing program (NOICC, 1989a). This statement presupposes that there is some form of career development program in existence, which is usually the case. However, the NCDG guidelines (1989a, b) suggest that there are seven basic processes that should be employed in the program:

1. Classroom instruction
2. Counseling
3. Assessment
4. Career information
5. Placement
6. Consultation
7. Referral

The following list is presented as a means of demonstrating how these processes might be employed in the development of student competencies. Some of these processes presuppose that a counselor will be present in the school. However, many of the processes can and probably will involve teachers.

Elementary School Competencies to Be Developed:
1a. Identify positive and negative ways to express and deal with feelings
1b. Implement plan of action for improving academic skills

Processes Used to Develop Competencies
Consultation:
1a. Parent consultation
1b. Parent/teacher consultation

Classroom Instruction:
1a. Classroom activity; my emotions
1b. Study skills units

Assessment:
1a. Informal assessment of outcomes
1b. Informal

Career Information:
1a and 1b not used with these competencies

Counseling:
1a. Individual counseling for students having problems
1b. Individual and group counseling for students with low achievement

Placement:
1a. Not used with this competency
1b. Place cross-grade tutoring program

Referral:
1a. More severe problems referred to Community Mental Health Center (CMHC)
1b. Referred private groups that provide remedial tutoring work program

Middle School Competencies to Be Developed:
1a. Identify skills that are transferable from one occupation to the other
1b. Identify strategies used in decision making
1c. Describe changing life roles of men and women in the family

Processes Used to Develop Competencies
Consultation:
1a. Teacher consultation
1b. Teacher consultation
1c. Teacher consultation

Classroom Instruction:
1a. Units on occupational clusters
1b. Units on decision making
1c. Units on male/female relationships

Assessment:
1a. Informal
1b. Informal
1c. Informal

Career Information:
1a. Cluster information
1b. Not addressed
1c. Information on nontraditional careers

Counseling:

1c. Small group guidance on male/female roles

Placement:

1a. Placement for job shadowing activities

1b, c. Not used for these competencies

Referral:

Not used for this competency

THE INSTITUTIONS

At one point in educational history, it was decided that the middle years of schooling should be preparatory for high school, and the junior high school was established to emulate the high school. Less than a decade ago, when numerous educational problems began to manifest themselves, the junior high school came under fire and middle schools became more prevalent. These schools typically enroll students in grades 6, 7, and 8 and are fashioned along lines similar to elementary schools. Elementary schools and middle schools are intended to provide a nurturing atmosphere where students can receive emotional and educational support. In the early elementary school years, self-contained classrooms are not uncommon. In these classrooms one teacher provides most of the basic instruction, with support in some instances from art, music, physical education, and special education teachers and in some instances from counselors.

As students progress in school, typically in the intermediate years (grades 3 and 4), they are exposed to a number of teachers who possess specialized knowledge in areas such as mathematics, science, social studies, and so forth in addition to music and physical education teachers, special education teachers, and counselors. At the upper elementary and middle school levels, the pattern remains essentially the same although middle schools are typically larger; specialization in instruction occurs and the curriculum becomes more diverse. For example, some students may be taking algebra in the eighth grade while others are enrolled in pre-algebra and general mathematics courses.

Career development activities in elementary and middle schools may be delivered in several ways: by the teacher in regular units much like social studies; by the teacher through infusion into the curriculum (e.g., careers related to science may be discussed in each science unit); by special teachers who teach careers, usually on a day, week, or semester basis; by counselors who teach special units on careers and plan activities such as career days, when workers representing various occupations visit the school and meet with students to discuss their jobs; through parent-directed activities typically designed by school counselors; and by personnel external to the school (usually from the central administrative offices of the school district) who perform some combination of the foregoing activities. The exact nature of the program, including its staffing and delivery, will depend on the philosophy of the school district, the availability of personnel, and the financial resources available to support various activities.

Background

Elementary school youngsters bring to the classroom attitudes and ideas that have developed as a result of the interaction of their background or environment and their experiences (Super, 1990). Since both are necessarily limited in the early years of elementary school, they reflect primarily attitudes of the adults with whom students have contact. Thus in many ways their ideas and concepts may be a generation out of date. During each generation, tremendous changes occur, especially in areas such as the world of work.

Early in the elementary school, each child should be helped to grasp the idea that much of what happens to her in the future will be of her own making and will depend to a large extent on how she uses abilities in the opportunities encountered. Long before entering school, every child will have made fantasy occupational choices such as teacher, police officer, mechanic, or secretary. During the early school years, the child will have matured to the point of recognizing that these are fantasy choices and nothing more. As this realization develops, children can begin to comprehend what factors are involved in the choices faced as they complete an educational program. Children need to understand the extent to which all choices—recreational activities, hobbies, reading materials, clubs, and others—ultimately influence major choices and decisions. They should also realize that career choice is always evolving and changing, throughout the entire life span.

In other words, if elementary school students are helped to develop an awareness of the world of work and to develop a more acute sensitivity to themselves as individuals with differing interests, abilities, and motivations, we may reasonably expect some understanding of how they as individuals function. Two opposing dangers exist that underscore the importance of focusing attention on this goal at the elementary level. One danger is assuming that an automatic connection between work and self will be made; this leaves too much to chance. The other danger is that elementary students may attempt to move too far toward closure and make definite choices prematurely. The goal lies between these two extremes. Students should be taught early that they do make decisions that affect their lives. This involves at least two aspects—namely, how decisions are made and how, once made, those personal choices influence their lives.

Nelson (1980) describes the CREST program as a technique that helps elementary children become aware of the choices they make and the impact of these choices in establishing insight. Since self-understanding is fostered early, the pupils benefit not only in establishing better relationships with others but in many other ways. For example, as self-understanding improves, the child is likely to understand others better. It is an easy step from understanding self and others to understanding how different kinds of people can make different contributions to their groups as a result of special knowledge, skill, or experience.

Using career-oriented materials in the elementary classroom may help many children build positive self-concepts. Too often success in the classroom may be based on activities that are academically oriented but have less direct relationship to the world of work. Of course, it is important for academically able youngsters to experience success; but all youngsters should have those experiences. Learning that is related to the real world and solving problems in that world is likely to have greater value for the child than an activity that is carried out to please the teacher. Cross (1974) proposes that children need a human "home base," someone they can depend on to be available and understanding and who does not have to be impressed. Further, he suggests that teachers must provide a secure place for every child with the other children in the classroom and that all school personnel must work toward the goal of building a sense of membership in the school within each child.

Approximately 20 years ago, Hansen (1972) proposed a career development model that is incorporated into the school curriculum. She assumed that career development *is* self-development—in other words, a process of developing and implementing a self-concept satisfying both the individual and society. By providing for exploration of self, particularly in educational and vocational pursuits, the system suggests that vocational maturation will develop. Hansen (1972) identifies objectives for this approach that will parallel those we have been considering. These goals propose that students will

1. Be aware of their own preferred life styles and work values.
2. Exercise some control over their own lives through conscious choice and planning.
3. Be familiar with the occupational options available to them.
4. Know the educational paths to preferred occupations and the financial requirements for entry.
5. Be familiar with the process of career decision making.
6. Know the major resources available in the school and community and be able to use them.
7. Be able to organize and synthesize knowledge of self and the world of work and to develop strategies. (p. 244)

McGee and Silliman (1982) describe a group of activities for fourth-, fifth-, and sixth-grade students using an interest-related inventory. Although there is general agreement that interests at these grade levels are very immature, they can still be used as a basis for increasing an awareness of individual differences and of one's own characteristics at this time.

Wernick (1972) describes the use of an adult from the community as a nucleus for building classroom activities that not only involve basic learning skills but also develop attitudes toward a wide range of occupations. The T4C project in New Jersey places a complete set of hand tools in the elementary school classroom along with a set of learning guides for 47 different learning episodes (Leonard, 1972). These experiences help the child feel the role of the various workers who use those tools in their jobs. Rost (1973) relates the building of a "career pyramid" by selecting any occupation suggested by an elementary class member and then constructing the pyramid of jobs, identified by the class members, that support that job.

Thompson and Parker (1971) report a study in which fifth graders were taught a unit based on learning objectives related to occupations. They found that the youngsters gained insight and knowledge of work from the unit. After completing the unit, they could identify better reasons for working and could identify a broader range of occupations, thus apparently understanding better the system by which individuals move into occupations.

Healthy attitudes toward work also require the recognition and elimination of gender-role stereotypes. Miller (1977) found that gender-role stereotyping already existed among 9-year-olds. Navin and Sears (1980) and Wolleat (1979) confirm the early appearance and restrictive results of such attitudes. Hageman and Gladding (1983) studied the attitudes of third- and sixth-grade students, and found that there was increasing stereotyping as youngsters advanced in school and that a majority of girls at both grade levels did not feel free to pursue nontraditional careers. The elementary school years provide a time to build open attitudes in both boys and girls through exposure to role models, field trips where both sexes can be seen in positions that might easily be stereotyped, and similar experiences.

Many myths and attitudes impede the development of respect for all kinds of work. Unfortunately, the school has sometimes contributed to these fallacies rather than helped to overcome them. This is not surprising because teachers are drawn primarily from the middle class and bring to the classroom ideas and concepts typical of the middle class. The family backgrounds and previous experiences of teachers have made them more familiar with white-collar workers than with skilled and semiskilled workers. The youngsters with whom they work in the classroom, however, may be drawn from a much wider sociological spectrum, with attitudes and viewpoints quite different from those of the teacher. Teachers should avoid developing or supporting biases and prejudices toward various types of work. Instead, they should teach that all work is important and that the worker who uses unique skills and abilities effectively in any field makes an important contribution to all members of society.

Several studies have looked at the vocational values held by elementary school children. For example, Cooker (1973) reports differences across both grade level and gender on values concerning altruism, control, and money. He reports fourth-, fifth-, and sixth-grade girls scoring higher on altruism as a vocational value and boys in those grades scoring higher on control and money. Hales and Fenner (1973) report similar differences across gender but no differences across social classes.

Bailey and Nihlen (1989) report that many children are quite willing to ask questions about careers after being exposed to nontraditional occupational role models and conclude that "elementary school children are indeed interested in the world of work" (p. 143). They suggest that elementary school career development contain the following elements:

1. Information about the responsibilities of various occupations
2. Opportunities for children to share their knowledge of and experience with work
3. Opportunities to interact with workers and to find out how workers feel about their jobs
4. Activities that counteract gender-role stereotyping

Interestingly, the Bailey and Nihlen (1987) study, which was done with elementary school children, supports at least one of the findings of Rubinton (1985), who concludes that middle school children benefit from activities that allow them to engage in self-expression and share their own experiences and concerns.

Seligman, Weinstock, and Owings (1988) conclude, on the basis of their research with young children, that "promoting a positive home environment as well as strong parent-child relationships is critical not only for its own sake but as a determinant of the children's career development" (p. 229).

Middle School Years: Beginning Exploration

The increasing academic skills required in most occupations have further persuaded the general public that all youth should be encouraged to continue their education as far as possible. The trend toward greater percentages of our youth completing secondary school is clear. Minimum school-leaving-age requirements and employment restrictions keep almost all youth in school at least through the middle school years. One can expect that present pressures to keep them in school for longer periods not only will continue, but will increase, with the result that very few youth will withdraw before completing high school.

For most youth, the middle school years are stormy and hectic as students enter adolescence and move toward greater independence and self-direction. Self-awareness becomes more pronounced, and the youth's concept of self as an individual independent of parents and family takes shape. As this distinctiveness of self becomes more apparent, the adolescent inevitably moves toward a view of self in terms of the world of work. Many of the career information activities of the middle school must be keyed to this transitional phase, to provide the adolescent an opportunity to try out self-concept and to modify, refine, and expand his view of self as a person. The junior high school came into being largely as an effort to provide this opportunity for tryout and exploration, and it is at this level in most school systems that the pupil encounters the first opportunity to make educational choices. In addition to the curriculum, the junior high school provides clubs and other activities that serve the purpose of exploration.

Most pupils entering middle or junior high school are still many years removed from full-time activity in the world of work. Similarly, the majority are still many years away from such activity when they move on to high school. Nevertheless, they are on their way toward the world of work, and during these years most become aware of this and develop a greater concern with the occupational world and their personal relationship to it. Although they are, for the most part, still concerned with work in the future, the realization of that future involvement enhances their awareness of it and focuses their attention on it to a much greater extent than previously. Students who are likely to be school dropouts may already have passed this point and may be concerned with thoughts of work in an immediate and specific sense.

By middle or junior high school age, most youngsters have had casual work experiences such as babysitting and newspaper routes. Even though these occasional bits of employment have little direct vocational significance, they do provide further contact with the world of work. Incidental employment not only helps youngsters gain some insight into why and how people earn a living, but also makes them more aware of an ultimate relationship to work. This new awareness usually stimulates concern for information about occupations generally. Often involvement in casual work provides an opportunity to encounter some of the experiences of adult workers—for example, receiving a paycheck and deciding how to use the money.

Jessell and Boyer (1989) surveyed 5,464 seventh and eighth graders to determine the extent to which educational and vocational plans have been developed. They found that 94 percent of those surveyed expected to finish high school, 14 percent expected to enroll in vocational technical school after high school, and 67 percent said they intended to complete college. Many of these same students had made career decisions. Twenty-six percent said they had made a decision and were reasonably confident that the decision was final. An additional 41 percent reported that they had made a decision but suggested that it might change later. Only 6 percent of the students in the survey reported that they had given career choice no consideration.

McDonald (1989), also studying seventh- and eighth-grade students, concludes on the basis of the results from 857 students that level of self-esteem, capacity to interpret complex occupational information, being female, relatively high socioeconomic status, and coming from a family with two parents present were favorably related to positive attitudes toward careers. Obviously, the school can only have an impact on two of these variables, self-esteem and the interpretation of information.

THE PROGRAM

To avoid redundancy in activities, the overall organization of the program needs to be organized around a theme. A common theme used in elementary schools could be characterized as proximity—that is, activities are designed initially to focus on workers who are closest to the child, gradually expanding as the child grows older. An example of this organizational theme would be as follows:

> Kindergarten: Workers at home and in my neighborhood
> First grade: Workers in my community
> Second grade: Workers in my county
> Third grade: Workers in my state
> Fourth grade: Workers in my nation
> Fifth grade: Workers of the world

The middle school then could be a continuation of the proximity or geographic theme simply by regarding the process and focusing on jobs of interest to the student in the neighborhood, community, state, etc. It is more likely that middle school activities will be organized around an occupational theme, however. Some school districts give an interest inventory and then organize their program around the occupations suggested by the inventory. The occupational classifications system of 15 occupational clusters developed by the U.S. Department of Education is likely to be the basis for the organization of the middle school program. These clusters are as follows:

1. Agribusiness and national resources occupations
2. Business and office occupations
3. Communication and media occupations
4. Commercial and homemaking occupations
5. Occupations related to the environment
6. Fine arts and humanities occupations
7. Health occupations
8. Hospitality and recreation occupations
9. Manufacturing occupations
10. Marine science occupations
11. Marketing and distribution occupations
12. Personal services occupations
13. Public services occupations
14. Transportation occupations
15. Construction occupations

Whether the middle school decides to organize its program around Holland's (1985) interest categories (Realistic, Investigative, Artistic, Social, Enterprising, Conventional), the foregoing occupational cluster system, or some other system, it is important to make sure that students are given a comprehensive, realistic look at the occupations available to them. It is also important that the program be integrated and fully coordinated with the elementary school and high school programs. Once an organizational theme has been selected, activities must be designed within the organizational theme to meet the objectives of the program. The following are some activities that might be used to develop various career development competencies.

Competencies of Elementary School Students

Be able to describe work of mother and father (if both in home)

Geographic Theme
Grade Activities

K. "What do you do, mother?"

1. Spend half an hour observing a community worker and give verbal report

2. Write brief report and give verbal report

Identify skills learned in school that are used in jobs

3. Class telephone call using speaker phone to "visible" (e.g., governor) state official

4. Analyze jobs of congressional representative

5. Study educational skills of workers in industrialized versus nonindustrialized countries

Competencies of Middle School Students

Demonstrate understanding of self

Interest Theme

6. Have students estimate interests; then give interest inventory with follow-up discussions

Identify at least five changes in society that affect work

7. Bring in old copies of *USA Today* and have small groups compete for number of trends that can be identified

Identify sources of employment in the community

8. Have job service counselor or personnel manager speak

It is also possible to organize the activities "vertically" (that is, by grade level) so that certain vital competencies and attitudes are developed.

Competency to Be Developed

Students will understand gender-role stereotyping and broaden their own view of their potential in nontraditional occupations.

Grade Activities

K. What kind of jobs do men and women hold? Start with mom and dad. Spontaneous discussion focusing on community.

1. Cut pictures out of old magazines that show men and women working. Discuss stereotyping. Build collage to show nontraditional careers.

2. Men and women working in our county. Discuss why men and women hold certain types of jobs. Bring in some nontraditional role models.

3. Focusing on state government, look at the number of men and women in government. Discuss reasons.

4. Focus on roles of women and men in national government. Why have we never had a woman president? What factors limit women in politics?

5. Get figures for males and females in various jobs throughout the world. Why the discrepancy? What is the impact on men and women?

6. Study social occupations. Why are they predominantly made up of women? Also look at realistic occupations. Why are they predominantly made up of men? Bring in nontraditional role models. What problems/rewards have resulted in holding nontraditional jobs?

7. Using the interest inventory as a guide, have each person identify three or four nontraditional occupations. Do in-depth papers about one or two.

8. Identify potential nontraditional career options. Assign job shadowing, filmstrip review, or interviews with workers in that field. Have students ask friends, "What would you think of me if I entered _____ (nontraditional career option)?" Have students discuss rewards of their traditional and nontraditional jobs.

Once all activities are developed for all competencies at each level, the result will be substantial. Typically these guides are organized by grade level, identify the objectives that are to be achieved, specify how attainment of each objective is to be measured, provide a detailed outline of the activities that are to be employed to accomplish that objective, and list the materials such as books and filmstrips that are to be associated with the activities. Some school districts have comprehensive guides that counselors and others can use when planning a program for an individual school. Other districts, such as the Wake County North Carolina schools, have prescribed minimal programs that must be delivered by counselors.

The literature suggests that the opportunities to integrate career awareness and exploration with other learning experiences abound.

Donahue and Woodcock (1985) describe how eighth-grade students interviewed workers and prepared occupational profiles for 30 local occupations in the process of preparing a career-oriented mathematics book. Workers were asked how they used math in their everyday work and to provide samples of the kinds of problems they solved. The result was a 92-page workbook used as a supplementary textbook. Hill (1981) describes a shadowing experience in a group of stores in a nearby mall. Staley and Mangieri (1984) provide a bibliography identified by level (K–3, 4–6, 7–9) for each of the 15 career clusters of the U.S. Office of Education and discuss strategies for using books to help elementary students increase their career awareness. Innis (1982) provided sixth graders experience in obtaining jobs, working, and receiving "pay" by developing an "employment service" within the school. Christopher and Blocker (1980) describe using a fourth-grade social studies unit on the environment to acquaint students with environmental- and recycling-related occupations using AV materials, interviews with experts, and field trips. Both Montimurro (1980) and Isaacson and Hayes (1980) describe adaptations of the career day format used with elementary-age students.

A WORD ABOUT ROLE RELATIONSHIPS

It is perhaps obvious from the foregoing discussion that counselors and teachers are expected to carry the burden for the elementary and middle school career development program. Detailed consideration of the role, function, and relationship of the teacher and the counselor lies beyond this book. Excellent discussions of this topic can be found in several books concentrating on the organization and administration of guidance services, as well as in books dealing more broadly with public school administration. A team approach is essential if the interests of students, school, and community are to be served effectively. It has long been understood that teachers alone are not prepared or able to carry out the career development activities of the elementary school (e.g., Clapsaddle, 1973; Roberts, 1971). Our discussion of teacher-counselor relationships is not intended to exclude other team members who may be found in some school systems. Since the majority of schools at present provide only teachers and counselors for career development activities, our discussion has been limited to these two groups.

The commonly expressed function of the school is to provide instruction. All other activities in the school are designed to help accomplish this function with maximum effectiveness. The underlying purpose is to create an opportunity for the optimum development of the individual. This basic purpose is usually interpreted broadly, recognizing that the classroom alone cannot bring about this optimum development. To accomplish this, other activities and personnel are brought into the operation of the school.

Ordinarily, school personnel are classified, according to the function they primarily perform, into three categories—administrative, instructional, or service. The administrative staff is responsible for the planning, executing, evaluating, and interpreting activities of the school. It provides the leadership that helps foster individual development. The instructional staff is responsible for inculcating skills, knowledge, and behavior that is important to the development of the individual. The service staff, including counselors, is responsible for activities that aid the individual youngster in the maximum development of potentialities. The three functions performed by school personnel pervade the entire structure and operation of the school. That is, each staff member is usually involved, to some extent, in all of the functions, although one can usually identify the area in which she has primary responsibility and others in which she has only secondary involvement.

Within this general structure, the teacher, whose primary function is instruction, and the counselor, whose primary function is service, must work closely together if each student is to gain the maximum growth in career development. Both teacher and counselor are inevitably involved in this process; neither alone can do all that must be accomplished. Each can contribute uniquely to the process. At the same time, although the work of each complements that of the other, it is not easily divided into two discrete units. Rather, one would expect to find in most school settings some variability in actual roles, since the skills and proficiency of each will determine how they can best work together.

Over the years, as guidance has expanded in schools, two contradictory and fallacious positions have developed concerning the relationship of teacher and counselor. One position implies total overlap in the work of the two and suggests that a good teacher can perform all the guidance services needed by the students in a school. This position has been supported by such slogans as "Every teacher a guidance worker," and "Guidance is just good teaching." This is an indefensible position because of the student load that each teacher carries and the lack of specialized preparation in such crucial guidance activities as psychometrics, counseling techniques, and career information.

The other position implies a false dichotomy, with the suggestion that the teacher has responsibility for instructional activities only, and the counselor has responsibility exclusively for guidance services. Perhaps one could bring about such a division of activity, albeit with considerable effort and resultant inefficiency. In any case, it would be most undesirable, since many guidance activities can be accomplished more effectively through instructional techniques and services; similarly, many instructional goals can be reached through guidance activities. Further, even though specialized skills are certainly required in both functions, neither the teacher nor the counselor is totally lacking in the basic skills of the other.

These extreme positions are erroneous and, instead, both counselor and teacher are involved in instructional and guidance responsibilities. The teacher plays a crucial role in the guidance activities of the school. No other staff member has as much direct contact with the student. No one else is in as strategic a position to observe individual growth and development and to see the first glimmerings of interest in new areas or the beginnings of concern about future problems. No one else has as many opportunities for brief informal contacts with the student and for encouraging the student to explore new areas or to open new vistas. The teacher's daily contact with the student does more to develop and influence the student's attitude toward the school than anything done by all the rest of the staff. This contact provides the greatest opportunity to create a working climate in which each student can feel that he has the chance to grow and develop as an individual. The teacher, then, is instrumental not only in giving instruction but also in obtaining information about the individual, establishing a favorable working environment, identifying students who need special help, building attitudes toward the guidance program and other services of the school, and participating with the counselor in the guidance program.

Counselors, on the other hand, can make many direct contributions to the instructional program. They are able to provide teachers with deeper understanding of the students so teachers can adjust the instructional program to meet students' needs and characteristics. They can help teachers with students whose problems cause them to be disruptive in the classroom. Counselors' frequent contacts with parents should help teachers by making the objectives of the instructional program clearer to community members. Counselors work directly with most of the students in the school in a counseling relationship or in other aspects of the guidance program, thereby helping them to progress in the instructional program.

Since both teacher and counselor are involved in guidance, it is logical to conclude that both the instructional and guidance functions of the school are best served when counselor and teacher work together cooperatively. Both the instructional and guidance functions are deeply and extensively involved in the career development process. Continuous teamwork between the two is necessary if this portion of individual development is to be advanced effectively. Within the school at least three situations bear on the individual as he is involved in the career development process: (1) the individual in the formal, structured classroom; (2) the individual in other group situations that may or may not be formal and structured; and (3) the individual in the face-to-face contact of the counseling relationship. In the first situation, we would expect the teacher to make the major, but not the exclusive, contribution; in the second, both teacher and counselor should be continuously involved; and in the third, the counselor should make the major, but not the exclusive, contribution. The specific involvements should be worked out in terms of personal qualifications, available time, and other factors related to the local situation.

HELPING PARENTS UNDERSTAND AND ACCEPT THEIR ROLE IN CAREER DEVELOPMENT

The emergence of concern about career development has reemphasized a reality that has often been overlooked or ignored: that the school is not the sole agent responsible for the development of the child. Career development concepts stress the role of the rest of the community, clearly including the family as well as other adults. School personnel, especially teacher and counselor, have a responsibility to create a cooperative working relationship with these individuals to maximize the child's opportunity to develop.

Parental ambition for a youngster may affect how she looks at the world and at occupations specifically. Deprecating one's own work in an effort to motivate the child toward something "better" may not help the youngster to develop a base for decision making where crucial factors can be weighed objectively. Parental pressures that push a child of limited ability toward academically competitive areas are just as harmful and wasteful as those that encourage academically able children to leave school and go to work as soon as possible. Similarly, parental attitudes toward various occupational fields may influence the child's view of these fields. This is particularly true of attitudes that certain jobs are "men's work" or "women's work."

The elementary teacher has a special advantage in his relationship to the parents of the children in his class. The teacher is often the first adult outside the family circle to spend a considerable period of each day with the youngster. Parents accept the teacher in this role and usually recognize the concern and interest that the teacher shares in the development of the child. This closer relationship between teacher and parents makes it possible for the teacher to help the parents see how their behavior and attitudes relate to the child's behavior in school, and in turn to ultimate development as an individual. The teacher can help the parents discover how they can be most helpful in the maturational process. Navin and Sears (1980) list several ways that teachers can include parents in planning and providing career development experiences.

Earlier, we considered the use of parents as an information resource to help youngsters learn about occupations. Almost every elementary teacher already uses the variety of job holders within the parental group in this way. Bearg (1980) discusses the use of parents as role models in developing career awareness, by using parents as classroom visitors to explain their occupation. The value of this simple activity should not be discounted. It provides an opportunity for the other children in the class to learn about a particular job by listening to Johnny's mother or Mary's father tell about what they do, how, and why. It also may help Johnny and Mary to see their parent's work from a different viewpoint than the random, end-of-the-day remarks that may have been the major basis for their view. Many peripheral values in school-home relationships may accrue from such an activity. There are, of course, numerous ways in which the school can involve parents in classroom activities as well as in school functions outside the classroom. If these are organized to maximize contact between the participating parents and children, both their own and others, many opportunities to learn adult roles, attitudes, and values will ensue.

Both teacher and counselor can help parents see the unlimited opportunities within the home for children to learn about work. Unfortunately, many parents have developed the attitude that parental success is accomplished by making the life of their children easier than the life they experienced as children. Such a distorted view prevents capitalizing on home-based circumstances to learn about work. The assignment of regular home tasks to each child helps the child learn necessary work-related attitudes such as punctuality, reliability, efficiency, and responsibility. It also helps children learn the rewards of work—satisfaction in a job well done, service to others, a feeling of worth and accomplishment, and comradeship with fellow workers. Some families have found it helpful to develop family projects such as do-it-yourself home improvements, gardening projects, or similar tasks that also teach much about work and create family togetherness.

Parents sometimes are unaware of the attitude toward work that they reflect in the family setting. Teachers and counselors can help parents identify the extent to which they emphasize the negative aspects of their jobs—boredom, weariness, discontent, conflict, pressure, competitiveness—during family conversations. If only these aspects are revealed, the child will have difficulty in seeing the positive values that the job provides. Children whose classroom view of work seems heavily negative may be reflecting parental comments and behavior of this type, although the parents may be unaware of the impact of their words and actions. Elementary-age youngsters are not yet mature enough to recognize that for every job holder the advantages of the job exceed the disadvantages. This is especially true if they are taught only the disadvantages. Parental work values are the primary base on which the youngster begins to build a personal view of work.

The family also can provide many decision-making experiences that will help the child build these essential skills. Parents can help the child build self-confidence as well as responsibility by encouraging the child to make choices rather than usurping decisions. As the child makes decisions, she learns the consequences of good and bad choices. Study after study has consistently shown that parents exercise more influence on the eventual educational and vocational choice of children than any other adults. If parents view occupations in limited ways, the child is likely to do so as well. Parents who see only a few occupations as suitable for their daughters limit girls' ability to see wider opportunities. Parents who insist that their children follow parental patterns or ambitions may build frustration, dissatisfaction, and failure.

SUMMARY

The elementary and middle school years are crucial in the career development process, particularly since crucial attitudes, values, and stereotypes are developing. Career development programming must be geared to broaden students' views of themselves as their perceptions relate to careers as well as to enhance their self-esteem. However, because of the diversity of institutions, students, and personnel each school must develop its own program to accommodate these factors. Since each school functions in the context of a larger system, the school district, it is essential that the program be articulated with other schools at levels within the system. The final result should be a program that addresses the needs of the students, that is endorsed within the school and by the school district, and that involves parents and the community in which the school is located.

REFERENCES

Bailey, B. A., & Nihlen, A. S. (1989). Elementary school children's perceptions of the world of work. *Elementary School Guidance and Counseling, 24,* 135–145.

Bearg, E. (1980). Parental role modeling as a career awareness tool. *Elementary School Guidance and Counseling, 14,* 266–268.

Brown, D., Pryzwansky, W. B., & Schulte, A. (1991). *Psychological consultation: Introduction to theory and practice* (2nd ed.). Boston: Allyn & Bacon.

Burck, H. D. (1978). Evaluating programs: Models and strategies. In L. Goldman (Ed.), *Research methods for counselors: Practical approaches in field settings* (pp. 177–197). New York: Wiley.

Burns, R. W. (1972). *New approaches to behavioral objectives.* Dubuque, IA: Wm. C. Brown.

Christopher, C., & Blocker, J. (1980). Career awareness through school and community activities. *Elementary School Guidance and Counseling, 14,* 281–285.

Clapsaddle, D. K. (1973). Career development and teacher inservice preparation. *Elementary School Guidance and Counseling, 8,* 92–97.

Cooker, P. G. (1973). Vocational values of children in grades four, five, and six. *Elementary School Guidance and Counseling, 8,* 112–118.

Cross, F. R. (1974). *Elementary school career education.* Columbus, OH: Charles E. Merrill.

Donahue, M., & Woodcock, G. (1985). Project math-co. In C. L. Thompson (Ed.), Idea exchange. *Elementary School Guidance and Counseling, 19,* 238–240.

Ginzberg, E., Ginzburg, S. W., Axelrad, S., & Herma, J. L. (1951). *Occupational choice: An approach to a general theory.* New York: Columbia University Press.

Hageman, M. B., & Gladding, S. T. (1983). The art of career exploration: Occupational sex-role stereotyping among elementary school children. *Elementary School Guidance and Counseling, 17,* 280–287.

Hales, L. W., & Fenner, B. J. (1973). Sex and social class differences in work values. *Elementary School Guidance and Counseling, 8,* 26–32.

Hansen, L. S. (1972). A model for career development through curriculum. *Personnel and Guidance Journal, 51,* 243–250.

Herma, J. L., Morris, L. L., & Fitz-Gibbon, C. T. (1987). *Evaluators handbook.* Beverly Hills, CA: Sage.

Herr, E. L., & Cramer, S. H. (1988). *Career guidance and counseling through the life span: Systemic approaches* (3rd ed.). Glenview, IL: Scott, Foresman and Co.

Hill, P. L. (1981). Career education at Meadowbrook Mall. In H. H. Splete (Ed.), Career guidance in the elementary school. *Elementary School Guidance and Counseling, 16,* 47–50.

Holland, J. L. (1985). *Vocational choices: A theory of vocational personalities and work environment* (2nd ed.). Englewood Cliffs, NJ: Prentice Hall.

Hoyt, K. B. (1977). *A primer for career education.* Washington, DC: Office of Career Education.

Hoyt, K. B. (1985). Career guidance, educational-reform, and career education. *Vocational Guidance Quarterly, 34,* 6–14.

Innis, J. (1982). Operation employment: A taste of the world of work. In C. L. Thompson (Ed.), Idea exchange column. *Elementary School Guidance and Counseling, 16,* 235–240.

Isaacson, L. E., & Hayes, R. (1980). Adapting career day to the elementary school. *Elementary School Guidance and Counseling, 14,* 258–261.

Jessell, J., & Boyer, M. (1989). *Career expectations among Indiana junior high and middle school students: A second survey.* Terre Haute, IN: Indiana State University.

Leonard, G. E. (1972). Career guidance in the elementary school. *Elementary School Guidance and Counseling, 7,* 234–237.

Lippitt, G. L. (1973). *Visualizing change.* La Jolla, CA: University Associates.

Lippitt, G. L., & Lippitt, R. (1986). *The consulting process in action* (2nd ed.). La Jolla, CA: University Associates.

Marland, S. P., Jr. (1974). *Career education.* New York: McGraw-Hill.

McDonald, J. (1989). *The influence of selected variables in career attitudes and perceived abilities of young adolescents* (doctoral thesis in preparation). Terre Haute, IN: Indiana State University Department of Counseling.

Miller, J. V. (1977). *Career development needs of nine-year-olds: How to improve career development programs.* Washington, DC: National Advisory Council for Career Education.

Montimurro, T. (1980). A career day for elementary school students? *Elementary School Guidance and Counseling, 14,* 263–265.

Morris, L. L., Fitz-Gibbon, C. T., & Lindheim, E. (1987). *How to measure performance and use tests.* Beverly Hills, CA: Sage.

Navin, S. L., & Sears, S. J. (1980). Parental roles in elementary career guidance. *Elementary School Guidance and Counseling, 14,* 269–277.

Nelson, R. C. (1980). The CREST program: Helping children with their choices. *Elementary School Guidance and Counseling.*

NOICC. (1988). *National career counseling and development guidelines: Elementary schools.* Washington, DC: Author.

NOICC. (1989a). *The national career development guidelines: Local handbook for elementary schools.* Washington, DC: Author.

NOICC. (1989b). *The national career development guidelines: Local handbook for high schools.* Washington, DC: Author.

NOICC. (1989c). *The national career development guidelines: Local handbook for middle/junior schools.* Washington, DC: Author.

NOICC. (1989d). *The national career development guidelines: Local handbook for postsecondary institutions.* Washington, DC: Author.

Roberts, N. J. (1971). Establishing a need for a vocational guidance program at the elementary and middle school level. *Elementary School Guidance and Counseling, 6,* 252–257.

Rost, P. (1973). The career pyramid. In G. E. Leonard (Ed.), Career guidance in the elementary and middle school level. *Elementary School Guidance and Counseling, 8,* 50–53.

Rubinton, N. (1985). Career exploration of middle school youth: A university school cooperative. *Vocational Guidance Quarterly, 33,* 249–255.

Seligman, L., Weinstock, L., & Owings, N. (1988). The role of family dynamics in career development of 5-year-olds. *Elementary School Guidance and Counseling, 22,* 222–230.

Staley, N. K., & Mangieri, J. N. (1984). Using books to enhance career awareness. *Elementary School Guidance and Counseling, 18,* 200–208.

Stecher, B. M., & Davis, W. A. (1987). *How to focus an evaluation.* Beverly Hills, CA: Sage.

Super, D. E. (1957). *The psychology of careers.* New York: Harper & Row.

Super, D. E. (1990). Career and life development. In D. Brown, L. Brooks, & Associates, *Career choice and development* (2nd ed., pp. 197–261). San Francisco: Jossey-Bass.

Thompson, C. L., & Parker, J. L. (1971). Fifth graders view the work world scene. *Elementary School Guidance and Counseling, 5,* 281–288.

Walz, G. R., & Benjamin, L. (1984). Systemic career guidance programs. In N. C. Gysbers (Ed.), *Designing careers* (pp. 336–360). San Francisco: Jossey-Bass.

Wernick, W. (1972). The ABLE model. In G. E. Leonard (Ed.), Career guidance in the elementary school. *Elementary School Guidance and Counseling, 7,* 150–155.

Wolleat, P. L. (1979). School-age girls. *Counseling Psychologist, 8,* 22–23.

10

Career Development in the High School

In Chapter 9, a general model for developing career development programs was delineated along with the National Career Development Guidelines model. In this chapter, some of the specific aspects of developing a career development program at the high school level are discussed along with some strategies that may be useful in fostering the career development of high school students. However, before discussing program development, some background information and some of the unique characteristics of high schools and high school students are presented.

BACKGROUND

The idea of individual differences suggests that each person will grow at his or her own pace. Therefore, we must expect some variation in the rate of career development that we encounter in our schools. The U.S. educational system provides considerable latitude for this diversity of growth; nevertheless, the passage of time and progression through the grades bring all individuals to certain crucial points in their educational experience. Decisions must be made, and the individual must pursue the consequences of each decision.

Mitchell (1977) reports the results of the survey of the career development of 17-year-olds (described in Chapter 1). Briefly, the data revealed the following:

1. Most had discussed future plans, twice as often with parents as with counselors.
2. Most could match five out of nine occupations with the physical characteristics or skills required, but less than 10 percent could do all nine correctly.

3. Only 2 percent saw school and academic areas as activities that would be useful for a job.
4. Most recognized that at least one course taken in high school might be useful on a job; most named a vocational subject.
5. Most felt that the best way to find out job requirements was by observation.
6. Nearly all had thought about the job they would like to hold in the future.
7. When identifying important elements of a letter applying for a job, most failed to include educational and training qualifications.

Several more recent studies provide supporting evidence to Mitchell's findings. Noeth, Engen, and Prediger (1984) found that a group of 1,200 college-bound high school juniors reported that interesting classes and their own families (92 percent and 90 percent) were most helpful in terms of assistance with career decisions. Next highest were grades (86 percent) and friends (73 percent). Counselors and out-of-school activities ranked at the bottom (52 percent and 53 percent) in terms of providing assistance with career decision making. Lee (1984) studied 520 rural tenth graders and found that parental influence varied by ethnic group but was the major factor in career development. McNair and Brown (1983), in a related study of 259 tenth graders, also found parental influence to be stronger than any other factor in the career development of this group. Dillard and Campbell (1981) found that parental aspirations for their high schoolers' careers influenced aspirations among African Americans and Puerto Ricans but not Anglos. These studies appear to emphasize the importance of an effective career guidance program in the school that involves parents.

Unfortunately, helping students plan for their work roles after high school seems to be a low priority in high school guidance programs. Moles (1991), reporting the results of a national survey of guidance program directors, indicates that helping students with academic achievement, planning postsecondary schooling, and promoting personal growth all receive more emphasis than career development activities. Not surprisingly, this emphasis is in agreement with the wishes of school counselors according to these program leaders. Moles's findings suggest that school counselors spend approximately 9 to 13 percent of their time in activities that are directly related to career development. These activities include career days, career seminars featuring speakers from specific occupations, visits to job sites, promoting the use of career information, and placement for exploratory work experience.

A fundamental goal of the high school career guidance program should be to alert the student to each impending decision sufficiently far enough in advance to permit the student, and parents when appropriate, to prepare for a wise choice. Only rarely do elementary or middle school students face educational and career decisions of major importance. These situations ordinarily begin to occur near the end of middle or junior high school and then appear with increasing frequency for the next several years. In Chapter 9, we discussed the importance of developing readiness for decision making among elementary and middle school students. The interaction of human development and educational organizations coincides in a way that confronts high-school-age students with a continuous network of situations in which decisions must be made.

Decision making during the high school years can only be as good as the information on which the process is based and the students' ability to interpret and use this information. Students, parents, teachers, and counselors will all need access to comprehensive career information centers stocked with current, accurate information. Career information, its collection, storage, and dissemination have been discussed extensively in Chapter 7 and elsewhere, and here we reinforce the importance of information in the overall career development program. Apparently, most schools have "an abundance of occupational information available to U.S. high school students if they want it" (p. 73), according to a survey by Chapman and Katz (1983). These authors conclude that students do not access the information available to the extent they should. Nearly 20 percent of the students studied had never used reference books, 33 percent had not used occupational books, and in those schools having computerized systems, 50 percent of the students had not used them. Clearly career development programming is needed to change this situation.

A meta-analysis of 18 career development programs by Baker and Popowicz (1983) suggests that, generally speaking, career development programs can be effective. The developers of the National Career Counseling and Guidance Guidelines for high schools (NOICC, 1988) conclude that these programs would have several positive outcomes—on students, their parents, and their schools—based on the literature reviews of Campbell, Connell, Boyle, and Bhaerman (1983), Crites (1987), Herr (1982), and Spokane and Oliver (1983). These benefits are listed in Figure 10.1.

While there may not be unanimous agreement that career development programs in high schools will produce the outcomes identified in Figure 10.1, there is widespread agreement that the high school years are crucial and that many activities that occur routinely in the high school lend themselves to fostering career planning and development. For example, students are confronted with numerous curricular choices, and it is not unusual for counselors to engage students in consideration of the occupational implications of their educational courses. Certain entire programs of study, such as auto mechanics, business education, and construction trades, have dramatic implications for career choice making, and the choice of these curricula is typically accompanied by a discussion of the occupational consequences of the choice. Similarly, students' desires to get part-time jobs and make postsecondary educational plans have tremendous implications for career choice making.

Continuation of the exploratory activities initiated at earlier levels should be maintained, with major attention during the high school years on

FIGURE 10.1   *Expected Benefits of High School Career Development Programs*

Student Benefits
   Decreased dropout rates
   Higher self-esteem and self-concept
   Improved school attendance
   Better social adjustment
   Lower rates of delinquency, truancy, and running away
   Understanding of the relationship between education and employment
   More competent decision making
   Improved information-seeking and information-use skills
   Awareness of changes in the world of work
   Greater independence in decision making
   Improved academic achievement
   Increased appreciation for the value of education
   Increased motivation resulting from personal career goals
   More realistic selection of courses of study

Benefits to Parents
   Greater parental involvement in students' career planning
   Increased parental satisfaction with students' career plans

Benefits to Schools
   Program goals stated in terms of student outcomes (thus accountability enhanced)
   Student achievement assessed regularly
   Program components evaluated in relationship to student outcomes
   Student outcomes and program components clearly specified at each level
   Reinforcement of learning from previous levels
   Student competency assessment that provides basis for individualized career planning assistance
   Individualized career plans that provide continuity of career planning at various levels

narrowing and clarifying students' goals. Identification of specific career options should not be expected for most high school students; and those students who are likely to pursue a baccalaureate degree may be least inclined to engage in career planning. The refining of choice to the point of naming a specific goal is not a function of age, grade level, or ability but rather should be directly related to the imminence of entry into the world of work or into a specific preparatory program. That choice should precede the entry point by sufficient time for the student to acquire the specialized training that the chosen occupation requires. For example, the scientific and technical professions generally require a specific, detailed baccalaureate program for admission. College prep for these fields often specifies a program heavily loaded with high school mathematics and science. A decision to move toward occupations in this general cluster would have to be made early enough in high school to ensure completion of these preparatory courses. On the other hand, some professional occupations require specialization only in the final year or two of college. In these fields, the student could remain unfocused until the college sophomore year and still encounter no delay in preparation.

Teachers and counselors have a crucial responsibility in the career development process: to help students develop awareness of the prerequisites for entry. Unless the students are willing to sacrifice the time needed to make up missed prerequisites, the opportunity to choose an area (e.g., engineering) is lost when the student passes the point at which the first required prerequisite (e.g., introductory algebra) ordinarily is started.

HIGH SCHOOL STUDENTS

As suggested earlier, high school students undergo a number of transitions including preparing for the transition from high school to work. Unfortunately, as many as 25 percent leave school prior to graduation. Although 40 percent of these return to school through alternative high school programs, community college programs, and other means, the economic consequences for those who do not are dramatic. For example, in 1985 a 25-year-old who had finished high school earned over $4,000 per year more than students who had not and could expect to earn over $250,000 more during his life span (Pallas, 1986).

Students who are planning to graduate from high school are also making important educational decisions that have economic, psychological, and sociological consequences. In 1985, 58 percent of high school graduates enrolled in some type of postsecondary institution. However, the enrollment of African-American students in postsecondary institutions in 1985 was 42 percent, down from 50 percent in 1977 (Wetzel, 1987). As noted earlier, high school graduates can expect to earn $250,000 more during their lifetime than high school dropouts. College graduates can expect to earn $450,000 more than high school graduates and $700,000 more than high school dropouts over their lifetime (W. T. Grant Foundation, 1988).

Minorities face a particularly difficult situation if they leave school prematurely since there is every indication that they generally fare less well in the labor force than their white counterparts. Unemployment data suggest that the employment ratio of minority youths to white youths has risen to 2.4 to 1 in the last 30 years (W. T. Grant Foundation, 1988). Almost one in two African-American high school dropouts is likely to be unemployed (U.S. Bureau of Labor Statistics, 1986).

A study by Post–Kammer (1987) shows that eleventh-grade girls' work values tended to run contrary to gender stereotypes in some instances. For example, girls valued achievement and variety to a higher extent and security to a lesser extent than did boys. However, boys valued management, economic returns, and independence more highly, and girls valued altruism and way of life more highly, which is in accordance with traditional gender stereotypes. These values and their implications for career planning need careful consideration, particularly for young women. Substantially more young women enter the labor force early and remain there longer than they did a generation ago. Moreover, both the entry rate and the proportion remaining in the labor force indefinitely will increase probably to the point that it approximates that of men (W. T. Grant Foundation, 1988).

During their high school years many students will gain their first experiences as a worker. In 1986, 41 percent of 16- and 17-year-old students were in the labor force (W. T. Grant Foundation, 1988). Most of the jobs held by these young workers are entry-level service jobs such as those in fast-food restaurants. These work experiences provide students with valuable (if sometimes negative) work experiences that can be capitalized on when exploring career options.

We also know that students with various types of disabilities enter high school. One estimate is that the number of students enrolled in special education programs from preschool through high school is approximately 4 million. During the high school years, students with learning disabilities make up the largest group (about 50 percent) while mentally retarded students constitute the second largest group (about 35 percent) (Office of Special Education and Rehabilitation Services, 1988). The consequences of not maximizing these students' educational potential and failing to make well-considered career plans is potentially more disastrous for students with disabilities than for any other group because of the biases that exist in our society regarding the potential of these students as workers.

As noted earlier, parents are an important influence in the career development of adolescents. Many adolescents do have difficulty communicating with their parents, according to a study of 11,000 eighth, ninth, and tenth graders (Bensen, Mangen, & Williams, 1986). Only 25 percent of these students said they would go to their parents if they were having trouble with alcohol or sex. However, it seems clear that many students do talk directly to parents about careers or are influenced indirectly by them. What is not clear is whether parents are maximizing their impact, but it is unlikely that this is occurring.

THE INSTITUTION

High schools are more diverse than either elementary or middle schools. For example, there are comprehensive high schools that offer a wide variety of programs including academic, vocational, and general courses of study. However, some high schools are specialized with regard to curricular offering. For example, it is not unusual to find vocational-technical high schools, high schools that emphasize the arts (music, dance, etc.) and mathematics and science preparatory schools. So-called alternative high schools may offer daytime or evening programs for potential dropouts or reentry opportunities for students who have already left school.

Types of students and their backgrounds will be major determiners of the career development program, as will the philosophy and objectives of the school itself. In the next section, we consider the unique aspects of developing a comprehensive career development program in a high school.

DEVELOPING THE PROGRAM

In Chapter 9, the process of developing a comprehensive career development program was outlined, a process that is identical for each level. What varies are the competencies that are to be developed for the high school. These are listed in Figure 10.2 (NOICC, 1989b, pp. 5–6) along with some sample indicators.

As was the case with the guidelines for elementary and middle schools, the competencies and indicators shown in Figure 10.2 are general guidelines, and it is expected that school staffs will develop their own competencies and skills based on the needs of the students. Obviously, the competencies outlined in Figure 10.2 will need to be translated into a series of specific objectives and programs or delivery mechanisms developed to achieve these objectives. Delivery mechanisms are discussed later in this chapter.

One task involved in planning and implementing a comprehensive career development program for an individual school not discussed in Chapter 9 is articulation. Articulation can be roughly defined as the process of coordination both within and across program levels (NOICC, 1988). The obvious purposes of program articulation, whether it be within a school or among school levels, are to ensure that the districtwide program is comprehensive, free from unneeded redundancy, and to plan so activities will be sequenced properly. In Chapter 9, we briefly discussed articulating the elementary school career development program with curricular offerings as well as sequencing activities so they will add to students' knowledge and skill level in a logical fashion. As was stated at the outset of this chapter, the elementary and middle school programs should prepare the student for career development activities in the high school. Numerous states have developed comprehensive, carefully sequenced, and articulated models of career development programs that can be used as models in this planning process. A list of these programs is presented at the end of this chapter.

DELIVERY MECHANISMS

The processes identified in the local handbooks for the *National Career Development Guidelines* for elementary and middle/junior high schools (NOICC, 1989a, c) were presented in Chapter 9. The discussion that follows identifies processes that can be used to develop career development competencies in high-school-age students.

FIGURE 10.2 *Competencies to Be Developed in High School Students and Sample Indicators*

Competencies	Sample Indicators: The student will
1. Understanding of the influence of a positive self-concept on career development	1. Demonstrate the ability to manage her/his behavior in developing and maintaining a healthy self-concept
2. Interpersonal and social skills required for positive interaction with others	2. Describe appropriate employee-employer interactions in varying situations
3. Understanding of the interrelationships of emotional and physical development and career decision making	3. Exhibit behaviors that are important to good physical and mental health
4. Understanding of the interrelationship between educational achievement and career planning, training and placement	4. Identify essential learning skills required in the work environment
5. Positive attitudes toward work and learning	5. Demonstrate positive work ethic and attitude
6. Skills for locating, evaluating, and interpreting information about career opportunities	6. Describe the impact of factors such as population, climate, and geographic location on local job opportunities
7. Skills for preparing for, seeking, obtaining, maintaining, and advancing in a job	7. Develop skills in preparing a resume and completing a job application
8. Understanding of how societal needs and functions influence the nature and structure of work	8. Demonstrate an understanding of the global economy and how it affects each individual
9. Skills in making decisions and choosing alternatives for and pursuing educational and career goals	9. Project and describe factors that may influence educational and career decisions
10. Understanding of the interrelationships of life roles and career	10. Describe the ways career choice may influence lifestyle
11. Understanding of the continuous changes in male/female roles and how they relate to career decisions	11. Develop attitudes, behaviors, and skills that contribute to the elimination of sex stereotypes and sex bias
12. Skills in career exploration and planning	12. Develop career plans that include the concept that a changing world demands lifelong learning

Source: National Career Development Guidelines: Local Handbook for High Schools. (1989). Washington, DC: NOICC, pp 5–6.

Classrooms and Groups

Let us first consider educational situations, in which the teacher is likely to be responsible for the career development program. We focus most of our attention on classroom and group-related activities. When considering the teacher's involvement in career development, however, one must not think only of the classroom. Nor should one think that only the teacher works with students in groups. The counselor often may teach a class or lead a group, and the teacher often is involved with students out of class in career exploration activities such as field trips and visits to training programs.

The development of the self-concept is a continuing, lifelong process that begins with the individual's first awareness of self as a person. Continuous though this process is, there are periods of particular intensity. The secondary and postsecondary school years comprise one of these periods, in which the individual is deeply involved in learning to understand the self in relationship to others and to the world.

The school provides the principal setting in which the elementary and early secondary student encounters the world outside the close family circle. In this setting, the student usually establishes the first prolonged contacts with adults and with peers who are not a part of the family group. It is entirely normal to select some of these people as models and ideals. As the student experiments with the different roles perceived as possibilities, he encounters varying degrees of gratification and satisfaction. Some of the roles played may be at variance or even in conflict with the roles that would be encouraged and approved within the family circle. Thus, inevitably, the school setting helps the student to broaden his development.

Most secondary and postsecondary schools attempt to assist students in the career development process by using portions of regular academic classes for special units related to the general topic of educational and vocational planning. There are certain obvious advantages to this approach. First, the administrative difficulties of staffing and scheduling are reduced since the work is simply incorporated into a regular course. Second, if a required course is used, all students at a given grade level are reached automatically, thus providing the broad coverage that the administrator usually desires. Third, the use of certain courses for special units leads to involvement of those teachers in the guidance program.

These advantages, unfortunately, have corresponding disadvantages. Attaching a special unit to a subject-matter class may solve the staffing problem, but in an unfortunate way. The subject-matter teacher may lack preparation or background for such teaching, with the result that she will feel both unhappy and threatened. Subject-matter teachers, naturally, have an affinity for their own subject area and see so much in their own field that they need to teach students that they are often reluctant to give up any sizable portion of that subject time for a special unit. Similarly, even though scheduling problems are resolved by the special unit, designating time in one subject area for a special unit may cause difficulties with accrediting agencies or may result in student deficiencies in that subject area.

Even though a guidance unit in freshman English will reach all freshmen enrolled in that course, this may not be the best or most appropriate time to present the unit to all freshmen. Individual differences in development and in personal plans may make the unit appropriate for some students, but perhaps premature for others. Placing the course arbitrarily at a given grade level may meet the needs of the average students but may fall seriously short for the others.

Balancing the advantages and disadvantages of using subject-matter time for guidance units must be resolved by the administrator. Resolving the problem requires careful consideration of many factors, including assessment of student needs, teacher abilities and interests, guidance staff utilization, and various other components.

Guidance units incorporated into regularly scheduled courses may be either general or specialized in nature. A general guidance unit usually is complete in itself, with little or no direct connection to the subject area into which it is inserted. A specialized guidance unit usually has a direct relationship to the subject area.

General guidance units may be found at any grade level of the secondary school. Because of the desire to reach all students at that level, they are usually attached to courses such as English or social studies. The objectives of these courses are usually broad enough, especially in content, to make them more amenable to such adaptation.

At the upper junior high and lower senior high levels, the general units most frequently are related to such broad topics as orientation to school, educational and vocational planning, or personal adjustment. In the upper grades they may, instead, deal with selecting a college, applying for a job, military service, or some similar topic appropriate for the person about to complete high school work. The duration of units may vary from 1 to 4 weeks.

The purposes of general guidance units vary considerably. Usually the purpose is to encourage and stimulate occupational exploration and to help students see the relationship between school and later careers. When the purpose is limited in this way, there is usually a reasonable chance that the unit will be successful. If, on the other hand, the school attempts to meet its total obligation for career development through such a unit, the project is doomed to failure, since the total process is too large to be handled in such a manner. Close cooperation between teacher and counselor is essential, so the counselor can assist the teacher in developing and presenting the unit and so the unit can lead to individual counseling for students for whom it is appropriate.

Specialized units frequently are career oriented and therefore often focus on the career opportunities that relate to a specific area. Such units logically are a part of courses that have obvious career implications. They also may be relevant in courses that have broader, fundamental, general education value, since few occupations are filled any longer by workers with only a specialized preparation. Too often in the past such specialized units have concentrated on the related specialties and have overlooked the broader application that each subject may have. Thus, non-college-bound students may feel that, because college preparation is necessary to become a chemist or a physicist, science holds no opportunity for them. Understanding the interrelationships of occupations should help the teacher see the broader implications and provide an opportunity for students to grasp the vast range of openings at various levels in all fields. Career-oriented units not only assist the student in career development but also serve a special purpose in stimulating interest in a specific course. Close cooperation between teacher and counselor will be helpful to both and will provide maximum value to the student.

Career education advocates (Hoyt, Pinson, Laramore, & Mangum, 1973) staunchly support the idea of teacher involvement in the career development process. They contend that the activities just described inevitably include a degree of artificiality because the unit is laid on the ordinary subject-matter instructional efforts of the teacher. They propose that more could be accomplished if the attention to career-related aspects were totally infused into the day-to-day classroom activities. This would require the teacher continually to relate subject matter to the world of work, to use illustrations from work whenever possible, and to orient classroom learning to postschool plans of the students. While one can argue against this position in theory, most high school teachers never adopted this approach. Its successful implementation necessitates major curricular revision and joint effort by teacher, counselor, and administrator. Since curricular revision is not in the offing, the classroom teacher can use career units advantageously.

For many years, a number of schools have included regular courses in their curriculum, under various titles, often "Careers" or "Occupations." They are sometimes taught at either the ninth- or the twelfth-grade level. Grade placement of such a course always has presented a difficult problem. Placement in the ninth grade permits maximum opportunity for educational planning after that grade, but students often feel so far removed from the world of work that motivation may be difficult. If the course is taught at the twelfth-grade level, students are more likely to see its pertinence to their own lives, but the course may come too late in the educational career to permit capitalizing on it effectively. The difficulties at either level can be met best if the course is developed to meet the needs of the students involved. Obviously, the ninth grader is likely to be more concerned with exploring occupations broadly, as they affect educational planning for the years ahead, whereas the senior is more apt to be confronted with the specifics of job seeking and preparation for entrance into the world of work. Ideally, it should be a required course and carry credit.

Organized classes in careers permit more extensive consideration of the topic than is possible in the short unit studied in another class. Nevertheless, any course will not be of limited value to the student if it is approached in textbook fashion with the aim of thorough familiarization with the world of work. The goal of such a course should be to maximize self-actualization through the development of concepts appropriate to the student's level of maturity and proximity to the world of work.

One advantage of an organized course in "Occupations" or "Careers" is that it can be closely tied to the school's total guidance program and properly staffed. In some schools the course is taught by a member of the counseling staff, whose academic preparation may be more appropriate for teaching such a course than is that of a subject-area teacher. Even though this arrangement lets the counselor contact with students, it also reduces the time available for individual counseling and other activities.

A regularly scheduled course taught by a counselor may offer the best opportunity to meet the individual needs of the students enrolled. It should be possible to relate class activities to individual counseling and to develop an approach based on both group procedures and individual counseling, with the student being involved in both phases to whatever extent is appropriate. When this dual approach can be arranged, the student will have the maximum opportunity to benefit.

The adoption of an organized course may cause a school faculty to assume that it has met its responsibility for helping students in the career development process. When this happens, the course becomes a one-shot effort, and the basic axiom that career choice and development should start in the early years and continue throughout one's life is disregarded. Two- and four-year colleges often adopt this view by offering an elective course called "Life and Career Planning" or "Career Exploration." Although the course is useful to those who enroll, it is not enough to meet the needs of all students.

Another aspect of this problem occurs when the careers course is organized on the premise that each participating student will make a career choice during the course. This approach disregards the developmental aspect of career development and may lead the student to the unwarranted view that a vocational choice is static and permanent rather than dynamic and flexible. Even in adulthood, the possibility of modification and revision of choice—because of change in self-concept, technological developments, and other factors—is so likely for most people that any implication of early permanent choice is not only misleading but also likely to make later adjustment difficult. A much more realistic approach is to help the student see vocational choice as a continuing series of choices, each of which is likely to be revised, thus leading to a new choice that may similarly be modified.

A final disadvantage can exist in the regularly scheduled careers course if it focuses only on the occupational aspects and disregards the educational factors. Educational and vocational planning and development are so closely interrelated, both during formal schooling and later, that it is inappropriate to consider one without the other. This is especially important in a society in which we can expect increasing numbers of adults to need continuing education and retraining beyond the regular school years to prepare them for occupations that did not exist when they were in school. As technological changes eliminate and modify existing occupations and create new ones, more adults become involved in further education to fit them for new jobs. The school can serve this group better if it helps them accept and understand the inevitability of change rather than leading them toward a specific niche as a definite and final goal.

Concern for the career development of the individual should have a natural and normal place within any classroom. Each member of the instructional staff has a responsibility in this area of student growth and maturity.

This responsibility probably can be met best by an awareness by all staff members and a concerted effort by all, led by the administration and the guidance staff, to develop an approach that permeates the school program with sufficient breadth and depth to meet the varying needs of all students.

Small Groups

Group procedures may enable the school or other agency to work with all or many of these individuals collectively on certain aspects of their development. The commonality of the problem may make it easier for more to become involved with members of their peer group in seeking information or understanding that will help them resolve their problems. This attitude may also lead them to accept suggestions and reactions from the peer group that they would be inclined to resist from others. The recognition that their peers face similar problems and uncertainties may help them obtain a different perspective on their own concerns, and this may encourage more independence and initiative on their part in seeking information and solution. In addition, an inevitable sharing of knowledge and information leads to a broader foundation for ultimate decision making.

Certain disadvantages or limitations exist in group procedures, and care must be taken to ensure the accrual of advantages and the avoidance of negative experiences. One individual within the group may be ahead of the others in personally acquiring the information or resolution that the group is seeking. Even though no loss may result from being part of the group, this individual's personal progress may be slowed by group participation. It also is possible for specific individual problems to be overlooked or sidetracked while the group focuses on a broader, more general concern. Thus either the individual does not acquire what she had hoped to gain, or the rest of the group marks time while attention is given to the individual's specific concern. Finally, there is always the possibility of loss of status by an individual within the group, since it may be difficult to develop a totally accepting group.

Even though a school goes to great pains to provide career information in class situations, it should not disregard out-of-class group activities led by the counselor. Class activities usually are oriented toward the general needs of the class, even in schools that make every effort to individualize instruction. Within each class, one can expect to find individuals whose particular needs scatter around the general mean for the class. Some individuals will obviously be farther from the mean than others. For those whose needs are quite different from those of majority, the general class activity will have less significance. In many situations, these special needs can be met more adequately by out-of-class groups. For example, students already planning to terminate their formal education shortly confront quite different questions than do students who anticipate continuing to graduation or beyond. A senior class unit on how to apply for a job is of no help to the early dropout, who expects to be gone from school before then. Unless she can be helped before leaving school, the unit is wasted. Further, she may need help in acquiring information about specific job opportunities available locally to young work-ers with limited education. However, exploration of this topic in sufficient depth to be meaningful to a potential dropout may not be of crucial impor-tance to the rest of the group.

Group career development activities may be quite varied. For example, it is possible to hold career seminars where a representative of an occupation such as insurance sales or over-the-road truck driving can discuss the nature of his job, the training, requirements, hiring requirements, lifestyle advan-tages and disadvantages, and so forth with a small group of interested stu-dents. Groups can also be organized for exploratory purposes, to focus on the career decision-making process, or for field trips to explore hospitals, indus-trial sites, and so forth.

Dropout prevention groups that center on career development activities are increasingly popular. In *Dropping Out or Hanging In* (Brown, 1990), which is a manual for students to use in dropout prevention groups, students are first taken through a series of self-awareness activities. These are fol-lowed by activities designed to teach decision-making skills, and then stu-dents are encouraged to practice using their skills in setting career, education, and other life goals. The culmination of these small groups is preparing students to "drop into" school if they do drop out and decide that they have made an error.

Prior to involving students in a group activity, a screening interview should be held to determine the students' objectives, degree of motivation, and the extent to which they will work collaboratively with other group members. Unmotivated students and potential discipline problems may be precluded from groups unless the counselor feels that the problems can be corrected in the group setting.

Life Planning Classes and Groups

The focus throughout much of this chapter has been on career exploration experiences. However, there is increasing support for broader career experi-ences that involve integrating career planning with other life roles. Brown (1980) outlines what he terms a life planning workshop for high school students, which consists of seven components: (1) understanding human behavior, (2) conceptualizing one's self as a winner, (3) the importance of fantasy in planning, (4) matching fantasy and reality, (5) setting goals, (6) short-term planning, and (7) long-term planning.

Amatea, Clark, and Cross (1984) evaluated a two-week course for high school students, called Lifestyles, aimed at (1) increasing students' aware-ness of their values and their preferences for various life roles; (2) increasing students' awareness of the costs and benefits associated with various life-styles; and (3) helping students establish life role priorities. They found that their course did seem to increase students' decisiveness about their career choice. They also found that at the end of the group sessions, males and females did not vary in their attitudes toward the family role.

RESOURCES FOR CLASSES AND GROUPS

It seems appropriate to review various resources that can be used with groups, with major emphasis on awareness and exploration objectives. We briefly consider publications, resources within the school, and community resources. Sources of occupational information have already been discussed in Chapter 7.

Publications

The school newspaper offers almost unlimited opportunity for passing information to students, arousing their interest, informing them of services that are available, or in other ways involving them in acquiring career information. It has many built-in advantages and should be used regularly to communicate with the student body.

The news columns of the newspaper can be used to inform the students of career conferences, scheduled field trips, visits to the school by industrial or educational representatives, and other newsworthy events that relate to career information. Feature pages are logical spots for stories such as reports from recent graduates or reviews of new career books available. Many aspects of career information lend themselves to a regular column presentation; for example, nearby colleges can be described in a continuing series, as can jobs available locally or nearby nonacademic training programs.

Special issues can be used to inform students of a major activity such as a Career Day. Details of the event and supplementary information about the topics to be included in the program can be published so students may participate more intelligently in the event.

Local daily newspapers provide additional access to student readers. Already rich with information about what is happening in the community, many also carry special business or financial pages that feature stories about employment opportunities or new and expanding business or industry. The classified advertisements, a convenient barometer of job openings in the community, can be used to build realistic concepts of the local world of work.

Besides being an excellent source of local information, the newspaper usually provides some coverage of school activities. This offers a means of keeping parents and other school patrons aware of the school program of career education and information. Special events in the school always warrant coverage in the local press. Keeping the community informed in this way can lead to closer cooperation between school, students, and parents.

Many schools regularly prepare a student handbook. Intended basically as an orientation device for new students, it has considerable potential as an instrument for transmitting educational information and materials about services available to students. Most handbooks include a section that presents the various curricula offered in the school. To be of maximum utility for students and parents, this section should include the educational and vocational goals to which each curriculum leads. Examples of employment opportunities, further schooling available, and future advanced career fields should be discussed here. A brief survey of occupational fields related to each subject should be discussed here as well as a brief survey of occupational fields related to each subject.

The handbook is probably more practical if arrangements are made for its use in a series of orientation sessions for new students, either within the framework of regularly scheduled classes or in special groups created specifically to help students adjust to their new environment. Group discussion of the contents should emphasize the importance of the information in the book.

School Resources

Even the most circumscribed and isolated school often has resources of which most staff members are unaware. This is especially true of career information resources, often because no one has attempted to determine and evaluate the information existing beyond the career resource center.

Useful resources include the educational and occupational experiences of the school staff. A simple inventory of the institutions attended by staff members probably will reveal a fairly adequate representation of many nearby colleges and universities—often including the schools in which most of the college-bound students ultimately will enroll. Obviously, a staff member who has attended "school X" can help students who are interested in the institution. Impressions of types of students, institutional goals and standards, student life, living accommodations, standards of dress, major activities, and similar information that usually cannot be assessed accurately from the printed page are particularly helpful.

Similarly, the typical school staff will have experienced a wide variety of part-time or full-time work during their high school and college years and later. In addition to their direct experiences, one is likely to find additional occupations with which they have had indirect contact through family, close friends, or other personal contact.

Another often overlooked built-in resource is the student body itself. Many young people have had opportunities to observe or experience a specific occupation, or they have become knowledgeable in some other way.

Community Resources

Outside the school, but within the local community, are many resources that can build insight into and understanding of career fields. Almost everyone is a potential resource who can be used to help students. Many local agencies recognize a responsibility in this area and are willing to assist the school in activities related to career choice.

Schools that maintain a file of community resources will have on hand an extensive listing of agencies and individuals that can be used in a variety of ways. Schools that do not have such a file may want to consider some of the following nearby resources.

In most cases, local businesses and industries already have close ties with the school. They have a continuing interest in the students of the local school, which is often their main source of employees, particularly for positions that do not require post-high-school training. Because of this natural relationship, they are usually interested in cooperating in any way possible to improve the quality of those students. This provides the school with an entree to representatives of local businesses and industries, who may be able to inform students about their fields of activity. Local professional groups may also be eager to render the same kind of service to interested students.

Local service clubs, whose members are drawn from local businesses, industries, and professions, are also frequently eager to provide assistance to the school or to specific students in problems related to career information. They can be helpful in organizing career day conferences or community occupational surveys. Members often are encouraged to make themselves available to students to discuss career opportunities in their fields.

Local labor union representatives or officials can provide information on training requirements, apprenticeship programs, employment opportunities, membership requirements, and benefits.

Government offices located in the community, at the local, state, or national level, often can provide information that will assist students. Government service opportunities and requirements are areas that can be covered by such representatives. Agencies such as county extension offices and employment services already are involved, by the nature of their work, in career information activities.

Every community includes some social agencies that are involved in career information activities. Particularly likely to be involved are agencies whose services are directed primarily at youth, such as Boy Scouts, Girl Scouts, YMCA, YWCA, and 4-H clubs. Many of these serve the same young people as the school. Special career information projects that they may develop can be of genuine assistance to the school. They may also have access to information in specialized fields that can help the school in its career information program.

Many churches organize special activity programs for school-age youth. Often these programs focus on the concerns and problems of the age group involved; for teenagers, this inevitably includes career-related problems. Many churches support or maintain church-related colleges or other educational institutions that may be of particular significance to members of the church's youth group. A number of churches operate summer camping programs for school-age youth, thus providing an additional means of reaching young people.

The importance of the local library to the career information program already has been mentioned. Cooperation with the library often will lead to a more comprehensive collection of career information materials as well as to the development of special services that will be of assistance to school-age youth.

Many resources cut across more than one of the categories we have considered. In many ways, these may be the most valuable of all. Counselors and teachers may find it advantageous to establish networks involving contact with as many school and community resources as possible so that each of those contacts can provide information on new resources.

OTHER INTERVENTIONS

Career Counseling

The career counseling process is discussed in detail in Chapter 14 and thus is not examined in detail here. It is worth noting that career counseling with high school students typically involves *initial* choice as opposed to adjustment within the current occupation or job loss. Many students who come to counselors for career counseling have little or no work experience, have developed few if any salable skills, may have a very limited understanding of their interests, values, and aptitudes, and probably have a very limited understanding of the skills needed to acquire and successfully perform a job. As a consequence of their limited exposure to the real world and often to other types of career information, experiences that can be provided through various types of information, including job shadowing, interviews with established workers, print, and audiovisual materials, are very important.

Career planning, as opposed to career counseling, may also be (and probably will be) a longer term process. Many high schools require counselors to discuss current career interests as they relate to current educational objectives each time counselors meet with students to engage in course selection or longer term educational planning. Career counselors need to be prepared to work with a wide variety of situations including various mental and physical disabilities, being mentally or artistically gifted, lack of motivation or educational achievement, and so forth.

As mentioned earlier, the label *talented* need not be restricted to students with high levels of academic ability. Dayton and Feldhusen (1989) identify two types of talented students enrolled in vocational educational programs; academically talented and vocationally talented. "Vocationally talented students are students who demonstrate exceptional capability within one of more vocational areas" (p. 357). Vocational education directors surveyed identified a number of special needs of both the academically and vocationally talented students, including the need for self-evaluation, in-depth career development activities, seminars, use of community resources, and the ability to interact with others who have similar intellectual capacity and interests.

In Moles's (1991) study of high school guidance programs, he found that helping students with academic achievement and planning for postsecondary schooling were the areas most emphasized by high school counselors according to program directors. It is suggested here that these two activities be integrated with career planning. As students are seen for course planning activities, counselors can explore interests and perceptions of aptitudes, review achievement test information, and discuss the implications of this information and the courses that are being selected for career choice. Students and counselors may wish to complete an Individualized Career Plan using a form such as the one shown in Figure 10.3 (NOICC, 1989b, pp. 81–87).

Involving Parents

A number of studies were cited at the outset of this chapter that strongly suggest that parents should be an integral part of the career development process. Another example of this type of information came out of a study by Palmer and Cochran (1988), who found that the Partners Program—which consists of the *Parent Career Guidance Manual* (Cochran, 1985), three workbooks that help parents facilitate self-awareness and the development of occupational information, and a planning manual—improved career development scores as measured by the *Career Development Inventory.*

The outcome of the *Going Places* program described by Amatea and Cross (1980) was not as carefully evaluated as that of the Partners Program, but it had similar components. These components were: compiling self-evaluation data (awareness), systematically exploring careers, developing the skills to acquire occupational information, matching self and occupational information, exploring educational alternatives, and developing decision-making skills. However, unlike the self-directed Partners Program, students and parents were involved in six two-hour counselor-led sessions to consider each of the careers mentioned. Evaluation data suggested that students and parents approved of the group format and appeared to benefit from the program.

Programs for Special Students

Gifted

It is probably a truism that counselors consistently underestimate the needs of students who are gifted, or as Pask-McCartney and Salomone (1988) termed them, multipotentialed students, because they have so many avenues to pursue. It is also the case that having so many career avenues open is a curse of sorts. Post–Kammer and Perrone (1983) report that over 30 percent of the gifted students in their study felt unprepared to make career decisions when they left high school. It is probably the case that the types of programs needed by these students do not vary dramatically from those required by their less talented counterparts, although a report by Borman, Nash, and Colson (1978) suggests that the gifted students in their program did not like the testing component. It is certainly possible that these students have been tested so extensively that they are alienated from the formal assessment process.

FIGURE 10.3 *Individual Career Plan Form: High School Level*

This activity suggests a technique to help staff monitor and strengthen student achievement of the career guidance and counseling competencies and to assist in developing an educational and career plan.

Instructions
1. It is recommended that an Individual Career Plan be maintained for each student throughout the high school experience.
2. The counselor or counselors to whom a student is assigned will be responsible for meeting with that student to develop, review, revise and implement the plan.
3. As product evaluation is completed, an individual profile of student attainment of the standards will be added to the plan.

Name _____
            Last   First   Middle

School _____

1. My interests are:

9th Grade	10th Grade	11th Grade	12th Grade
_____	_____	_____	_____
_____	_____	_____	_____
_____	_____	_____	_____

2. My abilities and skills are:

9th Grade	10th Grade	11th Grade	12th Grade
_____	_____	_____	_____
_____	_____	_____	_____
_____	_____	_____	_____

3. My hobbies and recreational/leisure activities are:

9th Grade	10th Grade	11th Grade	12th Grade
_____	_____	_____	_____
_____	_____	_____	_____
_____	_____	_____	_____

4. The school subjects in which I do best are: _____

9th Grade	10th Grade	11th Grade	12th Grade
_____	_____	_____	_____
_____	_____	_____	_____
_____	_____	_____	_____

5. I have explored careers in the following occupation clusters: _____

9th Grade	10th Grade	11th Grade	12th Grade
_____	_____	_____	_____
_____	_____	_____	_____
_____	_____	_____	_____

FIGURE 10.3 *Continued*

6. I have worked part time or had some experience with the following jobs or work tasks:

9th Grade	10th Grade	11th Grade	12th Grade
_____	_____	_____	_____
_____	_____	_____	_____
_____	_____	_____	_____

7. My tentative career goal(s) is (are): _____

9th Grade	10th Grade	11th Grade	12th Grade
_____	_____	_____	_____
_____	_____	_____	_____
_____	_____	_____	_____

8. I have chosen the following curriculum to study in high school. Courses are outlined on my high school studies plan, which is part of my cumulative record.
   (*20*) Credit Diploma _____
   (*22*) Credit Diploma _____
   Other _____

9. I plan to pursue further training beyond high school in the following programs, schools, or colleges:

   _____
   _____
   _____
   _____

OR

   I plan to obtain work in one of the following jobs (businesses, industries):

   _____
   _____
   _____
   _____

10. I have attained the indicators specified in the local student career development standards. If not, I have met with my counselor to determine activities I can do to strengthen each indicator that I have not attained. Also attach individual profile summarizing student attainment of indicators each year.

	Grade			
Competency	9th	10th	11th	12th
Understanding the influence of a positive self-concept.	____	____	____	____
Skills to interact positively with others.	____	____	____	____
Understanding the relationship between educational achievement and career planning.	____	____	____	____

(continued)

FIGURE 10.3   *Continued*

	Grade			
Competency	9th	10th	11th	12th
Understanding the need for positive attitudes toward work and learning.	____	____	____	____
Skills to locate, evaluate and interpret career information.	____	____	____	____
Skills to prepare to seek, obtain, maintain and change jobs.	____	____	____	____
Understanding how societal needs and functions influence the nature and structure of work.	____	____	____	____
Skills to make decisions.	____	____	____	____
Understanding the interrelationship of life roles.	____	____	____	____
Understanding the continuous changes in male/female roles.	____	____	____	____
Skills in career planning.	____	____	____	____

SIGNATURES:

Student _____

Parent _____

Counselor _____

Source: National Career Development Guidelines: Local Handbook for High Schools. (1989). Washington, DC: NOICC, pp. 81–87.

Physically Disabled

As Lombana (1979, 1980) aptly notes, the main barrier to entrance to various careers for students with visual and auditory disabilities is not their disability; it is the mistaken beliefs of employers, teachers, counselors, family members, and members of the general public regarding the potential of these clients. Her statement can be extended to all but students with the most severe disabilities. These students need the typical career development program, including activities to foster self-awareness and information about work. However, the career development program must be extended to include building self-confidence and the remediation of the negative attitudes of others (Lombana, 1980).

Students with disabilities, like other students, need to have an opportunity to observe models similar to themselves. These observations can come through discussions for visually impaired students (Lombana, 1979, 1980) or through firsthand observations for students with disabilities who are not visually impaired. Self-esteem development can be facilitated by making sure that the environment in which the students go to school has been adapted to meet their needs and that learning opportunities are developed and taught so these students can experience success. Counselors may need to become more actively involved in the career placement process so they can work to offset the negative attitudes of employers.

Emotionally Disabled

Levinson (1984) suggests that career development programs for emotionally disturbed students will necessarily have to be more extensive and intensive than those for typical students. He suggests that a comprehensive program would involve a simulated employer-employee program in the school in which the student would have the opportunity to try out several jobs, be evaluated, and receive pay in the future of a better job for adequate performance, academic training, vocational skills development, and the development of work adjustment skills. Work adjustment skills include occupational social skills and the development of work habits (Levinson, 1984) such as punctuality, following through, and meeting performance standards.

School counselors are routinely faced with assisting students with mental disabilities in career planning. Their potential, like that of students with physical disabilities, is often misunderstood by teachers, parents, and employers. They need assistance in maximizing their educational skills, developing an awareness of their potential as workers, and developing occupational social skills, employability skills, and some basic life skills such as budgeting, planning, and decision making. With the possible exception of occupational social skills, students who can be mainstreamed into regular classroom environments need programs similar to those required by other students. However, counselors may need to be more involved in the job placement process and assist in combating negative attitudes against these students, who are potentially very valuable workers. It may also be the case that the intensity and duration of some aspects of the program, such as the development of employability skills, may need to be increased.

Roessler, Johnson and Schrimmer (1988) summarize the characteristics of effective programs for all students with disabilities, which they characterize as enhancing vocational potential by developing good basic educational skills, developing career awareness, and developing marketable skills by carefully coordinating the Individualized Educational Plan required by PL 94-142 (and some state statutes) and the Individualized Written Rehabilitation Program, which focuses on job skills, on employability skills, and ability to interact with nondisabled peers. Roessler (1988) recommends that schools adopt Brolin & Kokaska's (1979) Life-Centered Career Education program by focusing on daily living skills, personal/social skills, and career development. Among the daily living skills addressed in this curriculum are raising children, managing a household, citizenship, and using recreational facilities and leisure time. Developing self-confidence, interpersonal skills, and making good decisions are among the areas covered in personal social skills. Finally, finding a job, applying and interviewing for a job, maintaining occupational adjustment, meeting competitive standards, and knowing how to make a job adjustment or career change are considered in the career development component of the curriculum.

Roessler (1988) identifies several barriers to the implementation of a comprehensive program for career development for students with disabilities: "assessment, planning, curriculum materials, generalization and maintenance (from the school to the community), and system commitment" (p. 24). The process outlined in the *National Career Development Guidelines: Local Handbook for High Schools* (NOICC, 1989b) could be used as a guide to overcoming the planning and school system commitment barrier if applied appropriately. Measures for assessing the occupational potential of students with disabilities are improving steadily, and Roessler and his colleagues (Roessler et al., 1988) validate materials that can be used in the assessment of students with disabilities. Roessler also concludes that the Life-Centered Career Education curriculum materials may solve the heretofore deficit in this area. Some of the guides listed at the end of this chapter may be helpful in this endeavor, particularly those from Virginia.

Part-Time Job Placement

Formal job placement activities are discussed in detail in Chapter 16. However, it is worth mentioning that many high schools operate rather informal job placement services where a secretary or volunteer accepts job orders from businesses and citizens from the community, posts these on bulletin boards, and circulates them to counselors and teachers. For example, the Youth Employment Service and Chapel Hill High School operate on this informal basis. The school asks the potential employer to identify the nature of the job, the skills required to perform the job, the salary, the dates/hours when the job is to be performed, and the name, address, and telephone number of the potential employer. This information is recorded on job order forms and circulated. The job placement service, whether formal or informal, can be a useful means of promoting career development by providing work experience.

Assessment

Standardized tests are given to school-age youngsters often beginning in kindergarten as a part of the screening process for first grade. Achievement testing typically begins in the third grade and continues through high school. Some schools administer special aptitude tests, such as those designed to measure clerical speed and accuracy or spatial relations, in the late middle school years or the early high school years so the data will be available to these students as they engage in career and educational planning. Interest inventories may also be included as a part of this overall assessment process, again being administered as a stimulus for career and educational planning. Additionally, high school students may be given tests and inventories selected to meet their special needs. Finally, thousands of students take a variety of specialized tests, such as the Scholastic Aptitude Test (SAT), American College Test (ACT), and the Armed Services Vocational Aptitude Battery (ASVAB), that may provide information both to the student and a college admissions office (in the case of the SAT and ACT) or a military recruiter (in the case of the ASVAB).

Tests and inventories administered by schools serve two basic purposes: monitoring educational progress and promoting self-awareness. Tests given to groups of students often ignore the fact that few students possess the psychological readiness needed to use the data generated. It is common practice in some school districts to administer an interest inventory *and* a special aptitude battery in the eighth grade so students and parents can use the information provided as one basis for selecting a high school curriculum and begin to engage in some preliminary planning. However, high school counselors report that few students actually remember what their scores were or how they related to careers, primarily because they were unready to engage in meaningful career planning at the time the tests were administered.

Counselors can and should engage in awareness activities that may promote readiness in students to use information about themselves, such as offering units on the changing work force, decision making, or the importance of self-awareness. Chapter 13 presents a more in-depth look at the types of tests and inventories available and how these might be used.

Consultation

The *National Career Development Guidelines: Local Handbook for High Schools* (NOICC, 1989b) manual suggests that consultation is a skill to be used to facilitate career development. Given the importance of parents and teachers in the career development process, it seems that consultation with teachers and parents is indeed an essential aspect of the program. Teachers may require assistance in finding and using occupational information or in discovering the implication of their subject matter for careers. Parents often need assistance in facilitating the career exploration of their children and helping them make well-considered educational and career choices. Munson and Manzi (1982) suggest that young children first be involved in watching and listening, then in assisting, then in participating, and then in performing jobs. It seems reasonable to suggest that this same approach might also be used with adolescents. Mangum (undated) also suggests that parents need to be made aware of their influence and be taught labor market information and decision-making skills so these can be passed on to their children.

SUMMARY

The high school career development program's central aim is to continue the developmental processes begun in the preceding grades. However, because many students are nearing the end of their educational career, the process takes on a new urgency because of the need to help students make the transition from school to work. For some students this means formulating concrete educational plans and developing the skills to implement them. For others it means setting educational goals and adopting preliminary career goals based on the educational plans that have been laid out. Careful and comprehensive planning is required if career development competencies are to be developed in the diverse students who attend our schools. While it is difficult to identify a single group of students as the neediest, high school dropouts and minorities have traditionally fared the least well in the workplace and are perhaps the most deserving of attention. Certainly, any student who is without a supportive home environment should be targeted in a career development program.

STATE-LEVEL GUIDES FOR CAREER GUIDANCE PROGRAM DEVELOPMENT

Alabama State Department of Education. (1984). *The guidance and counseling state plan for excellence in Alabama's public school.* Montgomery: Author. (53 pp.)

Alaska State Department of Education. (1981). *Promising practices: Criteria for excellence in guidance and counseling.* Juneau: Author. (10 pp.) (ERIC Document Reproduction Services No. ED 218 560).

California State Department of Education. (1981). *Guidelines for developing comprehensive guidance programs in California public schools: Kindergarten through adult school.* Sacramento: Author. (54 pp.) (ERIC Document Reproduction Services No. ED 217 337).

Colorado State Board for Community Colleges and Occupational Education. (no date). *Unified state plan for guidance, counseling, and placement in Colorado—Grades 7–12.* Denver: Author. (67 pp.) (ERIC Document Reproduction Services No. ED 236 487).

Florida State Department of Education. (1986). *Linking education and work.* Tallahassee: Division of Vocational and Technical Education, Bureau of Program Improvement. (57 pp.)

Idaho State Department of Education. (1985). *Guidance and counseling program review instrument/quality indicators.* Boise, ID: Author, Division of Guidance and Counseling/Testing. (16 pp.)

Illinois State Board of Education. (1986). *Illinois counseling and guidance by objectives handbook.* Springfield: Department of Adult, Vocational and Technical Education, Research and Development Section. (128 pp.)

Iowa State Department of Education. (1986). *The Iowa K–12 career guidance curriculum guide for student development.* Des Moines: Author, Guidance Services. (223 pp.) (ERIC Document Reproduction Services No. ED 273 973).

Kansas State Department of Education. (1982). *The Kansas guidance program evaluation guide and resource packet.* Topeka: Author, Educational Assistance Section. (24 pp.)

Maryland State Department of Education. (no date). *Standards for school guidance programs in Maryland.* Baltimore: Author, Division of Compensatory, Urban, and Supplementary Programs. (13 pp.)

Michigan State Department of Education. (1986). *State career guidance plan—Secondary level.* Big Rapids, MI: Ferris State College, Center for Occupational Education. (34 pp.)

Minnesota State Department of Education. (1981). *Career education: Some essential learner outcomes (K–12).* St. Paul: Author, Career Education Division. (28 pp.) (ERIC Document Reproduction Services No. ED 220 571-574).

Mississippi State Department of Education. (1984). *Standards for vocational guidance programs.* Jackson: Author, Board of Vocational and Technical Education. (12 pp.)

Missouri State Department of Education. (no date). *Missouri comprehensive guidance: A model for program development and implementation.* Jefferson City: Author. (13 pp.)

Nevada State Department of Education. (1987). *Guidance and counseling program.* Carson City: Author, Occupational and Continuing Education Branch. (4 pp.)

New York State Education Department. (1985). *Guidance and counseling: Ensuring the rights of students.* Albany: Author, Occupational Education Civil Rights Technical Assistance Unit. (5 pp.) (ERIC Document Reproduction Services No. ED 270 685).

North Carolina Department of Public Instruction. (1981). *Guidance services evaluative criteria.* Raleigh: Author. (23 pp.)

North Dakota State Board for Vocational Education. (1986). *Program standards for vocational guidance.* Bismarck: Author. (3 pp.)

Ohio State Department of Education. (no date). *Career education in Ohio.* Columbus: Division of Vocational and Career Education, Career Development Service.

Oklahoma State Department of Education. (no date). *Oklahoma standards for career guidance programs.* Stillwater: Author. (1 p.)

Oregon State Department of Education. (1986). *Oregon integrated career guidance model: Assessment and planning instrument—Grades 9–12.* Salem: Author. (15 pp.)

South Carolina State Department of Education. (1985). *Vocational guidance and placement planning guide.* Columbia: Office of Vocational Education, Vocational Guidance and Placement Unit. (454 pp.)

South Dakota Department of Education. (1983). *South Dakota standards for guidance and counseling.* Pierre: Author, Division of Elementary and Secondary Education and Cultural Affairs. (8 pp.)

Texas Education Agency. (1979). *Occupational orientation: Program standards for public schools.* Austin: Author. (35 pp.)

Vermont Department of Education. (1983). *Vocational guidance in Vermont—Five-year plan 1984–1989.* Montpelier: Author. (20 pp.)

Virginia Department of Education. (1984). *A monograph on career guidance and counseling.* Richmond: Author, Division of Special Education Programs and Pupil Personnel Services. (36 pp.)

Virginia Department of Education. (no date). *Virginia career guidance model.* Richmond: Author, Division of Special Education Programs and Pupil Personnel Services. (11 pp.)

Washington State Department of Education. (1980). *Guidelines for a vocational guidance system.* Olympia: Division of Vocational-Technical and Adult Education Services, Program Development Section. (9 pp.)

Wisconsin Department of Public Instruction. (1986). *School counseling programs—A resource and planning guide*. Madison: Author. (114 pp.) (ERIC Document Reproduction Services No. ED 275 925).

Wyoming State Department of Education. (1985). *Proposed standards for counseling programs*. Cheyenne: Author.

REFERENCES

Amatea, E. S., Clark, J. E., & Cross, E. G. (1984). Life-styles: Evaluating a life role planning program for high school students. *Vocational Guidance Quarterly, 32*, 249–259.

Amatea, E. S., & Cross, E. G. (1980). Going places: A career guidance program for high school students and their parents. *Vocational Guidance Quarterly, 28*, 274–287.

Baker, S. B., & Popowicz, C. L. (1983). Meta-analysis as a strategy for evaluating effects of career education interventions. *Vocational Guidance Quarterly, 31*, 178–186.

Bensen, P. L., Mangen, D. J., & Williams, D. L. (1986). *Adults who influence youth: Perspectives from 5th and 12th grade students*. Minneapolis, MN: Search Institute.

Borman, C., Nash, W., & Colson, S. (1978). Career guidance for gifted and talented students. *Vocational Guidance Quarterly, 27*, 72–76.

Brolin, D. L., & Kokaska, C. J., (1979). *Career education for handicapped children and youth*. Columbus, OH: Merrill.

Brown, D. (1980). A life-planning workshop for high school students. *Vocational Guidance Quarterly, 29*, 77–83.

Brown, D. (1990). *Dropping out or hanging in*. Lincolnwood, IL: National Textbook Center.

Campbell, R. E., Connell, J. G., Boyle, K. K., & Bhaerman, R. D. (1983). *Enhancing career development: Recommendations for action*. Columbus, OH: NCRVE, Ohio State University.

Chapman, W., & Katz, M. R. (1983). Career information systems in secondary schools: A survey and assessment. *Vocational Guidance Quarterly, 31*, 165–177.

Cochran, L. (1985). *Parent career guidance manual*. British Columbia, Canada: Bachanan-Kells.

Crites, J. O. (1987). *Evaluation of career guidance programs: Models, methods, and microcomputers*. Columbus, OH: NCRVE, Ohio State University.

Dayton, J. D., & Feldhusen, J. F. (1989). Characteristics and needs of vocationally talented high school students. *Career Development Quarterly, 37*, 355–364.

Dillard, J. M., & Campbell, N. J. (1981). Influences of Puerto Rican, black, and Anglo parents' career behavior on their adolescent childrens' career development. *Vocational Guidance Quarterly, 30*, 139–148.

Herr, E. L. (1982). The effects of guidance and counseling: Three domains. In E. L. Herr & N. M. Pirson (Eds.), *Foundations of policy in guidance and counseling* (pp. 22–64). Alexandria, Va: American Association of Counseling and Development (formerly APGA).

Hoyt, K. B., Pinson, N. M., Laramore, D., & Mangum, G. L. (1973). *Career education and the elementary school teacher*. Salt Lake City, UT: Olympus.

Johnson, W. F., Korn, T. A., & Dunn, D. J. (1975). Comparing three methods of presenting occupational information. *Vocational Guidance Quarterly, 24,* 62–67.

Lee, C. C. (1984). Predicting the career choice attitudes of rural black, white, and native American high school students. *Vocational Guidance Quarterly, 32,* 177–184.

Levinson, E. M. (1984). A vocationally oriented secondary school program for the emotionally disturbed. *Vocational Guidance Quarterly, 33,* 76–81.

Lombana, J. H. (1979). Facilitating career guidance of deaf students: challenges and opportunities for counselors. *Vocational Guidance Quarterly, 27,* 350–359.

Lombana, J. H. (1980). Career planning with visually handicapped students. *Vocational Guidance Quarterly, 28,* 219–224.

Mangum, G. L. (undated). *Youth transition from adolescent to the world of work.* Washington, DC: W. T. Grant Foundation Commission on Work, Family, and Citizenship.

McNair, D., & Brown, D. (1983). Predicting the occupational aspirations, occupational expectations, and career maturity of black and white male and female 10th grade students. *Vocational Guidance Quarterly, 32,* 29–36.

Mitchell, A. M. (1977). *Career development needs of seventeen year olds: How to improve career development programs.* Washington, DC: National Advisory Committee for Career Education.

Moles, O. C. (1991). Guidance programs in American high schools: A descriptive portrayal. *School Counselor, 38,* 163–175.

Munson, H. L., & Manzi, P. A. (1982). Toward a model of work task learning in the home. *Vocational Guidance Quarterly, 31,* 5–13.

Noeth, R. J., Engen, H. B., & Prediger, D. (1984). Making career decisions: A self-reporting of factors that help high school students. *Vocational Guidance Quarterly, 32,* 240–248.

NOICC. (1988). *The national career counseling and guidance guidelines: High schools.* Washington, DC: Author.

NOICC. (1989a). *The national career development guidelines: Local handbook for elementary schools.* Washington, DC: Author.

NOICC. (1989b). *The national career development guidelines: Local handbook for high schools.* Washington, DC: Author.

NOICC. (1989c). *The national career development guidelines: Local handbook for middle/junior high schools.* Washington, DC: Author.

Office of Special Education and Rehabilitative Services. (1988). *OSEP State Reported Data, 1986–87 School Year.* Washington, DC: U.S. Office of Education.

Pallas, A. M. (1986). *School dropouts in the United States.* Washington, DC: U.S. Office of Education.

Palmer, S., & Cochran, L. (1988). Parents as agents of career development. *Journal of Counseling Psychology, 35,* 71–76.

Pask–McCartney, C., & Salomone, P. R. (1988). Difficult cases in career counseling III: The multipotentialed client. *Career Development Quarterly, 36,* 231–240.

Post–Kammer, P. (1987). Intrinsic and extrinsic work values and career maturity of 9th and 11th grade boys. *Journal of Counseling and Development, 65,* 420–423.

Post–Kammer, P., & Perrone, P. (1983). Career perceptions of talented individuals: A follow up study. *Vocational Guidance Quarterly, 31,* 203–211.

Roessler, R. T., Johnson, J., & Schrimmer, L. (1988). Implementing career education: Barriers and potential solutions. *Career Development Quarterly, 37,* 22–30.

Spokane, A. R., & Oliver, L. W. (1983). The outcomes of vocational interventions. In W. B. Walsh & S. H. Osipow (Eds.), *Handbook of vocational psychology* Vol. 2. Hillsdale, NJ: Lawrence Erlbaum and Associates.

U.S. Bureau of Labor Statistics. (1986). *Employment and earnings.* Washington, DC: U.S. Department of Labor.

Wetzel, J. R. (1987). *American youth: A statistical snapshot.* Washington, DC: W. T. Grant Foundation Commission on Work, Family, and Citizenship.

W. T. Grant Foundation. (1988). *The forgotten half.* Washington, DC: Author.

__11__

Career Development in Four-Year Colleges, Community Colleges, and Vocational-Technical Schools

Over half of the students who graduate from high school attend some form of post-secondary educational institution, including 4-year colleges, community colleges, or vocational-technical schools. While one of the primary reasons for pursuing a college education is to train for a career, only approximately 60 percent of college graduates report being in their present career as a result of following a conscious plan. Of those adults who either did not finish college or attended a 2-year institution, about 43 percent followed a conscious plan into their current careers. Approximately 15 to 20 percent of those who attended some form of postsecondary education had never used any occupational information (Brown & Minor, 1991).

A study by Hatcher and Crook (1988) suggests that certain aspects of the career development of students are not being addressed. They surveyed graduates of a small liberal arts institution to determine what surprises they had encountered on their jobs. They found that students were better workers than they expected to be, criticism for poor work was greater than expected, and the organization's demand for good work was greater than expected. They also found that when expectations regarding work did not coincide with reality, particularly if that was a negative reality, students expressed intentions to leave their current jobs.

While not every student pursuing postsecondary education does so for the sole purpose of preparing for a career, many expect this to be a product of their educational experience. It is important that the career development needs of these students be met. Healy and Reilly (1989) tried to determine if career development needs of vocational-technical students enrolled in 10

California community colleges varied by age level. Older students indicated that they have less need to set career goals, become certain of career plans, explore career-related goals, select courses relevant to career goals, develop employability skills, and obtain a job than did younger students. However, about 25 to 50 percent of all age groups studied rated these needs of major concern. They also rated knowing more about their interests and abilities as an important need. The authors report that the finding that older students have less need for career development activities was not unexpected. However, one suspects that the reason that more younger respondents did not rate their needs for career development activities higher was because of lack of awareness of the problems encountered by college graduates.

Nearly 60 percent of college graduates would try to get more information about careers if they could start over, and only about 55 percent of those who graduated from college or received some college training feel that their skills are being well used in their current job. Also, 6 to 7 percent of those with at least some college expected to be forced to leave their current job in the year following the 1989 Gallup survey (Gallup Organization, 1989). Finally, while it is expected that the number of jobs requiring a college degree will increase as we move toward the year 2000, there will be increasing unemployment and underemployment among college graduates because of an oversupply and because of a mismatch between the education received by graduates and the demands of the work force (Johnston & Packer, 1987).

THE STUDENTS

The stereotype of community college, vocational-technical school, and 4-year college students is that they are 18 to 22 years of age and pursuing their first postsecondary educational experience. However, it has been estimated that there will soon be as many nontraditional students as those who fit this stereotype (Healy & Reilly, 1989). Nontraditional students are those who are older than 22, reentering after a previous academic failure, international students, women who have been displaced from their homemaking careers by divorce or economic necessity or who have decided to pursue a career after they complete child-rearing responsibilities, students with physical disabilities such as visual impairment, and students with learning disabilities such as dyslexia.

Within both the traditional and nontraditional groups, various subgroups need special attention. Griff (1987) suggests that returning students do so to make career changes, to ready themselves for a choice made earlier but postponed for various reasons, or because of transitions in family and leisure patterns. He suggests that all of these reasons for returning are often related to unmet career development needs and that the services available to these students should include the following:

1. Career and self-awareness activities
2. Exploration of interests, values, goals, and decisions

3. Realities of the current job market and failure trends
4. Collection of career resources and materials including updated practical information about careers
5. Telephone advising network
6. Topical workshops (e.g., risk building learning skills, resume writing, interviewing) (p. 470)

Student athletes are another group that may require some individualized attention because of their failure to set academic and career goals (Blan, 1985; Lanning, 1982). Wilkes, Davis, and Dever (1989) describe a joint planning effort between career planning and placement and the athletic department that resulted in a career planning seminar followed by a job search seminar that was offered to senior athletes. Other groups such as African Americans, Native Americans, Asian Pacific Islanders, educationally disadvantaged students, gay and lesbian students, and others have special career-related needs that should be met by the career development specialist.

THE INSTITUTIONS

Three general types of institutions are of concern here. The first of these, vocational-technical colleges, are extensions of high school vocational education programs and provide skills training in a variety of careers ranging from semiskilled to professional (such as heating and air conditioning equipment installation and maintenance, licensed practical nurses, registered nurses, and drafters). Because of the vocational nature of these programs, students often select an area of study at the time of entry and pursue it to completion. In many instances the necessity to make an early decision has led to mistakes.

Community colleges often have a vocational-technical component along with a college transfer program. In many states the college transfer program is coordinated with the programs in colleges and universities so that students transferring to 4-year institutions do so as "junior transfers." Students select community colleges because of financial reasons (they can live at home and thus save money), because of the need for remedial study to make up for academic deficits, because they want to explore whether post-high-school study is actually something they want to pursue, and for a variety of other reasons. Students who have had academic difficulty may also regain their eligibility to reenroll in 4-year institutions by demonstrating their competencies in community college courses. A remarkable aspect of community colleges is their open-door admissions policy, which enables students to begin at their academic competency level and advance their education. This open-door policy does not extend to all programs offered in these institutions, however. Vocational-technical programs as well as programs such as nursing, accounting, and others have established standards that must be met prior to entry.

Four-year colleges and universities are nearly as diverse as vocational-technical schools and community colleges. Highly prestigious colleges such as Harvard, Stanford, Yale, Williams, and Brown turn away hundreds and in some instances thousands of highly qualified applicants while some other colleges are barely able to attract sufficient numbers of minimally qualified applicants to maintain their enrollments. Some colleges are predominantly female, while others are comprised largely of males. Predominantly African-American colleges like Howard University have led the way in providing quality education to African-American students, while Gallaudet has focused on students with hearing impairments. Enrollments range from a few hundred to over 50,000, and the cost can vary from $5,000 a year to over $25,000 a year. Not surprisingly, the curriculums can vary widely. Some colleges emphasize liberal arts preparation, which focuses on the arts, sciences, and humanities, while others may concentrate on technical areas such as engineering or on preparing people for educational careers.

Resources, philosophy, mission, size and characteristics of the student body, curriculum offerings, location, and a variety of other factors influence the career development program. Career development specialists in liberal arts institutions must be prepared to help students choose careers that appear to have little relevance to their majors. Law schools give preferential treatment to English majors, all other things such as grades and Law School Aptitude Test (LSAT) scores being equal. Psychology majors may be able to use their skill in a variety of related areas, but they will need to know that personnel officers, human services workers, and researchers draw on psychological principles in their work.

CAREER DEVELOPMENT PROGRAMS

Johnson and Figler (1984) suggest that there are many issues confronting career development specialists as they plan programs for postsecondary institutions. Among these are philosophical issues of whether to (1) emphasize counseling or placement, (2) send clients out on their own to collect information, (3) focus students on the "vocational" aspects of their training, (4) involve significant others such as parents in the career planning process, and (5) emphasize risk taking or security in the career planning process. They also suggest that in the future the demand for career development services will increase and that services will expand. Dealing with the issues identified by Johnson and Figler and planning to meet new demands will require programming decisions that must be considered carefully.

The *National Career Development Guidelines* for postsecondary institutions (NOICC, 1989) lay out a process for developing a comprehensive program which is quite similar to the processes outlined in Chapters 9 and 10 for building or improving programs in elementary, middle, and high schools. In the document *The National Career Development Guidelines: Local Handbook for Post-Secondary Institutions*, two sets of competencies are laid out: those for young adults and those for adults. The young adult competencies include skills needed to make a career decision and to implement that decision by pursuing a proper educational training program and then enter the chosen career. The adult competencies include skills needed to continue to make career decisions, plan for and pursue education and programs needed, and implement these decisions. They also include skills needed for reentering the work force and for withdrawing from the labor force at retirement time. The young adult and adult competencies, along with the sample indicators that they have achieved these competencies, are shown in Figures 11.1 and 11.2, respectively.

In Figure 11.1 the first two competencies listed for young adults relate to maintenance of a healthy personal perspective and need for a high degree of self-awareness. The inclusion of competency 2, "ability to assess self-defeating behaviors and reduce their impact on career decisions," is particularly noteworthy since it explicitly recognizes the link between good mental health and successful career planning and implementation. For the most part, competencies 3 through 8 pertain to more traditional career development concepts such as relating educational and career planning, using career information, the development of employability skills, and developing skills in career planning. One exception to this is competency 7, which deals with the

FIGURE 11.1 *Competencies and Sample Indicators—Young Adults*

Competency	Sample Indicator: The Young Adult Will
1. Maintenance of a positive view of self in terms of potential and preferences and assessment of their transferability to the world of work.	1. Identify his/her abilities, interests, values, and needs and state their influence on educational and career choices.
2. Ability to assess self-defeating behaviors and reduce their impact on career decisions.	2. Identify strategies for reducing discriminatory attitudes and behaviors.
3. Ability to relate educational and occupational preparation to career opportunities.	3. Develop an action plan to achieve an educational goal.
4. Skills for locating, evaluating, and interpreting information about career opportunities.	4. Understand the uses and limitations of occupational outlook information.
5. Skills required for seeking, obtaining, keeping, and advancing in a job.	5. Establish a job search network through personal contacts with friends, family members, and others.
6. Skills in making decisions about educational and career goals.	6. Make and implement effective career and educational decisions.
7. Understanding of the impact of careers on individual and family life.	7. Describe the interrelationships among work, family, and leisure and career roles.
8. Skills in developing career plans.	8. Define both long- and short-range career goals based on information about self and the world of work.

Source: The National Career Development Guidelines: Local Handbook for Post-Secondary Institutions. (1989). Washington, DC: NOICC, pp. 50–52.

development of skills in relating career and family roles, and to a lesser degree leisure roles. While there are certain aspects of these ideas in the indicators suggested for other competencies, competency 7 makes it clear that young adults need to understand the interrelationships among life roles and act on this knowledge when they plan their careers.

The adult competencies and indicators outlined in Figure 11.2 parallel those for young adults. More pronounced differences between the competencies for young adults and adults can be seen in competencies 8 and 9, however. Competency 8 deals with the skills needed to make career transitions, while competency 9 addresses the competencies needed to move from

FIGURE 11.2   *Adult Competencies and Indicators*

Competency	Sample Indicator: The Adult Will
1. Maintenance of a positive view of self in terms of potential and preferences and assessment of their transferability to the world of work.	1. Identify achievements related to work, learning, and leisure and state their influence on his/her perception of self.
2. Ability to assess self-defeating behaviors and reduce their impact on career decisions.	2. Understand physical changes that occur with age and adapt work performance to accommodate these.
3. Skills for entering, adjusting to, and maintaining performance in educational and training situations.	3. Document prior learning experiences and know how to use their information to obtain credit from educational institutions.
4. Skills for locating, evaluating, and interpreting information about career opportunities.	4. Assess how skills used in one occupation may be used in other occupations.
5. Skills required for seeking, obtaining, keeping, and advancing in a job.	5. Develop a resume appropriate for an identified career objective.
6. Skills in making decisions about educational and career goals.	6. Develop skills to assess career opportunities in terms of advancement, management styles, work environment, benefits, and other conditions of employment.
7. Understanding of the impact of careers on individual and family life.	7. Describe how family and leisure roles affect and may be affected by career roles and decisions.
8. Skills in making career transitions.	8. Accept that career transitions (e.g. reassessment of current position, job changes, or occupational changes) are a normal aspect of career development.
9. Skills in retirement planning.	9. Recognize the importance of retirement planning and commit to early involvement in the retirement planning process.

Source: The National Career Development Guidelines: Local Handbook for Post-Secondary Institutions. (1989). Washington, DC: NOICC, pp. 53–55.

work to retirement. Clearly, if the NCDG model is followed, programs for young adults will have many similar components as well as several unique features.

As noted in Chapters 9 and 10, the process of organizing and developing the career development program is essentially a five-step process: organizing for program development, establishing expected student outcomes for the institution, acting to improve the existing program by determining strengths and making additions or deletions as needed, implementing the new program, and evaluating the outcomes (NOICC, 1989).

It is expected that the career development plan will contain a statement of the purpose of the program as well as the competencies that are to be developed as a result of the program. Like the elementary, middle/junior high school, and high school plans the processes (e.g., counseling, placement) that will be employed in the program along with specific activities should be included in the plan, along with the staff who are expected to deliver the activities and a timeline for delivery (NOICC, 1989).

Conducting a needs assessment is the first step in developing local standards. Evans (1985) compared two general approaches to needs assessment in postsecondary educational institutions: interviews and questionnaires. Within these general categories, Evans also tried to discern whether questionnaires and interviews based on developmental theory were superior to needs assessment procedures that had been empirically derived. She concluded that questionnaires provided a more efficient means of collecting and tabulating data about needs while interviews produced a richer database that provided more insight into the individual's concern. However, data for all the approaches suggested the same areas of need, including academic performance, career and lifestyle concerns, and issues relating to personal identity.

Once needs are identified, indicators should be selected and then standards of performance established. This process is as follows:

Needs Assessment: Sixty percent of sophomores uncertain about the relationship between their educational and career plans

↓

Develop Competency 3   **Ability to relate educational and occupational preparation to career opportunities**
                             Processes

Indicators	*Involved*	*Activities*	*Standard*
1. Assess education and training alternatives and selected field of study or training post	Information	Advising begins at matriculation	100% by end of sophomore year
2. Identify education or training requirements of specific occupations that are related to field of study	Classroom instruction	Required class on careers	100% will select appropriate occupation

3. Develop an action plan to achieve educational goal	Classroom instruction	Required class on careers; counseling	100% will develop action plan
4. Not chosen			
5. Develop long- and short-range plans to achieve identified career goals	Classroom instruction; counseling information	Required class; counseling, advising	100% will develop short- and long-range plan

Develop Competency 6 — **Skills in making decisions about educational and career goals**

Processes

Indicators	*Involved*	*Activities*	*Standard*
1. Establish personal criteria for making decision about educational and career goals	Classroom instruction	Required class on careers	100% will meet criteria
6. Make and implement effective career and educational decisions	Classroom instruction, information counseling	Career Information Center (CIC) advising, career counseling, required class	100% will complete

The actual competencies to be developed in the career development program, the processes to be used, and the specific activities will be dependent on the overall philosophy and the nature of the school itself. Because students in vocational-technical schools begin specific vocational preparation immediately, it is important that their ability to relate educational and occupational preparation to career opportunities (competency 3) and use skills in making decisions about educational career goals (competency 6) be developed early, perhaps prior to beginning the training program. Orientation, initial advising, and perhaps screening devices might be relied on to develop these competencies. Some suggested activities that may be used in conjunction with each of the processes identified in the postsecondary career development guidelines (NOICC, 1989) are listed in Figure 11.3.

SPECIFIC ACTIVITIES

Advising

Advising is the backbone of the educational planning process in postsecondary institutions, and it appears that the quality of this process varies greatly. If competencies dealing with the integration of educational and career planning are to be developed, it seems logical that one goal must be the develop-

FIGURE 11.3   *Processes/Approaches to Career Development*

Outreach
1. Career seminars in housing units
2. Informal rap sessions in housing units to establish contacts
3. Activities designed for special groups delivered at their meetings (e.g., international students)
4. Mentoring programs using alumni or upper classmen
5. Parent involvement such as career development seminars

Classroom Instruction
1. Required classes for credit
2. Optional classes for credit
3. Noncredit, short-term classes
4. Employability skills training classes
5. Units in regular classes dealing with careers

Counseling
1. Individual career counseling
2. Group career counseling
3. Employability skills groups
4. Special programs for alumni such as group counseling activities
5. Support groups for job hunters

Assessment
1. Screening examinations given at entry to focus on career/decision making
2. Ongoing assessment offered to students in counseling/career planning and placement center
3. As part of career counseling
4. Computer-assisted services
5. Self-directed assessment (e.g., Self-Directed Search)
6. Needs assessments

Information
1. Orientation sessions/information
2. Catalogs
3. Advising information/careers
4. Career information center
5. Articles in student newspapers
6. Computer-assisted systems
7. Handouts that relate educational programs to career opportunities
8. Alumni newsletters

Placement
1. Regular job placement activities for students
2. Job fairs to link employers and workers

Work Experience
1. Internship programs
2. Placement for part-time work

(continued)

FIGURE 11.3   *Continued*

---

3. Cooperative educational/work programs
4. Work-study programs

Consultation
1. With faculty advisors to make them aware of education-career connection; needs of certain students
2. With residence hall assistants and directors to provide assistance
3. With instructors who wish to infuse more career information
4. With club/social activities advisors to suggest career-related activities

Referral
1. To workers in the community for career information
2. To mental health professionals to get assistance with personal problems blocking career-related decisions

---

ment of an outstanding advising system. Dailey (1986) suggests that advisors use decision trees to aid in the academic/career planning process at the time the student must select a major. A decision tree is little more than a graphic representation of life decision points, with the branches of the tree representing options. The process of decision making using a decision tree approach is illustrated in Figure 11.4. Dailey believes that the decision tree approach may be particularly applicable for use with business majors because they have probably been oriented to this approach in their courses. However, use of the tree concept should not be limited to business.

Advisors need to be oriented to the implications of educational programs for careers. This can be done through consultation (if advisors are open to this process). However, advisors need data from follow-up studies that examine the career success of graduates. They also need information from recruiters who come on campus. Recruiters should be invited to provide seminars for advisors that focus on the criteria used by their institutions to make difficult admissions decisions. Finally, advisors should receive information regularly about the jobs entered by graduates of various programs.

Courses

As noted in Figure 11.3, there are numerous approaches to delivering career exploration courses to students, including modules, credit courses, and noncredit courses. Quinn and Lewis (1989) found that certainty of career choices was increased by inserting career-related material into a traditional academic course.

Savickas (1990, p. 278) designed and field tested a career exploration course that tried to develop the following attitudes and concepts: (1) Become involved now, (2) Explore your future, (3) Choose based on how things look to you, (4) Control your future, (5) Work: A problem or opportunity, (6) View work positively, (7) Conceptualize career choice, (8) Clear up career choice

FIGURE 11.4 *Decision Tree of College Sophomore's Decision-Making Process*

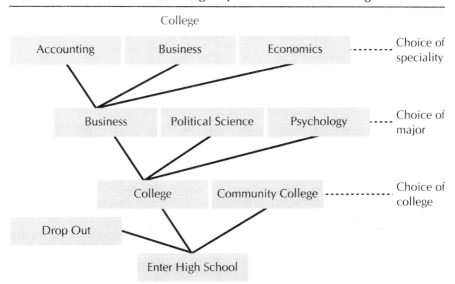

misconceptions, (9) Base your choice on yourself, and (10) Use four aspects of self as choice bases. He found support for the idea that the course generally had a positive impact on ability to engage in career decision making and on long-term time perspective, with students enrolled in the course being somewhat more oriented to a future time perspective. Savickas's findings generally support the earlier research of Lent, Larkin, and Hasequa (1980), who found that a 10-week career planning course focusing primarily on technical and scientific careers was helpful in facilitating career planning.

The availability of career planning classes is widespread. Goodson (1982) found that 64 percent of samples of institutions enrolling more than 2,000 students offered such a course over a decade ago. Typically, these courses focused on career exploration and development, career decision making, employability skills, and to a lesser extent on careers for special groups, field experiences, and self-assessment. Allyn (1989) describes a departure from this traditional curricular approach. She tried to "focus on the learning styles associated with the left and right hemispheres" (of the brain) (p. 281) and to apply the 4MAT System, which attempts to capitalize on learning styles using an experiential approach. The objectives of her course were to have students learn more about themselves, discover their support system, and to learn about careers that might be of interest. The first step in the course was to have students deal with the *why* of the course goal (e.g., "Why is this important?"). Then she focused on the *what* question, that is, "What is the content of the course?" After the *what* question is answered, students engaged in hands-on activities to determine how they would answer the question, "How will I fit into the world of work?" The *if* question was answered next, that is, "What if the information I have learned applies to me (or doesn't), What are the consequences?" The content of Allyn's (1989) course does not vary greatly from that covered in other courses described earlier, but the techniques, which include guided imageries and avoid lecture/discussion approaches and traditional assessment techniques because they foreclose career options, are worth serious consideration.

Brief Interventions

Goodson (1982) found that relatively short interventions, such as workshops and seminars, were available on 87 percent of the campuses surveyed. Pickering and Vacc (1984) reported, after a review of the literature on career-related interventions, that the most commonly researched areas were those with six sessions or less, including a variety of activities. They also reported that longer term interventions (more than five sessions) were usually more effective than short-term interventions. However, in a recent study, Buescher, Johnston, Lucas, and Hughey (1989) reported that a brief intervention consisting of a 1.5-hour meeting with a career counselor, the completion of an occupational card sort, a discussion of career options, and a tour of the career center resulted in positive changes for undecided students.

Kahnweiler and Kahnweiler (1980) report on a dual-career-family workshop that has particular relevance given the likelihood that married couples are likely to face this situation. The workshop was divided into didactic input, models of dual-career families, and discussion. In the didactic phase the benefits (e.g., extra income) and liabilities (e.g., gender-role conflicts) were presented. In the modeling section the workshop leaders, who were involved in a dual-career marriage, discussed the pros and cons of their relationship. Finally, students were engaged in a discussion focusing on their backgrounds and the problems they might have with dual-career marriages.

Unfortunately, many career seminars and other more didactic career interventions are not evaluated systematically. However, if the needs of the target audience are clearly identified and seminars and other experiences are carefully designed to meet these needs, these approaches can be highly effective for students who do not have decisional anxiety or other personal problems that preclude them from benefiting from the experience.

An example of a carefully designed and evaluated seminar that addressed specific student needs is presented by Robbins and Tucker (1986). Their concern, like that of many career counselors, was career goal instability, and they tried to discern whether small groups that were primarily self-directed were more effective than those involving leader-directed interaction. They found that students with high and moderate goal instability engaged in greater numbers of career information-seeking behaviors as a result of the interactional groups than those who participated in the self-directed groups. On the other hand, the type of group appeared to make little difference on the information-seeking behaviors of students with low goal instability. Students enrolled in the groups that were interactionally oriented were more satisfied with their groups than those where the leaders emphasized self-direction.

Self-Directed Activities

Many colleges provide opportunities for students to engage in self-directed activities including assessment, computer-assisted career exploration, and career exploration books. Pickering (1984) compares the results of a career planning seminar run by career counselors, a similar seminar run by peer tutors, and a self-directed group where students were oriented to using a career exploration workbook. The analysis of the outcome yielded no significant differences among the treatment groups. Unfortunately, Pickering did not include a no-treatment control group in the design. However, Pickering concluded that the self-study method was the most cost-effective method, an influence that must be interpreted very cautiously since Pickering and Vacc (1984) had earlier concluded that self-help approaches were the least effective approaches based upon their review of the research literature.

For those individuals who wish to establish a self-help section in their career information centers, Nachreiner's (1987) description of the material housed in the University of Wisconsin Madison Center is instructive. Their materials are placed in four color-coordinated stations:

Station I: Who Am I—Includes materials about life transitions, values, interests and skills

Station II: Job Search—Includes information about employability skills, such as resume development

Station III: Education and Career Research—Includes study skills information as well as educational and career information

Station IV: Bibliographies—Includes lists of readings on various topics

Information

Chapters 7 and 8 were devoted to discussions of various informational approaches, including types of information and the establishment and operation of a career information center. That discussion is not duplicated here. However, the *Career Line* approach developed at Michigan State University is worth consideration (Forrest & Backes, 1988). *Career Line* is a weekly career information column that appears in the student newspaper at Michigan State. It is a 300- to 400-word column that appears weekly and addresses such topics as planning for summer jobs, various types of careers, and related topics. One byproduct of the program has been the development of a *Career Line* booklet that includes some of the better columns.

Consultation

Spokane (1991) discusses career development consultation and prevention together, and while he does not link them directly, he suggests that both are linked to promoting career competence. Brown, Pryzwansky, and Schulte (1991) go one step beyond Spokane's position and link consultation to the prevention process, asserting that consultants can be instrumental in preventing problems from arising if they can effectively intervene in programs and activities that promote developmental processes. As suggested in Figure 11.3, consultation from internal consultants can be offered to advisors, residence hall advisors, instructors who wish to make their courses more career relevant, and the advisors of students who may wish to promote career development. Campus activities from the ski club to the student newspaper can have relevance to career and lifestyle decisions and should be pursued by career development consultants.

Career development specialists have numerous opportunities to engage in consultation with faculty members, club sponsors, resident assistants, and others to assist them in planning programs that will facilitate career development. However, one variant on this is to use alumni to consult with students about their career options. Willamette College developed such a program by creating a file of alumni who would be willing to consult with students and then providing their names to interested students (Bjorkquist, 1988). The staff at Willamette College also uses this alumni file as a basis for securing speakers for on-campus seminars. Ohio State University has also developed a program of this type.

Career Counseling

Chapter 14 is devoted entirely to the career counseling process, and thus this discussion is brief. However, many colleges and universities now offer career counseling services to alumni and some, like the University of South Carolina, devote a great deal of attention to this area. It is also noteworthy that some colleges and universities have developed cooperative arrangements with other institutions to provide counseling and informational services when geographic location makes it impossible for alumni to return to their alma mater.

Career counseling is probably the most widely offered of the career-related services (Goodson, 1982). Typically, career counseling services are offered through specialized agencies called career planning and placement, the university counseling center, or both. Magoon (1989) reports that over one fifth of the counseling centers offered no career counseling, while 40 percent of the counseling centers in large universities and 53 percent of the centers in small universities reported sharing the responsibility of offering career counseling with another agency on campus. Career counseling is offered exclusively at the remaining counseling centers (30 percent of the large and 24 percent of the small centers). If Stone and Archer (1990) are correct, there is decreasing interest among the counselors and counseling psychologists who have traditionally offered career counseling in university counseling centers. This may result in career counseling services being offered more frequently through career planning and placement centers.

Career counseling is offered in three modes: individual, group, and computerized services. Some career counselors would take exception to including computerized services in this listing, and perhaps they have a legitimate case since counseling has traditionally been viewed as a person-to-person process. However, computerized programs such as SIGI-Plus and DISCOVER do approximate traditional career counseling in many respects. Most career counseling is offered in the form of individual career counseling, which is, from a program planning perspective, the most inefficient approach in terms of cost or use of counselor time.

Some agencies that provide career counseling services have developed intake procedures in an effort to identify the best approach to dealing with students' problems. Intake interviews are conducted by counselors to determine students' needs and expectations. After this interview, students are referred variously to a psychometrician for testing, individual counseling, group counseling, or group guidance activities such as developing employability skills. The goal of the intake process is to deliver career development services effectively and efficiently.

Group career counseling has not received the same degree of investigation or discussion that individual career counseling has, although Oliver and Spokane (1988) concluded after a review of the literature that group interventions are as effective or more effective than other types. However, Butcher's (1982) suggestion that students be carefully screened prior to group counseling seems appropriate. She recommends that students need to be ready to engage in counseling, by which she means they are prepared to accept the responsibility of the process. She also suggests that some determination be made as to whether students have pervasive decisional problems (they are indecisive), since students who have decisional problems must have that concern addressed prior to engaging in the decision-making process.

One additional suggestion should be added to those advanced by Butcher: Students placed in groups should be at the same relative developmental level. For example, students who are just beginning to explore the relationship between educational and career goals should not be placed in the same groups with English majors who are determining potential career paths growing out of their major. However, a senior majoring in English who has decided that he made an error in choosing English as a major might very well be at the same place developmentally as a freshman or sophomore exploring all possibilities.

Butcher (1982) indicates that career counseling groups move through three distinct phases—exploration, transition, and action—and that understanding these stages along with the dynamics associated with them is a prerequisite for leading groups. It seems likely that not all counselors possess the skill to fully assess career maturity (readiness) or decisional problems (indecisiveness) or to lead groups, which requires a full understanding of group dynamics as well as career development issues. This suggests that some differential staffing may be required when deciding who should conduct career counseling.

Kivlighan (1990) reviewed the literature to determine whether the therapeutic factors believed to be necessary in group therapy had been studied in group career counseling studies. He concluded that the role of "self disclosure, catharsis, guidance, universality, altruism, vicarious learning, cohesion, interpersonal learning, self understanding, and instillation of hope" (p. 64) in the change process had gone largely unexamined. He also concluded that males and females come to career groups with different expectations, react differently to the group experience, and have different outcomes. Women seem to broaden their career horizons as a result of the group experience, while men tend to get confirmation for their plans. Finally, Kivlighan reported that two variables that have long been viewed as important factors in group therapy—group composition and leadership style—have been largely unexamined as factors in career group outcomes.

Career Resource Centers

Reardon, Zunker, and Dyal (1979) surveyed 4-year institutions of higher learning to investigate whether institutions had a separately budgeted career resource center. At that time, 51 percent responded affirmatively. This number has grown dramatically in the time since the survey, although exact percentages are not available. However, it is noteworthy that college graduates list the college career center as the second most often used source of information about careers, followed by newspapers. Nearly 48 percent of the college-educated adults in a Gallup poll (Gallup Organization, 1989) indicated that they had used the College Career Center, as it was termed in the survey. Clearly, the career resource center is the key to the dissemination of career information on the campus.

Major Fairs

Elliot (1988) describes a Pennsylvania State University program aimed at fostering educational planning. Undecided students, along with faculty representatives of various academic programs, were invited to attend an evening program in which students and faculty could interact about major areas of study. While no formal evaluation was conducted, those involved believed that the program was an effective way to stimulate educational exploration.

Peer Counseling Programs

Postsecondary institutions facing personnel shortages have at times turned to peer programs of various types, including tutorial and counseling programs. As Holly (1987) notes, careful screening and training of counselors is an essential aspect of a successful program. Screening criteria should include motivation, psychological openness, freedom from psychological concerns, communications skills, and interpersonal style. The nature of the training program will be dependent on the goals of the program, but with proper supervision, peer counselors might orient students to computer-assisted career planning systems, assist students to locate and interpret occupational information, train students in job shadowing and information interviewing, and answer questions about self-directed self-assessment devices. It is imperative that supervisors be available to answer immediate questions and that regular, ongoing supervision is established to protect both the client and the peer counselor. It is also important to note that serving as a peer counselor can provide a valuable career development experience for students who aspire to careers in the mental health field. The University of Maryland, Cornell University, and Dickinson College have developed exemplary peer counseling programs (Johnson & Figler, 1984).

Assessment

Many of the indicators that competencies have been developed require self-knowledge. For example, one indicator that the young adult is maintaining a positive view of self in terms of potential and preferences in the world of work is the ability to identify factors such as interests and values and indicate how they influence choice making. In some instances, this competency could be partially developed by the administration and interpretation of interest and values inventories as part of an ongoing career counseling process. In other instances, self-directed assessment may be all that is required and thus a student might take either a paper-and-pencil or computer-administered form of an interest inventory or a values survey.

Postsecondary institutions offer career-related assessment in numerous ways, including the aforementioned approaches. However, some include interest and personality inventories and aptitude tests as part of the orientation programs. Others support psychometric centers where students can go to take various types of inventories, usually after an intake interview. Students who enroll in career classes or volunteer for career groups are also likely to find that assessment plays a prominent role in the process of these experiences.

PROGRAM EVALUATION

Evaluation of the outcomes of career development programs was discussed in Chapters 9 and 10. We have provided the findings of studies evaluating the impact of career development intervention throughout this chapter. Obviously, the success of a program will depend on the extent to which students attain the competencies listed in Figures 11.1 and 11.2. The indicators listed are measured separately and collectively as a means to infer competency acquisition. The standards associated with these indicators tell us in a relative sense how well the program has succeeded. For example, if all students are expected to understand the uses and limitations of occupational outlook information (Figure 11.2, Competency 4) we must establish criteria by which to judge that success. We might, for example, use a paper-and-pencil test where students are asked to identify the three uses and three limitations of occupational outlook information and expect that 100 percent of the students would be able to answer this question correctly. If only 80 percent do answer it correctly, we can either accept this result, judge our programs accordingly, or reteach the competency. What is actually done will depend on resources and the importance attached to the competency. As the reader may recall from previous chapters, this type of evaluation is called product or outcome evaluation.

Mines (1985) suggests that measuring certain developmental phenomena poses difficulty because students do not "develop" at the same rate, even given identical experiences and backgrounds, and because students respond to their experiences differentially. For example, all students may participate in a course on career development, but because readiness (developmental stage) varies, the course will have differential impact. Also, because of learning styles and environmental variables (e.g., parent's demands), students will absorb the material at differential rates.

As noted in Chapter 9, process evaluation looks at decision making, staffing, resources, management variables, and other program process variables that may contribute to, or detract from, attainment of program goals. If these processes are perfect (which they will not be) and if the programs themselves are perfectly designed (which they will not be), some failure will occur because of the interaction of development and the environment. An example of the results of a process evaluation is presented by Reardon and Regan (1981). The objective of their evaluation was to determine student reactions to a career development course at Florida State University. The course, which consisted of three units (Self and Environmental Analysis, Decision Making, and Job Acquisition), was evaluated by two types of student rankings and by looking at academic records. Reardon and Regan found that students learned about the course from friends, faculty advisors, and the schedule of classes. They also discovered that students enrolled in the class to develop a fuller understanding of the career planning and decision-making process, to increase their motivation to engage in career planning, to find out more information about careers, and to determine how careers and majors are linked. Finally, they found that students valued the organization of the course and the level of instructor-student interaction. Reardon and Regan concluded that the information resulting from their evaluation was helpful in determining how the course could be marketed and as an aid in course redesign.

SUMMARY

Career development activities in postsecondary educational institutions can assist students to crystallize their career plans and begin the process of implementing them by linking education and career. However, not all students perceive that they need these activities; many hold the opposite view. In some instances, students do not need career development activities, but in others it is just as obvious that students' perceptions of the relevance of career development activities is based on naivete, not information. It is also clear that students enrolled in postsecondary institutions are diverse, both by virtue of their development and because of their age, ethnicity, and reasons for being in college. Good programming requires that these needs be carefully considered and attempts be made to meet them. It is likely that only those programs that use multiple approaches—including information, career counseling, classes, small groups, and units in classes—and that link advising and career planning will be successful.

REFERENCES

Allyn, D. P. (1989). Application of the 4MAT model of career guidance. *Career Development Quarterly, 37,* 280–288.

Bjorkquist, P. M. (1988). Creating an alumni career consultant program in a liberal arts college. *Journal of College Student Development, 29,* 77–78.

Blan, F. W. (1985). Inter-collegiate athletic competition and students' educational and career plans. *Journal of College Student Development, 26,* 115–118.

Brown, D., & Minor, C. W. (Eds.). (1991). *Minorities' perceptions of career planning and work.* Alexandria, VA: National Career Development Association.

Brown, D., Pryzwansky, W. P., & Schulte, A. (1991). *Psychological consultation: Introduction to theory and practice* (2nd ed.). Boston: Allyn & Bacon.

Buescher, K. L., Johnston, J. A., Lucas, C. B., & Hughey, K. F. (1989). Early interventions with undecided college students. *Journal of College Student Development, 30,* 375–377.

Butcher, E. (1982). Changing by choice: A process model of group counseling. *Vocational Guidance Quarterly, 30,* 200–209.

Dailey, M. J. (1986). Using decision trees to assist students through academic and career advising. *Journal of College Student Development, 27,* 457–458.

Elliot, E. S. (1988). Major fairs and undergraduate student exploration. *Journal of College Student Development, 29,* 278–280.

Evans, N. J. (1985). Needs assessment methodology: A comparison of results. *Journal of College Student Development, 26,* 107–114.

Forrest, L., & Backes, P. (1988). CareerLine: Career resources delivered to students. *Journal of College Student Development, 29,* 165–166.

Gallup Organization. (1989). *A Gallup survey regarding career development.* Princeton, NJ: Author.

Goodson, W. D. (1982). Status of career programs on college and university campuses. *Vocational Guidance Quarterly, 30,* 230–235.

Griff, N. (1987). Meeting the career development needs of returning students. *Journal of College Student Development, 28,* 469–470.

Hatcher, L., & Crook, J. C. (1988). First-job surprises for college graduates: An exploratory investigation. *Journal of College Student Development, 29,* 441–448.

Healy, C. C., & Reilly, K. C. (1989). Career needs of community college students: Implications for theory and practice. *Journal of College Student Development, 30,* 541–545.

Holly, K. A. (1987). Development of a college peer counselor program. *Journal of College Student Development, 28,* 285–286.

Johnson, C. A., & Figler, H. E. (1984). Career development and placement services in post-secondary institutions. In N. C. Gysberg (Ed.), *Designing careers* (pp. 458–481). San Francisco: Jossey-Bass.

Johnston, W. B., & Packer, A. E. (1987). *Workforce 2000: Workers and work for the twenty-first century.* Indianapolis, IN: Hudson Institute.

Kahnweiler, J. B., & Kahnweiler, W. M. (1980). A dual-career workshop for college undergraduates. *Vocational Guidance Quarterly, 28,* 225–230.

Kivlighan, K. M. (1990). Career group therapy. *The Counseling Psychologist, 18,* 64–79.

Lanning, W. (1982). The privileged few: Special counseling needs of athletes. *Journal of Sports Psychology, 4,* 19–23.

Lent, R. W., Larkin, K. C., & Hasequa, C. S. (1980). Effects of a "focused" interest career counseling approach for college students. *Vocational Guidance Quarterly, 34,* 151–159.

Magoon, T. M. (1989). *The 1988/1989 college and university counseling center data bank.* College Park, MD: University of Maryland Counseling Center.

Mines, R. A. (1985). Measurement issues in evaluating student development programs. *Journal of College Student Personnel, 26,* 101–106.

Nachreiner, J. A. (1987). A self-help education and career planning resource for adult students. *Journal of College Student Development, 28,* 277–278.

NOICC (1989). *The national career development guidelines: Local handbook for post-secondary institutions.* Washington, DC: Author.

Oliver, L., & Spokane, A. R. (1988). Career intervention outcome: What contributes to client gain? *Journal of Counseling Psychology, 35,* 447–462.

Pickering, J. W. (1984). A comparison of three methods of career planning for liberal arts majors. *Career Development Quarterly, 35,* 102–111.

Pickering, J. W., & Vacc, N. A. (1984). Effectiveness of career development interventions for college students: A recovery of published research. *Vocational Guidance Quarterly, 32,* 149–159.

Quinn, M. T., & Lewis, R. J. (1989). An attempt to measure a career-planning intervention in a traditional course. *Journal of College Student Development, 30,* 371–372.

Reardon, R., & Regan, K. (1981). Process evaluation of a career planning course. *Vocational Guidance Quarterly, 29,* 265–269.

Reardon, R., Zunker, V., & Dyal, M.A. (1979). The status of career planning programs in career centers in colleges and universities. *Vocational Guidance Quarterly, 28,* 154–159.

Robbins, S. B., & Tucker, K. R., Jr. (1986). Relation of good instability to self-directed and interactional career counseling workshops. *Journal of Counseling Psychology, 33,* 418–424.

Savickas, M. L. (1990). The career decision making course: Description and field test. *Journal of College Student Development, 38,* 275–284.

Spokane, A. (1991). *Career interventions.* Englewood Cliffs, NJ: Prentice Hall.

Stone, G. L., & Archer, J. A., Jr. (1990). College and university counseling centers in the 1990s: Challenges and limits. *The Counseling Psychologist, 18,* 539–607.

Wilkes, S. B., Davis, L., & Dever, L. (1989). Fostering career development in student-athletes. *Journal of College Student Development, 30,* 567–568.

__12__

Needs of
Special Groups

For most people, the theories of career development discussed in Chapter 2 and the developmental experiences described in Chapters 9, 10, and 11 are generally applicable. The early years are devoted primarily to physical and psychological maturation. During that period, one becomes aware of occupations and gradually matches one's understanding of self with what is visualized as existing in various occupations. In the teens and early twenties, most individuals make tentative choices and select preparatory programs that relate to those goals. By the middle twenties, most are beginning what Super (1990) calls the establishment stage. For some, the sketch can be completed with the phrase "and they lived happily ever after." But for many that would not be true.

The goal of this chapter is to consider some of the groups for whom circumstances or conditions require a modification in the usual career development process. We have assumed that career development is a unique, individualized process for every person, and it depends on all of an individual's personal attributes and characteristics interacting with the environment, the times, and the people who make up that person's world. Nevertheless, within that uniqueness one can find certain commonalities that are generally shared by others, and this provides the basis for the group activities that are used to educate, civilize, and socialize the person. Ideally, these are supplemented with personal experiences that aid the person in uniquely maximizing his total development. In parallel fashion, one can consider groups of people who share certain conditions or characteristics that necessitate or suggest a certain kind of response, and at the same time maintain respect for the individual.

Many types of classification could be used to identify representative groups that face somewhat different circumstances in career development experiences. This chapter considers five of these without any claim that these are all inclusive; rather, they have been chosen because they are representative of groupings to which career information and counseling can be related in special ways. We consider the following groups:

1. Special-needs groups, particularly those that are often described as disabled or disadvantaged
2. Culturally different groups, including minority ethnic groups, the geographically or socially isolated, and immigrants
3. Delayed entrants, such as displaced homemakers or those who elect to enter or return to work later than the usual entry time, returning military personnel, and prior offenders
4. Midlife changers, including those who either voluntarily or involuntarily turn in another direction
5. Late-life changers—those who reach or approach the retirement period with a desire to continue some kind of relationship with work

One purpose of this chapter is to increase awareness of differences among various clients and how some of these differences are shared by groups. Some counselors and helpers may have relatively little contact with several of the groups, perhaps even all of those identified here. Others may be deeply, or at least occasionally, in contact with members of one or more categories. Because of this variation in needs among readers, our discussion does not extend beyond the familiarization level. Each section of the chapter includes a listing of recent books or articles that will help the reader acquire a more complete understanding of that subgroup. Usually one can find these references in the early paragraphs of the section. Most articles included have been selected from readily available professional journals.

SPECIAL-NEEDS GROUPS

In the truest sense, everyone qualifies for this category because each person does have special needs that make him or her unique. Here, however, the term is applied in a slightly different way. Two groups are considered in this category: those individuals who have a physical or mental disability and as a result encounter handicaps, and those individuals who are disadvantaged because of education, language, or economic factors. For this chapter's discussion, the terms *disabled* and *disadvantaged* are restricted to those individuals for whom the disability or disadvantage clearly intrudes on the career development process to a degree that demands special attention to that characteristic.

Clients with Disabilities

The term *disability* is often misunderstood or misused. The *Chartbook on Disability in the United States* (Kraus & Stoddard, 1989) recommends the definition adopted by the World Health Organization, that is "a disability is any restriction or lack (resulting from an impairment) of ability to perform an activity in the manner or within the range considered normal for a human being." Hadley and Brodwin (1988) and Grealish and Salomone (1986) discuss the impact of imprecise terminology on the lives of people with disabilities. We often incorrectly use the terms *disabled* and *handicapped* synonymously. Fagan and Wallace (1979, p. 216) distinguish between the two terms as follows:

> The disability may be considered as the person's observable, measurable characteristic that is judged to be deviant or discrepant from some acceptable norm. In contrast, the handicap may be considered as the barriers, demands, and general environmental press placed on the person by various aspects of his or her environment, including other persons. Thus the absence of legs is a disability, whereas the presence of stairs, as the only means of access to a goal, is a handicap.

This definition suggests that a physical or mental condition becomes a handicap or impairment when the disability limits one or more major life activities. Public Law 93-112 defines a handicapped person in this way, and further states that physical or mental impairment means

> any physiological disorder or condition, cosmetic disfigurement, or anatomical loss affecting one or more of the body systems: neurological, musculoskeletal; special sense organs; respiratory—including speech organs; cardiovascular; reproductive; digestive; genitourinary; hemic and lymphatic, skin or endocrine; or any mental or physical disorder, such as mental retardation, organic brain syndrome, emotional or mental illness, and specific learning disability.

Because our attention is directed toward career and career development, we are concerned only with impairment as it limits or interferes with work-related activities—in other words, vocational handicap. To return to the original differentiation proposed by Fagan and Wallace, a disability is a handicap only if it limits or impedes the person's work involvement. Thus their illustration of disability—the absence of legs—is a handicap if legs are necessary for successful work involvement. Therefore, a paraplegic desk worker might not be handicapped, whereas a similarly disabled mail carrier definitely would be handicapped.

Kraus and Stoddard (1989) report that an estimated 14.1 percent of the 231.5 million noninstitutionalized U.S. residents have an activity limitation. Of these, 8.8 million are unable to perform their major activity, 13.6 million are limited in the kind and amount of major activity they can perform, and 10.1 million are limited in other activities. Of the 13.3 million people who are considered to have a work disability, 33.6 percent are in the labor force and 15.6 percent are unemployed; thus roughly half of those with a work disability are outside the work structure (neither employed nor classified as unemployed). These figures contrast with the population without disability, where 78.5 percent are participating in the labor force and 6.8 percent are unemployed.

The term *rehabilitation* is gradually being broadened in concept to apply to the overcoming of many kinds of disabling human problems, including physical disability, mental illness, mental retardation, alcoholism, drug addiction, delinquency, and crime. Specifically, rehabilitation may refer to special services such as education, physical functioning, psychological adjustment, social adaptation, vocational capabilities, or recreational activities.

Vocational rehabilitation traditionally has referred to the process of returning a disabled worker to a state of reemployability. In at least two major ways, however, this concept is unnecessarily narrow. First, it implies that a person must have acquired certain marketable skills before eligibility for help can be established; second, the idea of employability as a product of the service may make ineligible for help those for whom employability may be uncertain or unlikely. Fortunately, there has been some movement toward reducing both of these restrictions, so that people who face handicaps but have never worked may qualify and even those for whom assistance may result in greater self-esteem and self-satisfaction without clear certainty of employment may be included. More recognition is now being given to the impact of disability on family life as well as on the individual. This has placed greater emphasis on the need for independence, self-regard, and integration within the total society rather than on separation and isolation from it.

Public Law 93-112, the Rehabilitation Act of 1973; Public Law 94-142, the Education for All Handicapped Children Act (1975); Public Law 95-602, the Rehabilitation, Comprehensive Services, and Developmental Disabilities Amendments of 1978; Public Law 101-476; the Education of the Handicapped Amendments of 1990; and Public Law 101-336, the Americans with Disabilities Act of 1990 have reinforced and expanded existing laws to produce greater public concern for disabled individuals as well as more adequate programs of assistance. One result has been an increasing quantity of helpful material in the professional literature.

Literature on the general topic of vocational rehabilitation ranges from articles in professional counseling journals to special issues of those journals to journals that focus on rehabilitation to professional books on the topic. Examples of the first type (articles in professional journals) include articles by Chubon (1985), Curnow (1989), Dahl (1982), Hagner and Salomone (1989), and Roessler (1987). A special issue of the *Journal of Counseling and Development* (November/December 1989) devotes 40 pages to "Counseling Persons With Disabilities: A 10-year Update." Journals that concentrate on rehabilitation topics include *Career Development for Exceptional Individuals, Journal of Applied Rehabilitation Counseling,* and *Rehabilitation Counseling Bulletin.* Recent books in the field include Berkell and Brown (1989), Parker (1987), Rubin and Roessler (1987), and Rubin and Rubin (1988).

Rehabilitation services are provided by a number of professions—counseling, medical, nursing, psychological, social work, and others. Career counseling services are most frequently provided by rehabilitation counselors, whose counseling preparation has also usually included the medical and social aspects of various disabilities and their relationship to work. Thomas and Berven (1984) estimate there are presently about 25,000 rehabilitation counselors employed in the United States. In addition to the state vocational rehabilitation offices, they are employed in a number of national, state, and local public and private social agencies. Among the well-known organizations involved in vocational rehabilitation are Goodwill Industries, Jewish Vocational Service, and the Department of Veterans Affairs. Public schools play a significant role, especially for those of school age. Postsecondary schools are also involved in providing not only educational services but other types of programs as well.

Like other federal and state programs, public vocational rehabilitation programs exist in every state and are operated by state personnel under state policies within broad guidelines and provisions established by the federal agency. Funding for state services is provided on a shared or matching basis, with the formula used being a four-to-one ratio of federal to state funds. In other words, within the limits established by congressional authorization, for every $20 provided by state funds, the federal government matches with $80. The state first must make its funds available, and then federal dollars are allocated. Despite the generous matching formula, many states do not appropriate enough money to claim all the federal funds available to them. In these circumstances, unclaimed funds are reallocated to other states that are willing to provide additional matching monies. The obvious result is considerable variation in the quality and scope of public rehabilitation services from state to state. Costs vary greatly from one rehabilitation case to another, with some simple cases requiring small amounts of money to resolve the problem, while other cases require much time and money. In general, data from annual federal reports show that the average age for rehabilitants stays under 40, and the average client pays in federal income taxes within 3 years as much as the rehabilitation services cost. Thus an overwhelming case could be made in support of rehabilitation services on economic terms alone.

Fagan and Jenkins (1989) report the number of rehabilitation cases successfully closed in 1985 by type of disability. Of the more than 424 thousand cases, almost 54 percent were individuals who were blind, 11 percent lacked an extremity, 9 percent were cases of alcoholism, 7 percent had epilepsy, 3.5 percent were drug abuse victims, and the other disabilities were each less than 2.5 percent of the cases. A word of caution is necessary to emphasize that these figures include only successfully completed cases; often these numbers were served in various ways by the state and federal rehabilitation program.

Thomas and Berven (1984) describe the career counseling process for clients with disabilities. They propose a sequence consisting of assessment, occupational exploration and choice, vocational training, placement, and follow-up. The presence of a disability may require adjustment of some of the steps.

The purpose of assessment is to help the individual (and the counselor) understand the client as completely as possible. As with any client, tests and other techniques are used to obtain needed information not readily available. Also as with any client, the counselor must determine the appropriateness of the test for the specific client and judge the likelihood that the needed information can be obtained in this way. Guidubaldi, Perry, and Walker (1989) stress the importance of proper assessment procedures with students with disabilities. Zunker (1986) describes a number of assessment devices appropriate for many clients with disabilities. There are several indicators that nontest techniques may be more useful for clients with disabilities; for example, the disability may have isolated the client from experiences customary for her age group, or the impact of the disability on the client's physical and mental abilities may be such that psychometric measurement is inappropriate or produces imprecise results. The use of interview procedures with the client or with physicians and therapists may provide better evaluation of the disabling condition and its effect on the client. Work samples and job tryouts may be much more significant in evaluating the individual than in ordinary circumstances. Evidence of what the client *can* do, such as strength factors or aptitudes, is even more important than accurate identification of what she cannot do.

The occupational exploration process is similar to that followed by clients without disabilities except for greater emphasis on identifying occupations that meet the client's physical and mental abilities. *Selected Characteristics of Occupations Defined in the Dictionary of Occupational Titles* (described in Chapter 5) is the logical volume to use during the expanding phase of occupational exploration. Some of the computer-based career guidance systems (for example, Guidance Information System, described in Chapter 8) include evaluations of physical demands and environmental conditions of occupations similar to what can be found in *Selected Characteristics*. Visits to work sites and actual tryout experiences may often be of special significance because client and counselor would be dealing with reality rather than conjecture. In the past, workers with disabilities were often restricted to narrow segments of the world of work by the interaction of public attitudes and their own self-image. Nevertheless, the range of suitable work for workers with disabilities should be nearly as wide as the universe of jobs. Cook, Dahl, and Gale (1978) found workers with serious disabilities in 64 of the 82 two-digit *DOT* Occupational Divisions and in every one of the nine one-digit *DOT* Occupational Categories. Dahl (1982) states further that this does not suggest that each person with a disability can qualify for every job—nor can the rest of us.

Vocational training for individuals with disabilities involves the same choices and decisions faced by clients without disabilities. One additional factor must be considered by some clients with disabilities—accessibility. Training and educational institutions are modifying facilities to ensure accessibility by all individuals, but the task has not been completed. Younger individuals with disabilities will find increasing attention given to vocational training at the high school level as a result of recent legislation. Levinson (1984) describes such a program for emotionally disturbed students. Humes and Hohenshil (1985) urge establishing adequate career counseling and career education for students with disabilities. Some clients with disabilities, like some clients without disabilities, may need special training in nonskill aspects of work such as hygiene and grooming, punctuality and regularity of attendance, getting along with others, and so on.

Placement services for workers with disabilities, described in more detail in Chapter 16, involve more complexity than those for workers without disabilities. The added complications arise from attitudes of employers and fellow workers, as well as those of the client. Job club techniques, also described in Chapter 16, are appropriate. When the disability is severe, job modification may be necessary to permit full participation in work.

Follow-up activities with recently placed workers with disabilities provide a service similar to that performed by the work experience coordinator. The major function is to facilitate satisfactory adjustment between the worker and the work site. When identified early and solved rapidly, problems tend to be less severe and less disruptive. Sometimes minor adjustments in the work site are all that is needed to ensure that the worker can be as productive as workers without disabilities.

Economically Disadvantaged Clients

The term *disadvantaged* can be interpreted very broadly, in its usual dictionary sense, to include everyone who is in an unfavorable economic or social circumstance. Certainly almost everyone in the category just discussed would fit this description, as would many members of minority groups, women, the poor, dropouts, and several other large segments of the population; even left-handed individuals occasionally find themselves in awkward social circumstances. It can also be applied very legitimately in a restricted or narrow sense, as Miles (1984) uses it to describe the economically disadvantaged, equating the term with *economically deprived* or *poor.* Typically, two subgroups are included under this label because their circumstances often assign them here. These include those with limited education (in either quantity or quality) and those caught in geographic dislocation (often rural poor or urban unemployed who have moved elsewhere searching for something better).

Miles (1984) states that three groups make up the economically disadvantaged:

> *The Chronically Poor:* These are individuals born into poverty and raised in families with inadequate resources to meet basic needs.
>
> *The Unemployed or Newly Disadvantaged:* Some unemployed can bridge brief periods of unemployment by using savings and other available resources. It is probably fair to assume that unemployment, sooner or later, puts each victim in the disadvantaged group. The structurally unemployed are in the greatest

danger because they no longer have a job to which they can ultimately return. The cyclically unemployed can also be hurt if the economic recession outlasts their available resources.

The Underemployed: Miles calls these the working poor because they are found mainly in low-wage, marginal jobs that involve little skill. Their wages are not sufficient to exceed poverty standards. One unfortunate result of plant closing and plant exporting is likely to be a rapid increase in this category as structurally unemployed skilled workers settle into low-paying unskilled jobs. Miles states that approximately one sixth of the working population earn incomes that only barely exceed the poverty level; hence this group is constantly on the margin of falling into the poverty group. (pp. 386–389)

Some of the major problems faced by the disadvantaged in career planning may be lack of basic skills, unsuccessful vocational adjustment at early career entry stage, inability to obtain vocational training, low income levels, incongruity between self-concept and previously held low-level jobs, and periods of unemployment. Because of these needs, disadvantaged people often need career development programs that address both short-term and long-term goals. The counselor will need to involve the client in short-term planning accompanied by rewards and reinforcement to help the client reach a point where long-range goals and plans appear feasible.

It would appear that many of the career-related problems of the economically disadvantaged could be confronted with a four-part program including the following:

1. Access to basic adult education
2. Personal and/or career counseling
3. Information about the world of work
4. Access to appropriate vocational training and placement

Individuals with limited educational background are almost automatically relegated to the most marginal work opportunities. Literacy training, basic mathematics, and language proficiency are minimal essentials for almost every job in our society. Adult education programs exist in almost all metropolitan areas; however, individuals may be unable to capitalize on these services because of lack of transportation or unfamiliarity with local transportation systems, lack of child care, time schedule problems, and so forth. It is fairly safe to say that until basic educational skills are acquired, the individual has very little to sell to a prospective employer.

Personal counseling may be needed by disadvantaged individuals to clarify self-concept as well as to understand their circumstances. Several authors have emphasized the devastating impact that job loss has on feelings of self-worth. The chronically poor are likely to carry an even heavier feeling of worthlessness. The so-called American dream suggests that one's success in life is the product of hard work—the harder one works, the more one reaps in material rewards, status, and self-satisfaction. One frequent product is the feeling of guilt and failure by those without jobs or with only marginal jobs.

Marshall (1983) and Shifron, Dye, and Shifron (1983) describe ways to help such clients deal with feelings and values that may interfere with everyday life and often result from forces outside the individual's control.

Realistic and practical information about the world of work can be used to help the disadvantaged to see potential opportunities to break out of what is frequently viewed as a hopeless morass. Interviews with workers, work samples, plant visits, and synthetic work situations may help the person to understand the job, to relate that job to self, to see attainable goals, and perhaps to acquire usable role models.

Access to realistic skill training is necessary for all jobs but those at the lowest skill level. One problem is that many disadvantaged students withdraw from school before they reach the grade level where vocational skills are taught. This situation limits their access to skill training, to Job Training Program Administration (JTPA) programs, or to similar efforts provided at the local level. Compared with the numbers of people who truly need such preparation, the few training positions available are far too limited. Miles (1984) suggests that counselors must become change agents and assist clients in changing the system if this deficit is to be overcome.

CULTURALLY DIFFERENT CLIENTS

Some recent developments, such as multicultural education programs, bilingual classes for students, newspaper accounts of illegal immigrants, and new immigration laws, have helped some people realize that the United States includes more than the white, English-speaking middle class that many of them know best. The group of individuals labeled here as culturally different is no more all alike than a white, English-speaking group is all alike. Many of the subgroups (or at least individuals in each subgroup) are more like some of the white, English-speaking group than like any of the other people in the culturally different category. In many of the subgroups the range of economic, educational, and social differences is nearly as great as in the general population.

Casas and Arbona (in press), describing career-related issues faced by Hispanics, emphasize some of the factors that produce diversity within minority ethnic groups. Recognition of these variables may help counselors and others to be more cognizant of client individual differences, regardless of the person's ethnic background. Although the factors and percentages will likely vary across groups, the crucial aspect is recognition that each individual has a unique combination of these and many other unnamed factors. They point out that Hispanics, the second largest minority group in the United States, make up at least 8 percent of the population and because of enumerating difficulties may be considerably more than the 19 million counted in 1987.

Large subgroups within this ethnic group include those of Mexican origin (63 percent), Puerto Ricans (12 percent), Central and South Americans (11 percent), Cubans (5 percent), and other Hispanic groups (8 percent). The groups vary from a racial perspective, comprised of individuals who are of Caucasian, Mongoloid, and Negroid descent. There is also wide diversity within and across Hispanic subgroups in factors that can be labeled demographic, sociohistorical, sociopolitical, socioeconomic, and sociopsychological. Some of the subgroups, even though dispersed across the country, have high concentrations in certain areas. For example, Mexican Americans are numerous in the Southwest, many Cuban Americans are found in south Florida and near New York City, and many of Central American background are found in New York City, Los Angeles, and San Francisco.

Similarly, Fukuyama (in press) discusses Asian Pacific Islanders and career development. This ethnic minority includes a wide range of national origins, including Asian Indian, Pakistani, Thai, Chinese, Japanese, Filipino, Vietnamese, Laotian, Cambodian, Hmong, Hawaiian, Samoan, Guam, Korean, and others. Obviously, the cultural diversity within and across these national subgroups is wide.

The culturally different, for our purposes, include both recent legal and illegal immigrants and descendants of former immigrants who have lived in a subculture where family and community influences, language, ethnic factors, and religious practices have produced isolation and/or alienation from the dominant culture and have slowed the acculturation process. Also included in the group are those whose families may have been in this country for several generations but who, because of geographic or self-imposed isolation, have had limited contact with the general population. Another temporary part of this group includes foreign residents, such as the diverse foreign student population found on most major university campuses. Some individuals that we label culturally different may have limited English competency; atypical and/or limited educational experience; unfamiliarity with socially accepted practices in the United States; and a background that has produced values, viewpoints, and behaviors that some might think unusual. Cultural differences stem from adhering to customs, traditions, and values of the original culture.

Increasing attention is being given to preparing counselors to work with culturally different clients. Karayanni (1987) reports on the impact of modernization pressures on the vocational interests in a traditional-minded population. Articles by Ross (1984) and Webb (1983) focus on broad cultural factors such as adult development in different cultures and awareness of cross-cultural differences. Within the counseling literature one can find many articles that discuss the general problems produced by this impact of ethnicity and different cultural backgrounds on the counseling relationship and many articles that deal with preparing counselors to meet these challenges. Typical of articles that focus on cultural factors are those by Ahia (1984), Cheatham (1990), Giles (1990), Gim, Atkinson, and Kim (1991), Heinrich, Corbine, and Thomas (1990), Lee (1984), Leong and Hayes (1990), Sue (1978), and Sundal–Hansen (1985). Articles that stress counselor preparation for work with culturally diverse clients include those by Arrendondo–Dowd and Gonsalves (1980), Rosser–Hogan (1990), and Sue et al. (1982). Brown and

Minor (in press) report ethnic group responses to the Gallup survey reported in Chapter 1.

We must assume that culturally different clients have all the problems faced by other clients, with many of these having a different or unusual structure, and further problems created or accentuated by the cultural variances. Sue (1978) suggests a framework that can help counselors organize their approach to the counseling relationship, based on a two-dimensional concept with locus of control serving as the horizontal axis and locus of responsibility as the vertical axis. Thus the four quadrants represent the different combinations of internal-external control and internal-external responsibility. Sue believes that the internal control/internal responsibility quadrant represents the typically American outlook, reinforcement of behavior is primarily a product of our own behavior, and success or failure is primarily the result of our own skill and adequacy. This view also is basic to most philosophies of counseling. Many culturally different clients, however, would classify themselves in one of the other quadrants because of traditions and values. Understanding this difference, especially the factor of values, and adjusting one's approach appropriately may be the secret to successful counseling with these clients.

In addition to those factors that can be clearly labeled as cultural differences—such as importance of family group among Hispanics, unquestioning respect for elders and authority among Asians—other problems are faced by many in these groups. One of these is language and communication. Even the well-educated foreign graduate student often may find American vernacular and slang incomprehensible. Further, nonverbal communication is very different; for example, eye contact with a respected elder (the counselor, maybe), body contact such as handshaking, or the use of a negative may be considered rude or very difficult. A second difficulty arises from unfamiliarity with the system—not knowing how to do certain things that we take for granted. Sue et al. (1982) recommend that cross-cultural counselors maintain an open attitude that allows them to be aware of their cultural heritage and its values and biases, to recognize the differences that exist between counselor and client, and to be sensitive to the client's needs.

Clearly the counselor must bridge the chasm of cultural difference before career counseling or the use of career information can be effective. Initiation of solutions to problems of language, understanding and using the system, and other basic matters may be achieved through group procedures or the use of local social agencies; but they cannot be laid aside as inconsequential. Counseling culturally different clients is discussed further in Chapter 14.

DELAYED ENTRANTS

There are several factors that might cause an individual to enter the world of work later than immediately after completing education. Even today, the largest group who vary the pattern in this manner are women who marry near the time when they complete their education, or before, and elect to assume a homemaker role. Two other groups also can be considered delayed entrants. These include military personnel, who may spend from 3 to 30 years in the armed forces before entering civilian employment. Certainly it would be incorrect to imply that homemakers and military personnel do not work— they do indeed. The discussion here is limited to those whose entry into civilian, paid employment has been delayed beyond the usual point. A third group includes those who are incarcerated before acquiring significant work experience. There are others who are delayed for numerous personal or family reasons.

Late-Entry Women

One group of women, rapidly increasing in number, includes those who have acquired significant work experience before interrupting that work to devote their time to homemaking and mothering, and who after a period of time deliberately return to work. For the most part, these women are not the center of our concern in this section because they have both occupational skills and a career plan. Two other groups do exist that we consider here. One group, often referred to as *displaced homemakers*, includes those women who have considered themselves primarily to be homemakers but now, perhaps even unexpectedly, find that circumstances necessitate their working for pay. Their reasons vary: widowhood, divorce, illness or unemployment of spouse, abandonment, unexpected economic circumstances, and so on. The crucial aspect is the relatively sudden and unexpected—or at least unplanned—necessity of entering the labor market. The second group includes women who have deliberately planned to enter employment at a later time, after their children are all in school, or all in college, or all on their own, or when their parents no longer require full-time attention.

Increasing evidence shows that most women will fall into one of the three groups of women in the labor force—regular entrant, reentry worker, or delayed entrant. The Bureau of National Affairs (1986) reports that nearly 60 percent of mothers of children under age 18 were employed in 1985; the labor force participation rate for married women with children under 1 year old increased by 70 percent; and by 1995 more than 80 percent of women between ages 25 and 44 are expected to be working. Over two thirds of labor force entrants in the 1975–85 decade were women, and two-thirds of these had children.

The women's movement has helped direct attention to many of the inequities women face in the labor force—unequal pay, unfair employment practices, harassment, and so forth. In part, the still unresolved issue of comparable worth is a product of the pattern of unequal pay for women. All these problems confront most women who work to some extent, but they appear to be bigger problems for the two groups just described (delayed and late entry) than for other women. These two sets also face a number of other problems that we discuss shortly.

There is literature in the field for the counselor who assists women with work-related problems. More articles appear to be focused on the reentry worker than on the delayed entrant. Examples of available materials include articles by Ekstrom, Beier, Davis, and Gruenberg (1981), Farmer (1985), Gerson and Lee (1982), McGraw (1982), Pickering and Galvin–Schaefers (1988), Read, Elliott, Escobar, and Slaney (1988), Robinson, Rotter, and Wilson (1982), and Zawada (1980). More specialized discussions can be found in Bowen (1982), who describes career counseling with abused women; and Chusmir (1983), who describes women whose vocational choices are nontraditional. Slaney and Dickson (1985) have studied the effect of indecision on career exploration for reentry women workers, and Wade and Bernstein (1991) have examined counselor race and cultural sensitivity in dealing with African-American female clients. An issue of *The Counseling Psychologist* features a discussion by Astin (1984) of the meaning of work in women's lives, with responses by several well-known female psychologists.

The displaced-homemaker group will often need personal counseling because of the drastic, sudden, and sometimes traumatic events that have displaced them before they are ready for career counseling. Unfortunately, some decide that if they can leap into a full-time job or training program, their other problems will shrink or go away. Those other difficulties, however, must be resolved at least in part before any intelligent planning about education and/or work can take place.

Frequently, one of the problems that needs prior attention is the modifying of self-concept so the person can assume responsibility for decisions that previously may have been made jointly or by the absent partner. This may require both self-confidence building and access to basic information and knowledge needed for sound decisions. In some marriages, items often relegated to males include maintenance of property or living quarters, automobile purchase and care, and legal or financial matters. If these and other important areas are unfamiliar to a female client, she must either acquire that competence or deal with the problem in another way.

Displaced homemakers often face serious financial problems, either short term or long term. Referral to competent financial advisors may be necessary to resolve acquisition or disposition of property, relocation of residence, financial planning to cover a period of education or training, and so on.

A further common problem for the displaced homemaker is identifying and cultivating support systems to replace those that may have been lost. The counselor may be able to help the client explore the types of systems she needs and desires, how she might develop them, and specific groups and organizations that might facilitate this aspect.

After some of these problems have been sorted out or at least are headed toward solution, career problems can be considered. One issue that is likely to arise early is whether the woman is considering immediate employment only or is contemplating entry into some preparatory program. All the factors that bear on this decision for a teenager apply here, along with several additional ones—costs in time, effort, and money; whether the pay-back will justify those expenditures; opportunity; individual energy and psychological resources; and so on. If the person is thinking primarily of work, without specialized preparation, the counselor must help identify existing skills and ascertain the extent of job search skills. Identification of skills is obviously related to available or potentially available jobs; and occupational information, especially local labor market information, may be crucial in the early planning stages. The materials available in the career resource center may be particularly useful at this point along with referral to an agency that operates a job club that may offer experience in job interviews, help in searching, and other job-getting experiences. Kahn (1983) describes an employment counseling service that serves this group of reentry women.

The deliberate returner does not necessarily face the same problems that confront the displaced homemaker. Her decision is voluntary, although she may feel that economic factors or the desire for self-fulfillment require her to work. The basic support systems of family, friends, and organizations probably are intact, although the role she anticipates assuming may necessitate adjustments in all of these. Undoubtedly changes in lifestyle will and must occur, but they generally can be resolved without the pressure, grief, and uncertainty that confront the displaced person. Problems that are likely to be constant across both groups are those that relate to self-concept, development of independence, and assertiveness. The deliberate returner can undertake career planning more rapidly because she does not face the massive difficulties of her displaced counterpart. Financial pressures may be less, so the possibility of appropriate educational or training programs can be considered. Timing may be easier to handle, and often gradual reentry to work or preparation can be arranged.

Former Military Personnel

Individuals who return to civilian life after a period of military service can be divided into three groups: (1) those who have served their full time of 20 to 30 years and are now retiring from military duty and will draw pension benefits, (2) those who have incurred a disability that prevents continuing in military service and will now draw disability benefits, and (3) those who are leaving after a relatively brief period (often a single enlistment of 3 to 6 years). We consider the first group in the section "Midlife Changers." The second group, if they attempt to enter civilian employment, qualify for rehabilitation benefits as described earlier. Hence our concern here is primarily with the person who delays entrance into the civilian work force because of a period of military service long enough to justify the label of delayed entrant.

In addition to the customary reasons of patriotism and long-range career plans, many young people volunteer for military service for quite different purposes. The majority of voluntary enlistees are probably recent high schools graduates. Some, recognizing that they have no clear-cut educational or occupational plan, decide to enlist to give themselves time to decide what they want to do. Some, unable to obtain acceptable civilian employment because of either economic factors or the lack of salable skills, enlist as an alternative course of action. Others may volunteer to escape an array of problems—difficult family situations, unsatisfactory living conditions, or a desire for affiliation and belonging. Still others may have clearly formed long-range civilian goals in mind and may enlist to acquire specialized training that they expect to use in a civilian position, or to accrue educational benefits that will permit later completion of civilian college programs.

Many military occupations have equivalent civilian counterparts, and individuals who have acquired these skills in military service can transfer with little difficulty from one to the other, just as other workers move from one employer to another. There are, however, many other military occupations for which transferability of learned job skills is impossible.

Service personnel who elect not to reenlist or are not eligible to do so, and who have had military assignments where no transferable skill was acquired, are most likely to need career counseling. Like displaced homemakers, many in this group view themselves as disadvantaged because they are competing against younger individuals for entry-level jobs. Similarly, they may have only vague ideas about work values and occupational goals and may fail to see that, although they lack specific transferable skills, they may have generalized skills that employers value highly. Further, as a result of having lived in a tightly structured and directed environment, some will need help in assuming responsibility for decision making.

Whenever counselors identify the existence of problems involving self-concept, values, interpersonal relations, attitudes toward work and society, and similar personal attitudes or viewpoints, they must help the client focus on these factors first before proceeding to career choice. Added complications are sometimes encountered in former service personnel because they often feel that they are in a hurry to catch up with their age cohorts who have been in civilian jobs while they were in service, or because some fail to realize the extent of differences between life in military and civilian settings. Further, those who enlisted because of vocational uncertainty or various personal problems may find those difficulties still unresolved.

Those individuals who have completed periods of obligated service have usually incurred the obligation by accepting financial support from military sources for some portion of their advanced educational training—for example, scholarship support for advanced ROTC at the undergraduate level or a stipend or scholarship for completion of a professional school graduate program. Few of these people will need career counseling because the acquired preparation is ordinarily highly transferable. Those who have participated in such programs usually did so because they anticipated military careers or originally planned to transfer to civilian activity after satisfying the obligated period of service. Occasionally, a client who has followed this path may decide that the original choice of field was inappropriate or is no longer desirable and may wish to move to some other kind of work.

Many governmental agencies maintain special programs of assistance for former military personnel. Clients are sometimes unaware of the help that is available to them through various community resources. Among the best known of these programs are state service officers, state employment security agencies, state and federal civil service and personnel agencies, and the Department of Veterans Affairs.

Prior Offenders

Individuals released from penal institutions face the problems encountered by displaced homemakers and returning military personnel plus some others that are unique to their situation and previous experiences. It is probably safe to say that this group is at highest risk, and studies of recidivism show that overwhelming numbers soon find themselves incarcerated again.

State and federal penal institutions vary widely in fundamental philosophy with respect to the goal of rehabilitation versus custodial care. The range of variation is probably even greater when one examines the services actually provided in these two areas. Many prison officials confirm that even in those institutions that emphasize rehabilitation programs, the primary attention is still given to security and custody. One must conclude that very few inmates acquire significant occupational training during their imprisonment. Wendt (1980) points out that vocational programs in correctional institutions are aimed at inmates with low-level educational backgrounds and assume that any type of job, even broom pushing, is sufficient to keep the ex-inmate on the straight and narrow. A survey of educational programs in state and federal correctional institutions revealed that the average inmate is confined for 3 years, but that only one third are enrolled in academic programs (APGA, 1979). Deming and Gulliver (1981) describe an exemplary program in five New York correctional facilities aimed at helping inmates begin or complete college-level training that will prepare them for professional careers. There is an obvious need nationwide for vocational preparatory programs ranging from secondary through university level that can use the period of incarceration to help inmates acquire salable skills.

Most prior offenders will need extensive personal counseling before effective career counseling can be initiated. In many cases, the factors that originally led the person into difficulty may still exist. These have often been compounded by the experiences of confinement, producing an explosive mixture of hostility, anger, and frustration.

The former inmate faces new challenges and difficulties on release. Few communities provide any type of reentry assistance such as halfway houses or other organized social services. Prospective employers or educational institutions often react negatively to the individual on learning about the prior record. Probation and parole officers are usually overloaded and often provide only cursory assistance. The resources available to assist in this difficult transition are generally very few, frequently of limited quality, and rarely able to overcome the opposing pressures.

Many would agree that prior offenders can often be described as the most disadvantaged of all groups that might carry that label. Individuals in the disadvantaged group often encounter barriers such as poor job qualifications, conflicts with others, legal and/or financial difficulties, and emotional problems. Each, if it exists, must be dealt with in the counseling process before serious career counseling can be successful. Some of these problems can be relieved by focusing first on establishing a series of short-term goals, finding appropriate role models, and building self-directedness and personal responsibility.

MIDLIFE CHANGERS

So far in this chapter, our attention has been on groups of individuals who mostly have had little prior contact with the world of work. Workers with disabilities undergoing rehabilitation are the major exception. In this section we consider individuals who have had that contact, sometimes in highly responsible and financially rewarding assignments.

Like the other category labels used in this chapter, this one is ambiguous, ill defined, and variably applied. Levinson, Darrow, Klein, Levinson, and McKee (1978) report that they found about half of their sample involved in career advancement within a stable life structure in the 33–40 age period. Thus nearly half were classified in other categories, all of which suggests a high likelihood of major career change. Eighty percent of Levinson's sample of men also reported moderate or severe crisis during their early forties. We assume arbitrarily that midlife career change essentially occurs during the period of the middle thirties through the forties. Brown (1984) points out a further problem with the term—namely, how much change is considered to be a change. He concludes that the term should be applied when the new occupation requires mild, moderate, or extreme adjustments in training or experience.

Midlife career change has increasingly been the subject of research, especially during the last decade. Several authors consider causes and emerging patterns, including Schlossberg's (1984) book. Articles that deal more briefly with the topic include Armstrong (1981), Brown (1984), Kanchier and Unruh (1988), and Perosa and Perosa (1987). Stark and Zytowski (1988) provide a brief case study of a midlife counseling client's search for satisfying work. Finnegan, Westerfeld, and Elmore (1981) describe a workshop approach to helping midlife changers. Helping midlife individuals deal with job loss is discussed by Davenport (1984), Mallinckrodt and Fretz (1988), and Schlossberg and Leibowitz (1980).

In the previous section we contrasted the problems encountered by displaced homemakers with those of women who deliberately decide to go to work. One of the crises faced by the first group is recognition of tremen-

324 PART FOUR The Career Development Process

dous life change brought about by factors over which they had little or no control. It seems logical to consider midlife changers as being somewhat similar to these two groups of women. Some find themselves faced suddenly, often unexpectedly, by change they would like to have go away; others, often with careful thought and planning, initiate change by their own intentional action. We discuss the two groups separately because they appear to face quite different problems.

Voluntary Changers

The deliberate decision to redirect one's career goals can be caused by many factors. Some of these reflect increased maturity and self-understanding, clearer identification of values and goals, changing needs, or perhaps the appearance of new opportunities. Levinson et al. (1978) found that most of their sample reviewed their past during the early forties and began to make new plans or confirm already developed plans.

One aspect that is likely to transpire in a period of reevaluation is matching earlier dreams and aspirations against present and potential realities to judge the possibility of reaching those early goals. When the discrepancy seems insurmountable, change is likely to occur. Thomas (1979) found that many of his sample gave up high-status positions to search for "more meaningful" work. Closely related to this is the recognition of change in interest and needs within the individual: The youthful desire for travel may become less intense after years on the road; the need to maintain an income may become less pressing once the mortgage is paid off, the children are independent, and investments begin to pay dividends.

Changing circumstances in one's work may also lead the worker to consider change. For example, revision of one's assignment, changes in company management, failure to win a desired promotion, relocation of the work site, anticipated changes in process or quality, and similar factors can produce a desire for change. Feelings of dissatisfaction may lead the worker to look for other options. Sometimes those new opportunities appear even when the worker feels content with the present position—for example, when a new industry moves to town or new educational opportunities make options available that previously appeared closed. Snyder, Howard, and Hammer (1978) indicate that an occupational change will occur when the attractiveness of the new opportunity plus the expectation of successful entry exceeds the pressure to remain in the current position.

A further factor might be called an *enabling option*. The increase in the number of two-income families, with approximately half of U.S. wives now employed for pay, decreases the financial pressure that previously deterred many men from contemplating any type of occupational change. The presence of the second income allows some room for risk taking. Also, a spouse who finds self-satisfaction and fulfillment in work may encourage the partner to look for similar compensations.

Most counselors would concur that individuals who are motivated by factors such as these are mostly acting from positions of strength and are likely to need limited help, if any. Clarification of personal values, needs, and goals may help some, especially the worker who feels dissatisfied and has not focused on the causes of discontent. Some may desire information about job requirements and opportunities or educational preparation needed to qualify in a particular occupation. Others may want information about job search procedures or how to start a business.

Vaitenas and Wiener (1977) report a study that reveals some causes of mid-career change that may be less healthy than the aforementioned situations. They compared career changers and nonchangers in two age groups— a younger group (median age 29.4) and an older group (median age 43.0). They found significant differences between changers and nonchangers but not between age groups. The changers had less stable interest patterns, more emotional problems, and greater fear of failure. These results suggest that some changers are running away because of lack of self-understanding, inconsistent interest patterns, or concern that they will be unable to succeed in their job. Where these behavioral patterns are evident, there is need for personal counseling aimed at expanding self-understanding before any attention is given to career counseling.

Involuntary Changers

Like displaced homemakers, some workers suddenly find themselves in totally unexpected situations that they have never dreamed possible—their job is gone. Essentially, there are two conditions that account for most of the involuntary changers and a third, closely related, situation that we include here.

One example of involuntary change is that faced by the suddenly discharged worker. Some workers are fired because of incompetence or inability to meet the requirements of the job. Four out of five discharged workers are released because of their inability to get along with supervisors or fellow workers. Closely related to the discharged worker is the one who realizes that discharge is imminent and quits before the boss can fire her.

A second group of involuntary changers includes those whose job disappears because of technological change (structural unemployment), plant closing, or plant relocation. Whether the worker is fired from an ongoing job or caught in one that simply melts away, the result for the worker is the same.

Sandler (1988), responding to an earlier article by Kjos (1988), discusses her experiences with a 2-week workshop dealing with dislocated workers who ranged in age from 20 to 65. Although the workshop content focused on job-seeking skills and activities, one might reasonably expect that participation with a group in such activities might help to relieve some of the traumatic effects that job loss has on individuals. Hurst and Shepard (1986) describe the experience as an emotional roller coaster ride for the dislocated worker. They identify grief, anger, panic, depression, and denial as typical feelings experienced by the worker caught in a plant closing and resultant displacement.

A third group of involuntary changers includes those engaged in what might be called early-leaver occupations. These include many of those who participate in professional athletics, where the physical strength and stamina of youth is a crucial component and one is an oldtimer before age 40. Occupations in the public safety area involve high physical risk and therefore usually carry early compulsory retirement. Representative of these are occupations such as firefighter, police officer, and the military positions mentioned previously. Typically, workers in these positions qualify for retirement after 20 years of service, often by the time they reach 40. Although retirement may not be compulsory, and those who have advanced to managerial positions do stay on, the pension program is structured so that workers in lower-level positions cannot afford to continue.

Workers in early-leaver occupations have ample opportunity to anticipate departure from the job. Many plan their careers in patterns similar to those of the voluntary changers by anticipating when the event will occur, preparing for the change by developing educational or other transitional activities, and moving on easily to the next stage of their lives.

Change and readjustment are most difficult for the worker confronted with unexpected job loss. Not only must the grief process be managed, but the suddenness of the event must be handled. Further, not anticipating such a drastic change probably means that the person is totally unprepared for the whole affair of choosing a new field, perhaps preparing for it, engaging in the job-search task, and reestablishing oneself again. The available options are quite narrow for most involuntary changers, who frequently are not prepared to make the decisions required to resolve the dilemma. The choices include only the following:

1. Find a comparable job at another local establishment using the same skills.
2. Relocate to a site where there is a demand for the worker's skill.
3. Seek a job locally that involves other skills, usually at a lower level, possessed by the worker. (This is what happens to most structurally unemployed manufacturing workers who gain reemployment in low-paying service jobs.)
4. Enter an educational or training program that will create new salable skills.
5. Remain unemployed.

The counselor must help the involuntary changer to work through grief, blame, self-accusation, and defeat and then assist in the process of identifying appropriate options and developing plans to pursue those options.

LATE-LIFE CHANGERS

Early in Chapter 1, we examined some of the economic and social reasons that people work. Some people would emphasize the economic reasons—

people work to sustain themselves and their families and to acquire the things they need or want to make their lives comfortable and enjoyable. Others would stress social reasons: the feeling of contributing to society, social status in the community, desire to improve the quality of life for self and others, enjoyment of fellowship with other workers, and so on. Probably most people would select a combination of reasons to explain their personal involvement in work.

Regardless of their reasons, it is obvious that most people do work. Similarly, we see that the relationship to work follows a pattern similar to the life stages described by Super (1990), including a period of establishment in work followed by a maintenance period. Levinson et al. (1978) call the two periods "settling down" followed by "middle adulthood." Both see their latter period moving on to "decline," in Super's terminology, or "late adulthood" according to Levinson. In our everyday vocabulary we have a number of names for this time of life—golden years, senior citizenship, retirement, mature years, and so forth. There is considerable variability in when this period starts, although most people would probably say age 65. In recent years there have been two opposing trends that weaken the establishment of age 65 as marking this event. One trend is toward early retirement; in the past 20 years an increasing number of individuals have retired at 62, 60, or even earlier. More recently, legislation has eliminated compulsory retirement at 65, so workers who wish to do so may remain on their jobs longer than was possible previously.

Recent professional literature shows increasing attention to the late-life changer or postretirement worker—the individual we are discussing in this section. Good summaries of the general topic can be found in chapters written by Fox (1985), Ginzberg (1983), Lowry (1985), McConnell (1980), Sinick (1984), and Stumpf (1984). Articles on the general topic of aging and work include Babic (1984) and Lieberman and Lieberman (1983). Articles that focus on counseling aspects include Cahill and Salomone (1987), Hitchcock (1984), and Tolbert (1980).

Sinick (1984) describes a master's level preparatory program that prepares career counselors who will work with middle-aged and older workers. He points out that gerontological counselors understand the broad problems of aging and the difficulties encountered by older people, but they lack career and vocational expertise. One can expect that counselor education programs will add courses that emphasize the problems faced by older workers. There is already recognition of lifelong or life-span career counseling, but implementation has not kept abreast of that awareness.

Several factors suggest that increasing numbers of individuals may participate in paid employment after retiring from their regular job. Some of the more obvious reasons for this conclusion include the following:

1. Many individuals are in better health at retirement. They are more vigorous and wish to remain active.
2. Increasing costs of living raise concerns about the sufficiency of pension or retirement income. Rapidly rising health costs accompanied by

declining government Medicare benefits, and continued inflation accompanied by reduced cost-of-living adjustments are just two items that unbalance many carefully planned budgets.

3. An increasing number of jobs now lend themselves to the abilities, needs, and desires of older workers. Less strenuous physical activity is required, flexible hours and job sharing are available, and similar adjustments are becoming increasingly common.

4. The declining birth rate over 3 or 4 decades is rapidly graying the population. In 1900, 4 percent of the population was over 65; in 1980 that figure was 11 percent; and in 2030 it is estimated that almost one in five will be over 65.

5. Increasing numbers of currently employed workers expect to be involved in some kind of postretirement work. Harris and Associates (1981) state that 75 percent of those in the labor force want to work after they retire.

Ginzberg (1983) and other economists suggest that the issue may not remain a voluntary one of whether the older person wants to work, but may shift more heavily to economics as a result of the interaction between increased longevity and declining birth rates. A decreasing number of younger workers may be unable to support an increasing number of older people on the Social Security program. Further, the declining numbers of new entrants (beginning workers and women who have not previously been employed) may produce an imbalance between the numbers of positions that need to be filled and the numbers of workers available to fill those spots. If that imbalance begins to develop, more positions will be reengineered to fit older workers by adjusting schedules or hours and making other accommodations.

Hitchcock (1984) discusses the results of a study completed by Soumerai and Avorn (1983) which show that retirees engaged in part-time work reported better health, higher levels of happiness, and greater satisfaction than a comparable control group not engaged in work during the 6-month experimental period. These results show that work participation has a favorable effect on the older worker. However, Cahill and Salomone (1987) point to the absence of extensive research on the relationship between older workers and their job life. They also emphasize the need to extend most career theories into the upper age ranges.

Some of the problems that confront the older worker who considers reentry into the labor market are internal, whereas other problems are best described as external. *Internal* problems relate to the individual's personal motivation and attitude, health, and residual skills and capacities. *External factors*, those over which the individual has little personal control, largely derive from the stereotypes of older workers held by prospective employers and the general community. These often depict older workers as having slower reaction times; diminished physical strength, intelligence, and general alertness; lower productivity; greater likelihood of absences or accident; and so forth. Such negative stereotypes often result in employers being reluctant to hire older workers and, when they do hire, offering lower pay than other workers receive.

Much evidence already exists that contradicts the negative stereotypes, but stereotypical beliefs die slowly and more effective communication is necessary. Groups such as the Gray Panthers and the American Association of Retired Persons have helped raise the social conscience to some extent. The Age Discrimination in Employment Act, adopted in 1967 and amended in 1978, has also helped. Much still remains to encourage employers, as well as society generally, to assess more accurately what older workers can contribute.

From the standpoint of the counselor, there are several steps that can be taken to assist the older worker who wishes to reenter employment. Like first-time entrants, older workers may need to spend time in self-appraisal, investigating what they have to offer an employer. At least two factors have an impact at this point. The negative stereotypes mentioned here can be so pervasive in a community that they become self-fulfilling, and older workers may conclude from these public attitudes that they are less competent than they really are. The second factor relates to older workers' previous employment, wherein they performed a particular task for a long period and may be physically unable to do that job any longer or may have seen that job disappear as a result of technological modernization. Older workers may feel that since they cannot do that former job, there is nothing they can do (an attitude very close to that held by some displaced homemakers). Various activities to enhance self-understanding and self-concept may be required to establish positive views. Building self-confidence and assessing one's skills and competencies are parallel activities that can be pursued simultaneously.

Identification of potential occupations requires approximately the same steps as those faced by exploring youth. Many older workers are as unfamiliar with the world of work outside their previous experience as are young teenagers. Career resource centers and exploratory experiences, both group based and individual, can overcome this limitation. Exploratory experiences may reveal a need for education or training that can sharpen or enhance existing skills or facilitate new ones. Very few education and training programs have upper age limits, but many older people do not realize how open these opportunities are. Again, the career resource center and individual contact with institutions and programs can provide needed information.

Finally, older workers need help in the job search and placement process. Hitchcock (1984) describes a report by Gray (1983) of the results of using a job club with elderly job seekers. He worked with a group of 46 males and females, about half of them between 50 and 62, and half older than 62. The job club operated in the usual fashion. Individuals established concrete personal job goals, explained their goals to the group, reported regularly on achievement or failure in the search process, and maintained support from the group throughout their search. Gray reported that, at the end of the experiment, job club members had significantly higher employment rates than the control group, who had been referred to the state employment security agency.

Of course, a job club is not the automatic answer to placement of older workers. It is, instead, only one technique that is possible. The point is that older workers, like any other group of individuals who want to work and have usable skills, can be helped to find employment that is satisfying to them and to society.

SUMMARY

The focus in this chapter has been on several groups for whom the usual career development pattern does not apply. Consideration has been given to why the individual differs, as well as to how the career development helper can assist the individual.

Clients with physical or other restrictions find some occupations inaccessible because the work requires a physical act they are unable to perform. Vocational rehabilitation services can assist the person in preparing for activities that do not require that particular physical act. Economically disadvantaged clients can obtain training or other services to compensate for the restriction they are experiencing.

Individuals with different cultural backgrounds need counselors who can understand and help bridge the cultural differences, and who can assist the individual in recognizing and understanding the cultural climate of the workplace.

Some individuals enter the workplace at a later time in life than typical members of their age group. Examples include the woman who devoted her early post-education years to homemaking and child-rearing, the individual who spent some years in military assignments before moving to civilian life, and the individual who has been released from a penal institution. All must be helped to understand the world of work as it exists at the time of their entrance into it. They also usually need help in dealing with the age differential between themselves and other entering workers.

Other workers face major occupational change at mid-career periods. Those who initiate such changes voluntarily need primary help in the transitional process. Those who find themselves unexpectedly switching jobs may need help in dealing with factors related to the change process: grief over loss of the old job; readjustment to a new, undesired situation; and learning how to seek and find a new position.

The final group considered in this chapter was those who are approaching or have reached the usual retirement age, but who either wish to or are forced to continue to work. They may need help in developing realistic plans that fit their physical, emotional, and economic conditions.

Every person seeking career development help can be best served when attention is focused on the interaction between personal characteristics and the total environment in which that person exists.

REFERENCES

Ahia, C. E. (1984). Cross-cultural counseling concerns. *Personnel and Guidance Journal, 62*, 339–341.

American Personnel and Guidance Association. (1979). Of counseling interest. *APGA Guidepost*, December 13, p. 12.

Armstrong, J. C. (1981). Decision behavior and outcome of midlife career changers. *Vocational Guidance Quarterly, 29*, 205–212.

Arrendondo–Dowd, P. M., & Gonsalves, J. (1980). Preparing culturally effective counselors. *Personnel and Guidance Journal, 58*, 657–661.

Astin, H. S. (1984). The meaning of work in women's lives: A sociopsychological model of career choice and work behavior. *Counseling Psychologist, 12*, 117–126.

Babic, A. L. (1984). Flexible retirement: An international survey of public policy. *Aging and Work, 17* (10), 21–36.

Berkell, D. E., & Brown, J. M. (Eds.). (1989). *Transition from school to work for persons with disabilities*. New York: Longman.

Bowen, N. H. (1982). Guidelines for career counseling with abused women. *Vocational Guidance Quarterly, 31*, 123–127.

Brown, D. (1984). Mid-life career change. In D. Brown, L. Brooks, & Associates (Eds.), *Career choice and development*. San Francisco: Jossey-Bass.

Brown, D., & Minor, C. W. (Eds.). (in press). *Report of second Gallup survey: Focus on minorities*. Alexandria, VA: NCDA.

Bureau of National Affairs. (1986). *Source work and family—A changing dynamic*. Washington, DC: Author.

Cahill, M., & Salomone, P. R. (1987). Career counseling for worklife extension: Integrating the older worker into the labor force. *Career Development Quarterly, 35*, 188–196.

Casas, J. M., & Arbona, C. (in press). Hispanic career related issues and research: A diverse perspective. In D. Brown & C.W. Minor (Eds.), *Report of second Gallup survey: Focus on minorities*. Alexandria, VA: NCDA.

Cheatham, H. E. (1990). Afrocentricity and career development of African Americans. *Career Development Quarterly, 38*, 334–346.

Chubon, R. A. (1985). Career-related needs of school children with severe physical disabilities. *Journal of Counseling and Development, 64*, 47–51.

Chusmir, L. H. (1983). Characteristics and predictive dimensions of women who make nontraditional vocational choices. *Personnel and Guidance Journal, 62*, 43–47.

Cook, P. F., Dahl, P. R., & Gale, M. A. (1978). *Vocational opportunities*. Salt Lake City, UT: Olympus.

Curnow, T. C. (1989). Vocational development of persons with disability. *Career Development Quarterly, 37*, 269–278.

Dahl, P. R. (1982). Maximizing vocational opportunities for handicapped clients. *Vocational Guidance Quarterly, 31*, 43–52.

Davenport, D. W. (1984). Outplacement counseling: Whither the counselor. *Vocational Guidance Quarterly, 32*, 185–191.

Deming, A. L., & Gulliver, K. (1981). Career planning in prison: Ex-inmates help inmates. *Vocational Guidance Quarterly, 30*, 78–83.

Ekstrom, R. B., Beier, J. J., Davis, E. L., & Gruenberg, C. B. (1981). Career and educational counseling implications of women's life experience learning. *Personnel and Guidance Journal, 60*, 97–100.

Fagan, T. K., & Jenkins, W. M. (1989). People with disabilities: An update. *Journal of Counseling and Development, 68,* 140–144.

Fagan, T. K., & Wallace, A. (1979). Who are the handicapped? *Personnel and Guidance Journal, 58,* 215–220.

Farmer, H. S. (1985). Model of career and achievement motivation for women and men. *Journal of Counseling Psychology, 32,* 363–389.

Finnegan, R., Westerfeld, J., & Elmore, R. (1981). A model for midlife career—decision-making workshop. *Vocational Guidance Quarterly, 30,* 69–72.

Fox, J. H. (1985). Continuities in the experience of aging. In E.B. Palmore (Ed.), *Normal aging III.* Durham, NC: Duke University Press.

Fukuyama, M. A. (in press). Asian-Pacific Islanders and career development. In D. Brown and C. W. Minor (Eds.), *Report of second Gallup survey: Focus on minorities.* Alexandria, VA: NCDA.

Gerson, B., & Lee, S. (1982). Women and career competence: A theoretical and experiential model. *Personnel and Guidance Journal, 61,* 236–238.

Giles, H. C. (1990). Counseling Haitian students and their families: Issues and interventions. *Journal of Counseling and Development, 68,* 317–320.

Gim, R. H., Atkinson, D. R., & Kim, S. J. (1991). Asian-American acculturation, counselor ethnicity and cultural sensitivity, and ratings of counselors. *Journal of Counseling Psychology, 38,* 57–62.

Ginzberg, E. (1983). Life without work: Does it make sense? In H. S. Parnes (Ed.), *Policy issues in work and retirement.* Kalamazoo, MI: W. E. Upjohn Institute for Employment Research.

Gray, D. (1983). A job club for older job seekers: An experimental evaluation. *Journal of Gerentology, 38,* 363–368.

Grealish, C. A., & Salomone, P. R. (1986). Devaluing those with disability: Take responsibility, take action. *Vocational Guidance Quarterly, 34,* 147–150.

Guidubaldi, J., Perry, J. D., & Walker, M. (1989). Assessment strategies for students with disabilities. *Journal of Counseling and Development, 68,* 160–165.

Hadley, R. G., & Brodwin, M. G. (1988). Language about people with disabilities. *Journal of Counseling and Development, 67,* 147–149.

Hagner, D., & Salomone, P. R. (1989). Issues in career decision making for workers with developmental disabilities. *Career Development Quarterly, 38,* 148–159.

Harris, L., & Associates (1981). *Aging in the eighties: America in transition.* Washington, DC: National Council on the Aging.

Heinrich, R. K., Corbine, J. L., & Thomas, K. R. (1990). Counseling native Americans. *Journal of Counseling and Development, 69,* 128–133.

Hitchcock, A. A. (1984). Work, aging, and counseling. *Journal of Counseling and Development, 63,* 258–259.

Humes, C. W., & Hohenshil, T. A. (1985). Career development and career education for handicapped students: A reexamination. *Vocational Guidance Quarterly, 34,* 31–40.

Hurst, J. B., & Shepard, J. W. (1986). The dynamics of plant closings: An extended emotional roller coaster ride. *Journal of Counseling and Development, 64,* 401–405.

Kahn, S. E. (1983). Development and operation of the Women's Employment Counseling Unit. *Vocational Guidance Quarterly, 32,* 125–129.

Kanchier, C., & Unruh, W. R. (1988). The career cycle meets the life cycle. *Career Development Quarterly, 37,* 127–137.

Karayanni, M. (1987). The impact of cultural background on vocational interests. *Career Development Quarterly, 36,* 81–90.

Kjos, D. L. (1988). Job search activity patterns of successful and unsuccessful job seekers. *Journal of Employment Counseling, 25,* 4–6.

Kraus, L. E., & Stoddard, S. (1989). *Chartbook on disability in the United States.* Washington, DC: U.S. National Institute on Disability and Rehabilitation Research.

Lee, D. J. (1984). Counseling and culture: Some issues. *Personnel and Guidance Journal, 62,* 592–597.

Leong, F. T. L., & Hayes, T. J. (1990). Occupational stereotyping of Asian Americans. *Career Development Quarterly, 39,* 143–154.

Levinson, D. J., Darrow, C. N., Klein, E. B., Levinson, M. H., & McKee, B. (1978). *The seasons of a man's life.* New York: Alfred A. Knopf.

Levinson, E. M. (1984). A vocationally oriented secondary school program for the emotionally disturbed. *Vocational Guidance Quarterly, 33,* 76–81.

Lieberman, L., & Lieberman, L. (1983). The second career concept. *Aging and Work, 6* (4), 277–287.

Lowry, J. H. (1985). Predictors of successful aging in retirement. In E. B. Palmore (Ed.), *Normal aging III.* Durham, NC: Duke University Press.

Mallinckrodt, B., & Fretz, B. R. (1988). Social support and the impact of job loss on older professionals. *Journal of Counseling Psychology, 35,* 281–286.

Marshall, J. (1983). Reducing the effects of work oriented values on the lives of male American workers. *Vocational Guidance Quarterly, 32,* 109–115.

McConnell, S. R. (1980). Alternative work patterns for an aging work force. In P. K. Ragan (Ed.), *Work and retirement: Policy issues.* Los Angeles: Andrus Gerontology Center.

McGraw, L. K. (1982). A selective review of programs and counseling interventions for the reentry woman. *Personnel and Guidance Journal, 60,* 469–472.

Miles, J. H. (1984). Serving the career guidance needs of the economically disadvantaged. In N. C. Gysbers & Associates (Eds.), *Designing careers.* San Francisco: Jossey-Bass.

Parker, R. M. (Ed.). (1987). *Rehabilitation counseling: Basics and beyond.* Austin, TX: Pro-Ed.

Perosa, S. L., & Perosa, L. M. (1987). Strategies for counseling midcareer changers: A conceptual framework. *Journal of Counseling and Development, 65,* 558–561.

Pickering, G. S., & Galvin–Schaefers, K. (1988). An empirical study of reentry women. *Journal of Counseling Psychology, 35,* 298–303.

Read, N. O., Elliott, M. R., Escobar, M. D., & Slaney, R. B. (1988). The effects of marital status and motherhood on the career concerns of reentry women. *Career Development Quarterly, 37,* 46–55.

Robinson, S. L., Rotter, M. F., & Wilson, J. (1982). Mothers' contemporary career decisions: Impact on the family. *Personnel and Guidance Journal, 60,* 535–537.

Roessler, R. T. (1987). Work, disability, and the future: Promoting employment for people with disabilities. *Journal of Counseling and Development, 66,* 188–190.

Ross, D. B. (1984). A cross-cultural comparison of adult development. *Personnel and Guidance Journal, 62,* 418–420.

Rosser–Hogan, R. (1990). Making counseling culturally appropriate: Intervention with a Montagnard refugee. *Journal of Counseling and Development, 68,* 443–445.

Rubin, S. E., & Roessler, R. T. (1987). *Foundations of the vocational rehabilitation process* (3rd ed.). Austin, TX: Pro-Ed.

Rubin, S. E., & Rubin, N. M. (Eds.). (1988). *Contemporary challenges to the rehabilitation counseling profession.* Baltimore: Brookes.

Sandler, S. B. (1988). Dislocated workers: A response. *Journal of Employment Counseling, 25,* 146–148.

Schlossberg, N. K. (1984). *Counseling adults in transition: Linking practice with theory.* New York: Springer.

Schlossberg, N. K., & Leibowitz, Z. (1980). Organizational support systems as buffers to job loss. *Journal of Vocational Behavior, 17,* 204–217.

Shifron, R., Dye, A., & Shifron, G. (1983). Implications for counseling the unemployed in a recessionary economy. *Personnel and Guidance Journal, 61,* 527–529.

Sinick, D. (1984). Problems of work and retirement for an aging population. In N. C. Gysbers & Associates (Eds.), *Designing careers.* San Francisco: Jossey-Bass.

Slaney, R. B., & Dickson, R. D. (1985). Relation of career indecision to career exploration with reentry women: A treatment and follow-up study. *Journal of Counseling Psychology, 32,* 355–362.

Snyder, R., Howard, A., & Hammer, T. (1978). Mid-career change in academia: The decision to become an administrator. *Journal of Vocational Behavior, 13,* 229–241.

Soumerai, S. B., & Avorn, J. (1983). Perceived health, life satisfaction, and activity in urban elderly: A controlled study of the impact of part-time work. *Journal of Gerontology, 38,* 356–362.

Stark, S., & Zytowski, D. G. (1988). Searching for the glass slipper: A case study in midlife career counseling. *Journal of Counseling and Development, 66,* 474–476.

Stumpf, S. A. (1984). Adult career development: Individual and organization factors. In N. C. Gysbers & Associates (Eds.), *Designing careers.* San Francisco: Jossey-Bass.

Sue, D. W. (1978). Counseling across cultures. *Personnel and Guidance Journal, 56,* 458–462.

Sue, D. W., Bernier, J. E., Durran, A., Feinberg, L., Petersen, P., Smith, E. J., & Vasquez–Nutall, E. (1982). Position paper: Cross-cultural counseling competencies. *The Counseling Psychologist, 10* (2), 45–52.

Sundal–Hansen, L. S. (1985). Work-family linkages: Neglected factor in career guidance across cultures. *Vocational Guidance Quarterly, 33,* 202–212.

Super, D. E. (1990). A life-span, life-space approach to career development. In D. Brown, L. Brooks, & Associates, *Career choice and development* (2nd ed.). San Francisco: Jossey-Bass.

Thomas, K. R., & Berven, N. L. (1984). Providing career counseling for individuals with handicapping conditions. In N. C. Gysbers & Associates (Eds.), *Designing careers.* San Francisco: Jossey-Bass.

Thomas, L. E. (1979). Causes of mid-life change from high status careers. *Vocational Guidance Quarterly, 27,* 202–208.

Tolbert, E. L. (1980). Career development theories: What help for older persons? *Journal of Employment Counseling, 17,* 17–27.

Vaitenas, R., & Wiener, Y. (1977). Development, emotional, and interest factors in voluntary mid-career change. *Journal of Vocational Behavior, 11,* 291–304.

Wade, P., & Bernstein, B. L. (1991). Culture sensitivity training and counselor's race: Effects on Black female clients' perceptions and attrition. *Journal of Counseling Psychology, 38,* 9–15.

Webb, N. M. (1983). Cross-cultural awareness: A framework for interaction. *Personnel and Guidance Journal, 61,* 498–500.

Wendt, J. A. (1980). "Going straight" means bumpy road. *APGA Guidepost,* February 21, pp. 1, 7.

Zawada, M. A. (1980). Displaced homemakers: Unresolved issues. *Personnel and Guidance Journal, 59,* 110–112.

Zunker, V. G. (1986). *Using assessment results in career counseling* (2nd ed.). Monterey, CA: Brooks/Cole.

___13___

Testing and Assessment in Career Development

The original model of vocational development set forth by Frank Parsons in 1909 emphasized the importance of "personal analysis" to promote individual self-understanding. The trait and factor model of vocational development, which was built on Parsons's tripartite model, focused the science of psychology on the development of tests and inventories to promote personal analysis and became such a pervasive influence on vocational counseling that they became inextricably linked.

In 1972 Goldman observed that the marriage between testing and counseling had failed and that it was time to look for other approaches to facilitating growth and development. Specifically, Goldman raised concerns about the use of tests and inventories to predict vocational success and/or satisfaction. Goldman's criticism had been voiced earlier by Crites (1969) and has been rehashed since by Ivey (1982) and Weinrach (1979). However, Prediger (1974) took a different path. He discussed how the "failed marriage" between tests and inventories could be revived by using comprehensive assessment programs, providing test results to help those being tested bridge the gap between the tests results and career choice implementation, and relying more on self-administered and self-interpreted instruments. It appears that not everyone subscribes to Prediger's and Goldman's positions since the criticism of trait and factor approaches to measurement has continued.

Healy (1990) contends that the traditional trait and factor approaches to testing and assessment have had certain shortcomings that are inconsistent with the goal of promoting client growth and development. One of these inconsistencies is that people being assessed are placed in a dependent role since typically the assessment devices are selected by counselors. Healy also contends that trait and factor approaches to assessment do not strengthen clients' abilities to assess their own strengths and weaknesses, which he believes is inconsistent with the ideal of promoting independence. Moreover, relying on tests and inventories as the principal personal assessment tool

337

denies the influence of environmental and contextual (e.g., work setting) variables, such as qualities of supervision, that may interact with clients' characteristics. Finally, Healy criticizes traditional approaches to assessment because they emphasize helping clients find careers that "fit" them rather than actively involving them in identifying and implementing a career choice.

Healy enumerates certain remedies for the problems he sees with traditional approaches to assessment. For example, he suggests that clients be prepared to act as collaborators in the appraisal process by giving them more information about appraisal and its potential use in career choice and implementation. Counselors should also accentuate the development of self-assessment skills such as the ability to estimate aptitudes. Not surprisingly, Healy advocates that clients be made more aware of how their characteristics interact with workplace variables and how these interactions may influence their performance and ultimately their success or failure. Healy believes that in addition to the foregoing reforms in the appraisal process, there is a need to design new approaches to appraisal devices that will not only improve decision making but the implementation of decisions as well.

The degree to which clients are involved as collaborators engaged in developing self-evaluation skills, including the utilization of assessment data to make as well as implement choices, will depend on a number of variables. For example, one application of career development assessment is to facilitate exploration and planning over a period of time, as opposed to providing information for decision making at a specific point in time (Prediger, 1974). In the former, assessment is used to promote readiness by developing self-awareness, while in the latter the use of assessment data is to inform decision making and implementation of decisions once made. Prediger (1974) also points out that counselors may use assessment devices to diagnose various aspects of students' (and presumably nonstudents') career development for the purpose of designing programs to meet career needs. For example, counselors might give an interest inventory to ninth graders to stimulate self-awareness. This inventory might be selected, administered, and interpreted by counselors because only the most preliminary career decisions are being made at the time the inventory is administered and assessment of large numbers of students precludes the use of highly individualized strategies. On the other hand, a career counselor working with a college senior who is deciding among various career options should implement all of Healy's (1990) suggestions.

Criticisms of the philosophy and practice of traditional assessment have been prevalent. Goldman (1972, 1982) has criticized tests because they are mechanistic and reductionistic. Tyler (1978), another early proponent of tests, criticized them because they encourage competition rather than foster development. Tests and inventories have also been criticized because of gender and racial bias (Cronbach, 1984; Lonner, 1988) and for a host of other reasons. However, as Lonner concludes, psychologists counselors, and others have developed a large number of appraisal devices that are constantly being used to measure not only values, aptitudes, and personality variables but a host of other variables. The challenge is to be aware of the issues surrounding tests and use them for the benefit of those being served.

TYPES OF ASSESSMENT

Assessment procedures used in career development programming and career counseling can be classified as objective, qualitative, and clinical. In clinical assessment the counselor synthesizes data from various assessment sources and makes diagnoses and/or predictions. Clinical diagnoses are often based on a combination of objective and qualitative assessments as well as the counselor's hunches or intuition about the client (Goldman, 1961). In this chapter, only objective and qualitative assessment approaches are discussed, primarily because understanding these approaches is basic to career counseling and development. Clinical assessment is discussed in Chapter 14, so it is not discussed here.

Objective assessment devices are those most familiar to readers because they have taken achievement tests, the Scholastic Aptitude Test, or other similar tests as they progressed through public schools. Most readers will also have completed inventories that measure interests, values, or personality. These are also objective assessment devices. Tests are presumed to be measures of maximum or optimal performance, while inventories are presumed to measure typical performance. However, both tests and inventories have standardized administration and scoring procedures. Typically, tests are time limited, although power tests are not timed. Inventories are usually not time limited.

Tests and inventories may be paper-and-pencil tests or may have been adapted for computer administration and/or scoring. Today even paper-and-pencil versions of tests and inventories ar typically "machine" scored and the profile of results is computer generated. Sampson (1990) identifies a number of distinct trends as they relate to computer applications in testing. Among the most salient of these are the use of computer-based interpretational systems to support the interpretations made by practitioners, the use of computers to generate cutoff scores when aptitude tests are used as the basis for job or educational placement decisions, and the use of computer-controlled videodisk technology to reduce dialectic and language barriers in the interpretation process. Sampson also notes that adaptive devices such as braille keyboards are being used to enable some people with disabilities to take tests with relatively little assistance.

Qualitative assessment approaches, in contrast to objective approaches, are bound by less rigid parameters. For example, there may be no standardized set of directions and the "scoring" is more subjective; in fact, often there is no scoring at all. The results of these devices are not profiled, and they are interpreted idographically as opposed to normatively. Goldman (1990) points out that qualitative assessments tend to involve clients more actively than standardized or objective tests and inventories since the objective approach gives the client very little voice in where or how the instrument will be administered and scored. Goldman goes on to identify several qualitative assessment devices including card sorts, values clarifications exercises, simulations such as the use of work samples, and observations.

Some of the "qualitative" devices identified by Goldman (1990) can be developed into objective approaches to assessment. For example, Jones (1981) has developed a card sort, *Occ-U-Sort*, to measure Holland's (1985a) personality types that has a well-defined set of instructions and scoring procedures. Similarly, behavioral psychologists have developed highly sophisticated observational systems, as well as procedures for establishing interobserver reliability, that are as standardized as any test or inventory.

Throughout the history of the career counseling and development movement, objective or standardized tests have been emphasized (Brown, 1990). However, some of the earliest writings (e.g., Williamson, 1939) about career counseling also discussed qualitative methods of assessment such as job shadowing, which was used to help individuals "assess" their potential interests in, and aptitude for, a particular occupation. Perhaps what is different is that there are currently more qualitative assessment approaches available than ever before. Role play, self-efficacy assessment, and cognitive assessment are all strategies. Some of these qualitative assessment devices are potentially very useful.

Assessment is a major field of academic study with many facets. There are literally hundreds of quantitative and qualitative assessment approaches that could be included in this chapter. The question is, "What to include?" A few of the most useful qualitative assessment devices are discussed in this chapter. The qualitative assessment devices discussed were selected on the basis of the authors' perception of the utility of these devices in career development programming and counseling. The tests and inventories included were selected to a large degree on the basis of three surveys (Engen, Lamb, & Prediger, 1982; Kapes & Mastie, 1988, Zytowski & Warman, 1982). These authors examined the professionals' use and perceptions of various instruments used to assess interest, aptitudes, career development, and values. A few inventories that did not surface on any of these lists are also discussed, as are some instruments that may be useful in assessing certain decisional problems, such as career indecisiveness.

QUALITATIVE ASSESSMENT DEVICES

As noted earlier, qualitative assessment devices are those that do not possess a standardized set of directions and are not objectively scored. They are an extension of the counselor's clinical skill and to some extent require clinical skill to interpret. Four qualitative assessment devices are discussed in this chapter: (1) self-efficacy measurements, (2) role playing, (3) the genogram, and (4) card sorts.

Self-Efficacy Measurements

Self-efficacy is the individual's judgment regarding ability to perform a task at a certain level (Bandura, 1977). These self-efficacy cognitions mediate action with the result that individuals avoid tasks or activities that they believe are beyond their capabilities and engage in those that they judge themselves capable of performing (Bandura, 1982). Betz & Hacket (1981, 1986) were the first to emphasize the importance of self-efficacy expectations on career decision making and, drawing on Bandura's work (1977, 1982), set forth a model of career decision making based primarily on this construct. Self-efficacy has traditionally been measured by first identifying a task to be performed (e.g., complete algebra successfully), then asking clients to estimate the degree of difficulty of the task and the extent of their confidence that they can perform the task, and then estimating their performance in related situations (range) (Bandura, 1982).

The following is an example of how self-efficacy expectations might be assessed during career counseling.

Counselor:	We have been discussing engineering as a possible career option for you. On a one to ten scale, with one being extremely difficult, how would you rate the difficulty of engineering?
Client:	A ten—definitely a ten.
Counselor:	Then how confident are you that you can complete an engineering curriculum with at least a 2.5 GPA again using the one to ten scale, with one being very confident and ten being extremely confident?
Client:	That's tough. Probably a seven. I'm pretty good in math and science.
Counselor:	OK, just one more rating. We've discussed several options that are related to engineering, such as engineering technology, architecture, and industrial relations. Using the one to ten scale, how would you rate your confidence that you can enter and complete courses of study in these areas?
Client:	Engineering technology a ten, definitely; architecture, a five or a six. I'm just not sure I can do some of the things that are needed. Industrial relations probably a nine or a ten.

Self-efficacy ratings can be used on an ongoing basis to assess the clients' perceptions of their ability to find information about jobs, complete interviews with workers, or even complete career counseling successfully.

It is possible to measure self-efficacy more objectively, as Rotberg (1984, pp. 96-98) did. As can be seen in Figure 13.1, individuals were asked to rate their perceived ability to perform certain types of careers. The instru-

FIGURE 13.1 *A Career Self-Efficacy Rating Scale: Certainty of Performing Job Duties*

Please complete the following by indicating how certain you are that you could, if you elected to do so, perform the duties involved in the following occupations by circling a number on the scale provided. One (1) indicates that you are very uncertain that you could perform the task and five (5) indicates that you are very certain that you could perform the task.

1. *Secondary School Teacher:* Instructs junior or senior high school students, usually in a specific subject.

1	2	3	4	5
Very Uncertain		Somewhat Certain		Very Certain

2. *Psychologists:* Concerned with the collection, interpretation, and application of scientific data to human behavior.

1	2	3	4	5
Very Uncertain		Somewhat Certain		Very Certain

3. *Pharmacist:* Mixes and dispenses medicines, gives medication advice to health practitioners and the public.

1	2	3	4	5
Very Uncertain		Somewhat Certain		Very Certain

4. *Dental Hygienist:* Provides dental treatment, gives instruction on teeth care, takes x-rays, and assists dentists.

1	2	3	4	5
Very Uncertain		Somewhat Certain		Very Certain

5. *Buyer, wholesale or retail:* Purchases merchandise from manufacturers or wholesales merchandise that is then sold to the public.

1	2	3	4	5
Very Uncertain		Somewhat Certain		Very Certain

6. *Sales Manager:* Directs staffing and training of sales staff, and develops and controls a sales program.

1	2	3	4	5
Very Uncertain		Somewhat Certain		Very Certain

7. *Primary School Teacher:* Teaches elementary school students, teaching several subjects and supervising various activities.

1	2	3	4	5
Very Uncertain		Somewhat Certain		Very Certain

FIGURE 13.1 *Continued*

8. *Stocks and Bonds Salesperson:* Gives information and advice in the buying and selling of stocks and bonds.

1	2	3	4	5
Very Uncertain		Somewhat Certain		Very Certain

9. *Editor:* Assigns, stimulates, prepares, accepts or rejects, and sometimes writes articles for publication.

1	2	3	4	5
Very Uncertain		Somewhat Certain		Very Certain

10. *Registered Nurse:* Administers nursing care to the ill and injured, using skills, experience, and education.

1	2	3	4	5
Very Uncertain		Somewhat Certain		Very Certain

11. *Engineer:* Uses practical applications of mathematics, physics and chemistry to solve applied problems dealing with construction, use of chemicals, machine design, etc.

1	2	3	4	5
Very Uncertain		Somewhat Certain		Very Certain

12. *Personnel Relations:* Hires and assigns people to jobs that they can do, to benefit themselves and their employer.

1	2	3	4	5
Very Uncertain		Somewhat Certain		Very Certain

13. *Laboratory Technician:* Works with other health professionals in the laboratory analysis of biological materials.

1	2	3	4	5
Very Uncertain		Somewhat Certain		Very Certain

14. *Designer:* Creates original designs for new types and styles of clothing, leather goods, and textiles.

1	2	3	4	5
Very Uncertain		Somewhat Certain		Very Certain

15. *Librarian:* Maintains library collections of books and other materials, and aids people is using library material.

1	2	3	4	5
Very Uncertain		Somewhat Certain		Very Certain

Source: Rotberg, H. L. (1984). *Career self-efficacy expectations and perceived range of career options in community college students.* Unpublished doctoral dissertation. Chapel Hill: The University of North Carolina at Chapel Hill, pp. 96–98. Reprinted with permission.

ment shown in Figure 13.1 contains careers that are traditionally female, male, and androgenous; that is, occupations that have a balance of males and females in them. This type of assessment device could be used to determine if people perceive themselves in a stereotypical fashion.

Role Playing

Role playing can be used as both an intervention and assessment strategy, and while this discussion focuses largely on assessment, a brief description of the uses of role playing as an intervention is also presented. Role playing involves acting out a social situation to demonstrate how one would or has performed. For example, a career counseling client may report that she "blew her last job interview." The counselor needs to determine why the interview was blown and ask the client to report verbally what occurred. Verbal reports may be enlightening, but situations involving social skills are rarely described accurately.

Role playing represents an alternative to verbal descriptions. The career counselor may begin by asking the client to describe the interviewer or, better still, to imitate the interviewer's behavior. Once the counselor has a relatively full understanding of how the interview went, the client is asked to reenact the job interview with the counselor acting as the interviewer. If the client agrees to reenact the interview, she should be asked to illustrate through her behavior how she actually performed in the job interview. Then the role playing begins.

During the role-playing situation, the counselor observes the client, making mental notes about strengths and weaknesses. After the interview is completed, these observations may be shared with the client, or if the counselor wishes to "clench" the assessment, he may engage in role reversal. In role reversal, the counselor assumes the role of the client and the client assumes the role of the job interviewer, and the interview is repeated. Once completed, the interviewer asks the client if he has accurately depicted the client's behavior. If the answer is yes, then the client is asked to evaluate her own performances as observed in role reversal. The counselor then may provide any additional evaluations, and the client and the counselors can construct a list of interviewing strengths and weaknesses. Intervention follows. It usually entails presenting models of desired behaviors, practice through behavioral rehearsal, and feedback. Role playing can be used to assess clients' social skills in a wide variety of areas such as job interviews, telephone contacts, and employee-employer interactions (e.g., asking for a raise).

Card Sorts

Card sorts are devices that are typically designed by the counselor to assess a variety of variables such as values, interests, job skills, and lifestyle preferences. The potential options may be placed on 3" by 5" cards, and clients are asked to sort them into three to five stacks. For example, the following lifestyle variables could be placed on cards:

1. Ballet available
2. Symphony available
3. Theater available
4. Skiing within commuting distance
5. Short commute to work
6. High-quality schools for children
7. Golf courses nearby
8. Educational opportunities available for myself
9. Warm climate
10. Cold climate
11. Moderate climate (has all four seasons)
12. Close to parents
13. Intramural sports program for children
14. Near a large city
15. Near recreational water

The client could then be asked to sort these 15 cards into stacks of no importance, some importance, or of great importance while discussing the reasons for the selections with the counselor. Tyler (1961), Dolliver (1967), and Dewey (1974) pioneered the use of card sorts to measure interests. Gysbers and Moore (1987) provide a detailed discussion of how to construct card sorts.

Genogram

The genogram was developed for use in family therapy, and McGoldrick and Gerson (1985) have written an excellent book on its use with families. Essentially, in career counseling the genogram is used first to get a graphic representation of the careers of a client's family or a client's origin, namely grandparents, parents, aunts, uncles, and other relatives who might have influenced the client's career-related attitudes. If used correctly, it can be used to assess sources of self-limiting stereotypes, expectations about the outcomes of various career choices, and the source of career values and interests (Brown & Brooks, 1991; Okiishi, 1987).

The construction of a total genogram, as outlined by McGoldrick & Gerson (1985), is quite time consuming, but since the use of this device in career counseling has somewhat more limited objectives, an abbreviated version can be developed. Typically, generations of the family are listed on different lines with grandparents listed on line 1, parents and their brothers and sisters on line 2, influential cousins on line 3, and siblings on line 4. This organization is shown in Figure 13.2. It is also possible to add to this family tree other individuals outside the immediate family who had a significant impact on the "career thinking" of the client, such as teachers, early employers, and so forth.

Once the "family is placed on an organizational chart, occupations of each person (including homemaking) should be listed. Then clients should be asked to report how their relatives felt about their occupation, what values

FIGURE 13.2   *Organization of a Career Genogram*

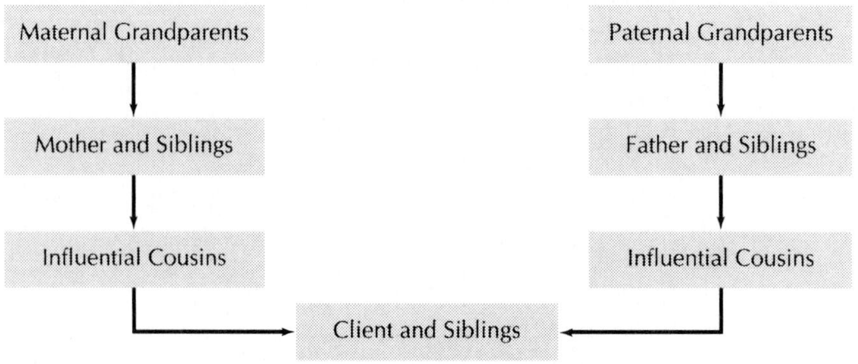

they tried to engender in the client, and why they believe each person in the chart influenced them either positively or negatively.

Support for Use of Qualitative Devices

Of the qualitative devices discussed here, only the use of self-efficacy measurement has been studied widely. Studies have demonstrated that self-efficacy is positively related to academic achievement (Lent, Brown, & Larkin, 1984), range of career options considered (Betz & Hackett, 1981; Lent, Brown, & Larkin, 1986; Rotberg, Brown, & Ware, 1987), and persistence in technical and scientific majors (Lent, Brown, & Larkin, 1984; 1986). To reiterate, self-efficacy expectations regarding one's ability to complete the academic and/or job requirements should be used at various stages of career counseling with some confidence that they will yield useful data. Empirical support for the use of the other devices discussed in this chapter is not as compelling, although there is widespread support for the use of card sorts (e.g., Gysbers & Moore, 1987) and role playing (e.g. Brown & Brooks, 1991).

QUANTITATIVE AND OBJECTIVE ASSESSMENT DEVICES

Needs and Work Values Inventories

Needs and values are sometimes confused in discussions, or the differences simply are not addressed. Similarly, values and interests are sometimes equated, although they are actually two separate constructs (Rokeach, 1979). Some needs are assumed to stem from the physiological functioning of the individual (e.g., need for air and water), and unless they are met the individual perishes. Psychological needs also stem from the functioning of the individual, and unless they are met the individual's development is arrested with various consequences (Rokeach, 1973, 1979). Values, on the other hand, are learned or may grow out of needs and are assumed to be a basic source of human motivation. Values may have either a positive or negative valence; that is, individuals are assumed to either seek or move toward values with a positive valence and away from those things that hold negative valences (Rokeach, 1973, 1979). Interests typically are viewed as less basic and as growing out of values (Holland, 1985a; Rokeach, 1979). The following is a description of three work values inventories that may be helpful in identifying areas for client exploration.

Minnesota Importance Questionnaire (MIQ)
David J. Weiss, René V. Davis, and Lloyd H. Lofquist

Background/purpose: The MIQ grew out of the trait and factor tradition and was designed to measure sources of worker satisfaction. It measures 20 worker needs and the six values associated with them. The needs scales include Ability Utilization, Achievement, Activity Advancement, Authority, Composing Policies and Practices, Compensation, Coworkers, Creativity, Independence, Moral Values, Recognition, Responsibility, Security, Social Service, Social Status, Supervision—Human Relations, Supervision—Technical, Variety, and Working Conditions. The values measured are Achievement, Altruism, Autonomy, Comfort, Safety, and Status Validity.

Target population: Males and females 16 years of age and older; reading level approximately fifth grade. Individuals' scores are compared to the ratings of supervisors and workers in 185 occupations (predominantly blue collar) to determine whether they might be satisfied in those occupations.

Dates of publication: User's manual, 1981; technical manual, 1971; counseling uses, 1975.

Publisher: Vocational Psychology Research, University of Minnesota, N620 Elliot Hall, 75 East River Road, Minneapolis, MN 55455.

Values Scale (VS)
Donald E. Super and Dorothy D. Nevill

Background and purpose: The VS is designed to measure what its authors term intrinsic and extrinsic values. Intrinsic values are those that are satisfied by actually performing the activity. Extrinsic values are those to be satisfied as an outcome of performing an activity. The scales of the VS are Ability Utilization, Achievement Advancement, Aesthetics, Altruism, Authority, Autonomy, Creativity, Economic Rewards, Life Style, Personal Development, Physical Activity, Prestige, Risk, Social Interaction, Social Relations, Variety, Working Conditions, Cultural Identify, Physical Prowess, and Economic Security.

Target population: Grade eight and up. Norm samples include high school students, college students, and adults.

Date of publication: Manual for VS, 1986.

Publisher: Consulting Psychologist's Press, 577 College Avenue, Palo Alto, CA 94306.

Salience Inventory (SI)
Dorothy D. Nevill and Donald E. Super

Background and purpose: The SI was developed to measure the extent of participation in, the degree of commitment to, and the values expectations attached to study (education), work, homemaking, leisure, and community service. It was designed to help clients and counselors answer one question: "What is the relative importance attached to these roles *at this time?*" The authors contend that the SI will help clients and counselors understand the readiness of the client to make certain decisions at a given time. Scale scores are provided for each of the five life roles for three areas: participation, commitment, and values expectations.

Target population: Grades nine and up. Norm samples include high school students, college students, and adults.

Date of publication: Manual for the SI, 1986.

Publisher: Consulting Psychologist's Press, 577 College Avenue, Palo Alto, CA 94306.

Support for the Use of Values Inventories

Cochran (1983) asked high school students to (1) generate and rank order a list of 10 occupational alternatives, and (2) to study and rank order a list of value-laden career constructs (e.g., higher salary). He concluded that their explicit ranking of career values did not correlate well with their implicit values that seemed to guide their selection of career alternatives. Pryor and Taylor (1980) also studied high school students in an effort to determine whether it was beneficial to use both values and interests measures. Their conclusion was that counselors are justified in using both. Their findings also support the conclusion of Knapp and Knapp (1979) that values and interests are two separate constructs. However, as we see in the next section, interest measures are the most widely used career counseling tools. This is probably because instruments measuring values have not received as much attention as have interest inventories.

Most practitioners use crude devices such as the checklists employed in Cochran's (1983) study to "measure" values, or they are measured using values clarification exercises or imagery (Brown & Brooks, 1991). Some practitioners may also infer values clinically from verbal reports. These approaches, as well as the use of psychometric instruments, appear useful as long as the limitations of the approaches used are kept clearly in mind.

Interest Inventories

Literally hundreds of thousands of interests inventories are administered each year. Regardless of the theoretical or empirical origin of these scales, they are presumed to measure liking or preferences for engaging in certain specific occupations.

Once scores on interest inventories are obtained, they may be compared to those of others in a reference or norm group, compared to some absolute criterion such as the interest levels of other pilots, or interpreted as raw scores (Blocher, 1987). Typically, inventories used in career development programs to promote awareness use either the normative or the raw score approach. For example, the individual's scores or the Strong Vocational Interest Blank are compared to a series of norm groups of successful workers in managerial, technical, and professional occupations. On the other hand, the raw scale scores on the Self Directed Search (Holland, 1985b) are used to construct a scale profile that is used to locate jobs of interest. Whether a normative approach is superior to a raw score approach to scoring and interpretation has been a hotly debated area (for a detailed discussion as this relates to the Self Directed Search see Weinrach, 1984).

Career Occupational Preference System (COPS)
R. R. Knapp and L. Knapp

Purpose: The COPS was designed to reveal preferences for job activities in the following areas: Science Professional, Science Skilled, Technology Professional, Technology Skilled, Consumer Economics, Outdoor, Business Professional, Business Skilled, Clerical, Communication, Arts Skilled, Service Professional, and Service Skilled.

Target audience: Junior high through college. Norm groups include junior high, high school, and college students.

Date of publication: Copysystem technical manual, 1984.

Publisher: EDITS, PO Box 7234, San Diego, CA 92107.

Self Directed Search (SDS)
John Holland

Purpose: The SDS was developed to be a self-administered, self-scored, and self-interpreted instrument to measure Holland's types: Realistic Investigative, Artistic, Social, Enterprising, and Conventional. Depending on the form, the inventory yields two- or three-letter personal profiles that can be used with an Occupations Finder to locate a career that should be of interest to the individual.

Target audience: Junior high through adult. Raw scores are reported. Inventory was developed using high school and college students as well as adults.

Dates of Publication:
   Regular form, 1985
   Form E (Easy), 1985
   Manual, 1985
   Occupations finder, 1985
   College major finder, 1987

Publisher: Psychological Assessment Resources, PO Box 998, Odessa, FL 33556.

Career Decision Making System (CDM)
Thomas F. Harrington and Arthur O'Shea

Purpose: The CDM is based on Holland's theory of occupational choice and yields six scores that are analogous to his types: Crafts (Realistic); Scientific (Investigative); the Arts (Artistic); Business (Enterprising), Clerical (Conventional), and Social (Social). The raw scores in the highest two or three interest scales are assessed to identify career clusters for exploration. Self-estimates of abilities, work values, future plans, and preferences for school subjects are incorporated into the overall career decision-making system.

Target audience: Junior high through adult. Norms drawn from junior high schools and senior high schools from across the country.

Dates of Publication:
   Self-scored and machine scored versions, 1982
   Users guide, 1982
   Technical manual, 1982
   College finder, 1991

Publisher: AGS, Publishers Building, Circle Pines, MN 55014.

Strong Interest Inventory of the Strong Vocational Interest Blanks (SVIB)
E. K. Strong, Jr., Jo-Ida C. Hansen, and David P. Campbell

Purpose: The SVIB was originally developed to help people interested in managerial, technical, and professional careers identify career options. It is now widely used in business and industry and adult counseling centers to assist people interested in making career changes as well as initial career choices. The SVIB yields a wealth of data including basic interest scales, general interest scales, general occupational themes, as well as administrative indices and special scales (e.g., Extoversion-Introversion). The basic interest scales and general occupational themes (GOT) are organized around Holland's types (RIASEC), and the 207 occupational interest scales (OIS) are also reported in this context.

Target audience: Late adolescents and adults. Norm groups for OIS were drawn from successful and satisfied people; those for GOTs were composed of women and men from each of six Holland types and from various educational levels.

Dates of publication: Latest revision form T325, 1985; manual, user's guide, 1985.

Publisher: Consulting Psychologists Press, 577 College Avenue, Palo Alto, CA 94306.

Vocational Interest Inventory (VII)
Patricia W. Lunneborg

Purpose: This inventory is based on Roe's classification of occupations and yields eight scale scores: Service, Outdoor, Business Contact, Science, Organization, General Culture, Technical, and Arts and Entertainment. The inventory was designed to help students identify job areas of highest interest and relate them to educational plans.

Target audience: Senior high students and college freshmen. Scores are compared to students who took the VII in junior and senior high and completed college successfully.

Dates of publication: Inventory, 1981; Manual, 1981.

Publisher: Western Psychological Services, 12031 Wilshere Boulevard, Los Angeles, CA 90025.

Kuder General Interest Survey (KGIS), G. Frederick Kuder

Purpose: The inventory measures interests in several broad fields including Outdoor, Mechanical, Computational, Scientific, Persuasive, Artistic, Literacy, Musical, Social Services, and Clerical.

Target audience: Grade 6 through adult. Norms were males and female grade 6 through adult.

Dates of publication: Latest revision, Form E, 1976; Manual, 1990.

Publisher: Science Research Associates, 155 N. Wacker Drive, Chicago, IL 60606.

Kuder Occupational Interest Survey Form DD (KOIS) G. Frederick Kuder

Purpose: The purpose of Form DD is to provide data on 104 occupational scales, 39 college major scales, 10 vocational interest estimates, as well as eight experimental scales to be used in educational and career planning using norms based on successful workers or graduating students.

Target audience: Grade 10 through adult. Norms provided for males and females on occupational and educational scales.

Dates of publication: Latest revision inventory, 1985; manual 1979.

Publisher: Science Research Associates, 155 N. Wacker Drive, Chicago, IL 60606.

Jackson Vocational Interest Survey (JVIS), Douglas N. Jackson

Purpose: This inventory is designed to assist in educational and career planning. The 35 basic interest scales include work role dimensions and work style scales. Scores on 10 general occupational themes, similarity to 17 educational major fields, and a ranking of 32 occupational clusters are available if the inventory is computer scored.

Target audience: High school to adult. Norm groups drawn from colleges and universities, students admitted to Penn State University, and a university in Ontario, Canada.

Dates of Publication: Latest revision of inventory, 1978; manual, 1977.

Publisher: Research Psychologists Press, 1110 Military Street, PO Box 984, Port Huron, MI 48061.

Reading—Free Vocational Interest Inventory—Revised (RFVII),
Ralph L. Becker

Purpose: The purpose of the revised RFVII is to determine the interests of mentally retarded and adolescents and adults with learning disabilities. It was developed to help these groups identify jobs in which they might gain proficiency and have productive lives. It yields scale scores in the following: automotive, building trades, clerical, animal care, food service, patient care, horticulture, housekeeping, personal service, laundry, and materials handling.

Target audience: 13- to 60-year-old people with mental retardation and learning disabilities. Norms drawn from mentally retarded; learning disabled; sheltered workshop adults; environmentally disadvantaged adults.

Dates of publication: Inventory, 1981; manual, 1988.

Publisher: Elbern Publications, PO Box 09497, Columbus, OH 43209.

Ohio Vocational Interest Survey: Second Edition (OVIS)
David Winefordner

Purpose: To provide students with information for career planning and to provide schools with summary data that can assist in the design of career development programs. It yields data on 253 jobs activities in the following work clusters: Manual Work; Basic Services: Machine Operation; Quality Control; Clerical; Health Services; Crafts and Precise Operations; Skilled Personal Services; Sports and Recreation; Customer Services; Regulations Enforcement; Communication; Numerical; Visual Arts; Agriculture and Life Sciences; Engineering and Physical Sciences; Music; Performing Arts; Marketing; Legal Services; Management; Education and Social Work; Medical Services.

Target audience: Grade 7 through adult. Norm groups are drawn from high school (8-12) students.

Date of publication: 1981.

Publisher: Psychological Corporation/HBJ, 555 Academic Court, San Antonio, TX 78204.

USES Interest Inventory (II)
United States Employment Service

Purpose: The II is used to identify areas highest of interest to focus career planning activities. It is typically given together with the General Aptitude Test Battery by employment counselors. The II yields scores in the following areas: Artistic, Scientific, Plants and Animals, Protective, Mechanical, Industrial, Business Retail, Selling, Accommodatory, Humanitarian, Leading-Influencing, and Physical Performing. The scores are used in conjunction with the *Guide to Occupational Exploration* to identify specific occupations.

Target audience: Grade 9 through adulthood. Extensive normative data are available including information on high school seniors, adults in occupational training programs, college students, and out-of-school job applicants.

Publication dates: All documents, 1982.

Publisher: United States Employment Service, 200 Constitution Avenue, N.W., Washington, DC 20210.

Support for the Use of Interest Inventories

Tittle and Zytowski (1980) estimated that 3.5 million people take interest inventories each year, and while there are no current estimates of the number, it seems unlikely that this number has decreased. Studies and opinion articles on the use of interest inventories abound. It also comes as no surprise that the Strong Vocational Interest Blank (SVIB), earlier called the Strong Campbell Interest Inventory (SCII), and the Self-Directed Search (SDS) are the object of much of this research since the SVIB is the oldest (and perhaps best) of the currently published inventories and the SDS is one of the most popular. Some of these studies are reported here.

Hansen and Swanson (1983) studied the validity of the SCII as a predictor of college majors and concluded that it was valid for this purpose, although slightly less so for males than females. Johnson and Hoese (1988) also studied the SCII and concluded that it cannot be used as the sole career planning device since many of the college students in this sample had a wide variety of personal and career development problems. The SCII was *not* developed as a stand-alone career planning instrument. Galassi, Jones, and Britt (1985) also studied the SCII along with six other inventories to determine to what degree they suggest nontraditional options for women. The instruments studied, in addition to the SCII, were the Kuder Occupational Interest Survey (KOIS), Career Assessment Inventory (CAI), Harrington–O'Shea Career Decision Making Systems (CDM), the Self-Directed Search (SDS), Non-Sexist Vocational Card Sort (NSVCS), and the Occ-U-Sort. The SCII suggested 46 nontraditional occupations, while the Occ-U-Sort guide suggested 382 jobs, the SDS Job Finder 327, the CDM 164, the KOIS 65, the CAI 50, and NSVCS 41. In another comparative study, the SCII was compared to the Vocational Card Sort (VCS) in order to compare expressed and inventoried interests of college women. Slaney and Slaney (1986) found that 42 percent of the expressed and inventoried interests were incongruent. They found that interests as measured by the VCS were more highly related to expressed interests than those of the SCII, suggesting that the VCS may be a superior means of measuring interests, at least for some groups. Finally, Borgen's (1988) comments on the SCII are noteworthy. He states that the latest revision of the SCII provides the counselor with even greater confidence and utility for the Strong.

The Self Directed Search, as an interest inventory, has also been explored extensively. For example, Gottfredson and Holland (1975) studied the predictive validity of the SDS and found it to be a moderately efficient predictor of choices for both men and women. However, the section of the SDS that asks for expressed career choice proved to be the best predictor of career choice. Numerous studies (e.g., Holland, Gottfredson, & Baker 1990; Noeth, 1983) have supported this finding.

Maddux and Cummings (1980) compared the test-retest reliability of the SDS and the SDS Form E (Easy) with high school students with learning disabilities and found that the Form E may be more appropriate because test-retest reliabilities are higher for the Form E for this group. In another comparative study, Jones, Gorman, and Schroeder (1989) compared the utility of the SDS with the Career Key (CK) in helping undecided college students choose academic majors. Students rated the CK more positively than the SDS and spent more time exploring career resources after testing than those taking the SDS. Finally, Gault and Meyers (1987) compared the SDS with the Vocational Interest, Experience, and Skills Assessment (VIESA) to determine which would best serve college and adult populations. In this study the SDS was rated more positively and as being more effective.

An argument arose about 20 years ago about the validity of using raw scores, particularly with women (e.g., Holland, Gottfredson, & Gottfredson, 1975; Prediger, 1981). This debate continued for nearly a decade and is still unresolved. For example, in 1981 Prediger questioned the validity of the SDS for females. His meta-analytic research suggested that using raw scores instead of normative scores restricted the range of occupations suggested for women and had less construct validity than when normed scores were reported. The crux of Prediger's arguments rests on the relative value of construct versus predictive validity. Holland (1982) asserted the importance of predictive validity in his reply, suggesting that "the depreciation of predictive validity [by Prediger] is a step backward" (p. 197).

The SCII and the SDS are not the only instruments that have received attention from researchers. For example, the Harrington–O'Shea has been shown to have moderate predictive validity for high school students' choice of a college major in a longitudinal study (Brown, Ware, & Brown, 1985). Generally speaking, research supports the continued use of these inventories.

Personality Inventories

Few personality inventories have captured the interest of career counselors, perhaps because many of those available were developed to measure abnormal behavior. As a result, only two personality inventories are discussed here.

Myers–Briggs Type Indicator (MBTI)
Isabel Briggs Myers and Katharine C. Briggs

Purpose: The MBTI was developed to provide a measure of Jung's types and yields scores of four dipolar scales: Extroversion-Introversion; Sensing-Intuition; Thinking-Feeling; and Judgement-Perception. A profile is constructed based on the person's highest score on each of the scales (e.g., ENTJ).

Target audience: High school students through adults. Norms available on junior high, high school, college, and various adult groups.

Publisher: Consulting Psychologists Press, 577 College Avenue, Palo Alto, CA 94306.

Dates of Publication: Standard Form (6), 1977; Revised Form (F), 1985; Abbreviated Form (AV), 1985.

Sixteen P. F. Personal Career Development Profile (16PFQ)
Verne Waller

Purpose: The interpretive profile (Personal Career Development Profile) provides an interpretation of personality and its potential influence on career choice and development. The profile is in actuality a computer-generated, occupationally oriented interpretation of the 16 personality factors measured by the Sixteen Personality Factor Questionnaire developed by Cattell (1969).

Target audience: High school through adult. Norms available for high school, college, and general adult population.

Dates of publication: 16 PFQ, 1969; 16 manual, 1980; PCDP manual, 1985.

Publisher: IPAT, 1801 Woodfield Drive, Savoy, IL 61874.

Support for the Use of Personality Inventories

Willis and Ham (1988) reviewed the MBTI and suggested that it has utility (1) in helping clients build a cognitive framework for organizing career information, (2) in work adjustment counseling, and (3) as a self-assessment device. They also provided some cautionary notes. For example, they suggested that the MBTI is not a comprehensive personality test and that it would be a mistake to overestimate the utility of the information gained from the scales. However, it is worth noting that the manual of the MBTI lists data on over 180 occupations. Perhaps the most striking feature of these tables is that most types are found in most occupations.

Wholeben (1988) suggests that the PCDP, which derived from the 1EPF, "is an excellent tool for career awareness in the high school curriculum and occupational exploration of adults" (p. 241). However, little construct or predictive validity information has been developed and thus much caution is in order.

It seems likely that the MBTI will receive increasing use in career counseling, although other personality inventories may not fare so well.

Multiple Aptitude Test Batteries

Theoretically, aptitude tests measure one's potential to acquire a skill or learn some specialized knowledge. In reality, they measure what has already been learned, which is an indicator of future performance. Unfortunately, not everyone has had the opportunity to acquire knowledge and/or skill to the same degree. However, when taken as *one* indicator of potential aptitude, tests can be of assistance to clients attempting to make career plans or can be simply one way of promoting self-awareness.

Differential Aptitude Test (DAT)
G. K. Bennett, H. G. Seashore, and A. G. Wesman

Purpose: Yields data that are potentially useful in the career/educational planning process. The subtests on the DAT are Verbal Reasoning, Numerical Ability, Abstract Reasoning, Clerical Speed and Accuracy, Mechanical Reasoning, Space Relations, Spelling, and Language Use.

Date of publication: Latest edition of all documents, 1981.

Target audience: Grade 8 through adult. Norms for grades 8-12.

Publisher: The Psychological Corporation, 655 Academic Court, San Antonio, TX 78204.

Armed Services Vocational Aptitude Battery (ASVAB)
Department of Defense

Purpose: This test provides data that may be useful to counselors and students in planning a military career. It is also used by military recruiters to determine applicants' potential for military careers. The ASVAB yields seven composite scores: Academic Ability, Math, Verbal, Mechanical and Crafts, Business and Clerical, Electronics and Electrical, and Health, Social, and Technology; as well as 10 subtest scores in General Science, Word Knowledge, Paragraph Comprehension, Numerical Operations, Arithmetic Reasoning, Math Knowledge, Auto and Shop Information, Mechanical Comprehension, Electronics Information, and Coding Speed.

Dates of publication: Counselor's manual, 1990; ASVAB test manual, 1984; student workbook, 1987.

Target audience: High school (10–12) and adults. Norms available for target groups.

Publisher: U.S. Military Entrance Processing Command, 2500 Green Bay Road, North Chicago, IL 60064.

General Aptitude Test Battery
United States Employment Service

Purpose: This battery measures nine vocational aptitudes including General Learning Ability, Verbal Aptitude, Numerical Aptitude, Spatial Aptitude, Form Perceptions, Motor Coordination, Finger Dexterity, and

Manual Dexterity. The inventory yields 59 Occupational Aptitude Patterns.

Date of publication: Most recent, 1982.

Publisher: United States Employment Service, 200 Constitution Avenue, N.W., Washington, DC 20210.

Support for the Use of Aptitude Batteries

Support for the use of all aptitude tests is probably summed up best by Anastasi's (1988) discussion of the Differential Aptitude Test (DAT). She observes that the support for the predictive validity of the DAT is relatively high when the criterion variable is success in high school, academic, and/or vocational education programs and quite modest when used to predict success in specific occupations. Ghiselli (1973) reviewed research prior to 1965 and concluded that the average correlation between test scores and educational performance was in the order of .30 and for occupational proficiency about .20. However, as Hogan, DeSoto, and Solano (1977) note, average correlations are of little value, and in some instances validity coefficients for occupational performance reach .60. Career counselors should carefully inspect validity studies to determine whether the test being used has adequate predictive validity generally and whether the norm groups are sufficiently representative to include the client with whom they are working. It is also important to keep in mind that even if a validity coefficient approaches .60, only 36 percent of the variance associated with performance is being accounted for by the test, and thus a combination of other variables such as work or study habits, motivation, family support, and person-environment are likely to be more important to the success of the individual than aptitude.

Diagnostic Inventories

A number of inventories have been developed to measure certain career development "problems." These inventories are often used in research but also have reliability in determining problems that may limit or retard the career development or career decision-making process.

Career Decision Scale (CDS)
Samuel H. Osipow

Purpose: The CDS was developed to provide explanatory information regarding failure to make career decisions. The CDS yields two scale scores: Certainty and Indecision. The scales provide an estimate of indecision; they also provide data regarding the antecedents of indecision.

Target audience: High school through adult. Norms available on high school students, college students, continuing education students, returning adults.

Date of publication: Most recent edition, 1987.

Publisher: Psychological Assessment Resources, PO Box 998, Odessa, FL 33566.

My Vocational Situation
John L. Holland, Denise C. Daiger, and Paul G. Power

Purpose: My Vocational Situation was developed primarily to identify lack of vocational identity, but it also provides information about lack of information and environmental or personal barriers to occupational choice. Three scale scores (Vocational Identity, Occupational Information, and Barriers) provide evidence regarding these areas.

Target audience: High school age through adult. Norm groups made up of high school through adult.

Date of publication: All information, 1980.

Publisher: Consulting Psychologists Press, 577 College Avenue, Palo Alto, CA 94306.

Career Development Inventory (CDI)
Donald Super, Albert S. Thompson, Richard H. Lindeman, Jean P. Jordaan, and Roger A. Myers

Purpose: The CDI was developed as a general measure of readiness to engage in career decision making and yields eight scale scores: Career Planning; Career Exploration; Decision Making; World of Work Information; Knowledge of Preferred Occupational Group; Career Development—Attitudes; Career Development—Knowledge of Skills; Career Orientation—Total.

Date of publication: School form, 1979; college form, 1981; user's manual, 1981.

Target audience: 8th graders through college age. Norms for high school students and college students.

Publisher: Consulting Psychologists Press, 577 College Avenue, Palo Alto, CA 94306.

Career Beliefs Inventory
John D. Krumboltz

Purpose: To assist individuals to identify problematic self-perceptions and world views.

Target audience: High school through adults.

Publication date: All documents, 1988.

Publisher: Consulting Psychologists Press, 577 College Avenue, Palo Alto, CA 94306.

Support for the Use of Diagnostic Inventories

The aforementioned diagnostic inventories fall into two categories: those that can be used to measure normal development, such as the Career Development Inventory, and those that can be used to diagnose some aspect of abnormal development, such as the Career Decision Scale. Psychologists and counselors have generally been concerned with both of these areas, although recent research has focused on diagnosing decisional difficulties.

Super and Thompson (1979) report that the CDI has three major uses: (1) to evaluate the outcomes of career development programs, (2) as a survey instrument to determine extent of information about careers and the sources of information being utilized, and (3) in individual counseling to determine decision-making problems or clients' knowledge of occupational information. What has not been demonstrated to this point is that this inventory is the most efficient means of collecting data about career development. The same is true of the various other instruments that purport to measure normal development, and thus, at least for the time being, their utility should probably be restricted to evaluation and research studies (Savickas, 1984).

With one exception, the diagnostic inventories described should probably not be used for any purpose other than research, since their authors and others have failed to produce the necessary empirical support to justify their usage. The exception to the recommendation is the *Career Decision Scale* (CDS). Numerous studies (Fuqua, Blum, & Hartman, 1988; Hartman, Fuqua, & Blum, 1984; Hartman, Fuqua, & Hartman, 1983b) have demonstrated that the CDS may be a useful tool when used as a preliminary screening device to differentiate undecided clients, who can benefit from traditional career counseling strategies such as testing and the provision of occupational information, and indecisive clients, who have decisional difficulties that must be addressed prior to the use of traditional strategies. Recent studies (Fuqua, Blum, Newman, and Seaworth, 1988; Larsen, Heppner, Harn, & Dugan, 1988; Vondracek, Hostetler, Schulenberg, & Shimiza, 1990), as well as some of the earlier studies, suggest that the constructs *undecidedness* and *indecisive* have correlates in other personality variables such as anxiety and locus of control; they have not provided evidence that the CDS may not be useful to practitioners.

Multipurpose Tests and Inventories

Most tests and inventories are designed to measure a single construct (e.g., career interests) or dimensions of a construct (e.g., aptitudes). However, a few tests and inventories have been developed to measure more than one construct (e.g., interests and aptitudes). A few of the potentially useful ones are presented here.

Occupational Aptitude Survey and Interest Schedule (OASIS)
Randall M. Parker
Purpose: The OASIS was developed to help junior and senior high school students engage in career planning. The instrument yields scores in 12 interest scales (Artistic, Scientific, Nature, Protestive, Mechanical, Industrial, Business Detail, Selling, Accommodating, Humanitarian, Leading-Influencing, and Physical Performing) and provides measures

of five aptitudes (General Ability, Perpetual Aptitude, Spatial Aptitudes, Numerical Aptitudes, Verbal Aptitude).

Date of publication: All documents, 1983.

Target audiences: Eighth through twelfth graders. Norm groups made up of twelfth graders.

Publisher: PRO-ED, 5341 Industrial Oaks Boulevard, Austin, TX 78735.

McCarron–Dial System (MDS)
Lawrence T. McCarron and Jack G. Dial

Purpose: The MDS was developed for use with special education and rehabilitation groups. It yields five scores: Verbal-Spatial-Cognitive, Sensory, Motor, Emotional, and Integration-Coping. The basic purpose of the MDS is to predict how clients will be functioning after training, and the instrument can be used in counseling or placement activities. The actual subtests included in the battery are The Peabody Picture Vocabulary Test, Bender Visual Motor Gestalt Test, Behavior Rating Scale, Observational Emotional Inventory, Haptic Visual Discrimination Test, and McCarron Assessment of Neuromuscular Development.

Target audience: Learning disabled, emotionally disturbed, mentally retarded, cerebral palsied, head injured, socially disadvantaged. Norms are available for target groups.

Date of publication: User's manual, 1986.

Publisher: McCarron–Dial Systems, PO Box 45628, Dallas, TX 75245.

Valpar 17-Pre-Vocational Readiness Battery (PVRB)
Valpar International Corp.

Purpose: The PVRB has four subtests—Development Assessment, Workshop Evaluation, Interpersonal/Social Skills, and Money Handling Skills—and was designed to measure functional skills that may transfer to educational or occupational settings. Its basic purpose is to identify people who may have functional problems as a preliminary step to in-depth diagnosis.

Target audience: High school age and adult. Learning disabled, educably mentally retarded, and trainable mentally retarded. Norms are available for people living in sheltered independent living groups and students in schools for exceptional children.

Date of publication: Most recent test, 1986.

Publisher: Valpar, PO Box 5767, Tuscon, AZ 85703.

Support for Using Multipurpose Tests and Inventories

Multipurpose inventories were developed for specific purposes and typically for use with specific populations. Test manuals should be consulted to determine whether the inventory is appropriate for one's client(s) and if the psychometric characteristics of the inventory justify its use.

SELECTING ASSESSMENT DEVICES

Career counselors may select from among hundreds of tests, inventories, and qualitative assessment strategies. For some of these, such as standardized tests and inventories, criteria have been developed that can be useful in the process. At present, only the ethical principles developed by the American Association for Counseling Development (AACD) and APA guide the selection of qualitative assessment approaches. Specifically, counselors must be competent in the use of any assessment device selected, the welfare of the client must be maintained as the uppermost consideration when selecting an assessment strategy, and cultural and gender issues must be carefully weighed prior to using an assessment approach with a client. Of course, these same ethical guidelines must be adhered to in the use of standardized inventories as well. However, the additional guidelines alluded are outlined below. These criteria are based to some degree on earlier discussions by Womer (1988) and Prediger and Garfield (1988).

Technical Qualities

The reliability, validity, and representativeness of the norm group (standardization) are of utmost importance in the selection of tests and inventories. The exact type of reliability (test-retest vs. internal consistency will, to some degree, be determined by the type of test or inventory, but test-retest reliability is generally preferred when measuring those traits of importance in career planning.

Predictive and construct validity are both of concern to career counselors, although the degree of importance of each will be determined by the purpose of the test. If the test is to be used for screening purposes or placement, predictive validity is of utmost importance. Construct validity becomes particularly important when one purpose of the assessment is to promote self-awareness. For example, the Self Directed Search was developed by Holland (1985a) to measure his theoretical personality types. These types and their descriptions became important aspects of the way students and adults see themselves, and thus any inventory puporting to measure Holland types should have construct validity. These inventories should also have predictive validity, but construct validity is the first consideration.

Not all inventories and tests compare the scores of the person tested to a norm sample. The SDS uses raw scores to determine a personality subtype without regard to how the individual compares to others. For those tests that do use norm-referenced comparisons, the representatives of the group becomes important. Obviously, in career planning and placement, the best comparison groups would be people with whom the client would be working or competing. When specific norm groups are unavailable, the value of the test is weakened.

Gender and Culture Bias

Gender and culture bias have received widespread attention in the counseling literature. For example, Tittle and Zytowski (1980) provide a full discussion of gender issues in assessing interest. More recently, Lonner (1988) discussed the cross-cultural issues in testing and assessment. At the center of these discussions is the question, "Do the tests used by career counselors produce information that may mislead either the person taking the test or persons (e.g., personnel managers) who may use tests to make a decision?" (Sundberg & Gonzalez, 1981, 222).

It is probably fair to say that tests and inventories are biased to some degree, but that most counselors attempt to use these products in a nondiscriminatory fashion. There are of course a number of legal prohibitions against the use of tests in a discriminatory manner, of which the most important is the Equal Employment Opportunity Act (Title VII of the Civil Rights Act of 1964 and its subsequent amendments) (Anastasia, 1988). Professional standards regarding the use of tests have also been developed and published (see listing at end of chapter).

Obviously, career development workers need to avoid using inventories and tests that have not been developed properly. However, even given the safeguards built into the development of tests and the legal prohibitions against using them inappropriately, subtle forms of bias do exist in the use of tests and inventories, particularly as they relate to minorities. The following concerns must be addressed in the assessment process if this is to be avoided.

> *The test or inventory itself:* The relevance of the content of the assessment device is a major concern when assessing minorities and women and clients who are culturally isolated, such as those from certain parts of Appalachia. If the following question is posed—"Are you more interested in going to an art gallery or reading quietly at home?"—a number of clients will have had no experience with art galleries, may never have had a quiet place to read, and as a result may begin to see the entire process as irrelevant to them. Similarly, if the question "Would you rather repair a small engine or complete a crossword puzzle?" is posed, not many females have been accorded the opportunity to repair a small engine, and those people who do not receive newspapers may have had little opportunity to do crossword puzzles. Careful examination of the content of tests and inventories as well as a thorough knowledge of the people to whom the devices are to be given is perhaps the only way to avoid this subtle form of bias.

> *The testing process:* Anastasia (1988) points out a number of factors that contribute to bias in the assessment process, including lack of

previous experience with assessment, lack of motivation to do well or to present a representative picture of self, and the inability of the test administrator to establish rapport, particularly with culturally different people. However, Anastasia states, "By far the most important consideration in the testing of culturally diverse groups—as in all testing—pertains to the interpretation of the test scores" (p. 66). The interpretation process is discussed in detail later in this chapter, but good test interpretation requires a thorough knowledge of the test or inventory and an awareness of the characteristics of the people taking the test, and how these might interact with the counselor and the assessment device.

In summary, when an inventory includes questions that are oriented to middle-class whites it is culturally biased (Lonner, 1988). There are numerous other sources of cultural bias, including language used and making assumptions about the motivation to take the test. The possibility that the norm group used is inappropriate because of underrepresentation of minorities (Lonner, 1988) can also be a problem. Moreover, when items are selected that are outside the experiences of females or, because of gender-role socialization interact negatively with past experiences, the test or inventory is gender biased.

Other Issues

The time needed to take the test or inventory, the cost, the reading level, the availability of computerized or hand scoring, and the counselor's preference are all factors to take into consideration when selecting tests or inventories. Prediger and Garfield (1988) suggest that career counselors need a high level of expertise in measurement and statistics as well as a thorough knowledge of various types of tests prior to using tests to promote career development.

INTERPRETING RESULTS

Goodyear (1990) reports, after an extensive review of the literature on career test interpretation, "Counselors can have some confidence that the interpretation of test results has a positive effect. Moreover there is little evidence that outcomes are differently affected by one treatment [interpretational approach] over another, although clients seem to *prefer* individual interpretations, and self-administered/interpreted measures offer a substantial cast scoring" (p. 246). He also reports that subjects in research studies tend to accept positively worded test results better than those that are couched in negative terms and that there seems to be no gender difference in the acceptance of results of generalized personality interpretations. Goodyear's summary probably represents the extent of empirically based knowledge about test interpretation. However, clinical experience and common sense provide some additional guidelines.

Tinsley and Bradley (1986, 1988) present a four-stage approach to test interpretation. The first stage, counselor preparation for test interpretation, involves counselors taking the time to make certain that they are thoroughly familiar with the test or inventory, the meaning of the scores, how the results can be integrated with other data such as educational history and family situation; determining the order of presentation if more than one assessment device is to be interpreted; and reviewing briefly interpretation plans.

All of the steps in the interpretation process stages are important, but one part that should receive particular attention is the integration of the data gained from more formal assessment devices with other sources of data. Do these data agree or conflict with other data? (Tinsley & Bradley, 1988). What are the implications of the agreement or disagreement? How will these implications be addressed?

The second stage involves preparing clients for test interpretation. As Tinsley and Bradley (1988) note, people who have taken tests are typically eager to get the results; however, it may be useful to review the purpose of the assessment device, how they "experienced it" when they were taking it, and ask clients to speculate scores or profiles.

During stage 3, the actual delivery of information, counselors are advised to keep the goals of the assessment in mind, to report scores but to explain measurement error, to avoid jargon, and to encourage reactions to the test results. Tinsley and Bradley also suggest that defensiveness should be minimized when providing "bad news." They suggest that one may do this by leaving the door open that the scores may not be totally accurate but, more importantly, by focusing on the meaning of the scores rather than the scores themselves. For example, a lower than expected score on an aptitude test may mean that the client will have to exert more effort than other individuals, not necessarily that the client is precluded from a field of study. It is also worth mentioning Goodyear's (1990) conclusion that clients more readily accept results that are positively phrased.

After the formal interpretation, stage 4, the counselor may wish to discuss the results in follow-up sessions, continue to check client's understanding of the results, and continue to help them integrate what they learned from formal assessment with informal data.

Finally, Bradley (1978) suggests that we use what he calls a "person referenced" approach to test interpretation. In this approach the counselor first determines whether the test is valid for the individual. This would be particularly useful when tests and inventories are administered to women, minorities, and people with disabilities. The counselor also determines, with the client, the strengths and weakness of the client's performance and determines means of dealing with the weaknesses. The counselor should also assist the client to determine how the information gained can be useful in decision making. The counselor and client should also look at the client's norm-referenced score if one is available. This approach to test interpretation fits with Healy's (1990) recommendation for reforming career assessment discussed at the outset of this chapter.

SUMMARY

Assessment is an essential ingredient in career counseling and other career development activities. However, unlike some activities associated with career development, the appropriate use of tests requires a high level of expertise that must be gained by careful training and supervision. It is inappropriate for untrained people to use tests and inventories for any purpose.

The two approaches to assessment discussed in this chapter, qualitative and quantitative, are both important approaches and have long been used by career counselors. It may be that the effective use of qualitative assessment procedures requires a higher level of clinical skill because fewer guidelines are provided to guide this work. However, both qualitative and quantitative approaches require counselors to be sensitive to issues related to race, ethnicity, gender, and socioeconomic status if they are to be used appropriately. Moreover, if these approaches are to be used effectively with the counseling process for any group, a high level of counseling skills is a prerequisite to administering and interpreting tests and inventories.

SOURCES OF INFORMATION ABOUT TESTS AND INVENTORIES

Standards and Guidelines

Standards for Educational and Psychological Tests. Washington, DC: AERA or APA.
Fairness in Interest Inventories. Washington, DC: NIE
Responsibilities of Users of Standardized Tests. Alexandria, VA: AACD.

Information/Reviews

The Ninth Mental Measurements Yearbook. Lincoln, NB: Buros Institute of Mental Measurements.
Tests: A Comprehensive Reference for Access in Psychology, Education and Business. Kansas City, MO: Test Corporation of America.
The ETS Test Collection Catalog: Volume I. Achievement Tests and Measurement Devices, and *Volume II. Vocational Tests and Measurement Devices.* Phoenix, AZ: ORNX Press.

Computerized Tests

Guidelines for Computer-Based Tests and Interpretations. Washington, DC: APA.
   Psychware Sourcebook, 1987-88. Kansas City, MO: Test Corporation of America.

REFERENCES

American Association of Counseling and Development. (1988). *Ethical standards.* Alexandria, VA: Author.

Anastasia, A. (1988). *Psychological testing* (6th ed.). New York: MacMillan.

Bandura, A. (1977). Toward a unifying theory of behavior change. *Psychological Review, 89,* 191–125.

Bandura, A. (1982). The assessment and predictive generality of self-percepts of efficacy. *Journal of Behavior Therapy and Experimental Psychology, 13,* 195–199.

Betz, N. E., & Hackett, G. (1981). The relationship of career-related self-efficacy expectations to perceived career options in college women and men. *Journal of Counseling Psychology, 28,* 399–410.

Betz, N. E., & Hackett, G. (1986). Applications of self efficacy theory to understanding career choice behavior. *Journal of Social and Clinical Psychology, 4,* 279–289.

Blocher, D. H. (1987). *The professional counselor.* New York: Macmillan.

Borgen, F. H. (1988). SCII review. In J. T. Kapes & M. M. Mastie (Eds.), *A counselor's guide to career assessment instruments* (2nd ed., pp. 121–126). Alexandria, VA: National Career Development Associates.

Brown, D., & Brooks, L. (1991). *Career counseling techniques.* Boston: Allyn & Bacon.

Brown, D., Ware, W. B., & Brown, S. T. (1985). A predictive validation of the career decision making inventory. *Measurement and Evaluation in Counseling and Development, 18,* 81–85.

Bradley, R. W. (1978). Person-referenced test interpretation: A learning process. *Measurement and Evaluation in Counseling and Development, 10,* 201–210.

Cattell, R. (1969). *The Sixteen Personality Factors Questionnaire.* Savoy, IL: IPAT.

Cochran, L. (1983) Implicit versus explicit importance of career values in making a career decision. *Journal of Counseling Psychology, 30,* 188–193.

Crites, J. O. (1969). *Vocational psychology.* New York: McGraw-Hill.

Cronbach, L. J. (1984). *Essentials of psychological testing.* New York: Harper & Row.

Dewey, C. R. (1974). Exploring interests: The non-sexist card sort. *Personnel and Guidance Journal, 52,* 348–351.

Dolliver, R. H. (1967). An adaptation of the Tyler Vocational Card Sort. *Personnel and Guidance Journal, 45,* 916–920.

Engen, H. B., Lamb, R. R., & Prediger, D. J. (1982). Are secondary schools still using standardized tests? *Personnel and Guidance Journal, 60,* 287–290.

Fuqua, D. R., Blum, C. R., & Hartman, B. W. (1988). Empirical support for the diagnosis of career indecision. *Vocational Guidance Quarterly, 36,* 363–373.

Fuqua, D. R., Blum, Newman, J. L., & Seaworth, T. B. (1988). *Journal of Counseling, 35,* 154–158.

Galassi, M. D., Jones, L. K., & Britt, M. N. (1985). Nontraditional career options for women: An evaluation of career guidance instruments. *Vocational Guidance Quarterly, 34,* 124–130.

Gault, F. M., & Myers, H. H. (1987). A comparison of two career-planning inventories. *Career Development Quarterly, 35,* 332–336.

Ghiselli, E. E. (1973). The validity of aptitude tests in personnel selection. *Personnel Psychology, 26,* 461–477.

Goldman, L. (1961). *Using tests in counseling.* New York: Appleton-Century-Crofts.

Goldman, L. (1972). Tests and counseling: The marriage that failed. *Measurement and Evaluation in Guidance, 4* 213–220.

Goldman, L. (1982). Assessment in counseling: A better way. *Measurement and Evaluation in Guidance, 4,* 213–220.

Goldman, L. (1990). Qualitative assessment. *The Counseling Psychologist, 18,* 205–213.

Goodyear, R. K. (1990). Research on the effects of test interpretation: A review. *The Counseling Psychologist, 18,* 240–257.

Gottfredson, G. D., & Holland, J. L. (1975). Vocational choices of men and women: A comparison of predictors from the self-directed search. *Journal of Applied Psychology, 22,* 28–34.

Gysbers, N. C., & Moore, E. J. (1987). *Career counseling: Skills and techniques for practitioners.* Englewood Cliffs, NJ: Prentice Hall.

Hansen, J. C., & Swanson, J. L. (1983). Stability of interests and predictive and concurrent validity of the 1981 Strong-Cambell Interest Inventory for college majors. *Journal of Counseling Psychology, 30,* 194–201.

Hartman, B. W., Fuqua, D. R., & Blum, C. R. (1984). A path-analytic model of indecision. *Vocational Guidance Quarterly, 33,* 231–240.

Hartman, B. W., Fuqua, D. R., & Hartman, P. T. (1983a). The construct validity of the career decision scale administered to high school students. *Vocational Guidance Quarterly, 31,* 250–258.

Hartman, B. W., Fuqua, D. R., & Hartman, P. T. (1983b). The predictive potential of the Career Decision Scale in identifying chronic career indecision. *Vocational Guidance Quarterly, 32,* 103–108.

Healy, C. C. (1990). Reforming career appraisals to meet the needs of clients in the 1990s. *The Counseling Psychologist, 18,* 214–226.

Hogan, R., DeSoto, C. B., & Solano, C. (1977). Traits, tests, and personality research. *American Psychologist, 32,* 255–264.

Holland, J. L., Gottfredson, G. D., & Baker, H. G. (1990). Validity of vocational aspirations and interest inventories, extended, replicated, and reinterpreted. *Journal of Counseling Psychology, 37,* 337–342.

Holland, J. L. (1982). The SDS helps both females and males: A comment. *Vocational Guidance Quarterly, 30,* 195–197.

Holland, J. L. (1985a). *Making vocational choices: A theory of vocational personalities and work environments* (2nd ed.). Englewood Cliffs, NJ: Prentice Hall.

Holland, J. L. (1985b). *Manual—Self Directed Search.* Odessa, FL: Psychological Assessment Resources.

Holland, J. L., & Gottfredson, G. D. (1975). Predictive value and psychological meaning of vocational aspirations. *Journal of Vocational Behavior, 12,* 290–296.

Holland, J. L., Gottfredson, G. D., & Gottfredson, L. S. (1975). Read our reports and examine the data: A response to Prediger and Cole. *Journal of Vocational Behavior, 7,* 253–259.

Ivey, A. E. (1982). Toward less of the same. Rethinking the assessment process. *Measurement and Evaluation in Guidance, 15,* 82–86.

Johnson, R. W., & Hoese, J. C. (1988). Career planning concerns of SCII clients. *Journal of Career Development, 36,* 251–258.

Jones, L. K. (1981). *Professional manual: Occ-U-Sort.* New York: McGraw-Hill.

Jones, L. K., Gorman, S., & Schroeder, C. G. (1989). A comparison of the SDS and career key among undecided college students. *Career Development Quarterly, 37,* 334–344.

Kapes, J. T., & Mastie, M. M. (1988). *A counselor's guide to career assessment instruments* (2nd ed.). Alexandria, VA: National Career Development Association.

Knapp, R. R., & Knapp, L. (1979). Relationship of work values to occupational activity interests. *Measurement and Evaluation in Guidance, 12,* 71–76.

Larsen, L. M., Heppner, P. P., Ham, T., & Dugan, K. (1988). Investigating multiple subtypes of career indecision through cluster analysis. *Journal of Counseling Psychology, 35,* 439–446.

Lent, R. W., Brown, S. D., & Larkin, K. C. (1984). Relationship of self-efficacy to self-efficacy expectation to academic persistence and achievement. *Journal of Counseling Psychology, 31,* 356–362.

Lent, R. W., Brown, S. D., & Larkin, K. C. (1986). Self-efficacy in the prediction of academic performance and perceived career options. *Journal of Counseling Psychology, 33,* 265–269.

Lonner, W. J. (1988). Issues in testing and assessment in cross- cultural counseling. *The Counseling Psychologist, 18,* 599–614.

Maddux, C. D., & Cummings, R. E. (1980). Alternate form reliability of the Self-Directed Search—Form E. *Career Development Quarterly, 35,* 136–140.

McGoldrick, M., & Gerson, R. (1985). *Genograms in family assessment.* New York: Mortin.

Noeth, R. J. (1983).The effects of enhancing expressed vocational choice with career development measures to predict occupational field. *Journal of Vocational Behavior, 22,* 365–375.

Okiishi, R. W. (1987). The genogram as a tool in career counseling. *Journal of Counseling and Development, 66,* 139–143.

Parsons, F. (1909). *Choosing a vocation.* Boston: Houghton Miffin.

Prediger, D. J. (1974). The role of assessment in career guidance. In E. L. Herr (Ed.), *Vocational guidance and human development* (pp. 325–349). Boston: Houghton Mifflin.

Prediger, D. J. (1981). A note on Self-Directed search validity for females. *Vocational Guidance Quarterly, 30,* 117–129.

Prediger, D. J., & Garfield, N. (1988). Testing competencies and responsibilities: A checklist for counselors. In J. T. Kapes & M. M. Matie (Eds.), *A counselor's guide to career assessment instruments* (2nd ed., pp. 47–54). Alexandria, VA: National Career Development Association.

Prediger, D. J., & Hawson, G.R. (1976). It's time to face some issues: A response to Holland, Gottfredson, and Gottfredson, *Journal of Vocational Behavior, 1,* 261–263.

Pryor, R. G. L., & Taylor, N. B. (1980). On combining scores from interest and value measures for counseling. *Vocational Guidance Quarterly, 34,* 178–187.

Rokeach, M. (1973). *The nature of human values.* New York: Free Press.

Rokeach, M. (1979). *Understanding human values: Individual an societal.* New York: Free Press.

Rotberg, H. L. (1984). Career self-efficacy expectations and perceived range of career options in community college students. Unpublished doctoral dissertation. Chapel Hill, NC: University of North Carolina–Chapel Hill.

Rotberg, H. L., Brown, D., & Ware, W. B. (1987). Career self-efficacy expectation and perceived range of career options in community college students. *Journal of Counseling Psychology, 34,* 164–170.

Sampson, J. P., Jr. (1990). Computer-assisted testing and the goals of counseling psychology. *The Counseling Psychologist, 18,* 227–234.

Savickas, M. L. (1984). Career maturity: The construct and its measurements. *Vocational Guidance Quarterly, 32,* 222–231.

Slaney, R. B., & Slaney, F. M. (1986). Relationship of expressed and inventoried vocational interests of female career counseling clients. *Career Development Quarterly, 35,* 24–33.

Sundberg, N. D., & Gonzales, L. R. (1981). Cross-cultural and cross-ethnic assessment: Overview and issues. In P. McReynolds (Ed.), *Advances in psychological assessment* (Vol. 5, pp. 475–491). San Francisco: Jossey-Bass.

Super, D. E., & Thompson, A. S. (1979). A six-scale, two-factor measure of adolescent career or vocational maturity. *Vocational Guidance Quarterly, 28,* 6–15.

Tinsley, H. E. A., & Bradley, R. W. (1986). Test interpretation. *Journal of Counseling and Development, 64,* 462–466.

Tinsley, H. E. A., & Bradley, R. W. (1988). Interpretation of psychometric instruments in career counseling. In J. T. Kapes & M. M. Mastie (Eds.), *A counselor's guide to career assessment instruments* (2nd ed., pp. 37–46). Alexandria, VA: National Career Development Association.

Tittle, C. K., & Zytowski, D. G. (Eds.), (1980). *Sex-fair interest measurement: Research and complications.* Washington, DC: Institute of Education, U. S. Government Printing Office.

Tyler, L. E. (1961). Research explorations in the realm of choice. *Journal of Counseling Psychology, 8,* 195–202.

Tyler, L. E. (1978). *Individuality.* San Francisco: Jossey-Bass.

Vondracek, F. W., Hostetler, M., Schulenberg, J. E., & Shimiza, K. (1990). Dimensions of career indecision. *Journal of Counseling Psychology, 37,* 98–106.

Weinrach, S. G. (1979). Trait and factor counseling: Yesterday and today. In S. G. Weinrach (Ed.), *Career counseling: Theoretical and practical perspectives.* New York: McGraw-Hill.

Weinrach, S. G. (1984). Determinants of vocational choice: Holland's theory. In D. Brown & L. Brooks and Associates, *Career Choice and Development,* (pp. 61–93). San Francisco: Jossey-Bass.

Wholeben, B. E. (1988). Sixteen PF personal career development profiles: Review. In J. T. Kapes & M. M. Mastie (Eds.), *A counselor's guide to career assessment instruments* (2nd ed, pp. 238–242). Alexandria, VA: NCDA.

Willes, C. G., & Ham, T. L. (1988). Myers–Briggs Type Indicator: Review. In J. T. Kapes & M. M. Mastie (Eds.), *A counselor's guide to career assessment instruments* (2nd ed., pp. 228–233). Alexandria, VA: NCDS.

Williamson, E. G. (1939). *How to counsel students.* New York: McGraw-Hill.

Womer, F. B. (1988). Selecting an instrument: Choice or challenge. In J. T. Kapes & M. M. Mastie (Eds.), *A counselor's guide to career assessment instruments* (2nd ed., pp. 25–36). Alexandria, VA: National Career Development Association.

Zytowski, D. G., & Warman, R. E. (1982). The changing use of tests in counseling. *Measurement and Evaluation of Guidance, 15,* 147–152.

__14_____

Career Counseling

BACKGROUND

It is likely that some form of career counseling has been provided in this country since the colonial period (Picchioni & Bonk, 1983). In 1883 Salmon Richards published *Vocophy*, which was a call for vocophers in every town. Vocophers, according to Richards, were to be trained in an institution established for the specific purpose of studying occupations and would be familiar with the moral and ethical standards of occupations as well as the requirements for performing them. Little response was immediately forthcoming from Richards's call, but by the turn of the century many high schools were offering some form of career guidance. In 1909 Frank Parsons set forth his tripartite model of career "counseling" in his classic, *Choosing a Vocation*. His model—develop self-awareness, provide information about occupations, and have individuals choose a career using true logic—became the cornerstone of the trait and factor approach to career development, an approach which may still be the most practiced approach to career counseling in this country (Srebalus, Maranelli, and Messing, 1982). However, as a number of authors have pointed out, career counseling is changing (e.g., Brown & Brooks, 1991; Gysbers & Moore, 1987).

In this chapter some of the current definitions of career counseling are presented and synthesized into a single definition, the process of career counseling is explored, the expected outcome of career counseling is discussed, a few of the techniques that are frequently used by career counselors are presented, and some of the special needs of various client groups are elaborated.

CAREER COUNSELING DEFINED

As noted, the earliest approaches to career counseling were based on trait and factor ideas. E. G. Williamson (1939, 1965) defined career counseling as a six-step process including (1) analysis, or collection of data about the

371

individual; (2) synthesis or summarizing the data that have been gathered; (3) diagnosis of the career problems (no choice; uncertain choice; unwise choice; discrepancy between interests and aptitudes); (4) prognosis or forecasting how successful the person will be if she has established goals; (5) counseling, which occurs if the person has not made a "good choice"; and (6) follow-up, which entails determining if the course of action taken as a result of the process is a viable one. If the choice turns out to be nonviable, the entire career exploration process needs to be recycled.

The National Career Development Association (NCDA) published a definition of career counseling which, like Williamson, focuses on career but expands on his ideas considerably. The authors state (NCDA, 1988) the following:

> Vocational/career counseling consists of those activities performed or coordinated by individuals who have credentials to work with other individuals or groups of individuals about occupations, life/career, career decision making, career planning, career pathing, or other career development related questions or conflicts. (p.3)

Obviously, the NCDA definition adds a wider array of career-related activities to the career counseling process than did Williamson's. It also alludes to, but does not spell out, that career counseling focuses on the interaction of career and other life issues and notes that counselors who conduct career counseling should be appropriately credentialled. The NCDA definition does not mention the relationship between career counseling and personal counseling, which are viewed by some as separate processes.

However, Crites (1981) notes the need for a rapprochement between counseling which focuses on career issues and personal counseling and suggests that career counseling not only facilitates career development but enhances personal development as well. Crites (1981) also suggests that career counseling is more difficult than therapy and that, in fact, career counselors need to be experts in psychotherapy as well as in career counseling. Many authorities who write about career counseling have agreed with at least one of Crites's positions: It is time to eliminate the dichotomy between career and personal counseling.

Yost and Corbishley (1987) state, "In the course of pursuing a career choice, clients often clarify values unrelated to careers, reassess general life goals, learn new interpersonal skills, and increase their self esteem" (p. 24). They point out that emotional constraints such as guilt and behavioral constraints such as nonassertiveness and cognitive constraints voiced in the form of "I can't," "I won't," "I shouldn't" statements all surface in the course of career counseling and must be dealt with if the process is to be successful.

Gysbers and Moore (1987) take a position similar to that of Yost and Corbishley (1987). They indicate that career counseling involves two phases, namely client goal or problem identification and resolution of the problem that has been identified. In phase 1 (goal or problem identification) they list the following subphases:

1. Establishing a working relationship and defining roles
2. Developing an understanding of the client's characteristics and environment
3. Making a diagnosis of the client's problem

In the problem resolution phase, the following subphases are listed (Gysbers & Moore, 1987):

1. Making an intervention
2. Evaluating the impact of the intervention
3. Terminating if the intervention is successful

On the surface, these phases and subphases appear somewhat analogous to Williamson's (1939) stages. However, Gysbers and Moore make it clear that career counseling involves such activities as identifying and eliminating irrational beliefs that may preclude career exploration, planning, or the establishment of career plans or distorted thinking that may result from filtering information (e.g., hearing only the negative or positive). They also provide guidelines for lifestyle analysis and looking at decisional problems that may grow out of faulty cognitions.

In what appears to be a radical departure from the traditional definitions of career counseling that focus on career choice, Kivlighan (1990) outlines a process that he refers to variously as career group therapy and career group counseling. He suggests that the same therapeutic factors that operate in therapy groups may be the curative factors in career group counseling as well. He also suggests that therapy and career counseling are analogous processes. However, he concludes that at this time we possess only rudimentary knowledge of the role of therapeutic factors and other group process variables in career counseling groups.

Brown and Brooks (1991) define career counseling as a process aimed at facilitating career development that involves choosing, entering, adjusting to, and advancing in a career. They also suggest that career development occurs over the life span and interacts with the development of other life roles (e.g., child, student, or leisurite). They define career problems as including areas such as undecidedness, indecisiveness (the inability to choose), work performance, incongruence between the person and the work role, job stress, and inadequate integration of work with other life roles.

The process of career counseling, according to Brown and Brooks (1991), involves establishing a relationship followed by evaluating the extent to which a client is able objectively to assess his personal characteristics and how they relate to potential occupations, and the client's motivation to engage in career counseling. If the counselor determines that cognitive clarity is lacking (inability to assess objectively self and environment), personal counseling may be necessary. If motivation is lacking, emphasis may need to be placed on preparing the client for the career counseling process. If cognitive clarity and motivation are present, the counselor can proceed with career counseling.

As stated at the outset, many career counselors see the relationship between personal and career problems. It is also the case that many career counselors adopt counseling approaches that integrate personal and career counseling aimed at helping their clients integrate work with other life roles. There are times when the counseling process focuses only on career choice or adjustment within the existing career. However, even in these moments, career counselors are alert to the possible impact of other life roles and/or mental health problems on work. It is also equally true that a process initiated ostensibly to correct career-related problems may have to be interrupted while personal problems are addressed. Finally, clients who come for personal counseling may actually need career counseling. For example, incongruence between people and their jobs and roles may result in job stress. This tension may in turn manifest itself as headaches, depression, insomnia, and lower back pains that may be treated by the novice as mental health problems (Brooks & Brown, 1986; Brown, 1985).

The career counseling definitions posed by Yost and Corbishley (1987), Gysbers and Moore (1987), and Brown and Brooks (1991) have focused to some degree on the relationships between mental health and career problems, work, and other life roles. These authors view career counseling as an interpersonal process aimed at fostering career development by identifying and eliminating mental health problems, if necessary, and by facilitating the development of personal awareness by eliminating cognitive and emotional barriers to self-exploration as well as enhancing knowledge of occupations, occupational mobility, the social and economic influences on careers, and the context in which people work (businesses, professions, etc.). It is also implicit in most definitions and explicit in two (Crites, 1981; NCDA, 1988) that career counseling requires specialized training in areas such as assessment and use of occupational information in addition to basic training in personal counseling.

THEORETICAL BASES

Early in this volume, several theories of occupational choice and career development were presented (see Chapter 2). Because of the rather brief treatment of these theories, it may not have been apparent that they would serve as a basis for career counseling. However, when many of the leading theorists were asked to apply their theory to a case description, most were able to do so without difficulty (Brown & Brooks, 1991). However, as Srebalus et al. (1982) point out, the study of theory in most instances is meant to be a stimulus for the trainee to develop her own personal theory. They also suggest that theories of occupational choice and career development may need to be integrated with general counseling theory, personality theory, and behavior-change theory, a recommendation that seems justified given the stage of evolution of theories of occupational choice and career development.

Most career counselors have developed their own approach to career counseling. Srebalus et al. (1982) suggest that the following factors should be considered as the counselor-trainee develops an approach to career counseling: foundation, description of clients, statements about client problems or goals, a conceptualization of career counseling clients, conceptualizations of the counseling relationship, beliefs about how problems are diagnosed, development of counseling strategies that will engender change, and approaches to evaluating counseling outcomes.

The foundation of most counselors' "theories" probably stems from two sources: formal theory and their informal theory of human functioning (Strohmer & Newman, 1983). All trainees come to counselor preparation programs with a set of beliefs about how people develop and change, although these may not have been carefully articulated. At the outset of most training programs, trainees are exposed to numerous theories including those that attempt to explain human development, personality formation, learning, change via counseling and therapy, and occupational change and career development. In well-conceptualized training programs, students are then assisted to integrate these formal theories with their personal belief system to develop their own model of counseling. More often, students are left to their own devices to develop a personal approach to counseling. It is suggested here that prospective career counselors begin to formulate their own model of career counseling by answering the following questions:

1. What are my personal beliefs about human nature? Are people essentially energetic and self-motivated or by nature lazy and in need of external motivation? What are the forces that cause people to grow and change? What retards that process?
2. With regard to formal theories of human development, how does normal development occur? What leads to abnormal functioning? How can abnormal behavior be changed? What circumstances may result in normal people becoming abnormal?
3. How do interests and work values develop? Why do they change? How can I measure them?
4. What are the indications of abnormal behavior? Why do they change? How can I measure them?
5. How does the work role interact with other life roles? How can they be interrelated? What happens when conflict between life roles occurs? How can the work role and other roles be brought into harmony?
6. How do I establish relationships with my clients?
7. How do I use information from tests and inventories in counseling?
8. How do I assess work satisfaction? How can I facilitate the process?
9. How do I motivate unmotivated clients?

10. What are the potential problems in providing career counseling to clients from other cultures? How can these be avoided? Remedied if they are used?
11. How can I evaluate the outcomes of my work?

To answer these questions adequately, career counselors need the following competencies (NCDA, 1991, unnumbered).

Individual and Group Counseling Skills

Individual and group counseling competencies considered essential to effective career counseling.

Demonstration of:

1. Ability to establish and maintain productive personal relationships with individuals.
2. Ability to establish and maintain a productive group climate.
3. Ability to collaborate with clients in identifying personal goals.
4. Ability to identify and select techniques appropriate to client or group goals and client needs, psychological states, and developmental tasks.
5. Ability to plan, implement and evaluate counseling techniques designed to assist clients to achieve the following:
    a. Identify and understand clients' personal characteristics related to career.
    b. Identify and understand social contextual conditions affecting clients' careers.
    c. Identify and understand familial, subcultural and cultural structures and functions as they are related to clients' careers.
    d. Identify and understand clients' career decision making processes.
    e. Identify and understand clients' biases toward work and workers.
    f. Identify and understand clients' biases toward work and workers based on gender, race and cultural stereotypes.
6. Ability to challenge and encourage clients to take action to prepare for and initiate role transitions by:
    a. Locating sources of relevant information and experience.
    b. Obtaining and interpreting information and experiences.
    c. Acquiring skills needed to make role transitions.
7. Ability to support and challenge clients to examine the balance of work, leisure, family and community roles in their careers.

Individual/Group Assessment

Individual/Group assessment skills considered essential for professionals engaging in career counseling.

Demonstration of:

1. Knowledge about instruments and techniques to assess personal characteristics (such as aptitude, achievement, interests, values and other personality traits).
2. Knowledge about instruments and techniques to assess leisure interests, learning style, life roles, self-concept, career maturity, vocational identity, career indecision, work environment preference (e.g., work satisfaction), and other related lifestyle/development issues.

3. Knowledge about instruments and techniques to assess conditions of the work environment (such as tasks, expectations, norms and qualities of the physical and social settings).

4. Ability to evaluate and select instruments appropriate to the client's physical capacities, psychological states, social roles and cultural background.

5. Knowledge about variables such as ethnicity, gender culture, learning style, personal development, and physical/mental disability which affect the assessment process.

6. Knowledge of and ability to effectively and appropriately use computer-assisted assessment measures and techniques.

7. Ability to identify assessment [procedures] appropriate for specified situations and populations.

8. Ability to evaluate assessment [procedures] in terms of their validity, reliability, and relationships to race, gender, age, and ethnicity.

9. Ability to select assessment techniques appropriate for group administration and those appropriate for individual administration.

10. Ability to administer, score and report findings from career assessment instruments.

11. Ability to interpret data from assessment instruments and present the results to client and to others designated by client.

12. Ability to assist client and others designated by the client to interpret data from assessment instruments.

13. Ability to write a thorough and substantiated report of assessment results.

Information/Resources

Information/resource base and knowledge essential for professionals engaging in career counseling.

Demonstration of:

1. Knowledge of employment information and career planning resources for client use.

2. Knowledge of education, training, and employment trends; labor market information and resources that provide information about job tasks, functions, salaries, requirements and future outlooks related to broad occupational fields and individual occupations.

3. Knowledge of the changing roles of women and men and the implications for work, education, family and leisure.

4. Knowledge of and the ability to use computer-based career information delivery systems (CIDS) and computer-assisted career guidance systems (CACGS) to store, retrieve and disseminate career and occupational information.

5. Knowledge of community/professional resources to assist clients in career/life planning, including job search.

Career Development Theory

Theory base and knowledge considered essential for professionals engaging in career counseling and development.

Demonstration of:

1. Knowledge about counseling theories and associated techniques.
2. Knowledge about theories and models of careers and career development.
3. Knowledge about differences in knowledge and values about work and productive roles associated with gender, age, ethnic and race groups, cultures and capacities.
4. Knowledge about career counseling theoretical models, associated counseling and information techniques, and sources to learn more about them.
5. Knowledge about developmental issues individuals address throughout the lifespan.
6. Knowledge of the role relationships to facilitate personal, family, and career development.
7. Knowledge of information, techniques, and models related to computer-assisted career guidance systems and career information delivery systems and career counseling.
8. Knowledge of the information, techniques, and models related to career planning and placement.
9. Knowledge of career counseling theories and models that apply specifically to women or are inclusive of variables that are important to women's career development.

Special Populations

Knowledge and skills considered essential in relating to special populations that impact career counseling and development processes.

Demonstration of:

1. Knowledge of the intrapersonal dynamics of special population clients while understanding resistances and defenses that may occur naturally during the counseling process.
2. Sensitivity toward the developmental issues and needs unique to minority populations.
3. Sensitivity toward and knowledge of various disabling conditions and necessary assistance and requirements.
4. Ability to define the structure of the career counseling process to accommodate individual cultural frames of reference and ethnic and racial issues.
5. Ability to distinguish between the special needs of the culturally different, immigrants, the disabled, the elderly, persons with the AIDS virus, and minority populations.
6. Ability to find appropriate methods or resources to communicate with limited-English-proficient individuals.
7. Ability to identify alternative approaches to career planning needs for individuals with specific needs.
8. Ability to identify community resources and establish linkages to assist clients with specific needs.
9. Ability to assist other staff members, professionals and community members in understanding the unique needs/characteristics of special populations with regard to career exploration, employment expectations and economic/social issues.
10. Ability to advocate for the career development and employment of special populations.

11. Ability to deliver and design career development programs and materials to hard-to-reach special populations.

Ethical/Legal Issues

Information base and knowledge essential for the ethical and legal practice of career counseling.

Demonstration of:

1. Knowledge about the code of ethical standards of the American Association for Counseling and Development, the National Career Development Association, NBCC, CACREP, and other relevant professional organizations.
2. Knowledge about current ethical and legal issues which affect the practice of career counseling.
3. Knowledge about ethical issues related to career counseling with women, cultural minorities, immigrants, the disabled, the elderly, and persons with the AIDS virus.
4. Knowledge about current ethical/legal issues with regard to the use of computer-assisted career guidance.
5. Ability to apply ethical standards to career counseling and consulting situations, issues, and practices.
6. Ability to recognize situations involving interpretation of ethical standards and to consult with supervisors and colleagues to determine an appropriate and ethical course of action.
7. Knowledge of state and federal statutes relating to client confidentiality.

THE CAREER COUNSELING PROCESS

As can be seen from the preceding listing of competencies, career counseling involves much more than matching a person to an occupation. Career counselors need to be prepared to identify "psychological states," understand cultural variables that may influence both career choice and the counseling relationship, and help clients consider career options in the context of other life roles. However, in the most simplistic terms, the career counseling process consists of five stages: (1) establishing a counselor-client relationship and structuring the relationship; (2) diagnosing the problem; (3) goal setting; (4) intervention, and (5) evaluation. As we have already seen from the definitions provided, some people writing about career counseling would elaborate on these stages, (e.g., Crites, 1981; Brown & Brooks, 1991) but most would accept this framework. In this section, the process of career counseling is described using these stages as the basic framework for the process.

Relationship/Structure

In this stage of career counseling, several tasks must be accomplished. Chief among these is the development of an open, trusting relationship based on mutual respect. Literally dozens of "how to" books have been written about how these steps are to be accomplished (e.g., Carkhuff, 1983; Hutchins &

Cole, 1986) and these should be consulted for further information. Structuring the career counseling process occurs simultaneously with relationship development and, while it is a separate process to some degree, is an integral part of the relationship development process. Yost and Corbishley (1986) indicate that the first task in structuring career counseling is to give the client a clear statement regarding the counseling process including goals, procedures to be used, risk to the clients, limitations of the process, possible outcomes, and cost if a fee is to be charged. Clients also have a right to know about the qualifications of the counselor and the role the counselor will assume.

One or two more aspects of structuring should probably be added to the Yost and Corbishley (1987) list. For example, in addition to making disclosures about the responsibilities of the counselor, some discussion of the counselor's expectations of the client are also in order (Brown & Brooks, 1991). For example, early in career counseling, perhaps in a discussion of the procedures to be used, the counselor will want to establish expectations about the client's responsibility in taking tests and inventories, homework assignments, interviewing workers or job shadowing, and disclosure of information about self.

Embedded in Yost and Corbishley's (1987) structuring statement about counselor responsibility is a statement about confidentiality. In most states, the clients of licensed counselors, psychologists, and social workers are accorded privileged communication in the laws that establish licensure requirements. The codes of ethics of all mental health professionals require practitioners to keep in confidence information disclosed in the course of counseling. Therefore clients' disclosures are protected both legally and ethically with certain limitations, namely if clients pose a threat to themselves or to others. These limitations should be explained along with the legal and ethical constraints on the counselor.

Structuring the career counselor relationship also involves establishing a time and place to meet and developing some preliminary expectations about how long the process is likely to take. Most career counselors working in college counseling centers have experienced the situation with the sophomore who, when confronted with the necessity of deciding a major in her sophomore year, concludes that she should also decide on her life's work. As one sophomore put it, "I only have 3 weeks until I meet with my advisor and I want to have both a major and a job picked out." It may be possible that a career can be selected in 3 weeks, but most career counselors find that it takes longer and should communicate to the client that the process may not be completed in 3 weeks.

Assessment

In Chapter 13, the general topic of assessment in career development was addressed. The primary focus of that chapter was on the use of tests and inventories to identify assessment strategies that may have relevance to career development. Certainly, formal assessment procedures will be employed to help clients develop an increased awareness of their interests, values, aptitudes, personality traits, and decisional style. However, much of the assessment that occurs in the career counseling process is based on the informal observations of the counselor. As noted in Chapter 13, this assessment is referred to as clinical assessment.

Clinical assessment of the client begins at the first contact and continues throughout the career counseling process. For many counselors, clinical assessment involves developing, and at times discarding and redeveloping, a hypothesis about the nature of the client's problem. In many instances, informal observations made during the course of the counseling interview are supplemented with data from the tests and inventories described in Chapter 13. If the hypothesis developed by the counselor suggests that a health problem may be involved, a physician may be consulted and the client may be asked to have a physical examination. The conclusion arising from all of the data gathered in the assessment process is the diagnosis.

Williamson's (1939) diagnostic system classified clients as having no choice, an uncertain choice, an unsure choice, or having a discrepancy between interests and aptitudes. Crites (1969) developed a comprehensive diagnostic system for career counselors that looked at interests and aptitudes as they related to three variables: adjustment, indecision, and realism. According to Crites, the adjusted person is in a field with appropriate interests and aptitudes and may simply come to career counselors for assurance. Maladjusted individuals are neither in a field of interest nor one that is commensurate with their aptitudes. Multipotentialed individuals may have many occupations that interest them and may have the aptitudes to pursue them all, while undecided individuals have no choice. Unrealistic individuals have a field of interest but do not have the aptitude to pursue that field. Unfulfilled clients have a field of interest, but it is below their measured potential. Coerced individuals are in an occupation where they can succeed because of aptitude, but they are not interested in it.

Contemporary career counselors are less likely to establish distinct nosological categories, choosing to look at certain distinct variables instead. Brown and Brooks (1985) identify cognitive clarity, informational deficits, client motivation, suitability of work environment (worker fit), interrelationship of work and other life roles, health factors, and the flexibility of significant others such as spouses as factors that should be assessed. Super (1990) assesses autonomy, time perspective, self-esteem, interests, vocational preferences, occupational self-concept, and a variety of other factors. Yost and Corbishley (1987) simply divide assessment into two spheres: psychological problems and work-related concerns. Regardless of the assessment categories, the end result is a diagnosis of the client's problem by the counselor. This diagnosis is shared with the client, and if there is consensus goal setting occurs.

Goal Setting

Gysbers and Moore (1987) prefer to describe the goal-setting stage as goal *or* problem identification, clarification, and specification, since they believe that having a counseling goal does not necessarily mean that the client has a problem. They refer specifically to clients who come to career counseling for self-improvement, not to solve problems. The term *goal setting* has been adopted here because it subsumes both situations where problems are to be resolved and where the client wants to pursue self-improvement.

Well-developed career counseling goals should be specific, feasible, desired by the client, and not dictated by the wishes of others and, if the counselor is to continue, compatible with the skills of the counselor (Brown & Brooks, 1991). Typically, clients pursue multiple goals during the process of career counseling. If it becomes apparent that this is going to be the situation, potential goals should be identified and prioritized. In many instances, circumstances dictate the priorities. Individuals who have lost their jobs will probably want to focus on getting another one, particularly if they have limited financial resources. Once a new job is secured, other more suitable occupations may be explored and additional choices pursued.

Intervention

Once goals are selected, the counselor suggests interventions that may be useful in helping the client attain the goal that has been set. It is undoubtedly true that all of the techniques explored in counseling are potentially useful in career counseling. However, a few of those techniques that are often used in career counseling are discussed here.

Gathering Occupational Information

Many clients who come for counseling simply lack occupational information. Others have the information but do not know how to use it in job planning. Twenty-five percent of American adults report that they have never used any form of occupational information (Brown, Minor, & Jepsen, 1991).

Occupational information can be used to clarify occupational alternatives, to generate new alternatives, or to eliminate some of the occupations currently being considered by the client. It can also be used to familiarize inexperienced clients with various occupations and to eliminate stereotypical perceptions of occupations and the people who hold various jobs. Occupational information can be used to motivate clients to make career choices by showing them the rewards associated with various careers (Brown & Brooks, 1991). Finally, occupational information is often used as a way to help individuals engage in reality testing by exposing them to the skills, aptitudes, and training required to prepare for and enter an occupation and the working environment for different types of jobs.

Identifying Transferable Skills

Displaced homemakers reentering the work force, students, people who have lost their jobs because of job termination, and many others find it necessary to find different jobs. Often career counselors engage in helping clients identify skills that have been acquired in their current job or in other jobs that will transfer to other jobs. These skills are typically not technical competencies, such as drafting, but are more general in nature (e.g., writing, communication, managing, scheduling, public speaking, fund raising).

Counselors typically use checklists (Figler, 1979), card sorts (Hampl, 1983), and logs of activities performed over a period of time (Yost & Corbishley, 1987) and then help the client organize them into clusters or patterns, perhaps using something like the Holland typology (e.g., RIASEC) as the basis for the organization (Brown & Brooks, 1991).

Facilitating Decision Making

Career decision making, whether it be making an initial choice, choosing a new career, or making an adjustment in one's current career, involves posing and answering a series of questions. To assist decision makers deal with the vast amount of data that is involved in the decision-making process, counselors often introduce decision-making aids that are generally of two types.

The first type is lateral decision-making aids. These were designed to increase both the quality and quantity of information available, by looking creatively at information that is available, and to create new ways of looking at job situations, even those that are satisfying. The lateral thinking techniques developed by de Bono (1970, 1985) can be used for these purposes.

While space does not permit an extensive discussion of de Bono's many and varied decision-making aids, his "six thinking hats" technique illustrates many of his ideas. When using this technique, the career decision maker is advised that creative decision makers wear six thinking hats: blue, white, red, black, yellow, and green. The counselor then suggests that the client wear each of the following hats:

White: Looks at only facts about self and careers

Red: Relies on intuition; follows unjustified hunches (e.g., I feel like I'd be a good mechanic)

Black: Figures how, why things do not work; is pessimistic and critical

Yellow: Is optimistic; figures out why things will work

Green: Brainstorms new alternatives, looks at problems differently

Blue: Is rational

The data generated by the client while wearing each hat are examined to determine what new or additional data about career choices are needed.

De Bono (1985) suggests that lateral thinking techniques are useful, but ultimately decision makers may need to turn to rational (wearing the blue hat) approaches. The several types of decision making which counselors offer are decision aids using rational procedures. These aids are, for the most part, based on scientific method: Identify the problem, generate alternatives, gather data, select an alternative based on the data, select and test the alternative, and recycle if necessary. However, many are much more complex.

The balance sheet decision-making aid (Janis & Mann, 1977) is an example of a fairly complex but highly useful decision-making aid. In this approach, the decision making begins by thoughtfully generating three to five career alternatives. Then the client makes a list of personal gains (e.g., money status) and losses (e.g., would be unable to participate in favorite leisure pursuit). These gains and losses are then weighted from +5 to –5. Lists of other gains and losses (e.g., spouse) that would accrue are then made and weighted in a similar fashion. This same procedure is followed with sources of self-approval and disapproval and with sources of social approval and disapproval. A brief version of the balance sheet technique is shown in Figure 14.1.

Once the totals in the balance sheet are compiled, the career decision maker examines the information that has been generated and, if appropriate, reevaluates the weights. Obviously, the balance sheet should not dictate the final occupational choice but may be helpful in weighing alternatives.

FIGURE 14.1 *Career Alternatives*

Personal Gains & Losses	Mechanic	Engineer
Training time	4	–5
Status	–3	4
Others Gains & Losses		
Girlfriend—I go away to school	1	–5
Parents' expenses	1	–5
Sources of Self-Approval/Disapproval		
Work with my hands	5	1
Can see finished product	5	2
Sources of Social Approval or Disapproval		
Parents' pride	0	5
Friends	4	2
Total	+15	–1

Improving Time Perspective

Clients may come to career counselors with three time perspectives: past, present, and future. It is essential to career planning that, at least with regard to career orientation, they have a future orientation (Savickas, 1991). It is also imperative, according to Savickas, that the "future" be viewed optimistically and that the future have density, that it is filled with a variety of events (e.g., choosing a career, completing preparations for the chosen career, getting hired, getting the first promotion).

Savickas recommends that techniques such as a birth-to-death lifeline be employed to assist clients to differentiate the future from the past and to anticipate future events and duties in the future to be established for anticipated events. Guided fantasy, a technique which is described in the next section, can also be used to "transport" the career client into the future and to have him "experience," via fantasies, certain events.

Guided Fantasy

Guided fantasy is a process that is structured and directed (guided) by the career counselor to enhance self-awareness, to help the client develop appreciation for his or her masculine and feminine side, to generate career alternatives, and, just as importantly, to solve anticipated problems.

Counselors design guided fantasies to fit client needs. Some clients, perhaps as many as 25 percent, have difficulty participating in guided fantasy (Richardson, 1981), and therefore it is imperative that before guided fantasy is employed that same exploration be conducted within the fantasy about the appropriateness of the procedure. However, once this is determined, the counselor should design the fantasy so that it relates to the goals being pursued. Some examples of fantasies that might be employed are shown in Figure 14.2.

After the suitability of guided fantasy has been determined, induction to fantasy should occur. This involves introducing the concept of fantasy to the client, gaining permission to use it, and providing an overview of the fantasy with statements such as, "After I get you relaxed, we are going to take a trip into your future where you will encounter some surprises. None of these will be unpleasant, but they may be perplexing." Clients should also be told that fantasy is natural: Almost everyone fantasizes; some people fantasize in color; others in black and white; you are in control of your fantasies; and it is possible that even the most innocuous fantasy will arouse powerful emotions (Brown & Brooks, 1991).

Induction is followed by relaxation (e.g., deep breathing), the fantasy itself, reorientation to the here and now, and processing what was experienced in the fantasy. Of these stages, reorientation is most critical. The client may be reoriented by touching objects in the immediate surrounding and perhaps doing mild physical exercise. Failure to reorient the client properly can have negative effects (e.g., feeling that the counselor is still in control; Heikkinon, 1989).

FIGURE 14.2 *Design Fantasy for Career Clients*

Problem	Fantasy
Cannot decide between two goals, one set of values or outcomes	A winding path, one leading to the other to a second set
Stuck in an appropriate career; designs a way out	Client treads into tar pit
Client fearful about job change, but also fearful of outcomes of risk taking	Fantasy involves unpleasant tasks of old job, pleasant tasks of new job

Homework

One of the most often used techniques in career counseling is homework. Homework assignments are developed collaboratively by the client and counselor (Brown & Brooks, 1991) and generally are engaged in to extend the learning that has begun in the counselor's office. For example, clients may be assigned to interview workers after developing a tentative job choice.

According to Shelton and Ackerman (1974), homework assignments should be specific in that they include what is to be done and how it is to be done. Homework assignments should also include components of where and when (e.g., "Please interview two nurses this week, in their work settings if possible, and try to determine why they selected their jobs, how they trained for them, what their duties are, the satisfying and dissatisfying aspects of their work, and where they hope to be in 5 years careerwise"). Brown and Brooks (1991) adopted the following formula for remembering the components of a well-designed homework assignment: 3 W H S S (what is to be done, where it is to be done, when it is to be done = 3W; how often it is to be done = H; self-statements = SS). Self-statements are self-reinforcing statements that are included when the client finishes her work. An example might be, "I feel good because I completed my homework assignment!"

There are literally dozens of other techniques that can be employed during the course of career counseling. Books by Gysbers and Moore (1987), Yost and Corbishly (1987), and Brown and Brooks (1991) should be consulted for a more elaborate discussion of the techniques listed in this section as well as discussions of other techniques.

CLIENTS

The foregoing discussion was intended to serve as a general orientation to career counseling regardless of the clients involved. However, all groups of clients require special considerations, preparation, and sensitivity. This section presents a brief overview of some of the special needs of various client groups.

Women

Women bring approximately the same general types of career problems to counselors as do men, with a few exceptions. For example, because of socialization influences, women have had lower career aspirations than men (Kerr, 1983), have entered a more restricted range of careers (Astin, 1984; Brooks, 1988; Hansen, 1984), and tend to put family concerns before career issues (Coombs, 1979; Di Benedetto & Tittle, 1990). Career counselors must be aware of the self-limiting stereotypes that restrict women's choices and be sensitive to the importance placed on families. They should also be aware that certain life experiences, such as sexual and physical abuse, may have severely lowered some women's self-esteem (Bowen, 1982). This is not to suggest that counselors must accept these stereotypes or should let the consequences of putting family ahead of career go unexplained. In short, good counseling strategy dictates that self-limiting stereotypes and inability to attribute success to one's own efforts (Stonewater, Eveslage, Dingerson, 1990) should be challenged and the impact of placing the family first in life planning should be fully explored. It also means accepting and supporting the decisions that are needed. Career counselors should also be prepared to accept various lifestyles and to explore the potential impact on careers of remaining single, lesbian relationships, single parenthood, and cohabitation. Career counselors also need to be aware of career options for women in the military (Lange, 1982), high-level government service, consulting, self-owned businesses, and occupations where telecommuting is possible.

Men

Even a casual observer of male-female relationships is aware that role relationships are changing, with men filling many of the roles that women have filled when women enter the work force out of choice and necessity. Just as women must plan for multiple roles, so too must men, even though there is some evidence that men are still planning careers without consideration of their family role (Di Benedetto & Tittle, 1990). Unfortunately, there is also some evidence that mental health professionals impose negative stereotypes on men who might opt for these nontraditional roles (Robertson & Fitzgerald, 1990). Again, career counselors must be prepared to challenge the self-limiting stereotypes of men, to explore the interaction of work and other life roles, and to examine alternative lifestyles (e.g., never marrying, gay relationships, cohabitation, and single parenthood).

The selection of, and adjustment to, nontraditional careers may increasingly be a reality for men as women fill spots in occupations traditionally held by men. Chusmir's (1990) review of the literature in this area suggests that men who have selected nontraditional careers in the past possess many of the same characteristics of women in those careers and are comfortable with their masculinity. However, his review also suggests that there are strong negative perceptions of men in occupations such as nursing, child care, and early childhood education, although there appears to be some evidence that attitudes are changing.

Minorities and Majorities

White counselors often find themselves faced with the prospect of understanding cultural values and behaviors that are somewhat at variance with their own values and standards. Conversely, counselors from minority groups who work with whites may be confronted with the same problem. While little research has focused on the problems of minority counselors faced with majority clients, the reverse has been discussed extensively and explored to some degree, with the conclusion that these relationships are at times less than optimal (e.g., Sue & Zane, 1987).

Minorities, like women, are concentrated in a restricted range of occupations, are more likely to be unemployed, earn less, and consequently are more likely to live in poverty (Arbono, 1989, 1990). Even the "model" minority, Asian Pacific Islanders, find themselves stereotyped as good at science and math, nonassertive, and nonexpressive, with the result that they are underrepresented in top management positions (Fukuyama, 1992). Career counselors need to be aware of their own stereotypes of minorities, be sensitive to the cultural norms of each minority group, and be prepared to deal with the anger, frustration, and even apathy that may result from being discriminated against and living in poverty (Brown & Brooks, 1991).

Smith (1985) makes a number of more specific suggestions for counseling minority clients. She suggests that the process should begin by identifying the sources of stress being experienced by the client, particularly those that are resulting from the minority status, and the client's reaction to these stressors particularly if it has led to social isolation and alienation.

For example, Palacios and Franco (1986) suggest that family conflict, interpersonal relationships, absence of working skills, low problem-solving ability, and low stress tolerance may contribute to the problems of Hispanic women, while Asamen and Berry (1987) suggest, on the basis of their research, that perceptions of prejudice may be more problematic for Japanese Americans than for Chinese Americans.

Once stressors associated with racial status have been determined, stress related to work and family roles should be assessed (Smith, 1985). When these and other stressors are identified, the counselor should help clients develop a sense of internal control and develop a support network. In designing specific strategies, the counselor must take into consideration the values pattern of the client's culture, the extent to which the client has adopted the values pattern of the dominant culture, the points of conflict between mainstream values and the client's values, and then work with the client to resolve values clashes.

People at Midlife

Bradley (1990) observes that relatively little is known about the actual number of people at midlife who are engaged in making career transitions and cites one estimate that approximately 10 percent of adults between 30 and 44 are in transition. The Gallup poll (1989) commissioned by the NCDA sheds some light on this question. For example, 21.8 percent of the 26–40-year-olds surveyed indicated that they would choose to change jobs in the 3 years subsequent to the poll, and nearly 10 percent believed that they would be forced to change jobs within 3 years. These figures for the 41–55 age group were 9.4 (choose to change) and 7.3 (will be forced to change) percent. While neither of these groups matches Griffin's 30–44 category, they indicate that the estimate that 16 percent of people at midlife are involved in some type of career transition is probably conservative.

The midcareer changer who chooses to change jobs presents a somewhat different problem than the worker who is forced to change jobs, particularly if the worker's job has been terminated suddenly. As Bradley (1990) notes, "Psychologically, the loss of a job can be devastating, as a job is closely linked to one's identity, self esteem, and self worth" (p. 7). Typically, career counseling for this group begins with providing emotional support, but it may turn quickly to finding immediate employment, depending on the financial circumstances of the client.

People who are electing to change jobs are less likely to be experiencing stress than are clients who are forced to change jobs. This is not to suggest that some of those career changers who are electing to change jobs do not feel the same sense of urgency as that experienced by their counterparts who have lost their jobs and, if retraining is involved, have many of the same concerns.

Counselors working with midlife career changers need to be prepared to develop (1) employability skills (e.g. job search, job interviewing, etc.) and (2) time management skills, particularly if the client will have heavy child care or family responsibilities, and to utilize those techniques already described in this chapter. If clients are depressed, angry, or frustrated because of the loss of their jobs, the counselor must also be prepared to deal with those concerns.

Adolescents and Young Adults

Many career counselors are engaged in helping high school and college students make initial career choices. Career development programs to help these groups are discussed in more detail in subsequent chapters. However, these clients usually need a great deal of emphasis on developing self-awareness, exploring career options, acquiring employability skills, and matching educational options to career choices. It is also true that this group needs to reorient its time perspective from the present to the future in many instances. Another common problem that arises when working with younger clients is that they have no well-articulated set of interests or work values. This problem is often related to lack of experience with career-related activities; psychological problems such as low self-esteem and perceived environmental constraints ("I'll never be able to get an education because we are poor") can also be at the heart of this problem (Brown & Brooks, 1991).

Interventions for clients who lack experience include the use of occupational information (bibliotherapy), interviews with workers, visits to job sites to observe workers (shadowing), and attending career seminars. When the problems are based on psychological problems, these will need to be addressed prior to, or simultaneously with, career exploration.

Multipotentialed Clients

Multipotential clients are those that, because of superior intellect, physical ability, artistic or other talents, have a variety of viable career options open to them. Perhaps the most publicized of these people are the few athletes that have the potential to pursue two or more professional careers. However, there are literally thousands of gifted individuals who can enter and succeed in almost any career of their choice. This potential, while apparently a blessing, can be quite frustrating.

Pask–McCartney and Salomone (1988) suggest that, in dealing with multipotential clients, the counselor should begin by ascertaining that the client is truly multipotential. This process may begin with the administration of an interest inventory but must ultimately be determined by "measures" of aptitudes. These measures are most readily available in the intellectual areas. Artistic and physical attributes will in all likelihood have to be determined by experts since there are no objective measures that can accurately predict who will be a star athlete or a ballerina.

Kerr (1988) also asserts that feeling that you have too many options can be a problem and suggests that a program be used such as the one developed at the University of Iowa (Kerr, Hood, & Wollison, 1987), which helps clients identify careers that are aligned with their values, interests, and abilities and ultimately helps them make career choices on the basis of their values. It may also be useful to advise these types of clients that being multipotentialed means they do in fact have multiple pathways to successful careers.

Clients with Disabilities

Clients with physical, emotional, or mental disabilities present the career counselor with a series of challenges. As Zunker (1991) notes, these clients may have limited interpersonal skills because they have limited (or others have limited) their social lives to interactions with other people with disabilities. They may also have lowered self-esteem, limited skills for independent living (perhaps because of a desire to be dependent), and limited career options, perhaps because of employers' perceptions of how well they can perform in various careers.

The career counseling process for clients with disabilities will involve addressing all of the aforementioned issues and may very well begin with an extensive psychological and vocational assessment (Zunker, 1991). The purpose of the psychological assessment will be to pinpoint debilitative psychological problems so these can be ameliorated and do not interfere with career planning or functioning on the job. Vocational assessment may involve routine interest, value, and aptitude testing along with involvement in work samples from various careers. In many instances, actual preparation for careers may take place in the same institutions as it does for clients without disabilities. In other instances, specialized training programs, sheltered workshops, and carefully supervised on-the-job training experiences will be necessary.

Finally, career counselors who work with clients with disabilities will need to stay apprised of the technological breakthroughs (e.g., scanners that can read and "verbalize" written documents) that open up increasing numbers of educational and career opportunities for people with disabilities every year.

Dual-Earner and Career Clients

Technically speaking, dual-career couples are those where both the husband and wife have a high level of commitment to work and where work is continuous for both parties. Dual-earner (Rapoport & Rapoport, 1971) or dual-work families are those where one spouse, typically the mother, works primarily for economic reasons and has a lower commitment to work (Gilbert & Rachlin, 1987). In the 1970s and 1980s, the dual-career/dual-earner family replaced the traditional family, where one spouse, typically the husband, was the sole wage earner. For a number of reasons, these families present unique problems for the career counselor.

Perhaps the major problem confronting dual-earner and dual-career families is role differentiation. Gilbert and Rachlin (1987), drawing on Peplau (1983), suggest that there are three types of role relationships that may be assumed by these families: traditional, modern, and egalitarian. Gilbert (1985) studied dual-career families and found three types of role relationships, which she labeled traditional, participant, and role sharing. These categories correspond quite closely to those established by Peplau (1983) and can be described as follows:

> Traditional: Female spouse adds the work role to her traditional role; male role little affected
>
> Participant: Parenting role is shared; woman retains responsibility for household chores
>
> Egalitarian: Gender has no impact; specialization eliminated

The specific problems growing out of dual-career and dual-earner families involve (1) role overload, more typically for the wife; (2) individual and couple role conflicts often revolving around caring for the children and careers; (3) secondary importance attached to wife's career by husband; (4) competition between spouses; (5) deciding when (or whether) to have children; and (6) occupational mobility (Gilbert & Rachlin, 1987).

Helping clients from dual-career families often requires that the couples be seen together, thus requiring the counselor to have some knowledge of couples counseling. More specifically, career counselors need to do the following:

1. Help spouses examine their assumptions about their roles (Parker, Peltier, & Wolleat, 1981; Wilcox–Mathews & Minor, 1989)

2. Engage in role adjustment such as renegotiating work role to increase role compatibility (Thomas, 1990)
3. Identify strategies for coping with stress (Gilbert & Rachlin, 1987)
4. Help couples plan and implement career goals and job shifts (Wilcox–Mathews & Minor, 1989)
5. Reduce role overload by redistributing work (Sunby, 1980; Wilcox–Mathews & Minor, 1989)
6. Teach time management skills
7. Foster basic marital communication skills
8. Help African-American couples who live in predominantly white areas deal with feelings of social isolation (Thomas, 1990)
9. Help African-American couples deal with feelings of guilt because they have achieved a higher level of affluence than relatives (Thomas, 1990)
10. Help lesbian (Hetherington & Orzek, 1989) and gay couples deal with issues such as whether to acknowledge the relationship and, if so, how best to handle the situation

CASE STUDY

The *Career Development Quarterly* publishes a case study of a career counseling client in each issue and then asks two or three career counselors to react to that case by telling how they might approach the counseling process with that client. The case of Jessie, which follows, is one of those cases (Kearney, 1988 pp. 5–8).

Jessie was referred to a rehabilitation counselor working in a mental health clinic. The clinic social worker felt that Jessie needed vocational counseling and, because she was unemployed, Jessie was amenable to such services.

The counselor's first impression of Jessie (in September, 1987) was that she was poor, not well educated, and personable. She appeared to be her stated age of 45. Her hands were black from picking walnuts, her hair was somewhat disheveled, and her polka-dotted pants did not match her striped blouse. When she spoke, she would sometimes misuse a word; for example, she said "insex" for incest.

During the first session, Jessie indicated that she would like to finish her second year in a food preparation course at a small vocational training school. She felt that she needed to learn how to use commercial ovens and how to cook large quantities of food for groups of people. She was convinced that without additional training no employer would hire her.

Jessie noted that even though she received a grade of 80 in her first year at the training school, she was told that she could not return to complete the program. Jessie stated that she did not get along with the other students because they were young and immature. She alleged that these students took her shoes and other items from her locker. (At that time, she was 42 and most of the other students were in their late teens.) Jessie also indicated that she often had car problems and, as a result, was absent from school 20 days and was late 38 days during the school year.

When the rehabilitation counselor called the school (with Jessie's permission), the cooking instructor implied that Jessie's behavior was improper because she would often compete with the teacher in conducting the class. The instructor felt that Jessie was trying to prove that she knew more than did the teacher. Also, she stated that Jessie's marginal personal hygiene was not appropriate for a cooking class.

In the next session, Jessie talked about her husband. She married John in 1965 and they have four children: three girls and a boy. Jessie declared that her husband was often unfaithful to her and that she still resented the physical abuse and personal mistreatment experienced in her marriage. She is still seeking advice from her legal assistant (who works for a community legal agency) regarding the separation from her husband in 1982 because she is not convinced that they were legally divorced in 1985. Because she has never received alimony payments, she is convinced that her husband bribed the lawyer. (Because they live in a rural area in the Northeast, somehow they both had the same lawyer.) Jessie stated that she went before a legal grievance board to complain about the quality of the legal services she had received, but one of the lawyers who had previously represented her was a member of the board. She is still trying to contest the negative alimony decision.

When Jessie reviewed her work history, she noted that following her high school graduation in 1960, she worked for 5 years in a garment factory (in a small town) as a seamstress. She enjoyed the work and felt that she developed a valuable skill. She did not work out of the home for many years after she was married.

Recalling an incident when she made her first pie, she said that her husband took a bite and immediately discarded it because of the displeasing taste. Afterwards, she learned how to bake and began to improvise with some of her recipes. She also grew some of the necessary baking ingredients (e.g., rhubarb) from her own garden.

In 1980, she started specializing in baking small pies and selling these to a local business. Jessie noted that she prospered in this situation until her husband became involved. She indicated that John wanted her to sell the pies for more money and that this action resulted in the termination of the business relationship between Jessie and a store owner in town. Two years later, Jessie started working with the store owner again, but her husband interfered and damaged her friendly association with the owner.

In a later session, Jessie indicated that she would like to start her own baking business and not give all of her profits to a "middle man". She expressed fear, however, that her ex-husband might jeopardize her future business dealings by his malicious gossip.

After giving further thought to her occupational plans, Jessie decided not to go back to the vocational school, but to consider starting a baking business within the next few months. Her plan was to sell her usual baked goods, special breads, and other foods (such as canned pickles) at farmer's markets, flea markets, and other shows. She realized that she would have to pay entrance or space fees, but she was pleased with the prospect of keeping the total profits.

Noting that because she had sold some of her baked goods at the local farmer's market 2 years ago, Jessie had learned to estimate the prices for which she could sell her goods. She stated that she had a large freezer for the storage of baked goods and that she had an adequate baking oven. Jessie thought that she needed to take a bookkeeping course because she did not know how to keep financial records.

In a later session, she indicated that she would also want to sew children's clothes and sell them at the various markets. Jessie preferred to set her own pace by having a baking and sewing business rather than working for someone else. Eventually, she would like to buy a specialized van out of which she could sell her goods or start a catering business.

The rehabilitation counselor spoke with Jessie's case manager to inquire about her community reputation regarding her bakery products. The case manager, who lived in the same area as Jessie, stated that Jessie was highly regarded for her baking. She remarked that the store owner, with whom Jessie had worked, had commented favorably about Jessie's baked goods.

Jessie's social worker indicated, in case notes, that Jessie is having difficulty coping with the stresses of being a single parent and managing a household. She also seeks assistance from service providers in the department of social services, at the legal assistance agency, and from a pastor. She continues to have numerous conflicts with her ex-husband, but has some emotional support from her mother and mother-in-law. She has a case manager helping her to locate a new living situation.

From Jessie's viewpoint, the immediate problem is her health. When she first saw the rehabilitation counselor, she complained of back pain. She visited an orthopedist but was not satisfied because, she said, he could not find anything wrong with her. She went to a neurologist for a second opinion because she also had numbness and tingling sensations in her arms and legs, especially in her right hand. When the counselor telephoned Jessie following her medical examinations, she read the results of her tests. She had plantar spurs on both feet and arthritic degeneration of the lumbosacral spine at C5–C6, and C6–C7. These physical conditions, Jessie indicated, are the reasons that she wants to work in her own home. She implied that she would be able to rest when needed and would have the help of her oldest daughter, if necessary.

Jessie defined another problem as not living in an adequate home. She would like to rent a three-bedroom apartment with a kitchen (in a frame house) that would be approved to standard health and commercial regulations. Her current apartment has not been so approved. Jessie was adamant that she would not leave the local area even though there are few apartments available. She was approved by HUD (Housing for Urban Development) for reduced rental payments in government-sponsored housing. She was advised by her case manager, however, to improve the condition of her current apartment substantially. According to her case manager, her home is disgraceful. Her porch and front yard are cluttered with junk and the inside is "total chaos." Jessie has a poor reputation as a tenant in her small town and, apparently, no apartment owner is willing to rent to her.

Jessie has been applying for Social Security disability benefits because of her physical condition. She has been denied benefits twice and recently had a hearing to determine if she is eligible. She is currently receiving social services assistance.

The clinic rehabilitation counselor has referred her to the Office of Vocational Rehabilitation, and they are currently reviewing her medical condition to determine service eligibility. If she is accepted, the OVR counselor has indicated a willingness to help Jessie learn bookkeeping for her new business venture. Jessie stated that she would also like help from OVR to purchase some of her business equipment.

Jessie sees the clinic rehabilitation counselor about twice a month and occasionally speaks to the counselor by phone. Jessie's always open to suggestions from the counselor and follows through on any assignments given to her. Her goals are that she will (a) discover what is wrong with her physically, (b) have an apartment soon, and (c) be accepted for services by OVR and be able to start baking and sewing by spring 1988—in time for the opening of the local farmer's market.

MacKinnon–Slaney (1988) was one of the career counselors who outlined the approach that she would use with this client. She suggests that the information provided in the case study would need to be supplemented with additional information, such as a history of sexual or physical abuse, an assessment of her coping strategies, and information about why she is not receiving alimony.

In approaching the case, MacMinnon–Slaney suggests that, through assessment, she would want to provide Jessie with a greater awareness of her general strengths and weaknesses as well as a heightened sense of her vocational personality. The goal of this assessment would be to confirm Jessie's expressed choice as well as develop a greater sense of self-awareness.

Other interventions suggested by MacKinnon–Slaney (1988) would involve helping Jessie improve her management skills, perhaps through a mentoring program, assist her to gain the capital she needs to start her business and to gain the knowledge she needs to succeed at that business. In related interventions, Jessie would need to improve her own housekeeping and personal hygiene skills.

Ursprung (1988), also reacting to the case of Jessie, emphasized the need to give Jessie feedback about her personal hygiene and appearance, simply because to be successful Jessie must convince others that she will produce clean products. In addition, Ursprung suggests that more information is needed about Jessie's current situation (e.g., medical state), that she requires supportive counseling as a means of helping her overcome her feelings of low self-esteem, and that she needs assertiveness training and work adjustment counseling to develop job survival skills (e.g., time management and punctuality).

Two important points need to be made about the reactions to Jessie. First, while there are similarities in the reactions, there are also differences in the approaches. Second, even though the present problem is a career problem, the personal concerns relating to self-esteem and family relationships would be addressed in the context of the counseling process.

CREDENTIALING CAREER COUNSELORS

Increasingly, the credentials of people who are providing career counseling services are questioned. Whether or not one accepts Crites's (1981) assertion

FIGURE 14.3 *Criteria for Certification as a National Certified Career Counselor*

Eligibility criteria for National Certified Career Counselors listed in this register include:

1. Certification as a National Certified Counselor.
2. Graduate degree in counseling or a closely related professional field from a regionally accredited university. Completion of the required coursework with a minimum of three semester hours per course in the areas of Lifestyle and Career Development and Assessment/Tests and Measurement.
3. At least three years post-master's professional career counseling experience.
4. A documented supervised practicum which includes a minimum of 25% time focused upon career counseling OR equivalent experience in a work setting under the direction of a counselor educator or a university counseling center staff supervisor.
5. Assessment of career counseling skills by two professionals in the field.
6. Successful completion of the Career Counseling Specialty Exam.

Source: NBCC. (1988). *National Directory of Certified Counselors* (p. 250). Alexandria, VA: Author. Reprinted with permission.

that career counseling is more difficult to conduct than psychotherapy, it should be apparent that specialized training is required if career counseling is to be delivered competently. Some mental health professionals, such as school counselors, mental health counselors, rehabilitation counselors, and counseling psychologists, routinely receive training in career development theory and career counseling practice. Typically, this training is restricted to a single didactic course and may or may not be accompanied by supervised field work involving actual career counseling. In 1981, the National Career Development Association established a certification program for career counselors as a means of recognizing individuals who meet minimum training, knowledge, and skill requirements to practice career counseling. This certification, Nationally Certified Career Counselor (NCCC), has been administered by the National Board of Certified Counselors (NBCC, 1988) in Alexandria, Virginia, since 1985 and remains as the single credential designed for career counselors. The qualifications for the NCCC are outlined in Figure 14.3. At the time of this writing, other forms of credentialing for career counselors, such as specialty provisions for licensed counselors, are being discussed and at least one state, Maryland, has a provision in its licensing law for counselors which has not been activated. Psychologists must be licensed in their states before they can practice career counseling presently. Unfortunately, NBCC certification and licensing laws for counselors and psychologists do not preclude untrained people from offering career counseling services. Credentialing is discussed in more detail in Chapter 16.

SUMMARY

Until recently, trait and factor approaches to career counseling dominated. Increasingly, career counselors are rejecting this simplistic approach in favor of models that incorporate theoretical constructs and techniques from personal counseling. These new approaches call for the use of more diverse assessment strategies that allow the counselor to determine the presence of mental health problems simultaneously with the determination of career development problems. These new models demand that career counselors first be skilled in personal counseling and then develop a set of additional skills to deal with career concerns.

At the time when career counseling practice is changing, the demand for the service is increasing and is likely to continue to do so. Unfortunately, this has led to the entrance of some poorly trained professionals into practice. For the moment *caveat emptor,* or let the buyer beware, is the watchword. The future is likely to bring new credentialing requirements for career counselors, however. The standards established by the National Board for Certified Counselors and the National Career Development Association for Nationally Certified Counselors seem to be the most viable at this time.

REFERENCES

Arbono, C. (1989). Hispanic employment and the Hollonil typology of work. *Career Development Quarterly, 37,* 267–268.

Arbono, C. (1990). Career counseling research and Hispanics: A review of the literature. *The Counseling Psychologist, 18,* 300–323.

Asamen, J. K., & Berry, G. L. (1987). Self-concept, alienation, and perceived prejudice. Implications for counseling Asian Americans. *Journal of Multicultural Counseling and Development, 15,* 146–160.

Astin, H. S. (1984). The meaning of work in women's lives: A sociopsychological model of career choice and work behavior. *The Counseling Psychologist, 12,* 117–126.

Bowen, N. H. (1982). Guidelines for career counseling with abused women. *Vocational Guidance Quarterly, 31,* 123–127.

Bradley, L. J. (1990). *Counseling midlife career changers.* Garrett Park, MD: Garrett Park Press.

Brooks, L. (1988). Encouraging women's motivation for nontraditional career and lifestyle options: A model for assessment and intervention. *Journal of Career Development, 14,* 223–241.

Brooks, L., & Brown, D. (1986). Career counseling for adults: Implications for mental health counselors. In A. J. Palmo & W. J. Weikel (Eds.), *Foundations of mental health counseling* (pp. 95–114). Springfield, IL: Charles C. Thomas.

Brown, D. (1985). Career counseling: Before, after, or instead of personal counseling. *Vocational Guidance Quarterly, 33,* 197–201.

Brown, D., & Brooks, L. (1985). Career Counseling as a mental health intervention. *Professional Psychology: Research and Practice, 16,* 860–867.

Brown, D., & Brooks, L. (1991). *Career counseling techniques.* Boston: Allyn & Bacon.

Brown, D., Minor, C. W., & Jepsen, D. (1991). The opinions of minorities about preparing for work. *Career Development Quarterly, 40,* 5–19.

Carkhuff, R. R. (1983). *The art of helping* (5th ed). Amherst, MA: Human Resource Development Press.

Chusmir, L. H. (1990). Men who make nontraditional career choices. *Journal of Counseling and Development, 69,* 11–16.

Coombs, L. C. (1979). The measurement of commitment to work. *Journal of Population, 2,* National Institute of Education.

Crites, J. O. (1969). *Vocational psychology.* New York: McGraw-Hill.

Crites, J. O. (1981). *Career counseling: Models, methods, and materials.* New York: McGraw-Hill.

de Bono, E. (1970). *Lateral thinking: Creativity step by step.* Boston: Little, Brown.

de Bono, E. (1985). *Six thinking hats.* Boston: Little, Brown.

DiBenedetto, B., & Tittle, C. K. (1990). Gender and adult roles: Role commitment of women and men in a job family trade-off context. *Journal of Counseling Psychology, 37,* 41–48.

Farmer, H. (1980). *The importance of family and career roles for high school youth.* Paper presented at a symposium. APA annual convention, Montreal.

Figler, H. (1979). *The complete job-search handbook.* New York: Holt, Rinehart & Winston.

Fukuyama, M. (1991). Report of the 1989 NCDA Survey. In D. Brown & C. W. Minor (Eds.), *Working in America.* Alexandria, VA: National Career Development Association.

Gallup Organization. (1989). *A Gallup Survey Regarding Career Development.* Princeton, NJ: Author.

Gilbert, L. A. (1985). *Men in dual career families: Current realities and future prospects.* Hillsdale, NJ: Lawrence Erlbaum.

Gilbert, L. A. & Rachlin, V. (1987). Mental health and psychological functioning of families. *The Counseling Psychologist, 15,* 7–49.

Gysbers, N. C., & Moore, E. J. (1987). *Career counseling: Skills and techniques for practitioners.* Englewood Cliffs, NJ: Prentice Hall.

Hampl, S. P. (1983). The skills sort: A career planning tool. *Journal of College Student Personnel, 24,* 463–464.

Hansen, L. S. (1984). Interrelationships of gender and career. In N. C. Gysbers & Associates, (Eds.), *Designing careers* (pp. 216–247). San Francisco: Jossey-Bass.

Heikkinon, C. A. (1989). Reorientation from attend states: Please, more carefully. *Journal of Counseling and Development, 67,* 520–521.

Hetherington, C., & Orzek, A. (1989). Career counseling and life planning with lesbian women. *Journal of Counseling and Development, 68,* 52–57.

Hutchins, D. E., & Cole, C. G. (1986). *Helping relationships and strategies.* Monterey, CA: Brooks/Cole.

Janis, I. L., & Mann, L. (1977). *Decision making: A logical analysis of conflict, choice, and commitment.* New York: Free Press.

Kerr, B. A. (1983). Raising the career aspirations of gifted girls. *Vocational Guidance Quarterly, 32,* 37–43.

Kerr, B. A. (1988). Career counseling for gifted women and girls. *Journal of Career Development, 14,* 259–268.

Kerr, B. A., Hood, A., & Wollison, A. (1987). *Attracting and retaining academically talented students.* American College Personnel Association Convention, Chicago.

Kivlighan, D. M., Jr. (1990). Career group therapy. *The Counseling Psychologist, 18,* 64–79.

Kuney, D. (1988). Poverty and its manifestations: The case of Jessie. *Career Development Quarterly, 37,* 5–8.

Lange, S. (1982) Ten-hut! Careers for women in the military. *Vocational Guidance Quarterly, 31,* 118–127.

MacKinnon–Slaney, F. (1988). Overcoming poverty: Female persistence and determination. *Career Development Quarterly, 37,* 9–12.

NBCC. (1988). *National Directory of Certified Counselors,* Alexandria, VA: National Board of Certified Counselors.

NCDA. (1988). *The professional practice of career counseling and consultation: A resource document.* Alexandria, VA: National Career Development Association.

NCDA. (1991). *Career counseling competencies memograph.* Alexandria, VA: Author.

Palacios, M., & Franco, J. N. (1986). Counseling Mexican-American women. *Journal of Multicultural Counseling and Development, 14,* 124–131.

Parker, M., Peltier, S., & Wolleat, P. (1981). Understanding dual career families. *Personnel and Guidance Journal, 60,* 14–18.

Parsons, F. (1909). *Choosing a vocation.* Boston: Haughton Mifflin.

Pask–McCartney, C., & Salomone, P. R. (1988). Different cases in career counseling III: The multipotentialed client. *Career Development Quarterly, 36,* 231–240.

Peplau, L. A. (1983). Roles and gender. In H. H. Kelley, E. Berscheid, A Peplau, & D. R. Peterson. *Close Relations* (pp. 220–264). New York: Freeman.

Picchioni, A. P., & Bonk, E. C. (1983). *A comprehensive history of guidance in the United States.* Austin, TX: Texas Personnel and Guidance Association.

Rapoport, R., & Rapoport, R. N. (1971). *Dual career families.* Middlesex, England: Penguin Books.

Richardson, G. E. (1981). Educational imagery: A missing link in decision making. *Journal of School Health, 51,* 560–564.

Robertson, J., & Fitzgerald, L. F. (1990). The (mis) treatment of men. Effects of client gender role and life-style on diagnosis and attribution of pathology. *Journal of Counseling Psychology, 18,* 352–357.

Savickas, M. L. (1991). Improving career time perspective. In D. Brown & L. Brooks (Eds.), *Career counseling techniques* (pp. 236–249). Boston: Allyn & Bacon.

Shelton, J. L., & Ackerman, J. M. (1974). *Homework in counseling and psychotherapy.* Springfield, IL: Charles C. Thomas.

Smith, E. M. J. (1985). Ethnic minorities: Life stress, social support, and mental health issues. *The Counseling Psychologist, 13,* 537–580.

Srebalus, D. J., Maranelli, R. P., & Messing, J. K. (1982). *Career development: Concepts and procedures.* Monterey, CA: Brooks/Cole.

Stonewater, B. B., Eveslage, S. A., & Dingerson, M. R. (1990). Gender differences in career helping relationships. *Career Development Quarterly, 29,* 72–85.

Strohmer, D. C., & Newman, J. L. (1983). Counselor hypotheses testing strategies. *Journal of Counseling Psychology, 30,* 557–565.

Sue, S., & Zane, N. (1987). The role of culture and cultural techniques in psychotherapy: A critique and reformulation. *American Psychologist, 42,* 37–47.

Sunby, D. Y. (1980). The career quad: A psychological look at some divergent dual-career families. In C. F. Derr (Ed.), *Work, family and career* (pp. 329–353). New York: Praeger.

Super, D. E. (1990). A life-span, life space approach to career development. In D. Brown, L. Brooks, & Associates (Eds.), *Career choice and development* (pp. 197–261). San Francisco: Jossey-Bass.

Thomas, V. G. (1990). Problems of dual-career black couples: Identification and implications for family interventions. *Journal of Multicultural Counseling and Development, 18,* 58–67.

Ursprung, S. L. (1988). Counseling toward clarification and skill building: The case of Jessie. *Career Development Quarterly, 37*, 13–16.

Wilcox–Mathews, L., & Minor, C. W. (1989). The dual career couple: Concerns, benefits, and counseling implications. *Journal of Counseling and Development, 68*, 194–198.

Williamson, E. G. (1939). *How to counsel students.* New York: McGraw-Hill.

Williamson, E. G. (1965). *Vocational counseling: Some historical, philosophical, and theoretical perspectives.* New York: McGraw-Hill.

Yost, E. B., & Corbishley, M. A. (1987). *Career counseling: A psychological approach.* San Francisco: Jossey-Bass.

Zunker, V. G. (1991). *Career counseling: Applied concepts of life planning* (2nd ed.). Monterey, CA: Brooks/Cole.

__15

Preparing for Work

In Chapter 1 we divided training time into two broad types, general education and specific vocational preparation. The first includes all the general academic preparation that develops reasoning and adaptability; ability to understand and follow directions; and basic tool skills such as mathematics, language, reading, and writing. Acquisition of these skills starts no later than an individual's first day of school and, in most cases, many months earlier. Although much general education is acquired outside the classroom and supplements the school curriculum, most is learned in school.

Specific vocational preparation, on the other hand, is training directed toward learning techniques, knowledge, and skill needed for average performance in a specific job-worker situation. In general, an individual is concerned with obtaining specific vocational preparation after a tentative career decision has been made and the person recognizes (usually in the planning period) that she must acquire certain skills and knowledge to implement the decision.

Every occupation requires some combination of these two types of preparation. Continued attendance in the formal school setting inevitably exposes the person to general education development. On the other hand, specific vocational preparation must usually be sought out, although it can be obtained in a number of different sites. In this chapter, we consider those situations where the person obtains the combination of preparation that the selected occupation requires. For some students, the preparation is included in the high school program; others elect to leave school before graduation and enter a training program; many select a nonclassroom training program that follows high school graduation; and some go on to postsecondary educational programs that may or may not include a college degree.

HIGH SCHOOL PREPARATION FOR WORK

School enrollment statistics in every state show us that a sizable fraction of students who enter high school will discontinue their education before they graduate, and nearly half of those who do graduate will seek no further education immediately. Obviously, if the goal of making work possible and meaningful is to be met for these two groups, it must be done within the high school years. Many believe that no one should complete grade 12 without being ready to enter higher education or enter useful and rewarding employment. We consider those going on to higher education in later sections of this chapter. At the moment we are concerned with those who plan no further training and must acquire specific vocational preparation during their high school years. We discuss briefly two types of high school preparation—vocational education and work experience programs.

Vocational Education

The direct antecedents of the modern high school, the grammar schools and the academies, were started for the explicit purpose of preparing students to enter and succeed in the institutions of higher education. Thus, at least presumably, all students were college bound. As the modern, publicly supported high school appeared a century ago, it enabled many non-college-bound individuals to extend their educations beyond grade school level. Many schools soon added a general curriculum to meet the needs of this noncollegiate group. A few years later, some schools began to offer vocational courses, and national legislation during the World War I era established vocational education in the high school curriculum across the country.

This long history has established vocational education solidly in practically every high school in the nation. State departments have provided support staff and funding programs as well as many other advantages. The need for high-quality work-preparation programs to serve almost every student is overwhelmingly obvious, and career education principles have emphasized that need even further. Many factors and events have interfered to prevent vocational education from being a broadly based program that can be used advantageously by most of the students. Instead it has often been narrowly defined and rigidly limited to a small portion of the student body. These restrictive influences have sometimes been self-imposed by vocational educators; but more frequently they have been introduced by other school staff (including counselors and administrators), local school boards, community attitudes, state-level regulations, occupational groups, or other sources.

The point to be emphasized here is that there is a clear need to revamp vocational education and its role in the U.S. high school so that it can serve effectively all students without clearly established postsecondary educational plans and most of that other group as well. One might reasonably expect all individuals by high school graduation to have encountered realistic contact with work to an extent that permits them to develop career plans for themselves, as well as acquiring usable, salable skills that adequately qualify them to participate in meaningful and satisfying work experiences. The logical place for this to occur is in the high school vocational education program.

Beale and Jacobs (1982) discuss the importance of cooperation between school counselors and vocational educators to facilitate maximum student development.

High school students are usually restricted to attending high schools within the school district in which they reside. Thus their access to appropriate vocational education largely depends on what is offered within that district. Two slight modifications to this barrier can be found in some states. One of these permits school systems to work out cooperative tradeoffs when an occasional student in one district needs access to a program available in another district. The second is the trend toward voluntary grouping by two or more districts to provide a broader based vocational education program. In most cases this cooperation has resulted in building a vocationally oriented facility that serves students as well as postsecondary enrollees from all the cooperating districts.

Work Experience Programs

Many secondary schools include in their curricula some opportunities for students to combine study in the classroom with experience in an employment situation. These opportunities vary slightly from school to school and are known by a range of titles—cooperative work experience, distributive education, office practice, job experience, diversified training. The programs are usually incorporated into the school's vocational curriculum.

The general purpose of the program is to prepare selected students for employment while they complete their high school education. As a result of successful participation, a student graduates with her class, completing a basic general education and being prepared for full-time employment in her chosen occupation.

Operationally, these programs depart somewhat from traditional high school instructional procedures. Often the students in the group are involved in widely varied occupations; in fact, one of the titles used for this type of program—Diversified Cooperative Education—stresses the variety. The program requires cooperation of the high school and local employers, who divide instructional and supervisory responsibilities to assist the student in gaining occupational competence. In general, then, this is a school-community program of vocational instruction that uses the training and educational resources, facilities, and personnel of both the local school and the community.

The program is expect to accomplish the following:

1. The student establishes an occupational objective consistent with abilities and interests.
2. The student develops skills necessary for full-time employment as a worker or as an apprentice in a chosen occupation.
3. The student acquires related and technical information necessary for intelligent occupational practice.

4. The student develops appropriate attitudes and personal characteristics enhancing adjustment, success, and progress in the occupational field.
5. The student becomes increasingly mature in her relationship to school, economic, social, and home life.

The specific objectives can be thought of in terms of (1) the job skills that the student will need to master, (2) the knowledge that must be gained to perform the work with intelligence and judgment, and (3) the personal and social traits one must develop to get along well on the job and in the community.

The instruction in job skills is provided by the employer under actual employment conditions, according to the program developed jointly by the school representative and the employer. Students usually work a minimum of 15 hours a week, mostly scheduled during the regular school day.

The typical program permits a student, usually in the junior or senior year, to attend classes half time and work in an assigned employment position the other half. In a few large city systems, the student spends 1 week in school and the following week at work, alternating with a fellow student who is on a reverse schedule. The most common situation, however, has the student in school in the morning and on the job in the afternoon. The student is supervised by the employer in the work assignment, but a school staff member serves as liaison agent between the school and the employer and maintains close contact with both the student and the employer. The student earns academic credit for the work assignment as a part of the school's vocational curriculum.

All participants are enrolled in a related study class that meets for at least one regular class period each school day. The class is conducted by the school staff member responsible for the program—usually designated as a coordinator. Most of the instruction is technical and has a direct relationship to the student's work assignment. The study provides the trainees with information that will help them in their work. Because the students are usually involved in a wide range of occupational assignments, they have a similar variety of individual training plans; so the class work is necessarily provided on an individual basis, using special instructional materials.

General information for beginning workers is included in the study class. Subjects covered usually include units on employer-employee relations, Social Security provisions, money management, income tax problems, personality and work, and labor organizations. This material is usually provided to all students in the program and often is called *general related* instruction. Some schools arrange their program so that each day includes one period of general related instruction and another period of specialized or individualized instruction.

The development of desirable personal-social traits needed by young workers is more difficult to approach directly. Although the general related instruction helps to meet this objective, direct contact with the employment assignment also contributes. Finally, the coordinator aids the development of the desired traits through individual contacts with the student.

Work experience is totally realistic—it has every characteristic of a regular job, including pay. The student has an opportunity to face the same situations that every worker encounters, with the added advantage of having a coordinator to assist in making adjustments or solving the problems encountered in the position.

Students who enroll in the work experience program are normally placed in an assignment appropriate to their vocational aims. Because of limited placement possibilities, distances involved, or other factors, the relationship between assignment and vocational goal may be only indirect. Even in such a situation, participation in the program has many advantages for youth not contemplating further formal education. They are provided an opportunity to gain insight into the working situation and their responsibility in it. They must adjust to the employer, fellow workers, the public related to the job, and the demands of the work situation. They learn the importance of punctuality, cooperation, responsibility, paths for advancement, and similar factors that lie beyond simple vocational skill. It is not unusual for participants, on completing their schooling, to accept full-time employment with the companies in which they were placed for work experience, even when such an arrangement was not planned in the original placement.

The major advantages of the work experience program are immediately obvious. The experience is totally realistic, with none of the artificialities thought by students to exist in the school setting. There is a direct relationship between school and work, with the study course serving as the connecting link. The participant gains an additional advantage later, since one can claim actual experience when seeking full-time placement.

Inevitably, the program also has some disadvantages. It is not always possible to arrange the ideal placement that would provide the maximum in training and in experience. Some employers are primarily concerned with obtaining inexpensive workers, when they should be fundamentally interested in training them. Similarly, students may enter the programs principally for the financial benefits rather than for vocational preparation. Some communities have no available employment settings that offer a wide range of experiences. Some programs have such strict admission requirements that the student who most needs assistance is ineligible to participate. Because of the time consumed in field supervision, consultation with employers, and observation of student workers on the job, each coordinator can handle effectively only a limited number of students; consequently, the program is rarely as extensive as it should be to meet the needs of most non-college-bound students in a given high school.

Though rarely used to the fullest extent, the work experience program appears to offer an opportunity for most secondary schools to render a service to both students and community by helping students prepare themselves realistically for postschool employment. Closer cooperation between the coordinator and the school counselor should bring more effective selection and placement in the program and more satisfying results to the student, school, and community.

Career education advocates point to the work experience program as illustrative of the close school-community cooperation considered essential for effective career education. They suggest that all students, from high school entrance onward, should have related experience in the work setting. This should be part time, perhaps even intermittent, not necessarily for pay, but clearly significant and participatory. Early assignments would be expected to be essentially exploratory in purpose, whereas later assignments would be considered more preparatory in nature, providing a practical laboratory experience with maximum realism. Extending over several school years and incorporating a variety of work assignments, such a program would clearly provide students with a better understanding of the world of work as well as with a set of marketable skills. Inevitably, the school and local employers would be drawn together into cooperative relationships of mutual benefit.

Implementation of a full-scale program involving all upper level students would necessitate major changes in the educational program, but fundamentally that is what career education is all about. Other countries have already adopted versions of this kind of activity with obvious benefits for participating students. Several high-level leaders of government and industry have suggested that child labor laws should be revised and possibly modified to encourage and permit more work participation by school-age individuals. One can only agree that exploration and preparation would be strengthened if students could share actively in work experiences.

OUTSIDE THE CLASSROOM— NO DIPLOMA REQUIRED

Few if any school systems succeed in retaining all students until they graduate. The group usually referred to as high school dropouts includes many who might more appropriately be labeled "pushouts" or "lost-outs." Some individuals decide that the school program has nothing to offer them and voluntarily leave when they reach the legal age or shortly thereafter. Others, confronting difficult problems—poverty, parental discouragement, lack of family, pregnancy, personal adjustment or behavioral problems, addiction, and so forth— do not receive sufficient help from the school to overcome the difficulties they face. With some obvious exceptions, most of those who leave before graduation are likely to face the greatest problems in finding, obtaining, and keeping a job. At the same time, the least amount of help is usually available for this group. Often these individuals have no career plan or goal, no specific vocational preparation, and only marginal general education. Unfamiliarity with the world of work makes them ignorant of how to seek work, what kinds of jobs might fit their qualifications, and where those jobs are. Those who find their way to state employment security agencies are helped by referral to other local agencies that may be able to provide some of the needed services or by referral to employers who are seeking unskilled entry-level workers. In general, two possibilities are available for this group—on-the-job training, or skill acquisition through programs such as the Job Training Partnership Act.

On-the-Job Training

Some employment situations require neither specialized educational preparation nor specific vocational experience as a prerequisite. The absence of such requirements usually means that the work either can be learned readily during a brief demonstration period or is such that only a minimal general education is sufficient to prepare the worker. Such a conclusion is not always precise. The employer may prefer, for a variety of reasons, to hire inexperienced workers who can be trained as desired.

Frequently, large companies employ training directors and extensive staffs who operate elaborate programs, including class instruction, to prepare new employees for their future assignments. Such companies prefer to start with totally inexperienced workers so that they can be taught the exact procedure to follow on the job. Previous experience may have taught the worker different techniques or methods that the employer wishes to avoid. The employer prevents such "contamination" by providing a training program. In some cases, such a supervised training program may be quite lengthy and detailed and may require at least a high school diploma.

More commonly, employers offer on-the-job training when the essentials of production can be learned in a relatively brief period of time, so that the worker is soon assigned to the task for which he was employed. Where the basic operation is performed by a team or crew of skilled workers, the new employee may be assigned to a skilled worker or to a team as a helper, where he learns a complex task by observing and assisting skilled practitioners for a specified period. Some employers may rotate the beginner's assignment so that he serves a period with several teams involved in different aspects of the work, thus becoming familiar with several phases before assignment to a specific job. Frequently, however, the rotation does not give the trainee comprehensive preparation for all parts of the work.

This type of training is sometimes found in occupational fields that also involve apprenticeship. On-the-job training frequently lacks the careful organization involved in apprenticeship, thus producing workers who may not have the thorough preparation that goes with the latter.

Job Training Partnership Act (JTPA)

Since World War II, the United States has attempted to develop a system for training or retraining workers needed in certain parts of the economy. The Manpower Defense Training Act served this purpose during the war years to train workers to fill positions in rapidly expanding defense and war-related industries. This was followed by the Manpower Development and Training Act (MDTA) to provide workers with skills needed in new and expanding industries. Training was aimed especially at unemployed or underemployed individuals. Next, the Comprehensive Employment and Training ACT (CETA) was developed to provide a decentralized program in which state and local units of government could develop training programs to meet local conditions and the needs of prospective employers as well as those of unemployed or underemployed workers. CETA was replaced by the Job Training Partnership Act in 1982.

The major differences between CETA and JTPA are that JTPA provides for more input from prospective employers in the private sector concerning the kind of job training to be provided locally. Second, those obtaining training or education under JTPA are not paid during the learning period, as trainees were under CETA. One intent of JTPA is to shorten the training time and to direct it toward specific occupations.

JTPA provides authority for state-level officials to designate "service delivery areas," geographic regions that consist of contiguous counties or other political units that constitute a "labor market." Within each service delivery area a Private Industry Council is created, consisting primarily of representatives of businesses or industries in the area, with responsibility for policy guidance and administrative oversight of job training in the area. The Private Industry Council and local government officials must concur on the local plan and its administration; this local plan then must be approved by the state governor's office. The law requires that 70 percent of the funds available to a service delivery area be spent on training. Each state, through the governor's office, is required to monitor programs in the service delivery areas.

The program authorizes a wide range of training activities aimed at economically disadvantaged youth and adults to prepare them for unsubsidized employment. Programs may include on-the-job training, classroom training, remedial education, basic skills training, job search assistance, and exemplary youth programs. At least 40 percent of the funds must be spent for disadvantaged youth between the ages of 16 and 21. Ninety percent of the participants must be economically disadvantaged. The other 10 percent must have identifiable labor market disadvantages, and might include individuals with disabilities, prior offenders, displaced homemakers, older workers, teenage parents, and others.

JTPA authorizes a state-administered program to assist dislocated workers, including workers from permanently closed plants, those unlikely to be returned to previous employment, and the long-term unemployed who have little prospect of obtaining local employment. Services provided may include job search assistance, retraining, prelayoff assistance, and relocation.

The law, as passed in 1982, provides for continuation of the Job Corps program. The Job Corps was originally established under provisions of the Economic Opportunity Act of 1964 to assist the most underprivileged youth by providing training and supportive services in residential sites where they could be assisted in a transition to a productive life. It was primarily intended for those youth who had dropped out of school and were in the greatest need of remediation to become employable. Some Job Corps centers have operated essentially as civilian conservation centers in national parks and forests; others have been located near large urban areas. Educational and vocational programs have covered a number of occupations. Both residential and non-residential centers have been operated. All centers provide the following services:

1. Intensive individual and group counseling intended to improve the enrollee's self-concept and to raise motivation and expectation
2. Medical attention and fundamentals of personal health care
3. Remedial education for enrollees, 45 percent of whom are either illiterate or poor readers on enrollment
4. Vocational training geared to realistic standards, which prepare enrollees for employment on completion
5. Activities designed to develop behavior patterns that will improve the enrollee's chances of obtaining and keeping a job
6. Courses leading to a high school equivalency certificate
7. Opportunities for learning and assuming the responsibilities of a contributing member of society

The educational program is organized to meet the needs of enrollees and comprises reading, mathematics, the "world of work," an advanced general education program, and health education. Some centers offer supplementary programs of physical education, driver education, language and study skills, English as a second language, home and family living, and tutorial programs. The advanced general education program provides the information and knowledge required to pass the High School General Education Development test for high school equivalency. The vocational preparatory program provides instruction and practical experience and may include on-the-job training.

Programs established under CETA for Native Americans and for migrant and seasonal farm workers have been continued under JTPA. The amount of funding for this portion of the program is very small.

Information about JTPA programs must be obtained within the local service delivery area because there is no state or national pattern. This is also true for on-the-job training.

OUTSIDE THE CLASSROOM—HIGH SCHOOL DIPLOMA PREFERRED OR REQUIRED

High school graduates, of course, have access to on-the-job training, and in some situations they may also be eligible for certain training programs under

JTPA. In addition, there are at least two other types of nonclassroom training situations where a high school diploma increases the likelihood of qualifying. Both provide some opportunities for the person without a diploma, but it is safe to say that many more opportunities are available for high school graduates. We consider apprenticeship programs and military training.

Apprenticeship Programs

The use of apprenticeships for transmitting knowledge and skills to new workers dates back at least to the Middle Ages. The various guilds of skilled craftsmen developed the regular practice of indenturing young workers to master craftsmen. During the period of indenture, often 7 years, the young worker served or worked for the master; in return, the master provided food and lodging for the boy, usually in the master's own home, and taught him the skills and secrets of the craft. On successful completion of the indenture, the worker was accepted by the guild as a journeyman or independent craftsman. As the practice of his craft grew and expanded, he in turn later became a master and took into his shop apprentices to whom were taught the necessary skills.

The general use of apprenticeships has continued since those early days. The experience of Ben Franklin, an apprentice printer under his older brother, is part of our own colonial history. During the 1800s, as our industrial development mushroomed, thousands of workers were attracted to the United States from Europe. Many were skilled craftsmen, and for nearly a century immigration was the major source of the mechanics and craftsmen needed to operate our growing industries. Following World War I, changes in immigration laws seriously restricted the movement of many European skilled workers to this country, thus necessitating the development of other sources of labor that this country needed in increasing numbers.

The National Apprenticeship Program was established by Congress in 1937 with the support of both labor and management organizations. The Fitzgerald Act authorized the Secretary of Labor to set up standards to guide industry in employing and training apprentices; to bring management and labor together to work out plans for training apprentices; to appoint such national committees as needed; and to promote general acceptance of the standards and procedures agreed on.

The agency now known as the Bureau of Apprenticeship and Training was created to put the program into effect. A committee representing management, labor, and government was appointed, known as the Federal Committee on Apprenticeship, to develop standards and policies.

A basic policy of the Bureau of Apprenticeship and Training has been that programs for employment and training of apprentices should be jointly developed by and mutually satisfactory to both employers and employees. Because apprenticeship programs exist in a wide range of trades, the standards recommended by the Federal Committee on Apprenticeship are quite general, thus permitting the employer and employee groups in the various trades to work out the details for the training programs. Under the provisions of the Bureau of Apprenticeship and Training, an apprentice is a person at least 16 years of age (most programs require 18 years of age) who works under a written agreement registered with the state apprenticeship council (or with the Bureau of Apprenticeship and Training if there is no state council). The regulation provides for a specified period of reasonably continuous employment for the person, and for her participation in an approved schedule of work experiences supplemented by at least 144 hours per year of related classroom instruction.

The bureau has established certain basic standards under which an apprenticeship program can function:

1. An apprenticeable occupation usually requires from 1 to 6 years of employment to learn. Most last about 4 years.
2. The employment must be organized into a schedule of work processes to be learned so that the worker will have experience in all phases of the work in the apprenticeship. This prevents assignment to only one or a few specific details for the period of training, and is intended to ensure the development of skill and knowledge in all aspects of the work.
3. There should be a progressively increasing wage scale for the apprentice, starting at about half the regular journeyman's rate.
4. Related classroom instruction should amount to at least 144 hours per year.
5. A written agreement, including the terms and conditions of employment and training of each apprentice, is registered with the State Apprenticeship Council.
6. The State Apprenticeship Council provides review of local apprenticeships.
7. Programs are established jointly by employer and employees.
8. Adequate supervision and records are required for all programs.
9. Full and fair opportunity to apply for apprenticeship is provided, with selection made on the basis of qualifications alone without discrimination.
10. Periodic evaluation of the apprentice's progress is made, both in job performance and in related instruction.
11. Recognition of successful completion is provided.

There are several easily identified advantages in apprenticeship programs:

1. They provide the most efficient way to train all-around craftspeople to meet present and future needs.
2. They ensure an adequate supply of skilled tradespeople in relation to employment opportunities.

3. They assure the community of competent craftspeople, skilled in all branches of their trades.
4. They assure the consuming public of those high-quality products and services that only trained hands and minds can produce.
5. They increase the individual worker's productivity.
6. They give the individual worker a greater sense of security.
7. They improve employer-employee relations.
8. They eliminate close supervision because the craftsperson is trained to use initiative, imagination, and ability in planning and performing work.
9. They provide a source of future supervision.
10. They provide the versatility necessary to meet changing conditions.
11. They attract capable young people to the industry.
12. They generally raise skill levels in the industry.

State departments of labor were asked to establish apprenticeship councils at the state level. Such councils were intended to serve as liaison agencies between federal local levels and to encourage cooperation of state agencies and employers and employee groups with the state. Where formed, these groups include an equal number of representatives of employers and employees, and representatives from appropriate state agencies. The state organization, using standards recommended by the federal committee as guides, set up state standards and procedures to be followed by industry with the state in employing and training apprentices. Once established and recognized by the bureau, the state council becomes a part of the national apprenticeship program.

In some industries, national employer groups and national trade unions have appointed apprenticeship committees. These committees meet as joint management-labor groups to develop national apprenticeship standards and to encourage the establishment of training programs in accordance with the adopted standards. These organizations grow out of specific industries and are concerned with programs within the specific industry; they are, therefore, independent of the Bureau of Apprenticeship and Training. The usual practice has been for a close relationship to develop between the national committees and the federal bureau, with each assisting the other through the sharing of information and consultation.

Both the federal and the state organizations are primarily concerned with the establishment and development of standards. The actual employment and training of apprentices occurs at the local level. Local joint apprenticeship committees are established to organize the development of standards for employment and training for all apprentices in the specific trade by employers who are members of the local groups and other employers who subscribe to the program.

Qualifications for employment, such as age, education, aptitude, wages, hours of work, the term of the apprenticeship, the schedule of job processes, and the amount of class time required, are usually spelled out in detail in the local standards. Also included are procedures for executing and registering the agreement and methods of supervising apprentices at work and at school. The classroom instruction is provided by local and state vocational schools. The local committee often serves as an advisory group in developing an appropriate program of instruction.

Admission requirements are set by the local apprenticeship council in compliance with general standards set at the state and national level. Considerable variation can be found from trade to trade and even within a particular trade among geographic regions. Although the majority of apprenticeships require a high school diploma, some programs require less. The number of applicants usually far exceeds the number of vacancies. For example, in the construction trades, applicants usually exceed openings about 8 to 1.

There are registered programs for apprenticeships in over 800 occupations (USDOL, 1987). The precise number is difficult to ascertain because, like occupational names, some general names in one locality may be broken into several more specific titles elsewhere. Figure 15.1 provides a partial list of apprenticeable occupations. Though not comprehensive, the list does show the range of programs that can be included.

The Bureau of Apprenticeship and Training (BAT, 1990, 1991) indicates that there were 283,352 registered apprentices at the end of 1990, 22.4 percent of which were filled by minorities and 7 percent of which were filled by females. The largest numbers of apprentices were in the construction trades of electrician (35,387), carpenter (25,795), and plumber (12,671). However, the figures available from BAT do not include California, the District of Columbia, Puerto Rico, Hawaii, Rhode Island, and the Virgin Islands. What is obvious is that there are women and minorities in *almost* every apprenticeship, although women in particular are decidedly underrepresented in some groups. For example, there were no women in the apprenticeship program for horticulturist, chef, welder-fitter, and office machine services, which are all small apprenticeship programs. Moreover, women make up less than 5 percent of the apprenticeships for electrician and carpenter and only about 2 percent of the apprenticeships in plumbing. Minorities, on the other hand, make up slightly less than 15 percent of the apprentices in the largest building trades and are overrepresented in apprentices such as correction officer, cook, and radio station operator, with about 50 percent of these apprentices coming from minority groups. Unfortunately, the ethnicity and race of the apprentices were not identified in the report.

Information about apprenticeships can be obtained from several sources. Locally, labor unions can provide information about programs in their occupation, and local offices of the state employment security agency can usually provide names, addresses, and telephone numbers of nearby resources. The state or regional office of the Bureau of Apprenticeship and Training (usually listed in the directory of state offices) can provide information on programs within the state or region. The national office (Bureau of Apprenticeship and Training, U.S. Department of Labor, Washington, DC 20210) can provide national information.

FIGURE 15.1 *Apprenticeable Occupations*

	DOT Code
1. Airframe-and-Power Plant Mechanic	621.281-014
2. Automobile-Body Repairer	807.381-010
3. Automobile Mechanic	620.261-010
4. Baker	313.281-010
5. Biomedical Equipment Technician	719.261-010
6. Boatbuilder, Wood	860.381-018
7. Boilermaker I	805.261-014
8. Boiler Operator	950.382-010
9. Butcher, Meat	316.681-010
10. Bricklayer	861.381-018
11. Cabinetmaker	660.280-010
12. Car Repairer (Railroad)	622.381-014
13. Carpenter	860.381-022
14. Cement Mason	844.364-010
15. Compositor	973.381-010
16. Computer-Peripheral-Equipment Operator (Clerical)	213.382-010
17. Construction-Equipment Mechanic	620.261-022
18. Cook	313.361-014
19. Coremaker	518.381-014
20. Cosmetologist	332.271-010
21. Dairy Equipment Mechanic	629.281-018
22. Dental Laboratory Technician	712.381-018
23. Drafter, Architectural	001.261-010
24. Drafter, Mechanical	007.281-010
25. Drilling-Machine Operator	007.281-010
26. Electrician	824.261-010
27. Electrical Repairer	829.281-014
28. Electronics Mechanic	828.281-010
29. Electronics Technician	003.161-014
30. Emergency Medical Technician	079.374-010
31. Environmental-Control System Installer-Servicer	637.261-014
32. Farm Equipment Mechanic I	624-281-010
33. Fire Fighter	373.364-010
34. Fire Medic	373.364-014
35. Furniture Finisher	763.381-010
36. Glazier	865.381-010
37. Heavy Forger	612.361-010
38. Instrument Mechanic	710.281-026
39. Insulation Worker	863.364-580
40. Legal Secretary	201.362-010
41. Line Erector	821.361-018
42. Line Maintainer	821.261-014
43. Machine Repairer, Maintenance	626.281-010
44. Machinist	600.280-022
45. Maintenance Machinist	600.280-042
46. Maintenance Mechanic	638.281-014
47. Medical Laboratory Technician	078.381-014
48. Millwright	638.281-018
49. Mine-Car Repairer	622.381-030

FIGURE 15.1 *Continued*

50. Miner I	939.281-010
51. Model Maker	693.361-010
52. Mold Maker Die Casting & Plastic Molding	601.280-030
53. Office-Machine Servicer	633.281-018
54. Offset-Press Operator I	651.482-010
55. Ornamental-Ironworker	809.381-022
56. Painter	840.381-010
57. Patternmaker, All-Around	693-280-560
58. Patternmaker, Wood	661.281-022
59. Pipefitter	862.381-018
60. Plumber	862.381-030
61. Powerhouse Mechanic	631.261-014
62. Precision Lens Grinder	716.382-018
63. Programmer, Business	020-162-014
64. Programmer, Engineering and Scientific	020.167-022
65. Refrigeration Mechanic	637.261-026
66. Sheet-Metal Worker	804.281-010
67. Shipfitter	806-381-046
68. Shoemaker, Custom	788.381-014
69. Stationary Engineer	950.382-026
70. Structural-Steel Worker	801.361-014
71. Television and Radio Repairer	720.281-018
72. Tool Maker	601.281-042
73. Tool-and-Die Maker	601.280-046
74. Water Treatment-Plant Operator	954.382-014
75. Welder, Combination	819.384-010
76. Welding-Machine Operator, Arc	810.382-010

Source: USDOL. (1987). *The National Apprenticeship Program* (pp. 5–9). Washington, DC: Author.

Military Training

In this section, we consider the opportunities for occupational training within the military services. Although the military includes a number of specialized occupations that actually exist only within the military—infantryman is a prime example—there are many more military occupations that have civilian counterparts to which military training and experience are directly transferable. Of the approximately 3,500 occupational specialties in the military services, 2,600 have civilian equivalents. Those that do not have civilian counterparts are primarily combat specialties. We consider programs for enlisted personnel in this section.

We exclude from our discussion in this section two military programs that may be important for some individuals. One of these is college-level training, either in one of the service academies, where a 4-year program leads to both a commission and a degree, or in a civilian college or university, where a 4-year ROTC (Reserve Officer Training Corps) program can produce the same results. The second is a matched savings program in which enlisted personnel can designate pay set-asides that are supplemented by additional two-for-one grants from the military to pay for college education after completing the military enlistment.

Baxter (1983) describes the various programs available to enlisted personnel in all branches. Enlistment periods can be as brief as 2 years in the Army, 3 years in the Navy, and 4 years in all other branches. Six years is the maximum commitment in all branches except the Coast Guard, where the ceiling is 4 years. Pay and allowances are uniform through the branches. High school graduation is preferred for all recruits and is required for all women, for all Coast Guard recruits, and for some training programs. Some high school seniors who want to acquire specialized occupational training in a specific occupation can assure themselves of this by participating in the delayed-entry program, in which they enlist for a specific training program with reporting to active duty delayed until high school graduation is completed.

Typically, new enlistees complete a basic training program that ranges from 6 to 10 weeks and consists of rigorous physical training along with classroom study and field work on weapons, military law, drill, and so on. After completing basic training, the person enters the training program for the selected occupation. This is usually a classroom-based program, but it may combine classwork with field experience or may even be primarily practical training. Figure 15.2 lists the occupations for which apprenticeships are available in the military services.

In addition to job-oriented training, the military services provide several other educational advantages. These include tuition assistance (up to 90 percent) for off-duty study at accredited schools, payment of fees for tests that establish college credit such as CLEP or SAT, independent study courses, and similar programs.

Information is easily obtained from recruiting offices that exist throughout the country. There are also toll-free telephone numbers that can be used to obtain information. *Profile* is a high-school-oriented magazine-format publication issued six times each year to provide information about the military services; it is available free to all senior high schools, colleges, or universities requesting it.

POSTSECONDARY NONDEGREE SCHOOLS

Career education advocates envision education as a lifelong process with the individual moving back and forth from classroom to work to classroom to work again, and even combining the two at times. Certainly most astute viewers of the U.S. scene would argue that the old concept of *commencement* as the end of education and the beginning of life is gone forever. The increasing complexity of life in our society, especially the impact of technological developments, requires every worker to keep abreast of change in some way. Furthermore, the changes are broader and require more than just routine updating—new jobs appear, old fields melt away or are combined

FIGURE 15.2 *Apprenticeable Occupations in the Military Services*

Apprenticeships in the following occupations are offered in the military. All are available in the Army unless otherwise indicated.

Air-Traffic communication technician (Marine Corps only)

Air-Traffic control radar technician (Marine Corps only)

Air-Traffic navigational aids technician (Marine Corps only)

Aircraft electrical mechanic

Aircraft engine mechanic (turbine)

Aircraft mechanic, armament

Airplane mechanic

Artillery repairer

Automatic equipment technician

Automobile body repairer and painter

Automobile mechanic (Marine Corps only)

Automotive electrical systems repairer

Baker (Marine Corps only)

Cable splicer

Camera repairer (Navy only)

Carpenter (Marine Corps only)

Central office telephone installer and repairer (Marine Corps only)

Construction equipment mechanic (Marine Corps only)

Cook (Marine Corps and Navy)

Drafter (architectural)

Electrical instrument repairer

Electrical mechanic (aircraft)

Electrical repairer (Marine Corps also)

Electrician (Marine Corps and Navy)

Electrician, radio

Electro-mechanical technician

Electronic mechanic (Marine Corps also)

Electronic mechanic (radar)

Electronic technician

Electronic technician (communications)

Electronic technician (radar)

Electronic technician (radio/TV)

Electronic warfare intercept systems repairer

Field engineer (microwave)

Fire control instrument repairer

Fire control system repairer

Firefighter

Fuel systems repairer

Grading and paving equipment operator

Heavy-duty equipment mechanic

Heavy-duty repairer (construction equipment)

Helicopter mechanic

Hydraulic equipment mechanic

Illustrator

Industrial electrician/repairer

Industrial welder

Instrument repairer (electronic)

Laboratory technician (petroleum)

Land surveyor (Marine Corps only)

Line installer/repairer

Lithographer (offset press operator)

Lithographer platemaker (Navy only)

Machinist (Navy also)

Maintenance mechanic (Navy only)

Maintenance mechanic, hydraulic equipment (aircraft)

Marine heavy-duty mechanic (heavy-duty mechanic—diesel)

Marine hull repairer, ironworker (boatbuilder—steel)

Meteorologist (Navy only)

Molder (Navy only)

Office machine servicer (Navy also)

Off-set press operator (Marine Corps only)

Ordnance artificer

Photograph interpreter

Photographer, motion picture

Photographer, still (Navy also)

Photographic equipment maintenance technician

Plant equipment operator

Plumber (Marine Corps only)

Plumber, pipefitter

Powerhouse electrician/repairer

Production coordinator (radio/TV broadcasting)

Pumper-gauger (petro-chemical)

Radio communications technician

(continued)

FIGURE 15.2   *Continued*

Radio mechanic (Marine Corps also)	Rigger	Stationary engineer (Navy only)	Truck mechanic
Radio operator	Sewing machine repairer	Surveyor (artillery)	Universal equipment operator (construction equipment)
Radio/Television repairer	Sheet metal worker (aircraft)	Surveyor, engineering	
Refrigeration/air-conditioning repairer/servicer	Small weapons repairer	Telegraphic-teletypewriter operator	Welder, combination (Marine Corps only)
Refrigeration mechanic (Marine Corps only)	Station installer/repairer (wire systems)	Television cable installer	

with others. Workers who need education to qualify originally for employment also must continue education to maintain their qualification, to master new procedures or developments, and to move to new fields that offer greater opportunity.

The greatest change in U.S. education since the end of World War II has been the expansion of postsecondary schools offering programs shorter than the traditional baccalaureate degree. The expansion has occurred in both the trade/vocational/technical schools and community/junior colleges. We consider both groups.

Trade, Vocational, and Technical Schools

One byproduct of the increased emphasis on career education and alternative educational programs has been the focus of greater attention on vocational preparation. During periods of economic downturn, high unemployment rates, and general uncertainty, there is a frequent upsurge in vocational school enrollment. Some of this is a search for security or a grasping for any help that might ensure employment or even an opportunity for employment.

A technical society, growing constantly more complex, underscores a continuing need for expanded opportunities for such preparation. The increasing emphasis on more varied forms of postsecondary education and the continuing technological thrust of our society undoubtedly will encourage many youth and adults to seek specialized education of one sort or another, often in vocational and technical schools, either public or private.

In many states, the expansion of the community college program or the establishment of publicly supported technical schools has met the major need in specialized education. Such expansion has not been uniform across the nation, however. Some states have established public area vocational schools; other states have established programs of postsecondary public specialized education through contractual arrangements with local secondary schools, universities, or other agencies equipped to offer vocational training to groups of students. Part of the impetus producing these rapid changes has come from the Vocational Education Amendments enacted by Congress, which broadened and redefined vocational education.

We are concerned here with schools whose programs generally are shorter than those offered by community colleges. Obviously, there is considerable overlap, since one type of program offered by 2-year schools is the short-course program to meet local needs. Some schools within the group are publicly supported by local, regional, or state tax units. Most, however, are private, proprietary schools; the extent of this aspect of education is often surprising. Wilms (1975) points out that there are more than 10,000 such schools in the United States, enrolling more than 3,000,000 students annually and producing gross annual revenues beyond $2.5 billion.

Obtaining accurate, usable information about a vocational school is often much more difficult than finding similar information about a degree-granting institution, for several reasons. Teachers and counselors, having been professionally prepared in colleges and universities, are more aware of the baccalaureate schools. Intercollegiate athletics and other activities publicize the colleges and universities locally, regionally, and nationally. The prestigious or high-status occupations in society mostly require a college education and focus public attention on schools providing such an education. In addition, vocational schools usually offer shorter training programs in less conspicuous quarters, have often been in existence for shorter periods, and rarely attract public attention.

Private proprietary vocational schools, like any other type of business, can include establishments that do their best to deliver a high-quality product for the lowest possible price, shoddy merchandise at exorbitant prices, or something between these two extremes. Belitsky (1970) suggests that private vocational schools provide an excellent opportunity for motivating and preparing unemployed older workers who do not expect to be able to return to their former occupations. Ressing (1974), on the other hand, emphasizes the importance of care and caution in dealing with private vocational schools. He urges prospective students, before enrolling for training in such an institution, to check first with potential employers by asking such questions as these:

1. Would you hire graduates of this school?
2. How many did you hire last year?
3. Were they hired because of their training?
4. Did the training make a difference in their starting salary?

Of the approximately 10,000 private proprietary vocational schools in the United States, Wilms states that about one third are cosmetology schools, one third are trade and technical schools, and one third are business schools and correspondence schools. Although the correspondence schools make up less than one tenth of the total group, they enroll two thirds of the students and generate more than one half of the total income.

Wilms (1975) has reported a research study that bears significantly on the status of private vocational schools. Funded by the National Institute of Education, his study sampled 4,800 students and graduates of 50 public and proprietary schools in San Francisco, Chicago, Boston, and Miami in six occupations—accounting, programming, electronic technician training, dental assisting, secretarial, and cosmetology. He reports that both groups of schools tend to serve the least advantaged of the students in postsecondary education; yet even so, the proprietary students were "the least advantaged of the least advantaged," more likely to be high school dropouts or products of general or vocational curricula, more likely to be from an ethnic minority group, and having lower verbal skills than public school counterparts. He explains the paradox of the least advantaged students paying high fees for education that is almost free in the public schools by pointing to the single-purpose nature of the private school, which has a shorter, more intensive program, with more flexible starting dates, and which is more actively advertised.

Wilms's findings included the following:

1. Little or no difference was found in the occupational success of public and proprietary graduates.
2. Only 2 out of 10 graduates from both groups who trained for professional or technical-level jobs ever got them. Most became clerks or took low-paying unrelated jobs.
3. Almost 8 out of 10 graduates in both types of schools who prepared for lower level clerical or service jobs got them, but except for secretaries barely earned the federal minimum wage.
4. Neither type of school fully compensated for less-advantaged students' backgrounds.
5. Proprietary graduates were generally less satisfied with their training than their public school counterparts and had paid 20 times more for it.

Wilms recommends that federal and state governments should be more actively engaged in protecting consumers of vocational programs in both public and proprietary schools by doing the following:

1. Ensuring that potential students have access to reliable information on the school's education program
2. Developing standards for vocational program effectiveness
3. Ensuring that all schools adhere to truth-in-advertising requirements
4. Auditing information given to prospective students to ensure accuracy
5. Ensuring that graduates of occupational programs receive equal pay for equal work

6. Encouraging experimentation on ways to use institutional resources for postsecondary occupational training
7. Encouraging both kinds of schools to evaluate objectives of programs and how they are being met

The need for current, reliable, and useful information about vocational schools is emphasized in several of the recommendations, clearly underscoring the greater difficulty in obtaining it. Publications similar to the catalog or bulletin of the college or community college are unusual rather than customary. Information is often in the form of brochures, briefs, flyers, or other sketchy statements. In vocational schools, new programs are established and old programs disappear more rapidly than in traditional 2-year and 4-year institutions, which, of course, affects routine publication of informational materials. The counselor who needs current information about vocational schools may find it helpful to check with the state office of education about opportunities with her state. Now that almost every state career information delivery system incorporates current data about education opportunities within the state, this resource can be very helpful to the person interested in trade or technical schools. Directories of national information about these schools are listed in Chapter 8.

Community Colleges and Junior Colleges

Junior colleges have existed in this country for many years. Some states—California, for example—have included junior colleges as an integral part of the statewide education program for over 50 years. Of more recent origin is the community college now found in most states. The two institutions are increasingly serving the same purposes and are therefore largely synonymous.

The junior college originally was developed essentially as a downward thrust of the college or university. Often established in populated areas not conveniently close to baccalaureate institutions, the junior college provided a means of delivering the first 2 years of several degree programs to students who, for varying reasons, could not attend a residential college or university. Since the curriculum consisted largely of introductory, or at least lower level, college courses, it needed neither elaborate facilities nor senior faculty members. Costs were often considerably less than those charged at 4-year campuses. The underlying idea was that the increased accessibility and the lesser costs would permit greater numbers of high school graduates to undertake baccalaureate programs, which could then be completed by transfer.

For 20 years or more after World War II, the expanded interest in college programs added further pressure for the development of new postsecondary opportunities for education. Changing interests, vocational goals, and lifestyles as well as increased mobility, new teaching procedures, and other factors led to the creation of an institution somewhat different from the junior college. The junior college function of bringing the college or university to "Main Street" was usually incorporated in the structure, but ordinarily as only one part of a broader program serving a much wider segment of the community population. Thus the community college often is considered to be an upward thrust of the secondary school, incorporating extensive offerings not necessarily leading to the traditional baccalaureate degree. Instead, many community college programs are designed to be terminal in nature, sometimes vocationally oriented, but also based on local needs and interests. Many junior colleges have moved to meet more effectively a wider range of local needs; hence the two titles are now often used almost interchangeably, and one would be hard pressed to establish clear-cut differential criteria. Probably they are now more commonly known as community colleges or as 2-year colleges.

Whether called community college or junior college, most of the public institutions, as well as most of the independent schools, provide a four-part program that includes the following:

1. The traditional college-related program for students who plan to transfer to a 4-year institution to complete a baccalaureate degree
2. A technical-terminal program to prepare students to enter employment on completion of the 2-year, or shorter, curriculum
3. Short courses of various sorts needed locally for retraining or further education
4. An adult education program of either formal or informal courses

Church-supported schools normally include the first two types of programs, but less often the latter two. A few of the private schools offer only a 2-year liberal arts program that provides for transfer to another institution.

Among the four types of programs, the greatest expansion has been in the technical-terminal area. This growth of the occupationally oriented part of the curriculum will increase the significance of the institution as a part of the educational plans for students who are not interested in the formal 4-year degree programs of the traditional baccalaureate institution. Its significance in the educational structure will be further increased as the concepts of career education are more widely adopted. It is entirely logical that this school can be expected to become the local skills center that will provide basic employment competencies through training and/or retraining programs. In some geographic areas, it will assume the role of the area vocational school. The place of the 2-year school in U.S. education is now firmly established; one should not expect, however, that these schools will assume a uniform organization, curriculum, or clientele. One of their greatest advantages may well be the flexibility that permits them to respond to local needs and interests.

The 2-year transfer programs and those technical-terminal programs that extend over two academic years often provide for the granting of an Associate in Arts degree on satisfactory completion. Programs that ordinarily are completed in less than this amount of time recognize successful completion with a certificate or other credential.

As with baccalaureate institutions, variation in admission requirement is common. Schools offering only college-related programs may establish entrance requirements parallel to those used by the schools to which their graduates transfer. Technical-terminal programs are more likely to have skill-based or experience-based requirements and are unlikely to specify particular academic records as prerequisites for admission. Terminal programs and adult education programs often operate on a totally open admission plan within the community served by the school. As a generalization, admission requirements usually are less stringent in the 2-year schools than in the 4-year schools, in keeping with the broader education function of the 2-year school.

Some students will have a special interest in certain 2-year schools with college-related programs for many different reasons—church affiliation, family ties, special programs available, geographic location, or other reasons. In these situations, the student may need the same kind of assistance in planning the other college-bound students require. Often, however, the choice is based on local accessibility or a similar factor, and obtaining the information needed to aid the student may be easy.

Responsibility for accreditation of 2-year schools rests primarily with state and regional agencies. Originally, accreditation was focused on the state department of education, the state university, or an organization of colleges within the state. In recent years, there has been a trend toward establishing regional accreditation, and most schools are moving toward such recognition if it has not already been acquired.

Financial aid at institutions that basically emphasize college-related programs is usually structured in a fashion similar to that at 4-year schools. Schools that emphasize other programs often have different plans for financial aid of students. Since students who attend 2-year schools often reside at home, one of the biggest expenses in college attendance is drastically reduced. Furthermore, because many schools are tax supported, tuition and fees are frequently modest. Some programs that lead to specific employment opportunities may be further subsidized with private, local, state, or federal funds.

The most reliable source of information about any school is the school itself. Direct contact with appropriate officials is most likely to result in up-to-date, correct answers to questions. The next best source of information is the bulletin or other publications of the school—also subject to the inevitable time lag and the danger that change has occurred. Because data in most state Career Information Delivery System (CIDS) are revised at least annually, these materials may be more current than institutional publications. Typical directories of information about 2-year schools that should be available in the career resource center are listed in Chapter 8.

COLLEGES AND UNIVERSITIES

From the early colonial beginnings of this country, there has been a continuing and increasing emphasis on the acquisition of as much formal education as possible. The history of our national development is studded with events that demonstrate this trend—including the founding of colleges almost with the beginning of the colonies, the "old deluder Satan" act of the Massachusetts Bay Colony establishing compulsory schooling in the towns, the Northwest Ordinance providing land for support of local schools, the Morrill Act establishing land grant colleges and universities, the Kalamazoo decision endorsing tax support for secondary schools, and the GI Bill, which has sent thousands of veterans on to higher education—to name only a few.

As our society has increased in complexity and become more dependent on technological development, the need for education beyond minimal levels also has become more apparent. Although the legal school-leaving age is still set at 15 or 16 in most states, the majority of youngsters now stay in school beyond this point. The proportion completing high school has increased steadily, doubling almost every decade in recent years. Not too long ago, the high school graduate was considered to have a very real educational advantage on entering the labor market, and many employers gave priority in hiring to such individuals. More recently, high school graduation is considered as minimal educational preparation, and the person who wishes to be in a position of advantage in the labor market now thinks of further preparation beyond high school.

We can expect the school-leaving age to continue to rise in all industrialized societies, since the increasing complexity of living makes more education imperative for the typical citizen. Further, the ideal of completing one's education with graduation from high school or college is now obsolete. The impact of technology on the world of work will emphasize a pattern in which individuals regularly return to school for either new or refresher training. For example, the rapid development of new scientific knowledge and its application is sometimes reputed to make an engineer's preparation obsolete within 5 years of graduation.

In times of drastic social and scientific change, the traditional degree-granting higher educational institutions find themselves between a rock and a hard place. The need for improved facilities, better programs, and higher quality faculty comes at the same time as leveling or declining enrollments, increasing costs, decreasing funding, and greater competition from other educational options. Eurich (1985) reports that educational programs operated by various U.S. corporations and associations for their employees are now educating almost as many people (8 million) as the number of students enrolled in 4-year colleges and universities in the United States. Further, the budget for these special educational programs amounts to about $40 billion per year, about two thirds of the total budgets for colleges for colleges and universities. Increasing numbers of these corporate programs are gaining accredited status from the same regional accrediting associations that evaluate the colleges and universities. Eurich reports that in 1984 there were 18 business-operated colleges that granted degrees, and plans were under way by eight other companies to have an additional 19 degree programs operational by 1988. Some programs are as brief as 1 to 7 weeks in length and are highly job oriented; others parallel traditional baccalaureate programs, with a special company-aimed emphasis; and several are graduate programs.

In addition to competition from the new corporate educational programs, 4-year schools also risk losing students to the vocational and technical schools and the 2-year schools that we have considered in previous sections. We focus the remainder of our discussion on the degree-granting colleges and universities.

Kinds of Programs

The variety of degree programs in colleges and universities has developed in many ways from numberless roots. Some of these simply developed; others originated from legislated prescriptions, pressures of professional groups, public insistence, or national emergencies. Higher education in the United States has followed a pattern permitting more flexibility and more breadth than is ordinarily encountered in the rest of the world. One result has obviously been greater variations in the nature and quality of educational programs and in the size and organization of the institutions. Because of this dispersion, any general statement is subject to exceptions in one or many schools.

In general, programs leading to a bachelor's degree are most frequently about 4 years in length. Recent years have shown movement in both directions from that base point, with programs in some technical areas, such as pharmacy or engineering, tending to climb upward toward 5 years. At the same time there has been increasing pressure to recognize the improved quality of secondary education in the United States by reducing the bachelor's degree to a 3-year program. Advocates of this proposal were heartened when the Carnegie Commission endorsed this plan.

Unlike most of the rest of the world, U.S. colleges and universities view college study as a cumulative process, with students earning credits, course by course, on a time-period base that may be a quarter, semester, term, or trimester. Degrees are most frequently granted when the requisite number of credits have been attained with a satisfactory level of quality. Most institutions use a letter-grading system; some use a numerical system; and a very few, usually small colleges, use a narrative report system. The pass/fail grading system has been adopted by very few schools on an across-the-board basis; many schools, however, use it as an adjunct or supplementary plan, permitting students to take a restricted number of hours, ordinarily outside of their basic program, with pass/fail grades.

Programs may range from the broad, liberal arts option originally developed to produce the "educated man" in early American colleges to the narrow, intense, professional preparation requiring almost all of the student's allotted schedule. Most matriculations fall between these extremes and provide that part of the student's time be devoted to broad, foundational, or enriching study and part of the work be focused on a subject or area major or professional specialty. Except in those programs controlled by law, licensure or certification requirements, or professional organizations, the degree of variation is probably greater than most people realize. The plan used at one's own alma mater is not necessarily the universally accepted one.

Admissions Requirements

The restriction of admission by a school, either because of its desire to maintain a student body size that it considers desirable or because it wishes to limit its faculty or facilities, at once creates a competition among applicants. If the school has a generally favorable reputation, the competitiveness is accentuated and the school's prestige is enhanced. Unfortunately, many prospective applicants and their parents assume that limitation of enrollment automatically reflects a high-quality educational program. Often one can find academic opportunities of equality at nearby public or private institutions that have not yet enforced limited admission policies.

Again, generalizations are risky. Different institutions are moving in opposite directions on admission policies for various reasons. Some schools are establishing enrollment ceilings as a means of maintaining what the school views as an ideal size for its purpose, faculty, and facilities. Often, when such ceilings are set, admission requirements may become more specific to narrow the range of clientele served by the school. Other institutions have moved in exactly the opposite direction, with some schools now adhering to a policy of open admissions, under which anyone with a high school diploma or other basic qualification may be permitted to enroll. Many institutions, even before the recent emphasis on career education, had established means by which individuals whose schooling had been interrupted at high school graduation or earlier could qualify for admission on the basis of signficiant employment, examination results, or other criteria.

For many years, most institutions have asked applicants to support the usual application data and transcript of high school or preparatory school record with admissions test data. Colleges and universities require test scores for many reasons. Most large schools serve students from wide geographic regions, often nationwide or worldwide. In such a broad area, considerable difference in academic standards of high schools can be anticipated; as a result, high school grades are difficult to compare, and the college or university may elect to require test scores in order to provide some uniform basis on which applicants' potential ability can be compared. Other schools may seek to serve a particular type of student. For example, they may choose to focus on the development of writing skill; such schools would be anxious to identify those students with high verbal skill. Some schools, in which enrollment restrictions limit the number of students, may wish to give priority only to the most able students; such a school may feel that a uniform testing program will provide the information it needs to select the students it wishes to admit. On the other hand, a school may wish to diversify the group it admits and may use test results as an additional means of ensuring the variety it wishes to include in its student body. Many schools base their financial aid programs partly on consideration of ability and therefore require scholarship applicants to submit test scores for this purpose.

Most degree-granting schools now require applicants to submit, with their application materials, scores obtained on either the College Entrance Examination Board (CEEB), Scholastic Aptitude Test (SAT), or the American College Test Program (ACT). Most schools specify the test they require, but some institutions will accept either. Both tests are now so widely used and are so generally available in U.S. high schools that they require no special discussion here. Some colleges and universities using SAT scores also may ask applicants to submit scores on achievement tests in subject areas relevant to the field the applicant plans to study.

The College Level Examination Program is one method used by many colleges and universities to determine if an applicant qualifies for advance standing and college credit. The program consists of a group of achievement tests more difficult than those we have just discussed. The basic assumption of this program is that there are many ways in which an applicant might acquire the knowledge or competencies taught in beginning-level college courses. Many high schools now provide advanced study for highly motivated students; some students undertake self-teaching projects because of interest or other reasons; tutorial assistance may push other students beyond the levels usually accomplished in high school; and some students may acquire these skills through travel, employment, or other out-of-school activity. Assuming that many colleges would willingly recognize such claims for advance standing as legitimate if properly documented, the CEEB established the CLEP plan. This program enables the student to move ahead to an appropriate level in those areas in which advanced skill has been developed and to obtain credit for the bypassed courses. CEEB reports at least two separate studies demonstrating that students given CLEP advanced standing do as well or better in advanced courses as students who have completed the usual prerequisite courses.

The Financial Aid Form is another program operated by the CEEB. This service is designed to simplify the process of providing family financial information to colleges and universities by applicants for financial aid. It provides a Parents' Confidential Statement that the applicant's parent completes, describing the family's financial situation. The report is analyzed, and a copy of the form and the analysis are forwarded to the schools specified by the applicant. A comparable form, the Family Financial Statement (FFS), is provided by the American College Testing Program. These forms are used by scholarship program sponsors as well as by financial aid officers in colleges and universities.

Factors to Consider in Choosing a College

School administrators, teachers, and counselors can anticipate a greater demand for accurate, usable information about college preparation. Inevitably, concerned students and parents will expert greater effort by the secondary school to assist its graduates in preparing for college and in gaining admission. This will likely require planning over a longer period as well as developing more extensive information about available institutions and greater staff involvement in the transitional process.

Since institutions of higher education come in an almost limitless variety of size, kind, and purpose, one can find almost as many individual differences here as among people. One can properly conclude, then, that specific schools will better fit the particular needs of certain students than will others. If an appropriate matching process is to occur, accurate information is imperative.

Many high school students assume that there is one perfect college that exactly fits their needs and personality. Such a romantic notion is comparable to similar ideas on finding the one perfect mate that often are prevalent in the same age group. It is more likely that for most individuals there are several colleges or universities that will suit them equally well.

Even students who are motivated to make careful educational plans may feel frustrated when confronted with an array of educational institutions numbering in the thousands and varying in many important characteristics that can have tremendous effects on their future. Just as the occupational world is too vast to consider job by job, so too is the range of colleges and universities. Some methodical approach is necessary to help the student understand the educational world. Since it can be assumed that it is impossible to study every school, some procedure must be applied that will help identify certain institutions for careful consideration.

Although the selection of a few schools for final consideration by a specific student depends on a great many factors, several general characteristics can be used in reducing the number of schools to be studied in detail. Among these are the following:

1. *Type and compatibility of program:* Does the college offer the major that the student intends to study in a package that matches the student's plans and expectations?
2. *School environment:* The geographic location and the size of the community should meet the student's needs.
3. *Admission requirements:* Can the student meet the institution's demands, and do they reflect the level of rigor desired?
4. *Size:* Many students have preferences for a general category such as small, medium, or large.
5. *Type of school:* A school may be tax supported, church supported, or independent; each type may offer particular advantages desired by the student.
6. *Type of student body:* Several factors need to be considered here, such as gender, geographic range, cultural homogeneity, and degree of competitiveness.
7. *Expenses and financial aid:* Costs vary extensively, with public schools usually less expensive than private institutions; however, financial aid may help balance some of these differences.

8. *Student activities, social, and cultural life:* If desired by the student, are these other aspects of college life available?
9. *Campus facilities:* Are the facilities adequate to provide the program and educational experience desired?

The student can consider many factors in the preliminary selection process. In some cases, such items as the availability of military training, extent of campus housing, fraternities and sororities, placement facilities, and success of graduates may be of greater importance than the items enumerated here. Certainly there are particular items that may be of relatively less importance to a specific student. Probably one of the first factors for a student to decide is the type of education desired; then she should decide which of these items, or others, apply to the situation. These selected factors then can be used in completing the preliminary screening.

Accreditation

Much of our time is spent in a world in which regulation and control are very obvious—speed limits, building permits, Social Security numbers, consumer protection agencies. We sometimes forget the ancient warning, *caveat emptor.* The commitment to a college education, in terms of time, effort, and money, is so great that both student and parent need to be assured that value will be received. Accreditation is one means by which the potential purchaser of a college education can have some assurance about the quality of the purchase.

Accreditation of colleges and universities is usually accomplished by two different kinds of organizations. In some academic areas, programs are evaluated by established groups of agencies formed by the appropriate professional organization into which graduates of the program ultimately will be received. The second type of accrediting agency is an association of educational institutions organized on a geographic basis, either national or regional. The National Council for the Accreditation of Teacher Education (NCATE) is an example of the first type, and the North Central Association of Colleges and Secondary Schools is an example of the second type.

Many prospective students or their parents raise questions about the ranking of a college or university or of a specific department or section within the school. It is often difficult to convince them that such rankings are not made by the accrediting agencies or other national groups. Generally, the accrediting groups simply list schools that meet certain levels of standards. Occasionally, this listing is arranged into appropriate groupings related to the scope of the program, the areas included, or similar factors, but a numerical listing in order of quality is seldom made. The variety of programs among schools, even in highly specialized subject areas, precludes the possibility of such ranking in terms of quality.

Public conviction that such rankings exist stems primarily from two sources. Many loyal alumni remember their alma mater as "the best in the country," "tops in such and such," or "highly recognized." Such evaluation is, of course, subjective and not based on comparative criteria. Second, many popular magazines, newspapers, and Sunday supplements run feature stories based on the judgment of a single person or a panel of so-called experts who often purport to evaluate institutions in various subject fields or by type of school. Again, the published judgments may be made by highly knowledgeable individuals who have a wide acquaintance with many schools; nevertheless, these reports are subjective in nature and are not based on detailed study of the type and scope that would justify a precise ranking.

Accreditation must be understood by the prospective student. The accreditation process is usually quite involved, relatively expensive, and highly demanding of faculty time to prepare materials, reports, and other studies for review. If a school has been accredited by a recognized agency, this indicated that the school has demonstrated to the satisfaction of that agency that it meets the minimum standards established by the agency. If the school is not accredited, one cannot automatically assume that it falls short of the minimum standards. There are sometimes valid reasons that a school with high quality and standards is not accredited, including the desire of the school to maintain a position of independence, the newness of the program, or a reluctance to expend the time and funds required to establish accreditation. An applicant should ascertain that nonaccreditation is for some reason other than quality of program.

Financial Aid

As the costs of higher education increase steadily, many students and their families need accurate information about the sources and extent of financial assistance available. Frequent change in federally funded and state-funded programs not only affects specific programs included in federal and state support but impinges on all other aid programs as well. Consequently, the basic data needed for planning are seldom available far enough in advance to permit broad publication of the information. Even the institution's financial aid office often encounters difficulty in answering questions about next year's aid.

There are a number of directories about financial aid and scholarships available that can be placed in career resource centers or in counselor's offices. Students should be alerted to the changes that occur with respect to financial help and the need for direct contact, at an early date, with the financial aid office in the institution they are planning to attend. Directories provide useful *general* and *supplementary* information. Examples include the following:

1. *Meeting College Costs: A Guide for Students and Parents*, The College Scholarship Service, College Board Publications Orders, Box 2815, Princeton, NJ 08541.
2. *Scholarships, Fellowships, Grants and Loans*, Macmillan Information, Division of Macmillan, 866 3rd Avenue, New York, NY 10022.

3. *Scholarships, Fellowships and Loans* (6 volumes), Bellman Publishing Co., PO Box 164, Arlington, MA 02174.
4. *Student Aid Annual,* Chronicle Guidance Publications, Inc., Moravia, NY 13118.

Sources of Information

Historically, one of the major tasks of U.S. high schools has been preparing students to continue their education at a degree-granting institution. Because of that historical tradition, one might expect the high schools to have information about colleges and universities in sufficient depth, breadth, and currency to meet the needs of most students. Unfortunately, this is only partly true. The importance of this kind of information was discussed in Chapter 8, along with the listing of commonly used directories that provide brief sketches and basic information on many schools. As mentioned previously, most state CIDS have at least statewide educational information, and many systems include national educational information. If these files are updated frequently (many are revised on an annual basis), the computerized information may well be more current than shelved copies of college catalogs and far more current than the directories.

High school students and adults seeking information about colleges and universities often need to be reminded that even a system with annual revision can still be nearly a year out of date. The basic source for accurate information must remain the college itself.

SUMMARY

Students and adults have a variety of educational options open to them once they make a career choice. Choosing from among these options may in fact be as bewildering as choosing a career itself. The ultimate option chosen will depend on a variety of factors including the career chosen, the wishes of the student, the ability of the student to finance his occupation, the academic record of the individual, and so forth. A carelessly chosen preparation program can lead to personal dissatisfaction and even to a change in career plan. Thus it becomes incumbent on career counselors to be fully abreast of educational information and to develop the skills necessary to facilitate educational exploration, because career and educational choices are inextricably linked.

REFERENCES

Apprenticeship. (1983). *Occupational Outlook Quarterly, 27, 4,* 18–30.
BAT. (1990). *National apprenticeship statistics ranked by DOT (mimographed).* Washington, DC: USDGL Bureau of Apprenticeship and Training.

BAT. (1991). *Registered apprentices on workload of bureau of apprenticeship and training (BAT) and state apprenticeship councils (SAC) mimeographed.* Washington, DC: USDOL.

Baxter, N. (1983). Job training for enlisted personnel in the military. *Occupational Outlook Quarterly, 27,* (3), 2–13.

Beale, A. V., & Jacobs, B. C. (1982). Hand in hand or a fist in the teeth: Counselors and vocational educators working together. *Vocational Guidance Quarterly, 31,* 21–27.

Belitsky, A. H. (1970). Private vocational schools: An underutilized training resource. *Vocational Guidance Quarterly, 19,* 127–130.

Eurich, N. (1985). *Corporate classrooms: The learning business.* New York: Carnegie Foundation.

Ressing, A. H. (1974). The uncertain promise of private vocational training. *Vocational Guidance Quarterly, 23,* 6–8.

USDOL. (1987). *National apprenticeship program.* Washington, DC: USDOL Employment and Training Administration.

Wilms, W. W. (1975). Protecting the vocational ed. consumer. *The Research Reporter, 9,* whole issue.

16

Job Placement, Outplacement, and the Job Search Process

In the wonderful world of make-believe, there is always a job for everyone who wants to work. Not only is there a job for everyone, but it is challenging, interesting, and rewarding. As we smile at this happy thought, we must ask ourselves why so many others are underemployed or dissatisfied with the jobs they have, and why some are gritting their teeth hoping they can keep the job they have. The easy answer is that in a society as complex and massive as ours, we will always have people who are looking for their first job or are between jobs as they leave one they do not like to search for one they think is better (frictional unemployment). Moreover, there are others who are caught in a temporary economic downswing in their industry, on temporary layoff of a few weeks or months (cyclical unemployment). Finally, there appear to be increasing numbers whose jobs have been eliminated by technological progress, industrial relocation outside the country, or similar causes (structural unemployment).

In Chapter 1, we discussed why people work and the role that work plays as individuals relate to society and to important other people in their lives. It was proposed that people without work often feel lost, unattached, sometimes disoriented, and worthless. Others report that their self-concept is damaged (Lopez, 1983) and they feel they have no dignity or place in everyday affairs. One also can see easily the economic loss to individuals and to society when an individual does not work. A day's work undone is lost forever; as a society we lose the goods or services the person might have produced, while the individual loses the rewards those goods or services would have provided.

Evidence substantiating the claim that we must develop more effective ways to help new entrants find work and to help displaced workers move to new jobs is rapidly accumulating. The increased amount of structural unemployment in the 1980s has underscored this need. Taber, Walsh, and Cooke

(1979) describe the impact on workers when a plant announced its plan to close. They found that workers did not have job-seeking skills, did not know what agencies could help them, did not recognize the scope of their problem, waited too long to seek assistance, and did not understand how to access existing community assistance services. Many services are available to assist displaced workers such as those described by Tabor et al. Some communities and companies have developed outplacement counseling programs in cooperation with state agencies, such as state employment security agencies and the Job Partnership Training Act (JTPA). However, Ferrin and Arbeiter (1975) point out that the problems faced by recent graduates and first-time workers are just as difficult. They identify several of the barriers that impede easy transition from education to work and suggest some mechanisms that might simplify the process.

Whether we focus our attention on the new entrant, the late entrant, the prospector for a better job, or the displaced worker, we can see certain basic problems involved in finding and obtaining a position. All career development specialists involved in helping relationships with individuals who are 16 or older will find that their clients are caught up in the job search process at least occasionally and probably frequently. In this chapter, we consider three main aspects of helping these individuals:

1. Job placement services
2. Helping groups with placement
3. Helping individuals execute a job search

JOB PLACEMENT SERVICES

A few individuals may have no contact with placement services at any time in their working life. Most, however, will use these services several different times. At least three types of placement services are generally available, and we consider all of them: public agencies, private agencies, and school-based services.

Public Employment Services

Every state has a state employment security agency (SESA). In some states it is called the Job Service; in others it is referred to as the Employment Service. It is a state-operated service that works within the general structure, regulations, and operating procedures established by the United States Employment Service (USES).

Public employment services in the United States have a history that spans over a century and a half. New York City organized a municipal service as early as 1834, and San Francisco established programs before the turn of the century. Ohio did so in 1890, Montana in 1895, New York in 1896, Nebraska in 1897, and Illinois and Missouri in 1899. The federal government entered the scene in 1907 with the formation of the United States Employment Service to help arriving immigrants find jobs across the country. During World War I, its task was changed to assist all unemployed people seeking work and to help employers find needed workers. After the war, many local offices were closed; and the agency was relatively inactive until the impact of the Great Depression in the 1930s resulted in reestablishment of a federal system of state offices. These state offices were nationalized during World War II and returned to state control in 1946.

Because each SESA is state operated, one finds some variation in structure and in operating procedure from state to state. Overall, however, there are far more similarities than differences, and most SESAs offer parallel services. Most states have established local offices in all metropolitan areas and conveniently located regional offices that serve less populated areas. The services usually provided include the following:

1. *Placement:* Applicants are registered, classified, selected, and referred to prospective employers. Orders for workers are received, and applicants' qualifications are matched with the employer's specifications so that referrals can be made.
2. *Counseling:* Applicants without previous work records or with inadequate experience are provided assistance through aptitude testing and counseling, so that appropriate classification and referral can be made.
3. *Service to veterans:* Each office is charged with providing special assistance to veterans seeking employment.
4. *Service to applicants with disabilities:* Each office is also responsible for providing placement assistance to people with disabilities.
5. *Collection of labor market information:* Changes and trends in the local employment situation are assessed regularly; pooling this information at the state and federal level increases the service available to those seeking work and provides a current picture of employment across the nation.
6. *Cooperation with community agencies:* The local office helps to keep the public informed, attracts applicants and possible employers, and maintains close contact with local employment conditions.

In addition to the foregoing, the SESA handles the registration and processing of unemployed workers who qualify for unemployment compensation payments. It also cooperates in the operation of the Job Bank, a computerized listing of hard-to-fill jobs across the nation. Further, in those states where the state Career Information Delivery System (CIDS) has incorporated statewide job vacancy information, it provides the basic input and monitors the recency of these data.

Because of the specific responsibilities assigned to the local public employment agency, it offers many services and advantages to the person attempting to obtain employment. Liaison with other local offices through the state provides useful information to workers on employment opportunities at both a statewide and nationwide level. The services of the local office are available without charge to applicants seeking work, who will be served by a professional staff concerned with matching applicants' abilities to employers' needs.

Besides providing direct service to the individual job seeker and the unemployed worker, the SESA is a prime source of information that can be used by counselors and those in charge of career resource centers. Because the SESA is the basic collecting unit for local labor market information, its staff is usually more knowledgeable about local job conditions and trends than any other agency. Since local data are pooled at the state level and, in turn, at the national level, the SESA has access to the latest available data on the employment situation at these broader levels as well. Most state offices issue regular labor market information reports as part of the occupational employment survey; and local, current data are available in frequently published newsletters and in radio and television reports in some cities. The career resource center should maintain a file of recent copies of both local- and state-level publications.

Private Employment Agencies

Probably every metropolitan area has several private employment agencies. A quick survey of the telephone directory's yellow pages will usually reveal more listings than most people would expect. Because they have many different purposes, it is difficult to provide a simple classification system. Some are regular profit-seeking businesses. Some serve the general public; others limit their clientele to a particular occupational group. Some work primarily for the job seeker; others serve the employer. Some list only regular, full-time positions; others handle only short-term, temporary jobs.

For-profit job placement organizations serve a role similar to the agent who represents a popular entertainer. The agency contracts with the job seekers to assist them in finding a satisfactory position with the understanding that a fee will be charged for the service if the person accepts a job. Some businesses contract with for-profit agencies to screen prospective employees and thereby reduce the load on the company's personnel office. When this arrangement exists, the employer often pays the fee charged by the private agency. As with any other group of businesses, the quality of service ranges widely. Lilley (1978) describes some of the problems that arise from involvement with unethical private placement agencies, and during the 1980s thousands of complaints were lodged against some of these agencies. However, it would be unfair to label all agencies as fraudulent. Fees may be on a sliding scale, with higher paying positions carrying a decidedly heavier fee. As a rough rule of thumb, most fees will approximate at least 1 month's pay, due in full the moment the individual accepts a position. The exact fee should be determined in advance.

Special-purpose placement agencies may restrict their clientele to a specific occupational or professional group. For example, some agencies serve only technical occupations at the professional or subprofessional level; others may handle only educational positions such as teachers, school administrators, and related jobs. Closely related to this type of placement agency is the union hiring hall, which serves only members of the organization, or the professional registry, like those found in some metropolitan areas for nurses who accept private cases.

A few placement agencies limit their activity to what they label as executive searches, or what others may call head hunting. These companies are employed by organizations to find a person for a specific position rather than the more customary reverse situation. The position to be filled is usually top-level management or some particularly sensitive position where those most qualified would be reluctant to be identified as candidates because of the impact that information would have on their present position. Fees are typically paid by the employing organization for these services.

Secondary and Postsecondary Placement Services

The most obvious time for individuals to need placement assistance is at the point when they complete their preparatory programs. Thus logically one would expect placement services to be an automatic adjunct of the educational system. We consider school involvement in terms of both secondary and postsecondary institutions.

Odell, Pritchard, and Sinick (1974) describe early relationships between state employment services and secondary schools. It has been an inconsistent and variable relationship, with both sides probably falling short of what might have been an unusual opportunity for close cooperation.

The school has several options available in organizing a placement service, ranging from transferring full responsibility to the local public employment security office to retaining total responsibility within the school itself. We consider each option briefly.

The major arguments for full use of the local public employment agency to meet the placement needs of the local school usually are as follows:

1. The state employment service, including the local office, is set up uniquely for placement services, with a trained staff, close contact with employers, and current and accurate local information on the labor market.
2. It is uneconomical to operate two parallel systems.
3. Development of a competing placement service within the school would arouse ill will among the public, who would oppose duplication.
4. The state employment service is where workers go to get a new job, so this facility might just as well be available in looking for a first job.

In spite of the foregoing points, a strong argument can be made in support of job placement services within the school. Advocates of this position usually argue as follows:

1. Our educational institutions are responsible for the adjustment of the individual. Changing from the classroom to the job is part of the adjustment of the individual.
2. Placement, to be best, should be made with consideration of the individual's previous experience and abilities. The educational institution is in the best position to know these.
3. If the school provides vocational education, it should logically include placement as part of the total process.

Of special importance in school-based placement activities is the opportunity to help students obtain part-time and vacation employment. Valuable experience, as well as a more realistic understanding of the relationship of worker to job, can be acquired by teenagers and young adults who engage in work after school hours, on weekends, or during vacations. These experiences can be helpful to students in their career planning. Often, part-time placements can be arranged that give students exploratory experiences that have a direct relationship to career fields. Even when this is not possible, the student can expect to profit in various ways from participation in work experience, such as becoming familiar with supervisory styles.

Some of the reasons that high school students and recent graduates encounter failure in obtaining positions include unsatisfactory appearance, attitude, and behavior; unrealistic wage demands; insufficient training; insistence on the job though unqualified; impatience and unwillingness to adapt to entry requirements; insistence on own concept of job duties; and ignorance of labor market facts. Many of these problems, prevalent in many young, inexperienced job seekers, can be reduced or even eliminated by an effective combination of counseling and placement. The recognition and eradication of possible problems is more likely to occur in the school setting, where the young person is better known and where time for counseling is available.

If the school assumes that the student needs special assistance as major changes are encountered in the educational experience, such as moving to junior high school and on to senior high school, it is certainly logical to expect that help will be needed in moving from school to job. The school can strongly contend that the student will learn most effectively if the change from school to job is correlated with experiences in the school that have been organized to prepare and assist in making the transfer. A school placement program would presumably provide this assistance. The discussion of the work experience program in an earlier chapter pointed out that a major advantage of the program was the availability of the coordinator as a liaison between school and employer, thus helping the student adjust to the demands of the work situation. A school placement officer can serve this function for students not enrolled in the school's work experience program.

Another argument for providing placement services within the school is the basic philosophic position that must be taken by each agency to perform its responsibility to society. The employment service has a primary responsibility for meeting the communities' needs for workers. The school, however, to meet its share of the responsibility, must give preeminence to the long-range development of the individual. It must consider the individual as a unique person with particular needs and goals, and its efforts should be to maximize the development of that person.

To some extent, the question of whether the school should be involved in placement services is an academic one, since inevitably the school is involved. In every school, staff members are contacted by employers seeking applicants for positions. Probably this happens most frequently in the vocational departments of the school, where commercial and shop teachers are asked to recommend possible candidates for existing vacancies. The basic question is whether the school wishes to continue an informal, unorganized placement service or whether it prefers to recognize a responsibility to all students who may seek work, regardless of the curriculum in which they are enrolled, and to organize a program to meet the needs of all students. Harris (1977) describes the program available on a statewide basis in Virginia schools. This program offers year-round service and helps students during the year after they leave school.

School districts that elect to provide placement services to their students have several options available. They can create a decentralized system, a centralized program, a combination of the two, or a cooperative program with the local SESA office.

The decentralized plan places responsibility at the lowest functional level. In a small school system involving only one high school, this probably would simply extend the informal placement efforts in which teachers or school departments already engage. In large school systems with more than one high school, placement would operate at the school level. The advantages are that students are in familiar surroundings, with staff members who probably already know them well, so little or no delay is involved in the referral process. The disadvantages of such a system are also obvious. The program serves a smaller group of students and may not be able to supply the best applicants; little time is available for developing employer contacts and conducting follow-up; there is duplication of effort and competition among the schools in the system; and employers are uncertain about which school staff member to contact or must make several calls to reach the proper person without a central clearinghouse.

In a centralized program, a single office is established that develops pertinent information about students desiring placement and employers who may send notification of job openings. The advantages of this approach are convenience and efficiency, with the likelihood of better staff, uniform policies, and better community relations. The disadvantages are that student records are not as readily available to placement, and the staff usually does not know the student personally.

Larger school systems may find it advantageous to develop some combination of the two basic systems, in order to capitalize on local situations or to meet particular needs. For example, a school system might establish a central office for employer contacts but use separate school offices for developing student records, or a central office might be used to coordinate the activities in the various schools.

A cooperative program involving both a school placement service and the local public employment service may provide the best opportunity to secure the advantages of each and to minimize the disadvantages. Several variations are possible in building such a service. The appointment by both agencies of liaison persons, who work together to accomplish the desired goals, is probably the first step. Both offices can focus on those parts of the work they can handle best, information can be shared as needed, and skills can be developed mutually. The likelihood of having a program that meets local needs seems greater when the two agencies effectively combine their efforts.

Odell et al. (1974) agree that a cooperative plan offers many mutual advantages to both school and employment service and also increases the provision of effective service. Odell suggests that schools could improve their lack of occupational information by drawing on the services of the local employment service office, which has much local information at hand. He further describes an arrangement in which an employment security counselor might be placed in a school assignment, either part time or full time, to assist both in placement and occupational information and in vocational guidance of students and to provide access to SESA operations such as the Job Bank. Pritchard emphasizes that placement programs need to be school based and community linked as well as to provide opportunity for follow-through, for helping the individual adjust to the job and develop in it.

Postsecondary schools are involved in placement, and many of them operate placement offices for their students and alumni. Typically, these offices operate as part of the services provided by the educational institution and charge either no fee or a very modest registration charge. Two types of placement offices can be seen on most university campuses.

Many university placement offices operate placement activities in a way that might be compared to a dating bureau, where the major objective is to facilitate the meeting of two people—the student and an employer's representative. In these situations the agency focuses its attention on inviting employer representatives to campus and establishing interviewing schedules so that as many students as time permits can have an opportunity to meet with that representative. Minimal student records are maintained, at most a resume, and more likely only a registration card. When they register, students may be asked to identify type of company or industry, geographic preference, or occupational goal. Then a notification system alerts students when representatives of companies that relate to their indicated preferences will be on campus, and a sign-up system provides an opportunity to register for an interview.

Other postsecondary placement offices may develop personal files for each student applicant, including a resume, personal statement about career plans, academic record, letters of recommendation, and similar supporting evidence. At the student's request, the file, or a copy of pertinent data, is made available to prospective employers.

Both types of postsecondary placement offices may offer workshops, training sessions, or other learning experiences to acquaint prospective users with current labor market information and develop techniques for improving personal placement possibilities, such as networking with other job hunters. Several of these programs were described in Chapter 7 and include using alumni (Heppner, 1981) and nontraditional role models (Plotsky & Goad, 1974, Self & Lopez, 1982).

OUTPLACEMENT SERVICES

Outplacement involves providing assistance to workers whose jobs have been terminated because of technological advances, business mergers, relocation of businesses outside this country, the need to increase competiveness by reducing costs, because an employee has been dismissed for poor performance, or for a number of other reasons. Outplacement services are most often provided to exempt employees (salaried; not reimbursed for overtime) but are also provided to nonexempt (salaried; reimbursed for overtime) and hourly workers. One study (Bohl, 1987) found that almost 55 percent of the companies sampled offered some form of outplacement service to their employees.

The source of assistance with outplacement can come from an external consulting firm such as Drake Beam Morin, The Redford Group, or Hickey & Associates or from within as an extension of the career development program. Outplacement firms typically charge a fee equal to 15 to 25 percent of the employee's salary and are therefore generally more expensive than internally located services (Bohl, 1987). However, Morin and York (1982) argue that externally located services have higher prestige and signal to employees that a serious effort is being made on their behalf. They also suggest that externally located services may be better able to gain the confidence of the employee who is to be outplaced, since they are not employees of the company that has terminated them.

While some companies offer internally located outplacement services and others contract with external outplacement firms, others offer what they term assistance for displaced workers which includes paid time off for conducting job searches, relocation opportunities with other units in the company, job fairs, job market data, liaisons with public employment agencies such as SESA, and opportunities to network with other managers to develop job opportunities. None of these activities meets the specific requirements of a comprehensive outplacement program.

Morin and York (1982) suggest that a comprehensive outplacement counseling service should be aimed at diffusing the employee's feelings of frustration, depression, and anger, establishing a contract with the employee to proceed with a job search, helping employees develop a job search plan and the skills to implement it, and following up with employees as they search for a job. Brammer and Humberger (1984) offer a similar outline, although they place more emphasis on assisting workers to engage in self-assessment strategies as prequisites to establishing career goals, than do Morin and York (1982).

The intensity of the outplacement process is reflected in Brammer and Humberger's (1984) observation that a counselor may spend 30 to 65 hours for each candidate for outplacement. The counselor may spend 5 hours orienting the candidate to the process of outplacement; 20 hours helping the candidate conduct a self-assessment of interests, values, and attitudes; and 40 more hours helping with job selection and mounting the job search campaign. Brammer and Humberger (1984) note that the candidates may spend 310 hours on these same activities.

Brammer and Humberger suggest that much of outplacement work is necessary because adequate counseling services regarding career opportunities, retirement, performance, and similar topics is not provided on an ongoing basis. Regardless, the process begins soon after the termination conference, and in some instances immediately after the conference. After an initial period of shock, ventilation of feelings often occurs followed by a typical career counseling process including assessment, goal setting, the development of employability skills, and the job search.

If the outplacement program is internally located, the resources to support it are probably already on hand. These resources include occupational and training information, duplication equipment, telephones, training space, and access to a computerized database. If an external placement firm is involved, these facilities may have to be created, sometimes at a cost of up to $1,500 for each employee involved (Bohl, 1987).

Finally, offering an outplacement service is not a guarantee of a job, only the guarantee of assistance in finding a new position. The quality of the personnel and the availability of a full support system including stationery, clerical help, occupational information, message services, and other similar services seem to be the most important features involved when outplacement agencies are being selected. Having a full support service and the quality of the experience will be key factors in the success of these programs.

EMPLOYABILITY SKILLS

Groups

In times of rapid technological and economic change, we realize a fact that really is true all the time—that many people encounter great difficulty in successfully executing the transition into employment whether they are coming from an educational institution, displaced homemaker status, or have recently lost a job. The popular perception has been that novices might be expected to have some difficulty because they are inexperienced and inse-cure, but everyone else is an "old pro" and knows exactly how to operate the system—if they do not have a job, they obviously do not want one. Recent plant closings have shown how false this perception is.

All phases of the career and development process can be addressed in either individualized or group settings. This is also true of the job search and placement phase of career development. In this section, we consider group activities that assist in this process; and in the next section, we consider individual activities.

The present Job Training Partnership Act (JTPA) include provisions for supplying *transitional activities*—a term that includes teaching and helping individuals to find and obtain jobs. JTPA programs are in a position to provide this type of group help to disadvantaged individuals, including school dropouts, displaced homemakers, dislocated workers, and some others. Ob-viously, secondary and postsecondary institutions are in a position to provide such help to enrollees who are about to complete their educational programs. Community agencies often sponsor support groups or directly operate pro-grams that provide this assistance to other members of the community who need and want such help.

The principal difference among these various settings is that in educa-tional institutions the emphasis is on teaching skills and techniques for application in the future—usually short range, from 6 to 12 months in ad-vance. In JTPA and community agencies, the emphasis is on an immediate problem: Enrollees are trying to find a job *now*. The difference is deeper than appears on the surface. In the school setting the process is somewhat ab-stract and future oriented, whereas in the community the participants are in crisis, often accompanied by personal concerns and financial emergencies that can affect the process.

At the high school level, units on job search techniques can be incorpo-rated into several courses, established as electives or offered as special activities during or outside of regular school hours. The content is usually based either on a brief textbook or, more often, on a workbook or manual. Examples of the materials available for this purpose include those by Bloch (1989), Wegman, Chapman, and Johnson (1989), and Farr (1989). The range of materials available for use with college-level students is much broader than that aimed at high school students. Many of these publications can be used by higher education students either on an individualized self-help basis or in a workshop or elective-course setting. Typical publications for this group include books by Bolles (1990), Figler (1979), and Blocher (1989).

A recent development that is being used in JTPA and community groups to help those actually engaged in the job search process is the formation of a job club, as described in step-by-step detail in a handbook by Azrin and Besadel (1979). They propose the formation of a group that not only provides support and encouragement but also helps members to improve their inter-view skills through role playing; clarifies and sharpens their goals through group efforts; shares tips with other members as possible leads appear; and seeks group solutions to problems facing individual members—child care, transportation, and so on. The more obvious advantages to this approach are found in the support group whose members face a common problem, in the resolution of those problems that frequently cause failure in the job search, in improved access to information about possible openings through networking, and in skill building in job-seeking techniques. The approach is clearly appropriate not only for the so-called disadvantaged groups but also for dislocated workers, the structurally unemployed, and late entrants.

Local labor market information is particularly useful with job clubs because members are seeking jobs within the local area. Some communities have formed advisory committees consisting of representatives of local employers who are able to add further realism to job club activities in several ways, such as role-playing application interviews, alerting members to potential vacancies, and helping members know what employers look for in applicants.

People with Disabilities

The process of placing people with mental and physical disabilities is essentially the same as that for those without disabilities when considered in general terms. However, when clients with disabilities have limited potential for competitive employment, two options exist. One is to develop sheltered workshops which subcontract with other businesses to produce various products. The second alternative is to develop job skills through supported work programs that include job-site training, job coaching, placement, and long-term follow-up to determine work adjustment. In both types of programs extensive assessment, including medical and psychomotor, intellectual, academic, interests, interpersonal skills, and work skills (Kanchier, 1990) must be conducted. This is followed by training, coaching, counseling, observation, and evaluation. People in supported work programs typically work in restaurants, motels, hospitals, and similar situations (Lam, 1986). Lam found that the supported work program is a more cost-effective means of servicing clients with mental retardation, while sheltered workshops may be more cost effective with those clients with moderate to severe mental retardation.

When clients with disabilities have the potential for competitive employment, such as is the case with many individuals with physical disabilities, additional support in the form of counseling, training, and work with employers to overcome stereotypes will be necessary, much as it is for clients with mental disabilities (Jones, Ulicny, Czyzewski, & Plante, 1987).

Executing the Job Search

In most settings, such as educational institutions, JTPA retraining centers, and community agencies, job search training can be handled in a group situation. There appear to be some definite advantages to the individual when this is possible, as well as more efficient use of staff time. It is not always possible to form a group, however, because of time schedules, too much variation in prospective members, unique problems faced by some people, or other reasons. In this situation the appropriate alternative is individual assistance. In general, the steps to be followed, either one on one or in a group, are comparable. We identify them and discuss each briefly.

The first step is essentially one of inventory taking—that is, establishing what one has for sale. If the counselor has been working with the client in a career counseling process, this step has already been identified and clarified. If the counselor or helper is starting at the job search stage, some backtracking is necessary to be sure that the client does know self thoroughly and accurately and can identify personal strengths and weaknesses. Identifying personal skills and strengths may be difficult for the individual with limited work experience. For example, the displaced homemaker may discount or overlook skills that were used in homemaking responsibilities but did not produce a paycheck. The period devoted to clarifying self-knowledge should be expanded to include consideration of goals and longer range views of self in order to provide a rationalization against which possible openings can be evaluated. Though often postponed until later, a basic resume can be prepared at this stage, since fundamentally the resume is simply an inventory of personal characteristics and accumulated experiences that relates to what one wants in work. Zunker (1990) suggests that a client can use self-estimates to classify work skills as functional, adaptive, or technical and, then, to identify the types of positions for which he is best qualified. Feild and Holley (1975) report the reactions of personnel managers to resumes and their place in the job search process.

The second step is to identify the individual's job market. Here we are concerned first with circumscribing a geographic area and, second, with identifying information sources within that specified territory. An individual's labor market area ordinarily must be described in terms of personal factors. Influencing items include one's access to transportation; how long and far one is willing to travel to and from the work site; whether restricting factors such as geographic, personal, or family barriers exist; and similar items that relate to the individual. Next the person can begin to identify how he can obtain information about possible job openings. Actually there are several sources available to the individual, who may often overlook some of the possibilities. One source, often disregarded, is the hidden job market that exists almost everywhere. The jobs consist of vacancies that are about to develop, perhaps through promotion, retirement, reorganization, or some similar influence. The individual who can capitalize on this situation is the one who has access to learning about such positions before they become public knowledge. Perhaps the basic question for many might be, "How well do you know what is happening inside the companies you are interested in?"

The second source of information is closely related to the hidden market and consists of the network of acquaintances in the local area where a job is sought. Those who are employed in sites that are potential sites for the client may know the hidden market in their company. They may also know what trends are beginning to influence the industry and how competing companies may plan to respond. The job clubs proposed by Azrin and Besadel (1979) emphasize the networking search. Other sources of information include the local state employment security agency; newspaper want ads; local newspaper stories of business activities; professional or occupational connections (organizations, union, professional societies); and private or school-based employment agencies.

The third step in the job search process is developing a strategy for selling oneself to prospective employers and polishing the skills needed to complete this phase. The appropriate strategy depends on many factors and must be developed essentially according to rules set by the employer. If the potential position has been identified, a properly written, well-stated letter containing a resume should be sent to the employer. If the advertisement asks applicants to telephone for an appointment, telephone manners may become quite important. The immediate goal is to secure an interview; the long-range goal is to complete that interview in a way that produces a job offer. Clients may need assistance in translating want ads in order to understand what is being said about the job. Clients almost certainly will need help in preparing letters of application, resumes, and interviewing skills. Many job applicants, especially first-timers, may be unaware of the influence of such items as personal grooming, appropriateness of attire, eye contact, proper grammar and self-expression, how one sits, and the ability to explain what one can give to a job and what one expects in return. Role playing and practice interviews are the most common techniques for sharpening these skills. Many of the workbooks listed earlier include sample questions that are likely to be asked in the interview.

The job-hunting process is generally outlined as we have done here: establish career goals; develop employability skills such as resume development, letter writing, networking, and interviewing; and finally wage the job search campaigns. However, both research and the experience of job hunters give us some additional clues about how to make this process more successful. For example, Helwig (1987) surveyed career and placement specialists to rate what they perceived as the most important information needed by job hunters. The 15 items rated (1–7 scale) most important and 15 rated least important information needed (out of 99 items) can be seen in Figure 16.1. Perhaps the most obvious finding, as Helwig notes, is that all items in his questionnaire were viewed as at least somewhat important by the respondent.

Yates (1987) took a somewhat different approach in her research than Helwig in that she asked job seekers to rate the information and skills they needed during the job search. She found that generally among job hunters self-assessment skills, decision-making skills, and job-hunting knowledge and skills were considered most important, while occupational and educational information were considered less important. The top 10 needs of job seekers, according to their own ratings, are (1) selling yourself, (2) preparing

FIGURE 16.1   *Counselors' Perceptions of Most and Least Important Information Needed by Job Seekers (N = 1,121)*

Most Important:
 1. Ability to identify one's aptitudes (6.35)
 2. Ability to identify one's skills (6.34)
 3. Ability to identify one's interests (6.31)
 4. Knowledge of the importance of personal appearance and hygiene in getting a job (6.29)
 5. Ability to sell one's skills to get a job (6.28)
 6. Awareness of the importance of a properly completed application (6.28)
 7. Ability to relate one's skills, interests, aptitudes, and values to a job (6.26)
 8. Knowledge of how to participate in a job interview (6.23)
 9. Ability to prepare for an interview (6.18)
10. Knowledge of the personal characteristics that are considered important by employers (6.17)
11. Knowledge of the importance of proper language and dress in the workplace (6.13)
12. Knowledge of the importance of personal responsibility in finding a job (6.11)
13. Ability to understand the employer's expectations for a specific position (5.99)
14. Knowledge of the steps in job hunting (5.97)
15. Knowledge of where to find job openings (5.97)

Least Important:
 1. Knowledge of military information (4.01)
 2. Knowledge of labor organizations (4.27)
 3. Knowledge of the regional history of employment changes and attitudes (4.28)
 4. Knowledge of how the natural environment influences the jobs that are available (4.40)
 5. Knowledge of seasonal jobs (4.52)
 6. Information about starting one's own business (4.58)
 7. Knowledge of the relationship between work and leisure time (4.58)
 8. Knowledge of the General Educational Development (GED) certificate (4.63)
 9. Knowledge of how cycles in the economy affect the number of job openings (4.63)
10. Knowledge of the different parts of a cover letter (4.67)
11. Knowledge of how public transportation may affect job choice (4.74)
12. Knowledge of how family and friends may influence occupational choice (4.74)
13. Ability to use the *Dictionary of Occupational Titles* and the *Occupational Outlook Handbook* (4.75)
14. Ability to ascertain employer differences regarding worker benefits (4.76)
15. Knowledge of illegal questions which may occur during the interview (4.78)

for a typical interview, (3) writing a resume, (4) self-assessment skills, (5) salary information, (6) budgeting until a job is found, (7) legal and illegal questions that may be posed by interviewers, (8) understanding the career decision-making process, (9) how to use skills acquired in past jobs in a new occupation, and (10) information about entry-level requirements of various jobs.

The interview has also been the focus of some important and enlightening research. Atkins and Kent (1988, p. 102) asked 95 business recruiters at

FIGURE 16.2   *College Recruiters' Rankings of the Most Important Consideration in the Employment Interview*

1. Overall oral communication skills	11. Overall appearance
2. Enthusiasm	12. Assertiveness
3. Motivation	13. Manners
4. Credentials	14. References
5. Degree	15. Preparation or knowledge of employer
6. Career maturity	16. Sense of humor
7. Initiative	17. Report-writing skills
8. Grade point average	18. Summer or part-time job experience
9. Listening skills	19. Abilitiy to resolve conflict
10. Punctuality	20. Extracurricular activites

West Virginia University to rate the most important variable involved in the job interview. The recruiters' rankings can be seen in Figure 16.2.

Riggio and Throckmorton (1987) examined the nature of errors in oral communication committed during the mock job interviews and found that the most common problem was responses that failed to provide enough information. Other errors identified were extreme difficulty in answering a question, complaining about either their employer or the quality of their education, providing negative personal information, lack of emphasis on their career, too much emphasis on salary, inability to communicate skills, and poor grammar. Often oral communication problems included answers that were too long, too vague, or bizarre such as thinking of committing suicide. Riggio and Throckmorton (1987) also found that students who received a 40-minute lecture on interviewing skills did no better in their oral communication than did those who had not been exposed to the lecture.

Some empirical guidelines for resume and cover letter preparation have also come forth. Feild and Holley (1975) found that personnel managers almost unanimously preferred that cover letters be typed and no longer than one page in length. They also found that personnel managers wanted a clear statement of the applicant's career objective, indication of why the applicant was seeking the job, and some statements indicating that the applicant understands the organization.

Helwig (1985) surveyed 71 recruiters from 50 corporations and found that they had a clear preference for a resume that was one page in length, was clearly labeled, had headings on the left side, used action verbs in describing work experience, and looked uncluttered as opposed to other one- and two-page resumes. Neatness, use of proper English, and correct spelling have also been found to be important to corporate recruiters, as has the order of presentation of data (Stephens, Watt, & Hobbs, 1979).

In a particularly significant study, Ryland and Rosen (1987) found that 230 personnel professionals preferred the functional resume format as compared to the standard chronological format (see Figure 16.3). Ryland and Rosen also found that functional resumes are particularly helpful when applying for highly skilled careers.

Apparently, personnel managers want to see education listed first and work experience second, while they have mixed opinions about the presentation of personal data, according to Stephens et al. (1979). How should the resume be structured? With regard to the importance attached to items on the resume, current address, past work experience, major in college, job objectives, permanent address, tenure on previous jobs, colleges attended, and specific physical limitations were rated as the most important items to include on the resume, while religious preference, race, personal data on parents, high school transcripts, photograph, sex, spouse's education, spouse's occupation, typing skills, and number of children were listed as the least important items.

SUMMARY

Placement has traditionally been viewed as the culmination of either the career counseling or vocational training process. While this is still true to a degree, many individuals are in need of job placement because they lost their current jobs. In some instances, these individuals will engage in some type of career planning; in other situations, they will be more concerned about getting the first available job. It is apparent that regardless of the reasons for undergoing a job search, modern-day job hunters must be properly equipped with a definite set of skills if they are to be successful. Personnel officers have definite preferences regarding resumes and certain biases against certain types of interview behavior. Unless job hunters have the skills to search out available jobs, write appropriate letters, develop attractive resumes, and interview properly, they will be severely limited in the job search. Fortunately, career development specialists have the tools they need to develop job-hunting skills and have proven to be effective in this area.

It is also clear that several different types of placement operations will be needed in a work force where literally millions of people seek to enter first jobs or find replacements for old ones. Part-time placement offices in high schools and postsecondary institutions can not only provide students with jobs but can facilitate their career development. Private placement agencies can provide specialized job placement services, and outplacement operations can help to relocate the displaced worker. Placement offices in high schools, vocational-technical schools, colleges, and elsewhere can help students find that critical first job. These job placement agencies working independently, but with the same purpose, can alleviate much of the anxiety of being without a job.

FIGURE 16.3 *Two Resume Formats*

Chronological

Jane E. Taylor
105 Oakdale Road
Columbus, Ohio 45710
614-554-3934

JOB EXPERIENCE: Sales representative for large pharmaceutical company

WORK EXPERIENCE:
1980 to present: APEX OFFICE FURNITURE AND SUPPLY COMPANY
Wage and Salary Specialist: Evaluate jobs for manufacturer office
furniture and supplies, determine job grading system, gather
wage survey data, determine and justify merit increases and
adjustments, approve job descriptions, establish salary ranges,
and counsel employees.

1976–1980   APEX OFFICE FURNITURE AND SUPPLY COMPANY
Personnel Assistant: Studied jobs, categorized positions,
interviewed prospective applicants, conducted exit interviews,
assisted with annual employee attitude survey and with
administration of pension programs.

1974–1976 $-MARK DEPARTMENT STORES
Assistant Store Manager: Assisted store manager with
maintaining stock, supervising sales clerks, ordering inventory,
developing displays for new merchandise, and handling
customer returns and complaints.

1971–1973   ABC DRUGSTORES
Sales Clerk (summers): Sold merchandise in busy neighborhood
store, handled purchase orders for stock, and trained three other
successful sales clerks.

EDUCATION: B.A. in Business Administration, Florida State University
  1974

INTERESTS: Tennis, Photography

References available upon request   Willing to relocate

FIGURE 16.3 *Continued*

Functional

Jane E. Taylor
105 Oakdale Road
Columbus, Ohio 45710
614-554-3934

JOB OBJECTIVE: Sales representative for large pharmaceutical company

SALES
Sold merchandise in busy neighborhood store, handled purchase orders for stocks, and trained three other successful sales clerks

MANAGEMENT
Assisted store manager of large discount department store with maintaining stock, supervising sales clerks, ordering inventory, developing displays for new merchandise, and handling customer returns and complaints.

Founded amateur photographers' club, increasing membership to 103 in one year. Coordinated convention for national photographers' organization, and organized and implemented photo show, featuring 30 artists.

ADMINISTRATION
Evaluated jobs for manufacturer office furniture and supplies, determined job grading system, gathered wage survey data, determined and justified merit increases and adjustments, approved job descriptions, established salary ranges, and counseled employees.

Studied jobs, categorized positions, interviewed prospective applicants, conducted exit interviews, assisted with annual employee attitude surveys and with administration of pension programs.

EDUCATION AND EXPERIENCE:

1980 to present	APEX OFFICE FURNITURE AND SUPPLY COMPANY Wage and Salary Specialist
1976–1980	Apex Office Furniture and Supply— Personnel Assistant
1974–1976	$-Mart Department Stores—Assistant Store Manager
1971–1973	ABC Drugstores—Sales Clerk (summers)
1970–1974	B.A. in Business Administration, Florida State University
INTERESTS	Tennis, Photography

References available upon request   Willing to relocate

Source: Ryland, E. K., & Rosen, B. (1987). Personnel professionals reactions to chronological and functional resume formats. *Career Development Quarterly,* p. 231. By permission.

REFERENCES

Atkins, C. P., & Kent, R. L. (1988). What do recruiters consider important during the employment interview? *Journal of Employment Counseling, 25,* 98–103.

Azrin, N. H., & Besadel, V. B. (1979). *Job club counselor's manual: A behavioral approach to vocational counseling.* Baltimore, MD: University Park Press.

Bloch, D. (1989). *The job winning resume.* Lincolnwood, IL: VGM Books.

Blocher, D. H. (1989). *Career actualization and life planning.* Denver, CO: Love.

Bohl, D. L. (Ed.). (1987). *Responsible reduction in force.* New York: American Management Association Publication Division.

Bolles, R. N. (1990). *A practical manual for job-hunters and career changers: What color is your parachute?* Berkeley, CA: Ten Speed Press.

Brammer, L. M., & Humberger, F. E. (1984). *Outplacement and inplacement counseling.* Englewood Cliffs, NJ: Prentice Hall.

Farr, J. M. (1989). *Getting the job you really want.* Indianapolis, IN: JIST Works.

Feild, H. S., & Holley, W. H. (1975). Resume preparation: An empirical study of personnel managers' perceptions. *Vocational Guidance Quarterly, 24,* 229–237.

Ferrin, R. I., & Arbeiter, S. (1975). *Bridging the gap: A study of education-to-work linkages.* New York: College Entrance Examination Board.

Figler, H. (1979). *The complete job-search handbook.* New York: Holt, Rinehart and Winston.

Harris, T. L. (1977). Employment counseling and placement services for secondary school students. *Vocational Guidance Quarterly, 26,* 166–173.

Helwig, A. A. (1987). Information required for job hunting: 1121 counselors respond. *Journal of Employment Counseling, 24,* 184–190.

Helwig, A. D. (1985). Corporate recruits preferences for three resumé styles. *Vocational Guidance Quarterly, 34,* 99–105.

Heppner, M. J. (1981). Alumni sharing knowledge (ASK): High quality, cost-effective career resources. *Journal of College Student Personnel, 22,* 173–174.

Jones, M. L., Ulicny, G. R., Gzyzewski, M. J., & Plante, T. G. (1987). Employment in care-giving jobs for mentally disabled young adults: A feasibility study. *Journal of Employment Counseling, 24,* 122–129.

Kanchier, C. (1990). Career education for adults with mental disabilities. *Journal of Employment Counseling, 27,* 23–36.

Lam, C. S. (1986). Comparison of sheltered and supported work programs: A pilot study. *Rehabilitation Counseling Bulletin, 30,* 66–82.

Lilley, W. (1978). Job hunters, beware. *Canadian Business, 51,* 36–37, 99–100.

Lopez, F. G. (1983). The victims of corporate failures: Some preliminary findings. *Personal and Guidance Journal, 61,* 631–632.

Morin, W. J., & York, L. (1982). *Outplacement techniques: A positive approach to terminating employees.* New York: AMACON.

Odell, C., Pritchard, D., & Sinick, D. (1974). Whose job is job placement? *Vocational Guidance Quarterly, 23,* 138–145.

Plotsky, F. A., & Goad, R. (1974). Encouraging women through a career conference. *Personnel and Guidance Journal, 52,* 486–488.

Riggio, R. E., & Throckmorton, B. (1987). Effects of prior training and verbal errors on students' performance in job interviews. *Journal of Employment Counseling, 29,* 10–16.

Ryland, E. K., & Rosen, B. (1987). Personnel professionals' reactions to chronological and functional resume formats. *Career Development Quarterly, 35,* 228–238.

Self, C., & Lopez, F. (1982). Women in nontraditional fields: A career development seminar for college women. *Journal of College Student Personnel, 23,* 545–546.

Stephens, D. B., Watt, J. T., & Hobbs, W. S. (1979). Getting through the resume preparation image: Some empirically based guidelines for resume format. *Vocational Guidance Quarterly, 28,* 25–34.

Taber, T. D., Walsh, J. T., & Cooke, R. A. (1979). Developing a community-based program for reducing the social impact of a plant closing. *Journal of Applied Behavioral Science, 15,* 133–155.

Wegman, L., Chapman, I., & Johnson, T. (1989). *Work in the new economy.* Indianapolis, IN: JIST Works.

Yates, C. J. (1987). Job hunters' perspective on their needs during the job search process. *Journal of Employment Counseling, 24,* 155–165.

Zunker, V. G. (1990). *Career counseling: Applied concepts of life planning* (3rd ed.). Monterey, CA: Brooks/Cole.

__17__

Career Development in Business and Industry

The term *career development* takes on a more circumscribed meaning in the business context. Thus far, we have discussed career development as a lifelong process that results in the choice, entrance, and adjustment to a series of occupations that together can be characterized as a person's career. Hall (1990) points out the fundamental difference between the vocational psychologists, such as Donald Super, and organizational psychologists such as himself who are concerned with business and industry. Vocational psychologists are more concerned with the individual processes of development, while industrial psychologists focus more on the situational variables associated with adjustment in the business setting. Job performance, commitment to the organization, job mobility, family-work interactions, and other similar variables are of greatest concern to career development specialists in business and industry (Hall, 1990).

Gutteridge (1986) depicts career development in business and industry as being comprised of two processes: "career planning which is an individual process, and career management, which is an institutional process" (p. 55). Career development, according to Gutteridge, is a joint process, or perhaps more appropriately, *should* be a joint process. Many businesses engage in career management without reference to the employee's career needs. Gutteridge indicates that in the past, businesses have not typically integrated career planning and career management in a manner that is either responsive to the career needs of the employees or the staffing needs of the corporation. As we see in the next section, the rationale for coordinating these two processes is becoming more compelling.

It is also useful to consider the potential services that may be offered by career counselors in business settings. Osipow (1982) elaborates a list of services that includes the following: (1) help employees assess their work styles and help them change those aspects of their styles that may be ineffective; (2) help managers identify the negative effects of repetitive work, forced

455

relocation, and job loss; (3) identify the strains associated with two-career families and presumably help ameliorate the stresses growing out of those relationships; (4) help managers identify the hazards associated with stress and work; (5) prepare people for retirement; (6) improve the process of performance appraisal; and (7) identify the special concerns of professionals such as scientists.

Osipow (1982) indicates that his "shopping list" is not exhaustive. In fact, several potential functions of the career counselor should be added: building effective work teams, designing and implementing substance and alcohol abuse programs and treatment programs for abusers, and designing and implementing programs to improve employees' health (Wilbur & Vermilyea, 1982).

While there is little doubt that improving physical health, mental health, and dealing with substance and alcohol abuse programs are related to improved work performance, these roles usually fall to health educators, directors of occupational health and safety, psychologists, counselors, and others involved with the employee assistance program. This chapter focuses on enhancing individual career planning and organizational career management processes and not on health-related issues.

Finally, just as the meaning of career development changes somewhat in an organizational context, so must the philosophy of the career counselor. Wilbur and Vermilyea (1982) suggest that this shift must occur along four lines: identity, profit motive, emphasis on organizational development, and level of evidence acceptable for decision making. These authors suggest that career counselors must take on the identity of businesspeople first and counselors or psychologists second. In individual counseling, the only concerns are client satisfaction and change. As a career counselor in business and industry engaged in designing and selling services, "operational quality, and efficiency, customer satisfaction, market penetration, resource allocation, and demonstration of impact" (pp. 31–32) become concerns. These are of concern because every business is dedicated first to making a profit. Counselors who are accustomed to putting individual growth first will somehow have to reconcile these two goals, just as they will the idea that organizational development takes precedence over individual development. This is not to suggest that these two areas are incompatible, but if one must be emphasized, individual development will typically be given a lower priority. Also, counselors and psychologists are systematically trained to look for scientific proof that an intervention works. Business decisions are usually not based on hard evidence, and managers are much more likely to rely on their intuition and experience to make decisions (Wilbur & Vermilyea, 1982), something that may be frustrating to the person trained to think more scientifically.

PROGRAMMING FOR CAREER DEVELOPMENT

Knowdell (1982, 1984) traced the origins of career development programs in business to the early 1970s, when governmental regulation placed pressure on businesses to provide equal employment opportunity. While Knowdell is undoubtedly correct about the development of comprehensive career development programs for all employees, specialized programs aimed at orienting, socializing, and enhancing the careers of managers probably began much earlier (Hall, 1990). However, the focus of this chapter is on the generalized programming efforts aimed at promoting the careers of employees.

In 1987 Keller and Piotrowski reported that 10 percent of the *Fortune* 500 companies had initiated formal career development programs. Citicorp, General Electric, AT&T, and NASA were among the first corporations to implement comprehensive programs. Ford Motor Company, American Airlines, Glaxo, Pfizer, and numerous other companies have initiated programs in the last few years. The number is increasing steadily, albeit relatively slowly, if one uses as the criterion for inclusion in the list that the program be comprehensive. It is likely that all major corporations in this country have a program aimed at orienting new hires to the business that has employed them and to their specific job, and socializing the employee by imparting the corporation's values. Many corporations also provide extensive educational programs aimed at assisting their employees to function more effectively in their current positions and to acquire new job skills that will enhance their opportunity for advancement. It is possible for employees in a few corporations to earn baccalaureate and advanced college degrees with the assistance and support of their businesses. However, what distinguishes these rudimentary career development programs from those that are more highly developed is that comprehensive programs are systematic and focused. A career development system within a business is "an organized, formalized, planned effort to achieve a balance between the individuals' career needs and the organizations' work force requirements" (Leibowitz, Farren, & Kaye, 1986, p. 4). The remainder of this chapter focuses on the rationale for design and implementation of comprehensive career development systems.

Rationale

As Knowdell (1982, 1984) suggested, one of the primary forces behind the development of career development programs in business and industry has been external pressure to provide equality of employment opportunity. Many businesses have been pressured to demonstrate fairness in their recruitment, retention, and promotion procedures. Career development programs that make employees aware not only of their own potential but of job openings with the company have been seen as one means of enhancing equal employment.

London and Stumpf (1986) note that the impetus for career development programs in the 1990s and beyond may be primarily internal to the business. They suggest that career development programs are needed to develop career motivation that they believe is based in career resilience, career insight, and career identity. Career resilience is workers' ability to keep a positive perspective even when their careers are not going as well as they would like. Career insight has to do with personal realism about one's own career potential and requires feedback about performance to develop.

Career identity is the extent to which workers' personal identity is related to their careers and is reflected in their career directions and goals.

Leibowitz, Farren, and Kaye (1986) also suggest that the current rationale for developing a career development program grows out of meeting internal needs rather than succumbing to external pressure. Career development programs allow businesses to make better use of their employees' skills, increase the loyalty of employees, enhance communication, increase employee retention, contribute to the effectiveness of personnel systems such as performance appraisal and promotion, and help to classify organizational goals. These organizational benefits accrue because managers and employees learn how to manage their own careers, increase their understanding of the organization and its policies, are better able to give and receive feedback about their performance, establish realistic goals about their careers, and increase the sense of personal responsibility for themselves.

Reports from business organizations such as the National Alliance of Business (1986) have made corporate executives aware that it will become increasingly important for corporations to develop and enhance their current employees' work-related capabilities if they are to remain competitive. It is a truism that the labor force of most businesses for the next 10 to 15 years is in place and that well-conceived corporate strategies designed to orient, train, and promote current workers will enhance organizational functioning. In short, corporate executives are concluding that career development programs are good business.

INITIATING THE PROGRAM

Early Steps

There are certain prerequisites to initiating a successful career development program. Among the more important of these are sanctions from top-level executives. Career development programs require various types of organizational changes, and without support from the power structure these changes are unlikely to occur. One CEO sent a memorandum to all managers that "career development will be our number one priority." Not surprisingly, that corporation has one of the finest career development programs in existence.

Establishing a budget to support the program is also an important early step. Choosing a manager who can develop the program is also an important prerequisite to change. The credentials of the manager and the amount budgeted for the development of the program will depend on the type of program to be developed. The manager should be knowledgeable about career development, testing, and career counseling. Moreover, a successful manager needs a basic understanding of organizational functioning, management principles and practices, as well as the general area of human resource planning and development. Specialized knowledge of management information systems, performance appraisal systems, personnel selection and development practices, instructional technology, and a whole host of other skills would of course be useful to the manager of a career development program.

Budgeting for the career development program requires setting forth a developmental budget as well as an operating budget. The initiation of a program in a major corporation can easily cost $300,000 to $400,000, again depending on the nature of the program. A budget for the development of a career development program should include the following lines:

- Manager's salary
- Support personnel salaries
- Consultant's fees/expenses
- Travel to model programs
- Materials acquisition
- Furnishings—desks, bookcases
- Equipment, including computers, printers, and typewriters
- Computer programming assistance
- Printing in-house materials, brochures, etc.
- Training expenses (orienting managers, training workshop leaders)

The actual cost of operating the program may actually be quite modest depending on the size of the corporation and the type of programs to be delivered. The budget for the program will contain many of the aforementioned budgetary lines, although the amounts for consultant's fees, travel, materials acquisition, equipment procurement, furnishings, printing, and training should be reduced greatly. However, an additional line—evaluation costs—should be added to the operating cost budget.

One additional step should be taken at the outset of the program: determining an organizational niche for the career development program. Typically, these programs are placed under the umbrella of the vice president or director of human resource development (HRD). Leibowitz, Farren, and Kaye (1986) note the importance of the current HRD effort in most corporations, which involves activities such as training new hires and veteran employees, posting job vacancies, evaluating the compensation plan, enhancing employee performance appraisal, and designing a career development program that enhances all of these efforts. For example, one of the jobs assigned to HRD is inventorying the available labor supply (i.e., determining the skills available to focus on the mission of the organization). The career development program can be designed in a manner that will enhance the assessment of employees' skills and thus improve this effort. The career development program can also be instrumental in identifying which employees are engaged in acquiring various types of new skills and thus make the forecasts of needs to recruit employees outside the corporation more accurate.

Needs Assessment

Accurately assessing employee needs is another important early step in the design of a career development program. The needs assessment should be designed in a manner that will answer several key questions such as, "What is the extent of our need for career development programming?" and "What type of program should we have?" However, several questions must be answered prior to embarking on a needs assessment. These questions include, "What data collection procedure should be employed?", "What domains of employee concerns should be sampled?", and "How will the needs of special groups of employees be identified?"

Data Collection Procedures

Some corporations have used employee interviews to determine their need for a career development program. This may be satisfactory as a means of ascertaining top-level management's perceptions of needs but is generally too time-consuming and expensive to use with all employees. A questionnaire should be sent either to a random sample or to all employees, depending on tradition and preference. Obviously, sampling reduces the cost, but if the corporation routinely surveys all employees in its data-gathering efforts, a census should be conducted.

The extent to which follow-up procedures will be employed to increase return rates will be dependent on such factors as the availability of funds and representatives of return rates. Every effort should be made to ensure that returns are both representative of the employees and accurate in their portrayal of employee attitudes. With regard to the latter, every effort should be made to guarantee employee anonymity if the returns are to accurately reflect employee career development needs. Some corporations utilize outside firms for data collection as one means of ensuring confidentiality. If this is not possible, questionnaires and return envelopes should be designed in a manner that they can be returned without identifying the respondent. Unmarked envelopes that can be placed in central (as opposed to departmental) receptacles can help protect the identity of respondents.

Domains to Be Sampled

The needs assessment questionnaire should be designed to collect information in the following domains: (1) desire for assistance with career planning; (2) preferred source of assistance with career development (e.g., manager, career counselor); (3) preferences for types of career development activities; (4) aversions, if any, to career development activities; and (5) evaluation of current career development activities (if they exist).

Desire for Assistance: While research has shown that as many as 77 percent of employees may participate in some aspects of the career development program (Wowk, Williams, & Halstead, 1983), it is important for program design purposes to know how many people expect to participate and to be able to estimate when they might participate if various types of career development activities are made available. Thus, direct questions regarding employees' interest in participating in the career development program should be included in the instrument. So should indirect indicators of interest such as degree of satisfaction with current position. People who are dissatisfied with their current jobs may very well be the first to volunteer to participate in the program. Sample items follow:

1. Rate your interest in exploring other career opportunities within the company.
2. Indicate the extent to which you are satisfied in your current position.

Source of Assistance: It is possible to deliver career development services through managers, career counselors employed by the corporation, external consultants, computerized programs, and so forth. Employees should be queried with regard to the people and/or delivery services they would prefer to provide career development services. If an outside firm is being considered, reactions to this option should be explored. All possible options considered feasible by the managers in charge of program development can be presented on the questionnaire for reaction. Some sample items are as follows:

1. Indicate the extent to which you would find each of the following people acceptable as sources of assistance with your own career planning:
   a. Your immediate supervisor
   b. A professional career counselor employed by the corporation
   c. A career counselor outside the corporation who would be brought in to provide assistance to employees
   d. Other—please specify

Types of Career Development Activities Preferred and Aversions, If Any: Recently, at a meeting of representatives from a corporation considering the implementation of a career development program, a debate about the wisdom of utilizing a particular personality inventory as a part of a career development program developed. This debate highlighted that some individuals are uncomfortable with values and personality inventories and perhaps other activities that are often included in career development programs. It is therefore important to ascertain how employees feel about such activities as discussions of interests, values, personality, decision-making style, and career change. If there is widespread aversion to activities such as taking and discussing work values inventories, either among managers or employees, these should either not be included in the program or they should be designed as optional activities. If employees feel uncomfortable with an activity, it is unlikely that their responses to questions or their participation in the activity will reflect their true values or attitudes. Items for sampling attitudes in this domain might include the following:

1. The following is a list of activities that are often included in career development programs. Please rate the extent to which you would feel comfortable participating in each of them:
   a. Completing an interest inventory

   b. Completing a personality inventory
   c. Discussing my work values
   d. Discussing long- and short-term career goals
   e. Discussing my ideal work setting
   f. Etc.

Evaluation of Existing Efforts: Most companies have some aspects of a career development program, usually in the form of job-related feedback during the performance evaluation. All aspects of a program currently in place should be evaluated in the needs assessment process so decisions can be made about their retention and/or modification. It is also useful to ascertain whether or not employees are aware of the opportunities that are now being offered by the corporation, such as paid educational experiences, in-house staff-development sabbatical programs, and so forth. These activities will become more important as the career development program evolves and people take an active role in managing their own careers. The needs assessment may point to an increased need for information about these programs or even to modifications that need to be made in them. Sample items might include the following:

   1. To what extent has your performance appraisal been useful to you in your career planning?
   2. Rate the degree to which the corporate educational leave policy is useful to you.

Identifying Special Needs

The design of the career development program can be enhanced by sampling the aforementioned five domains. However, the needs assessment will not be complete unless it focuses on the special needs of various subgroups of employees such as women, minorities, and new hires.

   The purpose of a career development program is to benefit both the company and the employee by helping to develop employee potential. As noted earlier, corporations that fail to develop talent from within will find themselves hard pressed to compete (e.g., National Alliance of Business, 1986). The career development program must be designed not only to identify talent but to help develop that talent.

   The needs assessment questionnaire should be designed to determine the extent to which new hires and others understand the corporate occupational structure and the degree to which it offers them opportunity for advancement. These data may be useful in designing employee recruitment and orientation programs as well as in providing information to employees who have considerable tenure with the company.

   The career development needs assessment should also be structured so that it identifies barriers to career mobility. Women may have child care problems. Minorities and poor whites may have had poor educational opportunities or have attended substandard schools. Both groups may have observed or experienced discrimination. For example, a recent Gallup survey revealed that 62 percent of the African Americans had observed discrimination in the workplace, either directed toward themselves or others (NCDA, 1988).

Many corporate executives are extremely sensitive about asking questions on the employee survey about emotionally laden issues such as discrimination. While this is understandable, if a decision is reached not to ask these questions on the needs assessment questionnaire, other means of ascertaining this information should be devised, such as hiring external consultants to conduct interviews with various groups of employees.

The special needs of subgroups of employees can be determined if employees are asked to provide certain types of demographic data (e.g., gender, race, employment status, type of job held, years of employment, etc.) and if questions are included in the data collection process that highlight potential problems. Literature reviews of the career development programs encountered by various subgroups can be a useful way of identifying needs that should be addressed.

It would not be unexpected to determine that not only do male and female employees have different career development needs, but that employees working in different departments or units have differing concerns as well. For example, it is literally impossible for the sales staff of many corporations to attend career development workshops, but they can utilize audiocassettes and workbooks that address career development issues. Some departments may have provided every employee with a personal computer and, thus, would prefer an interactive career development computer program to a workbook or workshop.

It is also likely that the desire for career development activities will vary across departments and units, and the types and levels of activities desired will be markedly different. These and the other factors mentioned affect the design of the career development program and should, therefore, be anticipated in the development of a needs assessment questionnaire.

A Word about Mechanics and Planning

As noted earlier, the needs assessment survey may be embedded in a routine employee opinionnaire or administered separately. Such typical issues as concerns about confidentiality must be attended to if results are to accurately reflect employee opinions. One atypical concern that arises in the assessment of career development needs is that some managers are concerned that the data collection process itself will raise false expectations about career development programming (Leibowitz, Farren, & Kaye, 1986, p. 36). This can be avoided in two ways: through a disclaimer and/or item selection.

If the career development needs assessment survey is conducted as an exploratory step to provide data for the planning of a career development program, this should be stated in the introduction to the questionnaire. If timelines have been established for the initiation of a program, then these should be stated as well. By telling employees that the company is soliciting employee input as one way of informing the decision-making process regarding the implementation of a career development program, raising false expectations can be avoided. Similarly, if the company plans to implement a career development program 2 years hence, indicating this on the questionnaire will lead to realistic expectations about when the program will be implemented. Also, no questions should be placed on the career development needs assessment questionnaire that are not realistic alternatives for inclusion in the program. For example, if no consideration is being given to the development of a computerized career development systems, this should not be posed as an option for delivering the program.

DESIGNING THE PROGRAM

The California Lawrence Livermore National Laboratory program has served as the prototype for many career development programs in other organizations (Knowdell, 1982). This program focuses on career and life planning and has three major components. The first of these is the Career Information Center (CIC), which contains college catalogs, career information, self-help books, and other information. In the "Livermore Labs" program, CIC personnel also assist employees in developing internal or external resumes. The internal resume is developed for use in pursuing job changes within the organization, while the external resume is used in pursuing a new job outside the corporation. Understandably, many corporations have not included an external resume development service as a part of their program.

The second component of the Livermore Labs program is individual career counseling. However, the counselors who provide this service also provide assistance with financial planning, preparation for retirement, family problems, and a host of other concerns (Knowdell, 1982).

Career assessment workshops constitute the third component of the Livermore Labs program. These consist of 40 hours of intensive career exploration. The content of the workshop sessions at the Livermore Labs program is as follows (Knowdell, 1984):

Week 1—Orientation to career planning (4 hrs)

Week 2—Assessment of work values, personality style, interests; also training in career decision making (16 hrs)

Week 3—Individual interview—a structured interview focusing on past achievements is videotaped (1 hr)

Week 4—Mini seminars made up of small groups of employees work to identify "motivated skills" and effective work style (10 hrs)

Week 5—Individual counseling session focuses on developing an individual career development plan (1 hr)

Week 6—Individuals independently gather information and work on career development plan (varies)

Week 7—Each person presents the what, how, when, and where of their career development plan to other seminar participants (8 hrs)

The actual content of individual seminars may vary to some degree in other corporations. For example, resumes may be developed, interviewing skills may be practiced, and organizational needs may be discussed. But generally speaking, the outcome hoped for in most of these programs is the development of a career development plan for each individual.

One type of information that can be used in developing a career plan is career paths. Career paths represent sequential lines of career progression in an organization (Leibowitz, Ferren, & Kaye, 1986). As can be seen in Figure 17.1, the entry job for administrative support personnel may be as an office assistant, and the corporate accountant (see Figure 17.2) typically enters the system as a financial systems analyst. These and other career paths are developed on the actual experience of employees who have moved to supervisory and managerial experience and thus reflect the promotion practices of the corporation.

Glaxo, the second largest pharmaceutical company in the world (located in Research Triangle Park, NC), has developed a program that is parallel in many ways to the Livermore Labs program. However, Glaxo, as a part of its occupational information, has provided employees with career pathing information for many of the top supervisory and management positions.

American Airlines elected not to offer workshops as a part of its career development program. However, career development specialists have made access to information about jobs and job vacancies readily available to employees. They have also developed policies that enable employees to shadow other employees in jobs of interest. For example, if a reservation agent wished to explore the duties of flight attendants, it would be possible for that agent to take a 2- or 3-day trip with a crew of flight attendants to gain firsthand information about their job responsibilities.

Ford Motor Company, in conjunction with the United Auto Workers (UAW-Ford, 1987), has developed what it terms an employee development and training program. This program uses a series of Life/Education Advisors who conduct one-on-one advising sessions with employees to assist them with educational and personal development planning and goal setting. These advisors also conduct life/education planning workshops; provide information to employees regarding educational, career, and personal growth needs; and collect material about training opportunities.

One of the expected outcomes of the UAW-Ford program is personal growth. A second is career development. However, it is relatively clear that in this program less emphasis is placed on career exploration, interests, and decision making and more emphasis is placed on educational planning than in the other programs discussed.

FIGURE 17.1 *Administrative Support*

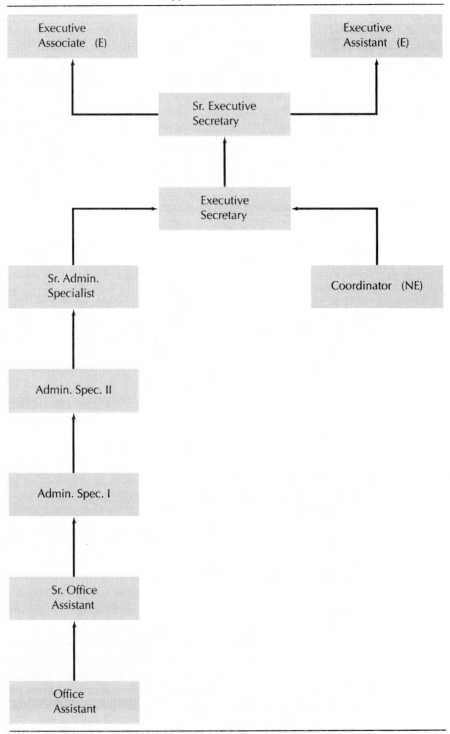

FIGURE 17.2 *Career Path: Corporate Accounting*

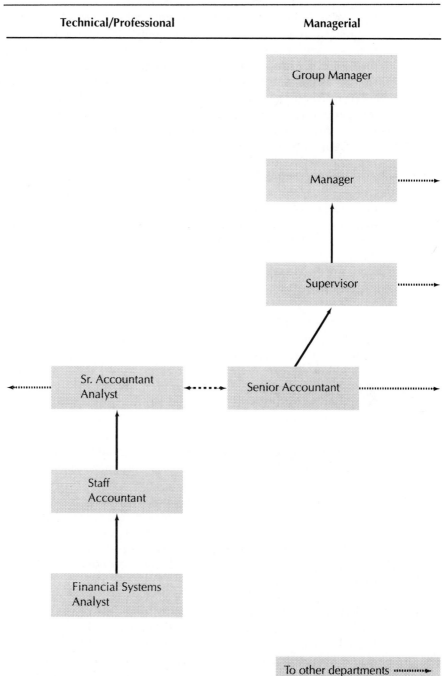

The Essential Components

Gutteridge (1986) lists five general types of organizational tools: (1) self-assessment tools, (2) individual counseling, (3) internal labor market information/placement exchanges, (4) organizational potential assessment processes, and (5) developmental programs. The Livermore Labs program uses workshops as its essential self-assessment tool. Glaxo Corporation offers workshops in which assessment devices are administered, scored, and interpreted. It also provides workbooks that assist in self-assessment. The UAW-Ford program relies on workshop activities for assessment.

Many corporations provide no individual career counseling using trained career counselors. Frequently, supervisors or managers provide "career counseling," coaching, or advice as a part of their performance appraisal meetings. As Gutteridge (1986) notes, this is one of the more controversial aspects of the program, and as Brooks (1984) states, "Despite claims that managers can or should provide career counseling for employees, managers seldom have either the skill or the inclination to provide these services" (p. 397).

Effective career development programs must have an adequate description of the duties performed by the workers in their organization and the minimum requirements (education and skills) for performing those duties. It is also important that information about career ladders/paths be provided and that all information be readily accessible to employees. For those companies that are prepared to assist workers seek employment outside the corporation, information about careers in the local area, state, and region must be made available. Educational information, like occupational information, may be of two types: internal and external. Most corporations offer ongoing training to employees. Many also offer the opportunities to explore additional education and training outside the corporate structure. Information about these opportunities must also be readily available.

Communicating information about job openings via job posting is one aspect of helping employees identify and pursue career opportunities. Helping employees develop internal resumes and job interviewing skills is another important aspect of this function. Often a CIC is established and staffed to provide these services. However, some companies rely on employee newsletters, bulletins posted in employee lounges and other places, and computerized systems to help employees identify job opportunities and to pursue them.

Every successful organization has an ongoing program to assess the potential of its employees to fill key roles in the organization. In the case of upper level management, succession planning is engaged in to make sure that there is continuity in organizational leadership. Promotability forecasts are also developed, partially on the basis of performance appraisal information. In some instances, promotability forecasts are developed on the basis of performance in assessment centers, although these centers are primarily used to assess potential for supervisory and managerial positions (Gutteridge, 1986). When assessment centers are used, corporate assessors design a variety of individual and group exercises that are related to functioning as a manager. This assessor then constitutes a panel, usually made up of managers who observe and evaluate employees' performance. As Gutteridge (1986) notes, the panel's recommendation is typically in the form of a "go–no go" recommendation. Skills inventories, which are detailed descriptions of the employee's work history, training, and accomplishments, may also be used in making a final decision.

Developmental programs such as the American Airlines "walk in my shoes" program help employees implement their plans. As already noted, internal and external training programs are also important in this regard as are mentoring systems, training reimbursement, and job rotation programs. Job rotation involves the systematic rotation of an employee through a number of careers, which may be lateral moves designed to introduce variety into the career or develop those skills needed to move vertically in the organization (Gutteridge, 1986).

Of the developmental programs that are offered in various organizations, perhaps none has received more attention than mentoring. Kram (1986) suggests that mentoring, which she defines as "relationships between junior and senior colleagues that contribute to career development" (p. 161), serves two functions: psychosocial and career. Career functions are those that help the junior members of the relationships prepare for advancement in their organizations, while psychosocial functions enhance their feeling of competency and clarify their identify.

To fulfill the career function, mentors "sponsor" junior members by helping them make interpersonal connections, give feedback about relevant job performance, provide support, create opportunities to demonstrate competence, and provide challenging work opportunities. The psychosocial function is fulfilled by role modeling of appropriate organizational behaviors of personal and professional concern, providing ongoing support and reinforcement, and acting as a friend (Kram, 1986).

While the obvious beneficiary of the mentoring relationship is the junior member, Kram (1985, 1986) also suggests that the senior member benefits as well. Feelings of involvement, making a contribution to the organization, the reciprocal support from the junior member of the dyad, and reliving earlier trials and successes are all benefits of being a mentor.

Mentoring is not without its pitfalls, particularly in cross-gender situations. Martin, Harrison, and Di Nitto (1983) report that cross-gender mentoring can reduce performance as well as feelings of competence and well being. Kram (1985, 1986) identifies five reasons for these outcomes:

1. Anxiety about the boundaries of the relationships, particularly concerns about intimacy and sexual attraction
2. Reliance on traditional sex roles, which results in a protective attitude by the male and a failure to establish independent roles
3. Ineffective role modeling by males because of different expectations for females in male-dominated organizations.

4. Cross-gender mentoring relations are often viewed suspiciously by managers and employees, with the result that the public image of the relationship becomes of primary concern rather than the well-being of the female.

5. When a woman working in a male-dominated organization is given special attention, peer resentment results because of concern about "unfair" competition. The result is that the woman is forced to choose between her mentor and her peers, with either choice being detrimental to her development.

Bowen (1985) also enumerates many of Kram's (1985, 1986) concerns about cross-gender mentoring. He concludes from his study that gender-related problems may not be as great as some might anticipate although envy, jealousy by spouses and others, and snide remarks by colleagues can all result from cross-gender mentoring relationships.

Almost everyone agrees that some form of mentoring occurs within most organizations and that it generally facilitates career development, a point that has been substantiated in a number of research studies which examined the careers of managers (e.g., Reich, 1985). Formal mentoring programs where junior hires are linked to senior mentors are increasingly popular, but it seems that the process of assigning mentors to protégés is tantamount to program failure (Kram, 1986). Instead of involuntary assignment, which often leads to resentment and role confusion, carefully screening potential mentors, enlisting their voluntary participation in the program, preparing them to become mentors through formal training about the role of the mentor, developing mentoring skills, orienting them to the relationship of the mentoring program to the organization and acquainting them with the potential problems associated with cross-gender and cross-cultural mentoring processes, and allowing the mentoring process to occur normally instead of forcing it seems best (Kram, 1985, 1986).

The actual design of each program will be dependent to some degree on employees' needs. It will also be related to the resources available, the culture of the organization, the goals of the organization, and the extent to which the program has been integrated with the other HRD functions.

Integration with HRD

The career development program should be designed in a manner that will enhance the overall function of the human resources development program. The following are examples of how this may be accomplished:

Performance Appraisal: This HRD function can be enhanced by designing activities that prepare employees to ask specific questions of their supervisors at the time of the performance appraisal. For example, employees may want to ask
- How does my current performance affect my promotability?
- What are my deficiencies and how can I remediate them?

- Based on your knowledge of the company, how can I best prepare myself for advancement?
- What are the strategies that I can employ that will most enhance my current job performance?

Many employees report that their managers are uncomfortable in their performance appraisal sessions, with the result that the sessions are brief and the feedback terse. Of course, managers can also be trained to be more specific in their feedback and in discussing the implications of the employee's performance and to provide "advice" regarding the directions the employee should take.

Training: Materials about the company's training policies should be included in the CIC and distributed in career counseling sessions as well as in workshops.

Job Posting: Employees who participate in the program should be made aware of the job posting procedure as well as general hiring practices.

Skills Inventories/Promotability Forecasts: The results of skills profiles developed in workshops can be placed in employees' records and thus help managers gain a more complete picture of the availability of talent and the potential promotability of various employees.

Compensation Systems: Information gained in workshops regarding employees' perceptions of the fairness and adequacy of the compensation system can be communicated to managers.

PROGRAM IMPLEMENTATION

Leibowitz, Farren, and Kaye (1986) recommend that a career development program be built on existing programs and practices. As has already been stated, for maximum effectiveness not only should the program be built on existing programs, but it should be carefully integrated with them (Gutteridge, 1986; Mirabile, 1986). Mirabile (1986) also points out that while methodology and program design are important, unless managerial and employee ownership of the program are gained, the program is likely to struggle. Leibowitz, Farren, and Kaye (1985, 1986) suggest that advisory groups made up of managers and employees may be an effective way of gaining the support that is needed to make the career development program viable. Mirabile (1986) provides even more specific suggestions, such as meeting with the executive vice president of the organization to clarify the organization commitment, to solicit input regarding the program's content, and to clarify the goals of the program as they relate to the organization's goal. He also suggests similar meetings with divisional vice presidents, a cross-section of employees, and other key personnel in the HRD organization.

After the program has been designed, a small pilot program should be implemented and evaluated (Gutteridge, 1986; Leibowitz, Farren, & Kaye, 1985, 1986; Mirabile, 1986). The evaluation of the pilot must necessarily have a focus: employee and organizational needs. Early research (Wowk, Williams, & Halstead, 1983) suggests that when formal career development programs are offered, well over 60 percent of the employees participate in some aspect of the program, with the heaviest participation being by accessing career information. They also report that managers' perceptions of the benefits of the programs include reduced turnover and increased productivity and profitability. However, it has been suggested repeatedly (e.g., Brooks, 1984; Hall, 1986; Hall & Lerner, 1980) that we need better designed evaluation studies that will produce information that relates to both managerial and employee needs.

The needs assessment discussed at the outset should be one of the reference points in designing the evaluation of the pilot programs. If the program has not met the needs of the participants, it cannot be deemed effective. It is also true that records of attendance, turnover, performance, productivity, and profitability are regularly kept by all organizations, and all existing data sources can be monitored as a source of evaluative data.

Finally, with regard to evaluation, these studies need not always be elaborate. Moravec (1982) reports that a career counseling program saved one bank nearly $2 million in 1 year by reducing employee turnover, increasing productivity, and enhancing promotability. It seems likely that both managers and employees would be quite satisfied with a program of this type.

Once evaluative data of the pilot program are collected, the program will need to be fine tuned and offered to employees throughout the organization. Perhaps the only cautionary word that should be added at this juncture is that widespread participation can be expected and that programming for full implementation should take this into account. To reintegrate and expand on the earlier report of the Wowk et al (1983) study, 77 percent of the employees in organizations that offered formalized career counseling programs had participated by accessing career information, 74 percent had participated in human resource planning, 70 percent had taken advantage of training and workshops, 61 percent had been involved in career evaluation, 60 percent had engaged in career counseling, and 47 percent had participated in special groups. While Wowk and her associates did not specify the time period in which the participation occurred, 71 percent of the programs surveyed had been implemented in the 5 years prior to their survey, and for most the participation in the programs occurred within a relatively short period of time.

BENEFITS

Even though career counselors in business and industry may need to concern themselves more with profit, they should still be concerned with the impact on individuals of the programs they design. Knowdell (1982) reports that the results of the follow-up of managers and supervisors in Livermore Labs revealed that 66 percent of both groups believed that employee morale had improved, 88 percent of the supervisors felt that the company would recoup the costs associated with the program, and 73 percent of the employees reported making significant changes in their careers or lives as a result of the program.

Schmidt (1990) summarizes the evaluation results from a number of programs in her review of the literature on the effectiveness of career development programs in business and industry. For example, in evaluations of the IBM career development program in San Jose, California, employees reported improvement in their ability to engage in self-assessment and planning. They also reported higher acceptance of responsibility and ownership of their career plan and increased awareness of career opportunities within the company. Schmidt also reports on the successes of programs located in two banks. The managers of the Third National Corporate program reported that the career development program was worthwhile but time consuming (Goodstein, 1987), while employees seemed to have experienced major improvements in their attitudes as a result of the program in the National Bank of Washington. Managers in both banks also reported a dramatic improvement in customer deposits, return on assets, and stock returns, which was one of the reasons for promoting career development (Johnson & Bell, 1987). The Dow Jones & Company employees and managers reported that communication had improved and that job changes were now viewed more positively by employees (Brozeit, 1986) as a result of their program. None of these reports is as dramatic as the 1-year saving of $2 million that resulted from the implementation of a career development program in a bank reported by Moravec (1982). However, they are generally supportive of the idea that both organizational and individual goals are enhanced.

SUMMARY

Career development in business and industry is a relatively new phenomenon, one that is likely to continue and expand. Increasingly, evidence suggests that both employer and employees benefit from these programs. As documentation of the benefits increases, so should the number and scope of these programs.

The exact nature of career development programs in business and industry will vary with the needs of the employees and the resources of the business and, just as is the case in other institutions, some programs will be minimal while others will be exemplary. However, the central elements in all programs will be accurate information about the jobs in the business, mechanisms to communicate this information, and a system that will allow employees to traverse organizational boundaries to pursue, train for, and enter new careers within the organization. Some organizations will undoubtedly rely on technology such as computerized systems to deliver these components, while others will depend more on people-oriented approaches. It is probably the case that both technology and people are needed to deliver high-quality career development programs in business and industry.

REFERENCES

Bowen, D. D. (1985). Were men meant to mentor women? *Training and Development Journal, 44,* 30–34.

Brooks, L. (1984). Career planning in the work place. In D. Brown, L. Brooks, & Associates (Eds.), *Career choice and development: Applying contemporary theories to practice* (pp. 386–405). San Francisco: Jossey-Bass.

Brozeit, R. K. (1986). If I had my druthers. *Personnel Journal, 65,* 84–90.

Goodstein, H. (1987). Career planning. *The Bunker's Magazine, 170,* 58–64.

Gutteridge, T. G. (1986). Organizational career development systems: The state of the practice. In D. T. Hall & Associates (Eds.), *Career development in organizations* (pp. 50–94). San Francisco: Jossey-Bass.

Hall, D. T. (1986). Career development in organization: Where do we go from here? In D. T. Hall & Associates (Eds.), *Career development in organization* (pp. 332–351). San Francisco: Jossey-Bass.

Hall, D. T. (1990). Career development theory in organizations. In D. Brown, L. Brooks, & Associates (Eds.), *Career choice and development* (2nd ed., pp. 422–454). San Francisco: Jossey-Bass.

Hall, D. T., & Lerner, P. (1980). Career development in work organizations: Research and practice. *Professional Psychology, 11,* 428–435.

Johnson, P., & Bell, D. (1987). Focused vision for focused performance. *Training and Development Journal, 45,* 56–59.

Keller, J., & Piotrowski, C. (1987). Career development programs in Fortune 500 firms. *Psychological Reports, 16,* 920–922.

Knowdell, R. L. (1982). Comprehensive career guidance programs in the workplace. *Vocational Guidance Quarterly, 30,* 323–326.

Knowdell, R. L. (1984). Career planning and development programs in the workplace. In N. C. Gysbers & Associates (Eds.), *Designing careers* (pp. 482–507). San Francisco: Jossey-Bass.

Kram, K. E. (1985). *Mentoring at work.* Glenview, IL: Scott, Foresman.

Kram, K. E. (1986). *Mentoring in the workplace.* In D. T. Hall & Associates (Eds.), *Career development in organizations* (pp. 160–201). San Francisco: Jossey-Bass.

Leibowitz, Z. B., Farren, C., & Kaye, B. L. (1985). The 12-fold path to CD enlightenment. *Training and Development Journal, 43,* 29–32.

Leibowitz, Z. B., Farren, C., & Kaye, B. L. (1986). *Designing career development systems.* San Francisco: Jossey-Bass.

London, M., & Stumpf, S. A. (1986). Individual and organizational career development in changing times. In D. T. Hall & Associates (Eds.), *Career development in organizations* (pp. 21–49). San Francisco: Jossey-Bass.

Martin, P. Y., Harrison, D., & DiNitto, D. (1983). Advancement for women to hierarchical organization: Analysis of problems and prospects: *Journal of Applied Behavioral Science, 19,* 18–33.

Mirabile, R. J. (1986). Designing CD programs the OD way. *Training and Development Journal, 44,* 38–41.

Moravec, M. (1982). A cost effective career planning program requires a strategy. *Personnel Administration, 27,* 28–32.

National Alliance of Business. (1986). *Employment policies: Looking to the year 2000.* Washington, DC.: Author.

National Career Development Association. (1988). *Planning for and working in America: Report of a national survey.* Alexandria, VA: Author.

Osipow, S. H. (1982). Counseling psychology: Applications in the world of work. *The Counseling Psychologist, 10,* 19–25.

Reich, M. H. (1985). Executive views from both sides of mentoring. *Personnel, 62,* 42–46.

Schmidt, S. (1990). Career development programs in business and industry. *Journal of Employment Counseling, 27,* 76–83.

UAW-Ford. (1987). *Life education planning program.* A status report in the UAW-Ford program. Dearborn, MI: UAW-Ford National Development and Training Center.

Wilbur, C. S., & Vermilyea, C. J. (1982). Some business advice for counseling psychologist. *The Counseling Psychologist, 10,* 29–30.

Wowk, R., Williams, D., & Halstead, G. (1983). Do formal career development programs really increase employee participation? *Training and Development Journal, 44,* 82–83.

__18__

Career Counselors
in Private Practice

There are literally thousands of counselors, psychologists, social workers, and other mental health professionals in private practice delivering a variety of mental health services. It is likely that a few hundred of these professionals, primarily counselors and counseling psychologists, provide some form of career counseling services to the public. It is also likely that this number will grow. In the 1989 NCDA survey of American adults conducted by the Gallup Organization, 7 percent of those surveyed reported that they had needed assistance in selecting, changing, or getting a job in the year prior to the survey. This percentage represents nearly 10 million adults. Of those people needing help, about one-third went to job service counselors (Employment Security) and a few more than one fifth, or nearly 2 million, reported seeking assistance from a professional counselor. Because of the nature of the question on the Gallup survey, it is uncertain whether assistance was sought from private practitioners, but it seems reasonable to assume that a large number used the resources of the career counselor in private practice.

In this chapter, several issues regarding private practice are addressed, including qualifications for career counselors, how private practitioners are regulated, consumer guidelines for selecting a private practitioner, and some recommended steps for establishing a private practice.

QUALIFICATIONS

In Chapter 14, the basic qualifications for practice as a career counselor were outlined. That discussion is not repeated here. However, it is important to note that many states have licensure, certification, and registry laws that regulate the practice of psychologists, counselors, social workers, and others. For example, all 50 states have licensure laws for psychologists, and approximately 40 states have licensure laws or some form of regulatory

477

statute for counselors. For the most part, the licensure laws for psychologists require that people who purport to be psychologists must be licensed whether they practice in public institutions or are engaged in private practice. On the other hand, the regulatory statutes for counselors are primarily aimed at regulating practice in the private domain. Unfortunately, these laws often have loopholes that allow some private practitioners to evade regulation (Brown & Srebalus, 1988). For example, a North Carolina statute established a registry for counselors which permits professionals interested in becoming registered to meet the requirements (e.g., meeting the training and supervision requirements and passing a test to demonstrate knowledge) and call themselves Registered Practicing Counselors. However, counselors who wish to enter private practice, including offering career counseling services, do not have to be registered and may use the titles counselor, career counselor, career consultant, along with any other title as long as they do not call themselves registered practicing counselors. While the regulatory statutes for counselors are much more stringent in states such as Mississippi, Virginia, and Florida, the extent of regulation varies considerably in other states, with at least 10 states having no regulation.

One state, New Jersey, has recently (1990) adopted a statute that requires employment agencies and employment agents to be licensed and career consulting and outplacement firms to be registered with the Chief of Bureau of Employment and Personnel Services. Admittedly, the New Jersey statute establishes a minimum criteria for providing placement and counseling services, but it is a landmark effort to regulate a wide range of services. It seems likely that specialty standards for career counselors will evolve in the near future in many states and that some will adopt statutes similar to New Jersey's. The only reliable means of determining the nature of the regulatory statutes in your state is to contact the licensing boards and get copies of the regulatory statutes as well as the rules established by the board to govern practitioners in your specialty.

GUIDELINES FOR CONSUMERS

Caveat emptor, or "let the consumer beware," is probably the best advice for consumers who are seeking assistance with career-related problems. The reason for this, as has already been noted, is that in many states career counselors are unregulated by statute. To assist consumers to make wise choices, the National Career Development Association has issued consumer guidelines for selecting a career counselor (NCDA, 1988). These guidelines are paraphrased as follows:

Credentials
Career counselors should have an earned graduate degree in an appropriate mental health specialty such as counseling, counseling psychology, or social work.

As a part of their training they should have completed a supervised field experience which involved career counseling.

They should have appropriate work experience.

They should have developed a knowledge base that will support their activities as a career counselor, including knowledge about career development, assessment, occupational information, employability skills, the integration of life roles, and the stresses of working, job loss, and/or career transitions.

Fees

Career counselors should have established fees and allow clients to choose services, terminate whenever they deem appropriate, and pay for only those services that have been provided.

Promises

Professional career counselors should refrain from making claims such as promising careers that have higher salaries or that they can provide immediate resolution to career problems.

Ethics

Career counselors follow ethical codes such as those published by the American Psychological Association or the American Association for Counseling and Development.

Even if consumers were aware of the guidelines developed by the National Career Development Association, it is likely that they may still be confused by the number of people who call themselves career counselors. For example, there are job placement counselors who offer resume preparation services, outplacement counselors who assist people whose jobs have been terminated find suitable employment, and a variety of other people offering "career counseling." Unfortunately, some of these people have little training in career counseling, while others may have completed a 1- or 2-week training course and received impressive certificates from what appear to be creditable organizations.

As suggested earlier, many states are considering more stringent legislation to regulate career counseling because it is virtually impossible to sort out qualified from unqualified practitioners. Until professional organizations can inform the public and stringent legislation can eliminate the unqualified people, "let the consumer beware" is the best advice that can be offered.

ESTABLISHING A PRIVATE PRACTICE

Almost everyone who has been involved in setting up a private practice will attest to the difficulty involved in the process, particularly if the practitioner chooses not to join a group practice where referrals are immediately available from other professionals. Many psychologists and counselors who enter private practice enter a group practice, and then choose to offer both personal and career counseling. Often they find that their group practice colleagues refer their "career cases" to them because they lack the skill to provide the service themselves. Other career counselors choose to set up independent practices and offer only career development services. In this section some of the general concerns regarding establishing a private practice are discussed.

Types of Services

Career counselors often offer a wide variety of services, including career counseling with individuals and groups, consultations, job placement, testing, outplacement, resume development and the development of other employability skills, retirement planning, career/life role integration counseling, spousal relocation, training, program evaluation, work adjustment counseling, and vocational appraisal services. Since marketing is a critical part of a successful private practice, practitioners must realistically determine if they have the skills to offer a service and whether there is a market for that service. The following are potential clients for each of the aforementioned services:

Service	*Potential Clients*
Individual and group career counseling	The general public; may target specialized groups such as transitional workers, women, or retirees
Testing	The general public; may target high school students doing career planning or other groups
Outplacement	Business and industry involved in reducing their work force and seeking placement services; often specialize in white-collar workers
Job placement	Members of the general public; specialization often occurs in that some agencies specialize in clerical, technical, or other types of workers (see Chapter 16)
Head hunters	A specialized form of job placement; often involves recruiting and placing corporate executives, school superintendents, scientists
Resume and employability skills development	General public; often targets young workers (e.g., college students), workers in transition, and those who have lost their jobs
Retirement planning	Workers preparing for retirement; may target military or other people from a specific industry

Career/life role integration	General public; may target workers at mid-life or new entrants to labor force
Training	Other professionals who want to upgrade their skills in various areas; may target those interested in setting up a private practice
Consultation	Businesses, governmental agencies, schools, colleges and universities, federal programs (e.g., JTPA)
Career development program evaluation	Businesses, governmental agencies, schools, colleges and universities, federal programs with career development programs
Work adjustment counseling	The general public; on a contract basis to businesses
Spousal relocation	Businesses; primarily those businesses interested in transferring executives who have employed spouses who are seeking careers
Vocational appraisal	Social Security administration; insurance companies; others interested in establishing extent of vocational disability
Career information	Develop customized information packets for clients who do not wish to pursue information independently

In addition to determining whether they have the skills to offer a service and whether there is a client group available in their area, practitioners must assess the degree to which competition is available. For example, outplacement has become highly competitive, and large outplacement firms such as Drake Beam Marin not only have well-developed outplacement programs but they have a national network of offices that can be called on to assist workers find jobs in a wide variety of job markets. These same firms often offer a spousal relocation service that not only is lucrative but helps them establish corporate contacts. Only a few individuals can compete with the large outplacement firms. However, a number of career counselors have developed outplacement services for small companies in areas where relocation does not entail extensive geographic relocation.

Location of the Office

Many private practitioners find it convenient and less expensive to use portions of their residence for their office. Obviously, this eliminates commuting, rental fees, janitorial services, etc. Some parking must be provided for clients, and this may become a major issue in some areas, particularly if group counseling is provided for 8 to 12 clients at a time. Using one's residence as a business office is impossible in some residential areas because of zoning restrictions.

Many counselors locate offices in settings that cater to professionals because of accessibility, the availability of parking, opportunities to share experiences with other professionals regarding the services of a receptionist or a telephone answering service and perhaps billing services, and opportunities to increase the likelihood of referrals. An office located in a professional office building also helps to project the professional image that many career counselors desire, particularly if they are involved with consultation in business and industry. The exact location and nature of the office will depend on the types of services to be offered, costs, desire for professional image, and convenience.

Services to Be Offered

As has already been noted, career counselors may offer a variety of services to the public. The backbone of most private practices is career counseling, but many practitioners are engaged in many other services. While it is probably true that many private practitioners simply begin their business and let it evolve, a careful plan should be developed to offer services and market them to the public.

In deciding what services to offer, the following questions should be posed (Ridgewood Financial Institute, 1990). First, "Am I really in business?" It is certainly the case that many private practitioners hedge on this question simply because their private practice is a part-time practice. Before deciding what type of services are to be offered, the response to this question must be in the affirmative and must be followed by the obvious question, "If I am in business, what business am I in? Will I specialize in career counseling? If yes, which services will I offer? Are there any underserved groups in my community? Are there career development services being offered that could be offered more effectively? At less cost?" Once private practitioners decide if they are really in business, that their private practice is really more than a hobby, and decide the business that they are in, it is time to ask a series of other questions.

Chief among the other questions to be answered is, "Am I projecting the right image?" (Ridgewood Financial Institute, 1990). It is certainly possible to build a successful private practice that specializes in career counseling operating out of an office in the home. It is less likely that a private practitioner can build a highly successful consultation or outplacement out of a home office, primarily because of the need to establish an image that will attract potential clients. For example, it may be difficult for a corporate executive to have confidence that a "shoestring" operation can provide services to 20 executives who need to be relocated because their jobs have been terminated. In real estate, there are three rules for selecting property: location, location, location. In private practice, particularly if there is an expectation of competing with well-established outplacement and corporate counseling firms, the three rules may well be image, image, image. Credentials, office space, stationery, business cards, personal dress and demeanor, and written and verbal presentations are all a part of one's business image and must be attended to in building a practice.

To assess image, compare facilities, equipment, stationery, dress, etc. to those of the competition and ask, "Which would I choose?" Some potential private practitioners, after making this comparision, have decided to join group practices so that they can learn to project the "right" image. Others have elected not to compete for business in certain arenas.

In the following section, marketing a private practice is discussed. However, in assessing whether to start or expand a current practice, the question arises, "Do I know how to market my current services, or if I elect, to expand a new service?" (Ridgewood Financial Institute, 1990). There are literally dozens of ways to market services. Private practitioners must be aware of these and, perhaps more importantly, be apprised of which ones are actually cost effective. If a knowledge of marketing strategies and their effectiveness has not been developed, marketing consultants may be contacted.

Ultimately a business plan must be developed with specific objectives. Marketing, selection of office space, image, and a host of other decisions and activities grow out of the objectives that are established.

Marketing the Service

Most career counselors working in public institutions are aware of the need to market their programs, but because they are paid regularly by a public or private institution, the immediate need to market is less pressing. Private practitioners are paid by their clients, and thus no clients—no income. This is precisely the reason why many private practitioners start working in institutional settings, initiate part-time private practices, gradually expand their practices, and once a client base is built, sever their relationships with their employers. These successful private practitioners have learned to market their services successfully. There are many strategies that can be employed to market career development services. But before any strategy is employed, the first step is to get comfortable with the idea of advertising. Many counselors who have worked in public institutions have an aversion to advertising (Ridgewood Financial Institute, 1990) because it almost seems unprofessional. Advertising is legal, it is professional, and it is essential to the establishment and maintenance of your private practice. Obviously, advertisements should be tastefully done, but there are no limitations on where they can be placed. Newspapers, newsletters, magazine ads, billboards, television and radio spots, and posters are a few of the potential ways of advertising a service. Another way to advertise your service is a tasteful brochure that outlines your services and solicits business (see Figure 18.1).

FIGURE 18.1   *Portions Taken from the Brochure Layout of Career Directions, Hackensack, New Jersey*

Is Career Counseling or Planning for You?
- I would like to examine my career options
- I would like to assess my abilities and interests
- I am not satisfied with my present position
- I cannot decide on a career
- I am uncertain how to change my career after the age of 35
- I am registered with fifteen employment agencies and not one has contacted me for an interview
- I don't know how to set up a complete employment search campaign
- I feel nervous and uncomfortable in an interview
- I want to return to school but cannot decide on a course of study

About Career Directions
- Career Planning and Decision Making
- Preretirement
- Midcareer Change
- Job Market Reentry
- Employment Search Skills
- Job Campaign Strategy
- Complete Resume Writing Service
- Interview Skills
- Aptitude, Achievement, and Interest Testing
- Advanced Educational Planning

One of the best types of advertisements is the nonad. One psychologist in private practice writes regularly for an airlines magazine. Because of the exposure he has received, he is invited to conduct more than 100 workshops per year. Another prepares a weekly column for a local newspaper. Still others serve in high-visibility volunteer positions where their names will be mentioned frequently in the local news media. Making appearances at several clubs, parent groups, and professional associations to discuss career counseling and development is another nonad marketing strategy employed by many practitioners. To use this strategy effectively, the private practitioner must have good public speaking skills and must be able to project a professional image. Name recognition is an important part of marketing any service, and depending on the nonad activity, the service provided can help build the desired image.

A marketing campaign may begin with nonads, but soon a target group must be developed, a list of the strategies to be employed must be compiled, an advertising budget must be developed, and an advertising calendar must be laid out. This campaign will be tied to what services are to be offered. For example, a private practitioner might decide to run weekly advertisements in the local newspaper to publicize a resume development service in January through May, because many high school and college students are beginning the job hunt at this time. These advertisements might be supplemented with posters placed in dormitories and on high school bulletin boards. The following are tips from successful practitioners about marketing a private practice.

> Private career counseling demands flexibility on the part of the owner/counselor along with creativity since private practice income fluctuates. Career counseling expertise needs to be marketed to several sectors other than private clients. Seminars, consulting, writing newspaper columns, teaching, and outreach counseling for nonprofit groups are necessary in order to advertise the practice, "grow the business," and make an adequate income.
> Joan F. Youngblood,
> Creative Career Counseling

> In order to make a private career counseling practice thrive, you need to attract clients. Advertising and publicity are two ways of attracting clients. Know the difference between advertising and publicity. Advertising costs you money. Publicity brings you money.

> To get your private career counseling practice going, (i.e., making money), you will need to spend up to 50 percent of your time in marketing and sales activities. Marketing and sales are *not* like counseling activities. If marketing and sales are not activities that you enjoy, you should think long and hard about spending so much time in an activity that you don't like. Think about this—Would *you* advise a client to spend 50 percent of his or her time in an activity that the client dislikes?
> Richard L. Knowdell,
> National Certified Career Counselor

> Networking and visibility within the communities you are planning to serve is essential. Because counselors are often uncomfortable doing marketing, they often do too little to promote themselves. Referrals come from a broad marketing campaign, encompassing contact development with friends, colleagues, and other professionals who potentially serve your client profile in other capacities. Initially, 50 percent of your time should be spent in marketing activities to generate referrals and a client base. Advertising, workshops, and community service are other techniques that are essential in your marketing plan to increase credibility and visibility as an expert in your field.
> Barbara Tartaglione,
> Career Connection

Networking is a process by which counselors interact with other professionals for the purpose of gaining access to business opportunities and/or referrals. Career counselors often attend local, regional, and statewide professional meetings for counselors to develop and reinforce their own expertise and to enhance the likelihood that clients will be referred to them by other professionals. Career counselors who offer consultation to business and industry should probably extend their networking to organizations like the American Society for Training and Development along with local meetings of counselors and psychologists, because people employed in local businesses belong to this association.

Direct solicitation of services via mail, telephone, or personal contact is also a method of gaining clients, particularly if consultation services are offered. These types of contacts can also be used to extend networks and perhaps gain referrals for other services offered, such as career counseling. Some career counselors believe that the best contacts are made in informal meetings, such as over lunch. While there is no data to support this supposition, the business lunch seems to be widely employed as a marketing strategy.

All forms of advertisement should adhere to the ethical guidelines of the practitioner's profession. Generally speaking, advertisements may contain a listing of the person's highest relevant degree, licenses and certifications, and professional services offered. Advertisements may not include endorsements for past clients and may not make claims of likely success, even if these statements do represent the facts (NBCC, 1992). Sample advertisements are shown in Figure 18.2.

It is also worth noting that networking strategies, advertisements, public appearances, direct solicitations, and other marketing strategies, while they do yield immediate results, do not necessarily result in great numbers of clients or multiple offers to engage in lucrative counseling jobs. The marketing of a private practice can take months and perhaps years. Moreover, marketing *never* stops. Clients terminate and consultation contracts end. To continue to earn, clients must be found and new contracts negotiated. Marketing may become easier, but it always remains as an essential task for private practitioners.

BUDGETING

A private practice is a for-profit business which requires a great deal of planning, including the development of a careful budget. Figure 18.3 shows a budget planning sheet utilized by Frank Karpati of Career Directions.

It is also imperative that careful logs be kept if kept for income tax purposes and many commercially developed log books are available. Any type of record, including ordinary date books, will suffice so long as the records are backed up by receipts for all expenses. In determining whether a deduction is legitimate the IRS expects the taxpayer to establish a clear relationship between the expense and the business. An emergency room physician successfully argued that a garage door opener allowed him to get

FIGURE 18.2   *Sample Telephone Directory Advertisement for Career Directions, Hackensack, New Jersey*

Professional RESUMES

CONSULTATION ● DESIGN ● PRINTING

Career Counseling, Testing
Interviewing Skills Training
Employment Search Strategy
Planning
BY NATIONAL CERTIFIED
Professional Career Counselor

(CAREER DIRECTIONS)

THE PROFESSIONAL RESUME PEOPLE
NO FEE for Initial Consultation

(DAY OR EVENING APPOINTMENTS)

487-0808

Professional CAREER COUNSELING & TESTING SERVICES RESUMES

Employment Search,
Interviewing & Salary
Negotiating Skills Training
by NATIONAL CERTIFIED
Professional Career Counselor

(CAREER DIRECTIONS)

NO FEE for Initial Consultation

487-0808
(Day or Evening Appts.)

CAREER DIRECTIONS

PROFESSIONAL RESUMES
CAREER COUNSELING TESTING
INTERVIEWING SKILLS, TRAINING &
Employment Search Strategy Planning

by NATIONAL CERTIFIED
PROFESSIONAL CAREER
COUNSELOR

No Fee For Initial Consultation
DAY OR EVENING APPOINTMENTS

Hackensack Area 487-0808

Professional RESUMES

CONSULTATION ● DESIGN ● PRINTING

Career Counseling, Testing
Interviewing Skills Training
Employment Search Strategy
Planning

Frank S. Karpall, M.A., N.C.C., N.J.C.C., N.C.C.C., ABVE-Diplomate
NATIONAL CERTIFIED
professional career counselor

(CAREER DIRECTIONS)

NO FEE for Initial Consultation
(DAY OR EVENING APPOINTMENTS)

487-0808

FIGURE 18.3   *Annual Budget Planning/Expenses; Professional/Business Expenses*

Advertising			**Outside Contractors**		
Yellow Pages	_____		Administrative Services	_____	
Other Printed Material	_____		Consultants & Training	_____	
Mailing/Postage	_____		Total	$ _____	
Total	$ _____				
			Rent		
Automobile			Total	_____	
Purchase	_____				
Depreciation	_____		**Office Equipment**		
Insurance/Registration	_____		Service Contracts	_____	
Repairs/Maintenance	_____		Computer	_____	
Fuel	_____		Depreciation	_____	
Total	$ _____		Typewriter	_____	
			Depreciation	_____	
Professional Membership			HP Laser	_____	
and Dues			Depreciation	_____	
Total	$ _____		Copier	_____	
			Depreciation	_____	
Publications			Total	$ _____	
Library	_____				
Depreciation	_____		**Office Furniture**		
Total	$ _____		Desks	_____	
			Depreciation	_____	
Professional Liability			Chairs	_____	
Insurance			Depreciation	_____	
Total	$ _____		Filing Cabinets	_____	
			Depreciation	_____	
Computerized Services			Other	_____	
Software	_____		Total	$ _____	
Supplies	_____				
Printing	_____				
			Telephone	_____	
Business Travel			Office	_____	
Air Transportation	_____		Home	_____	
Ground Transportation	_____		Total	$ _____	
Lodging	_____				
Meals	_____		**Public Relations/Entertainment**		
Miscellaneous	_____		Total	$ _____	
Total	$ _____				

to emergencies sooner. A noted speaker who gives 100 to 150 speeches per year also argued that a jacuzzi was essential to help him deal with the stresses of travel. However, both these cases are on the "fringes of acceptability" and might have been disallowed by another auditor. Entertainment, travel, meals, equipment purchases, furniture, malpractice insurance, and continuing education are all legitimate expenses if records are kept properly. However, a consultation with a knowledgeable accountant may be the first step to take in setting up a private practice, and continuing consultation regarding the legitimacy of expenses may be the best means of avoiding problems with the IRS.

Fees

The guideline established for fee setting by the National Board of Certified Counselors (1992) suggests that the career counselor must take into account the financial status of the client. While this is the guideline most practitioners adhere to, it does not answer the question, "Assuming that the client has adequate financial resources, what should I charge?" There are several possible answers to this question. One of the most common ways of setting fees in career counseling is to look at the fees of competitors and establish a commensurate fee schedule (Ridgewood Financial Institute, 1990). Another is to set fees in accordance with those being charged for psychotherapy, apparently based on the assumption that the practitioner's time and services are as valuable as those of the psychotherapist. A common fee-setting strategy is to charge less for group counseling than for individual counseling. Unfortunately, there are no data that provide definitive answers to the question, "What are career counselors charging for various services?"

There are surveys that provide data about the cost of psychotherapy (Ridgewood Financial Institute, 1990), which suggest that fees ranging from $35 to $150 per hour and beyond are charged by various mental health practitioners for psychotherapy. As suggested earlier, some practitioners gear their fee structure to that of psychotherapy. Most clients are probably paying $60 to $80 per hour for career counseling based on this one source. However, many career counselors also charge assessment fees for interest inventories, personality assessments, and aptitude tests, and these can run to $300 and beyond in some instances.

If the data about the fees for career counseling are unclear, those regarding career development consultation are simply unavailable. While some consultants who work with business and industry to set up career development programs, design performance appraisal systems, and improve employee-employer relations charge $1,000 to 1,200 per day based on private feedback to the authors, it is likely that the range of fees for consultation service is much broader—perhaps ranging from $500 to $5,000 per day, depending on the problem and the reputation of the consultant.

In addition, relatively little information about fees is available in the area of outplacement work. Outplacement firms and individual practitioners have demanded and received a fee based on the employee's salary for 3 months (see Chapter 16). Therefore, if the employee is paid $5,000 per month, the outpatient fee would be $15,000. However, these fees have been charged for outplacement of middle and upper management personnel. When businesses hire outplacement firms to work with blue-collar workers, the fee is typically much smaller, although the number of employees is usually larger.

The fee schedule should be established at the time the service is initiated along with the method of payment. The following statement appears in the contract signed by each client of Career Directions.

Fee Schedule
The fee for a 70–120 minute consulting is $180.00 payable at the time of the conference. This fee also includes counselor research, preparation and testing services. Therefore, for the fee the client should expect to receive 2-1/2 to 3 hours of professional services. Although the exact number of sessions cannot be initially determined, counseling is usually completed within *four* to *six* sessions.

In order for the counseling service to maintain its ability to function and provide the services you need, it is necessary to require of all clients that they be responsible for the time set aside for their consultation. This is particularly essential since a counselor's time is allotted to you alone for the duration of your session, and cannot be used in any other way. In the event that illness or emergency prevents your coming for counseling, you must notify the agency at least 24 hours in advance. The counselor will be happy to discuss this matter with you at length if you deem it appropriate.

One factor that plays a major role in the establishment of fees for psychotherapy that cannot be counted on in providing reimbursement for career counseling is health insurance. Many clients who come for psychotherapy have health insurance that pays some or all of the expense of the treatment. In those instances where insurance pays a portion (80 percent) of an established fee (perhaps $70 per hour) or any established fee ($50 per hour), psychotherapists often charge more for the service since the out-of-pocket cost to the client is not great. However, unless the client also has a mental health problem that can be treated simultaneously with the career problem, health insurance will not pay for the service. This fact alone may dictate that fees for career counseling be lower than those for psychotherapy.

Billing

One inevitable aspect of all forms of private practice is the need to collect fees. Many practitioners request that payment by check or credit card be made at the time the counseling is provided. However, whenever bills are unpaid, regardless of the circumstances, billing agencies and even collection agencies are often utilized to collect overdue accounts. The amount of money spent on collection and lost as a result of unpaid bills will vary with the situation. However, bad debts are a realistic part of all business and reduce expected income.

The Ridgewood Financial Institute (1990) suggests that there are several ways to increase payment for services. For example, collect complete information on every client including name, address, telephone number, and Social Security number so that collection can be expedited. Perhaps more importantly, when clients fill out information forms about themselves they should also be informed of their financial obligation, how payment is expected (cash, check, or credit card), and what will happen on past-due accounts. Some practitioners charge late fee penalties, sometimes labeled as business costs. Payment at time of service delivery is a means of lowering unpaid bills. This will not prevent receipt of bad checks, but it will probably reduce the number of outstanding bills to be collected.

Many practitioners have a series of "collection letters," with the message ranging from a friendly reminder that payment is past due to a warning that the bill is about to be turned over to a collection agency. The use of a collection agency is a last resort, since their fees often run to 50 percent of the debt and ultimately many of these agencies rely on threats to credit ratings as a basic collection strategy. Finally, some practitioners bring suit in small claims courts, have office assistants telephone people in arrears, and even accept in-kind services (such as repairs to home or office) as payments. While none of these methods is particularly desirable, they all result in increased income and should be considered as alternative methods for increasing the profitability of the practice.

Other Business Details

The establishment of a private practice involves dealing with a host of other details including establishing a recordkeeping system, considering the possibility of using an answering service (versus an answering machine), hiring assistants and/or clerical workers, choosing an appropriate liability insurance policy, and selecting an accountant. Some of these decisions are relatively simple. For example, most practitioners purchase liability insurance from companies that offer group rates through professional associations such as the American Association for Counseling and Development and the American Psychological Association. Other decisions will depend on costs, the image that is being projected, and the personal preference of the practitioner.

Developing a Testing File
One detail that deserves special consideration is the establishment of a testing file. All private practitioners are faced with identifying and securing a set of tests and inventories that can be used to facilitate their clients' career development. The first consideration in this process is to "qualify" to purchase tests. Publishing companies that produce, distribute, and in many instances score the results require that people who order tests provide proof that they are qualified by virtue of training, licensing, and/or certification to administer and interpret the tests that they wish to purchase. Professional ethics also dictate that competence be considered as a primary consideration when using tests and inventories. Finally, the potential for malpractice suits against people who carelessly use tests and inventories is considerable.

Establishing a Career Information Center

Earlier, the importance of a career information center was discussed as well as some guidelines for establishing a center. The National Career Development Association publication *Designing and Implementing a Career Information Center* (Brown & Brown, 1990) can also serve as a useful guide. However, an objective for the private practitioner must be to minimize costs while providing an adequate information source to meet client needs. Answering the questions "Who are (or will be) my clients?" and "What will their informational needs be?" is the starting place for establishing the center. The next step is probably to determine what information can be obtained inexpensively through your state Career Information Delivery System (CIDS) and through government publications such as *Occupational Outlook Handbook*, the *Guide to Occupational Information*, and special publications from the Department of Labor's Bureau of Labor Statistics. Once this process has been completed, materials can be purchased from the numerous commercial publishers to complete the library.

SUMMARY

Career counseling in private practice offers a rewarding if challenging career option. However, it also requires a set of skills in addition to those taught in most graduate programs. Career counseling in private practice requires that counselors be able to conceptualize and market a business operation, which involves everything from selecting an office to designing a marketing comparison. Individuals considering this option must carefully consider whether they are equipped personally and professionally to take on such an enterprise. The professional and economic rewards will probably be substantial for those who successfully develop a private practice, although as is the case with most small businesses, the risk of failure measured in economic terms will be high.

REFERENCES

Brown, S. T., & Brown, D. (1990). *Designing and implementing a career information center.* Alexandria, VA: National Career Development Association.

Brown, D., & Srebalus, D. J. (1988). *Introduction to the counseling profession.* Englewood Cliffs, NJ: Prentice Hall.

Gallup Organization. (1989). *A Gallup survey regarding career development.* Princeton, NJ: Author.

NBCC. (1992). *Certification information and application.* Alexandria, VA: National Board for Certified Counselors.

NCDA. (1988). *The professional practice of career counseling and consultation: A resource document.* Alexandria, VA: National Career Development Association.

Ridgewood Financial Institute. (1990). *Guide to private practice.* Hawthorne, NJ: Author.

19

Trends and Issues in Career Information, Career Counseling, and Career Development Programming

Chapter 1 discussed some of the trends influencing career development. In this chapter, we again turn to the future and try to identify the trends and issues that will affect career development theory, research, and practice in the 1990s and beyond. Of course, predicting the future can be risky as well as rewarding. For example, Herr (1974), writing in the National Vocational Guidance Association's decennial volume *Vocational Guidance and Human Development*, made the following predictions for the decade following the publication of the volume: (1) There will be increased specificity in the objectives of vocational guidance programs; (2) the counselor will increasingly act as an agent of change, and "he or she will proffer his (or her) skills indirectly rather than directly in behalf of those he (or she) serves" (p. 564); and (3) the emphasis of vocational guidance in the next decade will be on prevention rather than remediation. History has documented the accuracy of Herr's prediction that career development programs are designed to produce specific results, and they are currently more likely to be evaluated on their ability to produce specific outcomes. However, the predicted shift in counselors' roles from working with individuals to functioning as environmental agents of change has never materialized. We have seen a rise in the number of preventive career development programs in the career education movement of the 1970s, but by 1981 when Ronald Reagan assumed the presidency, the back-to-basics educational movement had all but eliminated these programs in most of our country's schools. There are still preventive career development programs in place, but in 1987 and 1989 only about 40 percent of American adults were in their current positions because of planning (Gallup Organization, 1987, 1989), which suggests that large numbers of people are not being affected by any type of programs. These same Gallup surveys suggest that 10 to 12 million adults each year need assistance in finding jobs, again suggesting that preventive programs are either not in place or are not working.

Ten years after Herr's (1974) projections, Gysbers (1984) took on a similar task, again writing for the National Vocational Guidance Association. He made the following projections regarding career development theory and practice:

1. The meanings given to career and career development continue to evolve from simply new words for vocation (occupation) and vocational development (occupational development) to words that describe human careers in terms of life roles, life settings, and life events that develop over the life span.
2. Substantial changes have taken place and will continue to occur in the economic, occupational, industrial, and social environments and structure in which the human career develops and interacts and in which career guidance and counseling take place.
3. The number, diversity, and quality of career development programs, tools, and techniques will continue to increase in almost geometric progression.
4. The population served by career development programming and the settings where career development programs and services take place have increased and will continue to do so. (p. 619)

Gysbers's (1984) predictions are somewhat more general than those set forth by Herr (1974) and as such had a higher probability of being accurate when they were cast. However, at this writing it is still unclear whether the meaning of career development is actually going to broaden, as Gysbers (1984) suggests. Some, like McDaniels (1989), certainly seem to be pushing in that direction by defining *career* as something other than the occupations held over the life span. Others, like Holland (1985), seem to be more in favor of the traditional idea of career. However, economic, social, and industrial change has been accelerated, the number and diversity of career development tools (although *not* the quality) has increased rapidly, and the populations and settings served by career development specialists certainly has increased since 1984.

Both Herr (1974) and Gysbers (1984) made relatively few predictions about the future of career development and, as has already been noted, took somewhat different approaches to doing so (general vs. specific). Zunker (1990), on the other hand, made nearly two dozen projections, focusing primarily on the issues that will confront workers in the future. For example, he projected that the future would provide alternative work patterns such as job sharing and telecommuting (working in the home on a computer), trends that are well documented by McDaniels (1989). However, he also predicted that the job market of the future would make some dramatic shifts, a prediction that is clearly contradicted by the data presented earlier in this volume.

Similarly, Zunkers's (1990) projection that workers would place less value on financial rewards seems not to be well founded, probably because the "data" that he used seem to be drawn from armchair philosophy rather than empirical sources.

For the most part, Herr (1974), Gysbers (1984), and Zunker (1990) were on target with their projections. When they became quite specific in their projections or relied on "faulty" databases, predictions appeared to be less accurate. The projections of trends and issues that follow are, like those of others, likely to be subject to error. However, they are made in an attempt to prepare readers to anticipate those forces which will impinge on them and their clients.

TRENDS: CAREER INFORMATION

1. There will be a continuing effort to improve the delivery of occupational information. The National Occupational Information Coordinating Committee (NOICC) was established in 1976 as an interdepartmental federal agency for the purpose of improving the quality and delivery of occupational information. A part of the enabling legislation that established NOICC also provided monies to set up state affiliates (SOICCs), although several states (e.g., Oregon, Ohio, Washington, and Wisconsin) had organized efforts prior to the establishment of NOICC. The SOICCs consist of representatives from vocational education, state economic development agency, employment security agency, job training council, and vocational rehabilitation agency. Each state has established a career information delivery system (CIDS), and these in turn have developed mechanisms to transmit labor market information to career decision makers. Importantly, these agencies have not restricted themselves to occupational information per se but have chosen to disseminate educational and occupational information as well as information about employment rates and job trends. For example, the Washington SOICC maintains state and local files that include job descriptions; salary information; job outlook data; information about vocational-technical schools, community colleges, 4-year colleges, and graduate schools; and information about the military. The information delivery systems vary by state but may include time-share on-line computer services, microcomputer programs, tabloids, microfiche systems, books of information, or all of these. Some SOICCs, such as the one in South Carolina, have entered into contracts with businesses to develop internal labor market information systems which contain job descriptions, training requirements, and other information that would be essential to setting up an in-house career development program.

   Currently, secondary schools, vocational-technical schools, 2- and 4-year colleges, private schools, employment security offices, rehabilitation agencies, correctional institutions, libraries, businesses, Job Training Partnership Act programs, and various types of counseling agencies access the information provided by CIDS in various states. It is expected that the SOICCs will continue to expand and improve the CIDS in the foreseeable future.

2. There will be an increased sensitivity to, as well as increased efforts to meet, the occupational information needs of adults. The national survey commissioned by the National Career Development Association in conjunction with NOICC (Gallup Organization, 1989) suggests that 25 percent of adults have never accessed any type of occupational information. The problem is most acute among those adults who never finished high school (40 percent reported using no source) and Hispanics (35 percent reported using no source), but even one fifth of college graduates reported using no source of occupational information. When these data are paired with other information (e.g., only 41 percent of the employed respondents reported being in their current jobs because they followed a definite plan, and 27 percent felt they needed assistance finding occupational information), the problem of helping adults access and use career information seems acute.

3. Interactive, computerized informational systems will become more widely utilized. The provisions for designing and implementing a comprehensive career information program at any level are fraught with problems (Brown & Brown, 1990). For example, information must be continuously updated, stored to maximize access, and selected so that the target audience will be motivated to use it. Print materials, needle sorts, microfiche, and other mechanical systems are difficult to keep up to date, store, and often are not highly attractive to the reader. Some of the early computerized systems produced data too slowly because of the capacity of the computers and did not allow for random assess and thus were rigid. With the introduction of laser technology, compact disks are being developed that contain both visual and audio messages. Interactive systems provide users the opportunity to respond to questions posed by the informational system as well as pose questions to the system. The introduction of visual images of college campuses, workers, technical training faculties, work settings, etc. will increase motivation to use these systems. Perhaps just as importantly, subscriber services will update these systems routinely. Currently, career counselors are largely relying on print materials, traditional audiovisual materials, and computerized systems that, while interactive, are still somewhat slow and devoid of a visual dimension. The future will see a decreasing reliance on print material and outdated computerized programs as technology advances and the cost of interactive compact disks decreases.

4. Graduate school courses emphasizing career information will continue to decrease. A survey of counselor education programs (Sampson & Liberty, 1989) suggests that the textbooks used in the preparation of

counselors in the area of career development increasingly emphasize career counseling and focus on occupational information. At the time when members of our society need more career information, training programs appear to be placing less emphasis on orienting counselors and psychologists to identifying, evaluating, and using information. This is partially why the NOICC (1986) commissioned the development of *Using Labor Market Information in Career Exploration and Decision Making: A Resource Guide* and developed an extensive in-service training program to help counselor educators and counseling psychologists enhance their ability to train career counselors.

The reduction in time spent on career information is partially due to the recognition of the need to pay more attention to career counseling, which is a healthy sign. However, since most counselors and counseling psychologists are required to take only one course that deals with the various aspects of career development, career counseling coverage is replacing time spent on career information. The result of all this is that career counselors and career development specialists will increasingly have to rely on their own study and in-service training for their knowledge of career information.

5. Our basic understanding of how to select and use occupational information will continue to receive a low priority by researchers. Except for Krumboltz and Associates (e.g., Krumboltz & Schroeder, 1965; Krumboltz & Thoresen, 1964), few researchers have made attempts to identify factors that lead to the effective uses of occupational information, and with a few exceptions (e.g., Brown, 1990; Prediger, 1974) the entire area has received little comment. Perhaps researchers assume that career development specialists understand how to select, evaluate, and use career information. Regardless of the reasons for omission, it is expected that career development specialists will continue to ignore the general topic of career information.

6. Career counselors will have to work harder in the future to keep abreast of information about a rapidly changing workplace. McDaniels (1989) reports the changing nature of the workplace, including job sharing, telecommuting, computer supervision, utilization of part-time or temporary help to reduce costs, the increasing importance of small businesses as employers, the decline in job opportunities for college graduates, and so forth. He also suggests numerous means by which career counselors and others can familiarize themselves with the shifts in the workplace that are occurring. For example, counselors may have to spend more time in direct conversations with employers and acquainting themselves with alternative sources of information about emerging work settings such as franchises and entrepreneurial enterprises.

Career counselors working with adults will certainly have to shift their emphasis from information about entry-level positions to information about midlevel positions. They will also have to become increasingly aware of information about fringe benefits, long-range retirement planning, and a related issue, tax laws, as well as a host of other information. The NOICC, the National Career Development Association, the U.S. Department of Labor, and other similar organizations may step in to help solve this problem, but ultimately the responsibility will fall most heavily on the counselor.

TRENDS: CAREER COUNSELING

1. Career counseling will be increasingly recognized as a counseling specialty that requires expertise in personal counseling as well as career-related assessment and intervention specialties. Recent books (e.g., Brown & Brooks, 1991; Gysbers & Moore, 1987; Spokane, 1991) have emphasized the interrelationship of mental health problems and career problems, suggesting that the stereotypical concept of career counselors who provide rather simplistic career counseling services (i.e., intake, select tests, give career information) is becoming less influential. Some of these books (e.g., Spokane, 1991) offer specific models of career counseling integrating personal and career concerns. However, even those contemporary books that do not offer specific models of career counseling (e.g., Herr & Cramer, 1988; Zunker, 1986) discuss the impact of mental health problems and how they interact with career development.

    It is difficult to discern the impetus for the current trend. Certainly, for over a decade Crites (1981) has been advocating that we not view career problems narrowly. It may very well be that this is an area where practice ran well ahead of academic thinkers. During the past 3 years, the second author of this book has conducted workshops for several hundred counselors from across the United States and Canada and, almost without exception, their first concern is that mental health problems may be interfering with clients' basic career development processes, such as decision making. Regardless of the source, the unanimity of opinion among practitioners and academics assures that this trend will continue.

2. Certification of career counselors will become an increasing concern among counselors and psychologists. To date, most psychological licensure laws provide licenses with a generic license to practice and, for the most part, psychology has not been concerned about the credentials of career counselors. On the other hand, the very first licensing law passed for counselors (Virginia) contained a provision for recognizing career counseling specialists. Similarly, the national effort to develop certification standards for counselors was initiated primarily for the purpose of recognizing specialists (Brown & Srebalus, 1988). Currently, the National Board of Certified Counselors (NBCC, 1991) certifies career counselors. One of the requirements for obtaining and becoming recog-

nized as a National Certified Career Counselor is that one must first become a NCC (National Certified Counselor), which is a generic certification. There are currently approximately 1,000 NCCs, and the number is expected to grow.

3. There will be a convergence of thinking about the career counseling practices for men and women. Most current career counseling books contain sections on the special career counseling needs of women (e.g., Herr & Cramer, 1988). A few (e.g., Zunker, 1986) also contain chapters on the special needs of men, while others consider the topic of gender simultaneously (e.g., Brown & Brooks, 1991). A few of the contemporary books (Gysbers & Moore, 1987; Yost & Corbishley, 1987) address this issue only to a slight degree.

   The biological fact that women bear children and men do not must be a consideration in career counseling. So must the socialization of gender roles and the impact this makes on career development and career choice. The point here is not that men and women are not different, they are. The point is that the basic counseling processes, including assessment and intervention strategies, used to help males and females are essentially the same. What career counselors require is a sensitivity to and respect for the differences, an ability to adapt techniques to males and females, not a different set of approaches.

4. There will be a convergence of thinking about the career counseling practices for whites and members of various ethnic minorities born and reared this country. Sociologists have long held that there are no distinct subcultures in this country. Except for recent immigrants, we speak the same language, go to the same schools, watch the same television programs, and generally live in the same culture. This is not to say that there are no cultural variations in our society except in the immigrant population. Ethnic origin plays a distinct role in our development, but our cultural experiences are overwhelmingly similar. Atkinson, Poston, Furlong, and Mercado (1989) found that African Americans, whites, Asian Americans, and Mexican Americans enrolled in introductory business classes had very similar preferences with regard to preference for counselor characteristics and that counselor characteristics may be more important than ethnicity to these groups. However, they also concluded that the students they studied preferred counselors with attitudes and values similar to their own. To some degree, one can argue that counselors and clients from similar ethnic background are more likely to have similar attitudes.

   Career counselors must become sensitive to the needs, values, and preferences of their clients. If language is a barrier to career counseling, then referral to a counselor who can speak the clients' language will be necessary. However, there is little in the counseling literature that suggests that highly different career counseling strategies need to be developed for ethnic minorities.

5. The number of people seeking help from career counselors will increase dramatically. The 1989 Gallup Organization survey of adults in the United States found that 7 percent of those interviewed had needed help in selecting, changing, or getting a job in the year prior to the survey. Of those needing help, 55 percent sought assistance from a job service worker (33 percent) or a professional counselor (22 percent). While these figures are subject to some error, they translate into 12.5 million people who needed help with some aspect of career planning and over 2.5 million who sought help from a professional counselor. It is also important to note that when employed adults were asked to project their employment future over the 3 years subsequent to the data of the survey (October, 1989), 20 percent said they expected to change jobs voluntarily and 9 percent expected their jobs to be terminated permanently. Employment Security counselors, private practitioners, private employment counselors, and counselors in business and industry helping with outplacement or relocation will all be influenced by the sheer numbers of people changing jobs.

6. The formulations of Holland (1985) and those based on social learning theory (Betz & Hackett, 1981; Mitchell & Krumboltz, 1990) will be the only current occupational choice and career development theories that have a significant impact on career counselors in the future. Holland's theory, as set forth in Chapter 2, has been and is currently a highly influential force in career counseling. His ideas have been widely incorporated into books, assessment devices, and career development programs. It seems likely that this will continue in the future.

It is not clear whether Krumboltz's social-learning-based theory will have an impact on practice or research (Brown, 1990), but Hackett and Betz's (1981) has already had an impact on the research on career choice (Brooks, 1990). It seems likely that the wide aspects of Bandura's (1977, 1986) formulations will influence career counseling, particularly as personal counseling is integrated with career counseling into unified systems of counseling. Other less well-articulated theories, such as Bordin's (1990), or more cumbersome theories, such as Super's (1990), are likely to decline in importance generally and as they relate to career counseling specifically. It is probable that eclectic career counseling systems such as the one posed by Gysbers and Moore (1987) will replace the strict trait and factor approaches or the atheoretical approaches (Yost & Corbishley, 1987).

TRENDS: CAREER DEVELOPMENT PROGRAMMING

1. As noted earlier, Gysbers (1984) predicted that the populations served by career development programing will continue into the late 1990s and beyond. Only about 10 percent of the *Fortune* 500 companies have

career development programs (Keller & Piotrowski, 1987). Many elementary, middle, and senior high schools are either without programs or have programs that are clearly deficient. Dropouts, students at risk, minorities, and many other groups are not well served by public school career development programs. Alumni are returning to colleges and universities seeking career development services when their jobs are terminated or they decide to make career changes. Immigrants from Central America and the Pacific Rim countries are struggling to find a place in our occupational structure. This list could be expanded almost indefinitely, but the need for career development services is clear, and in many places programs are being developed and expanded to meet this need. Lack of money, skeptical leaders, and other counterforces will certainly provide barriers to the development of these programs but, inevitably it seems, they will grow in numbers and become more functional.

2. There are several specific corollaries of the aforementioned trend. One of these is that, while the number of career development programs in business and industry will continue to grow, there will be an increasing emphasis on contracting with outside agencies for these services. A recent study of employee assistance programs (EAPs) (Hosie, West, & Mackey, 1988) across the country suggests that career development assessment is provided more frequently by EAPs external to the corporation than those internal to them. At the time of the survey, relatively small numbers of EAPs were providing this service, a not unexpected finding since EAPs and career development programs are not typically included in a single program. However, career development counseling is being provided by a substantial percentage of EAPs, with 67 percent of the agencies external to the corporations reporting that they provide this service.

   Many corporations have entered into contracts with external agencies of various types to provide mental health services (Hosie et al., 1988). Many of these agencies provide what was termed in their study career development counseling, and a few offer career assessments. It may well be that the respondents believed that the type of counseling they were providing would foster career development, even though it was not directly related to career decision making given the fact that so few provided related assessment services (35 out of 148). But even the suggestion that 81 of the 148 external EAP programs responding reported providing career counseling represents a significant trend. It is suggested here that business managers are increasingly recognizing the need for career counseling and will increasingly contract with external agencies for the service.

3. A second corollary of the first trend identified in this section is that a wider range of mental health professionals will become interested in career counseling and career development, with the result that programming for career development will increasingly occur in mental

health agencies (e.g., community mental health centers and substance abuse centers) that have traditionally focused only on personal counseling/psychotherapy. Hosie, West, and Mackey (1988) surveyed substance abuse centers to determine what competencies administrators expected of master's level counselors and found that nearly half expect counselors to have "vocational skills counseling." Developing career development programs and providing career counseling for substance abusers makes intuitive sense, but unfortunately Hosie et al. (1988) did not examine whether this occurred. It is expected that increased emphasis will be placed in this area.

4. A third corollary of the first trend is that career development programs in business and industry will expand, primarily because of the increasing recognition that career problems can increase stress, family problems, and contribute to other mental health concerns (e.g., substance abuse), and these in turn reduce productivity. Twenty percent of the employed workers interviewed by the Gallup Organization (1989) reported that job stress had interfered with their ability to do their job in the year prior to the interview. Approximately 35 percent of this same sample reported experiencing conflict between the demands of their work and family or interpersonal relationships a "great deal" or "quite a lot." Prevention of burnout, depression, and stress is a major function of EAPs (Hosie et al., 1988), and as the linkages among job dissatisfaction, career, and other life roles and how they contribute to or attenuate stress are better understood, preventing mental health problems will become a source of motivation for installing career development programs in business and industry.

ISSUES IN CAREER DEVELOPMENT

1. The need to update the basic sources of career information, the *Dictionary of Occupational Titles (DOT)* and the *Guide for Occupational Exploration (GOE)*, will continue to be an issue among occupational information career development specialists. As noted in Chapter 5, the latest edition of the *DOT* was published in 1977, with supplements being published by the U.S. Department of Labor in 1979 and 1986. The *GOE* was published in 1979 and updated by Harrington and O'Shea in 1984, although the update was directed at utilization of the *GOE*, not at the basic occupational information it contains. There has been, and continues to be, a belief among occupational information specialists that the information contained in the *DOT* needs to be continuously updated. At this writing, Congress has authorized some of the needed money and the *DOT* has been updated, as noted earlier. The *GOE* has not been redone, however. Perhaps more importantly, the ongoing job analysis

and collection of information about jobs is lagging behind because of lack of support.

2. Career counseling and career development programming will continue to operate without a solid empirical basis. Herr and Cramer (1988) identify a number of areas within the career development domain that need empirical investigation. In many ways, it would be easier to identify those areas that do not warrant additional research: none. Many of Holland's (1985) propositions have received widespread support, and we have found that almost any type of interpretation of tests and inventories improves client knowledge (Goodyear, 1990). However, we have not even begun to answer the classic question, "What types of intervention are most useful with which types of clients?" Neither have we answered basic questions about types of counselors or counseling that are most effective or begun to understand fully the interaction of human and computerized systems (Sampson, 1990). As Herr and Cramer suggest, there is much research that needs to be conducted.

3. In Chapter 2, several of the leading theories of career development were discussed briefly. None of these meets the standards of a "good" theory (Brown, 1990; Osipow, 1983). It has already been suggested that some of these theories will have less influence on career counseling in the future. Increasingly, there will be debates about whether these theories are necessary at all as the interaction of life roles and their development is considered. Some will argue that theories of career choice are still necessary, while others will argue that career development should be subsumed in comprehensive theories of human development. It also seems likely that the issue of separate theories for women will be a topic of debate well into the 1990s.

4. The use of tests and inventories in career counseling and development programs will be a subject of continuing debate. Women, minorities, and representatives of culturally disadvantaged groups will continue to argue that these inventories discriminate against, or at the very least are not helpful to, these groups. Others, relying on validity studies and tradition, will take the opposing view. While it is unlikely that these debates will have a widespread impact on the actual use of tests, the controversy will continue.

SUMMARY

A few of what are expected to be the most important trends and issues in career development have been outlined in this final chapter. At the outset, we stressed that prognostication is risky at best, and only time will tell about the accuracy of the predictions made here. It is unlikely that we have identified all the trends and issues that will arise in the decade to come. Career counselors need to learn to be their own futurists and to adapt to changes as they occur.

REFERENCES

Atkinson, D. R., Poston, W. C., Furlong, M. J., & Mercado, P. C. (1989). Ethnic group preference for counselor characteristics. *Journal of Counseling Psychology, 36,* 68–72.

Bandura, A. (1977). *Social learning theory.* Englewood Cliffs, NJ: Prentice Hall.

Bandura, A. (1986). *Social foundation of thought and action: A social-cognitive theory.* Englewood Cliffs, NJ: Prentice Hall.

Betz, N. E., & Hackett, G. (1981). The relationship of career-related self-efficacy expectations to perceive career operations in college men and women. *Journal of Counseling Psychology, 27,* 44–62.

Bordin, E. S. (1990). Psychodynamic model of career choice and satisfaction. In D. Brown, L. Brooks, & Associates (Eds.), *Career choice and development* (pp. 102–144). San Francisco: Jossey-Bass.

Brooks, L. (1990). Recent developments in theory building. In D. Brown, L. Brooks, & Associates (Eds.), *Career choice and development* (pp. 364–394)). San Francisco: Jossey-Bass.

Brown, D. (1990). Summary, comparison, and critique of the major theories. In D. Brown, L. Brooks, & Associates (Eds.), *Career choice and development* (pp. 338–363). San Francisco: Jossey-Bass.

Brown, D., & Brooks, L. (1991). *Career counseling techniques.* Boston: Allyn & Bacon.

Brown, D., & Srebalus, D. J. (1988). *Introduction to the counseling profession.* Englewood Cliffs, NJ: Prentice Hall.

Brown, S. T., & Brown, D. (1990). *Designing a career information center.* Garrett Park, MD: Garrett Park Press.

Crites, J. O. (1981). *Career counseling: Models, methods, and materials.* New York: McGraw-Hill.

Gallup Organization. (1987). *A Gallup survey regarding career development.* Princeton, NJ: Author.

Gallup Organization (1989). *A Gallup survey regarding career development.* Princeton, NJ: Author.

Goodyear, R. K. (1990). Research on the effects of test interpretation: A review, *The Counseling Psychologist, 18,* 240–257.

Gysbers, N. C. (1984). Major trends in career development theory and practice. In N. C. Gysbers and Associates, *Designing careers: Counseling to enhance education, work, and leisure* (pp. 618–632). San Francisco.

Gysbers, N. C., & Moore, E. J. (1987). *Career counseling: Skills and techniques for practitioners.* Englewood Cliffs, NJ: Prentice Hall.

Hackett, H. G., & Betz, N. E. (1981). A self-efficacy approach to the career development of women. *Journal of Vocational Behavior, 18,* 326–339.

Harrington, T. F., & O'Shea, A. J. (Eds.) (1984). *Guide for occupational exploration* (2nd ed.). Minneapolis: National Forum Foundation.

Herr, E. L. (1974). The decade in prospect: Some implications for vocational guidance. In E. L. Herr (Ed.), *Vocational guidance and human development* (pp. 551–574). Boston: Houghton-Mifflin.

Herr, E. L., & Cramer, S. H. (1988). *Career guidance and counseling through the life span: Systematic Approaches.* Glenview, IL: Scott, Foresman.

Holland, J. L. (1985). *Making vocational choices: A theory of vocational personalities and work environment* (2nd ed.). Englewood Cliffs, NJ: Prentice Hall.

Hosie, T. W., West, J. D., & Mackey, J. A. (1988). Employment and roles of counselors in substance-abuse centers. *Journal of Mental Health Counseling, 10,* 188–189.

Keller, J., & Piotrowski, C. (1987). Career development programs in Fortune 500 companies. *Psychological Reports, 16,* 920–922.

Krumboltz, J. D., & Thoreson, C. E. (1964). The effects of behavioral counseling on group and individual settings on information-seeking behavior. *Journal of Counseling Psychology, 11,* 323–333.

McDaniels, C. (1989). *The changing workplace: Career counseling strategies for the 1990s and beyond.* San Francisco: Jossey-Bass.

Mitchell, L. K., & Krumboltz, J. D. (1990). Social learning approach to career decision making: Krumboltz's theory. In D. Brown, L. Brooks, & Associates, *Career Choice and Development* (pp. 145–196). San Francisco: Jossey-Bass.

NBCC. (1991). *NBCC counselor certification, 1991.* Alexandria, VA: Author.

NOICC. (1986). *Using labor market information in career exploration and decision making: A resource guide.* Garrett Park, MD: Garrett Park Press.

Osipow, S. H. (1983). *Theories of career development* (3rd ed.). Englewood Cliffs, NJ: Prentice Hall.

Sampson, D. E., & Liberty, L. H. (1989). Textbooks used in counselor education programs. *Counselor Education and Supervision, 29,* 111–121.

Sampson, J. P., Jr. (1990). Computer-assisted testing and the goals of counseling psychology. *The Counseling Psychologist, 18,* 227–239.

Spokane, A. (1991). *Career Interventions.* Englewood Cliffs, NJ: Prentice Hall.

Super, D. E. (1990). A life-span, life-space approach to career development. In D. Brown, L. Brooks, & Associates, *Career Choice and Development* (pp. 197–261). San Francisco: Jossey-Bass.

Yost, E. B., & Corbishley, M. A. (1987). *Career counseling: A psychological approach.* San Francisco: Jossey-Bass.

Zunker, V. G. (1990). *Career Counseling: Applied concepts of life planning* (3rd ed.). Monterey, CA: Brooks/Cole.

___ Appendix _____

Directory of State Occupational Information Coordinating Committees (SOICCs)

Dr. Mary Louise Simms, Director
Alabama OICC
Bell Building, Suite 400
207 Montgomery Street
Montgomery, AL 36130
TEL: 205/242-2990

Ms. Sally Saddler, Coordinator
Alaska Department of Labor
Research and Analysis Section
Post Office Box 25501
Juneau, AK 99802
TEL: 907/465-4518

Mr. Patolo Mageo, Program Director
American Samoa State OICC
Office of Manpower Resources
American Samoa Government
Pago Pago, AS 96799
TEL: 684/633-4485

Mr. Stan Butterworth, Executive Director
Arizona State OICC
Post Office Box 6123
Site Code 897J
Phoenix, AZ 85005
TEL: 602/542-6466
FAX: 602/542-6474

Mr. C. Coy Cozart, Executive Director
Arkansas OICC
Arkansas Employment Security Division
Employment and Training Services
Post Office Box 2981
Little Rock, AR 72203
TEL: 501/682-3159
FAX: 501/682-3713

Mr. Sigurd Brivkains, Executive Director
California OICC
800 Capitol Mall, MIC-67
Sacramento, CA 95814
TEL: 916/323-6544

Mr. James L. Harris, Director
Colorado OICC
State Board Community College
1391 Speer Boulevard, Suite 600
Denver, CO 80204-2554
TEL: 303/866-4488

Dr. Prudence Brown Holton
Executive Director
Connecticut OICC
Connecticut Department of Education
25 Industrial Park Road
Middletown, CT 06457
TEL: 203/638-4042

Mr. James K. McFadden, Executive Director
Office of Occupational and LMI/DOL
University Office Plaza
Post Office Box 9029
Newark, DE 19714-9029
TEL: 302/368-6963
FAX: 302/368-6748

Ms. Etta Williams, Executive Director
District of Columbia OICC
Department of Employment Services
500 C Street, NW, Room 215
Washington, DC 20001
TEL: 202/639-1090

Mr. Robert Kessler, FLOIS Manager
Bureau of LMI/DOL and ES
Suite 200, Hartman Building
2012 Capitol Circle SE
Tallahassee, FL 32399-0673
TEL: 904/488-7397
FAX: 904/488-2558

Mr. Clifford L. Granger, Executive Director
Georgia OICC/Department of Labor
148 International Boulevard—Sussex Place
Atlanta, GA 30303
TEL: 404/656-9639

Mr. Jose S. Mantanona, Executive Director
Guam OICC
Human Resource Development Agency
Jay Ease Building, 3rd Floor
Post Office Box 2817
Agana, GU 96910
TEL: 671/646-9341 thru 9344

Mr. Patrick A. Stanley, Executive Director
Hawaii State OICC
830 Punchbowl Street
Room 315
Honolulu, HI 96813
TEL: 808/548-3496

Mr. Charles M. Mollerup, Director
Idaho OICC
Len B. Jordan Building, Room 301
650 West State Street
Boise, ID 83720
TEL: 208/334-3705

Mr. Jan Staggs, Executive Director
Illinois OICC
217 East Monroe, Suite 203
Springfield, IL 62706
TEL: 217/785-0789

Ms. Linda Piper, Acting Executive Director
Indiana OICC
10 N. Senate Avenue, Room 101
Indianapolis, IN 46204
TEL: 317/232-1898

Dr. Alan B. Moore, Executive Director
Iowa OICC
Iowa Department of Economic Development
200 East Grand Avenue
Des Moines, IA 50309
TEL: 515/242-4890
FAX: 515/281-7276

Mr. Randall Williams, Director
Kansas OICC
401 Topeka Avenue
Topeka, KS 66603
TEL: 913/296-1865
FAX: 913/296-2119

Mr. Don Sullivan, Information Liaison
Kentucky OICC
275 E. Main Street—2 Center
Frankfort, KY 40621-0001
TEL: 502/564-4528 or 5331

Mr. George Glass, Coordinator
Louisiana OICC
Post Office Box 94094
Baton Rouge, LA 70804-9094
TEL: 504/342-5149

Mr. Susan Brown, Executive Director
Maine OICC
State House Station 71
Augusta, ME 04333
TEL: 207/289-2331

Ms. Jasmin M. Duckett, Coordinator
Maryland SOICC
State Department of Employment and Training
1100 North Eutaw Street, Room 600
Baltimore, MD 21201
TEL: 301/333-5478
FAX: 301/333-5304

Mr. Robert Vinson, Director
Massachusetts OICC
MA Division of Employment Security
CF Hurley Building, 2nd Floor
Government Center
Boston, MA 02114
TEL: 617/727-6718

Mr. Robert Sherer, Executive Coordinator
Michigan OICC
Victor Office Center, Third Floor
Box 30015
201 N. Washington Square
Lansing, MI 48909
TEL: 517/373-0363
FAX: 517/335-5822

Mr. John Cosgrove, Director
Minnesota OICC
Department of Economic Security
690 American Center Building
150 East Kellogg Boulevard
St. Paul, MN 55101
TEL: 612/296-2072

Mr. William Caston, Executive Director
Mississippi OICC
Sillers Building, Suite 1005
Post Office Box 771
Jackson, MS 39205
TEL: 601/359-3412
FAX: 601/359-2832

Ms. Kay Raithel, Director
Missouri OICC
421 East Dunklin Street
Jefferson City, MO 65101
TEL: 314/751-3800
FAX: 314/751-7973

Mr. Robert N. Arnold, Program Manager
Montana OICC
1327 Lockey Street, 2nd Floor
Post Office Box 1728
Helena, MT 59624
TEL: 406/444-2741
FAX: 406/444-2638

Mr. Phil Baker, Administrator
Nebraska OICC
Post Office Box 94600
State House Station
Lincoln, NE 68509-4600
TEL: 402/471-4845

Ms. Valerie Hopkins, Director
Nevada OICC
1923 North Carson Street
Suite 211
Carson City, NV 89710
TEL: 702/687-4577
FAX: 702/883-9158

Dr. Victor P. Racicot, Director
New Hampshire State OICC
64B Old Suncook Road
Concord, NH 03301
TEL: 603/228-3349
FAX: 603/228-8557

Mr. Laurence H. Seidel, Staff Director
New Jersey OICC
1008 Labor & Industry Building
CN 056
Trenton, NJ 08625-0056
TEL: 609/292-2682
FAX: 609/292-6692

Mr. Charles Lehman, Director
New Mexico OICC
401 Broadway, NE—Tiwa Building
Post Office Box 1928
Albuquerque, NM 87103
TEL: 505/841-8636

Mr. David Nyhan, Executive Director
New York State OICC/DOL
Research & Statistics Division
State Campus, Building 12—Room 400
Albany, NY 12240
TEL: 518/457-6182
FAX: 518/457-0620

Ms. Nancy H. MacCormac, Executive Director
North Carolina OICC
1311 St. Mary's Street, Suite 250
Post Office Box 27625
Raleigh, NC 27611
TEL: 919/733-6700

Dr. Dan Marrs, Coordinator
North Dakota OICC
1600 East Interstate—Suite 14
Post Office Box 1537
Bismarck, ND 58502-1537
TEL: 701/224-2197
FAX: 701/224-3420

Mr. Konrad Reyes, Executive Director
Northern Mariana Islands OICC
Post Office Box 149
Saipan, CM 96950
TEL: 671/234-7394

Mr. Mark Schaff, Director
Ohio OICC/Division of LMI
Ohio Bureau of Employment Services
1160 Dublin Road, Building A
Columbus, OH 43215
TEL: 614/644-2689
FAX: 614/481-8543

Mr. Curtis Schumaker, Executive Director
Oklahoma OICC
Department of Voc/Tech Education
1500 W. Seventh Avenue
Stillwater, OK 74074
TEL: 405/743-5198

Ms. Nancy Hargis, Executive Director
Oregon OICC
875 Union Street, NE
Salem, OR 97311
TEL: 503/378-8146
FAX: 503/373-7515

Mr. Fritz J. Fichtner, Jr., Director
Pennsylvania OICC
Pennsylvania Dept. of Labor and Industry
1224 Labor and Industry Building
Harrisburg, PA 17120
TEL: 717/787-8646 or 8647
FAX: 717/772-2168

Mr. Jesus Hernandez Rios, Exec. Director
Puerto Rico OICC
202 Del Cristo Street
Post Office Box 6212
San Juan, PR 00936-6212
TEL: 809/723-7110
FAX: 809/724-6374

Ms. Mildred Nichols, Director
Rhode Island OICC
22 Hayes Street—Room 133
Providence, RI 02908
TEL: 401/272-0830

Ms. Carol Kososki, Director
South Carolina OICC
1550 Gadsden Street
Post Office Box 995
Columbia, SC 29202
TEL: 803/737-2733
FAX: 803/737-2642

Ms. Mary Sue Vickers, Director
LMI Center
South Dakota Department of Labor
420 S. Roosevelt Street
Post Office Box 4730
Aberdeen, SD 57402-4730
TEL: 605/622-2314

Dr. Chrystal Partridge, Director
Tennessee OICC
11th Floor Volunteer Plaza
500 James Robertson Parkway
Nashville, TN 37219
TEL: 615/741-6451

Mr. Richard Froeschle, Director
Texas OICC
Texas Employment Commission Building
15th and Congress, Room 526T
Austin, TX 78778
TEL: 512/463-2399

Dr. Reta Oram, Executive Director
Utah OICC
c/o Utah Department of Employment Security
Post Office Box 11249
174 Social Hall Avenue
Salt Lake City, UT 84147-0249
TEL: 801/533-2274
FAX: 801/533-2466

Mr. Robert Ware, Director
Vermont OICC
Green Mountain Drive
Post Office Box 488
Montpelier, VT 05601-0488
TEL: 802/229-0311

Ms. Dolores A. Esser, Executive Director
Virginia OICC/VA Employment Commission
703 E. Main Street
Post Office Box 1358
Richmond, VA 23211
TEL: 804/786-7496
FAX: 804/786-7844

Ms. Annie Smith, Coordiantor
Virgin Islands OICC
Post Office Box 3359
St. Thomas, US VI 00801
TEL: 809/776-3700

Mr. A. T. Woodhouse, Director
Washington OICC
212 Maple Park MS KG-11
Olympia, WA 98504-5311
TEL: 206/438-4803
FAX: 206/438-3215

Dr. George McGuire, Executive Director
West Virginia OICC
One Dunbar Plaza, Suite E
Dunbar, WV 25064
TEL: 304/766-8342
FAX: 304/766-7846

Ms. Maile Pa'alani, Administrative Director
The Wisconsin OICC/Division of E&T Policy
201 East Washington Avenue
Post Office Box 7972
Madison, WI 53707
TEL: 608/255-8012
FAX: 608/267-0330

Mr. Michael E. Paris, Executive Director
Wyoming OICC
Post Office Box 2760
100 West Midwest
Casper, WY 82602
TEL: 302/235-2642

___ Name Index ___

513

_____ Subject Index _____